A PRACTICAL COMMENTARY
ON THE CODE OF CANON LAW

A PRACTICAL TREATISE
ON THE CULTURE OF

A PRACTICAL COMMENTARY ON THE CODE OF CANON LAW

BY

Rev. STANISLAUS WOYWOD, O.F.M., LL.B.

WITH A PREFACE BY

Most Rev. PHILIP BERNARDINI, S.T.D., J.U.D.

VOLUME I

Sixth Printing

NEW YORK

JOSEPH F. WAGNER (Inc.)

LONDON: B. HERDER

1941

Nihil Obstat:

> FR. BENVENUTUS RYAN, O.F.M.
> FR. THOMAS PLASSMANN, O.F.M.

Imprimi Potest:

> FR. JEROME DAWSON, O.F.M.
> > *Minister Provincialis*

Nihil Obstat:

> ARTHUR J. SCANLAN, S.T.D.
> > *Censor Librorum*

Imprimatur:

> ✠ MOST REV. STEPHEN J. DONAHUE, D.D.
> > *Administrator of New York*

NEW YORK, JANUARY 3, 1939

PREFACE TO THE FIRST EDITION

The author of the two large volumes on the Code of Canon Law is well known to the English speaking public by his many contributions on questions of Canon Law in the Homiletic and Pastoral Review, by his pamphlet on the "Ne Temere" decree, and by the synopsis of the Code in his book "The New Canon Law." We believe that the new work will be a welcome help to all students of Canon Law and a source of information to the priests engaged in the active ministry. Every Canon of the Code is paraphrased, and most of the practical difficulties which arise under the law of the Code are discussed, special attention being given to those portions of the Code which are of more frequent and practical application, e.g., the Canons on the Sacraments and the Canons on Religious. The author realizes that the study of the Code is still in its infancy, and when he discusses the difficulties arising here and there, he gives the opinions of principal leading authors on either side of the controversy and indicates his own preference. The order of the Code in the treatment of the matter has been faithfully adhered to, the latest decisions and declarations of the Holy See have been inserted in their proper places and besides, a complete summary of these is given in one of the Appendices to the work.

We trust that the present work will further the knowledge and observance of the laws of Holy Mother Church, and wish the author all success in his noble endeavor.

MONSGR. PHILIP BERNARDINI
Professor of Canon Law at the
Catholic University of America.

Washington, October 26, 1925.

FOREWORD

When, in 1918, we prepared a paraphrased rendition of those parts of the Code which the clergy need to consult more frequently in their sacred ministry, we promised to write at a later date a more complete work on the Code. We have now done so, and offer it respectfully with the hope that the "Practical Commentary of the Code of Canon Law" may help in some slight measure to further the understanding and observance of the universal law of our Holy Mother Church.

Although several commentaries on the Code or on parts of it, have been recently published in English, and a goodly number have appeared in Latin, German, French, and Italian, we believe that our present work, in two volumes, is not untimely or superfluous, but that it answers a real need. Commentaries on the Code which extend over many volumes are not convenient for frequent and casual consultation, and those commentaries that deal with the entire Code in one volume are not sufficiently complete to offer explanation of important difficulties arising from the succinct texts of the Canons. Even a mere paraphrase of the Code, without any study of its problems, would make a large volume, so that at least two large volumes are needed to contain the entire text and the necessary discussion of the more important controversies.

Many commentaries do not strictly adhere to the order of the subjects and of the Canons in the Code, but dislocate certain topics and Canons for convenience' sake. The Holy See has commanded that the Code be the text-book of Canon Law in all theological schools and therefore does not favor any disarrangement of the order of the Code. Hence we have faithfully adhered to the Code in its sequence of books, titles, chapters, articles and Canons, and this will facilitate the use of our commentary as a reference work on the Code.

While it is impossible to treat all difficulties which arise from a careful perusal of the Code even in the space of a two-volume commentary, we have endeavored to give an explanation of all the important practical difficulties. In many instances we have consulted a large number of the available commentaries and summed up the opinions of authors who have dealt with the subject under discussion, indicating which of the opinions seemed preferable to us.

Since our commentary is intended chiefly for the clergy, secular and religious, of the United States, all or the vast majority of whom are very busy men engaged in parish work (which still has in many places the character of the pioneer work, including the building, or clearing from indebtedness, of churches, schools, parochial residences, School Sisters' convents, and charitable institutions of many kinds), we have thought it best not to overload our commentary with references to many works on Canon Law, but have merely given those necessary to indicate either as sources of the laws of the Code or as authorities whose opinions we discuss. We intend to publish, either semi-annually or annually, as the new matter may call for, decrees, decisions and official declarations affecting the Code, so as to keep this Commentary up to date. The supplements will serve also to correct any errors or faulty statements that may have crept into our Commentary.

That this work may aid in the furtherance of God's honor and glory, through a loving study of and faithful obedience to the laws of His Church of which He said: "He who heareth you heareth Me," is the hope and desire of

THE AUTHOR.

Written on the Feast of The Seraphic Doctor, St. Bonaventure, 1925.
St. Bonaventure's Seminary and College, Allegany, N. Y.

P. S.—Since the appearance of the Code the Holy See has issued many decisions and decrees which interpret or supplement its provisions. In cases where, because of their length or for other reasons, it was impracticable to insert these in the text, they have been given in Appendix III of Volume II.

CONTENTS

THE FIRST BOOK

THE SECOND BOOK

CONTENTS

CONTENTS

A PRACTICAL COMMENTARY ON THE CODE OF CANON LAW

THE FIRST BOOK

GENERAL RULES

These general rules (Canons 1–86) are introductory regulations affecting the entire Code. They explain the nature and extent of the laws of the Code and the effect of the Code on the former Canon Law, both universal and particular.

1. The first Canon of the Code states that its laws are obligatory for the Catholic Church of the Latin Rite exclusively, except in matters which of their very nature affect also the Oriental Church (**Canon 1**). It is evident that in matters of faith and morals all Catholics, without distinction of race, nationality or rite, are bound by the authoritative pronouncements of the Holy See. There can be but one rule in these matters for all who belong to the Catholic Church. In matters of discipline the Supreme Authority of the Church may sanction various rules for various countries, nations or rites. The Church takes into consideration the particular circumstances under which her children live in the different parts of the world—the manners, customs and habits of races and nations. The Oriental peoples differ widely in their national characteristics from the Western races. Besides, the ecclesiastical discipline of the Churches of the Oriental Rites has a venerable antiquity which the Supreme Authority of the Church is anxious to respect.[1] Therefore, the Code states that the disciplinary laws of the Latin Church are not to be extended to

[1] Benedict XIV, Encyclical "Allatæ sunt," July 26, 1755; Gasparri, "Fontes Cod. jur. can.," II, 456, n. 434.

the Oriental Rites.   To maintain the disciplinary laws of the Oriental Rites in their purity and in harmony with their ancient customs, the Holy See has established a special Sacred Congregation of Oriental Rites.[2]

2. All liturgical laws heretofore decreed for the celebration of Holy Mass, the recitation of the Divine Office, the administration of the sacraments and sacramentals and other sacred functions, retain their force, except in so far as the Code explicitly corrects these laws (**Canon 2**).   There are not many Canons which deal with liturgical matters.   Most of these are found in the section of the Code which deals with the sacraments and with sacred places.   The Sacred Congregation of Rites has jurisdiction over liturgical functions, and its decrees and declarations are published in the *Acta Apostolicæ Sedis*. At various intervals the Sacred Congregation of Rites publishes these decrees in its official collection called *Decreta Authentica,* of which six volumes have appeared up to the present time.

3. The agreements entered into between the Holy See and the various nations are not abolished or modified by the Code, but remain unaffected by the laws of the Code (**Canon 3**).   The relation between the Church and the State is a big and interesting subject of study.   Every Christian is necessarily subject to both the temporal or civil and the spiritual or ecclesiastical power.   Exercising authority over the same subjects under different aspects, the two powers naturally come into contact with each other in many matters.   Both authorities are instituted by God, and in that respect are alike competent and independent of each other, each in its proper sphere of jurisdiction.   If the two powers are compared in rank and importance, it is evident that the purpose for which God ordained the spiritual power is far above the purpose of the civil power.   The spiritual power should, therefore, get the preference in a conflict of jurisdiction. However, frequently the rights of the spiritual power have been disregarded by the civil authority, not only in heathen nations but also in Christian and Catholic nations.   For the sake of peace, the Church has been obliged to allow the civil power certain rights in ecclesiastical affairs to obtain assurance from the civil power of the free exercise of her most essential rights. Again, at times the civil authority has granted to the ecclesi-

[2] Motu Proprio of Benedict XV, May 1, 1917; *Acta Ap. Sedis*, IX, 529.

astical power certain rights of a purely civil nature. The written agreements between the Holy See and the civil power are usually called *concordats*. Here in the United States there have never been any permanent diplomatic relations between the Church and the civil power, and therefore we have no concordats with the Holy See.[3]

4. Acquired rights, privileges and indults which have been granted by the Holy See to individuals or organizations up to the present time, if they are still in use and have not been revoked, remain in force unless they are explicitly repealed in the Canons of this Code (**Canon 4**). Ecclesiastical legislation is usually conservative. Laws introducing sudden and far-reaching changes in the discipline of the Church are rare. A careful perusal of the Code will convince the reader that this monumental work contains a systematic summary of former laws rather than new laws. The changes, which in the course of time become necessary, are made slowly and with much deliberation. Just as the laws are not easily changed, so also the rights and privileges of individuals and organizations. The Holy See has its own special reasons in granting rights and privileges, and the Church does not lightly recall them, according to an ancient axiom of law: *Beneficium principis decet manere*. Therefore, rights and concessions rightfully obtained and enjoyed up to the time of the publication of the Code are not abolished unless some Canon of the Code plainly revokes them.[4]

5. Now existing immemorial customs, both local and universal, when at variance with the Canons of the Code, are abolished if the Code explicitly disapproves of them. In so far as they are not rejected by the Code, immemorial customs or those observed for a century may be tolerated if the Ordinaries judge that they cannot prudently be abolished because of the local circumstances and the peculiarities of the people. Customs disapproved explicitly by the Code are to be considered corruptions of law and must be abolished: they can never in future be revived and obtain the force of law. Ordinary customs at variance with the laws of the Code are to be considered suppressed, unless the Code explicitly states otherwise

---

[3] Coronata, ''Jus publicum ecclesiasticum'' (Turin, 1924).
[4] Avrinhac, ''General Legislation of the New Code,'' n. 84.

(**Canon 5**). This is the law in reference to customs before the promulgation of the Code. In Canons 25–30 the laws governing future customs are outlined.

6. In reference to the former Canon Law the Code states that, as a rule, the old discipline is retained though there are some modifications of the old law. The following rules are laid down by the Code:

(1) All laws, both universal and particular, which are opposed to the provisions of the Code are abolished, unless the Code explicitly rules otherwise in reference to some particular laws;

(2) Those Canons which re-state former laws in their entirety must be interpreted in accordance with the old law, and hence the interpretations accepted by approved authors are to be followed in the interpretation of these laws of the Code;

(3) Those Canons which agree only in part with the former law must be interpreted according to the old law in the part in which they agree with the former law; in the parts which differ from the old law, the Canons must be interpreted according to the meaning of the words employed;

(4) In case of doubt whether some provision of the Canons differs from the old law, one must adhere to the old law;

(5) All former ecclesiastical penalties of which no mention is made in the Code are abolished. This rule covers all classes of penalties, spiritual and temporal, corrective (*medicinales*) and punitive (*vindicativæ*), penalties incurred *ipso facto* (*latæ sententiæ*) and incurred after the sentence of the ecclesiastical judge or superior (*ferendæ sententiæ*);

(6) All other disciplinary laws of the old law which were in force until now, and which are neither explicitly nor implicitly contained in the Code, have lost all force of law with the exception of the laws contained in the approved liturgical books and laws derived from the natural and the positive divine law (**Canon 6**).

The student of Canon Law must keep in mind the rules of Canon 6 throughout the whole course of study of the Code, for these rules are the key to the correct interpretation of all the laws of the Code. When the Code states that all disciplinary laws not contained explicitly or implicitly in the Code are abolished, it speaks only of laws which were of universal application in the Church, and does not speak of particular laws (e.g., for a country, diocese, religious organization), for Canon 22 rules that a general law does not abolish particular laws unless the general law explicitly abrogates the particular law. Furthermore, the first rule of Canon 6 already states that particular laws opposed to the laws of the Code are abolished, not other particular laws. Therefore, the great bulk of particular laws remain in force, for generally the particular laws cover matters not covered by the universal law.

Here may be mentioned the declaration of the Sacred Congregation of the Holy Office, March 22, 1918, which ruled that the regulations concerning the oath against Modernism prescribed by Pius X are to remain in force until such time as the Holy See shall otherwise ordain. As the Code made no mention of the laws against Modernism, it was generally believed that the rule of Canon 6 applied, and that these laws were abolished.[5]

7. By the term "Apostolic See" or "Holy See," wherever it occurs in the Code, is meant not only the Roman Pontiff, but also, unless the context proves the contrary, the Sacred Congregations and the Roman Tribunals and Offices through which the Roman Pontiff usually transacts the affairs of the Universal Church (**Canon 7**).[6]

TITLE I

OF ECCLESIASTICAL LAWS

PROMULGATION OF LAWS

8. Laws become effective by their promulgation. Laws are not presumed to be personal but territorial, unless the law indicates that it is a personal law (**Canon 8**).

The promulgation of a law is the official act of the legislator, by which he makes the law known to his subjects. The manner of that promulgation depends on the will of the legislator. He

---

[5] Cfr. App. III, 4, a.
[6] Reorganization of the Roman Curia by Pius X, Constitution "Sapienti Consilio," June 29, 1908; *Acta Ap. Sed.*, I, 7.

must, however, promulgate his laws in such a manner that his subjects can with a reasonable effort acquire a knowledge of the law. Laws are territorial, as the Code states in conformity with the unanimous opinion of commentators on the old Canon Law. By residence in the territory persons become subject to the law. The universal laws of the Church affect the entire world, wherefore the distinction between the territorial and personal effect of law is of little practical value in universal laws. The territorial effect of law is of importance, not only in the particular laws of a diocese or a country, but also in the indults and dispensations granted by the Holy See to a diocese or country by which the universal law is modified. The universal law as modified in a particular place by the Holy See binds the residents of those places, and outsiders share in the indults and dispensations while they are staying in these places.[7]

9. The laws issued by the Holy See are promulgated by being published in the official organ of the Holy See, the *Acta Apostolicæ Sedis,* unless in particular cases another mode of promulgation is prescribed. The laws thus promulgated do not begin to bind in conscience until three months have elapsed after the date of the issue of the periodical containing the law, unless the nature of the law is such that its immediate enforcement is evident, or the law itself explicitly and specially provides for a longer or shorter period of suspension (**Canon 9**).

The publication of the *Acta Apostolicæ Sedis* began in January, 1909, and from the very beginning it was declared the official organ of the Holy See.[8] Prior to the appearance of this publication, the laws and declarations of the Holy See had been published in periodicals which did not bear an official character. Several of the Sacred Congregations have from time to time published their own decrees and declarations in official records usually called *Collectanea* (or Collections).

The provision of Canon 9 obviates to a great extent the former uncertainty about the existence of decrees and declarations of the Sacred Congregations. One difficulty remains, namely, to ascertain whether a given decree or declaration is

---

[7] Cfr. Canons 13 and 14 (see below, n. 12).
[8] The Constitution ''Promulgandi'' of Pius X, Sept. 29, 1908; *Acta Ap. Sedis,* I, 5.

of universal obligation or merely a particular answer which concerns only the diocese or country whence the inquiry was submitted to the Holy See. The mere fact that the decree or answer of the Sacred Congregations appears in the *Acta Apostolicæ Sedis* does not determine its universal character, for it is evident on inspection of the *Acta Apostolicæ Sedis* that many documents which have already appeared therein are entirely particular and do not concern the Church at large. The wording has to be carefully considered to determine whether a certain decree or answer of the Sacred Congregations is universally binding. If it is apparent from the tenor of the answer given to an inquiry that it is an interpretation of a former general decree or order, then, independently of the particular circumstances in the inquiry, the answer is to be understood as of universal application.[9]

The authentic interpretation of the laws of the Code is reserved exclusively to the *Commissio ad Codicis Canones authentice interpretandos*, by *Motu Proprio* of Benedict XV, Sept. 15, 1917.[10]

Laws Are Not Retroactive

10. Laws concern future actions and not acts done before the law was made, unless they make special mention of past actions (**Canon 10**).

Justice demands that the legislator abstain from subjecting persons to punishments for actions which were not against any law before the new law was promulgated. In this sense a retroactive law would be an unpardonable oppression. But the Code itself indicates that the law may have a retroactive effect if the law specially so provides. What retroactive effect is meant? It is certain that the new law cannot punish actions which were legitimate under the old law. In other respects, however, the new law may be retroactive as, for instance, by depriving persons of offices or of other acquired rights legitimately obtained under the former law or by other means. Laws, however, are not to be regarded as retroactive unless

---

[9] On the authority of the Decrees of the Sacred Congregations, cfr. Noldin, ''De principiis theol. mor.,'' I, 161; Wernz, ''Jus decretalium'' (2nd ed.), I, n. 146.

[10] Cfr. App. III, 2.

they explicitly state so. The public welfare demands that the Supreme Authority of the Church has the authority to pass such laws, though it causes hardship to individuals. The civil power proceeds in like manner in its legislation. It is but one of the instances where the rights of the individual have to be sacrificed for the sake of the common welfare.

Invalidating Laws

11. Those laws only are to be considered invalidating or inhabilitating which explicitly or equivalently state that an action is null and void, or that a person is incapacitated from acting (**Canon 11**).

Laws which annul an action for reason of certain formalities and requirements, or which render a person unqualified to act validly for certain specified reasons, are odious because of their severity. Therefore, the Code states that no law should be considered invalidating or inhabilitating unless the wording of the law plainly gives it this effect. From ancient times it has been an axiom of law that many things, though forbidden, are nevertheless valid when done against the law. Invalidity is not to be presumed, but must be clearly proven from the law.

Persons Subject to Ecclesiastical Laws

12. Laws which are purely ecclesiastical in their nature do not bind: (1) unbaptized persons; (2) baptized persons who do not have sufficient use of reason; (3) children under seven years of age, unless the law explicitly rules otherwise (**Canon 12**).

The general laws bind the persons for whom the law was made in any part of the world. Laws which were given for a particular territory, bind those for whom the laws were made and who have their domicile or quasi-domicile in that territory, while they actually stay in that territory (**Canon 13**).

Strangers are not bound by the particular laws of their regular place of residence during their absence from this place, unless their transgression of the law does harm in such place of residence, or unless the laws are personal. Nor are strangers bound by the particular laws of the place where they are actually staying except by the particular laws which concern the safeguarding of public order, or laws which determine the formalities of actions (for instance, in the matter of contracts). Strangers are bound by the general laws, though these laws are not in force in their own homes; but, if a general law is not in force in the strange place, though it is in force in their own homes, they may enjoy the exemption from the law. Persons with no domicile or quasi-domicile anywhere, called *vagi* in law, are bound by both the general and the particular laws in force in the place in which they actually stay (**Canon 14**).

Canon 8 stated that the laws of the Church are to be considered territorial. Canons 13 and 14 are particular applications of that principle to practical cases. Canons 92–95 treat of domicile and quasi-domicile (see below, nn. 69–72). A person becomes subject to the law in a certain place by establishing there his domicile or quasi-domicile, but he is held to the particular laws of his domicile only while he is actually in the place (that is, diocese or country). When a person who has a canonical domicile or quasi-domicile in some place is temporarily absent from that place, he is called a *percgrinus* (stranger or traveler) in the place outside his own diocese or country. The brevity of the time which the stranger stays in the strange place is immaterial; thus, he may cross over the boundary line merely to take a meal. The law does not oblige him to stay in his place of residence, and, if in the neighboring diocese or country some general law of the Church is dispensed with (e.g., a fast, holyday of obligation, etc.), and he wishes to be in that place on such a day, he participates in the indult or dispensation. On the other hand, if a stranger stays in a place where the universal law is observed, while in his own home that law is not in force, he must observe the law in the strange place. Thus, Americans traveling in Europe where there are more holydays of obligation in force than in the United States, must keep those holydays which are mentioned in the Code as days of obligation.

Strangers are generally free from the obligation of particular laws of places through which they travel or where they stay temporarily. The exceptions of the Code as to matters of public order and the formalities of actions are quite logical. Scandal must be avoided by strangers and that may be another reason why, in a particular case, they must conform themselves to some prohibition peculiar to the diocese or country where they are staying. Persons who have no canonical domicile or quasi-domicile are considered residents of the place where they actually stay, and they have the obligations and the privileges of residents as to the observance of laws. They are not exempt from the particular laws of the place where they stay, but they do participate with the residents in the indults and dispensations given to the place.

Force of Doubtful Laws

13. All laws including invalidating and inhabilitating laws lose their binding force in a *dubium juris*. In a *dubium facti* the Ordinary can dispense from the laws, provided there is a question of laws from which the Roman Pontiff usually dispenses (**Canon 15**).

When the existence, meaning, or extent of the obligation of a law is doubtful, it is called a *dubium juris;* when the existence of some circumstance relating to a person, his status, or his actions, or of any other fact under consideration is doubtful, it is called a *dubium facti*. The distinction between the two kinds of doubts often becomes very difficult in its application to concrete cases. Laws are necessarily based on facts, and in some instances it is difficult to determine whether the doubt is caused by the uncertainty of the meaning of the law as applied to the facts, or whether some circumstance or fact of the case is uncertain and causes the doubt. In the *dubium juris,* the facts of the case are clear and undoubted, but it is doubtful whether a certain law applies to the case. In the *dubium facti,* the law is clear, but some facts or circumstances of the case are doubtful.

The majority of moralists maintain that a doubtful law is no law, and has no force to bind in conscience. This is true if the existence, meaning, or scope of the law is in doubt, and the Code admits that a law in a *dubium juris* has no binding force. The moralists also hold that, in a *dubium facti,* the law does not bind, but they limit the exemption to cases where there is question only of the licitness of the act. They exclude cases in which, besides the action, a certain effect of the action has to be obtained or a certain evil has to be avoided. These exceptions they group under three heads: (1) where there is question of the necessary means of salvation; (2) where there is question of the validity of a sacrament, and (3) where the certain right of a third person is involved.

The Code, in Canon 15, indirectly denies the force of the axiom "lex dubia non obligat" in a *dubium facti*, for it grants to the Ordinaries power to dispense from the law, and it limits that power of dispensation to matters in which the Holy See usually dispenses. Some commentators on the Code hold that this ruling of the Code on the *dubium facti* has reference to matters of the external forum, and that in matters affecting the internal forum only we may follow the teaching of moralists, which holds that, with the exceptions enumerated above, a law does not oblige in conscience in a *dubium facti*.[11]

IGNORANCE OF THE LAW

14. No ignorance of invalidating or inhabilitating laws excuses from their observance, unless the law explicitly admits ignorance as an excuse. As a rule, ignorance or error is not presumed when it concerns the law or its penalty, or one's own action, or the notorious action of third persons; concerning the non-notorious action of third persons, ignorance is presumed until the contrary is proved (**Canon 16**).

Canon 16 rules that ignorance does not impede the effect of invalidating or inhabilitating laws. It does not make any difference whether such ignorance was culpable or without fault. The force of these laws is absolute as to their legal effect. The law does not decide whether a person is guilty of sin when violating these laws through ignorance. That is a moral question, and the answer depends on the fact whether or not his ignorance was morally culpable. Ignorance and good faith are immaterial, as far as the effect of invalidating and inhabilitating laws is concerned. The common welfare demands that these laws have absolute effect. Canons 2202 and 2229 speak of ignorance and of the effects of culpable and inculpable ignorance in reference to canonical penalties.

In the external forum everybody is presumed to know the law. Wherefore, Canon 16 states that ignorance of the law or

---

[11] Maroto, "Inst. Juris Can.," I, 242; Vermeersch, "Theol. Moral" (1922), I, 330.

the penalty is not presumed. It must be proved to the ecclesi-astical superior that one's inculpable ignorance was the cause for breaking the law. The law, furthermore, does not permit one to plead ignorance as to facts and actions of one's own, nor as to the notorious facts of third persons. The law pre-sumes knowledge, and he who denies having had such knowledge must prove this lack. The law presumes ignorance of non-notorious facts concerning third persons.

INTERPRETATION OF LAWS

15. Laws are authoritatively interpreted by the law-maker and his successor, and by those to whom the law-maker has committed the power to interpret the laws. The authoritative interpretation of the law given in the form of law has the same force as the law itself. If that interpretation merely declares the meaning of the words of law that were certain in themselves, the interpretation need not be promulgated, and it has retro-active effect. If the interpretation restricts or extends the orig-inal law, or explains a doubtful law, such interpretation does not have retroactive effect, and it must be promulgated to be binding. An interpretation of the law given by way of a judicial sentence, or by a rescript in a particular affair, has no force of law, and it binds those persons only to whom it is given and in the matters affected by the sentence or rescript (**Canon 17**).

Canon 17 speaks of the official interpretation of laws made by the competent authorities. The Committee for the Authentic Interpretation of the Code is the body which has been exclu-sively delegated to interpret officially the laws of the Code.[12] The Code states the various modes of authoritative interpreta-tion of the law and its effect. It is difficult to understand what is meant by an interpretation of "the words of a law certain in themselves," for, if the meaning of the words is certain, there is no need of an interpretation. Very likely that kind of in-terpretation which the canonists call *declaratio* or *interpretatio comprehensiva*, is meant.[13] It is an interpretation in other terms and clearer expressions of the words of a law sufficiently clear in itself. Such declarations are considered embodied in

[12] Motu Proprio of Benedict XV, Sept. 15, 1917; *Acta Ap. Sed.*, IX, 483.
[13] Wernz, "Jus Decretalium" (2nd ed.), I, 145.

the law from the beginning, and therefore need not be specially promulgated to obtain binding force; they have retroactive effect because the law-maker supposes that the meaning of the law was understood from the beginning in the sense in which it is now interpreted. If the official interpretation is a determination of a doubtful meaning of a law, or if the interpretation restricts or extends the law beyond the natural and obvious meaning of the terms of the law, such interpretation, being to all practical purposes a new law, must be promulgated and has not retroactive effect.

Judicial sentences determine the rights between the parties engaged in the litigation, and do not bind non-litigants. Incidentally, such sentences are at times a declaration of a disputed point of law, but they do not oblige other persons not concerned in the lawsuit to follow the interpretation of the law as given in a judicial sentence.

16. The ecclesiastical laws are to be interpreted according to the proper meaning of the terms of the law considered in their context. If the meaning of the terms remains doubtful or obscure, one must have recourse to parallel passages of the Code (if there are any), or to the purpose of the law and its circumstances, and the intention of the legislator (**Canon 18**). This Canon has reference to the private interpretation of the law. The manner of interpretation here indicated by the Code has been followed by canonists generally in the study of law before the Code appeared.

Laws which decree a penalty, or restrict the free exercise of one's rights, or establish an exception from the law, must be interpreted in a strict sense (**Canon 19**). These classes of laws are considered odious and according to the *Regula juris* 15, in the "Liber Sextus": *Odia restringi et favores convenit ampliari*. It may seem strange that a law which contains an exception from the general law is called odious, whereas in fact it may be very acceptable. However, it is a recognized principle of legislation to favor the universal or common law and to discourage exceptions.

If there is no explicit provision concerning some affair either in the general or in the particular law, a norm of action is to be taken from laws given in similar cases, from the general principles of law applied with the equity proper to Canon Law, from the manner and practice of the Roman Curia, and from the common and constant teaching of doctors (**Canon 20**). In the matter of canonical penalties, one may not apply the rule of the similarity of cases, because according to the *Regula juris* 49, in the "Liber Sextus": *In pœnis benignior est interpretatio facienda.*

Laws made for the purpose of safeguarding the public against a common danger bind, even though in a particular case there is no danger (**Canon 21**). The teaching of canonists generally agrees with the teaching of the Code in Canon 21. Thus, for instance, in some mixed marriages there may be no danger to the faith of the Catholic party and the children, and yet this absence of danger is no excuse from the laws concerning mixed marriages.

Abrogation of Laws

17. A more recent law given by the competent authority abolishes a former law, if the new law explicitly says so, or if it is directly contrary to the old law, or if it takes up and readjusts the entire subject matter of the former law. A general law does not abolish laws for particular places or the statutes of inferior legislators, unless the contrary is explicitly stated in the general law, or the particular law is directly contrary to the new general law, as was pointed out in Canon 6, n. 1 (**Canon 22**). The Church is conservative in her legislation. Changes in the universal law of the Church are made by the Holy See only for serious reasons and after mature deliberation. The presumption is in favor of the old law remaining unchanged, unless it is certain that the new law does intend to change the former law. Canon 22 gives the criteria by which we may know that a former law has been changed by a new law. These criteria are not new, but were known and commented on by the canonists of old. The laws of the Code are all to be considered as one law, and there can be no question of anterior and posterior law. If one law of the Code modifies another, the principle, *Jura juribus concordanda,* has to be employed. It is not permissible to interpret one Canon in such a manner as to make another Canon contradict it, or to make it useless or superfluous. In stating that particular laws are not abolished unless they are directly opposed to the laws of the Code, or unless

the Code explicitly abolishes them, this Canon refers to particular laws passed before the promulgation of the Code, for it is evident that, after the promulgation of the Code, no authority inferior to the Holy See can pass a valid law which is contrary to the Code.

In the case of a doubt whether the former law has been revoked, the repeal of the law is not to be presumed, but the more recent laws are to be, as far as possible, reconciled with the former laws so that one may supplement and not contradict the other (**Canon 23**).

Force of Precepts

18. Precepts given to individuals bind them wherever they go, but they cannot be urged in a canonical trial, and they expire with the expiration of the authority of the one who imposed the precepts, unless they were given in the form of a legal document, or before two witnesses (**Canon 24**). There is a difference between laws and precepts. The most obvious difference is that laws, as a rule, directly affect the territory and indirectly the persons resident in the territory, and they bind the persons only while they actually stay in the territory. Precepts are directly attached to the persons subject to the superior, and they bind the persons irrespective of the territory in which they stay. Laws are generally permanent obligations imposed on the public, e.g., the whole Church, a country, a diocese, or an autonomous body like the various religious organizations. Moreover, ecclesiastical jurisdiction in the external forum must be possessed by the person to empower him to make a law. Precepts are issued by superiors for the guidance of individuals primarily, and any superior who has authority over others may issue precepts, though such authority be merely private or domestic. In the case where a superior vested with ecclesiastical jurisdiction in the external forum issues an order to all his his subjects, it may be difficult to determine whether it is a law or a precept. Canonists explain that the temporary character of a precept distinguishes it from a law in such cases.[14]

The provision of the Code for the permanence of precepts after the expiration of the office or authority of the superior is

---

[14] Cfr. any of the leading canonists and moralists on the difference between law and precept.

new in Canon Law. The term "legitimum documentum" is difficult to understand. When is a bishop's letter a "legitimum documentum"? The general formalities as to place, date and signature are so common today that they cannot be a distinguishing mark between legal and non-legal documents. At the same time the law nowhere prescribes any further formalities in issuing a precept of the ordinary kind. In the canonical procedure special kinds of precepts are spoken of (e.g., the summons to appear in court), but these formalities are part of the procedural law, and have no application to Canon 24. It seems that, if the bishop's letter has the ordinary formalities required in all documents (place, date, signature), and if it is plain from the wording of the letter that the bishop means to use his authority to impose a precept on the subject to whom he gives his orders, such a letter can be called a "legitimum documentum" in the sense of Canon 24.

TITLE II

ON CUSTOMS

19. Custom can obtain the force of law in the Church only by the consent of the competent ecclesiastical superior (**Canon 25**).

A community which is capable of receiving a law can introduce a custom which obtains the force of law (**Canon 26**).

No custom can abrogate or modify the Divine law, either positive or natural. In order that a custom may have the power to change an ecclesiastical law, it must be reasonable and lawfully prescribed by a continuous and uninterrupted usage of forty years. Against a law of the Church which contains a clause forbidding contrary customs in the future, only a reasonable custom that is either immemorial or of a hundred years' standing can obtain the force of law. A custom which is explicitly reproved in the law, is not a reasonable custom (**Canon 27**).

A custom outside the law (*præter jus*), which has been knowingly introduced by a community with the intention of binding itself, obtains the force of law if it is reasonable and legitimately prescribed by having been observed for fully forty successive years (**Canon 28**).

Custom is the best interpreter of laws (**Canon 29**). This axiom is taken from the old law, and it is to be understood of customs *secundum jus* (i.e., in harmony with the law). Such customs are the practical applications of the law to the life and activity of the subjects of the Church.

In reference to customs which were in existence before the Code was promulgated, and which are contrary to the laws of the Code, Canon 5 stated that, if these customs are explicitly reproved by the Code, they must be abolished and may never in future be revived. Furthermore, the law of Canon 5 abolishes ordinary customs contrary to the Code. An exception is made in favor of existing immemorial customs and those of a century's standing in so far as they are not explicitly condemned by the Code. These the Ordinaries may allow to continue if their abolition does not seem advisable to them because of special circumstances connected with the place or people.

20. Customs against law and customs outside of law are revoked by contrary custom or by a contrary law. A law contrary to centurial and immemorial customs does not revoke these customs unless the law explicitly mentions these customs. A general law contrary to existing particular customs does not revoke these customs unless the law explicitly says so (**Canon 30**).

Canon 30 lays down the limits within which customs may develop after the promulgation of the Code, and has no application to customs in existence before the promulgation of the Code, for Canon 5 has already ruled on those customs.

Future customs contrary to the Code can be introduced under the limitations of Canon 27. The ordinary universal custom of forty years' standing is considered to have the same force as a common law, and it can be revoked in the same manner as common laws are revoked, namely, by contrary custom or by a contrary law. The immemorial and centurial customs are favored, inasmuch as they are not revoked by a contrary law unless the law explicitly states that they are revoked. A particular custom has the same force as a particular law, and the same rule applies to the revocation of a particular custom as to the repeal of a particular law. Therefore a general law con-

trary to a prior particular custom does not abolish that custom
unless the law explicitly revokes the custom.

21. All canonists and moralists treat of customs in their
commentaries, and, generally speaking, the rules of the Code
on customs are the same as in the former Canon Law. The
length of time required for ordinary customs has been definitely
fixed by the Code. On this point the commentators on the old
Canon Law did not agree. For other points concerning the
law of customs, the commentators on the old law can be read
with profit. It is important to remember that Canon 5 clears
the field as to customs in existence before the promulgation of
the Code, and Canons 25–30 state the law on future customs.
The Church by the institution of Christ is governed by the
hierarchy, not by the will of the majority of the members of
the Church. The subjects of the Church can, therefore, neither
introduce nor abolish a law. The Supreme Authority of the
Church, however, has granted that under certain conditions it
will give its consent to the customs introduced by the people,
and it is by this consent that the customs obtain the force of
law. The conditions under which the Church admits customs
are given in the Code. With the exception of the period of
time necessary for a legal custom, the other conditions of customs and their legal effect are the same as in the old law.

TITLE III

ON THE RECKONING OF TIME

22. Time is to be reckoned according to the following rules,
unless the Canons explicitly decree otherwise. The manner of
reckoning time in the liturgical laws is not changed (**Canon 31**).

A day consists of twenty-four consecutive hours to be
counted from midnight to midnight; a week consists of 7 days;
a month in law means a period of 30 days, and a year a period
of 365 days, unless month and year are said to be taken according to the calendar (**Canon 32**). If the month and year are to
be taken as in the calendar, they differ of course according to
the various months and years (e.g., leap years).

23. In reckoning the hours of the day, the common custom of the place is to be followed, but in the private celebration of Holy Mass, private recitation of the Divine Office, in receiving Holy Communion and in the observance of fast and abstinence, one may deviate from the common custom of the place and follow the local true time, or the mean time, or the legal time, or any of the several other ways of computing time. The time for determining the obligation arising from contracts is to be reckoned according to the rules of the civil law in each country, unless the contracting parties have made a special agreement on this point (**Canon 33**).

If it is twelve o'clock midnight according to the time commonly followed in a place, and according to some other system of marking time it is not yet midnight, one may take advantage of the difference in reference to the obligations spoken of in Canon 33. The introduction of daylight-saving time in many places in the United States during the summer months frequently gives occasion for the application of this Canon of the Code. Odd cases may arise under the concession of Canon 33. May a priest eat meat on a Friday night after midnight of daylight-saving time, because it is Saturday morning, and say part of his office of Friday because, according to Standard time, it is not yet midnight; and, furthermore, may he consider himself fasting from midnight so as to say Holy Mass on Saturday? If the priest eats meat on the assumption that Saturday has begun after midnight, daylight saving time, it seems correct to declare that he cannot say Mass on Saturday. In connexion with the same action or obligation, it would appear utterly inconsistent to consider the same period of time as part of both Saturday and Friday. Consequently, Maroto holds that one may not eat meat on Saturday morning (on the assumption that it is after midnight by daylight saving time) and then go to Holy Communion because it was not yet midnight by standard time. Toso does not admit that one can use the same hour for breaking the Friday abstinence and receive Holy Communion on Saturday. Leitner would allow the priest in the above illustration to eat meat and to say his office, but not to say Holy Mass on Saturday. Vermeersch-Creusen seem to agree with this opinion when they say: *Actiones formaliter diversæ, præcepta distincta, possunt eodem tempore diversis legibus regi*. Blat seems to agree, for he says for various obligations one can follow one **or the other** time.[15]

MEANING OF MONTH AND YEAR

24. If the month and year is designated in law by its own proper name or its equivalent—for example, "in the month of February," "the next following year"—they are to be taken as in the calendar having the precise number of days as the calendar of that year indicates.

If the day on which a certain period of time is to begin (*terminus a quo*) is neither explicitly nor implicitly determined —e.g., suspension from the celebration of Holy Mass for a month or two years, three months' vacation in a year, etc.—the time is to be calculated to the exact minute. If the time is continuous (as in the first example given), the months and years are to be taken as in the calendar. If the period of time is intermittent, a week means 7 days, a month 30 days, and a year 365 days.

If the time consists of one or several months or years, one or several weeks, or several days, and the starting point (*terminus a quo*) is explicitly or implicitly set in law, the following rules obtain:

(1) The months and years are to be taken according to the calendar;

(2) If the starting point coincides with the beginning of the day (e.g., two months' vacation from the fifteenth of August), the first day is to be counted in the number of days and the time expires with the beginning of the last day of the same number. In the given example, the vacation expires at midnight between October 14 and 15;

(3) If the starting point does not coincide with the beginning of the day (e.g., the fourteenth year of age, the year of novitiate, eight days after the vacancy of a bishopric, ten days for appeal, etc.), the first day is not to be counted and the time expires with the end of the last day of the same number; [16]

---

[15] Maroto, "Inst. Juris Can.," I, 281; Toso, "Comm. Minora," I, 104; Leitner, "Handbuch des kath. Kirchenr.," I, 16; Vermeersch-Creusen, "Epitome Jur. Can.," I, 56; Blat, "Comment. Textus Jur. Can.," I, 120.

[16] The Committee for the Authentic Interpretation of the Code declared that the year of novitiate is to be figured by this rule and that it is

(4) If the month in which the term expires has not a corresponding date (e.g., one month from January 30), the term expires either at the beginning or the end of the last day of such month. It expires at the beginning of the last day, if the starting point coincided with the beginning of the day; it expires at the end of the last day, if the starting point did not coincide with the beginning of the day;

(5) In the case of periods appointed for the renewal of acts of the same kind (e.g., the three years' interval between the taking of temporary and of perpetual vows, three years or any other period of time between elections, etc.), the time expires on the same day of the month on which it began, but the new act may take place throughout the entire day (**Canon 34**). The fact that the profession of temporary vows took place (e.g.) at 9 A.M., on August 15, 1920, does not oblige one to delay solemn profession or simple perpetual profession to a later hour, but it may take place at any hour on August 15, 1923.

The term, "tempus utile," means that the time for the exercise or prosecution of one's rights does not lapse if one was ignorant of his rights, or could not act at that time (**Canon 35**). For instance, ten days are granted in law for appeal from the sentence of a lower court or a decree of a superior. Now, if a person is prevented by sickness or other cause from availing himself of this concession of the law, or if he did not know of this privilege, the ten days begin only from the day on which he knew of such rights and was able to avail himself of them. The term, "tempus continuum," means in law a space of time which does not suffer any delay or suspension by reason of one's ignorance or inability to act during that interval.

---

obligatory for validity (Nov. 12, 1922; *Acta Ap. Sedis*, XIV, 661). In periods of eight or ten days one cannot properly speak of the day of the same number, but it is clear that the Code means to say that when the starting point does not coincide with midnight, the first day does not count and that one has eight or ten full days after the first day before the time expires. Concerning zone-time, cfr. App. III, 6.

TITLE IV

ON RESCRIPTS

25. Rescripts of the Holy See as well as of other Ordinaries may be freely petitioned by all who are not explicitly forbidden in law to make such petitions (**Canon 36,** § 1). Favors and dispensations of any kind granted by the Holy See are valid even for those who are under censure with the exception of the persons mentioned in Canons 2265, § 2, 2275, n. 3, and 2283 (**Canon 36,** § 2). An *excommunicatus vitandus,* and a person excommunicated by a condemnatory or declaratory sentence of the ecclesiastical judge, cannot validly receive any favor from the Holy See, unless the papal rescript states that it shall be valid notwithstanding the excommunication of the recipient by the court (cfr. Canon 2265). The same rule applies to those personally interdicted (cfr. Canon 2275), or suspended by sentence of an ecclesiastical court (cfr. Canon 2283). The terms, ''condemnatory'' and ''declaratory'' sentences, recur frequently throughout the Code. In the condemnatory sentence the court itself inflicts the penalty of the law, and for that reason these penalties are called *ferendæ sententiæ* (penalties to be inflicted by sentence of the court). In the declaratory sentence, the law itself has already inflicted the penalty immediately on the breaking of the law, and the court in which the offender is arraigned merely declares that it has found the person guilty, and that therefore he has incurred a certain penalty of the law. These penalties are called *latæ sententiæ* (sentence already pronounced). The law imposing a penalty usually makes it quite plain whether the penalty is incurred immediately on the commission of the offense, or whether the court is ordered to inflict the penalty when the offender is found guilty. Though declaratory and condemnatory sentences of censures and other penalties are usually issued by the ecclesiastical courts, superiors vested with external jurisdiction may (under the rules of Book V) also issue such sentences. A sentence of censure by any legitimate authority disqualifies one for a papal rescript.

26. Rescripts may be obtained for a third person without his consent. Though such a person is free to use or not to use

the favor granted by the rescript, it is nevertheless valid before it is accepted, unless the contrary appears from the clauses added to the rescript (**Canon 37**).

How long may one wait to decide whether one wants to accept the rescript or refuse it? The Code does not give a time limit. Can a rescript asked with the consent of the person in whose favor it is given, be refused when he receives the document? There is no Canon in the Code which obliges a person to accept a privilege or a dispensation granted exclusively in his own favor, but, as Canon 69 remarks, there may be an obligation from some other source. There is a recent illustration of this point in the decision of the Sacred Congregation of the Religious, August 1, 1922. The Sacred Congregation was asked whether a religious, who has asked either for an indult of secularization or a dispensation from simple vows, might refuse to accept the rescript even though the Superior General has already executed the same in accordance with Canon 56. The Sacred Congregation answered that he may refuse, provided the superiors have no grave objections against his change of mind; if they have, and he refuses to accept the rescript, they should refer the case to the Sacred Congregation.[17] It may be further noted that a rescript, which grants a dispensation extending for some length of time, ceases not only by the total failure of the motive reason, but also for the same reasons for which a privilege ceases. Among such reasons is a renunciation accepted by the competent superior, namely the one who issued the rescript or a higher superior.

27. Rescripts by which a favor is granted without requiring the ministry of an executor take effect from the moment at which the letters were issued [i.e., written and signed: the date which the rescript bears is presumed to be the date on which it was signed by the person competent to issue the document]; other rescripts take effect from the time of execution (**Canon 38**). The execution of such rescripts is regulated by Canons 51–59.

28. Conditions demanded in the rescripts are essential for their validity in those cases only where they are expressed by the particles "if," "provided" (*si, dummodo*), or any other particle of the same signification (**Canon 39**). This explicit rule that conditions obliging under pain of nullity in rescripts

17 *Acta Ap. Sedis*, XIV, 501.

are to be expressed by particles denoting a condition is important. Formerly, conditions were often expressed by the Latin
ablative absolute (e.g., *impleta pœnitentia, restitutione facta*),
which might or might not be a necessary condition.

29. All rescripts are considered as given upon the condition,
"provided the petition is truthful" (*si preces veritate nitantur*),
with the exception given in Canons 45 and 1054 (**Canon 40**).

30. In rescripts in which no executor is required, the petition must be true at the time when the rescript is issued; in
others at the time of execution (**Canon 41**). The Code takes
into account the possibility that a change of circumstances in
the interval between the time when the petition was forwarded
to the Holy See and the time of the signing of the rescript
(or the time of its execution), may change the situation of the
petitioner and make his petition untrue.

31. The concealment of truth (which is called in law *sub-
reptio*) does not invalidate the rescript provided those particulars are expressed in the petition which are demanded for validity
by the custom and practice of the Roman Curia (*de Stylo
Curiæ*). Nor is a rescript invalidated by adding reasons which
are not true (*obreptio*, in law), provided the one motive reason
is true, or at least one of the several motive reasons stated in the
petition is true. If the suppression of the truth or the statement
of a falsehood is found in one part only of the petition, this
fault does not invalidate another part of the rescript, if several
favors are granted by one and the same rescript (**Canon 42**).

Note that the Code does not speak of the subjective truthfulness of the reasons advanced in the petition, but rather of
objective truth of facts stated: good faith is immaterial, if in
fact the statement is untrue. Consequently, the rescript is invalid according to the foregoing rules, even though the mis-
statement was made in good faith. In matters of the internal
forum, where the motives for asking a favor from the Holy See
are to a great extent subjective (at least in many cases), good
faith is essentially the same as truth, for the only way of
ascertaining the truthfulness of the petition is the petitioner's
good conscience.

32. If any Roman Congregation or Office has refused a favor
asked of it, the same favor cannot be validly obtained from
another Sacred Congregation or Office or from the bishop of

the diocese (though they have ordinarily the power to grant the favor), unless the Congregation or Office from which the favor was first asked gives its consent. This rule does not deprive the Sacred Penitentiary of its right to grant favors in the internal forum independently of any previous application in the same matter to one of the Sacred Congregations (**Canon 43**).

This law is taken substantially from a decree of Pope Innocent XII, "Ut occurratur," June 4, 1692.

33. A favor which has been refused by one's own Ordinary shall not be asked from another Ordinary without making known the refusal of the first: if the petitioner informs the second Ordinary of the refusal, the latter shall not grant the favor until he has been informed by the first Ordinary of the reasons for the refusal (**Canon 44,** § 1). The Code does not attach the pain of invalidity to the violation of this rule.

A favor, which has been refused by the vicar-general, cannot afterwards be validly obtained from the bishop without mentioning the refusal by the vicar-general; a favor refused by the bishop cannot be validly granted by the vicar-general, even though the refusal by the bishop is mentioned in the petition to the vicar-general (**Canon 44,** § 2). If there are several vicars-general with equal powers in the diocese (as is the case in some dioceses in the United States), it seems that a favor refused by one vicar-general cannot validly be obtained from another vicar-general without mentioning the refusal, because there is the same (if not a stronger) reason for this procedure as in the law making the granting of the favor by the bishop invalid unless refusal by the vicar-general is mentioned.

34. If rescripts in answer to the petition of a person are given with the clause of *Motu proprio,* they are valid even though certain truths (or facts) which should otherwise have been stated are suppressed: they are, however, invalid if the only motive reason or principal cause alleged in the petition is false, the dispensation from impediments of marriage of minor degree (cfr. Canon 1054) being the only exception to this rule (**Canon 45**).

Though a rescript is given in the form of a *Motu proprio,* it is invalid if the person to whom the favor is granted is by the common law made incapable of receiving the favor. Furthermore, rescripts which grant favors contrary to the legitimate custom of some place, or against a particular law, or against the certain rights of a third person, are invalid unless the rescript contains a clause to the effect that, notwithstanding such contrary particular custom, law, or the right of third persons, the grantee may enjoy the favor (**Canon 46**). Canon 36 states, as we have seen, who may or may not obtain rescripts.

35. Rescripts are not rendered invalid by an error in the name of the person to whom or by whom they are issued, nor by a mistake in the place of residence of the petitioner, or an error concerning the subject matter of the rescript, provided that in the judgment of the Ordinary there is no doubt as to the identity of the person or the object of the favor (**Canon 47**).

36. If it happens that two mutually contradictory rescripts have been obtained in one and the same matter, the particular rescript prevails against the general rescript in the points which are specially detailed; if both rescripts are equally particular or general, the rescript issued first in the order of time prevails over the one issued on a later date, unless the second rescript makes mention of the first, or unless the first petitioner has not made use of his rescript either through guile or notable negligence; if both rescripts were issued on the same day, and it is not known which of the two rescripts was issued first, both are invalid and, if the occasion warrants, recourse must be had again to the superior (**Canon 48**).

37. Rescripts must be interpreted according to the proper signification of the words and the common usage of the language, and they may not be extended to other cases besides those expressed (**Canon 49**).

If the meaning of a rescript is doubtful, the following rescripts must be strictly interpreted: (1) rescripts which refer to litigations; (2) those which infringe on the acquired rights of third parties; (3) those which grant to private individuals favors against the law; (4) those which were obtained for the purpose of acquiring an ecclesiastical benefice. All other rescripts may receive a liberal interpretation (**Canon 50**).

EXECUTION OF RESCRIPTS

38. A rescript of the Apostolic See in which no executor is appointed need not be exhibited to the Ordinary of the petitioner unless this is demanded in the document, or there is a

question of public affairs, or it is an affair in which the Ordinary must examine certain conditions (**Canon 51**). Matters of the public forum are controlled by the bishop of the diocese as the one local authority vested with ecclesiastical jurisdiction in that domain. His government of the external affairs of the Church in the diocese is not to be interfered with, unless the law of the Holy See gives such authority to others. The Holy See does not readily grant to private individuals rights and powers in the external forum, and, when they are granted, the Holy See demands that, out of respect for the Ordinary, the rescript be shown to him, even though no clause to that effect appears in the document. The same rule applies to a subject of a religious organization and his superior of the rank of an Ordinary. The clauses of the rescript have to be observed, for they may stipulate (even in the case of a faculty of the internal forum) that the document be exhibited to the Ordinary, or that certain faculties cannot be used except with the consent of the Ordinary.

39. Rescripts which do not specify the time in which they must be presented by the petitioner to the executor, may be presented any time, provided there is no guile or fraud in the delay (**Canon 52**). The executor of a rescript cannot act validly before he has received the rescript, and has established its authenticity and integrity. The only exception to this rule is the case in which the superior who issued the rescript notifies the executor in advance of the contents of the same (**Canon 53**).

40. If in a rescript the mere office of execution is committed to a person (e.g., bishop, confessor, etc.), the execution of the rescript cannot be refused, unless it is evident that the rescript is null and void because of a suppression of facts or a statement of falsehood, or because there are conditions demanded in the rescript which the executor knows have not been complied with, or because, in the judgment of the executor, the recipient of the rescript is so unworthy of the favor that its concession would be a scandal to others. In the last-mentioned circumstance, the executor shall at once inform the superior who has granted the rescript, and meanwhile suspend its execution. If the rescript refers to the executor the granting of the favor, he shall follow his own judgment and conscience in granting or denying it (**Canon 54**).

This Canon distinguishes between two kinds of executors: one has merely ministerial duties, while the other has delegated powers and discretion to make use of them or to refuse to do so. The powers of the first are limited by this Canon; the powers of the second are largely at his discretion. The wording of the rescript must be consulted to decide what powers an executor has. Commentators on the old law speak of *executor necessarius* and *executor voluntarius*. The *executor necessarius* is ordered by the rescript to give the favor to the petitioner, and has no discretion in the matter, unless it is evident that the rescript is null and void or the conditions are not fulfilled, or the recipient is so unworthy of the favor that it would be a scandal to grant it to him (as is stated in the first part of Canon 54). The *executor voluntarius* is delegated to confer the favor, but it is left to his prudent judgment and conscience to grant or refuse the favor.

41. The executor must proceed according to the form of the mandate contained in the rescript, and the execution becomes invalid unless he conforms to the essential conditions expressed in the rescript, and observes the essentials in the manner of procedure (**Canon 55**). The execution of rescripts which deal with matters of the external forum should be done in writing (**Canon 56**). The writing is not demanded under pain of invalidity of the execution.

42. The executor of rescripts may substitute another person for the execution according to his prudent judgment, unless either the rescript or the law forbids such substitution, or the rescript itself determines the person who may be substituted; if, however, the executor has been appointed because of "personal qualifications," he may not entrust to another the execution, but only acts preparatory to the execution (**Canon 57**).

Any rescript may be executed also by the executor's successor in the dignity or office, unless the executor was appointed because of personal qualifications (**Canon 58**).

The Latin term "industria personæ," which we translate "personal qualifications," implies that because of special confidence placed in his ability the Holy See wants the executor to execute the rescript personally. The wording of the particular rescript has to be considered to determine whether the executor was appointed because of personal qualifications.

43. If the executor makes any mistake in the execution of

rescripts, he has the right to repeat the execution. In reference to the tax for the execution, the law of Canon 1507 is to be observed (**Canon 59**).

In that Canon it is stated that the tax for the execution of rescripts of the Holy See can be determined by a Provincial Council or by the bishops in convention, but that such regulation has no force until it has been approved by the Holy See, to which it must be submitted. See Canon 1056 in reference to the prohibition of tax for dispensation of marriage impediments. According to the *Normæ peculiares* for the Sacred Congregations, the tax which the bishop may collect for the execution and other taxes for the rescript are indicated in the rescript itself.

REVOCATION OF RESCRIPTS

44. If a rescript is revoked by a special act of the superior, it is valid until the one who obtained the rescript is notified of the revocation. Rescripts are not revoked by a contrary law, unless the law states otherwise, or unless it has been issued by an authority superior to the one who issued the rescript (**Canon 60**).

45. Rescripts of the Holy See or of an Ordinary are not rendered invalid by a vacancy of the Holy See or of a diocese, except in two cases: (1) if the clauses in the rescript indicate its cessation at the vacancy of the Holy See or the diocese; (2) if the rescript confers on some individual the power to grant a favor to particular persons mentioned in the document, and the one who has such power under the rescript has not yet begun to make use of it when the see becomes vacant (**Canon 61**).

The clause "ad beneplacitum nostrum" is the most common one of those which indicate that the rescript ceases when the grantor goes out of office. If the clause reads "ad beneplacitum Apostolicæ Sedis," or "ad beneplacitum Ordinarii pro tempore," the rescript does not cease when the grantor goes out of office. Usually rescripts of the Holy See in matters of the external forum give power to the Ordinary of the diocese to grant the favor. The death, transfer, etc., of the Ordinary do not affect the rescript, for the power goes to the successor in office. If the Ordinary has not yet begun to act on the powers given him by the rescript and the Holy See becomes vacant, the rescript ceases to exist. If the Ordinary has begun to act on the powers given him by the rescript before the vacancy of the Holy See, though he has not yet come to the final execution of the same, the rescript is not affected by the vacancy.

If a rescript contains, not merely a favor, but a privilege or a dispensation, the Canons of the Code on privileges and dispensations must be observed (**Canon 62**).

TITLE V

ON PRIVILEGES

46. Privileges may be acquired not only by the direct concession of the competent authority and by communication, but also by legitimate custom or by prescription. Possession of a privilege for one hundred years or from time immemorial justifies the presumption that a privilege has been granted (**Canon 63**).

A privilege may be defined "a private law conceding a favor which dispenses the privileged person from obedience to some law or gives him powers beyond those fixed by the ordinary provisions of law." A privilege is called a private law, because as a rule a privilege is perpetual like a law, and moreover a privilege indirectly forbids others to interfere with the rights of the privileged person. The term "private law" given by commentators in the definition of a privilege is not very correct (at least in the case of the privileges of individuals), for the idea of a law supposes a society or community to which a law is given.

47. Before we speak of the acquisition of privileges by communication, three more Canons must be considered. **Canon 64** states: In the communication of privileges, even *in forma æque principali,* those privileges only are considered communicated which have been conceded to the primarily privileged person directly and perpetually and without special relation to a certain place, object, or person. Moreover, the capacity of the person to whom the communication is granted has to be considered.

Canon 65 states: Privileges acquired by communication *in forma accessoria,* are increased, diminished, or lost *ipso facto,* if the privileges of the principally privileged person are increased, diminished, or lost; but privileges communicated *in forma æque principali,* are not affected by the increase, diminution or cessation of the privileges of the primarily privileged person. Canon 613 rules: Any religious organization has such privileges only as are contained in the Code, or have been granted to them directly by the Holy See, all communication of privileges being forbidden in future.

The laws of the Code on the communication of privileges repeat the old Canon Law in most of its provisions. The rule forbidding the future communication of privileges between religious organizations is new. The distinction between communication *in forma accessoria* and *in forma æque principali* is taken from the former law, and so are the different effects attributed to the two kinds of participation in privileges granted to another person. The communication in the accessory form gives to the participant the privileges of the first grantee in such a manner that those privileges suffer the same fate as the privileges of the first grantee. The communication which declares the participant a principal grantee equally with the person who first received the favor, makes the participant independent of the first grantee in the enjoyment of the privileges. There can be no communication of privileges granted to special places (e.g., a celebrated shrine), to special objects (e.g., relic of a saint in a certain place), or for personal reasons (e.g., exceptional services rendered to the Church).

48. The commentators on the Code are divided in their interpretation of Canon 613, which deals with the communication of privileges between religious organizations. Canon 4 states that the privileges granted by the Holy See to individuals or to organizations which were in force before the promulgation of the Code, remain unless they are explicitly revoked by the Code. One can only with difficulty construe Canon 613 as an explicit revocation, wherefore it should not be thus interpreted.[18]

---

[18] Cfr. Vermeersch-Creusen, ''Epit. jur. can.,'' I, 304, for a summary of the opinions on both sides.

FACULTIES

49. The habitual faculties which are granted either perpetually, or for a definite period of time, or for a certain number of cases, are considered privileges *præter jus* (**Canon 66, § 1**). Unless they contain a direct statement to the contrary, or were given to the bishop on account of personal qualifications, the habitual faculties granted by the Apostolic See to the Ordinaries and to others mentioned in Canon 198, do not lapse with the vacation of the See by the Ordinary to whom they were given (even though he had begun to make use of the faculties), but are transmitted to the succeeding Ordinary; moreover, the faculties granted to the bishop are also granted to the vicar-general (**Canon 66, § 2**).[18a] Faculties granted by the Holy See include also such other powers as are necessary for their exercise; wherefore, the faculty to dispense includes the power to absolve from ecclesiastical penalties if such happen to prevent the granting of the dispensation. This absolution, however, has no other effect than to take away the incapacity to receive the dispensation (**Canon 66, § 3**). The faculty to dispense in one certain case differs from the habitual faculties, and must, according to Canon 85, be strictly interpreted.

INTERPRETATION OF PRIVILEGES

50. The extent of a privilege must be judged from the wording of the document, and its scope must not be extended or abridged (**Canon 67**).

If there remains a doubt as to the meaning of certain terms, the rule of Canon 50 is to be followed—namely, those concessions which contain a mere favor are to receive a liberal interpretation, but privileges which infringe on the rights of third parties, or refer to ecclesiastical trials, or grant an exemption from the law in favor of private individuals, or deal with the acquisition of a benefice, must be strictly interpreted: in no case should the interpretation be so rigorous that the privilege confers no benefit, for some benefit must accrue from the privilege (**Canon 68**).

51. Nobody is obliged to make use of a privilege which has been conceded him for his own private benefit, unless the obli-

[18a] Concerning delegation of faculties, cfr. App. III, 11.

gation to exercise it comes from some other source (**Canon 69**). The *Regula Juris* 61, in the "Liber Sextus," states that what has been conceded in one's favor should not be turned into a burden. Wherefore, authors generally hold that one is not bound to make use of a privilege to fulfill some other ecclesiastical law which could not under the circumstances be observed except by the use of the privilege. When, therefore, the Code states that one may be held to use the privilege, if the obligation arises from some other source, we must infer that source to be either the natural or the Divine positive law, for it would be a strange kind of a privilege that bound one to observe an ecclesiastical law from which one would be otherwise excused. Thus, the privilege to anticipate Matins and Lauds on the previous day does not oblige the priest to anticipate even though he knows that he will not be able to say the office on the next day, or will have so much work as to excuse him from the obligation.

CESSATION OF PRIVILEGES

52. A privilege is to be considered perpetual, unless the contrary is certain (**Canon 70**). Thus, a privilege granting faculties for a certain number of cases, ceases of its very nature when the number of cases has been exhausted.

Privileges contained in the Code are revoked by a general contrary law; otherwise, the law of Canon 60 is to be observed which rules that privileges are not revoked by a contrary law unless the law explicitly states their revocation, or the law is passed by a legislator superior to the one who granted the privilege (**Canon 71**).

53. Privileges are terminated by renunciation after such renunciation has been accepted by the competent superior (**Canon 72**). The competent superior is the person who had the power to grant the privilege, or a higher superior. Any private individual can renounce those privileges which have been conceded in his own personal favor. A privilege which has been granted to some community, dignity or place, may not be renounced by a private individual. Even the community or body is not at liberty to renounce a privilege which was given in the form of law (e.g., the privileges contained in

the Code), nor can it renounce a privilege if such renunciation would be prejudicial to the Church or to other persons.

54. If the ecclesiastical superior who granted the privilege goes out of office, privileges conceded by him do not cease unless granted under the clause *ad beneplacitum nostrum,* or an equivalent phrase (**Canon 73**).

55. Personal privileges follow the person, and may be exercised wherever the person goes; they become extinct with the death of the person (**Canon 74**).

Real privileges which adhere to an object or place, lapse with its complete destruction. If the place (e.g., a church or monastery) is rebuilt in the same or about the same location (cfr. Canon 924) within fifty years, the privileges revive (**Canon 75**). The Code distinguishes between privileges adhering to objects and those adhering to places. Places may be rebuilt, and therefore provision is made for the revival of the privileges granted to a place. If the privileges adhere to an object (e.g., a miraculous image), they perish with the object when it is totally destroyed.

56. Privileges are not lost by non-use or by usage contrary to a privilege, if they are not burdensome to others; privileges which are a burden to others cease by non-use or contrary usage, if there is a legitimate prescription against them, or if the non-use is a tacit renunciation (**Canon 76**).

57. Privileges also cease if in the course of time circumstances change in such a way that, in the judgment of the superior, they have become injurious, or their use is illicit. If the privileges were granted for a definite period of time, or for a definite number of cases, they become extinct with the expiration of the period of time or the exhaustion of the number of cases (**Canon 77**). In matters of the internal forum, however, Canon 207 provides that if by inadvertence the priest has not noticed that the time of his faculties has expired, or that he has used the faculties to the limit of the number of cases, his action on the supposed faculties shall nevertheless be valid.

If a person abuses the power granted to him by a privilege, he deserves to be deprived of the privilege, and the Ordinary should not fail to notify the Holy See of the grave abuse of a privilege which it has conceded (**Canon 78**).

Though privileges which have been orally granted by the Holy See to some person may be made use of in the forum of conscience, no one may cite such a privilege in the external forum against anyone, unless he can furnish legal proof that he has received that privilege (**Canon 79**).

TITLE VI

OF DISPENSATIONS

NATURE OF DISPENSATIONS

58. A dispensation is a relaxation of the law in a particular case: it can be granted by the legislator, by his successor in office, by a superior legislator and by a person delegated by the foregoing (**Canon 80**).

Ordinaries other than the Roman Pontiff cannot dispense from the general laws of the Church, even in a particular case, unless (1) this power has been conceded to them explicitly, or (2) recourse to the Holy See is difficult, while there is danger of grave harm in delay, and the case is one in which the Holy See usually dispenses (**Canon 81**).

59. Bishops and other local Ordinaries can dispense from diocesan laws, from the laws of Provincial and Plenary Councils, according to the rule of Canon 291; but they cannot dispense from laws which the Roman Pontiff has specially passed for a particular territory, except in the case indicated in Canon 81 (**Canon 82**). Canon 291 states that the laws of a Provincial or Plenary Council, after the approval of the Holy See and promulgation of those laws, bind the respective territory, and that the local Ordinary can dispense from them only in particular cases and for a just cause.

60. Pastors cannot dispense either from a general law of the Church or from the particular laws of a diocese or country, unless this power has been expressly conceded to them (**Canon 83**). By custom introduced from time immemorial and confirmed by Canon 1245, pastors can dispense individual parishioners or families from the fast and abstinence and from the laws forbidding servile work on Sundays and holydays of obligation.

DISPENSATIONS NOT TO BE GRANTED WITHOUT A GOOD REASON

61. No dispensation from an ecclesiastical law should be granted without a just and reasonable cause, which should be in due proportion to the gravity of the law from which dispensation is given: otherwise a dispensation granted by an inferior is both illicit and invalid. When it is doubtful whether the reason for a dispensation is sufficient, one may licitly ask for the dispensation, and the superior may validly and licitly grant the same (**Canon 84**).

62. Dispensations must be strictly interpreted as stated in Canon 50, as also must the faculty to dispense in a certain case (**Canon 85**).

63. Dispensations which have a recurrent application cease not only for the same reasons as a privilege, but also with the total cessation of the motive cause or reason for which they were granted (**Canon 86**). This Canon refers to dispensations which are virtually multiple—e.g., dispensations from the recitation of the Divine Office, from fast or abstinence, etc. In other cases—e.g., dispensations from marriage impediments, vows, etc.—the dispensation is granted once, and by it the status of the person is changed. It suffices in these dispensations that the reason for which they were granted existed at the time when the dispensation was granted. Canon 38 determines the moment when a dispensation is granted, namely: in dispensations which are granted directly to the petitioner without the intervention of an executor, the dispensation is granted at the moment when the document granting it was issued (usually the date which it bears); dispensations which are granted through the intervention of an executor take effect from the moment of execution.

The rules of the Code on the interpretation of dispensations are practically the same as in the old law. Therefore, the commentators on the old law may be consulted upon this subject in the many practical cases which are liable to arise in the matter of dispensations.

THE SECOND BOOK
LAWS CONCERNING PERSONS

64. By baptism a person becomes a subject of the Church of Christ with all the rights and duties of a Christian, unless, in so far as rights are concerned, there is some obstacle impeding the bond of communion with the Church, or a censure inflicted by the Church (**Canon 87**).

The Code simply states that all baptized persons are subject to the laws of the Church. There is but one baptism and one Church authorized by Christ. Consequently, all validly baptized persons are in principle subject to the Church. It does not depend on the person who administers baptism to determine whether or not the baptized person shall be a subject of the Church; wherefore, persons baptized outside the Church become subjects of the Church by baptism. Among Catholic authors there can be no controversy on the question whether baptized non-Catholics are in principle subject to the Church. Some authors, however, have maintained that the Church does not intend to bind non-Catholic baptized persons by those laws which are intended primarily for the sanctification of the individual. The Church has never exempted them from her laws in a general way; where she wants to grant an exemption, she states it plainly—for instance, in the law on the form of marriage and in the impediment of disparity of cult.

65. The question has also been discussed by commentators on the law whether persons whose baptism is of probable validity are to be considered subjects of the Church. This doubt may arise in two forms: whether the persons were baptized at all, and whether a certain ceremony of baptism which was administered is valid. If the fact of baptism is not certain, no obligation can arise. If the fact of baptism is certain and only the validity of its administration is in doubt, the validity must be presumed unless there are reasons which contradict this pre-

sumption. With the great disregard of the necessity of baptism in many non-Catholic denominations, the presumption that baptism was validly administered is very much weakened. In reference to marriage, Canon 1070 rules that, if at the time of contracting marriage one of the parties was generally considered baptized, or if his baptism was doubtful, the validity of the marriage must be upheld until it is proved with certainty that one party was baptized and the other was not.

CLASSIFICATION OF PERSONS BY AGE

66. A person who has completed his twenty-first year, is called a major; under twenty-one, he is called a minor. A boy is regarded as having reached the age of puberty when he completes his fourteenth year; a girl when she completes her twelfth. A child who is under the age of seven years (called *infans, puer, parvulus*), is not considered responsible for his actions. When fully seven years of age, the law presumes that the child has attained the use of reason. Persons habitually devoid of the use of reason are regarded by the law as equivalent to infants (**Canon 88**).

A person of major age is entitled to the full exercise of his rights; minors remain subject to their parents or guardians in the exercise of their rights, except in matters in which the law holds them exempt from the paternal power (**Canon 89**). The exemption from the paternal power refers mostly to matters touching the salvation of their own souls (e.g., reception of the sacraments, vocation for the priesthood or for the religious life).

CLASSIFICATION OF PERSONS, PLACE AND DOMICILE

67. By a child's place of origin, is meant that place where the father had a domicile or (failing a domicile) a quasi-domicile at the time of the birth of the child. This rule also applies to a convert. In the case of illegitimate or posthumous children, the domicile or quasi-domicile of the mother determines the place of origin. If the parents have neither domicile nor quasi-domicile, the child's place of origin is where it was actually born. A foundling's place of origin is where it was found (**Canon 90**).

The place of origin, or *locus originis* in Latin, is of importance especially in candidates for the priesthood. In most of the provisions in Canon 90 the Code repeats the former law. There are a few changes: first, under the old law the place of origin of children whose parents had no domicile or quasi-domicile at the time of the birth of a child was considered to be the same as the place of origin of the father. Second, in reference to converts, some canonists held that the place of baptism might be considered as their place of origin.

If a father has two domiciles at the time of the birth of a child, it seems that both places may equally be considered as the place of origin. If the father has deserted his wife and has no domicile or quasi-domicile, and the wife has obtained from the Ordinary a decree of separation, the child born under these circumstances probably can claim the domicile or quasi-domicile of the mother as his place of origin: for a wife who is legitimately separated from her husband by authority of the bishop can have a domicile of her own (Canon 93), and as a rule the innocent party has the custody of the children (cfr. Canon 1132).[1] As to foundlings, writers discuss the question whether a foundling's domicile is changed into that of his parent, if the parent later on claims the child as his own. Probably that is the case, because the fiction of law gives way to the reality, or rather he ceases to be a foundling.[2]

68. A person is called an *incola* in the place where he has a domicile; an *advena* in the place where he has a quasi-domicile; a *peregrinus*, while he is actually outside the place of his domicile or his quasi-domicile; a *vagus*, if he has nowhere a domicile or quasi-domicile (**Canon 91**).

69. A domicile is acquired by residence in any parish or quasi-parish (or at least in a diocese, vicariate apostolic or prefecture apostolic). This residence must either be associated with the intention to stay there permanently, unless something calls one away, or must extend over ten complete years. A quasi-domicile is acquired by residence in a parish, or a diocese, with the intention to stay there for the greater part

---

[1] The Committee for the Authentic Interpretation of the Code declared that a woman deserted by her husband cannot acquire a domicile of her own without authorization from the local Ordinary (July 14, 1922; *Acta Ap. Sed.*, XIV, 526.

[2] Vermeersch-Creusen, "Epit. jur. can.," I, 84, n. 164.

of the year unless something calls one away, or by having actually lived there for the greater part of the year. The domicile or quasi-domicile in a parish or quasi-parish is called parochial; residence in a diocese, vicariate or prefecture (though not in the same parish or quasi-parish), constitutes a diocesan domicile or quasi-domicile (**Canon 92**).

There is no doubt that a person acquires a domicile in a new place from the moment he arrives in the new place with the intention to stay there permanently. According to the common teaching of canonists, the intention must be unconditional to stay permanently or indefinitely in the place. Unforeseen circumstances, or causes which may make one change one's mind later on, are not conditions in the strict sense of the term. Temporary absence, whether for reasons foreseen or unforeseen, does not invalidate the intention to stay permanently. The intention must be manifested in some external way to be considered in the external forum. The explicit declaration to others of the intention to stay permanently is one way. Circumstances which show such intention without any explicit declaration may also prove the intention. Can a seminarian who is of age, and who wants to establish his domicile in the diocese of the bishop who has adopted him, do so by going to the diocese and there expressing his intention to stay permanently, and thus acquire a domicile so that the bishop becomes authorized, under Canon 956, to ordain him? Some writers on Canon Law hesitate to admit this manner of acquiring a domicile because the intention is conditional—viz, "if I shall be ordained." A conditional intention is not sufficient, as we stated above. However, is that intention *de facto* conditional? Assuming the previous agreement of the bishop to accept him for his diocese, it is no more conditional than any other intention in which there is always a possibility of circumstances arising which may make one change his mind. To all appearances, his ordination is certain, and therefore his intention cannot be called conditional.

70. A wife necessarily shares the domicile of her husband, unless she is legitimately separated from him; an insane person shares that of his guardian; a minor that of his parents or guardian. After the years of infancy, a minor can acquire a quasi-domicile of his own; likewise, a wife not legitimately sepa-

rated from her husband can acquire a quasi-domicile, and a legitimately separated wife can also acquire a domicile of her own (**Canon 93**).

It was not clear what was meant by ''legitimately separated,'' for Canon 1131 states that a husband or wife may for reasons assigned in that Canon separate privately without the intervention of the local Ordinary, if the case is urgent. Wherefore, some canonists held that a woman who lived separately for a canonical reason but without authorization from the local Ordinary, could acquire a domicile of her own. On being asked whether a wife deserted by her husband can obtain a domicile of her own, the Committee for the Authentic Interpretation of the Code answered: No, unless she has obtained from the ecclesiastical judge a perpetual separation or a separation for an indefinite length of time.[3]

71. Through domicile, or quasi-domicile, each of the faithful acquires his proper pastor and Ordinary. The proper pastor or Ordinary of the *vagi* is the pastor or Ordinary of the place where the *vagi* actually stay. Persons who have only a diocesan domicile or quasi-domicile, have for their proper pastor the pastor of the parish in which they actually stay (**Canon 94**).

72. Domicile and quasi-domicile are lost by the act of leaving the place with the intention of not returning, except in the cases mentioned in Canon 93 (**Canon 95**).

Thus, the necessary domiciles of minors and married women are not lost by leaving the place with the intention of not returning; the law provides that domicile, and it cannot be given up by the will of the minor during minority or a married woman. Canonists generally hold that one may have two canonical domiciles by living half the year continually in one place, and half the year in another. Some canonists hold that a person can have more than two domiciles if he lives annually for part of the year in each of several homes. Two quasi-domiciles are possible with minors and married women, who can have a quasi-domicile of their own and share also the domicile or quasi-domicile of parent or husband. Whether other persons can have two quasi-domiciles at the same time is controverted by canonists; some hold that one having acquired a quasi-domicile in one place, may leave that place intending to

[3] Cfr. App. III, 7.

return, and, if he stays for the greater part of the year in the other place, he acquires there a quasi-domicile, while the other was not lost because he intends to return. Other canonists maintain that the fact of his stay for the greater part of the year in the new place shows his intention not to return to the first quasi-domicile.[4]

CLASSIFICATION OF PERSONS BY BLOOD AND AFFINITY

73. Consanguinity is traced by lines of descent and degrees. In the direct line there are as many degrees as there are generations, or as many degrees as there are persons, not counting the *stipes* or ancestral head. In the collateral lines there are as many degrees as there are generations in one line, if the distance from the common parent or ancestor is equal; if the distance is not equal, there are as many degrees as there are generations in the longer line (**Canon 96**).

The Code repeats the former Canon Law on consanguinity, and any of the old commentators may be consulted on this subject. The only difference of the law on blood relationship between the Code and the old law is the manner of counting multiple consanguinity. The old law on that point was quite complicated. The Code in Canon 1076 simplifies the method by the rule that consanguinity is multiplied only when the common stock from which two persons descend is multiplied. This matter and the reduction of the impediment of consanguinity from the fourth to the third degree are discussed in the study of the marriage impediments.

74. Affinity arises from valid marriage, either consummated or unconsummated. Affinity exists only between the husband and the blood relations of the wife, and the wife and the blood relations of her husband. The degrees of affinity are counted in the same way as the degrees of consanguinity, so that the blood relations of the husband become the relations by marriage (*affines*) of the wife in the same line and degree as they are towards the husband, and *vice versa* (**Canon 97**).

The Code changes the law of affinity in the important point that it makes the basis of the affinity a valid marriage, not the

---

4 Maroto, "Inst. juris can.," I, 478, n. 413; Vermeersch-Creusen, "Epit. Iur. can.," I, 87, n. 167.

copula carnalis as in the old law. It follows that the affinity arising from illicit intercourse is abolished by the Code, and it further follows that the affinity is contracted immediately on the conclusion of a valid marriage, not only on the consummation of the marriage. Furthermore, the term *matrimonium ratum* means a marriage between two baptized people; wherefore, only such marriages produce the affinity, according to some writers.[5] We doubt whether the term "ratum" is used in Canon 97 in its technical meaning, for the position of the word in the Canon seems rather to indicate that it is employed merely to indicate non-consummation of the marriage. There are a few authors who take the term "ratum" merely in the sense of "non consummatum," and interpret the Canon to the effect that affinity arises from every valid marriage whether consummated or unconsummated (Noldin, "Theol. moral.," III, n. 598; Chelodi, "Jus matrim.," n. 99). Canon 1077 deals with affinity as an impediment of marriage.

CLASSIFICATION OF PERSONS ACCORDING TO THE VARIOUS RITES

75. A person belongs to that Rite by the ceremonies of which he was baptized, unless (1) the baptism was administered by a priest of another Rite, who had no right to baptize but did so fraudulently, or who baptized in a case of necessity where no priest of the proper Rite could be secured; or (2) by apostolic indult a person obtained permission to be baptized with the ceremonies of a certain Rite without the obligation of adhering to that Rite.

The clergy shall not presume to induce either Catholics of the Latin Rite to join an Oriental Rite, or Catholics of an Oriental Rite to join the Latin Rite. Nobody is allowed without permission from the Apostolic See to go over to another Rite or, after a legal transfer, to return to his former Rite.

The wife who belongs to a Rite different from her husband's may, at the time of marriage or any time during the marriage, join the Rite of her husband. When the marriage is dissolved, she is free to return to her own Rite, unless particular laws rule otherwise.

The custom, no matter of what duration it may be, of re-

[5] Vermeersch-Creusen, "Epit. jur. can.," I, 90, n. 173.

ceiving Holy Communion in another Rite does not entail a change of Rite (**Canon 98**).

Canon 756 contains further rules in reference to baptism, namely: the child is to be baptized in the Rite of its parents; if father and mother belong to different Rites, the child is to be baptized in the Rite of the father, unless particular laws rule otherwise; if one of the parents is a non-Catholic, the child is to be baptized in the Rite of the Catholic party.[6]

LEGAL OR MORAL PERSONS

76. Besides physical persons, there are also in the Catholic Church the so-called moral or legal persons instituted by the public authority of the Church: these artificial or legal persons are distinguished into *collegiate* and *non-collegiate* bodies—e.g., churches, seminaries, benefices, etc. (**Canon 99**).

The Catholic Church and the Apostolic See have the nature of a legal person by Divine ordinance. The other inferior legal persons get their personality either by the law itself, or by a special concession of the competent ecclesiastical superior through a formal decree, for the purpose of religion or charity. To constitute a collegiate moral person, there must be at least three physical persons or individuals. The legal or moral persons, both collegiate and non-collegiate, are regarded as equivalent to minors under the law (**Canon 100**).

The civil laws of the various States of the United States provide corporation laws by which legal persons or bodies are created, and their rights and duties defined. Since there is no official recognition of any church in the United States, the dioceses, parishes, and other institutes of the Church, must protect their rights by availing themselves of the right to incorporate. Generally speaking, little difficulty has been experienced in this matter, and the Church in the United States has been able to develop a marvelous activity in the short history of our country as is evidenced by the thousands of

---

[6] Litteræ Apost. "Ea Semper" of Pius X, June 14, 1907, by which the Ruthenian Rite was established in the United States; *Acta S. Sedis*, XLI, 3. Decree of the Sacred Congregation of the Propaganda on the spiritual administration of the Greek Ruthenian Church in the U. S., August 17, 1914; *Acta Ap. Sedis*, VI, 458.

churches, monasteries, convents, schools, hospitals, and all other kinds of charitable institutions.

77. The actions of collegiate legal bodies in the Church are subject to the following rules:

(1) Unless the common law or particular statutes explicitly prescribe a different course of action, that which has been voted for by the absolute majority of those who vote (not counting invalid votes), shall have force in law. [A vote may be invalid for various reasons given in law—e.g., the incapacity of the voter (cfr. Canon 167), voting for a person who is incapacitated for the office (cfr. Canon 170), or if a vote be blank, or not sufficiently explicit, etc.] If no absolute majority be obtained on the first ballot, a second is taken. If no absolute majority be obtained in the second, the relative majority decides in the third ballot. If there is no relative majority because the votes are equally divided in the third ballot, the president of the voters shall by his vote destroy the tie vote and thus decide the issue; if there is question of elections and the president does not want to destroy the tie by his vote, the person who is the senior in ordination, in the profession of the first vows after the novitiate, or in age, is to be considered elected.

(2) Matters which concern all as individuals, must be approved by all (**Canon 101,** § 1). This rule is taken from the *Regula Juris* 29, in the "Liber Sextus." In every community the individual has to sacrifice certain rights and assume certain obligations for the benefit of the entire body. Nevertheless, there remain to the individual other rights of which he may not be deprived even by the vote of the majority. There is an illustration of this principle in Canon 172 dealing with election by compromise. The right of the individual voter to his vote cannot be taken from him by a majority of the voters who vote in favor of the compromise; only unanimous consent can make a compromise legal.

78. If there is question of the actions of non-collegiate legal persons, the particular statutes and the rules of the common law regarding such persons are to be followed (**Canon 101,** § 2).

79. A legal person is of its very nature perpetual. However, it becomes extinct on suppression by the legitimate authority, or by having ceased to exist for a space of one hundred years. If at least one individual of a collegiate legal person

remains, the rights of all the others devolve on such survivor (**Canon 102**).

80. Actions which are done by either a physical or a moral person through extrinsic compulsion that could not be resisted, are considered as though they were not done. Actions based on great fear unjustly created or on deceit, are valid unless the law rules otherwise. They can, however, be declared null and void by the ecclesiastical judge, according to Canons 1684–1689, at the instance of the injured party, or even without such petition (**Canon 103**).

Error annuls an action, when the error concerns the substance of the action, or amounts to a *conditio sine quâ non*—that is to say, if the action would not have been done except for the error; otherwise the action is valid, unless the law states the contrary. In contracts, however, error may give the person contracting under such error the right to an action in court for the rescinding of the contract (**Canon 104**). The rules concerning actions done through physical compulsion or violence, moral force or fear, deceit or error, are all taken from long-standing rules of Canon Law and moral theology, and the commentaries of approved theologians and canonists may be consulted for a further study of these interferences with the free will and deliberation of human actions.

Legal Persons Acting through the Superior

81. Whenever the law requires the Superior to seek the consent or counsel of some persons before acting, the following rules obtain:

(1) If consent is required, any action taken by the Superior contrary to the vote of these persons is invalid. If consultation only is demanded (by words like *de consilio consultorum, audito capitulo, parocho,* etc.), it suffices for the validity of the action if the superior consults the persons specified. Though he is not obliged to follow their vote (even if unanimous), he should have great regard for a unanimous vote where several persons had to be consulted, and he should not without very good reason—of which he is the judge—act contrary to their counsel;

(2) If the consent or the consultation of several persons is required (not of one or other only), these persons must be

legitimately convoked, and thus assembled express their minds; the failure to convoke them, however, does not matter if those not notified were nevertheless present (cfr. Canon 162). The Superior may, if he thinks the matter of sufficient importance, oblige the councillors to take the oath of secrecy concerning the affair;

(3) All persons whose consent or counsel is required, must respectfully, truthfully and sincerely state their opinion on the matter (**Canon 105**).

PRECEDENCE AMONG THE VARIOUS PHYSICAL AND LEGAL PERSONS

82. In reference to the precedence between various physical or legal persons, the following rules are to be observed, subject to the special regulations which are given in various places of the Code:

(1) He who represents another person, takes precedence according to the rank of the person whom he represents. However, persons who are present as proxies in Councils and other similar meetings, take their places after the persons present in their own right and of the same rank as the principal of the proxy: thus, the proxy for a bishop takes his place after all the bishops who attend in person; a proxy for an archbishop takes his place after all the archbishops;

(2) He who has authority over either physical or legal persons, has the right of precedence over such persons;

(3) Between various ecclesiastical persons, none of whom have any authority over the others, the following rules obtain: Persons who belong to a higher rank precede those of an inferior rank. Persons of the same rank but of a different order, have precedence according to higher or inferior order. [The rank has reference to the hierarchical degrees of jurisdiction, the order means the same as ordination in the various degrees of the hierarchy of orders.] If several persons stand in the same degree of rank and orders, they precede in the order of time in which they were elevated to the rank; if they were promoted to the rank at the same time, seniority in the reception of the orders determines precedence, unless the junior was ordained by the Roman Pontiff; if they are equal in rank and in

time of promotion to orders, seniority of age determines the precedence; [6a]

(4) In the matter of precedence the diversity of Rites is not considered;

(5) Among various legal persons of the same kind and degree, that person precedes who is in undisputed quasi-possession of precedence. If there is no certainty about the right of quasi-possession, that person precedes which was first instituted in the place where the question arises. Among the members of the same college or body of men, the right of precedence is determined by their own legitimate constitutions or otherwise by legitimate custom; if there is no such custom, the rules of the common law decide the precedence;

(6) The local Ordinary has authority in his diocese to decide questions of precedence among his subjects with due regard to the principles of the common law, the legitimate customs of the diocese, and the offices committed to them. In more urgent cases the Ordinary has the right to decide all questions of precedence, even among exempt persons whenever they appear in a body with others. No appeal suspending the decision of the Ordinary is allowed in law, but any person whose rights are affected by such a decision retains the right of recourse;

(7) The precedence of persons attached to the papal household is regulated by the special privileges, rules and traditions of the papal palace (**Canon 106**).

DISTINCTION BETWEEN CLERGY AND LAITY

83. By divine ordinance the clergy are distinct from the laity in the Church, though not all of the orders of the clergy are of divine institution. Both clerics and laymen may be Religious (**Canon 107**).

[6a] Concerning precedence among suffragan bishops, cfr. App. III, 8.

PART ONE

LAWS CONCERNING THE CLERGY

SECTION I

OF THE CLERGY IN GENERAL

84. Those who have been assigned to the Divine ministry at least by the first tonsure, are called clerics.   They are not all of the same grade, for they form a sacred hierarchy in which some are subordinate to others. By divine institution, the sacred hierarchy of orders consists of bishops, priests and ministers; the hierarchy of jurisdiction consists of the Supreme Pontificate and the subordinate episcopate. By institution of the Church other degrees have been added (**Canon 108**).

The Code repeats the dogmatical teaching of the Council of Trent on the hierarchy of orders and of jurisdiction. It leaves unsettled the question as to what is meant by the ''ministers'' in the above enumeration of bishops, priests and ministers. The common teaching of theologians is that the deacons only are meant by the term ''ministers,'' and that the subdeacons are not included.

85. Persons who are received into the ecclesiastical hierarchy, are not accepted by the consent or at the call of the people or of the secular power, but are constituted in the degrees of the power of orders by sacred ordination. In the Supreme Pontificate, the person legitimately elected and freely accepting the election receives jurisdiction by the divine law itself; in all other degrees of jurisdiction by canonical appointment (**Canon 109**).

86. Though the Holy See gives some of the clergy the title of prelate without jurisdiction as a mere honorary title, the term ''prelates'' properly denotes in law clerics, either secular and religious, who have ordinary jurisdiction in the external forum (**Canon 110**).

OF THE MANNER OF ASCRIBING CLERICS TO A DIOCESE

87. Every cleric must belong either to some diocese or to some religious organization, and no recognition may be extended to vagrant clerics. By reception of the first tonsure, a cleric is ascribed to—or as it is called, incardinated in—the diocese for the service of which he was promoted (**Canon 111**).

Canon 956 determines what bishop has the right to promote a candidate to the clerical rank: it is the bishop where the man has a canonical domicile. Here are to be considered the rules of the Code on the acquisition of a domicile (Canon 92; cfr. above, nn. 69–72). Canon 969 rules that the bishop of domicile should promote to the ranks of the clergy only as many candidates as he needs for his diocese and no more. If another bishop needs men, and agrees with a bishop to take a certain number, the bishop of domicile may promote these men and later on transfer them to the bishop who wanted them: in this transfer the formalities of excardination and incardination are to be observed.

88. With the exception of the cases mentioned in Canons 114 and 641, the valid incardination of a cleric into another diocese requires that his own bishop issue letters of perpetual and unconditional excardination, and that the bishop receiving him likewise issue letters of perpetual and unconditional incardination. The letters of excardination and incardination must be signed by the respective bishops (**Canon 112**).

The vicar-general cannot grant excardination or incardination without a special mandate from his Ordinary, nor can the vicar-capitular do this except after one year's vacancy of the bishopric, and only with the consent of the Cathedral Chapter (**Canon 113**). In the United States and other countries where there are no Cathedral Chapters, the administrator takes the place of the vicar-capitular, and the diocesan consultors take the place of the Cathedral Chapter.

IMPLIED INCARDINATION

89. If the Ordinary gives to a cleric of another diocese a benefice requiring residence (e.g., a parish) with the written

consent of the proper Ordinary of that cleric, the cleric is incardinated in the new diocese. Likewise, if a cleric has obtained from his own bishop written permission to leave the diocese permanently, and another bishop gives the cleric a benefice requiring residence, the cleric is thereby incardinated in the new diocese (**Canon 114**). Another case of implied incardination is found in Canon 641. If a bishop accepts a secularized religious in major orders for three years' trial, he may prolong the period of probation for a second period of three years; but, if he does not dismiss the ex-religious before the second period has elapsed, the latter is automatically incardinated.

According to the law of Canon 585, a person making religious profession is thereby excardinated from his proper diocese (**Canon 115**).

GENERAL RULES GOVERNING EXCARDINATION AND INCARDINATION

90. Excardination may not take place without just reasons, and it does not take effect unless incardination into the other diocese follows. The Ordinary of the incardinating diocese must as soon as possible inform the first Ordinary of the accomplished incardination (**Canon 116**).

A bishop shall not incardinate a cleric of another diocese, except under the following conditions:

(1) The need or good of the diocese must demand it, and the rules of law concerning the canonical title of ordination must be observed;

(2) The bishop must have received through legitimate document notice of the legitimate excardination, and have moreover obtained from the Curia of the excardinating diocese letters (*sub secreto,* if necessary) concerning the birth, life, character and studies of the cleric, especially in case of a cleric of a different language and nation. The Ordinary who excardinates the cleric, has the grave obligation in conscience to see that the testimonials are truthful;

(3) The cleric shall under oath declare before the Ordinary or his delegate that he desires to be ascribed permanently to the service of the diocese according to the law of the sacred canons (**Canon 117**).

OF THE RIGHTS AND PRIVILEGES OF CLERICS

91. Only clerics can obtain the power of either orders or ecclesiastical jurisdiction, and ecclesiastical benefices and pensions (**Canon 118**).

All the faithful owe the clergy reverence according to their various degrees and offices, and they become guilty of sacrilege if they inflict personal injury on clerics (**Canon 119**).

92. All lawsuits against clerics, both civil and criminal, must be brought into the ecclesiastical court, unless other provisions have been legitimately made for some countries (**Canon 120, § 1**).

Cardinals, Legates of the Apostolic See, bishops (including titular bishops, abbots or prelates *nullius*), the supreme heads of religious organizations approved by the Holy See, and the major officials of the Roman Curia may not be sued in the secular courts in matters relating to their offices without permission of the Apostolic See. All others who enjoy the privilege of the forum, may not be sued in the secular courts without permission of the Ordinary of the place in which the case is to be tried. The Ordinary, however, should not refuse such permission without a just and serious reason, especially when the plaintiff is a lay person—all the more so, when the bishop has vainly endeavored to effect a friendly settlement between the parties (**Canon 120, § 2**).

If clerics are sued in the secular courts by one who has not obtained permission from the respective authority, they may through necessity and to avoid greater evil appear, but they must inform the superior from whom the permission should have been obtained (**Canon 120, § 3**).

93. All clerics are exempt from military service and from all civil duties and offices which are alien to the clerical state (**Canon 121**).

Clerics who are compelled to pay their creditors, may not be deprived of what is necessary for their decent maintenance, according to the prudent judgment of the ecclesiastical judge; but they remain under the obligation to satisfy their creditors as soon as possible (**Canon 122**).

94. A cleric cannot renounce the aforesaid privileges: he loses them, however, if he is reduced to the condition of the laity, or is punished by the perpetual deprivation of the ecclesiastical garb (Canons 213 and 2304); if the penalty is remitted, or if he is again received into the ranks of the clergy, the privileges are recovered (**Canon 123**).

The rights and privileges of the clergy enumerated here by the Code are but a restatement of the ancient law of the Church. The origin of these laws can be traced to the early centuries when the Church christianized the nations of Europe. The demand of the Church on the Christian nations to respect these rights and privileges of the clergy, is certainly reasonable and proper. The civil power of the State and the Church stand side by side, both having been instituted by the will of God; one power has charge over the temporal, and the other over the spiritual affairs of men, and each is independent of the other in its own sphere. The Church has as much right to demand what she thinks necessary and proper for carrying on the work that God has committed to her, as the civil power has to manage its own affairs. In those matters which bring the two powers into contact, mutual respect for each other's rights and good-will for each other's progress offer the only practical solution of difficulties which may arise between the two powers. However, there are few, if any Christian states today which recognize that the Church has her power and her constitution by the will of God; and that, in a comparison between the two powers, the Church is the superior, inasmuch as the purpose for which God instituted her is by far superior to the purpose for which He instituted the civil power. Owing to this unbelief and disregard of sound principles, the Church and her clergy have to suffer indignities at the hands of the State in many countries.

TITLE III

OF THE OBLIGATIONS OF CLERICS

95. Both the interior life and the exterior conduct of the clergy should be superior to that of the laity, to whom they should furnish an example of virtue and good deeds (**Canon 124**).

The Ordinary should take care: (1) that all the clergy go frequently to confession; (2) that they devote some time daily to meditation, visit the Blessed Sacrament, say the rosary and examine their conscience (**Canon 125**).

96. At least once in three years, all secular priests must make a retreat for an interval of time to be specified by the Ordinary in some pious or religious house designated by the bishop: no priest may be exempted from the retreat, except in a particular case for a just reason and with the explicit permission of the Ordinary (**Canon 126**).

97. All clerics, particularly the priests, are bound by a special duty to respect and obey their Ordinary (**Canon 127**). Any office assigned to clerics by the Ordinary, must be accepted and faithfully discharged as often and as long as the bishop judges that the needs of the Church demand it, unless a legitimate impediment excuses (**Canon 128**).

The extent of this so-called canonical obedience is defined nowhere in Canon Law. The various writers on Canon Law comment on canonical obedience, but nothing very definite can be gathered from their discussion of this obligation. The general understanding of this duty is that it extends to the purposes for which the Church demands the obedience—namely, for the regulation of the life and activities of clerics in their capacity of ministers of the Church. It would be preposterous to assert that a cleric has lost all his liberty and freedom of action by joining the clergy, but it is hard to draw the line of demarcation between a cleric's private rights as an individual and his duties as a minister of the Church and subject to his superior.

Clerics and Study of Sacred Sciences

98. After their ordination to the priesthood, clerics must not neglect study, especially that of the sacred sciences. In the sacred sciences, they must always follow the sound doctrines handed down by the Fathers and commonly accepted by the Church, and they must avoid profane novelties of expression and what is wrongly called scientific (**Canon 129**).

99. Even though they have a parochial or canon's benefice, all priests must for three years after their ordination undergo

an annual examination in various branches of the sacred sciences designated a sufficient length of time before the date of the examination: the manner of conducting the examination is to be determined by the Ordinary, who may for good reasons grant exemption from the examinations. In the appointment to offices and benefices those ought to be preferred who, other things being equal, excelled in the examinations (**Canon 130**).[6b]

100. The diocesan conferences shall be held repeatedly during the year in the episcopal city, and in each deanery; they shall deal with questions of moral theology and sacred liturgy, to which subjects the Ordinary may add other exercises which he thinks useful for the promotion of the learning and piety of the clergy. If it should be very difficult to hold the meetings, the answers to the cases or questions should be made in writing and sent by mail according to the directions of the Ordinary. All priests should attend the conference (or, failing the conference, make written answers), unless they have expressly been excused beforehand by the Ordinary. This rule applies not only to all secular priests, but also to exempt regulars who have the care of souls (even if they have conferences in their own house) and all other religious to whom the Ordinary has granted the faculty of hearing confessions in the diocese, if the religious do not have conferences in their own houses (**Canon 131**). According to the decision of February 12, 1935, the phrase "having the care of souls" applies to all assistants and other priests who take the place of the pastor and assist him in the entire parochial ministry (cfr. App. III, 9, 1).

Obligation of Celibacy of the Clergy

101. Clerics in major orders are forbidden to marry, and are so bound by the obligation of observing chastity that sins against chastity are also a sacrilege. However, Canon 214 rules that, if a cleric received major orders through grave fear or force, and did not ratify his ordination at least tacitly by the exercise of the orders, thereby freely assuming the obligations of the clerical state, he may bring his case before the bishop, and, if he can prove his case, he must be pronounced free from the obligations of the major orders. Clerics in minor orders may get married, but they cease to be clerics by the very fact

[6b] Concerning religious priests, cfr. App. III, 9, a.

of marriage; if such marriage was invalidated by the use of force or grave intimidation, they remain clerics. A married man who in good faith receives major orders without dispensation from the Holy See, is forbidden to exercise those orders (**Canon 132**).

102. Clerics should beware of having in their houses, or holding any intercourse with, women who may give reason for suspicion. They are allowed to reside only with women about whom there can be no suspicion, either because of a natural bond (as mother, sister, aunt) or of advanced age, combined in both cases with good repute. It is the Ordinary's prerogative to decide in individual cases whether the retention or further visitation of women (even of those who enjoy a good repute) may be the cause of scandal and a danger to continency, and to forbid the clergy to retain or visit such women in future. If the priest has been admonished repeatedly and yet continues to be obstinately disobedient in the matter, he is to be presumed guilty of concubinage (**Canon 133**). Suspension and privation of office are the penalties for concubinage. The manner of procedure is outlined in Canons 2176–2181.

Various Duties Affecting the Life and Conduct of the Clergy

103. The custom of the secular clergy to lead a community life is praiseworthy and is to be encouraged, and, where it is in vogue, it should be continued as far as possible (**Canon 134**).

104. Clerics in major orders are under the obligation to recite daily all the Canonical Hours according to their proper and approved liturgical books. Those clerics who have been reduced to the state of laics, as described in Canons 213 and 214, are not obliged to recite the Divine Office (**Canon 135**).

The obligation spoken of in this Canon is not new, for it was introduced by custom many centuries ago, and was commonly recognized as a law. Discussions on this duty may be found in all textbooks on canon law or moral theology, old and new. We only draw attention to the tendency of the modern world to get away from prayer or to hurry through it as much as possible. The priest must guard his soul against the subtle influence of the spirit of today; if he is not a man of prayer, he is no priest at heart, and, not being spiritually minded, he cannot make others spiritual. The successful management of a parish or other ecclesiastical establishment is not the only goal of a priest's life; the more important part of his life's work is of a spiritual nature.[7]

105. All clerics are bound to wear a becoming clerical garb according to the legitimate local customs and the regulations of the Ordinary. They shall also have the clerical tonsure, unless the custom of the country is against it, and must avoid vanity in the dressing of their hair. Clerics are not allowed to wear a ring, unless it is conceded to them either by law or by Apostolic privilege. Clerics in minor orders, who on their own authority and without a legitimate cause discard the ecclesiastical garb and the tonsure and, after being admonished by the Ordinary, do not obey within a month, forfeit by that very fact the clerical state (**Canon 136**).

The Code wisely leaves the matter of the clerical garb and the tonsure to the legitimate customs of the various countries, because a universal rule on these matters is impossible. For the United States the law of the Third Plenary Council of Baltimore, n. 77, regulates the clothing of the clergy. Cleanliness and neatness are in harmony with the dignity of the sacred ministers; any affectation in dress is absolutely unbecoming to their sacred calling.

106. Clerics are forbidden to give bail or be surety for any one, even with their own money, unless they have the permission of the Ordinary (**Canon 137**).

107. Clerics must absolutely abstain from all things that are unbecoming to their state: they must not practice unbecoming arts, nor play games of chance for money, nor carry weapons (unless there is just cause for fear), nor indulge in hunting (never in hunting associated with much display and publicity), nor visit saloons or other places of that nature except in cases of necessity or for any other just reason approved by the Ordinary (**Canon 138**).[7a]

---

[7] Pontifical functions and Divine Office, App. III, 9, b.

[7a] Concerning hunting, cfr. App. III, 9, d. Concerning wearing of beard, cfr. App. III, 9, c. Concerning conduct of priests on sick-leave, cfr. App. III, 9, e. Concerning immigration of priests from European countries to America and the Philippine Islands, cfr. App. III, 9, j.

108. Clerics must also avoid affairs which, although not unbecoming in themselves, are foreign to the clerical state. Without Apostolic indult, they shall not practice medicine or surgery; nor act as notary public, except in the ecclesiastical curia; nor accept public offices that entail secular jurisdiction or administrative duties (**Canon 139**, §§ 1–2).

109. Without permission from their Ordinaries the clerics shall not act as agents for the goods and property of lay people, nor assume secular offices that impose the obligation of rendering an account, nor exercise the office of solicitor or attorney, except in the ecclesiastical court, or in the civil court when there is question of their own case or church. Clerics shall not take any part at all—not even as witnesses, unless they are forced to act as such—in criminal cases in secular courts, if it is a case in which the criminal may be punished with a grave personal penalty (**Canon 139**, § 3).

110. Without permission of the Holy See, the clerics are not allowed to compete for, or accept, the offices of senator or representative in those countries where this is forbidden by the Holy See; in other countries they shall not seek or accept these offices without the permission of their own Ordinary as well as of the Ordinary of the place where the election is to take place (**Canon 139**, § 4). In the United States it is not the custom for priests to seek any public office, and the Third Council of Baltimore, n. 83, forbids the priests to meddle in political affairs unless the defense of morality and sound principles is at stake. Some States exclude clergymen generally from holding any public office.[7b]

111. The clergy must keep away from all theatrical performances, dances and shows (especially in public theatres), which are unbecoming to the clergy, and where their attendance might cause scandal (**Canon 140**). Much depends in this matter on the customs of particular localities and on the general reputation of a play-house or a theatre. As a rule, people in the United States regard theatre-going as a proper amusement and recreation, and take no offense at the clergy's going to respectable places of amusement or recreation. The Code does not absolutely forbid theatre-going, but qualifies its pro-

---

[7b] Declarations concerning secular public offices, cfr. App. III, 9, f. Concerning political activities of the clergy, cfr. App. III, 9, i.

hibition. The Ordinary has the right to prohibit the clergy from attending anything scandalous of this nature.[7c]

112. Clerics shall not volunteer for military service, unless they do so with the permission of their Ordinary for the purpose of getting free sooner from the service in countries where there is compulsory military service for all able-bodied men. Clerics must not take part in, nor help in any manner internal revolts or disturbances of public order. Clerics in minor orders who, in violation of this law, volunteer for military service, forfeit thereby their clerical rank (**Canon 141**).

113. Clerics are forbidden to engage either personally or through others in any business or trading, whether for their own benefit or for that of others (**Canon 142**). That the clergy must attend to their spiritual work, and not involve themselves in secular business, has been the law of the Church for many centuries, and the Code repeats the ancient law. The terms "business" and "trading" are well understood in their plain and ordinary meaning. One may not conduct a business of one's own through others, nor trade through others. It is generally held by canonists and moralists (with a few exceptions) that a cleric may buy shares of stock or bonds in corporations engaged in any legitimate business or trade. It is a common form of investing money, and the cleric may invest his own money without engaging in any business or trade. As nobody in modern times considers such investment as business or trade, it cannot be said to be forbidden by the Code. The directors of the corporation conduct the business for the corporation, and, though the directors are elected by the stockholders and the priest who holds stock may vote in this election, he cannot be said to engage in business, but rather to have lent his money in return for interest or dividends and certain rights for the safeguarding of the money thus invested. Trading may be done not only by a continuous series of actions (as in a store), but also by a single action (e.g., buying a piece of property to sell when the price advances). It is trading to buy shares of stock for the purpose of selling them at a profit. Business cares, trading with its hazards, speculations for profits —all these things are not becoming to clergymen, who must be

7c Decree concerning dances, cfr. App. III, 4, c.

satisfied with a safe and sane investment of their money so that their minds may be free to devote themselves undividedly to God and to the Church.

114. Clerics, including those who have no benefice or office which requires residence, are forbidden to be absent from their diocese for a notable length of time without at least the presumed permission of their own Ordinary (**Canon 143**). For absence of pastors, cfr. Canon 465.[7d]

Clerics who go into another diocese with the permission of their bishop, but are not excardinated, may be recalled for a just reason, but the laws of equity must be observed. Similarly the bishop of the other diocese may for a just reason deny a priest permission to prolong his stay in that diocese, unless he has given the extern priest a benefice (**Canon 144**). In the United States there are practically no other benefices than parishes, cfr. Canon 114.

TITLE IV

OF ECCLESIASTICAL OFFICES

115. In the broad sense of the term, an ecclesiastical office is any employment which is legitimately practiced for a spiritual purpose. In the strict sense, an ecclesiastical office means a stable position created either by the divine or the ecclesiastical law, conferred according to the rules of the sacred canons, and entailing some participation at least in ecclesiastical power, whether of orders or jurisdiction. In law, the term "ecclesiastical office" is used in its strict sense, unless the context clearly indicates the contrary (**Canon 145**).

In reference to offices which come under the name of benefices, the following Canons on the appointment to ecclesiastical offices are to be applied, and also the precepts of Canons 1409–1488 on ecclesiastical benefices (**Canon 146**).

Chapter I
OF APPOINTMENT TO ECCLESIASTICAL OFFICES

116. An ecclesiastical office cannot be validly obtained without canonical appointment. By canonical appointment is

[7d] Priests teaching at secular schools, App. III, 9, g. Clerics studying at laical universities, App. III, 9, h.

understood the conferring of an ecclesiastical office by the competent ecclesiastical authority in harmony with the sacred canons (**Canon 147**).

The appointment to an ecclesiastical office is made: (1) by free appointment on the part of the legitimate superior; (2) by the so-called "institution" in cases where a patron has the right to nominate or present to the ecclesiastical superior the person who is to obtain the office; (3) if the person is elected, the superior who accepts the result of the election is said to give the "confirmation"; (4) if the voters postulate the appointment of a person to a certain office, the superior who accepts the postulation is said to grant "admission"; (5) finally, an office may be obtained simply by election and acceptance of the election by the elected, if the law does not require confirmation of the election. In reference to the institution in office of a person presented or nominated by a patron, special laws are laid down in Canons 1448–1471 (**Canon 148**).

Candidates elected, postulated, presented or nominated by any persons for an ecclesiastical office shall not be confirmed, admitted or instituted by a superior below the Roman Pontiff, unless these persons have first been adjudged suitable by their respective Ordinary. The Ordinary thus has the right to subject them to an examination, if either the law or the nature of the office requires it, or the Ordinary judges it opportune (**Canon 149**).

117. The conferring of an office which is not legally vacant in the manner described in Canon 183, is *ipso facto* invalid, and the appointment is not validated by a subsequent vacancy. The promise of an office not legally vacant has no legal effect, no matter who makes the promise (**Canon 150**).

If an office is vacant by law, but is perhaps actually held in illegal possession by some one, it may be conferred, provided the declaration of illegal possession has been issued according to the sacred canons, and mention is made of this declaration in the letters of appointment (**Canon 151**).

ARTICLE I.—OF FREE APPOINTMENT

118. The Ordinary has the right to fill ecclesiastical offices within his own territory, unless a limitation of his power is

proved. The vicar-general does not possess this power, unless he has a special mandate to exercise it (**Canon 152**).

The candidate for promotion to a vacant office must be a cleric, and must have the qualifications which are demanded either by the common law, or the particular law, or the rules of the foundation of the office or benefice. Candidates are to be appointed for their merits, not for any human consideration. When the person appointed to an office lacks the requisite qualifications, the conferring of the office is null and void, if either the common or the particular law or the rules of the foundation contain this stipulation; otherwise, it is valid, but it may be declared void by the sentence of the legitimate superior (**Canon 153**).

119. Offices which entail the care of souls either in the external or the internal forum, cannot be validly conferred upon clerics who are not ordained priests (**Canon 154**). The former Canon Law did not insist on the priesthood at the time of appointment, but ruled that within a certain time after the appointment the cleric had to receive the priesthood.

Unless special laws specify the term of vacancy, the conferring of offices which have become vacant must never be deferred over six months from the time when the vacancy becomes known to the superior and he is able to act. In the appointment of pastors to vacant parishes, Canon 458 leaves it to the judgment of the Ordinary to defer the conferring of the pastorship, when special reasons make such delay advisable (**Canon 155**).

120. No one shall be given two incompatible offices—that is, offices which cannot be filled simultaneously by the same person. The concession of a second office by the Holy See is invalid, unless in the petition for such mention was made of a prior incompatible office, or unless a clause is added in the papal rescript dispensing with this rule of law in the case. Furthermore, in virtue of Canon 188, n. 3, a person who accepts and takes possession of a second office incompatible with the first, loses the first office *ipso facto* (**Canon 156**).

121. An office which has become vacant either through resignation or by the sentence of deprivation of the ecclesiastical court cannot validly be conferred by the Ordinary who accepted the resignation or issued sentence: (1) on members

of his own household or of the household of the recent incumbent of the office; (2) on his own blood relations or relations by marriage to the second degree inclusive, or the corresponding relations of the recent incumbent (**Canon 157**).

A person who confers an office which he ordinarily has no power to confer, but only acts for another to supply his negligence or his inability to make the appointment, does not thereby acquire any jurisdiction over the man thus appointed, and the legal status of the latter is the same as though the appointment had been made according to the ordinary process of law (**Canon 158**). Thus, for instance, Canon 432, § 2, ordains that if, when a see becomes vacant, the Cathedral Chapter does not elect within the prescribed time the vicar-capitular to take charge of the diocese, the archbishop has the right to appoint the vicar-capitular, but he does not thereby obtain any jurisdiction over the vicar or over the diocese.

122. The appointment to any office is to be made in writing (**Canon 159**). The Code does not say that the appointment to an office is invalid when made orally, but it commands that it be done in writing. In those cases only where the Code makes the appointment in writing necessary for validity, would an oral appointment be invalid.

ARTICLE II.—OF ELECTIONS

123. The election of the Roman Pontiff is governed exclusively by the Constitution of Pope Pius X, "Vacante Sede Apostolica," December 25, 1904.[8] In other ecclesiastical elections the laws of the following Canons are to be observed, and also such special regulations as may have been legitimately enacted for the election to individual offices (**Canon 160**). In reference to elections by the Chapters of religious congregations, the Code (Canon 507) rules that the special laws on election of the various organizations may be retained only in so far as they are not contrary to the general laws on election contained in the Code (i.e., Canons 160–182).

---

8 Amended by the *Motu Proprio* of Pius XI, March 1, 1922 (cfr. App. III, 10, a). The most important amendment is the extension of time for the holding of the election of the new Pope from ten to fifteen days after the death of the Pope and two or three additional days at the option of the members of the Conclave.

124. If the right to elect to a vacant office rests with an electoral college, the election, unless stated otherwise in the law, shall never be deferred for more than three months reckoned from the day on which notice of the vacancy was received. If the electoral college has neglected to hold the election within the three months, the superior who has the right of confirming the election, or to whom passes the right of appointment in default of the college, shall freely appoint a person to the vacant office (**Canon 161**).

The three months are called "trimestre utile" to indicate that the election may be held at a later date, if impossible within the three months. The Code uses the phrase "or to whom passes the right of appointment," because there may be elections in which no confirmation of the election is required by law. If the election was held within the prescribed time but did not take effect because the elected did not accept the election, or died, or if the election was annulled by the superior, or was invalid for some reason for which the law does not deprive the voters of the right of election, the election may be held again.

CONVOCATION OF THE VOTERS

125. Unless particular constitutions or customs regulate the manner of convoking the voters, the president shall convene all the members of the electoral college in the prescribed manner at a place and a time convenient to the voters. If the convocation is to be announced to each one personally, it suffices for validity, if the notice be addressed either to the place of domicile or quasi-domicile of the voters, or to the place where they actually stay. If one of the voters was neglected, and for that reason missed the election, the election is valid, but the person thus neglected may demand that the competent superior rescind the election provided lack of notification and absence from the election is proved. The party retains this right even after the election has been confirmed, provided he can furnish legal proof that he forwarded his objection to the competent superior within at least three days after obtaining knowledge of the election. If more than one-third of the voters were neglected in the convocation, the election is *ipso jure* invalid. The lack of notice

does not invalidate the election, if those who were not called are nevertheless present. If the election is to an office which is to be held for life, the convocation of the electors made before the office was vacant has no legal effect at all (**Canon 162**).

The Code uses the phrase "neglected" (*neglectus fuerit*) to indicate the intentional failure to send the announcement of an election to a voter. If the failure to notify a voter was accidental, the voter who did not get the notice has no right to demand an annulment of the election. The Code seems to suppose that the slighted voter will make his objection to the election by mail, as the term "forwarded" (*transmissum*) indicates. If it is done by mail or telegram, the letter must be posted (i.e., put into a mail box or post office), or the telegram given to the company for transmission, within three days after knowledge of the election was obtained from any source that gave certainty of the fact.

126. The convocation having been legitimately made, the right to elect rests with those who are present on the day fixed in the notice, and no one has a right to vote either by letter or by proxy, unless the particular law rules otherwise (**Canon 163**).

QUALIFIED VOTERS

127. Even though one and the same person may have the right to vote under several titles, he may nevertheless cast but one vote (**Canon 164**). No one who does not belong to the electoral college, may be admitted, except in virtue of privileges legitimately acquired; otherwise the election is *ipso facto* null and void (**Canon 165**). If laymen meddle in any way in the ecclesiastical election, or interfere with its canonical freedom, the election is *ipso facto* invalid (**Canon 166**).

128. The following persons may not cast a vote:

(1) Persons incapable of a human act;

(2) Persons under the age of puberty;

(3) Persons suffering from censure or infamy of law, if such censure or infamy has previously been inflicted by a declaratory or condemnatory sentence;

(4) Persons who have joined an heretical or schismatical sect, or publicly adhered to such. This refers to Catholics who

have fallen from the faith, as a similar phrase in Canon 542 was explained by the Committee for the Authentic Interpretation of the Code; [9]

(5) Persons deprived of the active vote either through legitimate sentence of the ecclesiastical judge or by the common or the particular law.

If any one of the aforesaid persons is admitted to the election, his vote is invalid, but the election is valid unless it is certain that the elected would not have had the required number of votes without the illegal vote; and the election is invalid if a person excommunicated by a declaratory or condemnatory sentence has knowingly been admitted to vote (**Canon 167**).

If any of the voters is present in the house in which the election takes place, but cannot be present at the election on account of ill-health, his written vote shall be taken by the tellers, unless particular laws or legitimate customs provide otherwise (**Canon 168**).

Manner of Voting

129. A vote is null and void unless it is: (1) *free,* wherefore a vote is null and void if, through grave fear or deceit, the voter was led directly or indirectly to cast his vote for a certain person, or for several persons separately; (2) *secret, certain, absolute,* and *determinate.* Conditions attached to a vote before the election are to be ignored (**Canon 169**). No one can validly vote in his own favor (**Canon 170**).

130. Before the election at least two tellers from among the voters are to be appointed by secret ballot, unless they are already appointed by the proper statutes of the organization. The tellers and the president, if the latter is one of the body of voters, must take the oath to discharge their office faithfully, and to keep secret the transactions in the assembly even after the completion of the election.

The tellers shall take care that the votes are cast secretly, faithfully, individually and in the proper order of precedence. After all the votes have been cast, they shall collect the same and shall in the presence of the president of the election ascertain whether the number of votes corresponds to the number

[9] October 16, 1919 (*Acta Ap. Sedis,* XI, 480).

of voters; then they shall open the ballots and make known to the voters how many votes each candidate received. In the inspecting and counting of the votes the particular constitutions or legitimate customs are to be followed.

If the number of votes be larger than the number of voters, the ballot is null and void.

The votes are to be burned immediately after each ballot, or, if there are several ballots in the same session, after the session. All the proceedings of the election shall be accurately recorded by the one who acts as secretary, and they must be signed by the secretary, the president and the tellers and kept carefully in the archives of the electoral college (**Canon 171**). Regarding the number of ballots, cfr. above, n. 77.

ELECTION BY COMPROMISE

131. Unless the law rules otherwise, the election may be made also by compromise, if the voters by unanimous and written consent agree to transfer for that one election the right of election into the hands of one or several qualified persons, either of their own body or outsiders, who shall by the power thus received hold the election in the name of all. If the electoral college be a clerical one, the persons chosen by compromise must be priests, or otherwise the election is invalid.

The persons appointed by compromise must, under pain of nullity of the election, observe the conditions attached to the compromise, if these are not contrary to the common law. If no conditions were attached, they must observe the common law regulating elections. Conditions contrary to the common law are considered as though not made.

If the voters by compromise appointed only one person, this one cannot elect himself; if several were designated, no one of these can add his vote to that of the others who vote for him in order to effect his election (**Canon 172**).

132. The compromise ceases and the right of election is returned to the voters: (1) by revocation of the body of voters before the persons appointed by compromise have begun to exercise their right; (2) if one of the conditions of the compromise was not fulfilled or observed; (3) if the election was held, but proved invalid (**Canon 173**).

Result of the Election

133. The person who obtained the majority of the votes (as defined in Canon 101, § 1, n. 1, cfr. above, n. 77), is considered elected and is to be proclaimed as such by the president of the electoral college (**Canon 174**). The election is to be made known at once to the person elected, and within eight days at the most from the time he received the notice he must declare whether he accepts the election or not; otherwise he loses every right acquired by the election (**Canon 175**). The period of eight days is called "octiduum utile" to indicate that the person elected does not lose his right to the election, if for any reason the notice did not come to him or was delayed, or if he was not able to answer within that time.

134. If the person elected renounces his election, he thereby forfeits all rights acquired by the election, even though he afterwards regrets his renunciation. He may, however, be re-elected. The body of voters must proceed with a new election within one month from the date on which they receive notice of the renunciation.

By the acceptance of the election the one elected obtains immediately the full right of the office, unless confirmation of the election is necessary. If the law requires confirmation, the elected acquires only a claim to the office. Before confirmation of the election has been received, the person elected is forbidden to meddle in the administration of either the spiritual or temporal affairs of the office under the pretext of his election, and any acts which he may execute are null and void (**Canon 176**).

135. A particular law, if approved by the Holy See since the promulgation of the Code, may deprive the person elected of the liberty to renounce the election, as is done by some of the constitutions of religious organizations. The old Canon Law gave the person elected one month's time to accept or refuse the election. If the elected first renounces his election and afterwards changes his mind and accepts the election, the matter is decided by whichever notice gets first to the president of the election. If he first accepts and afterwards refuses the election, the effect of such action depends on the nature of the election. If the election does not require confirmation, the

acceptance which has come to the president of the voters finishes the entire matter, for the law confers the office immediately when accepted: the laws on renunciation of offices govern after the acceptance. If the election needs confirmation, it seems that the elected may within the eight days withdraw his first acceptance, if the confirmation has not yet been requested of the competent superior. This is the opinion of commentators on the old Canon Law, and these same commentators state that, if the petition for confirmation has been sent to the superior and received by him, it is left to the judgment of this superior whether he will consider the resignation. The voters cannot in such a case elect another without permission from the superior.[10]

Confirmation of the Election

136. If the election needs confirmation, the person elected must, either in person or through another, ask the competent superior for such confirmation within eight days after acceptance of the election; otherwise he loses all right to the office, unless he can prove that he was prevented by some just impediment from asking for the confirmation within the appointed period.

The superior may not refuse the confirmation, if he has ascertained that the person elected is suitable, and that the election was conducted according to the rules of law. The confirmation must be given in writing. Upon the receipt of the confirmation, the person elected obtains full rights to the office, unless the law rules otherwise (**Canon 177**). In some offices the law forbids the person elected and confirmed to exercise any of the powers of the office until after the canonical installation in office.

137. If the election was not completed within the prescribed period, or if the body of voters has been punished with deprivation of the right to elect, the free appointment to the office devolves on the superior who would have had the right to confirm the election, or on him who succeeds to the rights of the voters to fill the office (**Canon 178**).

---

10 Wernz, ''Jus Decret.,'' II, 145, n. 380.

ARTICLE III.—OF POSTULATION

138. If the election of the person whom the voters think most capable and preferable, is obstructed by some impediment on the part of that person, and if the impediment is of a nature that it can be, and usually is dispensed from, the voters may by their votes request the competent superior to admit this person to the office, even when there is question of an office for which the elected person does not need confirmation (**Canon 179,** § 1). This is called postulation in law, and it is permissible under the above conditions unless the law rules otherwise. In the elections made by religious organizations, Canon 507 rules that election by postulation can be admitted only in extraordinary cases, and provided the constitutions of the particular organization do not forbid the postulation.

The persons appointed by compromise of the voters to make the election in the name of all, cannot postulate unless this is explicitly granted to them in the mandate or compromise (**Canon 179,** § 2).

In order that the postulation may be valid, the majority of votes must be in its favor, and, if it concurs with the election, there must be at least two-thirds of the votes in favor of postulation. The vote for postulation must be expressed by the term "postulo," or its equivalent; the formula, "eligo vel postulo," or an equivalent one, stands for election if there be no impediment, otherwise for postulation (**Canon 180**).

139. The Committee for the Authentic Interpretation of the Code has decided that if, in the third balloting (which is final), some voters postulate one person, while others elect another, and the one postulated does not have the required two-thirds of all votes, the other is elected on a relative majority of votes; he does not need an absolute majority. If votes are cast for one who is postulated, and also for two or more candidates who can be elected; then, in the third balloting, if the one postulated does not have two-thirds of all the votes cast, one of those who could be elected and who has a relative majority of votes, excluding the one who was postulated, is to be considered elected.[11] The person postulated must, therefore, have two-thirds of all the votes cast, and unless he has that number of votes at least

---

[11] Cfr. App. III, 10, b.

in the final balloting, one of the persons who could be elected is preferred to the one postulated on a relative majority of votes.

140. The postulation must be forwarded within eight days to the superior who has the power to confirm the election, if he has also the power to dispense from the impediment; otherwise to the Roman Pontiff or to another authority having the faculty to dispense. If the postulation was not sent to the superior within the prescribed time, it becomes *ipso facto* null and void, and the voters lose for this one election the right to vote or to postulate, unless they can prove that they were prevented by a just impediment from forwarding the postulation. By the postulation the person nominated for the office does not acquire any right, and the superior is free to reject the postulation. After the presentation of the postulation to the superior, the voters cannot revoke it except with the consent of the superior (**Canon 181**).

141. If the superior rejects the postulation, the right to elect rests with the body of voters, unless the voters knowingly postulated a person who was affected by an impediment of such a nature that the dispensation could not be, or usually is not granted; in that case the filling of the office in question rests with the superior. If the postulation is admitted, the person thus chosen for the office is to be notified of his admission to the office, and he must within eight days answer whether or not he accepts the appointment to the office, as is prescribed in Canon 175: if he accepts, he thereby at once acquires full right to the office (**Canon 182**).

CHAPTER II

OF THE LOSS OF ECCLESIASTICAL OFFICES

142. An ecclesiastical office may be lost by renunciation, by deprivation, by removal, by transfer and—in the case of offices to which one was appointed or elected for a definite period of time—by the lapse of this period. An ecclesiastical office is not lost by the fact that the superior who made the appointment goes out of office in any way, unless the law ordains otherwise, or the appointment to the office was made by the

superior under the clause: "ad beneplacitum nostrum" or an equivalent phrase (**Canon 183**).

RESIGNATION OF OFFICES

143. Anyone capable of performing a human act may resign an ecclesiastical office for a good reason, unless the resignation is forbidden to him by a special prohibition (**Canon 184**). The Code mentions several cases where resignation is forbidden or is subject to certain restrictions: for instance, the resignation of benefices by clerics in major orders (Canon 1484), the resignation of a benefice under the title of which a cleric was ordained (Canon 1485), the resignation of a cleric's benefice during his novitiate (Canon 568). In religious organizations the constitutions may forbid the resignation of offices conferred by election in the Chapter.

A resignation based on grave and unjust intimidation, or on deceit, substantial error or simony, is *ipso jure* void (**Canon 185**).

The validity of a resignation requires that it be made in writing, or orally before two witnesses, or by a proxy appointed by special mandate. A written statement of the resignation made in any of the foregoing ways is to be deposited in the respective Curia (**Canon 186**).

The resignation, to be valid, must usually be made to him who has the right to accept it, or, if it does not need acceptance, to him from whom the cleric received the office or who takes the latter's place. Wherefore, if the office was conferred by confirmation, admission, or institution, the renunciation must be made to the superior in whom the right to grant the confirmation, admission, or institution is vested by ordinary law (**Canon 187**).

144. All offices shall be vacant *ipso facto* by tacit resignation in the following cases:

(1) If a cleric makes religious profession, the rules of Canon 584 being observed in the case of benefices. That Canon states that one year from any religious profession parochial benefices become vacant, and after three years all others;

(2) If a cleric who has obtained an office neglects to assume the office within the time fixed by law, or, in default of a term

fixed by law, within the time determined by the Ordinary. The time is called "tempus utile" to indicate that the office is not lost by the lapse of time, if the cleric appointed did not receive notice or was unable to act during the specified period of time;

(3) If a cleric has accepted another office incompatible with the first, and has obtained peaceful possession of the second, in which case the first one is *ipso facto* vacant;

(4) If a cleric has publicly lapsed from the Catholic Faith;

(5) If a cleric has contracted marriage, though only by the ceremony of a so-called civil marriage;

(6) If a cleric has volunteered for military service contrary to the law of Canon 141;

(7) If a cleric has put aside his clerical garb on his own initiative and without a just cause, and has not resumed the clerical garb within a month from the warning of his Ordinary to do so;

(8) If a cleric has unlawfully deserted the residence to which he is bound, and, despite his Ordinary's warning, has neither appeared, nor answered within a reasonable time fixed by the Ordinary, without having a legitimate excuse for not appearing or answering (**Canon 188**).

145. The superiors shall not accept resignations unless there is a just and proportionate cause for them. The local Ordinary shall either accept or reject resignations within one month (**Canon 189**). The Committee for the Authentic Interpretation of the Code has declared that the Ordinary may accept a resignation even after the month has elapsed, unless the resigner has revoked his resignation and has notified the Ordinary to that effect before the latter accepted the resignation.[12]

146. The resignation having been legitimately made and accepted, the office becomes vacant after the resigner has received notice of the acceptance. The resigning cleric remains in office until he has received authentic notice of the acceptance of his resignation by the superior (**Canon 190**). Once the resignation has been legitimately made, there is no more time for reconsideration, but the resigning cleric may again acquire the office under another title (**Canon 191, § 1**). The Committee for the Authentic Interpretation of the Code in the decision just cited has declared that the resigning cleric may revoke the resig-

12 Cfr. App. III, 10, c.

nation before the superior has accepted it. The term "accepted" does not refer to the receipt of the letter or other instrument containing the resignation, but the statement of the superior that he accepts the resignation and releases the cleric from the office.

The notice of the acceptance of the resignation is to be sent promptly to those persons who have any rights concerning the appointment to that office **(Canon 191, § 2)**.

Deprivation of Office

147. The deprivation or loss of an office may be incurred either according to the law itself, or through the act of the legitimate superior. The Ordinary cannot deprive a cleric of an irremovable office, except by the process prescribed by law.

In the case of a removable office, the deprivation may be decreed by the Ordinary for any just reason according to his prudent judgment, even though there is no offense on the part of the cleric. While the Ordinary should observe natural equity, he is not bound to follow a certain form of procedure except in the removal of rectors from removable pastorates in which the Canons prescribe the manner of procedure (cfr. Canons 2157–2161). The deprivation of office has no effect until it has been communicated by the superior, and from the decree of the Ordinary recourse to the Apostolic See is granted "in devolutivo" only **(Canon 192)**. The recourse "in devolutivo" means that the decree of the Ordinary is not suspended by such appeal, and that the person removed has therefore to obey and vacate the office.

Transfer from One Office to Another

148. The transfer from one ecclesiastical office to another can be ordered only by him who has the right both to accept the resignation, to remove the incumbent from the first office, and transfer him to another. When the transfer is made with the consent of the cleric, any reasonable cause suffices. When the transfer is made against the will of the cleric, the regulations regarding the cause and procedure in the case of deprivation of office (Canon 192) should be observed. In reference to the transfer of pastors, Canons 2162–2167 are to be followed (**Canon 193**).

In the transfer, the first office becomes vacant when the cleric takes canonical possession of the second office, unless the law or the legitimate superior has provided otherwise. The transferred cleric receives the income of the first office until he has taken possession of the second (**Canon 194**).

The persons who elected, postulated or presented a cleric to an office cannot deprive him of the office, nor can they recall, remove or transfer him to another office (**Canon 195**).

TITLE V

OF ORDINARY AND DELEGATED POWER

149. The Catholic Church possesses, by divine institution, the power of jurisdiction or government. This power is two-fold: that of the external forum, and that of the internal forum, or forum of conscience. Finally, the internal form is subdivided into the sacramental and the extra-sacramental forum (**Canon 196**).

150. Ordinary power of jurisdiction is that which is automatically attached to an office; delegated power is that which is committed to a person. Ordinary power may be either *proper* or *vicarious* (**Canon 197**). Ordinary power is obtained through an office to which the law automatically attaches certain powers; the delegated power by commission from the superior (or in certain instances, from the law). The delegated power supposes a superior as the principal and the inferior acting in the name of the superior.

By *Ordinaries* are to be understood in law (unless explicitly excepted in individual instances) : the Roman Pontiff, within their respective territories the residential bishop, abbot and prelate *nullius* (and their vicar-general), administrator, vicar and prefect Apostolic. Furthermore, those persons are Ordinaries who, in case of vacancy of the above offices, succeed to the office during vacancy by the provisions of the law or of approved constitutions. In exempt clerical religious organizations, the major superiors are Ordinaries over their subjects. By the term

Ordinarius loci or *locorum* are meant all persons enumerated in this Canon with the exception of the religious superiors (**Canon 198**).

DELEGATION OF ORDINARY AND DELEGATED POWER

151. The person who has ordinary power of jurisdiction can delegate it to another, either totally or in part, unless the law explicitly restricts the power of delegation.

Jurisdiction delegated by the Holy See can be subdelegated, either for one act or even habitually, unless the first person was delegated for personal qualifications, or subdelegation was forbidden.

Jurisdiction delegated for a "universality of affairs" (i.e., all cases of a certain category) by an Ordinary inferior to the Roman Pontiff can be subdelegated in individual cases.

In all other cases, the delegated power of jurisdiction may not be subdelegated without explicit concession. Duties, however, which do not entail jurisdiction, can be subdelegated by delegated judges, even though subdelegation was not explicitly granted.

No subdelegated power can be further subdelegated, unless this faculty has been explicitly granted (**Canon 199**).

The general rule is that he who has ordinary power, can delegate the same, unless the law states otherwise. Sometimes the Code plainly forbids it; in other cases, the prohibition must be inferred from other Canons of the Code. Thus, the pastors have ordinary jurisdiction to hear confessions, and no express prohibition of delegation is found in the Code, but the Committee for the Authentic Interpretation of the Code declared that the pastors cannot delegate other priests.[13] The reason is that Canons 874 and 875 explicitly state who may delegate priests for the hearing of confessions, and the pastors are not mentioned.

152. The Code rules that one who is delegated by the Holy See can subdelegate his powers, not only for an individual case but also habitually, unless the delegation was given for reason of personal fitness of the one delegated, or the subdelegation was forbidden. With reference to the faculties granted to the

---

[13] Oct. 16, 1919; *Acta Ap. Sedis*, XI, 477.

bishops by the Code, the Sacred Penitentiary declared that the bishop cannot delegate these faculties to his priests.[14]   The reason evidently is that these faculties are privileges (which the Code calls them in Canon 349), given to the episcopal dignity; these faculties stand, therefore, in a class by themselves, and do not come under the delegated powers of jurisdiction of which Canon 199 speaks.

The delegate "ad universalitatem negotiorum" may subdelegate his powers in individual cases.   The "universality of affairs" does not necessarily mean a delegation of all the powers which a person vested with ordinary power possesses; it may be universal in reference to a certain part of the business of the superior.

Interpretation of Ordinary and Delegated Power

153. The ordinary power of jurisdiction and the delegated jurisdiction for a "universality of affairs" is to be interpreted liberally; all other jurisdiction strictly.   It is understood, however, that the person to whom jurisdiction has been delegated, has been granted all power necessary to make his jurisdiction effective.   He who claims to possess delegated jurisdiction, has the burden of proving the delegation (**Canon 200**).

How Jurisdiction is to be Exercised

154. The power of jurisdiction may be exercised directly over subjects only.   The judicial power, both ordinary and delegated, may not be exercised for one's own convenience nor outside the proper territory (**Canon 201, §§ 1–2**).   Exceptions to this rule are contained in Canons 401, 881, and 1637.   Canon 401 states that the canon penitentiary at the cathedral and at a collegiate church has ordinary power, and may absolve subjects of the diocese even outside the territory of the diocese.   Canon 881 extends this same ruling to one who has ordinary power to absolve.   Canon 1637 refers to an ecclesiastical judge who is either expelled from his territory or prevented from exercising his power, in which case he may exercise it in a

14 July 18, 1919; *Acta Ap. Sedis*, XI, 332.

territory outside his jurisdiction, notifying the local Ordinary of his action.

155. The non-judicial or so-called voluntary jurisdiction can be exercised even in one's own favor, and made use of even outside one's territory, and in favor of a subject who is outside the territory, unless the nature of things or the law forbid such use of jurisdiction (**Canon 201, § 3**).

156. Acts of jurisdiction based on either ordinary or delegated power granted for exercise in the external forum, are valid also in the internal forum; acts based on jurisdiction for the internal forum only, are not valid in the external forum. Power given for the internal forum can be exercised also outside of confession, unless the faculty is restricted to the sacramental forum. If the forum for which power was granted is not expressed, the power is considered granted for both the internal and external forum, unless the contrary is certain from the very nature of the power (**Canon 202**). The priest's faculties usually extend to the internal forum only. The internal forum deals with matters of conscience, with affairs which are not public; the external forum deals with matters of a public character, the public standing of persons in the Church.

The delegate who acts beyond his mandate, either as to the matters or the persons over which he received power, acts invalidly: a mere deviation from the method of transacting the affair as desired by the person delegating authority, is not considered a transgression of the limits of the delegation, unless the method was prescribed as a condition of the delegation (**Canon 203**).

157. If a person applies to a higher superior, passing over a subordinate, the so-called voluntary jurisdiction of the latter —whether ordinary or delegated—is not thereby suspended: he shall not, however, interfere in a matter submitted to the higher superior except for a grave and urgent reason, and in this case shall immediately notify the superior of his action (**Canon 204**). The term "voluntary jurisdiction" is used in contrast to "jurisdictio contentiosa or judicialis." The voluntary jurisdiction embraces the legislative and administrative power; the judicial, as the name suggests, has to do with the power exercised in the ecclesiastical court of deciding litigated

questions of rights by judicial procedure and punishing transgressions of the law after trial and conviction. Here must be noted the rules laid down in Canons 43–44 regarding favors asked from and refused by one of the Sacred Congregations (which cannot be obtained from another congregation without the consent of the first), and favors refused by the Ordinary (which may then under no condition be granted by the vicar-general).

SEVERAL DELEGATES IN THE SAME CASE

158. If several men have received delegated power over the same affair, and doubt arises whether the delegation was given *in solidum* (to each independent of the other) or *collegialiter* (to each as members of a body), it is to be considered given *in solidum* in matters which do not require judicial proceedings, and given *collegialiter* in matters which do require judicial procedure. If several persons are delegated *in solidum,* he who first makes use of his power in the case excludes the others from acting, unless the first delegate is afterwards impeded, or does not wish to continue to act in the affair. If several persons are delegated *collegialiter,* all must act together in the matter to make their action valid (cfr. Canon 207, § 3), unless the rescript of delegation provides otherwise (**Canon 205**).

If several persons have been delegated for the same affair successively, the first delegate in the order of time must transact the affair unless the later rescript of delegation given to another person explicitly revokes the power of the first delegate (**Canon 206**).

CESSATION OF DELEGATED AND ORDINARY POWER

159. The delegated power expires in the following cases: (1) when the mandate has been executed; (2) when the time of delegation has expired, or the number of cases for which it was given has been exhausted; (3) when the final motive or cause of the delegation ceases; (4) by recall of the delegation by the delegating superior conveyed directly to the delegate; (5) by renunciation of the delegate conveyed directly to the delegating superior and accepted by him. Delegated jurisdiction does not cease on the retirement from office of the delegating

superior, except in the two cases mentioned in Canon 61 (**Canon 207, § 1**; cfr. above, n. 45). Privileges granted *ad beneplacitum nostrum* cease when the superior who granted them goes out of office (cfr. Canon 73). The same rule applies in dispensations which extend over a certain length of time, if given *ad beneplacitum nostrum* (cfr. Canon 86).

Power granted for the internal forum is still validly exercised, if through inadvertence the priest has not noticed that the time for which the faculties were given has elapsed, or that the number of cases has been exhausted (**Canon 207, § 2**).

When several persons are delegated *collegialiter*, all lose their delegated powers if one fails to act (e.g., owing to death, absence, refusal), unless the contrary is stated in the delegation (**Canon 207, § 3**).

160. As stated in Canon 183, the ordinary power does not cease on the retirement of the superior who conferred an office to which ordinary power is attached: it ceases on the loss of office; it is suspended by legitimate appeal, unless the appeal is only *in devolutivo*, and its use is invalid in the cases specified in Canons 2264 and 2284 (**Canon 208**). The first of these Canons states that the exercise of power by a person excommunicated by condemnatory or declaratory sentence of the ecclesiastical court is invalid. Canon 2284 extends this ruling to suspensions which forbid acts of jurisdiction, and declares these acts invalid after the suspension has been inflicted by condemnatory or declaratory sentence.

Jurisdiction Supplied by the Church

161. The Church supplies jurisdiction both for the external and the internal forum: (1) in common error; (2) in a positive and probable doubt whether of fact or law (**Canon 209**). Common error consists in the erroneous belief of all or nearly all the people of a place, parish, community, that a man has jurisdiction. The fact that the person knows that he has no jurisdiction, does not interfere with the validity of his acts if by common error he is believed to have jurisdiction. In the old Canon Law the great majority of canonists and moralists did not admit that common error alone was sufficient to make the exercise of jurisdiction valid; they demanded in addition the

"titulus coloratus," that is to say, some act on the part of the superior which is ordinarily sufficient to confer jurisdiction, but which, on account of some secret impediment, was rendered invalid. That "color of title" is no longer required, and in the case of common error, no matter how created, the Church supplies the jurisdiction for the benefit of the people.[15]

162. The Church likewise supplies jurisdiction in a positive and probable doubt. Authors do not agree on the interpretation of the terms, "negative" and "positive" doubt. Generally speaking, a negative doubt means that one has no reason to serve as a basis for deciding a question, and it is about equal to ignorance on that question. A positive doubt means that one has a good reason for deciding a question one way, but that there is also a reason in favor of a contrary decision of the question. For example, the reasons for and against the existence of jurisdiction in a certain case create a positive doubt; and, if the reasons on both sides are of such weight so as to create a *bona fide* doubt, the Church supplies the jurisdiction, even though actually the person did not possess it.

THE POWER OF ORDERS MAY NOT BE DELEGATED

163. The power of orders which has been attached to an office by the legitimate ecclesiastical superior or has been committed by him to a person, cannot be delegated to others, unless the law or an indult explicitly allows such delegation (**Canon 210**). There are two distinct powers in the Church, the power of jurisdiction and the power of orders. The rules of the Code on ordinary and delegated power have reference to the power of jurisdiction only. As to the power of orders, both ordinary and delegated, the Code does not admit delegation or subdelegation except by explicit concession. The power of jurisdiction imports the government of the faithful, in its legislative, administrative and judicial functions; the power of orders refers to the sacred ministry and the divine cult. Some acts necessitate the exercise of both powers, as, for instance, the adminis-

---

[15] In a study of the question of the supplying of jurisdiction in common error to a priest for the hearing of confessions, Raus in the *Linzer Quartalschrift*, LXXV, 297, sums up the opinion of commentators of the Code, and states that they *fere communiter* require necessity or a grave reason to hear confessions *licitly* with jurisdiction supplied by common error.

tration of the Sacrament of Penance which partly partakes of the power of jurisdiction or government (since it involves the judgment of the conduct of the faithful), and partly pertains to the power of orders (because of conferring a sacrament).[15a]

TITLE VI

OF THE REDUCTION OF CLERICS TO THE STATE OF THE LAITY

164. Though sacred ordination once validly received cannot be invalidated, a cleric in major orders may be reduced to the state of the laity by rescript of the Holy See, by decree or sentence of the ecclesiastical court in the case mentioned in Canon 214, or by the penalty of degradation. A cleric in minor orders may be reduced to the state of the laity not only for reason of the causes laid down in law which *ipso facto* effect the reduction, but also by his own free will, after first notifying the local Ordinary of his intention. Furthermore, for a just cause, the local Ordinary may on his own initiative issue the decree of reduction when he prudently judges that, all things considered, the cleric cannot with due respect for the clerical state be promoted to sacred orders (**Canon 211**).

If a cleric in minor orders has for any reason returned to the state of the laity, he may again be admitted to the clergy with the permission of the Ordinary into whose diocese he was incardinated by ordination. The Ordinary shall grant the permission only after a diligent inquiry into the life and character of the individual, and after a test the length of which is to be determined by the judgment of the same Ordinary. A cleric in major orders who has returned to the lay state cannot be admitted again to the clerical state without the permission of the Holy See (**Canon 212**).

All clerics who have been legitimately reduced, or have returned, to the state of the laity, thereby lose the offices, benefices, rights and privileges of the clergy, and are forbidden to wear the cassock and the tonsure. A cleric in major orders, however, is bound by the obligation of celibacy, except in the case mentioned in Canon 214 (**Canon 213**).

[15a] Concerning bishops' faculties, App. III, 11.

165. A cleric who received a major order through grave fear may be reduced to the state of the laity by sentence of the ecclesiastical judge, provided he can prove that he was ordained out of grave fear and has not ratified the ordination afterwards, at least tacitly, by the exercise of the order with the intention of undertaking the obligations of the major orders. By the sentence of reduction he is freed from the obligation of celibacy and from the duty of saying the Divine Office. The compulsion and absence of ratification must be proved in the manner prescribed in Canons 1993–1998 (**Canon 214**).

Section II

OF CLERICS INDIVIDUALLY

166. The Supreme Authority of the Church has the exclusive right to erect ecclesiastical provinces, dioceses, abbeys and prelatures *nullius,* vicariates and prefectures apostolic, or to change their limits, divide, unite, and suppress them. In law, the term "diocese" refers also to abbeys or prelatures *nullius,* unless the nature of things or the context show the contrary (**Canon 215**).

167. The territory of every diocese shall be divided into distinct territorial sections, and each portion shall have its own proper church to which the Catholic population of the district shall be assigned. Such a church is presided over by a rector as the proper pastor for the necessary care of souls. The vicariates and prefectures apostolic shall be divided in like manner, where it can conveniently be done. The parts or sections of a diocese are called parishes; those of vicariates and prefectures apostolic are called quasi-parishes, and the priests assigned to the quasi-parishes are called quasi-pastors (**Canon 216,** §§ 1–3).[15b]

168. Without special permission from the Holy See, the constitution of parishes may not be based on the difference of languages of the people in the same town or territory. It is likewise forbidden to establish purely personal parishes for certain families or persons. Where such parishes have been already established, no change shall be made without consulting the Apostolic See (**Canon 216,** § 4). In the United States there

[15b] What are canonical parishes, App. III, 12, a and b.

are many parishes for people of different languages, and these do not as a rule have any boundary lines because such a division is practically impossible. For the efficient care of the foreigners such parishes are necessary in many places. The Code demands that the Holy See be consulted in future, before any others are established. It is evidently the intention of the Holy See to have one uniform system of parishes everywhere, and, if peculiar circumstances demand a deviation from the common system, the Holy See wants to be consulted concerning the matter.

169. By declaration of the Committee of the Authentic Interpretation of the Code, Sept. 26, 1921, the doubts as to the canonical standing of many parishes in the United States were settled. The Committee declares that: (1) no special or formal decree of erection of the parish by the bishop is required; (2) that it suffices for the erection of a parish that the Ordinary define the territorial limits and assign a rector to the people and the church; (3) in reference to parishes established by the bishop before the promulgation of the Code, these parishes became *ipso facto* canonical parishes, and no decree of erection is necessary beyond the definition of the territorial limits and the appointment of a pastor to take charge of such territories. The declaration was not published in the *Acta Apostolicæ Sedis,* but sent to the bishops of the United States by the Apostolic Delegate by letter of November 10, 1922. The decree does not speak of the status of the language parishes in the United States, but, as the Code recognizes the language parishes established before the Code was promulgated and does not allow the Ordinary to change them without consulting the Holy See (cfr. Canon 216, § 4), they may be considered canonical parishes.[16]

170. The bishop shall divide his diocese into regions or districts consisting of several parishes, which districts are known under the name of *vicariatus foranei, decanatus, archipresbyteratus,* etc.: if this division is impossible or impracticable for

---

[16] The Committee for the Authentic Interpretation of the Code declared that in countries of mixed languages which politically constitute one State, but where several so-called official languages are in use, an Apostolic indult is required, in virtue of Canon 216, to erect a language parish, though that language is one of the official languages and the parish has its own territorial boundaries (cfr. App. III, 12, c).

reason of peculiar circumstances, the bishop shall consult the Holy See, unless the same has already provided for such cases (**Canon 217**). The dioceses in the United States are usually divided into deaneries.

TITLE VII

OF THE SUPREME AUTHORITY AND THOSE WHO BY ECCLESIASTICAL LAW SHARE IN IT

CHAPTER I

OF THE ROMAN PONTIFF

171. As the successor to the primacy of St. Peter, the Roman Pontiff has not only the primacy of honor, but also supreme and full power of jurisdiction over the universal Church, in matters of faith and morals as well as in those pertaining to the discipline and government of the Church throughout the whole world. This power is episcopal, ordinary and immediate, and extends over each and every church, and over each and every pastor as well as over the faithful, and is independent of all human authority (**Canon 218**).

The Roman Pontiff legitimately elected obtains, from the moment he accepts the election, the full power of supreme jurisdiction by divine right (**Canon 219**). The position of the Roman Pontiff is altogether without parallel in the world. In all other independent human organizations and societies, the form of government is dependent on the will of the majority, but the form of government of the Church is fixed by Christ, and thus cannot be changed by men. The authority of the Supreme Pontiff does not come from the Church, but from Christ. All that the Church can do is to determine the manner of electing her Supreme Head. The power of the Pope comes directly from God, for he is not merely the representative of the people of the Church, but the representative of Christ. The Church has all the characteristics of an independent human society, but it has its own peculiar constitution, which is well adapted to its spiritual nature and purpose.

Affairs of greater importance, which are reserved exclusively to the Roman Pontiff either by their very nature or by the positive rulings of the law, are called *causæ majores* (**Canon 220**).

172. If it should happen that the Roman Pontiff wishes to resign his office, it is not necessary for the validity of the renunciation that the Cardinals or any other persons accept the resignation (**Canon 221**). The reason for this rule is that the Pope has no superior above him who could accept the resignation; neither the College of Cardinals, nor all the bishops as a body, nor the faithful have any authority over the Supreme Pontiff, who is, as his title indicates, supreme.

CHAPTER II

OF ŒCUMENICAL COUNCILS

173. There can be no Œcumenical Council unless it is convoked by the Roman Pontiff. It is the right of the Roman Pontiff to preside over the Œcumenical Council either in person or through others; to determine the matters to be discussed and in what order; to transfer, suspend, or dissolve the Council, and to confirm its decrees (**Canon 222**).

174. The following persons shall be called to the Council and have a decisive vote:

(1) The Cardinals of the Holy Roman Church, even though they are not bishops;

(2) The patriarchs, primates, archbishops, and residential bishops, even those not yet consecrated;

(3) The abbots or prelates *nullius;*

(4) The Abbot Primate, abbots who are superiors of monastic congregations, the supreme heads of exempt organizations of religious clergy. The superiors general of other religious bodies are not to be called, unless the bull of convocation explicitly states otherwise.

If titular bishops are called to the Œcumenical Council, they also have a decisive vote, unless it is otherwise provided in the decree of convocation. Theologians and experts in Canon Law who may be invited to the Œcumenical Council have but a consultive vote (**Canon 223**).

175. If any one of the above-mentioned clergy, who, according to the foregoing Canon must be summoned to the Council,

cannot come on account of some just impediment, he shall send a proxy and prove the impediment. If the proxy is one of the Fathers of the Council, he shall not have a double vote; if he is not, he shall be allowed to be present only at the public sessions, but without a vote. At the completion of the Council, he is entitled to subscribe his name to the acts of the Council (**Canon 224**).

176. No one of those who should be present at the Council is allowed to leave before the Council is lawfully finished, unless the President of the Council shall have approved of the reason for leaving and have granted permission to leave (**Canon 225**).

The Fathers of the Council may add other questions to those proposed by the Roman Pontiff, but they must have been previously approved by the President of the Council (**Canon 226**).

177. The decrees of the Council have no definite binding force, unless they shall have been confirmed by the Roman Pontiff and promulgated by his orders (**Canon 227**). The Œcumenical Council has supreme jurisdiction in the whole Church. From the judgment of the Roman Pontiff there is no appeal to the Œcumenical Council (**Canon 228**).[17]

If the Roman Pontiff should die during the celebration of the Council, the Council is by law automatically suspended until the new Pontiff shall have ordered its resumption and continuation (**Canon 229**).

CHAPTER III

OF THE CARDINALS OF THE HOLY ROMAN CHURCH

178. The Cardinals of the Holy Roman Church constitute the Senate of the Roman Pontiff, and assist him in the government of the Church as principal advisers and assistants (**Canon 230**).

The Sacred College is divided into three orders: the episcopal order, which includes only the six Cardinals appointed to the suburbicarian sees; the presbyteral order, consisting of

---

17 By Canon 2332 all persons of whatever rank, degree or dignity, including bishops and Cardinals, who appeal from the then reigning Roman Pontiff to an Œcumenical Council, are *ipso facto* excommunicated, which excommunication is reserved *speciali modo* to the Pope.

fifty Cardinal Priests, and the diaconal order, consisting of fourteen Cardinal Deacons. Each of the Cardinal Priests and Deacons is assigned by the Roman Pontiff a cardinalitial title or deaconry respectively in the City of Rome (**Canon 231**).

The name of Cardinal is derived from the Latin *cardo* (hinge), and the derived adjective, *cardinalis* (chief or principal), came to be applied to the head priest of a church; wherefore, in ancient documents, bishops and sometimes canons of a cathedral are called cardinals (cfr. *Decretum Grat.*, c. 3, D. 24). In the course of time the term was restricted to the principal priests at the seven ancient churches of Rome and to the head deacons of the seven *diaconiæ regionariæ* of the same city. Thus, in the sixth century, we have the titles *Cardinalis Presbyter* and *Cardinalis Diaconus Romanæ Ecclesiæ* (cfr. *Decretum Grat.*, c. 5, D. 93). The bishops of the towns in the vicinity of Rome were considered attached to the cathedral church of the Pope, the Lateran Basilica, and in the eighth century they came to be called Cardinals. By the law of Pope Pius V, the clergy of other churches were forbidden to assume the title of Cardinal, and of the Roman clergy only the suburbicarian bishops, fifty priests and fourteen deacons were permitted to use the title. By this Constitution of Pope Pius V, there are thus six Cardinal bishops, fifty Cardinal priests and fourteen Cardinal deacons. This number of the Sacred College has not since been changed, as the Code retains the three orders and the respective numbers of Cardinals, the Cardinal priests and deacons being assigned to certain presbyteral or diaconal churches in the City of Rome.

Creation of Cardinals

179. The creation of Cardinals is reserved to the free choice of the Roman Pontiff. The men must be at least priests, and be endowed with exceptional learning, piety and prudence. The following persons are barred from the dignity of the cardinalate:

(1) Illegitimates, though legitimized by subsequent marriage; men suffering from canonical irregularity or impediment to sacred orders (cfr. Canons 984, 985, 987), even though the Holy See has granted them a dispensation to receive orders and to be promoted to the episcopal dignity;

(2) Men who have a child or a grandchild, legitimate or illegitimate;

(3) Men who are related in the first or second degree of consanguinity to any living Cardinal (**Canon 232**).

180. The Cardinals are created and nominated by the Roman Pontiff in consistory, and by this creation and nomination obtain the right to vote in the election of the Roman Pontiff and the other privileges of Cardinals. If the Roman Pontiff announces in consistory the creation of a Cardinal, but reserves the name to himself (*reservatio in pectore*), the person thus promoted does not in the meantime enjoy any of the rights and privileges of Cardinals, but, after the Roman Pontiff has published his name, he partakes of the rights and privileges from the time of the publication, and takes precedence over other Cardinals created after the time of the reservation *in pectore* (**Canon 233**). If the person promoted to the dignity of the cardinalate is not at Rome, he must on receiving the red biretta take the oath that he will go to see the Supreme Pontiff within one year, unless he is legitimately excused by some impediment (**Canon 234**).

Unless the Holy See provides otherwise in particular cases, not only all dignities, churches or benefices which the new Cardinal held are *ipso facto* vacant, but also all ecclesiastical pensions are forfeited by the promotion to the cardinalate (**Canon 235**).

181. By option made in consistory and approved by the Supreme Pontiff, the Cardinals of the order of priests may choose another titular church, and the Cardinals of the order of deacons may change to another of the deacons' titular churches; the priority of order and of promotion to the cardinalate determine the precedence in this connexion. If a Cardinal Deacon has stayed in that order of Cardinals for fully ten years, he has the right of option also for a title of the order of Cardinal Priests. The Cardinal Deacon who by option transferred to the order of Cardinal Priests precedes in the Sacred College all those Cardinal Priests who were created Cardinals after him.

If one of the suburbicarian sees is vacant, the Cardinal Priests who are present at the Papal court at the moment when the vacancy occurs, or are absent for a while on account of some business committed to them by the Roman Pontiff, have an option in consistory for that see in the order of the priority of their promotion to the cardinalate.

The Cardinals who hold one of the suburbicarian bishoprics do not have an option for another see. When, however, a Cardinal succeeds to the title of Dean of the Sacred College, he combines his own diocese with the See of Ostia which see is therefore always united with one or another of the suburbicarian bishoprics in the person of the Cardinal Dean (**Canon 236**).

182. The Sacred College of Cardinals is presided over by the Cardinal Dean, that is to say, the Cardinal who is the oldest in promotion to a suburbicarian see, but the Dean has no jurisdiction over the other Cardinals, and is regarded merely as the first among equals. If the position of Dean is vacant, the subdean succeeds automatically by law, whether he is at the moment of vacancy present at the Papal court or absent at the time on account of some duty committed to him by the Roman Pontiff (**Canon 237**).

183. The Cardinals are obliged to reside at the Papal court, and they are not allowed to leave the City without permission of the Roman Pontiff with the following exception: Though the Cardinals who have a suburbicarian bishopric are also obliged to reside at the Papal court, they do not need permission to go to their dioceses whenever they deem it necessary. The Cardinals who are bishops of non-suburbicarian sees, are exempted from the obligation of residence at the Papal court; but, when they come to the City of Rome, they must visit the Roman Pontiff and cannot leave the City before they have obtained from him leave to go (**Canon 238**).

PRIVILEGES OF CARDINALS

184. Besides other privileges given to Cardinals in various Canons of the Code, all have the following faculties from the time of their promotion in consistory:

(1) to hear confessions anywhere in the world, even of religious of either sex, and to absolve from all reserved sins and censures, with the exception of the censures reserved *specialissimo*

modo to the Holy See and those attached to the breaking of the oath of secrecy of the Holy Office;

(2) to choose a confessor for themselves and the members of their household. If this confessor should not have jurisdiction, he obtains it automatically by his choice as confessor, and he has power to absolve from all reserved sins and censures with the restrictions mentioned in the preceding paragraph;

(3) to preach the word of God everywhere;

(4) to celebrate or to allow another to celebrate in their presence one Holy Mass on Holy Thursday and three Masses on Christmas Night;

(5) to bless everywhere merely by the sign of the cross and attach the indulgences usually granted by the Holy See to rosaries and other prayer beads, crosses, medals, statues and scapulars approved by the Holy See, without the obligation of having the names of those received into the scapular put on record;

(6) to erect the Stations of the Way of the Cross and bless them under one formula in any church, oratory (even private ones), and other religious places. The Cardinals may bless crucifixes with the indulgences of the Way of the Cross for the benefit of the faithful who, through illness or other legitimate impediment, cannot visit a place where the Stations are erected;

(7) to celebrate Holy Mass on a portable altar, not only in their own residences but wherever they are, and to allow another Holy Mass to be said in their presence;

(8) to say Holy Mass on the ocean, due precaution being taken not to upset the chalice;

(9) to say Holy Mass in all churches and oratories in conformity with their own calendar;

(10) to enjoy on any day the benefit of the personally privileged altar;

(11) to gain in their own private chapel those indulgences for which a visit to some church or sacred shrine is prescribed in the town or city in which the Cardinal actually stays. The members of the household participate in this privilege;

(12) to bless the people of any place after the manner of bishops; in the City of Rome, however, only inside the churches, pious places and meetings of the faithful;

(13) to wear the pectoral cross after the manner of bishops, even over the mozzetta, and to use the mitre and crozier;

(14) to celebrate Holy Mass in any private oratory without prejudice to the person having the privilege of the private oratory, so that if the privilege allows only one Mass a day, the Mass of the Cardinal does not take the place of that Mass;

(15) to perform pontifical functions with the throne and canopy in all churches outside the City of Rome, notifying the local Ordinary if he wishes to celebrate in the cathedral church;

(16) to receive the honors usually shown to local Ordinaries wherever the Cardinal goes;

(17) to authenticate for the external forum oral pronouncements of the Supreme Pontiff;

(18) to have a private oratory which is exempt from visitation by the local Ordinary;

(19) to dispose of the revenues of their benefices even by last will, with the exceptions mentioned in Canon 1298;

(20) to bless and consecrate anywhere churches, altars, sacred vessels, to bless abbots and perform similar functions—with the exception of the consecration of holy oils, if the Cardinal is not a bishop. In reference to the consecration of places, Canon 1157 must be observed which rules that the consent of the local Ordinary is always required for the blessing or consecration of a sacred place;

(21) to precede all prelates, even patriarchs and papal legates, unless the papal legate is also a Cardinal, in which case he precedes within the territory of his jurisdiction all the Cardinals. Outside the City of Rome, the Cardinal Legate *a latere* (i.e., a Cardinal sent by the Roman Pontiff to represent him in some affair) takes precedence of all other Cardinals;

(22) to confer first tonsure and minor orders, provided the candidates have dimissorial letters from their proper bishop;

(23) to confer the sacrament of Confirmation with the obligation, as prescribed by law, that the names of those confirmed be entered in the records of their respective parishes;

(24) to grant an indulgence of two hundred days, even *toties quoties*, in places and institutions and for persons under the Cardinal's jurisdiction or protection. He may grant these indulgences also in other places, but they can be gained only by those present and once only (**Canon 239, § 1**).

185. The Cardinal Dean of the Sacred College enjoys the privilege of ordaining and consecrating the elected Roman Pontiff, if he needs ordination and episcopal consecration, and in that case the Cardinal Dean has the right to use the pallium. In absence of the Cardinal Dean, this privilege devolves on the sub-dean, and if he also is absent, on the oldest suburbicarian Cardinal Bishop.

Finally, the Cardinal Proto-Deacon in the name of the Pope places the pallium on archbishops and bishops (who have the privilege to wear it) or on their proxies, and he announces to the people the name of the newly elected Roman Pontiff (**Canon 239, §§ 2–3**).

186. A Cardinal who has been promoted to a suburbicarian bishopric, and has taken canonical possession of the same, is truly a bishop of the diocese, and has the same powers over it which residential bishops have over their dioceses.

The other Cardinals, after having taken canonical possession of their titular churches, can perform in those churches all the functions which local Ordinaries perform with the exception of canonical trials and acts of jurisdiction over the faithful, but they have authority in matters pertaining to the discipline and correction of abuses and the service of the church. The Cardinal Priests may perform pontifical functions with throne and canopy in their titular church, and the Cardinal Deacons may assist in pontificals in their own titular church, but no one else can perform pontifical functions in that church without the consent of the respective Cardinal. In other churches of the City of Rome the Cardinals cannot make use of the throne and canopy without the permission of the Roman Pontiff (**Canon 240**).

During the vacancy of the Holy See, the Sacred College of Cardinals and the Roman Curia have no powers except those defined by the Constitution "Vacante Sede Apostolica," of Pope Pius X, December 25, 1904 (**Canon 241**).

CHAPTER IV

OF THE ROMAN CURIA

187. The Roman Curia consists of the Sacred Congregations, Tribunals, and Offices as described in the following Canons (**Canon 242**).

From ancient times the Roman Pontiffs employed the help of various colleges of clerics in the government of the Universal Church. Thus, in the time of Pope Clement (died 100), we read of seven notaries who originally had the duty of investigating and recording the acts of the martyrs, and who, after the cessation of the persecutions, were employed in the writing of the papal documents and in other affairs of the Holy See. Again, we read of seven defenders (*defensores regionarii*), who had the duty of defending the rights and property of the Church and of providing for the widows and the poor, and who, especially from the time of Pope Gregory I, were employed in other important affairs. Furthermore, there was the college of the *clerus palatinus,* whose members assisted the Supreme Pontiff in liturgical functions, in the affairs of the government of the Church, and in personal service. Of these the seven *judices palatini* were the most important up to about the thirteenth century.

With the rapid spread of the Church in Europe and in far distant countries, the business of the Holy See increased in proportion. While the Supreme Pontiffs had employed the help of the above-mentioned standing committees, and had called into council the clergy of the City of Rome, especially the heads of the ancient parishes of the city and the bishops of the suburban dioceses, it became necessary to establish standing committees of Cardinals and other dignitaries, each attending to a specific division of Papal affairs. Pope Paul III instituted the Sacred Congregation of the Inquisition on July 21, 1542. By the Constitution "Immensa," January 22, 1588, Pope Sixtus V, put the Roman Congregations on a basis which has practically been retained to this day, with some modifications as to the number of these Congregations and their various duties.

188. In each of the Congregations, Tribunals and Offices, that discipline shall be preserved and those rules for the transac-

tion of business followed which have been prescribed, either in general or particular, by the Roman Pontiff. All who belong to any of the Congregations, Tribunals and Offices of the Roman Curia are bound to secrecy within the limits and according to the laws laid down for each (**Canon 243**). The Constitution "Sapienti Consilio," of Pope Pius X, June 29, 1908, brought about a reorganization of the Roman Curia, and detailed the rules and regulations whereby the various branches of the Curia are governed.

189. Nothing of importance or of an extraordinary character is to be decided by the Sacred Congregations, Tribunals, and Offices without the president of the respective committee having first notified the Roman Pontiff. All concessions and resolutions need the Papal approval, except those affairs for which special faculties have been given to the presidents of the Offices, Tribunals and Congregations, and excepting the sentences of the Tribunals of the Roman Rota and Apostolic Signatura (**Canon 244**).

If any controversy concerning competency arises between the Sacred Congregations, Tribunals and Offices of the Roman Curia, a committee of Cardinals which the Roman Pontiff shall appoint in each individual case will decide the question (**Canon 245**).[17a]

ARTICLE I.—OF THE SACRED CONGREGATIONS

190. Each of the Congregations is presided over by a **Cardinal Prefect**, unless the Roman Pontiff himself is the Prefect of the Congregation, when it is directed by a Cardinal Secretary. With the prefect are associated as many Cardinals as the Pope may think fit to assign, together with other necessary assistants (**Canon 246**).

191. *The Congregation of the Holy Office,* of which the Supreme Pontiff is the prefect, guards the doctrine of faith and morals. It judges crimes which according to its own proper law are reserved to it, with the power to judge these criminal cases not only in the case of appeals from the court of the local Ordinaries, but also in the first instance, if the case has been brought directly before this Congregation.

It has *exclusive* jurisdiction in cases which involve directly

[17a] Decisions on competency, cfr. App. III, 13, a–d.

or indirectly the Pauline Privilege in marriage, disparity of cult and mixed religion, and to this Congregation belongs the power to dispense from these impediments. Wherefore every question of this kind must be submitted to the Congregation which may, according to its judgment and as the case demands, refer it to another Congregation or to the Tribunal of the Sacred Rota.

To it pertains not only the careful examination of the books denounced to the Holy See and, if necessary, their prohibition, but also the granting of dispensations from this prohibition to read forbidden books. It is its task also to investigate *ex officio* in the best available manner the censurable writings of any kind which are published, and to remind the Ordinaries of their duty to proceed conscientiously against pernicious writings and to denounce them to the Holy See in accordance with Canon 1397 (cfr. n. 1412). The Holy Office exclusively is competent in all matters which relate to the eucharistic fast for priests celebrating Holy Mass (**Canon 247**).

192. *The Consistorial Congregation* has the Roman Pontiff as prefect. The Cardinal Secretary of the Holy Office, the Prefect of the Congregation of Seminaries and Universities and the Secretary of State belong *ex officio* to this Congregation. Among the consultors of the Consistorial Congregation are numbered the Assessor of the Holy Office, the Secretary of the Congregation of Extraordinary Affairs of the Church, and the Secretary of the Congregation of Seminaries and Universities.

This Congregation not only prepares the *agenda* in Consistories, but also establishes in places not subject to the Congregation of the Propaganda new dioceses and provinces, cathedral and collegiate chapters; divides already existing dioceses; proposes bishops, administrators Apostolic, coadjutor and auxiliary bishops; gives orders for the canonical investigation or process concerning the men who are to be promoted to the aforesaid positions, carefully examines the acts of the process, and conducts the examinations of these men in regard to their knowledge. If in these appointments the Church has to deal with the civil governments, Canon 255 commits the proceedings relative to these appointments to the Congregation for Extraordinary Ecclesiastical Affairs.

On this Congregation depend all those matters which pertain to the establishment, conservation and state of dioceses. Wherefore, it inquires whether or not the Ordinaries fulfill their duties; examines the written reports of the bishops on the state of their dioceses, orders Apostolic visitations and examines the report of the same, and in both cases remands to the various Congregations for their deliberation those matters which particularly pertain to each (**Canon 248**).

193. *The Congregation of the Sacraments* has charge of the disciplinary regulations of the Seven Sacraments, with the exception of matters reserved to the Holy Office in Canon 247 and to the Sacred Congregation of Rites in reference to the sacred rites and ceremonies to be observed in their administration. Dispensations from marriage impediments and from other disciplinary laws in other sacraments are under the jurisdiction of this Congregation, except in cases expressly assigned to other Congregations. To it belong the dispensation from the *matrimonium ratum non consummatum* and the investigations necessary in the case. Also questions of the validity of marriage, sacred orders and other sacraments may be brought before this Congregation, which, according to its own judgment, may turn the cases over to the Roman Rota (**Canon 249**).

194. *The Congregation of the Council* has charge over the entire discipline of the secular clergy and the Christian people.

Wherefore, it has the duty to see that the precepts of Christian life are observed, and has the faculty to dispense, when advisable, the faithful from their observance. It has charge of affairs concerning pastors and canons, of pious sodalities and unions (even though they are dependent on religious or are erected in their churches or houses), of pious legacies and works, Mass stipends, benefices or offices, ecclesiastical goods both movable and immovable, diocesan taxes, taxes of episcopal Curias and other affairs of this kind. To it is reserved the faculty to exempt from conditions required for the obtaining of benefices, whenever the conferring of them belongs to the Ordinaries; to accept a settlement from persons who have taken possession of ecclesiastical goods (even though these belong to religious); to permit the faithful to acquire ecclesiastical goods which have been seized by the civil powers.

It also attends to all matters relative to ecclesiastical immunity, and to controversies over precedence without prejudice to the rights of the Congregation of Religious and the Ceremonial Congregation.

It has charge over all affairs relative to the holding of Councils and the approval of proceedings therein, and over meetings or conferences of bishops, outside the places which are under the jurisdiction of the Congregation of the Propaganda. In all controversies arising out of the affairs committed to the Congregation of the Council it is competent to render decisions if the cases are conducted in the disciplinary form; if they are to be discussed in the form of a canonical trial, the Congregation shall remand the cases to the competent court (**Canon 250**). In controversies arising out of the administrative acts, decrees, orders, etc., of Ordinaries no appeal to the Tribunal of the Roman Rota is permitted, but merely recourse to the Sacred Congregation of the Council (cfr. Canon 1601, n. 1585).

195. *The Congregation of Religious* has exclusive jurisdiction over the religious organizations of all kinds, even including communities or societies which have no vows but lead a community life after the manner of religious. Their government, discipline, studies, goods and property, privileges, dispensations from the common laws of the Church, with the exception of the eucharistic fast for the celebration of Holy Mass, are subject to this Congregation. In districts subject to the Sacred Congregation of the Propaganda certain of these matters come under the jurisdiction of that body.

While questions which are to be decided by canonical trial are to be turned over to the proper tribunal, and matters subject to the Holy Office and to the Sacred Congregation of the Council are to be referred to these Congregations by the Sacred Congregation of the Religious, the latter decides all cases of its competency in the disciplinary form. A controversy between a religious and one who is not a religious, may, especially if the non-religious requests it and the request seems fair, be referred to another Congregation or Tribunal (**Canon 251**).

By decision of a special Committee of Cardinals, it was declared: (1) that all questions in reference to any rights, privileges, etc., of religious either as a community or as individuals belongs exclusively to the Sacred Congregation of the Religious with the exception of matters proper to the Holy

Office (as the eucharistic fast, matters of faith, censure of objectionable books, etc.) ; (2) the fulfillment and administration of foundation Masses actually intrusted to the religious, and the granting of sanations and condonations for the past and reductions of Masses for the future, are subject to the Sacred Congregation of the Religious; (3) dispensations for the reception of sacred orders by the religious on account of defect of age, irregularities, or other conditions and the requisite number of years of study can be granted only by the Sacred Congregation of the Religious; religious priests who on account of sickness, or for any other reason, are physically or morally impeded from the celebration of Holy Mass, are to obtain dispensations from the Sacred Congregation of the Religious.[18]

196. *The Congregation of the Propagation of the Faith* has charge of the Catholic missions for the spread of the faith, and whatever is connected with and necessary for the management of the missions. Councils held in missionary districts are subject to the Propaganda. Its jurisdiction is limited to those districts where either the hierarchy is not yet established, or, if established, is still in its initial stage. Societies and seminaries founded exclusively for the training of missionaries are under the jurisdiction of the Propaganda. The Propaganda is bound to refer to the competent Congregations all cases concerning faith, marriage, and the general rules governing the sacred liturgy.

In reference to the religious in the mission territories, the Propaganda has jurisdiction in all matters which concern them as missionaries, whether individually and collectively. All matters that concern them as religious, whether individually or as a body, come under the jurisdiction of the Sacred Congregation of the Religious (**Canon 252**).

197. *The Congregation of Sacred Rites* has authority to supervise and regulate all matters pertaining directly to the sacred rites and ceremonies of the Latin Church. Matters which are concerned only remotely with the sacred rites (e.g., questions of precedence and other rights of that kind), are not subject to this Congregation. The Congregation grants exemptions from the liturgical laws, insignia to be worn at the sacred functions,

18 March 24, 1919; *Acta Ap. Sedis*, XI, 251.

and other privileges of honor. The causes of beatification and canonization, and all questions concerning sacred relics, are subject to the Congregation of Sacred Rites (**Canon 253**).

198. *The Ceremonial Congregation* regulates the ceremonies in the papal chapel and the papal court, and the sacred functions which the Cardinals perform outside the papal chapel. It decides also questions of precedence among the Cardinals, as well as among the legates whom the various nations send to the Holy See (**Canon 254**).

199. *The Congregation for Extraordinary Affairs* of the Church has jurisdiction to constitute or divide dioceses and appoint suitable bishops in countries where the civil governments have to be dealt with in doing these things. It also has to handle those matters which the Supreme Pontiff may refer to this Congregation through the Secretary of State, especially affairs connected with the civil laws and the agreements of the Holy See with the various nations (**Canon 255**).

200. *The Congregation of Seminaries and Universities* has jurisdiction over the government, discipline, temporal administration and studies in seminaries, except those in charge of the Propaganda. Its jurisdiction also extends to universities and faculties established with the authority of the Church, including those directed by some religious order or society. It approves new universities, gives authority to confer academical degrees, prescribes the conditions under which these degrees should be conferred, and, in the case of a man distinguished for exceptional learning, may itself confer the degrees. The Cardinal Secretary of the Consistorial Congregation is included among the Cardinal members, and the Assessor of the Consistorial Congregation among the consultors of this Congregation (**Canon 256**).

201. *The Congregation for the Oriental Church* has for its Prefect the Roman Pontiff. To this Congregation are reserved all affairs of every kind relating to persons, discipline, and Rites of the Oriental Churches, even those of a mixed nature —that is to say, such as affect partly a Catholic of the Oriental and partly a Catholic of the Latin Rite (e.g., marriages between a Catholic of the Latin Rite and a Catholic of an Oriental Rite; Oriental priests celebrating Mass in a church of the Latin Rite, and *vice versa*). This Congregation has all the powers of the

other Congregations combined in its jurisdiction over the Oriental Rites, subject however to the jurisdiction of the Holy Office, as stated in Canon 247 (**Canon 257**).

ARTICLE II.—OF THE TRIBUNALS OF THE ROMAN CURIA

202. *The Sacred Penitentiary* is presided over by a Cardinal called the *Major Penitentiary*. The jurisdiction of this tribunal is limited to affairs of the internal forum, both sacramental and non-sacramental. It grants favors for the internal forum exclusively, such as absolutions, dispensations, commutations, sanations, condonations. The Sacred Penitentiary, moreover, considers and decides questions of conscience.

All questions connected with the *use and concession of Indulgences* are also decided by the Sacred Penitentiary, subject to the rights of the Holy Office to decide dogmatic questions on Indulgences and to approve new indulgenced prayers and devotions (**Canon 258**).

203. *The Tribunals of the Sacred Roman Rota and the Apostolic Signatura* decide cases which must be settled by canonical trial, within the limits and according to the rules laid down in Canons 1598–1605. The rights of the Holy Office and of the Sacred Congregation of Rites in the cases proper to their jurisdiction are not affected by this Canon (**Canon 259**).

ARTICLE III.—OF THE OFFICES OF THE ROMAN CURIA

204. *The Apostolic Chancery,* in charge of the Cardinal Chancellor of the Holy Roman Church, has the duty of drawing up and mailing the Apostolic Letters or Bulls for the appointment to benefices and offices made in consistory, for the institution of new provinces, dioceses, and chapters, and for other very important affairs of the Church. Such letters and bulls are not to be issued except by orders of the Sacred Consistorial Congregation in those matters over which it has authority, or by order of the Supreme Pontiff in other affairs, and the instructions given in each individual case must be observed (**Canon 260**).

205. *The Apostolic Dataria,* which is in charge of the Cardinal Datary of the Holy Roman Church, has the duty of investigating the qualifications of candidates to be promoted to

non-consistorial benefices reserved to the Holy See. It draws up and sends out the Apostolic letters of appointment to these benefices, and may simultaneously grant exemptions from the conditions required by these offices, in so far as the conferring does not devolve on the Ordinary. It also provides for the pensions and the execution of the duties which the Supreme Pontiff may appoint in conferring these benefices (**Canon 261**).

206. *The Camera Apostolica,* in charge of the Cardinal Camerlengo of the Holy Roman Church, has the care and administration of the temporal goods and rights of the Apostolic See, especially for the time of vacancy, in which case the laws of the Constitution of Pope Pius X, ''Vacante Sede Apostolica,'' of December 25, 1904, must be observed (**Canon 262**).

207. *The Secretariate of State,* in charge of the Cardinal Secretary of State, consists of three divisions:

(1) The first division, presided over by the Secretary of the Congregation for Extraordinary Affairs, attends to those matters which must be subjected for examination to that Congregation according to Canon 255;

(2) The second division, under the direction of the *Substitutus,* attends to ordinary affairs;

(3) The third division is under the direction of the Chancellor of Apostolic Briefs and attends to the drafting and mailing of these documents (**Canon 263**).

The Secretariate of Briefs to Princes and of Latin Letters has the duty of writing in Latin the pontifical documents which the Supreme Pontiff commits to it (**Canon 264**).

CHAPTER V

OF THE LEGATES OF THE ROMAN PONTIFF

208. Independently of any civil power, the Roman Pontiff has the right to send legates to any part of the world, either with or without ecclesiastical jurisdiction (**Canon 265**). A Papal Legate is called ''Legate *a latere,*'' when the Supreme Pontiff sends out a Cardinal with this title to represent him personally (*tanquam alter ego*), and with such powers as the Pope may grant (**Canon 266**).

Legates who are sent with the title of Nuntius or Internuntius have the following rights and duties:

(1) To foster according to the usual rules of the Holy See the relations between the Holy See and the civil government of the country where they act as permanent legates;

(2) In the territory assigned to them they must watch over the condition of the Church, and report to the Roman Pontiff;

(3) Besides these two ordinary powers, they usually receive other faculties which are of the nature of delegated jurisdiction (**Canon 267,** § 1).

Legates who are sent with the title of Delegate Apostolic have but one ordinary duty or power, viz., that of watching over the condition of the Church and informing the Holy See. They have no official relations with the civil government of the territory. Other powers may be granted to them by the Holy See in the form of delegated faculties (**Canon 267,** § 2).

209. The office of the legates, with all the faculties committed to them, does not expire at the vacancy of the Holy See, unless the contrary is stated in the papal letters. It ceases, however, when the object for which they were sent is accomplished, by revocation conveyed to the legate, and by resignation accepted by the Roman Pontiff (**Canon 268**).

The legates shall not impede the free exercise of jurisdiction by the local Ordinaries. Even though perhaps the legates may not be consecrated bishops, they take precedence of all Ordinaries except Cardinals. If they are bishops, they may without the permission of the Ordinaries bless the people and perform the liturgical functions in pontificals in all churches, except cathedral churches, using also the throne and canopy (**Canon 269**). Bishops who on account of their see have the honorary title of Apostolic Legates, do not thereby acquire any special right (**Canon 270**).

CHAPTER VI

OF PATRIARCHS, PRIMATES, METROPOLITANS

210. The title of patriarch or primate does not confer any special jurisdiction, unless particular law rules otherwise in some affairs. They have, however, the prerogative of honor and precedence as specified in Canon 280 (**Canon 271**).

The distinction between bishops of higher and lower rank occurs as early as the Council of Nicæa (held in 325), where the Bishops of Rome, Alexandria and Antioch are distinguished by superior jurisdiction as well as by special prerogatives of honor. The same Council also confirms the special honor due to the Bishop of Jerusalem, based on custom and ancient tradition. In the First Council of Constantinople (381), the Oriental bishops conceded to the Bishop of Constantinople the place of honor immediately after the Roman Pontiff for the reason that Constantinople is the *New Rome*. Though the Pope did not for many centuries admit this ruling of the Council of Constantinople, the bishop of that city actually obtained soon after the Council the jurisdiction of an exarch over all the provinces of Thrace and over Proconsular Asia Minor and Pontus. The Bishop of Jerusalem secured independence from the Patriarch of Antioch, and, with the rights of a metropolitan, obtained the power of a primate over the three ecclesiastical provinces of Palestine. The Roman Pontiffs and the bishops of the West, however, did not recognize any patriarchs other than the Roman Pontiff and the Bishops of Alexandria and Antioch. On the invasion of the Arabs in the seventh century, practically all the patriarchates of the Orient disappeared. At present these patriarchates exist as mere titular ones. The conferring of these titles is reserved to the Roman Pontiff. After the dissolution of the ancient patriarchates of the Oriental Church, minor patriarchates arose of which several returned to communion with the Holy See—namely, the patriarchs of the Maronites, Chaldeans, Armenians, Melchites, Syrians and Copts.

211. The name "exarch," which corresponds to the Latin "primate," occurs in the first Council of Constantinople (381) and again in the Council of Chalcedon (451). In the Latin Church, the Primate of Carthage in Africa comes nearest to the Oriental exarchs, for, as St. Cyprian testifies (about 258), quite a few rights over the ecclesiastical provinces of Northern Africa had been conceded to the Bishop of Carthage. In the other countries of the Western or Latin Church, the dignity and jurisdiction of a primate was claimed by many bishops, and it thus came to pass that each country had at least one, and sometimes several primates. Their rights may be traced, not so much to ancient custom, as to a special concession of the Holy See.

212. The title of Metropolitan (now usually archbishop) occurs in the Council of Nicæa. The metropolitan had not only

the first place of honor, but also various powers of jurisdiction over the bishops of an ecclesiastical province. Though the rights of jurisdiction were gradually limited by the Supreme Pontiff, still the Decretals of Pope Gregory IX and the *Liber Sextus* of Pope Boniface VIII contain a number of powers proper to the metropolitan. In Canon 274, the Code finally specifies explicitly the rights which they have at present over the dioceses of the bishops of the province.

The metropolitan or archbishop presides over an ecclesiastical province, and this dignity is attached to that episcopal see which the Roman Pontiff has constituted or approved as the metropolitan see (**Canon 272**). Besides the special duties mentioned in Canons 275–280, the metropolitan has in his own archdiocese the same obligations and the same rights as the bishop in his diocese (**Canon 273**).

213. Over the dioceses of the suffragan bishops of the province the metropolitan has the following rights only:

(1) If a suffragan bishop, without a legitimate excuse, omits to put into office clerics presented by patrons for a benefice within the time fixed by law, the metropolitan has the right to canonically invest those presented with the benefice;

(2) He can grant an indulgence of one hundred days in the dioceses of the province as well as in his own;

(3) If the cathedral chapter (or, in dioceses without chapters, the diocesan consultors) neglect to elect a vicar-capitular (or, in dioceses without a chapter, an administrator) within the time prescribed in Canon 432, the archbishop has the right to appoint the vicar (or administrator);

(4) The archbishop has the duty to watch over the faith and ecclesiastical discipline of the Church in the province and to inform the Roman Pontiff of abuses;

(5) If a suffragan bishop neglects to hold the canonical visitation of his diocese, the archbishop is to supply the neglect, but, before he does so, the Holy See must first have approved of the reason;

(6) The archbishop has the right to hold the pontifical functions in all churches (even exempt) within the ecclesiastical province, notifying the bishop in advance if he wants to pontificate in the cathedral. He may bless the people, as the bishop does in his own diocese, and have the cross carried before him,

but he may not perform other acts importing jurisdiction in the dioceses of the suffragan bishops;

(7) The archbishop receives appeals from the judicial sentences of the suffragan dioceses, and acts as the judge of the second instance;

(8) He acts as judge of the first instance in cases concerning the rights or the temporal goods of the bishop, or the diocesan curia, according to Canon 1572, § 2. The bishop does not necessarily have to submit the case to the archbishop, but may appoint a committee of three judges (**Canon 274**).

214. Within three months from his consecration or, if he is already consecrated bishop, from his appointment in consistory, the metropolitan must ask the archiepiscopal pallium from the Roman Pontiff either in person or through a proxy. The pallium signifies the archiepiscopal power (**Canon 275**). Before the imposition of the pallium, the archbishop, unless authorized by special Apostolic indult, acts illicitly in exercising metropolitan jurisdiction or episcopal functions in which the liturgical laws demand the use of the pallium (**Canon 276**). The metropolitan can make use of the pallium in all churches of his province (both non-exempt and exempt) in the celebration of Solemn Holy Mass on the days designated in the *Pontificale Romanum* and other days that may have been conceded to him. Outside his province he cannot use the pallium even with the consent of the local Ordinary (**Canon 277**). If the archbishop loses the pallium, or if he is transferred to another archiepiscopal see, he must obtain a new pallium (**Canon 278**). The pallium may not be loaned or donated, or bequeathed to anyone by the dying archbishop, but all pallia which the archbishop got must be buried with him (**Canon 279**).

215. The patriarch precedes the primate, the primate precedes the archbishop, the archbishop precedes the bishop, but according to Canon 347, the bishop within his own diocese precedes all archbishops and bishops with the exception of Cardinals, Legates of the Pope, and his own proper archbishop. Canon 106 determines the rule of precedence outside the diocese (**Canon 280**).

CHAPTER VII

OF PLENARY AND PROVINCIAL COUNCILS

216. The Ordinaries of several ecclesiastical provinces may meet in Plenary Council, but they must first ask the permission of the Holy See, which will appoint a legate to convoke and preside over the Council (**Canon 281**).

At the Plenary Council should be present the following persons who have a decisive vote: besides the Papal Legate, the archbishops, the residential bishops (who may send coadjutor or auxiliary bishops to take their place), the Apostolic administrators of dioceses, the abbots and prelates *nullius,* vicars and prefects Apostolic, and vicars-capitular. If the titular bishops who are staying in the territory where the Council is held, are also summoned by the Papal Legate in accordance with his instructions, they should appear at the Council, and have a decisive vote, unless the document of convocation explicitly provides otherwise. Other members of either the secular or the regular clergy, who are invited to the Council, have only a consultive vote (**Canon 282**).

217. In each ecclesiastical province a Provincial Council shall be held at least every twenty years (**Canon 283**). The metropolitan chooses the place of the Council after having consulted all who are entitled to a decisive vote: ordinarily the metropolitan city should be the place, unless there are good reasons why that is inadvisable. If the metropolitan see is vacant, or the metropolitan is legitimately impeded from calling the Council, the suffragan bishop who is the oldest in promotion to a suffragan bishopric shall convoke the Council. The metropolitan is president of the Council, or otherwise the oldest suffragan who takes his place (**Canon 284**).

218. Bishops who are not subject to any metropolitan, abbots and prelates *nullius,* and archbishops who have no suffragan bishoprics shall choose permanently (if they have not already done so) one of the neighboring metropolitans with the approval of the Apostolic See, and they shall take part in the Provincial Council of that province and observe the laws made at the Council and see that these are observed in their respective territories (**Canon 285**).

219. Besides the dignitaries just mentioned, the suffragan

bishops, the vicars and prefects Apostolic and the vicars-capitular must be called to and must attend the Council, at which they have a decisive vote. The titular bishops staying in the province may be called with the consent of the majority of the members of the Council. If they are called, they have a decisive vote, unless the document of convocation states otherwise. The Cathedral Chapter, or the diocesan consultors of every diocese of which the Ordinary is of right invited to the Council, should be also invited to attend, and, if invited, should send two of their number selected by common vote, who shall have only a consultive vote in the Council. The major superiors of clerical exempt religious organizations and the superiors of monastic congregations who live within the province should be invited, and, when invited, should either appear or make known to the Council the reason that prevents them from taking part in the Council. These as well as other members from the secular or regular clergy who may be summoned, have only a consultive voice in the Council (**Canon 286**).

220. Persons who are under obligation to attend a Plenary or Provincial Council, and who have a decisive vote, shall send a proxy if they are legitimately impeded from coming in person, and they shall prove such impediment to the Council. The proxy, if he be one of the Fathers of the Council who has a decisive vote, shall not have a double vote; if he is not one of the Fathers of the Council, he has a consultive vote as proxy (**Canon 287**).

221. In a Plenary or Provincial Council, the president determines the order of business, opens the Council, and transfers, suspends, or closes it. In the Provincial Council these acts must be done with the consent of the Fathers of the Council (**Canon 288**). Once the Plenary or the Provincial Council has been opened, none of those who are obliged to be present may leave without a just cause which must be approved in the Plenary Council by the Papal Legate, or in the Provincial Council by the Fathers of the Council (**Canon 289**).

In Plenary and Provincial Councils are to be discussed and decided matters that serve for the increase of the faith, the guidance of morals, the correction of abuses, the settling of controversies, and the promotion of uniformity of discipline in the respective territory (**Canon 290**).

On the conclusion of the Plenary and the Provincial Council, the president shall submit all the acts and decrees to the Holy See, and these shall not be promulgated until the Sacred Congregation of the Council has considered and approved the same. The Fathers of the Council shall designate the manner of promulgation and the time when, after promulgation, the decrees are to go into force. The decrees of a Plenary or the Provincial Council, after their proper promulgation, bind all persons in the respective territory, and the Ordinaries of the dioceses cannot dispense from them except in individual cases and for a just cause (**Canon 291**).

222. Unless the Holy See has provided otherwise for particular places, the metropolitan (or the senior suffragan as pointed out in Canon 284) shall at least every five years arrange for a meeting of the local Ordinaries of the province to discuss the ways and means of promoting the cause of religion in the province and to prepare the matters to be treated in the next provincial Council. The bishops and other persons mentioned in Canon 285 are to be called, and should take part in the meeting. The Ordinaries shall in the meeting designate the place where the next meeting is to be held (**Canon 292**).

Chapter VIII

OF VICARS AND PREFECTS APOSTOLIC

223. Territories which are not erected into dioceses are governed by vicars and prefects Apostolic, whose nomination is reserved exclusively to the Holy See. Vicars and prefects Apostolic take possession of their territories by exhibiting, either in person or through a proxy, their credentials to the one who according to Canon 309 governs that district. The proper credentials of the prefects Apostolic are their letters of appointment from the Sacred Congregation of the Propaganda; the vicars Apostolic exhibit the Apostolic letters (**Canon 293**).

Vicars and prefects Apostolic enjoy in their respective territories the same rights and faculties as the residential bishops, unless the Apostolic See has made some restriction in a particular case.[18a] Within the limits of their territory and during the time of their office, they may perform all the blessings

[18a] Their names not to be put in Canon of Mass, cfr. App. III, 14, a.

reserved to the bishops (except the pontifical blessing), even though they may not be consecrated bishops; they can consecrate chalices, patens and portable altars with the Holy Oils blessed by a bishop; they can grant fifty days' indulgence, and confer confirmation, first tonsure and minor orders subject to the restrictions defined in Canons 782 and 957 (**Canon 294**). Canon 782 states that they can validly confirm only in their own territory.   Canon 957 rules that the conferring of tonsure and minor orders is limited to the lay subjects of their own territory, and, if they ordain men who are not their own subjects, these latter must produce dimissorial letters from their proper Ordinaries.   These conditions are required for validity.

224. Vicars and prefects have the right and duty to demand that all priests, secular and religious, show them their letters of appointment to the mission.   Priests who fail to produce such letters should be prevented from exercising any acts of the sacred ministry.   All missionaries, secular and religious, must ask the vicar or prefect for permission to exercise the sacred ministry, which permission should not be denied except in special cases and for grave reasons (**Canon 295**).   The missionaries of religious orders are also subject to the jurisdiction, visitation and correction of the vicar or prefect in matters pertaining to the management of the missions, care of souls, administration of the sacraments, direction of schools, alms given for the mission, fulfillment of pious bequests for the benefit of the missions.   The religious discipline depends on the religious superior, except in cases where the law provides otherwise.   If a conflict arises between the orders of the vicar or prefect and those of the religious superior in matters in which according to this Canon the vicar or prefect has jurisdiction, the order of the vicar or prefect must be obeyed. Recourse *in devolutivo* to the Holy See is open to the religious. If the religious have been conceded certain rights in special statutes approved by the Holy See, these must be respected by the vicar or prefect (**Canon 296**).

If there are not enough secular priests to do the work in the vicariate or the prefecture, the vicar or prefect can after consulting the superior oblige all the religious (both non-exempt and exempt) attached to the mission to exercise the care of souls. Any special statutes that may have been approved by the Holy See for the religious, must be observed (**Canon 297**). All differences regarding the care of souls that may arise between individual missionaries (secular or religious) or different orders, shall be decided by the vicar or prefect, and his decision must be followed. Recourse *in devolutivo* to the Holy See is open (**Canon 298**).

225. Vicars and prefects Apostolic are obliged to make the visit to the tomb of the Holy Apostles Peter and Paul at Rome by the same law which is laid down for residential bishops in Canon 341. If grave difficulties prevent them from coming in person or sending a proxy, they may appoint a proxy, even one residing at Rome (**Canon 299**). By Canon 340, vicars and prefects Apostolic are obliged to make the quinquennial report on the state of their mission district to the Holy See. That report must be signed by the vicar or prefect and at least one of their consultors spoken of in Canon 302. Moreover, at the end of each year, they shall send to the Holy See a statement of the number of converts, of baptisms, and of the sacraments administered during the year, together with other items of special importance (**Canon 300**).[18b]

Vicars and prefects Apostolic are obliged to reside in their respective territories, and are not permitted without a grave and urgent cause to be absent for a notable length of time without first consulting the Holy See. They should make the visitation of their district, whenever it is necessary—either in person or, if legitimately impeded, through a delegate. The visitation is concerned with the same matters as that of bishops in their dioceses (**Canon 301**).

226. Vicars and prefects Apostolic shall appoint a council of at least three of the older and more experienced missionaries whose opinion they shall seek, at least by letter, in more serious and difficult affairs (**Canon 302**). As far as circumstances permit, they should once a year call together at least the principal missionaries of their district (both secular and religious), so that they may ascertain from the experience and the counsel of these men what affairs need closer attention (**Canon 303**).

227. The laws of the Code in reference to the archives which bishops should establish, apply also to vicars and prefects

[18b] Concerning quinquennial report, cfr. App. III, 14, b.

Apostolic as far as the circumstances of the missions permit. Likewise, the rules of the Code on Plenary and Provincial Councils (Canons 281–291) apply to the Plenary or Regional and Provincial Councils in the districts subject to the Sacred Congregation of the Propaganda, in so far as they are applicable; and the laws on Diocesan Synods (in Canons 356–362) apply to the synods in vicariates and prefectures Apostolic. However, no time is fixed for Provincial Councils and for synods. Before promulgation, the laws of the Councils in mission districts must be submitted to the Sacred Congregation of the Propaganda for approval (**Canon 304**).

228. Vicars and prefects Apostolic are bound in conscience to make a zealous effort to provide from among the Christian natives or inhabitants of their district tested candidates for the clerical state, who should be properly trained and raised to the priesthood (**Canon 305**).

229. Vicars and prefects are obliged to apply Holy Mass for the people of their district at least on the feasts of Christmas, the Epiphany, Easter, the Ascension, Pentecost, Corpus Christi, the Immaculate Conception and Assumption of the Blessed Virgin, St. Joseph, Sts. Peter and Paul, and All Saints, observing the rules of Canon 339 (**Canon 306**).

Without consulting the Holy See, they may not grant any missionary sent by the Holy See permission to leave the vicariate or prefecture permanently, or to go elsewhere, nor may they expel them. In case of public scandal, they may, after consulting their Council, remove the missionary immediately; if there is question of a religious, his superior shall also be informed before action is taken, in so far as this is possible. The Holy See shall at once be informed of the removal (**Canon 307**).

230. Vicars and prefects Apostolic who are bishops are entitled to the same privileges of honor which the law gives to titular bishops. If they are not bishops, they have during their office and within their own territory the insignia and privileges of Prothonotaries Apostolic *de numero participantium* (**Canon 308**).[19]

---

[19] The rights and privileges of the class of Prothonotaries Apostolic here referred to are outlined in the *Motu Proprio* of Pope Pius X "Inter Multiplices," Feb. 21, 1905. In general, they are allowed to wear the episcopal apparel and to perform pontifical functions with certain restrictions. For

231. As soon as they come into their territory, vicars and prefects Apostolic shall appoint a qualified pro-vicar or pro-prefect from among either the secular or regular clergy, unless a coadjutor with the right of future succession has been appointed by the Holy See. The pro-vicar or pro-prefect has no power during the lifetime of the vicar or prefect, except such as is committed to him by his superior. When the vicar or prefect goes out of office, or when his jurisdiction is impeded in the manner described in Canon 429, the pro-vicar or pro-prefect must assume the entire government and retain it until the Holy See has made other provision. The pro-vicar or pro-prefect who succeeds in office, as said before, must immediately appoint an ecclesiastic who shall succeed him in case of death, etc. If perchance it should happen that nobody was appointed as administrator either by the vicar or prefect (or by the pro-vicar or pro-prefect), then the senior missionary present in the vicariate or prefecture is to be considered delegated by the Holy See to assume the government of the vacant vicariate or prefecture. Seniority is determined by the letters of appointment of a missionary to the district; if several were appointed on the same date, the senior in the priesthood is preferred (**Canon 309**).[19a]

232. The men who succeed to the government of a district in virtue of the laws of the preceding Canon must as soon as possible inform the Apostolic See of the vacancy. Meanwhile they can make use of all the faculties, both the ordinary ones mentioned in Canon 294 and the delegated ones which the vicar or prefect had, unless they were given to them for reason of personal qualification (**Canon 310**). He who is appointed to the government of a vicariate or prefecture for a certain length of time, must retain the government with all the faculties conceded to him, until the successor has taken canonical possession of his office, even though the definite period specified has elapsed (**Canon 311**).

instance, they cannot in a Pontifical Mass make use of the throne and crosier, and they must give the blessing to the people in the form of the priest's, not of the bishop's blessing (cfr. *Ecclesiastical Review*, XXXIII, 73).

19a Vicars and prefects Apostolic may appoint a vicar-delegate after the manner of a vicar-general (cfr. Vol. II, App. III, 14, d.).

CHAPTER IX

APOSTOLIC ADMINISTRATORS

233. The administrators spoken of in this chapter of the Code are men who for grave and special reasons are appointed by the Holy See to administer a canonically erected diocese, either while the bishop is still alive and in possession of the diocese, or during the vacancy; the administrators may be appointed either permanently or only for a certain length of time (**Canon 312**).

The Holy See may appoint an Apostolic administrator *sede plena* (i.e., while the Ordinary is in legal possession of the see) in case the Ordinary is incapacitated through old age or other habitual infirmities from governing the diocese, or in case of his expulsion, imprisonment, etc., by the civil power, or for any other reason that the Holy See thinks sufficient. The same authority may appoint an Apostolic administrator *sede vacante,* i.e., during the vacancy of the see, if (e.g.) the men who have the right to elect the diocesan administrator choose an unworthy or otherwise disqualified person.

234. Every Apostolic administrator who is appointed to govern a diocese while the bishop is still in possession of the see must for the purpose of taking canonical possession of the administration exhibit his letters of appointment to the bishop, if he is of sound mind and lives in the diocese, and also to the Cathedral Chapter or the diocesan consultors in the manner prescribed in Canon 334. If the see is vacant, or if the bishop is not of sound mind, or does not live within the diocese, the Apostolic administrator takes possession in the same manner as a bishop (**Canon 313**).

The rights, duties, and privileges of the Apostolic administrator are to be judged from his letter of appointment, or, if the letter does not expressly state otherwise, his faculties are to be determined by the following Canons (**Canon 314**). The Apostolic administrator whose appointment is perpetual enjoys the same rights and honors, and has the same obligations as the residential bishop. If he is appointed temporarily, (1) he has the same rights and duties as the vicar capitular (or the diocesan administrator, in countries where there are no Chapters), but if the bishop is still in possession of his see, the administrator may nevertheless hold the canonical visitation, but he is not bound to say Mass for the people, since this obligation rests with the bishop; (2) as far as privileges of honor are concerned, Canon 308 is decisive. A bishop who is transferred to another see, but retains the administration of his former diocese, can claim in this diocese also all the privileges of honor due to residential bishops (**Canon 315**).

235. When an Apostolic administrator is placed over a diocese while the bishop is still in possession of the see, the bishop's and his vicar-general's jurisdiction is suspended. Though the administrator is not subject to the authority of the bishop, he should not interfere in matters concerning the bishop personally, nor should he institute canonical procedure or otherwise punish the vicar-general for reason of acts done under the former administration of the diocese (**Canon 316**). If the jurisdiction of the Apostolic administrator is impeded, or if the administrator dies, the Holy See is to be informed immediately. Meanwhile, if the diocese is vacant or the bishop is not of sound mind, the law of Canon 429 is to be applied —namely, the Cathedral Chapter (or the diocesan consultors) shall elect an administrator; otherwise the bishop governs the diocese, unless the Holy See has in advance made other arrangements (**Canon 317**).

The jurisdiction of the Apostolic administrator does not expire at the death of the Roman Pontiff or of the bishop. It ceases when the new bishop takes legitimate possession of the vacant diocese in the manner prescribed in Canon 334 (**Canon 318**).

CHAPTER X

OF INFERIOR PRELATES

236. Prelates who rule over the clergy and people of a district that is separated from every other diocese are called either abbots or prelates *nullius* (i.e., of no diocese). They are called abbots *nullius*, if their church is an abbey, and prelates *nullius*, if their church is a secular prelacy. An abbacy or prelacy *nullius* that does not consist of at least three parishes is ruled by special laws, and to such does not apply what the Canons state concerning abbacies and prelacies *nullius* (**Canon 319**).

237. The abbots and prelates *nullius* are nominated and instituted by the Roman Pontiff, without prejudice to the right of election or presentation, if such legitimately belongs to anyone: in the latter case, the Roman Pontiff has the right of confirming the election or of instituting the one presented.   Clerics who are to be raised to an abbacy or prelacy *nullius* must have the same qualifications as the law requires for bishops (**Canon 320**). If an electoral college has the right to elect an abbot or prelate *nullius,* an absolute majority of votes is necessary for a valid election, not counting invalid votes.   If a particular law requires a greater number of votes than the absolute plurality—for instance, two-thirds of all the votes—that law shall stand (**Canon 321**).

Under no title whatsoever may the abbot or prelate *nullius* interfere in the government of the abbacy or prelature either personally or through others before he has taken canonical possession of his office as prescribed in Canon 334.   The abbots or prelates *nullius* who either by Apostolic precept or by the proper Constitutions of their Order must receive the abbatial blessing, are obliged to ask this blessing of any bishop of their choice within three months after the receipt of the Apostolic letters of appointment, unless they are prevented by a just impediment (**Canon 322**).

238. Abbots or prelates *nullius* have the same ordinary powers and the same obligations under the same penalties as a residential bishop in his diocese.   If they do not have episcopal consecration and have received the abbatial blessing (if bound to receive it), they have, besides the faculties mentioned in Canon 294, the power to consecrate churches and immovable altars.   In the matter of the appointment of a vicar-general they shall observe the rules of Canons 366–371, which speak of the appointment by the bishop of the vicar-general and the rights attached to that office (**Canon 323**).   The Chapter of the religious of an abbacy or prelature *nullius* is governed by its own laws and constitutions.   If the Chapter consists of the secular clergy, it is governed by the rules of the Code on cathedral Chapters (**Canon 324**).

An abbot and prelate *nullius,* though not possessing episcopal consecration, may use the pontifical insignia in his own territory of jurisdiction with throne and canopy, and celebrate there liturgical functions according to the pontifical rite. The pectoral cross, the ring with the gem, and the purple skull cap (*pileolus*) may be worn by these prelates even outside their territory (**Canon 325**).

239. If a secular prelacy *nullius* has no Chapter, consultors are to be elected as prescribed by Canons 423–428 (**Canon 326**). At the vacancy of the abbacy or prelature *nullius*, the Chapter of the Religious (if it is a religious abbacy or prelature *nullius*) succeeds in the government of the district, unless the Constitutions rule otherwise. If the prelature is a secular one, the Chapter of Canons succeeds. Either Chapter must within eight days after the vacancy elect a vicar-capitular, according to Canons 432 sqq.; and the vicar-capitular shall govern the abbacy or prelature *nullius* until the election of the new abbot or prelate. If the abbot or prelate *nullius* is prevented from exercising his jurisdiction, the precepts of Canon 429 are to be observed (**Canon 327**).

240. Regarding the clergy attached to the Papal Household, whether they enjoy the title of prelate or not, the special privileges, regulations, and traditions of the Papal Palace shall be observed (**Canon 328**).

TITLE VIII

OF THE EPISCOPAL JURISDICTION AND THOSE PARTICIPATING IN IT

CHAPTER I

OF BISHOPS

241. The bishops are the successors of the Apostles, and are placed by Divine institution over the individual churches, which they govern with ordinary power under the authority of the Roman Pontiff. They are freely appointed by the Pope. If some college has been granted the right to elect a bishop, the precepts of Canon 321 shall be observed, which requires an absolute majority of the votes of all those who have the right to vote (**Canon 329**).

In this Canon the Church repeats the dogmatic teaching on the nature of the office of bishops. They are the successors of the Apostles, and, as the latter had St. Peter as their head, so have the bishops the Roman Pontiff, the successor of St. Peter, as their head. Thus there is perfect unity of government. There is but one Supreme Head, the Roman Pontiff, who appoints the bishops to the various places, for to St. Peter and his successors was committed the care of the whole Church. The power, however, which the bishops exercise, they have in virtue of their office which was instituted by Christ Himself. The extent of the power which the bishops possess was not defined by Christ; it is left to the Supreme Head of the Church to determine the government of the Church. Here also the commentators of the old law consider the question of the difference between the episcopate and the priesthood, which is not properly a question of Canon Law, but rather one of dogmatic theology and church history.

242. Before a person is elevated to the episcopate, proof must be furnished in the manner prescribed by the Holy See that the individual is qualified for the office (**Canon 330**). The requisites of a candidate for the episcopate are: (1) he must be born of legitimate wedlock. Those legitimized by subsequent marriage are also excluded; (2) he must be at least thirty years of age; (3) he must have been ordained priest for at least five years; (4) he must possess good character, piety, zeal for souls, prudence and other qualifications to govern the diocese in question; (5) he should have obtained the degree of doctor or licentiate in theology or Canon Law from a school approved by the Holy See, or must at least be well versed in these sciences. If the candidate is a religious, he must have received from his major superiors a similar degree, or at least a testimonial certifying to his learning (**Canon 331**, § 1).

243. Also those who are elected, presented, or designated for a bishopric by persons who have the privilege from the Holy See to elect, present, or designate, must have the aforesaid qualifications. The Holy See has the exclusive right to pass judgment on the suitability of any candidate for the episcopate (**Canon 331**, §§ 2–3). Every candidate for the episcopate, even though elected, presented, or designated by the civil government, needs the canonical provision or institution in order to be the bishop of a vacant diocese, which institution is exclusively the right of the Roman Pontiff. Before the canonical institution, the

candidate must make the profession of faith mentioned in Canons 1406–1408, and take the oath of fealty to the Holy See by the formula approved by the Holy See (**Canon 332**).

244. Unless prevented by legitimate impediment, the person promoted to the episcopate, even though he be a Cardinal, must within three months from the receipt of the Apostolic Letters receive the consecration and go to his diocese within at least four months. A single exception is given in Canon 238, namely, that the bishops of the suburbicarian sees of Rome are obliged (as Cardinals) to reside at the Papal Court, not in their dioceses (**Canon 333**).

245. The residential bishops are the ordinary and immediate pastors in the dioceses entrusted to them. They cannot enter upon the government of the diocese either in person or through others or under any title until they have taken canonical possession of their diocese. However, if they were vicars-capitular, judges (*officiales*), or *œconomi* in the diocese before their appointment to the bishopric, they may continue to retain and exercise these offices even after the appointment. They take canonical possession of the diocese as soon as they exhibit, in person or by a proxy, the Apostolic Letters of appointment to the Cathedral Chapter, in the presence of the secretary or chancellor of the Chapter who shall make entry of the fact into the acts of the diocese (**Canon 334**). In countries where there are no Cathedral Chapters the letters of appointment must be exhibited to the diocesan consultors.

246. The bishop has the right and the duty to govern the diocese both in spiritual and temporal affairs, and to this end he possesses legislative, judicial, and coercive power which must be exercised according to the precepts of the Sacred Canons. The laws of the bishop begin to bind immediately when promulgated, unless he provides otherwise in the same laws. The manner of promulgation is determined by the bishop himself (**Canon 335**).

247. The bishop must urge the observance of the laws of the Church, and he cannot dispense with the common law except in so far as Canon 81 allows. (That Canon rules that the bishop cannot dispense unless the law or a special concession gives him power: in emergencies, however, where the good of souls requires immediate action, he may dispense in

those laws in which the Holy See usually dispenses, if recourse to the Holy See is difficult, e.g., because of great distance and the consequent delay in getting the dispensation).

The bishop has the duty to guard ecclesiastical discipline against abuses, especially in reference to the administration of the sacraments and sacramentals, the worship of God and the veneration of the saints, preaching, indulgences, and the fulfillment of last bequests in favor of pious causes. He must watch over the integrity of faith and morals, and must see that the people (especially the children and the illiterate) are properly instructed in Christian doctrine, and that the schools for children and young men and women are conducted according to the principles of the Catholic religion. In reference to preaching, Canon 1327 must be observed which states that the bishop's obligation to preach is personal, unless a legitimate impediment excuses him from this duty (**Canon 336**).

248. The bishop can in his diocese hold pontifical functions anywhere, even in exempt churches. Outside the diocese he cannot make use of the mitre and crozier except with at least the reasonably presumed consent of the local Ordinary, and, in the case of an exempt church, with the consent of the religious superior. The phrase, to "exercise the pontificals," means to perform those functions in which by the laws of the sacred liturgy the use of the pontifical insignia of the crozier and mitre is required. When one bishop grants another the permission to exercise the pontificals in his diocese, he may also allow the use of the throne with the canopy (**Canon 337**). The bishop who gives permission to a bishop of another diocese to hold some pontifical function in his own cathedral, may allow the visiting bishop the use of his own throne so that it is not necessary to erect another on the Epistle side. A bishop may not allow the use of his own throne to a dignitary of the same diocese (e.g., a coadjutor or an auxiliary bishop, or the vicar-general).[20]

249. The bishop is obliged to reside personally in the diocese, even though he has a coadjutor bishop. Absence from the diocese for at most three months a year, either continuous or interrupted, is allowed. Besides this, the bishop may be

20 Sacred Congregation of Rites, Nov. 29, 1919; *Acta Ap. Sedis*, XII, 177.

absent to make the prescribed visit *ad limina,* as the official visit to the tomb of the Apostles and to the Holy Father at Rome is called; he may be absent to take part in Councils which the law obliges him to attend, or to comply with the duties of the civil office which is legitimately attached to his bishopric. Except for these reasons, however, he must not be absent more than at most three months, continuous or interrupted, and the bishop must see to it that his absence does not injure the interests of his diocese. The time of absence to make the visit *ad limina,* or to attend a Council, or the duties of the civil office, may not be prolonged by adding the months of vacation; the vacation should be taken at another time. The vacation of two years may not be combined, nor may a newly appointed bishop delay for more than four months to take up his residence in the diocese by adding the months of vacation to the four months. The bishop may not be absent from his cathedral church during Advent, or Lent, or on Christmas, Easter, Pentecost, or Corpus Christi, except for a grave and urgent reason. If without a legitimate reason, he has been absent from his diocese over six months, the archbishop (or in case of illegitimate absence of the archbishop, the senior resident suffragan) shall denounce the one absent to the Holy See. Canon 274, n. 4, obliges the archbishop in general terms to inform the Holy See of abuses in the ecclesiastical province (**Canon 338**).

Application of Holy Mass for the People

250. After having taken canonical possession of his diocese, the bishop must apply Holy Mass for the people of the diocese on all Sundays and holydays of obligation, including the suppressed holidays; neither the small amount of revenue or salary nor any other reason excuses the bishop from this obligation. On Christmas, and on Sundays on which a holyday of obligation falls, it suffices to apply one Holy Mass for the people. If a holyday of obligation is transferred in such a way that, on the day to which it is transferred, not only the Mass and office but also the obligation of hearing Mass and the duty to abstain from servile work is transferred, Holy Mass is to be applied on the day to which the feast is transferred, otherwise on the day itself. (In the United States this case does not hap-

pen with any of the six feasts to which the holydays of obligation have been reduced by special concession.)

The bishop must on these days apply Holy Mass himself;
if he is legitimately prevented from saying these Masses, he
must have them said by another priest on these days; if this
also is impossible, he must as soon as possible make up these
Masses either personally or through another. If a bishop has
two dioceses which are united *æque principaliter* (by which union
each diocese retains its individual identity), or if in addition
to his own diocese he is administrator of another, he satisfies
his obligation by applying one Holy Mass for all the people
in his charge. If the bishop has not satisfied the obligation
spoken of in this Canon, he shall as soon as possible supply
the number of Masses omitted (**Canon 339**).

251. The obligation to say the Mass for the people is binding: (1) on all Sundays of the year; (2) on the ten holydays
of obligation stated in Canon 1247, namely, Christmas, Circumcision, Epiphany, Ascension, Corpus Christi, Immaculate
Conception, Assumption of the Blessed Virgin, St. Joseph
(March 19), Sts. Peter and Paul, and All Saints; (3) on the
suppressed holidays. There was some uncertainty as to the
number of suppressed holidays on which Holy Mass has to be
applied for the people, wherefore the Holy See issued an instruction on this matter,[21] enumerating the following:

1. Monday and Tuesday after Easter and after Pentecost;
2. Finding of the Holy Cross, May 3;
3. The Purification or Candlemas Day, February 2;
4. The Annunciation, March 25;
5. Nativity of the Blessed Virgin, September 8;
6. Dedication of St. Michael, September 29;
7. Nativity of St. John Baptist, June 24;
8. St. Andrew, Apostle, November 30;
9. St. James, Apostle, July 25;
10. St. John, Apostle, December 27;
11. St. Thomas, Apostle, December 21;
12. Sts. Philip and James, Apostles, May 1;
13. St. Bartholomew, Apostle, August 24;
14. St. Matthew, Apostle, September 21;
15. Sts. Simon and Jude, Apostles, October 28;
16. St. Mathias, Apostle, February 24;
17. St. Stephen, Protomartyr, December 26;
18. Holy Innocents, December 28;
19. St. Lawrence, Martyr, August 10;
20. St. Sylvester, Pope, December 31;

[21] Sacred Congregation of the Council, Dec. 28, 1919. Cfr. App. III,
15, a and b.

21. St. Ann, Mother of the Blessed Virgin, July 26;
22. Patron of the Country;
23. Patron of the Town or City.

In reference to the last two feasts in the United States, we have the Immaculate Conception as Patron Feast of the Church, and, this being already included in the list of days on which Holy Mass must be said for the people, there is no additional obligation for the Patron Feast. Patrons of towns and cities are practically unknown here in the United States, except in some places in the districts first settled by the Spaniards and the French where a patron of a town had been legitimately chosen.

REPORT ON THE STATUS OF THE DIOCESE AND VISIT TO ROME

252. Every bishop is bound to make a report on the status of his diocese every five years according to the formulas issued by the Holy See.[22] The five years' term is fixed for all dioceses, and runs from January 1, 1911. In the first year of each quinquennium reports must be made by the bishops of Italy, the islands of Corsica, Sardinia, Sicily, Malta, and the other small islands off the coast; in the second year the bishops of Spain, Portugal, France, Belgium, Holland, England, Scotland, and Ireland with the adjacent isles; in the third year the other bishops of Europe with the adjacent isles; in the fourth year the bishops of all America and the adjacent isles; in the fifth year the bishops of Africa, Asia, Australia and the islands in these parts of the world. If the year assigned for the report should fall entirely or in part within the first two years of the bishop's reign of the diocese, the bishop may for that term abstain from sending a report to the Holy See (**Canon 340**).

The bishops who are to make the report are to go to Rome that same year to venerate the tomb of the Holy Apostles, Sts. Peter and Paul, and to appear before the Roman Pontiff. The bishops, however, who are outside of Europe have permission to make the visit *ad limina* every ten years (**Canon 341**). The bishop should make the visit *ad limina* in person or through the coadjutor if he has one; for a just reason approved by

---

[22] For List of Questions to be answered in report, cfr. App. III, 15, c.

the Holy See, he may also delegate a qualified priest who resides in his diocese (**Canon 342**).

VISITATION OF THE DIOCESE

253. The bishop must visit at least part of his diocese annually so as to cover the entire diocese at least once in five years either in person, or, if legitimately excused, through his vicar-general, or another priest. The bishop has the right to take two of the clergy (even those of the Cathedral or Collegiate Chapter, or any others he may choose), as companions on his visitation. No contrary custom or privilege restricting the bishop's right of choice is recognized in law. If the bishop neglects to hold the visitation the archbishop has the right to interfere (according to Canon 274, nn. 4–5) by reporting the matter to the Holy See, and, if the Holy See approves of it, the archbishop then has the right to hold the visitation in such diocese (**Canon 343**).

To the visitation of the bishop are subject the persons, goods and pious institutions (even though exempt) within the limits of his diocese, unless special exemption is proved to have been granted them by the Holy See. The bishop can visit the exempt religious only in the cases explicitly stated in law (**Canon 344**). The Canons which have reference to the visitation and the religious are: Canons 512, 615–619, 631, 690, 1261, and 1491.

254. The bishop should proceed in a paternal manner concerning the object and purpose of the visitation. From the precepts and decrees given in the visitation, an appeal is allowed only *in devolutivo*—i.e., the orders must be obeyed until the Holy See grants relief. In other cases (i.e., matters outside the scope of the visitation), the bishop, even at the time of visitation, must proceed according to the rules of law which prescribe the manner of procedure (**Canon 345**).

The visitation must not be unduly prolonged, no unnecessary expense shall be put on the place visited, and no donation shall be accepted either by the bishop or any of his companions. All contrary customs are hereby condemned. Concerning the living and traveling expenses of the bishop and his companions, the legitimate custom of the diocese shall be adhered to (**Canon 346**).

PRIVILEGES OF BISHOPS

255. In his own diocese, the bishop precedes all archbishops and bishops, except his own archbishop, Cardinals and Papal Legates; while he is outside his own diocese, the rules of precedence of Canon 106 are to be observed (**Canon 347**).

Titular bishops cannot exercise any act of jurisdiction in the diocese of their title, neither do they take possession of that diocese. Charity should prompt them to apply sometimes Holy Mass for the titular diocese, but there is no obligation to do so (**Canon 348**).

256. The following privileges are granted to bishops, both residential and titular, from the time they receive authentic notification of their canonical promotion:

Besides other privileges mentioned in the respective titles of the Code, they enjoy many of the privileges of Cardinals enumerated in Canon 239: (1) the privilege to choose a confessor for themselves and their households, and, if such confessor has no jurisdiction in the place, he obtains it automatically for the confession of the bishop and his household, and has also the faculty to absolve from all sins and censures including the diocesan reserved cases, except the censures reserved *specialissimo modo* to the Holy See and censures inflicted for the violation of the secret of the Holy Office; (2) the privilege to preach in any place, with at least the presumed consent of the local Ordinary; (3) the privilege to celebrate, or to permit another to celebrate in their presence, one Holy Mass on Holy Thursday, and three Holy Masses at midnight on Christmas, provided they are not obliged to celebrate in their cathedral; (4) the privilege to bless everywhere with the prescribed rites of the Church beads, rosaries and other prayer beads, crosses, medals, statutes, scapulars approved by the Holy See, with all the indulgences usually attached by the Holy See; to erect the Way of the Cross, with the formula of the *Rituale,* in churches, oratories (even private ones), and other pious places, and to bless crucifixes with the indulgences of the Way of the Cross for those who through sickness or other legitimate impediment cannot make the Way of the Cross in places where the Stations are erected; [22a] (5) the

---

[22a] Cfr. Vol. II, App. III, 40 h, for recent decisions on form of blessing.

privilege to celebrate Mass on a portable altar not only in their own residence but wherever they travel, and to permit another Mass to be celebrated in their presence; to say Mass on the ocean, observing due precautions; to celebrate Holy Mass according to their own calendar in all churches and oratories; to have the benefit of the personal privileged altar every day; to gain in their own private chapel those indulgences for which the visit to a church or public place of worship is prescribed in the town or city where they actually stay (which privilege is shared by the members of their household); to bless the people after the manner of bishops, but in the City of Rome in churches, pious institutes and at gatherings of the faithful only (**Canon 349, § 1, n. 1**).

257. Bishops have the right to wear the episcopal insignia according to the liturgical laws. Residential bishops from the moment that they have taken possession of their diocese have the right: (1) to receive the income of the *mensa episcopalis;* (2) to grant fifty days' indulgence in places of their jurisdiction; (3) to erect in all churches of their diocese the throne with canopy (**Canon 349, § 1, n. 2, § 2**).[23a]

The Sacred Penitentiary has declared that the faculties of the bishop to bless the various religious objects, Stations, etc., are given as personal privileges in recognition of the episcopal dignity, and cannot be delegated to priests of the diocese, July 18, 1919.[23b]

CHAPTER II

OF COADJUTORS AND AUXILIARY BISHOPS

258. The Roman Pontiff only can assign to a bishop a Coadjutor. A Coadjutor is usually assigned to the bishop personally, with the right of succession; sometimes, the Coadjutor is given to the episcopal *see.* An assistant assigned to the person of the bishop without the right of succession is called by the special name of *auxiliary* (**Canon 350**).

The rights of the coadjutor given to the person of a bishop are to be learned from the Apostolic letters of appointment. Unless otherwise stated in these letters, the coadjutor given a bishop who is entirely incapacitated, has all the rights and

[23a] Concerning pontifical functions, cfr. App. III, 15, d.
[23b] Cfr. App. III, 11 and 15, e.

duties of the bishop; in other cases he can exercise only such duties as the bishop may commit to him. What the coadjutor can do and is willing to do, the bishop should not habitually delegate to another. Whenever the bishop requests him to do so, the coadjutor, unless prevented by some just impediment, is obliged to perform the pontifical and other functions which the bishop is bound to hold (**Canon 351**).

259. A coadjutor who is assigned to the episcopal see, may exercise the functions of the episcopate in the territory of the diocese, except sacred ordination. In other affairs he can do only as much as has been committed to him either by the Holy See or by the bishop (**Canon 352**). In order that the coadjutor may take canonical possession of his office, it is necessary that he show his Apostolic Letters of appointment to the bishop. A coadjutor with the right of succession and a coadjutor given to the see must show these Letters also to the Cathedral Chapter (or to the diocesan consultors in dioceses which have no Chapters), in the manner prescribed in Canon 334. The Chapter or the consultors are to be assembled, and the secretary or chancellor must be present and put the fact on record in the diocesan archives. If the bishop's condition of health is such that he is not capable of a human act, coadjutors of any kind need not show the letters of appointment to the bishop but only to the Chapter or the consultors (**Canon 353**).

260. Every coadjutor is bound, like the bishop himself, to reside in the diocese from which (outside the period of vacation as provided by Canon 338) he may not absent himself except for a short time and with the permission of his bishop. Canon 338 speaks only of the two or three months' vacation which the bishop may take each year, and does not there mention the coadjutor bishops. Canon 354 states that the coadjutors have the same vacation as that of the bishops in Canon 338 (**Canon 354**).

261. When the see becomes vacant, the coadjutor with the right of succession immediately becomes the Ordinary of the diocese, provided he has taken legitimate possession of his office, as demanded in Canon 353. The office of the auxiliary bishop expires with the death or removal of the bishop whose personal assistant he was, unless the Apostolic Letters of appointment provide otherwise. If the coadjutor was given to

the see, his office continues also during the vacancy of the see (**Canon 355**).

CHAPTER III

OF THE DIOCESAN SYNOD

262. The diocesan synod is to be held at least every ten years. In it should be treated only questions which touch the particular needs of the clergy and the people of that diocese. If the bishop governs several dioceses which are united *æque principaliter,* or if, besides his own diocese, he holds another as permanent administrator, he may convoke a common synod for these dioceses (**Canon 356**). The bishop convokes and presides over the diocesan synod; the vicar-general cannot preside except by special mandate of the bishop, nor can a vicar-capitular preside. It is to be held in the cathedral, unless there is good reason to have it elsewhere (**Canon 357**).

263. As to the history of the diocesan synod, we find that in the days when every town had its own bishop, and the diocese did not extend beyond the town, the clergy were naturally in close contact with their bishop. Later, when diocesan territories became large and parishes were established in the country districts, the contact of the clergy with the bishop was not so frequent, and consequently the bishops began to call meetings of the clergy. The first recorded instance of a diocesan synod is said to be that which Patriarch Alexander held at Alexandria in 321, in which synod he deposed Arius. In the Western Church the first synod on record is said to be that held at Auxerre, France, in 585. That synod ruled that each year in the middle of May all the priests shall assemble. Soon provincial councils passed the law that diocesan synods must be held yearly, that in these synods the bishop give an account of the administration of the diocese and that the decrees of the provincial council be promulgated in the synod. The Fourth Lateran Council (1215) passed the general law that diocesan synods were to be held yearly. That law was confirmed by the Council of Trent, and remained valid until the promulgation of the Code, although historians say that the law was never universally introduced in the Church. The Code insists that the diocesan synod be held at least once

in ten years, and leaves it to the discretion of the bishop to hold it more frequently.

Persons to be Called to the Synod

264. The following persons must be called to, and should attend the Synod: (1) the vicar-general; (2) the canons of the cathedral or the diocesan consultors; (3) the rector of the diocesan seminary, at least of the major seminary; (4) vicars-foranes or deans; (5) one deputy from each collegiate church to be chosen by the Chapter from among their own members; (6) the pastors of the city where the synod is held; (7) one pastor at least from each deanery to be elected by all the priests of the district who have care of souls, and such pastors must provide a priest to take his place in the parish during his absence; (8) the abbots who are actual superiors of abbeys, and one of the superiors of each clerical religious organization in the diocese to be designated by the provincial superior. If the residence of the provincial is in the diocese, he himself may go to the synod instead of sending one of the local superiors.

If the bishop wishes, he may also call others to the synod, namely, all the canons, pastors, religious superiors, any or all of the secular priests of the diocese, provided enough priests are left to attend to the care of souls. Those invited have the right to vote just as the others, unless the bishop in the invitations states otherwise (**Canon 358**).

Those who should come to the synod, but are impeded by some legitimate impediment, may not send a proxy to take their place at the synod, but they must notify the bishop why they cannot come. Those who neglect to attend (except exempt religious who are not pastors), may be compelled by the bishop with just penalties (**Canon 359**).

265. Before the synod the bishop may appoint committees to prepare the subjects for discussion in the synod. Before the sessions open, a schedule of the subjects to be discussed is to be given to all who answered the call to the synod (**Canon 360**). The proposed questions are to be submitted by the bishop, or the one presiding in his place, to the free discussion of the members of the synod in the preliminary sessions (**Canon 361**).

The bishop is the only legislator in the synod, the others having only a consultive vote. He alone signs the laws passed in the synod, which, if they are promulgated in the synod, go into force immediately, unless the bishop decrees otherwise (**Canon 362**).

CHAPTER IV

OF THE DIOCESAN CURIA

266. The Diocesan Curia consists of those persons who assist the bishop—or the prelate who takes the place of the bishop— in the government of the diocese. To the Curia belong the vicar-general, the judge (cfr. Canon 1573 as to his appointment and office), the chancellor, the promoter of justice, the *defensor vinculi,* the synodal judges and examiners, the parochial consultors, auditors, notaries, cursors and summoners (**Canon 363**).

The nomination of those who are to hold the aforesaid offices and appointments shall be done in writing, as Canon 159 demands. Those nominated must: (1) take oath before the bishop that they will faithfully discharge their office without respect to persons; (2) transact their respective duties under the authority of the bishop and according to the rules of law; (3) preserve secrecy within the bounds and in the manner prescribed by law or the command of the bishop (**Canon 364**).

Concerning the judge, the promoter of justice, the *defensor vinculi,* the synodal judges, the auditors, cursors and summoners, the laws of Canons 1573–1593 shall be observed; the other officials are to be guided by the following Canons (**Canon 365**).

ARTICLE I.—OF THE VICAR-GENERAL

267. Whenever the proper government of the diocese demands it, the bishop should appoint a vicar-general, who shall enjoy ordinary jurisdiction in the entire diocese. The vicar-general's appointment is left to the free choice of the bishop, who can also remove him at will. As a rule, there should be but one vicar-general, unless either the diversity of Rites or the size of the diocese demand otherwise. If the vicar is absent

or unable to act, the bishop may appoint a substitute (**Canon 366**).

In the early history of the Church we find that, as the dioceses became larger through the rapid conversion of the heathens at the beginning of the fourth century, the duties of the bishop increased in proportion, and it was then that the need of assistants in the government of the diocese made itself felt. Among those called to assist the bishop we find, in the fourth century, the archdeacon who was the head of seven deacons, which number was kept at many cathedrals in memory of the first seven deacons chosen by the Holy Apostles at Jerusalem. The archdeacon's duties were the supervision of the care for the poor, the distribution of the offerings of the faithful, assisting the bishop at ordinations, the government of the inferior clerics, the visitation and correction of the clergy generally. In the Decretals of Pope Gregory IX the archdeacon appears vested with ordinary jurisdiction as judge of the first instance in court proceedings and also in matters of administration of the diocese. At first the bishops had been entirely free in the choice of the archdeacon, but, in the course of time, some cathedral Chapters had obtained the right to elect the archdeacon, and in some countries the king nominated this official.

268. As a reaction against the almost independent power of the archdeacon, the bishops began, in the twelfth century, to appoint an *officialis* (later called vicar-general), who was dependent on the bishop in the exercise of the powers delegated to him by the bishop. In the *Liber Sextus* of Pope Boniface VIII these officials are recognized and their duties are defined. In some countries—for instance, England, Belgium, France, Germany—two officials were instituted, one called vicar-general for acts of the so-called voluntary jurisdiction (granting of favors and other affairs not connected with judicial procedure), and for the administration of the temporalities of the diocese; the other, called the *officialis*, vested with jurisdiction in court affairs, both civil and criminal. The archdeacon thus lost practically all the powers connected with his office in former times, and the Council of Trent explicitly deprived the archdeacon of the power to judge matrimonial cases (Session XXIV, Chapter 20, On Reformation) and of jurisdiction over criminal cases

of the clergy (Session XXV, Chapter 14, On Reformation), and limited his power of visitation (Session XXIV, Chapter 3, On Reformation). Finally, the archdeacon's office came to be nothing more than a dignity in the Cathedral Chapter without any ordinary jurisdiction.

269. In the old *Jus Decretalium,* the names of the *officialis* and vicar-general are used promiscuously to designate one and the same person. The new Code of Canon Law distinguishes between the vicar-general and the *officialis*: the latter has none of the duties of the vicar-general, but is the judge of the episcopal court with ordinary power to judge all cases except those which the bishop reserves to himself, or where the law demands a special court of three or more judges.

QUALIFICATIONS OF THE VICAR-GENERAL

270. The vicar-general must be a priest of the secular clergy, at least thirty years of age, a doctor or licentiate in theology and Canon Law, or at least highly skilled in these subjects, and conspicuous for sound doctrine, probity of life, prudence and experience. If the diocese has been committed to a religious organization, the vicar-general may be a member of that organization. The office of vicar-general must not be given to the Canon Penitentiary, or to a blood-relation of the bishop, especially one in the first or in the second degree mixed with the first, or, excepting the case of necessity, to a pastor or others having the care of souls. The bishop is not forbidden to take the vicar from his own diocese (**Canon 367**).

POWERS OF THE VICAR-GENERAL

271. The vicar-general has, by virtue of his office, jurisdiction over the entire diocese in spiritual and temporal matters to the extent of the bishop's ordinary jurisdiction, except in those affairs which the bishop has reserved to himself, or which by law require a special mandate from the bishop.

Unless it is explicitly stated otherwise, the vicar-general can execute the rescripts of the Holy See which are sent to the bishop or his predecessor in the diocese, and in general he has the faculties which are habitually given to the local

Ordinary by the Holy See, according to Canon 66. This Canon states that also the faculties for a certain number of cases and those for a limited length of time come under the name of habitual faculties. The same Canon rules that faculties given to the bishop personally can be exercised only by the bishop (**Canon 368**).

Many canonists who wrote before the promulgation of the Code maintained that the vicar-general should not be chosen from among the priests of the diocese, but should be an outsider. Their opinion was based on declarations of the Sacred Congregations, specially those of the Bishops and Regulars, which had been given to individual dioceses and for reason of special circumstances. The Council of the Roman Province, in 1725, passed a decree to that effect for the Province (cfr. Wernz-Vidal, II, n. 638).

272. The vicar-general needs a special mandate for the following affairs: (1) incardination and excardination (Canon 113); (2) appointment to offices (Canon 152); (3) acceptance of resignation of offices (Canon 187); (4) convocation of synods (Canon 357); (5) confirmation of persons elected, or institution of persons presented for office, appointment of pastors and parochial vicars and of assistants in parishes (Canon 455); (6) removal of parochial vicars (Canon 477); (7) erection of pious associations (Canon 686); (8) reservation of sins (Canon 893); (9) issuing dimissorial letters (Canon 958); (10) permission for *matrimonium conscientiæ* (Canon 1104); (11) consecration of sacred places (Canon 1155); (12) permission to build a church (Canon 1162); (13) authentication of relics (Canon 1283); (14) permission to expose for veneration relics lacking document of authenticity (Canon 1285); (15) permission to a poor church to collect from extern priests a small fee for the use of vestments, sacred vessels, etc., in celebrating Mass for their own devotion (Canon 1303); (16) erection, union, conferring, giving canonical institution, exchange of benefices (Canons 1414, 1423, 1466, 1487); (17) matters incumbent on the Ordinary in a process of canonization and beatification (Canon 2002); (18) inflicting of penalties *ab homine* (Canon 2220); (19) remission of penalty inflicted by judicial sentence (Canon 2236); (20) absolution in the external forum of apostates, heretics, schismatics (Canon 2314).

273. The vicar-general shall refer to the bishop the principal acts of the Curia, inform him of what has been, or should be done to safeguard discipline among the clergy and people. He must take care not to use his powers contrary to the good pleasure of the bishop. Canon 44, § 2, decrees that a favor asked of and refused by the vicar-general, cannot validly be granted by the bishop unless the refusal of the vicar is made known to the bishop; and a favor which the bishop has refused, cannot validly be granted by the vicar, even though the refusal of the bishop is made known to the vicar (**Canon 369**).

Within the diocese, the vicar-general has precedence over all other priests, even the dignitaries of the Cathedral Chapter. The only ones who precede him are those who have the order of the episcopate (e.g., a titular bishop). If the vicar-general is a titular bishop, he has all the privileges of honor of these bishops; if he is not a bishop, he has during the time of his office the privileges and insignia of a titular prothonotary Apostolic (**Canon 370**). It is disputed whether these prothonotaries have the title of *monsignori*. Their cassock is black as is also the silken sash which hangs down on the left side; this girdle may end in two tassels. They may wear the *rochettum* and black mantle. At Holy Mass and other solemn functions, they may use the extra candle on a small stand with a handle, called the *palmatoria*.[23c]

274. The jurisdiction of the vicar-general expires by resignation made according to Canons 183–191, or by the revocation of the bishop made known to the vicar, or by the vacancy of the bishopric. If the bishop's jurisdiction is suspended, that of the vicar is likewise suspended (**Canon 371**).

275. Recourse from the orders of the vicar-general to the bishop may be had by anyone who feels himself injured. The commentators of the old Canon Law do not admit appeal to the bishop, but they usually speak of the judicial power of the vicar-general and of the sentences pronounced by him. In former times the vicar-general had judicial power in all cases coming under the ordinary jurisdiction of the bishop, but by the Code the vicar-general has only the so-called voluntary jurisdiction, and Canon 1573 forbids the bishop to appoint the vicar-general as judge, unless the diocese is so small that it is

[23c] Concerning precedence, cfr. App. III, 16.

superfluous to have a special judge of the Curia. Canon 1573 states that the judge of the diocesan Curia constitutes one tribunal with the local Ordinary, and hence no appeal from judicial acts of diocesan judges (whether the vicar-general or the *officialis*) to the Ordinary is possible. That recourse from acts of the voluntary jurisdiction of the vicar-general is possible, seems to be indicated by the fact that the Code speaking of favors denied by the vicar-general (cfr. Canon 44) supposes the recourse to the bishop, and it states that the refusal of the vicar must be made known to the bishop, otherwise his granting of the favor would be invalid.[24]

276. Abbots and prelates *nullius* may appoint a vicar-general, but the Vicars and Prefects Apostolic do not have the power, as Canon 198 states; however, the Holy See has allowed them to appoint a *delegatus generalis*, with all the faculties of a vicar-general.[25]

ARTICLE II.—OF THE CHANCELLOR, OTHER NOTARIES AND THE EPISCOPAL ARCHIVES

277. In every Curia the bishop shall appoint a chancellor who must be a priest, and whose principal office is to keep the acts of the Curia in the archives, to arrange them in chronological order, and make an index of the same. If needs be, he may have an assistant whose title shall be vice-chancellor. The chancellor is by his very office a notary (**Canon 372**).

278. The bishop may also appoint other notaries besides the chancellor, and their signature will be recognized by the Church in her courts. The bishop may appoint a notary either in general (for all acts), or for specified acts or occasions only. He may also appoint laymen as notaries, if clerics are not available; but in criminal cases of the clergy, the notary must be a priest. The chancellor and the other notaries must be men of unblemished reputation and above all suspicion. Any of the notaries may be removed or suspended by the person who appointed them, or by his successor, or by a higher superior; but they cannot be removed by the vicar-capitular except with the consent of the Chapter (**Canon 373**).

[24] Chelodi, ''Jus de Personis, n. 200.
[25] Sacred Congregation of the Propaganda, Dec. 8, 1919; *Acta Ap. Sedis,* XII, 120.

The office of the notary is: (1) to write the acts and transactions in judicial proceedings; (2) to consign faithfully to writing the proceedings, adding place, day, month and year, and his own signature; (3) to show to those who have a right to see them the acts and documents on file and to attest that copies agree with the original. The notary cannot write acts outside the diocese where he is appointed as notary, nor draw up papers in affairs beyond his appointment (**Canon 374**).

The Diocesan Archives

279. The bishop shall provide a safe and convenient place for the archives of the diocese. A catalogue or index of all the documents with a summary of its contents shall be carefully made (**Canon 375**). Each year, within the first two months, the catalogue should be brought up to date, and all the documents of the past year classified. The Ordinary shall institute a careful inquiry about documents missing from the archives, and he has authority to use any necessary means to have them returned (**Canon 376**).

The archives shall be locked, and nobody shall be allowed to enter them without the bishop's or the vicar-general's and the chancellor's permission. The chancellor only shall have a key to them (**Canon 377**). Without the bishop's or the vicar-general's permission, no one is allowed to take any document out of the archives, and all documents must be returned after three days. The Ordinary only may allow a longer interval, and this favor should not be easily granted. He who takes any document out of the archives, must leave a signed receipt for it with the chancellor (**Canon 378**).

280. The bishop shall also have a special place for documents that must remain secret. Each year, as early as possible, the documents of trials for bad behavior, the subjects of which have passed this life, or in whose case ten years have elapsed since their sentence was pronounced, shall be taken out of the archives and burnt. A brief summary of the case and the text of the final sentence is to be kept for reference. A catalogue of the documents contained in the Secret Archives shall be drawn up and revised each year, as is demanded by Canon 375 for the general archives (**Canon 379, §§ 1–2**).

The Secret Archives should be so constructed that they can be opened only by the use of two different keys—one to be kept by the bishop (or administrator Apostolic) and the other by the vicar-general (or, if there is no vicar-general, by the chancellor). Only the bishop or the Apostolic administrator may ask for the other key to open, without any witness, the secret archives (**Canon 379, §§ 3–4**). Immediately after having taken possession of the diocese, the bishop shall designate a priest who, during a vacancy or during the time that the bishop is hindered from exercising his jurisdiction, shall keep the key of the secret archives which the bishop had (**Canon 380**).

281. Unless an Apostolic administrator has been appointed for the diocese, the priest designated as stated in the preceding Canon shall give the key to the priest delegated by the bishop to govern the diocese during the time that he is impeded from the exercise of his jurisdiction (cfr. Canon 429); if the vicar-general governs the diocese, the priest shall keep the key. If the bishopric becomes vacant, or the bishop is impeded and there is no one to take his place so that the Cathedral Chapter or the diocesan consultors must choose a priest to govern the diocese (cfr. Canon 429), the key must be given to the cleric chosen by the Chapter or the consultors. The vicar-general or the chancellor shall give the key he holds to the first dignitary of the Cathedral Chapter, or to the senior diocesan consultor. The secret archives are to be sealed with the seal of the Curia, and are not to be opened until a bishop or Apostolic administrator has taken over the government of the diocese (**Canon 381**). Only in case of urgent necessity, may the vicar-capitular or administrator chosen by the diocesan consultors break the seal and open the secret archives, and he must do so in the presence of two canons or two consultors. In their presence he may consult the documents, but may not take them away; after the consultation, he replaces them and seals the archives in the presence of the two witnesses. When the new bishop arrives in the diocese, the vicar-capitular or the diocesan administrator who opened the secret archives shall give the bishop an account of the reason for opening the archives (**Canon 382**).

ARCHIVES AT OTHER CHURCHES

282. The bishop shall insist that an inventory or catalogue be made in two copies of the documents of cathedral, collegiate and parochial churches and of confraternities and diocesan institutions. One copy shall be kept in the respective archives and the other in the episcopal archives. The rules of Canons 470, § 3, 1522, nn. 2–3, and 1523, n. 6, must herein be observed. Original documents shall not be taken away from any of the ecclesiastical archives, except under the conditions laid down by Canon 378 (**Canon 383**).

283. The documents of the parochial and of the diocesan archives which are not of such a nature that they must be kept secret, may be inspected by anyone who has an interest in them. Anyone may also ask that a legal copy be made at his expense and given to him. In the matter of exhibiting documents or issuing copies of the same, the chancellor of the Curia, the pastor and other custodians of archives shall observe the rules made by the legitimate ecclesiastical authority, and shall in doubtful cases consult the local Ordinary (**Canon 384**).

ARTICLE III.—OF SYNODAL EXAMINERS AND PAROCHIAL CONSULTORS

284. Every diocese should have synodal examiners and parochial consultors, of whom all are to be appointed in the synod, at the proposal of the bishop and with the approbation of the synod. There should be as many as the bishop judges necessary—however, not less than four nor more than twelve (**Canon 385**). If any of the synodal examiners or parochial consultors should die in the time between the synods, or otherwise go out of office, the bishop may appoint others (called pro-synodal) with the advice of the Cathedral Chapter or the diocesan consultors. The same shall be done in the appointment of examiners and parochial consultors, whenever the synod is not held (**Canon 386**).

The synodal examiners were created by the Council of Trent, and their principal duty was to assist the bishop in the *concursus* or examinations of men desiring to become pastors. The parochial consultors are first mentioned in the Decree of the Sacred Consistorial Congregation of August 20, 1910.[26] The duties of the synodal examiners are pointed out in Canon 389. The parochial consultors are employed in the proceedings for the removal of pastors, as stated in Canons 2147 sqq.

Synodal examiners and parochial consultors, whether instituted in the synod or outside of it, go out of office after ten years, or even sooner, when a new synod is held. They can, however, finish an affair of their office which they had begun to handle, and they may be reappointed, provided the rules of law are observed as to their appointment. Those who are appointed in place of examiners or parochial consultors who go out of office before their term expires, remain in office only as long as those would have remained in whose place they were chosen (**Canon 387**). They cannot be removed by the bishop except for a grave cause and with the advice of the Cathedral Chapter or the diocesan consultors (**Canon 388**).

The synodal examiners should faithfully give their services, especially in the examinations for the appointment of pastors and in the proceedings for the removal of pastors, as outlined in Canons 2147 sqq. In the examinations of the candidates for ordination and of priests who apply for faculties to hear confessions and to preach, and for the examinations of the junior priests (cfr. Canon 130), the bishop is at liberty either to employ the synodal examiners or others (**Canon 389**). One and the same person may be synodal examiner and parochial consultor, but not in the same case (**Canon 390**).

CHAPTER V

OF THE CHAPTERS OF CANONS

285. In the earliest days of the Church we read of priests and deacons at the church of the bishop, assisting the latter in the care of souls and in administrative duties and forming his council in important affairs. In Spain, Italy, England and France, church history tells of the community life of the cathedral clergy under the presidency of the bishop. St. Chrodogang, Bishop of Metz (d. 766), was a great promoter of the community life of the cathedral clergy. But the contrary

---

26 Council of Trent, Session XXIV, ch. 18, On Reform; Decree ''Maxima Cura,'' *Acta Ap. Sedis*, II, 636.

tendency to be independent and to have one's income at one's free disposal gained the upper hand and the common funds of the cathedral clergy came to be assigned in certain proportionate shares to the individual clerics serving at the cathedral.

From the twelfth century the clergy of the cathedral churches began to be formed into a legal body with certain honors and rights. In that body itself there were certain persons vested with powers of jurisdiction (*dignitates*), others with certain honors and precedence (*personatus*), others with offices importing certain rights and duties. Many of the Cathedral Chapters obtained the right to administer the diocese during the vacancy and to elect the bishop. The wars and disturbances caused by the Reformation and by revolutions brought about the dissolution of many Cathedral Chapters, and, in the reorganization of the affairs of the Church in the various countries, most of the Cathedral Chapters lost the right to elect the bishop of the diocese. Chelodi states that the right of election exists in Switzerland, Prussia, Hanover, in the provinces of the Upper Rhine and in the dioceses of Olmütz and Salzburg.[27]

286. A chapter of canons, of either a cathedral or a collegiate church, is a body of clerics instituted for the purpose or rendering the service of God more solemn in these churches, and the Cathedral Chapter has the additional purpose of assisting the bishop as his senate and council according to rules of Canon Law, and to administer the diocese during a vacancy. *Capitulum insigne* or *perinsigne* are titles obtained by Collegiate Chapters either by Apostolic privilege or by immemorial custom (**Canon 391**).

The creation, re-establishment and suppression of cathedral and collegiate Chapters is reserved to the Apostolic See (**Canon 392**). In every capitular church there shall be dignitaries and canons among whom the various offices of the Chapter are to be distributed. There may be also other minor benefices in one or more degrees. The Chapter consists of the dignitaries and canons, unless the constitutions of the Chapter rule otherwise regarding the dignitaries; the holders of inferior benefices (called *mansionarii*), who assist the canons, do not belong to the Chapter.[27a] Canonries without income attached to them shall

[27] *Jus de Personis*, n. 188, p. 286.
[27a] Cfr. App. III, 17, 1.

not be established without special permission of the Holy See (**Canon 393**).

287. In Chapters in which the number of canons is fixed, there shall be as many *prœbendœ* as there are canons. The *prœbenda* is the income or salary attached to the position of a canon. In Chapters where the number of canons is not limited to a definite number, there shall be as many canons as can be properly maintained from the revenues of the Chapter; the bishop, after having consulted the Chapter, may determine the number. The establishing of dignitaries is reserved to the Apostolic See. The bishop has the power, with the consent of the Chapter, to restore dignitaries which had become extinct and to add other canonries or mere benefices to the *prœbendœ* already existing in the Chapter. In cathedral and prominent (*insignia*) collegiate Chapters, where the salaries and distributions are so small that they do not suffice for the support of the canons, the bishop shall with the advice of the Chapter apply for permission from the Holy See to unite some simple benefices with the canonries, or to suppress some canonries. If lay patrons have the right to present persons for the canonries, the consent of these persons must be obtained before their suppression (**Canon 394**).

288. If a cathedral or collegiate church has no fund from which daily distributions can be made, or if they are so small that they are of no account, the bishop may set aside one third of the income of all dignitaries, canons, offices and other benefices of the cathedral or collegiate church and convert them into a fund for daily distributions. (Besides the salary of the canons, there was to be a fund from which a certain amount was given to those canons who attended faithfully to the duty of reciting the Divine Office in choir, those who absented themselves being deprived of their share in it.) If the distributions cannot for any reason be introduced, the bishop shall decree a money fine to be paid by all dignitaries, canons and other holders of benefices at that church for neglect of the choir, which fine should correspond to the distributions and it shall take their place (**Canon 395**, §§ 1-2).[27b]

289. The distributions go to those who are faithful in attending choir and all collusion or remission of the distributions is forbidden. If the salary of the dignitaries of the Chapter is

[27b] Concerning daily distributions, cfr. App. III, 17, a.

derived from a fund separate from that of the other canons, the distribution lost by them go to the other dignitaries who attended choir, otherwise to the church, or, if the church does not need it, to some other ecclesiastical institute specified by the bishop. Every Chapter must have one or more censors or so-called *punctatores,* who must each day mark down the names of those absent from choir; they must take the oath before the Chapter or its president that they will faithfully do their duty. The bishop may add a censor of his own choice. If no censor is present in choir, the senior canon present has the duty to record the absentees (**Canon 395,** §§ 3–4).[27c]

290. The conferring of dignities in cathedral and collegiate Chapters is reserved to the Apostolic See.[27d] The *option* is forbidden, and all customs favoring it are condemned.[27e] (By the option the senior canon could obtain the lowest dignity, and an inferior dignitary could rise to a higher dignity.) If the option exists in virtue of agreements with the founder of a dignity or canonry, the option continues. The first dignitary in the Cathedral Chapter should, whenever possible, be a doctor in sacred theology or Canon Law (**Canon 396**). Unless stated otherwise in the statutes of the Chapter, the dignitaries and canons in the order of precedence have the right and duty: (1) to supply the place of the bishop in holding the sacred functions on the solemn feasts of the year; (2) to give to the bishop pontificating the aspersorium at the entrance to the church and to act as presbyter assistant; (3) to give the last sacraments to the bishop, and to hold his funeral; (4) to convoke the Chapter, preside at it and ordain what refers to the direction of the choir, provided the dignitary belongs to the body of the Chapter (**Canon 397**). The dignitaries are of the body of canons unless the constitutions of particular Chapters rule otherwise (cfr. Canon 393).

291. Every cathedral church should have the office of "canon theologian," and, where possible, that of "canon penitentiary." Also in collegiate Chapters, especially in those having the title of *insigne capitulum,* the office of the canon theologian and canon penitentiary can be established (**Canon 398**). The canon theologian and canon penitentiary should be men specially qualified for their position, preferably doctors in sacred theology or Canon Law. The Code desires that the canon penitentiary should

---

[27c] Cfr. App. III, 17, c and d.   [27e] Cfr. App. III, 17, f–h.
[27d] Cfr. App. III, 17, e.

be at least thirty years of age. These offices should not be conferred without previous investigation of the character of the candidates. If the *concursus* or examinations are demanded by particular law, that law must be observed. The canon penitentiary is forbidden to accept or to exercise any other office to which jurisdiction in the external forum is attached (**Canon 399**).

292. The canon theologian has the duty of explaining the Sacred Scriptures publicly in church on the days and at the hour fixed by the bishop with the advice of the Chapter. If the bishop considers it more useful, he may order the theologian to explain other matters of Catholic doctrine. The canon theologian must attend to this duty personally; if he is impeded for more than six months, he must get another priest at his own expense to do the work; the bishop has the right to appoint such a priest. For a grave reason the bishop may appoint the theologian to teach the sacred disciplines in the seminary, instead of holding lectures in church (**Canon 400**).

293. The canon penitentiary of cathedral and collegiate churches obtains by law ordinary power to hear confessions and to absolve from the sins and censures reserved to the bishop. He can hear the confessions of persons from other dioceses coming into the diocese, and he can hear the subjects of the diocese even outside its limits. This ordinary jurisdiction cannot be delegated by the penitentiary. The bishop shall prescribe the days and hours when the penitentiary must be at the confessional in the capitular church; he may oblige him to be there also at the time of divine services (**Canon 401**).

If the care of souls is attached to the Chapter, the Chapter must elect, in the manner defined by Canon 471, a parochial vicar who is to take care of the parish (**Canon 402**).

294. With the exception of the dignities, the bishop has the right with the advice of the Chapter to confer each and every benefice and canonry in cathedral and collegiate churches. Contrary custom of any kind is rejected, and every contrary privilege is revoked. Contrary agreements with founders remain in force and the laws of Canon 1435 reserving the conferring of canonries and other benefices under certain conditions to the Holy See must be observed (**Canon 403**).[271]

The bishop must confer the canonries on properly qualified

[271] Concerning appointments, cfr. App. III, 17, j.

persons (**Canon 404**). As soon as the dignitaries, canons and other beneficiaries have taken possession in the manner pointed out in Canons 1443–1445, they obtain the rights and privileges proper to their respective benefices. Canon 1406, § 1, n. 5, requires that those promoted to a dignity or a canonry make the profession of faith before the local Ordinary or his delegate (**Canon 405**).

295. The Committee for the Authentic Interpretation of the Code has declared in reference to the "properly qualified persons" spoken of in Canon 404, that the particular laws, privileges and customs by which the canonries are to be conferred exclusively on natives or citizens born in the respective city in which the Chapter exists, or that they are to be preferred to others, are abolished by the Code. Only if by concordat or by the law of the foundation of a canonry such restrictions are made they continue in force but only under the condition that worthy candidates can be found among these persons; otherwise the canonries may and must be conferred on other worthy candidates.[28]

296. The bishop, not the vicar-general or the vicar-capitular, has the right to nominate honorary canons from among men of the diocese (or outsiders), having first consulted the respective Chapter. If he nominates a man from another diocese as honorary canon, the consent of the proper bishop is required for validity of the nomination. The nominating bishop should inform the proper bishop of the insignia and privileges which the honorary canon will have by the nomination. The honorary canons residing outside the diocese for which they are nominated must be one-third less than the actual canons (**Canon 406**).

Men who are made honorary canons of some basilica or collegiate church of the City of Rome, can make use of the privileges and insignia only within the territory of such basilica or collegiate church and its dependent churches or chapels. Men who are made honorary canons of churches outside of Rome may use the privileges and insignia only in the diocese where they are nominated—not outside the diocese except when they accompany the bishop on a journey or represent the bishop or the Chapter in councils and on other solemn occasions. Hon-

[28] November 26, 1922; *Acta Ap. Sedis*, XV, 128.

orary canons obtain together with the insignia and privileges a place in choir (**Canon 407**).

297. The Cathedral Chapter precedes all other Chapters of the diocese. Further rules on precedence of the various dignitaries, canons, honorary canons, and beneficiaries, are given in Canon 408 but this matter is largely regulated by particular law and particular customs which the Code allows to be retained (**Canon 408**).

In the cathedral and collegiate churches the dignitaries who are bishops wear in choir the episcopal garb; all others must wear in choir the garb assigned in the document of erection of the chapter or conceded by Apostolic indult; otherwise they are considered absent from choir. The canons may wear the choir garb and the special insignia of the Chapter in the whole diocese where the Chapter exists; outside the diocese they may not wear their insignia except when they accompany their bishop or represent the bishop in a council or on other solemn occasions. Every contrary custom is rejected (**Canon 409**).

298. Each Chapter shall have its own statutes, and all dignitaries and canons and beneficiaries are held to their observance. The Chapter can make its own statutes by legitimate common action. The statutes must be submitted for approval to the bishop, and they cannot afterwards be abolished or changed without his authority. If the bishop orders the Chapter to make the statutes and the Chapter neglects to do so, the bishop may after six months have elapsed make statutes and impose them on the Chapter (**Canon 410**). At stated times and at the appointed place, the Chapter shall meet to discuss the affairs of their church and of the Chapter. Besides the regular meetings, the bishop, or the president of the Chapter, or the majority of the canons may call for special meetings. For the ordinary meetings no special convocation is necessary; it is necessary for extraordinary meetings and shall be done in the manner pointed out by the statutes. In the meetings of the Chapter the canons, excluding honorary canons, have a vote and also the dignitaries if they are of the body of the Chapter. Canon 393 states that they are of the body of the Chapter unless the constitutions of the Chapter show the contrary (**Canon 411**).

299. The canons of cathedral and collegiate Chapters must assist the bishop at solemn services, not only in the respective church of the Chapter, but also in other churches of the city or its suburbs, if the bishop invites them. Enough canons must be left at the church of the Chapter for the divine worship. The bishop may take two men from the cathedral or the collegiate Chapter and retain them to assist him in the ecclesiastical ministry and the service of the diocese (**Canon 412**).

300. Every Chapter is under the obligation of performing daily the Divine Office in choir and the services demanded by agreements with founders. The Divine Office comprises the recitation of the canonical hours in choir and the celebration of the *Missa conventualis cum cantu,* besides other Masses required by the rubrics or by agreements with founders. The Chapter Mass may be a Low Mass on the days when the bishop, or someone else in his name, has a *Missa pontificalis* in the church of the Chapter (**Canon 413**). In a decision of March 13, 1921, the Sacred Congregation of the Council holds that the hebdomadarian must say the Mass, for the Mass of the bishop is not a *Missa conventualis,* nor is the Pontifical Mass which a dignitary of the Chapter says in place of the bishop. If, however, the dignitary by approved custom celebrates the Pontifical Mass on the days when the bishop should celebrate in the cathedral, it is a *Missa conventualis* and must be applied by the celebrant for the benefactors.[29]

Each and every one who holds a choir benefice is obliged to perform the Divine Office in choir daily, unless service in turn has been allowed by indult of the Holy See or by the conditions of the foundation (**Canon 414**).[29a]

301. If the cathedral or collegiate church is at the same time a parish church, the following rules apply unless an indult of the Holy See or particular agreements legitimately made and accepted by the Ordinary at the time of the erection of the parish provide otherwise. The pastor must apply the *Missa pro populo,* preach and hold catechetical instructions, keep the parochial books and attest copies of the records, and hold the parochial functions mentioned in Canon 462.

The pastor officiates at funerals, except those of dignitaries, canons, honorary canons and beneficiaries of the Chapter; he

29 Cfr. App. III, 17, m.
29a Concerning choir service ''per turnum,'' cfr. App. III, 17, b.

discharges other functions which are not strictly parochial but are usually held in parishes, provided they do not disturb the choir service, and the Chapter does not hold the same functions; the pastor may collect alms for the poor of the parish, accept those directly or indirectly offered, administer and dispense them according to the will of the donors.

To the Chapter belongs the custody of the Blessed Sacrament, but one key to the tabernacle must be in the hands of the pastor; the Chapter watches that the pastor in his functions in church keeps the liturgical laws; the Chapter takes care of the church building, administers its goods and pious legacies. The Chapter and the pastor should not interfere with each other's rights. If a controversy arises, the local Ordinary shall decide. He should specially see to it that the catechetical instructions are given at a time convenient for the people. The Chapter is in charity bound to help the pastor in his work, especially if he has no assistants, and the Ordinary shall determine the method in which this assistance shall be given (**Canon 415**).

302. The statutes of the Chapter should furnish the regulations whereby the canons and beneficiaries discharge in rotation the services at the altar, as celebrant, deacon or subdeacon. The dignitaries, the canon theologian, and the canon penitentiary should not be employed for the offices of deacon and subdeacon. In Chapters where there are distinct prebends for canons who are deacons and subdeacons, priests also should not be employed as deacon and subdeacon (**Canon 416**).[29b]

The Conventual or Chapter Mass must be applied for the benefactors generally. A canon who, on account of sickness, cannot say this Mass when his turn comes, need not give a Mass stipend to the canon who says Mass in his place, unless the statutes of the Chapter or particular customs rule otherwise. The custom of giving a stipend to the celebrant of the Conventual Mass out of the fund set apart for the daily distributions or out of the revenue of all prebends by contribution of all holders of the prebends may be continued (**Canon 417**).

303. Canons and holders of benefices who are liable for daily choir service, may not be absent for more than three months a year, either continuous or interrupted. Contrary custom allowing a longer absence is condemned. If the statutes

[29b] Cfr. App. III, 17, n.

of the Chapter or legitimate custom demand a longer service, the particular law governs. Without legitimate cause and special permission of the bishop, the vacation cannot be taken during Lent and Advent or on the principal feasts of the year enumerated in Canon 338, nor may more than one-third of the canons be absent at one and the same time. During the vacation every kind of distribution is lost to those absent notwithstanding any remission made by the other members of the Chapter. The revenue of the prebend is not lost during the vacation, and if all revenue of the prebends consists in distribution, two-thirds are received during the vacation (**Canon 418**).

In those churches where all are not obliged to attend choir at the same time, those whose turn it is cannot satisfy their obligation through a proxy, except in particular cases and for a just and reasonable cause, and provided the substitute is not bound to attend choir at that time. The substitute must be a canon of the same church if he substitutes for a canon, and a holder of a benefice if he substitutes for a holder of a benefice. During the days that the members of the Chapter are not obliged to be in choir, they are not obliged to reside in the place of the benefice. If one on the same day has the obligation of saying Mass for the people and also the Conventual Mass, he shall say and apply the latter Mass himself, and shall have the other said by another priest, or say it himself on the day following (**Canon 419**).[29c]

304. Excused from choir duty with the right to get both the income of the prebend and the daily distributions, are the following:

(1) Jubilarians of the Chapters, according to Canon 422;

(2) the canon theologian on the days only on which he fulfills his office of preaching;

(3) the canon penitentiary when he hears confessions during the choir service;

(4) the parochial vicar or another priest of the Chapter appointed by the bishop as pastor or assistant, while they are occupied in parochial duties;

(5) those who through sickness or other physical impediment cannot attend choir;

[29c] Cfr. App. III, 17, o.

(6) those who are sent elsewhere as Papal legates or actually are in the personal service of the Roman Pontiff;

(7) those who are making their annual retreat (only once a year does this excuse them from choir service);

(8) those who go with or in place of the bishop for the visit *ad limina;*

(9) those who are sent by the bishop or the Chapter to an Œcumenical, Plenary, or Provincial Council, or to the diocesan Synod;

(10) those who with the consent of the Chapter, and without the opposition of the bishop, are absent from choir to attend to affairs for the benefit of the Chapter or the capitular church;

(11) those who assist the bishop pontificating in some church of the same city or its suburbs;

(12) those who accompany the bishop in the visitation of the diocese, or make the visitation as his delegates;

(13) those who are occupied on a process of beatification or canonization, or are called as witnesses in these cases, are excused from choir for the days and hours during which they attend to this;

(14) parochial consultors, synodal examiners and judges while they attend to their duties. Distributions which by the statutes of the Chapter are to be made "inter præsentes," may be received by those absentees mentioned above under 1, 7, 11, and 13, unless the will of the founder expressly forbids even such absentees to get the distributions called "inter præsentes" (**Canon 420**).

305. Excused from choir duty with loss of the daily contributions but with payment of the income from the prebend are the following:

(1) those who, with the permission of the local Ordinary, teach sacred theology or Canon Law in a school recognized by the Church; [29d]

(2) those who, with the permission of the Ordinary, are engaged in the study of sacred theology or Canon Law in schools approved by the Church;

(3) the vicar-capitular, vicar-general, judge and chancellor, if they are of the body of the Chapter, while they are engaged in the duties of their respective offices;

[29d] Cfr. App. III, 17, p–r.

(4) canons who serve the bishop continually in the ecclesiastical ministry and the service of the diocese (cfr. Canon 412).

If the entire income of the prebend consists of daily distributions, or if the income from the prebend is so small that it does not amount to one-third of the daily distributions, then the persons mentioned shall get two-thirds of the distributions made up of the income of the prebends and the distributions (**Canon 421**). The principle is that the men mentioned here shall get two-thirds of the stipend of those who attend choir.

306. If a canon has served his church in a praiseworthy manner for forty successive years, or in various churches of the same city, or has done choir service for that length of time in the diocese, he can get from the Holy See the indult of an emeritus or jubilarian. No one else can grant this indult. By this indult the jubilarian becomes free from choir service, and retains the right to receive the income of his prebend and the daily distributions, including those "inter præsentes," even though he does not reside in the place of his benefice. If in reference to the daily distributions the laws of the foundation, or the will of those who gave the offerings for the daily distributions, or the statutes, or the custom of the particular church absolutely exclude from the distributions all who are not present in choir, these regulations prevail. If the right of option exists by the laws of the foundation, a canon jubilarian is excluded from the option (**Canon 422**).[29e]

CHAPTER VI

OF DIOCESAN CONSULTORS

307. In those dioceses in which it has not yet been possible to institute, or to revive former Cathedral Chapters of canons, the bishop shall appoint diocesan consultors, except where the Apostolic See has given special laws to some diocese. The consultors are to be priests commendable for piety, good character, knowledge and prudence (**Canon 423**). They are nominated by the bishop according to the rules of Canon 426 (**Canon 424**). There shall be at least six consultors, or, even in dioceses with few priests, at least four. All the consultors must live either in the episcopal city or in adjacent places. Before they

[29e] Cfr. App. III, 17, s.

enter upon their office, they must take an oath to perform their duties faithfully without respect for persons (**Canon 425**).

308. The office of consultors lasts three years. When the three years expire, the bishop shall either appoint others, or reappoint the same consultors for another term of three years. This rule shall be followed every three years. If any of the consultors retire from office for any reason before the three years expire, the bishop shall appoint others in their place, with the advice of the remaining consultors; these substitutes shall remain in office for the rest of the unexpired term.

If the three years' term expires during the vacancy of the bishopric, the consultors remain in office until the new bishop takes possession, and he must appoint successors within the first six months according to the rules of this Canon. If, during the vacancy, any one of the consultors dies or resigns, the vicar-capitular (or the administrator) shall, with the consent of the other consultors, nominate a substitute who needs the confirmation of the new bishop to continue in office after the bishop has taken possession of the diocese (**Canon 426**).

309. The body of diocesan consultors takes the place of the Cathedral Chapter as the council of the bishop. Wherefore, whatever part in the government of the diocese the Canons give the Cathedral Chapter during the reign of the bishop, during the time that the exercise of his jurisdiction is impeded, or during the vacancy of the bishopric, is also assigned to the body of consultors (**Canon 427**).

During their term of office the consultors shall not be removed except for a just cause and with the advice of the other consultors (**Canon 428**).

310. The Code does not prescribe any regular meetings of the diocesan consultors, but the Third Plenary Council of Baltimore demands that the bishop convoke them to meeting four times a year at stated intervals; only where this is impossible, may the bishop limit the meetings to two a year (no. 21). As to the matters in which the bishop must consult the diocesan consultors, and in a few cases get their consent, the Code refers us to the same cases in which the bishop must get the advice or consent of the cathedral chapter. The consultors' advice must be obtained in dismemberment, division and union of parishes (Canon 1428); the union of a parish with a religious

community requires both consultation of the bishop with the diocesan consultors and permission of the Holy See (Canons 452, 1423); the appointment of the two committees, one for the discipline and the other for the temporal administration of the diocesan seminary, is to be done with the advice of the diocesan consultors (Canon 1359); pro-synodal examiners and pro-synodal parochial consultors must be appointed with the advice of the diocesan consultors, and their advice is also required in the removal of synodal examiners and parochial consultors (Canons 386, 388); the alienation of church property of the value of one thousand and not over thirty thousand lire or francs needs the consent of the diocesan consultors (Canon 1532); and by the Third Plenary Council of Baltimore the bishop needs the advice of the consultors to make use of the indult of the Holy See (extended July 31, 1916, for ten years) to alienate church property of the value of over thirty thousand francs; the *consent* of the consultors required for from one thousand to thirty thousand francs by Canon 1532, is modified for the United States by the special indult which requires only the *advice* of the consultors. As the normal exchange rate is about five francs or lire to a dollar, this is the value according to which the francs or lire of the Code must be taken, for otherwise there is no firm basis for the laws of the Code in this matter. The tax to be paid on the occasion of funerals is to be fixed by the bishop with the advice of the diocesan consultors (Canon 1234); the consultors' advice is required in the erection of removable parishes and in raising removable to irremovable parishes (Canon 454); but the bishop does not need to consult them in the appointment of pastors (Canon 455). By the law of the Third Plenary Council of Baltimore (no. 273), the bishop must consult the diocesan consultors on the amount of the salaries of pastors and questions connected with the salaries. The consultors' advice is required for the making of diocesan reserved cases outside of a synod (Canon 895); also when the bishop wants to order extraordinary processions for public cause (Canon 1292). Their advice is required for fixing (outside of a synod) the tax which the bishop allows a poor church to collect from extern priests saying Mass there for their own convenience (Canon 1303); the committee for the administration of the diocesan church property consisting of the bishop and two or more men is to be established with the advice of the diocesan consultors (Canon 1520).[30]

CHAPTER VII

OF OBSTRUCTION IN THE GOVERNMENT OF THE DIOCESE, VACANCY, VICAR-CAPITULAR

311. If the bishop is in captivity, or banished, exiled, or otherwise inhabilitated, so that he cannot even by letter communicate with the people of his diocese, the government of the diocese shall rest with the vicar-general or another priest delegated by the bishop, unless the Holy See has made other provision. The bishop may in such circumstances for grave reasons delegate several persons who are to succeed each other in turn. If all of them fail, or are impeded in any of the ways described above, the Cathedral Chapter—or the diocesan consultors, where there is no Chapter—shall elect a vicar who shall assume the government with the powers of a vicar-capitular. Those called upon to take the government of the diocese in such circumstances, shall as soon as possible inform the Holy See of the state of affairs and of their having assumed the government.

If the bishop should have incurred excommunication, interdict, or suspension, the archbishop or—if the archbishop is under censure, or fails to act—the oldest suffragan bishop shall at once have recourse to the Holy See that proper provision may be made. The vicar-general's jurisdiction is suspended together with that of the bishop (Canon 371). In the case of bishops and prelates *nullius*, who belong to no ecclesiastical province, but who have to choose an archbishop to whose jurisdiction they wish to belong for the purpose of the Provincial Council (cfr. Canon 285), the archbishop thus chosen shall report to the Holy See (**Canon 429**).

VACANCY OF THE EPISCOPAL SEE

312. The episcopal see becomes vacant on the death of the bishop, on his resignation accepted by the Roman Pontiff, on his transfer, and on his deprivation of office made known to

---

[30] Klekotka "Diocesan Consultors," 112 sq. The right of the consultors to elect the administrator of the vacant diocese is treated in the next chapter.

the bishop. Nevertheless, all acts of the vicar-general are valid until he has received certain notice of the bishop's death; and, in the case of removal or transfer by the Holy See, all acts of the bishop or his vicar-general are valid until official notice from the Roman Pontiff has reached them. Only appointments to benefices and offices are excepted from this rule.

If a bishop is transferred to another diocese, he must within four months from the receipt of the notice take possession of the new diocese (cfr. Canons 333–334); the first diocese becomes fully vacant from the day the bishop takes possession of the new diocese. In the meantime, the bishop has the following powers in the diocese from which he was transferred: (1) he has the jurisdiction and obligations of a vicar-capitular, the jurisdiction of the vicar-general ceasing entirely; (2) he retains the honorary privileges of residential bishops; (3) he receives all the income of the *mensa episcopalis,* according to Canon 194 (**Canon 430**). In the United States, there is no *mensa episcopalis* as a distinct source of revenue, but the salary of the bishop is meant whether this is derived from the *cathedraticum* or from any other source.

313. In case of vacancy the government of the diocese devolves on the Cathedral Chapter (or on the diocesan consultors in dioceses where there are no chapters), unless there is an Apostolic Administrator or the Holy See has otherwise provided. If, by special arrangement of the Holy See, the archbishop, or another bishop, has the right to appoint an administrator for a vacant diocese, such administrator has all those —and only those—faculties and powers which the vicar-capitular has, and is subject to the same obligations and penalties (**Canon 431**).

Election of the Vicar-Capitular by the Chapter, or of the Administrator by the Diocesan Consultors

314. Within eight days from the notice of the vacancy of the episcopal see, the Cathedral Chapter must elect the vicar-capitular for the government of the diocese (**Canon 432, § 1**). In the United States and other places which have no chapters, the diocesan consultors have the same right and duty as the Cathedral Chapter. If the Chapter for any reason whatsoever

neglects to hold the election within that time, the archbishop has the right to appoint the vicar-capitular, and, in case of the vacancy of the metropolitan see, this right devolves on the senior suffragan bishop (**Canon 432, § 2**).

In case of the vacancy of an abbacy or prelature *nullius*, the Chapter must within eight days nominate the vicar or *œconomus*, and, if they neglect to do so, the metropolitan of the province which was legitimately chosen (according to Canon 285) by the abbacy or prelature for the purpose of taking part in the provincial council, has the right to appoint the vicar. However, if the constitutions of an abbacy or prelature *nullius* belonging to a religious organization have other provisions for the appointment of the vicar of the vacant abbey or prelature, those regulations govern (**Canon 432, § 3**).

The Chapter, or the diocesan consultors, shall as soon as possible notify the Holy See of the vacancy and of the election of the vicar-capitular, or the administrator (**Canon 432, § 4**).

315. There is no doubt that the diocesan consultors of the dioceses in the United States have the right to elect the administrator of the diocese in the case of a vacancy. In answer to doubts sent in by the Apostolic Delegate, the Holy See has explicitly declared [31] that, where there are at least five or six diocesan consultors, they elect the administrator. Where there are fewer, the archbishop—or, during vacancy of the archbishopric, the senior suffragan bishop—receives faculties for three years to nominate the administrator, with the approval of the Apostolic Delegate. If the number of consultors is increased to five or six before the three years expire, the faculty does not apply. The Code does not indicate which of the consultors should convoke the meeting for the election of the administrator. It may be safely said that the consultor first in precedence has the right to convoke the board; the precedence should be regulated by Canon 106. If there is an auxiliary bishop in the diocese and he does not belong to the consultors, he has no right to convoke them. Now, among the consultors themselves, one of a higher rank precedes the others of an inferior rank; if there are no prelates or digni-

---

[31] Cfr. App. III, 3, a. Extended to Dioceses in Canada and Newfoundland, May 8, 1919; *Acta Ap. Sedis*, XI, 233.

taries among them but all are merely priests, the **seniority** of ordination to the priesthood decides precedence, and, if several were ordained the same day, the senior in age precedes. **The** seniority in the office of consultor cannot be considered because all are supposed to be appointed at the same time and for three years only. The rules of the Code on election **(Canons 160–178)** must be followed by the consultors.

The chapter, or the consultors, may appoint **only one vicar-**capitular, all contrary customs being condemned; otherwise the election is null and void. The election of the vicar-capitular and the *œconomus* must be done by action in a body according to the rules on election of Canons 160–178, without prejudice to special rules of the respective chapter. An absolute majority of votes, not counting invalid votes, is required for validity. The same person may be elected vicar-capitular and *œconomus* (**Canon 433**).

The *œconomus* mentioned in Canons 432–433 appears only during the vacancy of an episcopal see and his office ends with the rendering of an account to the new bishop. He is to be elected by the Cathedral Chapter (or the diocesan consultors). His office is to take care of the revenues of the *mensa episcopalis* so that the income which belongs to the bishop may be kept for the successor. If there are no goods to be preserved for the successor (e.g., in dioceses where the government pay the salary of the bishop and where such payments are suspended during the vacancy), Cocchi remarks that the appointment of an *œconomus* is quite useless (Commentarium, III, n. 319). The Code suggests that he is to be appointed only when there are goods to be administered for the benefit of the successor to the episcopal see. The Council of Trent (Sessio **XXIV**, cap. 18, *De Reform.*) stated: "When a see is vacant, the chapter, in those places where the duty of receiving the fruits devolves upon it, shall appoint one or more faithful and diligent stewards to take care of the property and revenues of the church," which precept is repeated in Canon 432 of the Code.

Qualifications of the Vicar-Capitular

316. The vicar-capitular must be a priest, fully thirty years of age, and must not have been elected, nominated or presented

to the vacant see in question. These requirements bind under pain of invalidity. (In the United States the diocesan consultors have to attend only to the requirements of priesthood and age, because we have no dioceses where the bishop can be elected, nominated or presented.) The vicar-capitular should be a doctor or licentiate in theology or in canon law, or at least well versed in these sciences; his character must be blameless, and he must possess piety and soundness of doctrine combined with prudence. If the Chapter or the consultors choose a man who has not the requirements demanded for validity by the first section of this Canon, the archbishop—or, in case of the vacancy of the archbishopric, the senior suffragan bishop of the province—shall appoint a vicar as soon as he learns of the invalid choice. The acts of the invalidly elected vicar are absolutely invalid (**Canon 434**).

Powers of the Vicar-Capitular or the Administrator

317. At the vacancy of the bishopric, the ordinary jurisdiction of the bishop in temporal and spiritual affairs devolves on the Chapter or the diocesan consultors; after the election of the vicar or the administrator, that power is vested in the man elected, except in matters wherein his jurisdiction is expressly denied by the law. The Chapter and, after the election, the vicar can do all things which the vicar-general can do according to Canon 368. They can also allow any bishop to hold pontifical functions, and, if the vicar-capitular (or the administrator) is a bishop, he can himself hold pontifical functions, but he may not use the throne with the canopy.

The vicar-capitular (or the administrator) and the Chapter may not do anything which prejudices the rights of the diocese or of the future bishop. It is specially forbidden to the vicar-capitular or others (either of the Chapter or outsiders), clerics or laymen, by themselves or through others, to take away, destroy, conceal, or change any document belonging to the episcopal Curia (**Canon 435**).

318. During the vacancy no innovations shall be made (**Canon 436**). In the election of the vicar-capitular (or the administrator), the Cathedral Chapter (or the diocesan consultors) cannot retain for themselves any jurisdiction, nor fix

the duration of the office, nor attach any other restrictions (**Canon 437**). Once he has made the profession of faith before the Chapter or the consultors, as required by Canons 1406–1408, the vicar-capitular or administrator immediately obtains jurisdiction, and does not need confirmation of the election from any person (**Canon 438**). The vicar also enjoys the privileges of honor assigned to the vicar-general in Canon 370 (**Canon 439**). He is obliged to reside in the diocese and to apply Mass for the people in the same manner as the bishop is bound by Canons 338–339 (**Canon 440**). The vicar-capitular, or the administrator, and the *œconomus* have a right to a just salary, to be determined either by the Provincial Council or approved custom, which is to be taken from the revenue of the *mensa episcopalis* or from other sources. The rest of the income of the bishopric, which accumulates during the vacancy, shall be reserved for the future bishop for the needs of the diocese, if it would have gone to the bishop had he been in office (**Canon 441**). The *œconomus* shall have the care and administration of the ecclesiastical goods and their income, under the authority of the vicar-capitular (**Canon 442**).

Removal of the Vicar-Capitular and the Œconomus

319. The removal of the vicar-capitular (or administrator) and the *œconomus* is reserved to the Holy See. If they want to resign, they must present to the Chapter (or consultors) a written document in authentic form, but the acceptance of it by the Chapter (or consultors) is not necessary for its validity. After the resignation, the election of a new vicar-capitular (or administrator) or *œconomus* rests with the Chapter (or consultors). The new election must be held according to the same rules as the first election of the vicar and the *œconomus,* as outlined in Canon 432. The office of the vicar and *œconomus* ceases when the new bishop takes possession of the diocese by presenting in person or through a proxy the Apostolic Letters of appointment to the assembled Chapter or the diocesan consultors as stated in Canon 334 (**Canon 443**).

320. The new bishop has authority to demand from the vicar-capitular (or administrator), *œconomus* and all other officials constituted during the vacancy of the diocese an ac-

count of the administration of their respective offices. **The** bishop has the right to punish them for delinquencies in office, even though the Chapter (or consultors) may have exonerated them. They must also give an account of the documents pertaining to the diocese that arrived during the vacancy (**Canon 444**).

Chapter VIII

OF VICARS-FORANES OR DEANS

321. A dean (*vicarius foraneus*) is a priest who presides over a deanery by appointment of the bishop (**Canon 445**). Canon 217 demands that the bishop divide the territory of his diocese into districts, called deaneries. The bishop shall appoint to the office of dean worthy priests, especially from among the pastors. The bishop may at will remove a dean from office (**Canon 446**).

Rights and Duties of Deans

322. Besides the faculties which the Provincial Council, or the diocesan synod, or the bishop gives to them, they have the right and duty: (1) to watch over the clergy of their district so that they may live according to the laws of the Church, and attend to the duties of their respective offices; especially that they keep residence, attend to preaching and the instruction of the children and adults, and do their duty towards the sick; (2) to see that the clergy carry out the decrees and orders of the bishop issued at the time of his visitation; (3) to see that the rules about the reservation of the Blessed Sacrament are observed; (4) to see that the churches, vestments and sacred vessels are kept in proper condition; that the Church property is properly and faithfully administered, and the obligations attached to church endowments (especially foundation Masses) are fulfilled; that the church records of the parishes are correctly and properly kept.

323. To obtain information on these matters, the dean must at stated times (to be fixed by the bishop) visit the parishes of his district. It is the dean's duty, as soon as he hears of the serious illness of any pastor of his district, to see that such

a priest receives the necessary spiritual and bodily care, and, in case of death, a becoming funeral. He has, moreover, the duty to see that, during the illness or after the death of a pastor, the books, documents, sacred utensils and other objects belonging to the parish are not lost or taken away (**Canon 447**).

324. On the days appointed by the bishop the dean must summon the priests of his district for the conferences of which Canon 131 speaks, and preside over them. If they are held in various places of his district, he must see that they are properly attended. If the dean is not a pastor, he must reside in the territory of the deanery or in an adjacent place, according to the regulations to be made by the bishop (**Canon 448**). At least once a year the dean must submit a report to the bishop about his district, detailing not only the good that has been accomplished during the year, but also any evils that may have crept in, any scandals that may have arisen, what has been done to rectify them, and what he has to suggest for the complete eradication of the evils (**Canon 449**). The dean shall have a special seal for the deanery. He precedes all pastors and other priests of his district (**Canon 450**).[31a]

Chapter IX

OF PASTORS

325. The pastor is an individual priest or a "moral person" (college chapter, etc.), to whom a parish has been given "in titulum" with the care of souls to be exercised under the authority of the local Ordinary. (The phrase "in titulum" may be translated "with rightful possession," designating the office, rights and duties of the legal holder of the parish.) The following persons come in law under the name of and are held equal to pastors with all parochial rights and duties: (1) the quasi-pastors who are in charge of quasi-parishes in vicariates and prefectures Apostolic, where the territory has been divided into districts, and individual rectors have been appointed over the districts. In countries, like the United States and others which have been recently withdrawn from the jurisdiction of the Sacred Congregation of the Propaganda, there are no quasi-parishes, but parishes in the canonical sense of the term; (2)

[31a] Cfr. App. III, 18.

the parochial vicars, if they have full parochial charge of the parish during the time of their office. The Code treats of parochial vicars in the following chapter, Canons 471–478. Concerning the major and minor military chaplains, the special regulations of the Holy See determine the extent of their power (**Canon 451**).

326. Without an indult of the Apostolic See the bishop cannot unite a parish with a so-called legal or moral person (e.g., a monastery, college) so completely that the legal person itself becomes the pastor of a parish, as is stated in Canon 1423. The legal person to whom a parish has been given in full right, can retain only the habitual care of souls; the actual exercise of the pastoral rights rests with the parochial vicar who is presented by the legal person, and must be instituted by the bishop if he finds him duly qualified, as is stated in Canon 471 (**Canon 452**). The union in full right (i.e., with regard to both the spiritual and the temporal rights over the parish) is, in Canon 1425, contrasted with the union *ad temporalia tantum*. Since we have no parishes in the United States which are endowed in the manner of many European parishes, the union of a parish for the temporal goods only is not likely to occur. If a parish is given to a religious organization, the consent of the bishop cannot be given unless he first consults the diocesan consultors (cfr. Canon 1428), and the consent of the Apostolic See is likewise required. A union in full right transfers according to the common law the title of all property and income to the legal person to whom the parish is thus united.

327. In order that a cleric be validly appointed pastor, he must be a priest. He should, in addition, have those qualifications of character, knowledge, virtue, prudence and experience which will enable him to govern the parish properly, and which are demanded by both the common and the particular law (**Canon 453**).

Removable and Irremovable Pastors

328. Those who are appointed as the proper rectors for the government of a parish, should remain permanently in office. This rule, however, does not forbid the change of any pastor.

provided the rules of law are observed. Not all pastors have the same stability; those who enjoy greater stability are called *irremovable;* those who have a lesser degree of stability are usually called *movable* pastors. Irremovable parishes cannot be made movable without the *beneplacitum* of the Holy See. The movable parishes can be made irremovable by the bishop (not, however, by the vicar-capitular or administrator) with the advice of the Cathedral Chapter or the diocesan consultors. New parishes to be established should be made irremovable, unless the bishop, after consulting the chapter or the diocesan consultors, prudently judges that under the peculiar circumstances of the place and persons a movable rectorship is more advisable. All pastors of quasi-parishes are movable.

Pastors belonging to religious communities are always, as far as the individual person is concerned, movable, and they can be removed from the pastor's office both by the will of the bishop (notifying the religious superior), and also at the will of the respective religious superior (notifying the bishop). Both have equal rights, and the one does not need the consent of the other, nor has one to give to the other the reason for his action, much less proof of such reason. Both have the right of recourse *in devolutivo* to the Holy See in case of disagreement (**Canon 454**).

Right of Bishop to Appoint Pastors

329. The right to nominate and institute pastors belongs to the bishop, except for parishes reserved to the Holy See; all contrary customs impairing this right of the bishop are disapproved. Those, however, who have been legitimately granted the privilege to elect or present the pastor, retain this right (**Canon 455**, § 1).

330. When the diocese is vacant, or the bishop is prevented from exercising jurisdiction (as described in Canon 429), the vicar-capitular (or administrator) or whoever rules the diocese has the right: (1) to institute parochial vicars according to Canons 472–476; (2) to confirm the election or accept the presentation to vacant parishes and to grant the canonical institution to the men elected or presented to the pastorship; (3) to appoint pastors to parishes generally, if the see has been vacant for at least one year. The vicar-general has no

power to confer parishes without a special mandate from the bishop, except in cases where the bishop is in captivity, exile, inhabilitated to act, etc. (cfr. Canon 429) : in such cases, the vicar-general has the same powers as are given in this Canon to the vicar-capitular or the administrator (**Canon 455,** §§ 2–3).

In the United States all the secular pastors are freely appointed by the bishop, because we have no parishes that are reserved to the Holy See, nor have we any parishes where other persons have the right to elect or present the pastor.

331. In parishes given to religious organizations, the superior presents the pastor, and the bishop has the right to examine him as to his fitness for the position, but, if he finds him qualified, he must give him the canonical institution (**Canon 456**).

332. Quasi-pastors are nominated from the secular clergy by the local Ordinary with the advice of his council. These quasi-parishes are found only in vicariates and prefectures Apostolic, and in these the vicar or prefect Apostolic has, according to Canon 302, to appoint at least three of the older missionaries as his advisory board, and must consult these men in the appointment of quasi-pastors (**Canon 457**).

Manner of Appointment of Pastors

333. The bishop should not delay the appointment of a pastor to a vacant parish for more than six months, unless peculiar local or personal considerations seem to render a delay advisable (**Canon 458**). The local Ordinary is bound under grave obligation of conscience to give the vacant parish to the priest whom he judges best qualified, and to avoid all favoritism. In judging the qualifications of the candidates for the pastorship, he must consider not only learning, but also all the other qualities required for the proper administration of the parish (**Canon 459,** §§ 1–2).

Wherefore the Ordinary shall not neglect to (1) gather information prudently from every source as to the character of the priest; (2) refer to the examinations he passed when belonging to the junior clergy (cfr. Canon 130); (3) subject the candidate to an examination as to his theological knowledge before himself and the synodal examiners, unless there is question of a priest well known for his theological learning, in which case he may with the consent of the same examiners dispense him from the examination; (4) in countries where the conferring of parishes is done by a *concursus*—either in the form of the Constitution "Cum illud" of Pope Benedict XIV, Dec. 14, 1742, or by a general *concursus*—that form shall be retained until the Holy See shall have otherwise provided (**Canon 459**, §§ 3–4).

334. In the United States the Third Council of Baltimore requires the *concursus* in substantially the same form as the aforesaid Constitution of Pope Benedict XIV for all irremovable parishes (cfr. Chapter V, *De rectoribus inamovibilibus*, n. 36). In the dioceses which have a very extensive territory and where it would be difficult for all the priests to arrive in time for the examinations when a vacancy of an irremovable parish occurs, a general *concursus* is permitted by the Third Council of Baltimore (no. 59), to be held once a year. Those who pass the examinations may be appointed by the bishop to vacant irremovable parishes within six years from the examination.

335. In reference to the examination of candidates for the office of pastor, which is held before the Ordinary and the diocesan examiners, the Holy See has given the following declarations to various cases: (1) if a pastor is transferred from one parish to another because the bishop proposes and desires such a change, there is no need of a new examination; if the pastor himself requests the change, he is liable to a new examination, unless the bishop with the synodal examiners judge that the priest is absolutely qualified for the new position; (2) if an irremovable pastor is changed to another parish after proceedings of removal, he need not take a new examination; (3) in the case of a removable pastor who was transferred to another parish in the manner specified in Canons 2162–2167 (namely because the transfer is judged by the bishop to be to the advantage of the diocese), though against the wishes of the pastor, no new examination is required; (4) if none of the priests whom the Ordinary thinks fit for the office of pastor in a certain parish wish to undergo the examination, for the reason that the parish is very small, the Holy See desires that recourse be had to the Sacred Congregation of the Council; (5) the examination prescribed in Canon 996, § 2, for the reception of major

orders, when held in the presence of the **Ordinary** and the synodal examiners, may serve also for the examination for the first parish, provided it extends over the entire matter required in the examination for a pastorship; (6) the examination to which the junior priests must submit in accordance with **Canon** 130, is not sufficient for the conferring of a pastorship.[32]

336. A pastor may hold title to one parish only, according to Canon 156, unless there is question of two parishes which have been united *æque principaliter,* i.e., each parish retaining its legal personality or entity. Canon 1423 allows the Ordinary to unite parishes thus where necessity or great evident advantage justifies the union. In one and the same parish there can be but one pastor who has the actual care of souls; all contrary customs are disapproved and all contrary privileges recalled (**Canon 460**). The Holy See was asked whether this law applies only to parishes to be erected after, or also to those erected before the promulgation of the Code, and replied that it refers also to those erected before the Code. To the further question whether this Canon applies to parishes in which several pastors were introduced, not by custom or privilege, but by a legitimate statute, the answer was that it applies also to these parishes. To decide which of the several pastors is to retain parochial jurisdiction—whether the one in the more prominent parish or the oldest in possession—the Holy See wants the matter submitted to the Sacred Congregation of the Council in each case.[33] In the United States, we have several pastors in one district only in the case of the language parishes, and such parishes erected before the promulgation of the Code are sanctioned by the Holy See, as is evident from Canon 216.

Powers of the Pastor

337. The pastor assumes the care of souls in his parish from the moment of taking possession. The manner of taking possession may, according to Canon 1444, be regulated by particular law or by custom. Before taking possession, or in the act of taking possession, he must make the profession of faith prescribed by Canon 1406, § 1, n. 7 (**Canon 461**). In the United

32 Cfr. App. III, 19, a.
33 Cfr. App. III, 19, b.

States there is no form of taking possession of the parish prescribed by the Plenary Councils of Baltimore, wherefore it is left to the statutes or custom of the individual dioceses to determine the manner of taking possession.

338. The functions reserved to the pastor, unless the law states otherwise, are the following:

(1) to confer solemn baptism;

(2) to carry the Blessed Sacrament publicly to the sick within the parish. In the United States the Blessed Sacrament is not carried publicly to the sick. Canon 849 states that any priest may privately take Holy Communion to the sick;

(3) to administer the Holy Viaticum, whether publicly or privately, and to give Extreme Unction. The bishop receives the last sacraments from the canons of the cathedral chapter, or where there is no chapter, from the diocesan consultors; the order of precedence in these bodies determines who is to administer the last rites. In clerical religious communities the administration of the last rites to the religious and to all persons of the household of the monastery, abbey, etc., belongs to the religious superior. In case of necessity any priest may administer the last rites, and sometimes also by presumed permission;

(4) to announce the ordination of candidates from the parish and the marriage banns. To assist at marriages and give the nuptial blessing;

(5) to perform the funeral services of his parishioners unless they themselves selected before their death another church for burial;

(6) to bless the houses on Holy Saturday (or any other day according to local custom) with the blessing of the ritual. In the United States it is not the custom to bless the houses on Holy Saturday or any other fixed day. The ordinary blessing of houses is not reserved to the pastor;

(7) to bless the baptismal font on Holy Saturday, to hold public processions outside the church with great pomp and ceremony, unless in the case of a capitular church the Chapter performs such functions (**Canon 462**).[33a]

339. The pastor has the right to the revenue to which legitimate custom or legal taxation (cfr. Canon 1507) entitles

[33a] Concerning processions, cfr. App. III, 19, c.

him. If he exacts more than he is entitled to, he is bound to make restitution. If any of the parochial affairs are discharged by another priest, the fees or offerings belong to the pastor, unless it is certain that those making the offering wished otherwise concerning the sum that is over and above the ordinary tax. The pastor must not refuse to serve gratuitously those who are not able to pay for the services (**Canon 463**). The amount of the salary is not determined by the Code, and it is evident that such a law is practically impossible on account of the great difference of financial standing of the parishes in the various countries. The Third Plenary Council of Baltimore (no. 273) orders that the individual bishop fix the amount of the salary, and the same Council (no. 281) rules that the pastor who does not draw his salary within a year from the time it became due, loses the right to it, unless a written demand for it was submitted to and approved by the Ordinary or his chancellor.

340. The pastor is bound, in virtue of his office, to exercise the care of souls over all who are not legitimately exempt from his jurisdiction. The bishop may for just and grave reason exempt from the authority of the pastor a religious community or a pious institution located within the territory of a parish, though they are not exempted by the common law (**Canon 464**).

Obligations of the Pastor

341. The pastor is obliged to live in the parochial house, near his church. The Ordinary may permit him for a just reason to live elsewhere, provided the house is not so far away from the church that the attendance to the duties of his office suffers. He is allowed at most two months' vacation in a year (either continuous or interrupted), unless the Ordinary restricts or prolongs that period for a grave reason. The days spent in the annual retreat of the priests of the diocese do not count as part of the vacation (**Canon 465**, §§ 1–3).

342. Whether the pastor takes his vacation for two months in succession or with interruptions, the rule is that, whenever he goes away for more than a week, he must in addition to a legitimate cause of absence have the written permission of the

Ordinary. While away from his parish, the pastor must provide a substitute approved by the Ordinary. If the pastor is a religious, he must have also the consent of his superior, and the substitute must be acceptable both to the Ordinary and the religious superior (**Canon 465,** § 4).

343. If the pastor is obliged to leave his parish suddenly for some very urgent reason, and must be away for over a week, he shall as soon as possible inform his bishop by letter of the facts, and make known what priest he left in charge, and obey the orders of the bishop. Also when the pastor is away from the parish for less than a week he must provide for the wants of the people of the parish, especially if the peculiar circumstances of the place require constant attention (**Canon 465,** §§ 5–6). With reference to the pastor's substitute during his absence, several questions have been decided by the Holy See: (1) the substitute appointed by the pastor with the approval of the bishop may licitly and validly assist at marriages in the parish, if no limitation of his powers was made when he was appointed; (2) the substitute may not assist at marriages before his approval by the bishop; (3) the substitute of a pastor of a religious community may assist at marriages after the approval of the bishop and before the approval of the religious superior has been obtained; (4) the substitute of the pastor who has to leave the parish suddenly may, provided the Ordinary was notified by the pastor of the appointment, assist at marriages before he receives the approval of the Ordinary until he has ruled otherwise.[34]

344. Pastors are strictly bound to apply Holy Mass for their congregation on all Sundays and holydays of obligation, even on the abolished holydays, just as the bishop according to Canon 339 has to apply Holy Mass for the people of the diocese. The quasi-pastors, that is to say, pastors in districts subject to the Sacred Propaganda, are obliged to say Holy Mass for their congregation on the greater feasts of the year enumerated in Canon 306 (cfr. above, n. 229). In the United States there was considerable doubt whether the pastors were obliged to apply Holy Mass for the people as this Canon demands, because the canonical standing of many parishes in our country was doubtful; there did not seem to be the neces-

[34] Cfr. App. III, 20, a, and 47, a and b.

sary formalities demanded by the Code to make them canonical parishes. However, as we saw under Canon 216 (cfr. n. 169), there is now the official declaration that our parishes are canonical and that the pastors have the duty to apply the Mass for the people. The days of the official list of feasts will be found under Canon 339 (cfr. above, n. 251).[34a]

345. If the pastor is in charge of several parishes which are united *æque principaliter* (i.e., each parish keeping its separate legal existence), or if he is administrator of an additional parish (or parishes), he satisfies his obligation by saying one Mass for the several parishes. The Ordinary can for a just reason allow the pastor to apply Mass for the people on another day than that specified in law. The pastor should say the Mass for the people in his parish church, unless circumstances force him or make it advisable to say Mass elsewhere. If the pastor is legitimately absent, he may either himself say the Mass for the people in the place where he stays, or have it said by the priest who takes his place in the parish (**Canon 466**).

346. The pastor must hold the divine services, administer the sacraments to the faithful whenever they legitimately request it, get acquainted with his parishioners, admonish the erring with prudence, assist the poor and the suffering people, and give his special care to the instruction of the children in the Catholic faith. The faithful must be admonished to visit their parish church frequently, where this can be done conveniently, and to assist at the Divine services and hear the Word of God (**Canon 467**).

347. The pastor shall take special care of the sick, above all when they are near death, give them the Sacraments frequently, and commend their souls to God. The pastor, and any other priest assisting the sick, has the faculty to give the Apostolic blessing with a plenary indulgence at the moment of death according to the formula of the Roman Ritual (**Canon 468**).

The pastor must guard that nothing be done against faith or morals in his parish, especially in the schools whether private or public, and he must foster or institute the works of charity, faith and piety in his parish (**Canon 469**).

348. The pastor must keep the parochial records of Bap-

34a Concerning small parish churches, cfr. App. III, 19, d.

tism, Confirmation, marriage and the deceased. He shall take care to have the census book as correct as possible, and shall keep these books with great care and according to the approved custom of the Church or the regulations of the bishop. In the baptismal record shall be inserted also a notice about the Confirmation, marriage or subdeaconship, or solemn religious profession, saving the marriage of conscience discussed in Canon 1107 (q.v.). When issuing baptismal certificates these facts should always be mentioned in the certificates. At the end of each year the pastor should send an authentic copy of the records of the parish to the episcopal Curia with the exception of the census book (**Canon 470, §§1–3**). Various Canons of the Code demand that the notice of the Confirmation, marriage, subdeaconship, and solemn religious profession be sent to the pastor of the parish where the persons were baptized, and the pastor is to make an annotation of the fact in the baptismal record in the margin opposite the individual records. If, in some of the record books, there is no space left for the entry of such notice, a mark can be made at the name of the person's baptismal record and the notices can be kept in the appendix.

The pastor shall have a parochial seal and a safe place for the above-mentioned parochial books, where he should also keep the bishop's letters and other documents that it may be useful or necessary to keep (**Canon 470, § 4**). In dioceses with a large Catholic population this double record at the diocesan Curia would grow to an immense size within some twenty years. Yet, the advantage of having a double set is evident when one considers how easily the records in the parish rectory may be destroyed by fire. Loose-leaf files which could be inserted by the chancellor as he gets the blanks sent to the pastors filled out would make it possible to have a complete second set of the records of each parish at the diocesan Curia.

CHAPTER X

OF PAROCHIAL VICARS

349. If a parish is united to a religious house, to a capitular church, or to any other legal person in full right, a vicar must be instituted for the actual care of souls who shall receive a

suitable salary from the income of the parish according to the judgment of the bishop. The religious superior, or the Chapter, or other legal body to which the parish is attached, shall nominate the vicar and present him to the bishop, who must appoint him if he finds him qualified after having examined him (cfr. Canon 459). The bishop himself nominates the parochial vicar only in cases where he obtained that right by legitimate privilege or custom, or the endowment of the vicariate was provided by the bishop with the stipulation that he reserved to himself the right freely to nominate the vicar.

If the parochial vicar is a religious, he is movable like the religious pastor mentioned in Canon 454. All other parochial vicars are perpetual as far as the college or Chapter that presents him is concerned, but the bishop has the right to remove him in the same manner as pastors, notifying the one who presented the vicar. To the vicar exclusively belongs the care of souls with all the rights and duties of the common law and of the approved statutes of the diocese and laudable customs (**Canon 471**). Canon 454 speaks of a "parochus" belonging to a religious community, and Canon 471 calls the religious priest in charge of a parish belonging to a religious community a "vicarius," parochial vicar. It seems that the terms are applied synonymously by the Code. In any case, Canon 471 states that this parochial vicar has all the rights and obligations of a pastor.

ADMINISTRATOR OF VACANT PARISH

350. When a parish becomes vacant, the local Ordinary shall as soon as possible appoint an administrator, called a *vicarius œconomus,* who shall take charge of the parish during the vacancy and to whom the bishop shall apportion a part of the income of the parish for his proper maintenance. (If the Ordinary wishes to appoint a priest of a religious community as administrator, he must get the consent of the respective religious superior. There is question in this Canon of the ordinary secular parishes—not of parishes united to a religious community, a cathedral Chapter, or other legal person, for of these the preceding Canon spoke.)

Before the administrator is appointed, the assistant of the

former pastor shall assume charge of the parish, unless other provision has been made. If there are several assistants in the parish, the first assistant is to take charge; if they are all equal, the senior in office takes charge. If there are no assistants, the nearest pastor takes charge. If there is question of a parish belonging to a religious community, the superior takes charge. The bishop in the diocesan synod, or outside the synod, shall determine beforehand which parish is to be considered nearest. He who takes charge of the parish as said above, shall notify the bishop immediately of the vacancy of the parish (**Canon 472**).

351. The administrator has the same rights and duties as the pastor in all things concerning the care of souls.[34b] He must, however, do nothing that might be prejudicial to the rights of the pastor or the parish. The administrator shall in the presence of the dean or another priest appointed by the bishop hand to the newly appointed pastor or administrator the key of the parochial archives and the inventory of books and documents and all other things belonging to the parish, and give an account of the receipts and expenditures during the time of his administration (**Canon 473**). The parochial vicar who takes charge of the parish during the absence of the pastor, as stated in Canon 465, or who is appointed by the bishop to administer the parish of a pastor who has been deprived of the parish and has appealed to the Holy See (as stated in Canon 1923), has all the rights of the pastor in the care of souls, unless the Ordinary or the pastor has restricted his power (**Canon 474**).

352. If the pastor, through old age, mental debility, incompetence, blindness, or other permanent inability, is incapable of discharging his duties properly, the Ordinary shall give him an assistant vicar. If the parish is in charge of a religious community, the religious superior presents the vicar. The vicar must be given a sufficient portion of the income of the parish for his support, unless other provision has been made for him. The vicar who takes the place of the pastor in all affairs of the parish has all the rights and duties of a pastor, with the exception of the application of the Mass for the congregation which obligation rests with the pastor. If, however, he has only a part of the pastoral duties to attend to, his rights and

[34b] Concerning the "Missa pro populo," cfr. App. III, 19, e.

obligations must be learned from his letters of appointment.

If the pastor is of sound mind, the vicar must help him in the pastoral duties under his authority and according to the bishop's instructions. If the spiritual interests of the parish cannot be properly taken care of by an assistant acting as vicar, the bishop has the right to remove the pastor according to the formalities described in Canons 2147–2161 (**Canon 475**).

Assistant Priests

353. If the pastor alone cannot take care of all the work of the parish on account of the great number of parishioners or for other reasons, the Ordinary shall give him one or more assistants, called in law *vicarii cooperatores,* who shall receive a proper salary. The assistants may be appointed either for the entire parish or for a certain specified part of it. The bishop, not the pastor, has the right to nominate the assistants of the secular clergy, after having given a hearing to the pastor (**Canon 476,** §§ 1–4). The Holy See has declared that, notwithstanding any custom to the contrary, the rule of this Canon demanding that the Ordinary consult the pastor before assigning assistants to him must be observed.[35]

354. In parishes belonging to a religious community, the competent religious superior, after having consulted the pastor, presents to the bishop the religious priests who are to be assistants, and it is the bishop's duty to approve them.

355. The assistants are obliged to reside in the parish according to the diocesan statutes, or the laudable customs, or the law of the bishop. The bishop should prudently arrange that the assistants live in the same house with the pastor, as Canon 134 desires a community life of the clergy. The rights and duties of the assistants depend on the diocesan statutes, the bishop's letter of appointment and the commission of the pastor. Unless the contrary has been explicitly stated, the assistants must help the pastor in the general ministry of the parish, with the exception of the Mass for the congregation. The assistants are subject to the pastor who shall paternally instruct and direct them in the care of souls, watch over them, and send each year a report to the bishop concerning their

---

[35] Sacred Congregation of the Council, Nov. 13, 1920; cfr. App. III, 20, b.

conduct. If the parish is such that even the **appointment of** assistants does not properly provide for the spiritual welfare of the people, the bishop has the right to divide the **parish,** according to Canon 1427 (**Canon 476,** §§ 5–8).

356. Administrators and assistants, spoken of in Canons 472–476, who belong to a religious community may be removed at will by the bishop and by the religious superior, just as Canon 454 states about the religious pastor. The secular administrators and assistants may be removed at will by the bishop or the vicar-capitular or diocesan administrator; the vicar-general cannot remove them except by special mandate of the bishop. If a benefice is connected with the assistant's position, he can be removed by canonical trial, not only for reasons for which a pastor can be removed but also for grievous violation of the obedience due to the pastor in the exercise of his duties (**Canon 477**). In the United States there are no benefices connected with the assistant's position, but in Europe this is frequently the case.

357. In reference to the powers of the assistants, Father Augustine, O.S.B., in his recent commentary on the Code,[36] is of the opinion that the assistant is by reason of his office supposed to possess all the powers of the pastor, assistance at marriage not excluded. This does not seem to be correct, for the Code nowhere makes the office of assistant an office in the strict sense of the term so that by the very appointment to it certain powers are enjoyed. On the contrary, Canon 476 states that all his rights and duties must be determined by the diocesan statutes, the orders of the bishop, and by commission or delegation of the pastor. The rights are therefore not determined by the common law. After these words, the Code does indeed say that the assistant must help the pastor and take his place in the performance of the parochial ministry *ratione officii,* but the term *office* cannot be taken here in its technical sense, otherwise the second part of the same section would contradict the first which is against the recognized rules of interpretation. Canon 1096 seems to indicate that the assistant does not have parochial power to assist at marriages when it says that they may receive general delegation.

[36] Fr. Augustine, O.S.B., "A Commentary on the New Code," II, 576. Cfr. Declaration of Committee, May 20, 1923; cfr. App. III, 20, c.

358. As the pastor of the cathedral church precedes all other pastors and parochial vicars of the diocese, so does the parochial vicar of a Cathedral Chapter. The right of precedence of an administrator of a parish is governed by the rules of precedence of Canon 106 (cfr. n. 82): the vicar who acts as substitute of the pastor in his absence, etc., and the priest who acts as coadjutor of an inhabilitated pastor, precede while in office the assistant priests; the assistant priests precede other priests belonging to the parish church (**Canon 478**).[36a]

CHAPTER XI

OF RECTORS OF CHURCHES

359. By the term "rectors of churches" are meant here those priests who have charge of some church that is neither parochial, nor capitular, nor annexed to a house of a religious community which holds divine services in that church. Concerning chaplains of religious women, of laical communities of men, of confraternities, and other legitimate associations, the laws of the Canons dealing particularly with these subjects shall be observed (**Canon 479**).

The rectors of churches are freely appointed by the local Ordinary, except in places where certain individuals have the right to elect or present the candidate; the approval in that case rests with the bishop. Even if the church belongs to an exempt religious organization, the rector nominated by the religious superior must be approved by the local Ordinary. If the church is connected with a seminary or other college conducted by the clergy, the superior of the seminary or college is at the same time the rector of the church, unless the Ordinary directs otherwise (**Canon 480**).

RIGHTS OF THE RECTOR

360. In the church committed to him the rector cannot hold parochial functions (**Canon 481**). The rector can celebrate the divine services also solemnly, observing the laws of the foundation (i.e., such regulations as were drawn up and approved by the bishop and the patron who built or endowed the church). The services in the church of a rector may not

36a Precedence of pastor of cathedral church, App. III, 19, f.

be conducted so as to injure the parochial ministry of the parish within which the church is located, and the bishop has the right to judge whether injury is done to the parish church and to prescribe proper rules to remedy the matter (**Canon 482**). In the United States, this Canon is of rare application except in the case of religious communities who have a church but no parish attached to it. There are some of these in the country, though more frequently a parish is united to the churches of religious men. Since many of the religious orders have the Papal privilege to have a public church or oratory in connection with the religious house, and since it is evident that the parish church near which the .church of the religious is located would lose a great amount of the ordinary and necessary revenue if the people were free to attend Holy Mass in the church of the religious, it will be necessary that an agreement is drawn up in such cases between the bishop and the religious not to admit the public to Mass in their church on Sundays. Other accidental loss that may result to the parish church by donations and offerings made to the religious by the free-will of the people is not considered in law a sufficient reason for the pastor to make objection to the establishment of a religious house and church in his parish. It may need special approval of the Holy See for the renunciation of this privilege (cfr. Canon 72).

361. If the non-parochial church is so far away from the parish church that the parishioners could not be expected to go to the parish church for the divine services, the bishop may command the rector, even under grave penalties, to hold divine services at hours convenient for the people, to announce the feasts and fast-days of the Church, and to give catechetical instruction and explanation of the Holy Gospel. The pastor has the right to take Holy Communion to the sick from such a church, if, in accordance with Canon 1265, the Blessed Sacrament is kept there (**Canon 483**).

362. Without the permission of the rector or other legitimate superior, no priest may say Holy Mass, or administer the Sacraments, or hold other sacred functions in that church. This permission is to be granted or denied according to the rules of law. In reference to preaching in the church, the laws of Canons 1337–1342 must be observed (**Canon 484**).

The rector of the church, under the authority of the local Ordinary and with due regard to the legitimate statutes and acquired rights, must see that the divine services are conducted in orderly manner, according to the rules of the sacred canons; that the obligations resting on the church are faithfully complied with; that the goods are properly administered; that the sacred vessels and vestments and the building are kept in good condition, and that nothing shall be done there which is repugnant to the sanctity of the place and the reverence due to the house of God (**Canon 485**).

363. The Ordinary may at will remove the rector of a church for any just cause, though he was elected or presented by others. If the rector is a religious, the rule of Canon 454 in reference to his removal is to be observed, which states that the bishop and the religious superior have equal right independently of each other to remove a religious pastor (**Canon 486**).

PART TWO

OF THE RELIGIOUS

364. The religious state, by which is meant a stable manner of community life in which the faithful besides observing the common precepts bind themselves to the observance of the evangelical counsels by the vows of obedience, chastity and poverty, shall be held in honor by all (**Canon 487**).[37]

EXPLANATION OF TECHNICAL TERMS

365. The meaning of the following terms which are used frequently in the Canons on religious is laid down by the Code:

(1) *Religio* means a society, approved by the legitimate ecclesiastical authority, whose members strive after evangelical perfection by living according to the special laws of the society itself and by taking public vows, either perpetual or temporary,

[37] For an outline of the history of religious life, see Fr. Augustine, O.S.B., ''A Commentary on the New Code,'' III, 1–39; Wernz, ''Jus Decretalium,'' III, 264–276. Concerning translations of the law of the Code on Religious, cfr. App. III, 21, a.

and to be renewed, if temporary, when the time of the vows expires.

(2) *Ordo* denotes a religious organization in which solemn vows are taken; *congregatio monastica* is a combination of several independent monasteries of monks under one superior; *religio exempta* means a religious organization, of either solemn or simple vows, that has been withdrawn from the jurisdiction of the local Ordinary; *congregatio religiosa,* or simply *congregatio,* signifies a religious body in which only simple vows, either perpetual or temporary, are taken.

(3) *Religio juris pontificii* is a religious organization which has received from the Holy See either approval or at least the *decretum laudis; religio juris diœcesani* means a religious organization which has been created by the Ordinary, and has not yet obtained the *decretum laudis* from the Holy See.

(4) *Religio clericalis* means a religious body of men whose members are mostly priests; otherwise it is called *religio laicalis* (i.e., laical religious organization).

(5) *Domus religiosa* signifies the residence of any religious community; *domus regularis* is the house of an Order; *domus formata* means a religious house in which at least six professed religious reside, of whom, if there is question of clerical religious organizations, four at least must be priests.

(6) *Provincia* is a combination of a number of houses of religious under one superior, constituting a part of the same religious organization.

(7) *Religiosi* are those persons who have taken vows in any religious community; *religiosi votorum simplicium* are those who have taken vows in a religious Congregation; *regulares* are the professed members of an order; *sorores* are religious women who have taken simple vows; *moniales* are religious women with solemn vows, or also religious women whose vows from their institution are solemn vows, but who in some places must by order of the Apostolic See take simple vows. These latter are therefore comprehended under the term *moniales,* unless the nature of the law or the context show that only those nuns are meant who actually have solemn vows.[37a]

(8) *Superiores majores* are the Abbot Primate, the Abbot superior of a monastic congregation, the abbots of independent monasteries (though belonging to some monastic congregation),

[37a] Cfr. App. III, 21, c a.

the supreme head of any religious society, the provincial superiors, their vicars and others who have the power of a provincial (**Canon 488**).

Preliminary Rules

366. The rules and particular constitutions of individual religious organizations which are not contrary to the Canons of the Code remain in force. Those rules and constitutions which are opposed to the Canons of the Code are hereby abolished (**Canon 489**). The Holy See demanded that all religious orders and congregations which were under Papal law shall revise their rules and constitutions, making only such corrections as are necessary to bring them into harmony with the Code. Two copies of this revision had to be sent to the Sacred Congregation of the Religious for approval.[38] This order of the Sacred Congregation does not refer to diocesan religious communities. They certainly are obliged to revise their constitutions so as to make them conform to the laws of the Code, but their revision is not to be sent to Rome, but is to be inspected by the Ordinary of the diocese where the motherhouse is located.

The laws of the Code for the religious when expressed in the masculine gender, *religiosus, religiosi,* apply in the same manner to religious women, unless the context or the nature of the law prove the contrary (**Canon 490**).

367. The order of precedence is as follows: the religious precede the lay persons, clerical organizations precede laical, canons regular precede monks, monks precede other regulars, regulars precede religious congregations, congregations of Papal law precede diocesan congregations. Among religious bodies of the same kind in the same town or city precedence is regulated according to the priority of residence in the place, as is stated in Canon 106, n. 5. The secular clergy precedes both laical and clerical religious bodies outside their own churches, and the secular clergy precedes laical organizations even in their own churches. The cathedral or collegiate Chapter precedes the religious everywhere (**Canon 491**).

[38] Sacred Congregation of Religious, June 26, 1918, and Oct. 26, 1921; *Acta Ap. Sedis,* X, 290; XIII, 538.

OF THE ERECTION AND SUPPRESSION OF RELIGIOUS ORGANIZATIONS, PROVINCES, HOUSES

368. The bishop, but not the vicar-capitular, or administrator, or vicar-general, can create religious congregations. He shall not establish them, nor allow their foundation, without first consulting the Holy See. In the case of Tertiaries living in community, it is required, moreover, that the supreme head of the First Order aggregate them to that Order (**Canon 492, § 1**). In the new rules (*Normæ*) which the Holy See published to indicate the manner in which the Holy See proceeds in the approval of congregations and in what form the constitutions must be drawn, it also states the matters which the bishop has to submit to the Holy See before he creates a diocesan congregation.[39]

369. The Sacred Congregation of the Religious wanted to get a complete list of all the diocesan congregations, and ordered every bishop to make report on the number of such congregations which had their motherhouse in his diocese. The bishop must investigate when and by whom these congregations were approved, and if no document of approval could be found, he is to issue a document of recognition, according to the rules given in the decree. Bishops in whose diocese there was no motherhouse of any diocesan congregation were to make a statement to that effect to the Sacred Congregation. For the future, after the bishop has obtained permission from the Holy See to erect a diocesan congregation, he shall do so by means of a formal document of erection, and one copy of that document must be kept in the diocesan archives and another in the archives of the congregation. Furthermore, the Sacred Congregation of the Religious is to be informed of the formal erection, and a copy of the document is to be sent to the Sacred Congregation.[40]

370. A diocesan congregation retains that character though it has in the course of time spread to several dioceses, and it remains under the jurisdiction of the bishops, according to the

---

[39] Sacred Congregation of Religious, March 6, 1921; cfr. App. III, 21, b.

[40] Sacred Congregation of the Religious, Nov. 30, 1922; *Acta Ap. Sedis*, XIV, 644.

rules of the Canons, until it has obtained from the Holy See approval or, at least, the *decretum laudis*.

The title and religious habit of an established religious organization cannot be assumed by those not legitimately belonging to it or by a new organization (**Canon 492,** §§ 2–3).

371. Any religious organization, even a diocesan congregation, which has been legally established, cannot be dissolved, though it should consist of but one house, except by the Holy See, to which is also reserved the disposition of the goods of a suppressed organization, saving always the will and intention of the donors (**Canon 493**).

372. It also rests with the Holy See to divide a religious organization of papal law into provinces, to join provinces which have been established, or to change their boundaries, to establish new provinces and to suppress established ones, to separate independent monasteries from one monastic congregation and unite them to another.

When a province has become extinct, the right to dispose of its goods belongs to the General Chapter, or, outside the Chapter, to the superior general with his council, unless the constitutions provide otherwise; the laws of justice and the will of persons who have made so-called pious foundations must be considered (**Canon 494**).

DIOCESAN CONGREGATIONS ESTABLISHING HOUSES IN OTHER DIOCESES

373. A diocesan congregation cannot establish houses in another diocese except with the consent of both the bishop of the diocese where its principal house is located, and the bishop of the diocese to which it wishes to go. The Ordinary of the diocese of the principal house shall not deny permission without serious reasons.

If a diocesan congregation happens to have spread into other dioceses, changes in the laws of that congregation cannot be made except with the consent of each and every Ordinary of the dioceses in which it has a house. Matters which according to Canon 492 have to be submitted to the Holy See before a bishop can establish a diocesan congregation, may not be changed by the bishops (**Canon 495**).

The Code does not state whether the consent of the bishop of the motherhouse of a diocesan congregation is required each time that the congregation establishes a new house in another diocese, but it seems that his consent is required only for the first foundation in another diocese, and after that other foundations can be made with the consent of the bishop of the other diocese in which the congregation has once been legitimately established. If a diocese is divided by the Holy See, some of the houses of a diocesan congregation may be in the new diocese, and no further formalities are required for their continuance in the new diocese, since they were legitimately established there. If a diocesan congregation has houses only in one diocese, the bishop of that diocese may change the constitutions of the congregation with the exception of those points which the bishop had to submit to the Holy See before he obtained leave to establish the congregation. This restriction of the power of the bishop applies to all diocesan congregations established after the promulgation of the Motu Proprio, "Dei Providentis," July 16, 1906. As to diocesan congregations founded before that time, the bishop has complete control of the constitutions of the congregation which has houses only in his diocese.

374. No religious house shall be established unless it can be prudently judged that the community will be able to support itself properly, either by a fixed income, or the usual alms, or by other means (**Canon 496**).

375. For the erection of a house of exempt religious, whether it be a *domus formata* or *non formata* (cfr. Canon 488), for a monastery of nuns with solemn vows, and for any religious house in countries subject to the Propaganda, the *beneplacitum* of the Holy See is required, together with the written consent of the local Ordinary. For all other houses of religious the consent of the Ordinary suffices.

The permission to establish a house given to a clerical religious organization carries with it the right to have a church or public oratory, and to perform therein the sacred functions according to the rules of law; and for all religious the permission to establish a house includes the right to exercise the pious works proper to each, observing the conditions under which the permission to establish a house was granted. When religious intend to build a church, the bishop's approval of the location must be sought, according to Canon 1162, § 4.

For the building and opening of schools, hospices, or other houses separate from the religious house of either exempt or non-exempt religious, the written permission of the Ordinary is necessary and sufficient. (Therefore, the exempt religious communities do not need the permission of the Holy See for these additional houses, though they need that permission for establishing a new religious residence.)

For converting a religious house to other purposes than those for which the premission was given at the time of the establishment of the religious community in a place, the same formalities are required as in a new foundation. It is not considered a change to other purposes, if there is question of changing it for purposes belonging to the internal government and discipline—for example, to use the religious house, or build a new house, of studies for the religious themselves. If, however, contrary agreements between the bishop and the religious were legitimately made at the time of the foundation of the house, they must be kept. Likewise, if benefactors built a house for the religious or endowed it under certain conditions (e.g., to serve for a specified purpose), a change cannot be made without their consent (**Canon 497**, §§ 1-4).

376. In reference to the suppression of a religious house the Code has the following rules: A religious house, whether a *domus formata* or *non formata*, belonging to an exempt religious organization can be suppressed only with the permission of the Holy See; if it belongs to a non-exempt congregation of papal law, it can be suppressed by the supreme head of the congregation with the consent of the local Ordinary; if it is a house of a diocesan congregation, it can be suppressed by the sole authority of the Ordinary of the place where the house is located after having given a hearing to the head of the congregation. The congregation has the right of appeal to the Holy See, and that appeal suspends the order of the bishop. If the congregation has but one house, Canon 493 provides that it cannot be suppressed except by authority of the Holy See (**Canon 498**).

The Code uses the term "suppressio" in its widest sense, having in view the ultimate effect, namely, the abandoning of the religious house as a residence of religious, whether done voluntarily or against the will of the organization. Exempt communities and communities of papal law cannot be forced by the bishop to abandon the place where they were legitimately established. How far a community may change the location of their house without calling it a new foundation and an abandoning of the old one, is not clearly indicated in the Code. Commentators of the old law are quite in accord on the point that the change of location in the same city or town, provided the change does not prejudice the rights of others, is not such a change as to amount to a new foundation, and can therefore be done by the religious without being held to the formalities required for either new foundations or the abandoning of old foundations.

TITLE X

OF THE GOVERNMENT OF RELIGIOUS ORGANIZATIONS

CHAPTER I

OF SUPERIORS AND CHAPTERS

377. All religious are subject to the Roman Pontiff as their highest superior, whom they are bound to obey also in virtue of the vow of obedience. The Cardinal Protector of any religious organization has no jurisdiction over the community or over the individual members, unless the contrary has been ordained in particular cases, nor can he interfere in the internal discipline and the administration of property, it being his office only to promote the good of the community by his advice and patronage (**Canon 499**). St. Francis of Assisi says in his rule (Chap. XII): "I command the Ministers in obedience to ask of the Lord Pope one of the Cardinals of the Holy Roman Church as governor, protector, and corrector of this Fraternity." Other Orders followed the example of St. Francis and it became the general practice for religious Orders to have a Cardinal Protector, and in recent times also Congregations of papal law usually ask for a protector. The extensive powers enjoyed by the Cardinal Protector in former times were reduced by Pope Innocent XII, Constitution "Christi Fidelium," Feb-

ruary 16, 1694, to a general paternal interest in the welfare of the respective organization, and the Code agrees with that Constitution.

378. The religious are subject also to the local Ordinary, with the exception of those who have obtained from the Holy See the privilege of exemption; but even these are subject to the local Ordinary in those matters in which the law gives him jurisdiction over exempt religious. Nuns (Sisters with solemn vows, *moniales*), whose constitutions place them under the jurisdiction of the regular superiors, are subject to the local Ordinary in those cases only which are specified in law. Without a special papal indult, no religious organization of men can have under its jurisdiction religious congregations of women, or claim a special right to the care and direction of the members of such congregations (**Canon 500**).

The privilege of exemption of religious organizations from the jurisdiction of the bishop of the diocese has a long and complicated history upon which any of the larger works on Canon Law may be consulted. The policy of the Church since the Council of Trent has been rather to restrict the privilege of exemption. Generally speaking, the Code retains the privilege of exemption of those religious who legitimately had such privilege before the promulgation of the Code. The cases in which the Code subjects the exempt religious to the jurisdiction of the Ordinary of the diocese are scattered throughout the Code. We shall draw attention to them in the course of this commentary. A good summary of the cases is given by Fr. T. Schäfer, O. M. Cap.[41]

Jurisdiction of Superiors and Chapters

379. The Superiors and Chapters have the so-called *domestic* power over their subjects, according to the constitutions and the common law; in exempt clerical organizations, they have ecclesiastical jurisdiction for the internal as well as the external forum. All Superiors are strictly forbidden to interfere in cases pertaining to the Holy Office.

The abbot primate and the superior of a monastic congregation do not have all the power and jurisdiction which the

41 T. Schäfer, O. M. Cap., "Ordensrecht," 60–62.

common law attributes to major superiors; their power and jurisdiction must be gathered from their proper constitutions and the particular decrees of the Holy See, without prejudice to Canons 655 and 1594. Canon 655 refers to the dismissal of a solemnly professed religious or one with perpetual simple vows, which case is to be judged by the abbot superior of the respective monastic congregation, and Canon 1594 states that the abbot superior of a monastic congregation is the judge of the second instance for cases tried by the abbot (**Canon 501**).

The domestic power spoken of in this Canon is the same as that of the head of a family over the members of the household. Ecclesiastical jurisdiction is given only to clerics by the Church. The cases reserved to the Holy Office have to do with teaching or actions contrary to faith and morals in which the religious superiors may not exercise jurisdiction, but must refer the cases to the Holy Office.

380. The supreme superior of a religious organization enjoys power over all provinces, houses and the individual religious, to be exercised according to the respective constitutions; other superiors have power within the limits of their office (**Canon 502**). The major superiors in exempt clerical organizations can appoint notaries for the ecclesiastical affairs of their religious organizations only (**Canon 503**).

381. Unless the proper constitutions of individual religious bodies demand a more advanced age and other more stringent conditions, all religious are ineligible for the office of major superior who have not been at least ten years professed (the years to be counted from the first profession), and born in legitimate wedlock; and for the office of the supreme head of a religious body (or for abbess in monasteries of nuns), those under forty years of age; for the office of other major superiors, those under thirty years of age (**Canon 504**). The solemn religious profession heals the irregularity of defect from illegitimate birth (in virtue of Canon 984), but it does not take away the ineligibility for the office of major superior. Illegitimates who have been rendered legitimate by subsequent marriage of the parents according to Canon 1116, are by Canon 1117 freed from ineligibility for the office of a major superior.

382. The major superiors are to be temporary, unless the constitutions of a religious organization call for perpetual su-

periors; the minor local superiors, however, shall not be constituted in office for more than three years. After that term they may again hold office for a second term, but not for a third successive term in the same religious house (**Canon 505**).[42] Canonists had upheld the custom that the founders of a religious community remained superiors for life, even though the constitutions of the religious organization made the office of the supreme superior temporary. The Sacred Congregation of the Religious decreed that these founders cannot, without an Apostolic Indult, remain superiors for life.[42a]

The Holy See has also declared that, if the constitutions of a religious organization provide a term of several years of office for the supreme head of the organization and allow re-election for a second term only, the Chapter cannot elect the same superior for a third term without first obtaining a special faculty from the Sacred Congregation of the Religious.[43]

ELECTIONS IN CHAPTERS OF RELIGIOUS

383. Before the election of major superiors in religious organizations of men, each and every member of the Chapter must take an oath to vote for those only for whom he believes before God he should vote (**Canon 506, § 1**).

In the monasteries of nuns with solemn vows, which are subject to the bishop, he or his delegate, with two priests who act as tellers, presides at the election of the abbess, without entering the enclosure. If the nuns are subject to the superiors of a religious Order, the regular superior presides, but in this case also the bishop must be notified in good time of the day and hour of the coming election, and he may, together with the religious superior, be present or send a delegate; if the bishop assists, he presides (**Canon 506, § 2**). From the Latin reading of the Code it is not clear whether the delegate of the bishop also has the right to preside in preference to the religious superior. The Holy See, however, has since declared that the delegate of the Ordinary has the right to preside.[44] The

---

42 About superiors of ''domus filiales,'' cfr. App. III, 21, f, 4.

42a Cfr. App. III, 21, f, 1.

43 Cfr. App. III, 21, f, 2 and 6; concerning directors of schools, hospitals, etc., cfr. App. III, 21, f, 5.

44 Cfr. App. III, 21, f, 7.

business transactions of the Chapter are presided over by the
newly elected abbess. In the elections the ordinary confessors
of the nuns are not to be appointed as tellers (**Canon 506**, § 3).

384. In religious congregations of women the local Ordinary
of the place where the elections are held presides, either in
person or by his delegate, at the election of the superior general.
In diocesan congregations the Ordinary of the place where the
Chapter is held not only presides at the election of the superior
general, but has also the right to confirm or rescind the election, as he in conscience sees fit (**Canon 506,** § 4). The right
of annulling the election does not give the Ordinary the right
to appoint a superior general, but only to order a new election.
Only in cases where the law rules that the right devolves on
the ecclesiastical superior can he appoint the superior general.
In diocesan congregations the local Ordinary may preside also
over other elections and the business sessions of the Chapter.

As to diocesan congregations and their Chapters, the
Holy See has declared that if a congregation has houses in
several dioceses, the right to appoint the place for the Chapter
belongs to the superior general, not to the bishop of the diocese
where the motherhouse is located. The right to preside at the
election of the superior general does not belong to the bishop
of the diocese where the motherhouse is situated, but to the
Ordinary of the place where the Chapter is held.[45]

385. In the elections held by the Chapters of religious, the
common law (Canons 160–182) is to be observed, together with
the constitutions of the individual religious organizations, in
so far as they are not contrary to the Code (on elections, cfr.
above, nn. 123–137). All religious must beware of soliciting
votes, directly or indirectly, for themselves or for others. Election by *postulation* (cfr. above, nn. 138–141), can be admitted
only in an extraordinary case, and then only when not forbidden by the constitutions of the respective organization
(**Canon 507**).

OBLIGATIONS OF SUPERIORS

386. The superiors shall reside in their respective houses
and not leave them, except according to the rules of the con-

[45] Sacred Congregation of Religious, July 2, 1921; cfr. App. III,
21, f, 8.

stitutions (**Canon 508**). Every superior must promote among his subjects the knowledge and execution of the decrees of the Holy See for the religious. The local superiors shall see: (1) that at least once a year, on the prescribed days, the constitutions proper to the organization are read publicly, as also the decrees which the Holy See may order to be read publicly; (2) that at least twice a month an instruction on Christian doctrine is given to the lay religious and servants, adapted to the needs of their condition of life, and that, especially in laical organizations, pious exhortations are addressed to all the members of the community (**Canon 509**). Canon 565 also prescribes a careful training in Christian doctrine of the lay novices, brothers or sisters, and a special instruction at least once a week. The reading of several decrees of the Holy See at stated times before the assembled community is no longer of obligation. The Code says that the Holy See may prescribe such in future.[46] One obligation of all superiors in clerical organizations after their election—namely, to take the oath against modernism together with the profession of faith prescribed by Canon 1406—is not mentioned in the Code, but a Decree of the Holy Office states that this oath is to be taken.[47]

387. Every five years, or more frequently if the constitutions so demand, every abbot primate, superior of a monastic congregation, and supreme head of a religious organization of papal law must send to the Holy See a report concerning the state of the organization, signed by those superiors and their council—and, in case of a congregation of women, also by the local Ordinary of the place in which the superior general and her council reside (**Canon 510**).

The Holy See has made the following regulations in reference to this report: The report is to be made every five years, beginning with January 1, 1923, in the following order: in the first year by the religious orders and congregations of men (canons regular, monks, military orders); in the second year by the mendicant orders; in the third year by the regular clerics; in the fourth year by clerical and lay congregations

---

[46] Is the decree on Frequent and Daily Communion to be read annually? The great majority of commentators of the Code hold that there is no obligation, although a few say there is.

[47] Sacred Congregation of the Holy Office, March 22, 1918; *Acta Ap. Sedis*, X, 136.

with simple vows; in the fifth year by societies of men living after the manner of religious without vows or with private vows. The religious organizations of women shall make their report according to the various countries in which the principal house of the organization is located, or where the superior general has her residence *ex officio*: in the first year, Italy, Spain and Portugal; in the second year, France, Belgium, Holland, England and Ireland; in the third year, the other European countries; in the fourth year, North and South America; in the fifth year, all other countries in the world and also all societies of women living after the manner of religious without vows or with private vows.

If an organization has already made the report within five years preceding the year in which they would have to make the report according to this Decree, they are excused from making it for the first quinquennium. The report is to be made according to the list of questions published by the Holy See, March 25, 1922.[48]

VISITATION OF THE HOUSES OF RELIGIOUS

388. The major superiors on whom the constitutions impose the obligation of visitation at stated times, must visit all the houses subject to them either in person or, if they are legitimately impeded, through a delegate (**Canon 511**).

389. Every five years the local Ordinary must visit either in person or through a delegate: (1) every monastery of nuns (Sisters with solemn vows) subject to himself or immediately subject to the Holy See; (2) every house of the diocesan congregations of both men and women (**Canon 512, § 1**).

Within this same period the local Ordinary shall also visit: (1) the monasteries of nuns subject to the regulars, to inquire about the observance of the law of enclosure, and also about all other matters if the regular superior did not hold any visitation within the last five years; (2) every house of clerical congregations of papal law, even those enjoying exemption, the visitation to extend only to the church, sacristy, public

---

[48] Sacred Congregation of Religious, March 8, 1922 (*Acta Ap. Sedis*, XIV, 158); List of Questions, March 25, 1922 (*Acta Ap. Sedis*, XIV, 278–286). Official English translation of the list of questions in the issue of Sept. 1, 1923 (*Acta Ap. Sedis*, XV, 459–466; cfr. App. III, 23).

oratory, and places where confessions are heard; (3) every house of laical congregations of papal law, the visitation to embrace not only those points mentioned in the preceding instance, but also all other affairs concerning internal discipline —without prejudice, however, to Canon 618, n. 1, which provides that congregations of papal law are not subject to the bishop in matters concerning the economical affairs of the community (**Canon 512, § 2**).[48a]

The administration of goods and property of religious organizations shall be governed by the laws of Canons 532-535 (**Canon 512, § 3**). As will be seen later, certain rights are thereby given to the bishop over the finances of monasteries of nuns, the dowry, goods given to the religious for public charities, etc.

390. The visitor has the right and duty to interrogate any of the religious who he thinks should be questioned and thus to obtain knowledge of those matters which are within the scope of the visitation. All religious are bound to answer truthfully, and superiors are forbidden to dissuade them from this obligation, or in any other way to hamper the purpose of the visitation. From the decrees of the visitor there is allowed an appeal *in devolutivo* only, unless the visitor institutes a canonical trial (**Canon 513**). This means that the orders have to be obeyed, pending the result of the appeal; in the case of a canonical trial, however, an appeal *in suspensivo* is possible, which suspends the orders of the visitor. According to Canon 2413, interference with the visitation by transferring religious to another house after the visitation has been announced, or by intimidating or molesting the subjects, etc., may be punished by the visitor by removal of the superior from office and by declaring all subjects guilty of interference incapable of holding offices which entail power over others.

ADMINISTRATION OF THE LAST SACRAMENTS IN RELIGIOUS HOUSES

391. In all clerical religious communities the superior has the right and duty to administer, either in person or by another, the Viaticum and Extreme Unction to the professed, the novices, and to others who live day and night in the religious house, either as servants, or for the purpose of education, or

[48a] Concerning visitation of nuns, cfr. App. III, 21, f, 9.

as guests, or on account of ill health. In the house of nuns
(Sisters with solemn vows), the ordinary confessor, or the one
who takes his place, has the same right. In other laical organizations of religious this right and duty belongs to the
pastor, or to the chaplain to whom the Ordinary has given full
parochial powers, in accordance with Canon 464. Concerning
funerals from religious houses, the laws of Canons 1221 and
1230 are to be observed (**Canon 514**). From these Canons may
be gathered the general rule that he who has the right to
administer the last Sacraments, has also the right to bury
persons to whom he administered the last rites.

The Code says that these persons must be *in domo religiosa*
to come under the jurisdiction of the religious superior. It
need not be the same house, but it must be within the *septa
monasterii vel domus religiosæ* (i.e., the enclosure within which
the religious live). The length of time that guests, servants, or
sick persons must stay to come under the jurisdiction of the
religious superior is probably a day and a night, or they must
be received into the religious house for at least that length
of time, as authors usually explain, though they have not yet
stayed a full day when they become dangerously ill.

HONORARY TITLES FORBIDDEN TO RELIGIOUS

392. Merely honorary titles of dignities and offices are forbidden to religious, but, if the constitutions allow it, titles of
major offices which a religious has actually held in his own
organization are tolerated (**Canon 515**). Besides forbidding
the assumption of mere honorary titles of ecclesiastical dignities and offices, Canon 626 further declares religious ineligible
for promotion to dignities, offices or benefices which are not
compatible with the religious state, unless the Holy See authorizes such promotions. The Code does not forbid religious to
obtain academic degrees and titles.

COUNCILLORS, ŒCONOMI, PROCURATORS

393. The supreme superior of a religious organization or
monastic congregation, the provincial superiors and the local
superiors (at least those of a *domus formata*) must have their

council, the consent or advice of which they must ask in various affairs according to the regulations of the constitutions and the Sacred Canons (**Canon 516,** § 1).

The number of councillors and the manner of their appointment to office is not determined by the Code, but is decided by the constitutions of the various religious orders and congregations. When the law obliges a superior to get the consent or the advice of his council, he must consult them in a body (not separately): otherwise his act is invalid. If the consent of the councillors is required, it is not sufficient to consult them, but under pain of invalidity the superior is bound to follow the vote of the majority. If in the first ballot no majority is obtained, there must be a second and, if necessary, a third ballot. In the third ballot a relative majority decides the matter: if the votes are equally divided, the presiding superior has the right to break the tie vote by his vote (cfr. Canon 101).

394. In the law of the Code the consent of the council is required: (1) in the admission of novices to the first temporary vows; (2) in the appointment of the *œconomus,* if the constitutions are silent as to the manner of electing him; (3) in the dismissal of professed members (cfr. Canons 647 and 650); (4) in the alienation of goods and property (cfr. Canon 534).

395. The advice of the council is demanded in many affairs mentioned in various Canons of the Code. The individual constitutions must be consulted to ascertain whether the consent of the council may not be also required in other affairs besides those in which the common law demands it.

396. *Œconomi* shall be appointed for the administration of the temporal goods: a general *œconomus* to administer the goods of the entire religious organization, a provincial *œconomus* for the province, a local *œconomus* for each individual house: all these shall attend to their office under the direction of the superior. The superior general and provincial cannot be general or provincial *œconomi;* the office of local *œconomus* can be combined with that of local superior, if necessity demands, but it is preferable to have a separate official for the administration of goods. If the constitutions are silent as to the manner of electing the *œconomi,* the major superior shall select them with the consent of his council (**Canon 516,** §§ 2–4). Canon 2347

rules that superiors and *œconomi* are to be punished for violating the laws of the Code on the alienation of church property, and if they wilfully neglect to obtain the *beneplacitum* of the Holy See in cases where the Code requires it, those guilty fall into excommunication *latæ sententiæ nemini reservata.*

397. Every religious organization of men under papal law shall have a procurator general who is to be designated according to the constitutions, and whose office shall be to transact affairs of his organization with the Holy See. He shall not be removed before his term fixed by the constitutions expires, without consulting the Holy See (**Canon 517**). The procurator general must be a member of the organization and reside at Rome.[49] Before the Code became law, only the religious orders (not the congregations) were obliged to have a procurator at Rome.

398. Schäfer (*Ordensrecht,* 101) states that according to a declaration of the Sacred Congregation of Bishops and Regulars, January 15, 1907, the procurator general has the right to vote in the election of deputies to the general and provincial Chapters, and in the voting in the house of the Order where he stays for reason of his office. There is no such general law: if the procurator general has any privileges, he can have them only through the particular constitutions of his order or congregation. The decision cited is not general, but an answer to an inquiry of the Missionaries of the Sacred Heart as to their procurator general and the councillors of the superior general. Vermeersch (*De Religiosis, Periodica,* 1911, II–III, 252) says that, if the constitutions of an organization have no provision on this matter, one can recur to this decision. However, the particular law of one order or congregation can have no authority for any other religious organization.

CHAPTER II

OF CONFESSORS AND CHAPLAINS

399. In every house of a religious organization of clerics there shall be appointed several lawfully approved confessors (in proportion to the number of religious) with the faculty, if there is question of exempt religious, to absolve the religious

[49] Sacred Congregation of Religious, June 4, 1920; *Acta Ap. Sedis,* XII, 301.

also from the reserved cases of the organization. Provided they observe all the requirements of the law, religious superiors who have the faculty may hear the confessions of those of their subjects who of their own free will and choice ask to be heard, but without a grave reason they shall not do so habitually. The superiors must beware of inducing, either personally or through others, any of their subjects to come to them for confession, whether by force or fear, or by importune urging, or in any other way (**Canon 518**). In clerical exempt organizations, the superiors designated by the respective constitutions have power to delegate any priest, either religious or secular, to hear the confessions of their subjects. In laical exempt religious bodies, the superior proposes the confessor, but he must get jurisdiction from the Ordinary of the place where the religious house is located (cfr. Canon 875). The bishop has likewise the power to delegate priests, secular or religious (even exempt), to hear the confessions of all religious and seculars, making their confession in his diocese (cfr. Canon 874). Besides the superiors, the master of novices and the assistant master are also forbidden to hear the confessions of the novices (cfr. Canon 891).

400. Without prejudice to constitutions which require or urge the religious to make their confession at stated times and to certain specified confessors, if a religious (even of an exempt organization), for the peace of his conscience, makes his confession to a priest approved by the bishop of the diocese where the confession is made, even though such priest be not appointed by the superior of the religious for the confessions of his subjects, the confession is valid and licit; and that priest can absolve the religious even from sins and censures reserved in the order or congregation (**Canon 519**). All contrary privileges of exempt religious organizations by which their subjects could not validly confess to a priest not approved for their confessions by the superior, are hereby revoked.

The text of Canon 519 is clear and explicit in its provision in favor of the liberty of conscience. The phrase, "for the peace of his conscience" (*ad suæ conscientiæ quietem*), has caused some discussion among authors. The majority of the commentators on the Code rightly interpret this phrase as merely explanatory, and not as a condition strictly speaking, for they remark that every confession seriously made is made for the sake of obtaining peace of conscience. The Code rightly expects the religious to conform themselves ordinarily to the rules of their constitutions as to the days of confession and the appointed confessors in the community, but, notwithstanding such regulations, if they confess to any priest who has the faculties of the diocese, the confession is valid and licit.

Confessors of Religious Women

401. In every house of religious women there shall be appointed only one ordinary confessor for the whole community, unless on account of the large number of religious, or for any other just cause, two or more are necessary. If any sister, for peace of her mind and greater progress in spiritual life, asks for a special confessor or director, the Ordinary should readily grant the request, but he shall guard against any misuse of this concession. If abuses creep in, the bishop shall eliminate them cautiously and prudently without prejudicing the liberty of conscience (**Canon 520**). Several commentators of the Code state that, for small houses of Sisters (less than six), the bishop is not obliged to appoint confessors. However, the Code rules that the confessors be appointed for every house. A particular decision of the Sacred Congregation of the Religious, July 3, 1916, to the Bishop of Linz, cannot have the force of modifying the general law of the Code.[50]

402. Every community of religious women shall have an extraordinary confessor who shall visit the convent at least four times a year, and on these occasions all the Sisters shall go to him, at least to receive his blessing. The local Ordinary shall appoint several priests in the vicinity of every convent to whom the Sisters may have recourse freely in particular cases for the Sacrament of Penance, without approaching the Ordinary on every occasion. If a Sister asks for any of these priests, no superioress is allowed, either personally or through another, directly or indirectly, to inquire into the reason or to refuse the request in word or action, or to show displeasure in any way (**Canon 521**).

[50] Chelodi, ''Jus de Personis,'' 398, n. 257; cfr. App. III, 21, g, 1.

403. If, notwithstanding the concessions of the two foregoing canons, a Sister goes for her peace of conscience to any confessor approved by the local Ordinary for confessions of women generally in any church, public or semi-public oratory, the confession is valid and licit. Any privilege to the contrary of orders and congregations of women is revoked. The superioress cannot forbid the Sister to make use of this concession of the Code, nor is she allowed to inquire even indirectly into the reason, nor are the Sisters bound to make any explanation to the superioress (**Canon 522**).[50a]

Commentators on the Code point out the difficulty of reconciling Canon 522 with Canon 876, which states that, for the validity of the confessions, a special approval of the local Ordinary is necessary for a priest to hear the confessions of religious women. Undoubtedly Canon 522 is an exception to the general rule of Canon 876, and gives the Sisters liberty to confess to any priest who has the faculties of the diocese. By this privilege of the Sisters, the law grants faculties to the priest whenever the Sisters want to make use of the privilege and ask the priest to hear their confessions. There is nothing unusual about this manner of conferring jurisdiction on a priest. A superior who has jurisdiction in the external forum may grant his subject permission to choose any confessor, who by this choice gets jurisdiction in the case. The Code makes this concession to all bishops and Cardinals in Canons 239 and 349.

It is not the priest who has the faculty to act as confessor, but the Sister who has a right to ask the priest to hear her confession, and thus indirectly cause the priest to obtain the faculty to absolve her. Her request, or her approaching the priest to make her confession, is what gives the priest jurisdiction. The priest who is not specially approved for Sisters' confessions may not, for example, go to a convent instead of the appointed confessor to hear their confessions. However, a priest who comes to a convent—for instance to say Mass, to visit, etc.—may be requested by a Sister to hear her confession. Authors in general agree that it makes no difference whether the Sister makes use of the privilege in her own convent or while she is outside her house. The confessions of Sisters

[50a] Sisters **not** to leave convent without permission, cfr. App. III, 21, g, 3.

should be heard in churches, public or semi-public oratories, **or,** as a late declaration of the Holy See has it, in any place legitimately appointed by the bishop of the diocese for the hearing of confessions of women.[51]   There are several commentators who do not consider the place of confession, as specified in the Code and in the late decision, essential for validity—e.g., Schäfer, Chelodi, Vermeersch-Creusen, *Commentarium pro Religiosis,* and some others who wrote before the declaration of Nov. 24, 1920.[52]

Commentators explain the phrase ''for her peace of conscience'' in the same manner as the similar phrase in Canon 519, so that practically any confession seriously made is said to be for the peace of conscience.   The decree ''Cum de sacramentalibus'' of the Sacred Congregation of the Religious, Feb. 3, 1913, made it obligatory on the special confessor to see to it that the Sisters do not ask for him except for a good reason, and the Sisters were to be instructed that only for the good of their souls should they ask for a special confessor.   Canon 2414 rules that the bishop shall admonish a superioress who violates the regulations of Canons 521, 522 and 523: if she offends again, she shall be punished by removal from office, and the Sacred Congregation of the Religious then notified of the matter.

404. Whenever a Sister is seriously ill, even though there be no danger of death, she may call any priest approved for the confessions of women, though he is not approved for the confessions of Sisters, and she may confess to him during the grave illness as often as she desires.   The superioress may not either directly or indirectly prohibit the Sister from making use of this concession (**Canon 523**).

405. The bishop should appoint for every community of women an ordinary and an extraordinary confessor, either from the secular clergy or from the religious with the permission of their superiors.   The confessors should be priests who have no jurisdiction over the Sisters in the external forum; they should be forty years of age—unless the bishop for a

51 Cfr. App. III, 21, g, 2; recent decision settles controversy about place of confession.
52 Schäfer, ''Ordensrecht,'' 117; Chelodi, ''Jus de Personis,'' 400, n. 258; Vermeersch-Creusen, ''Epitome Jur. Can.,'' I, 221, n. 498; ''Commentarium pro Religiosis,'' II, 22, 37.

just reason thinks it well to dispense with the qualification—and men of great prudence and integrity.

The ordinary confessor cannot be made the extraordinary, nor, except in the cases mentioned in Canon 526, may he again be appointed as ordinary for the same community until at least one year has elapsed from the expiration of his term. When his term expires, the extraordinary confessor may immediately be made the ordinary confessor. The ordinary and extraordinary confessors of religious women shall not in any way interfere with the internal or external government of the community (**Canon 524**). According to a decree of the Sacred Congregation of Religious, April 22, 1917, the priest who has been ordinary confessor may immediately at the expiration of his term be appointed special confessor for an individual Sister (cfr. Canon 520).

Some commentators remark [53] that the pastor should not be appointed confessor of the Sisters who teach in his parochial school, because he has a certain amount of authority over the teachers in his school. Experience proves that it is not advisable to appoint the pastor as confessor, for to all practical purposes the pastor is their superior in the performance of their school work, and that position may hinder frankness and absolute confidence in the confessions. However, the Code cannot provide for all possible conditions, and we do not find this case discussed in the Canons. In most cases the bishop can prevent this embarrassment of the Sisters. In some isolated parishes where the pastor is the only priest, it may not be easy to get another priest as ordinary confessor.

406. If a house of religious women is under the immediate jurisdiction of the Holy See or of the local Ordinary, the latter chooses both the ordinary and extraordinary confessors. If the house is subject to a regular superior, he presents the confessors to the Ordinary, for it is the latter's prerogative to approve the confessors for these nuns, and, in case the superior neglects to present confessors, to choose them himself (**Canon 525**).

The ordinary confessor of religious women shall not hold this office for more than a single term of three years. The

53 Vermeersch-Creusen, "Epitome Jur. Can.," I, 218, n. 494; Schäfer, "Ordensrecht," 119.

bishop may, however, reappoint him for a second and third term, if on account of scarcity of priests qualified for this work he cannot provide new confessors every three years, or if the majority of the Sisters by secret vote petition the bishop to reappoint the same confessor. Even Sisters who otherwise have no voice in the affairs of the religious organization, participate in this voting. Those Sisters who dissent must be given another confessor if they so desire (**Canon 526**). The voting is to be secret so that nobody knows who voted for or against the reappointment of the confessor. All the Sisters, whether perpetually or temporarily professed, and even the novices have a vote in this matter, for, in reference to the confessions of novices in communities of women, Canon 566 rules that Canons 520–527 apply.

As stated in Canon 880, the local Ordinary may for a grave reason remove both the ordinary and extraordinary confessors of a community of Sisters, even if the convent is subject to a regular superior and the confessor be a regular; nor is the bishop bound to give any reason for the removal to anyone except to the Holy See, when requested by it. If, however, the nuns are subject to the regular superior, he must notify the latter of the removal of the confessors (**Canon 527**).

407. Also in houses of laical religious organizations of men, ordinary and extraordinary confessors shall be appointed according to the rules of Canons 874 and 875. If a religious asks for a special confessor, the superior shall grant the request and shall not in any way inquire into the reason, nor show displeasure at the request (**Canon 528**). Canon 874 states that the bishop has the right to give delegated jurisdiction for hearing the confessions of any religious in his diocese. Canon 875 states that, in exempt laical organizations, the religious superior has the right to propose the confessors to the bishop.

408. In the case of non-exempt laical religious, the local Ordinary has the right to designate the priests for the sacred ministry and for preaching; in the case of exempt, the regular superior has the right to designate those priests, or, in default of the superior, the bishop himself (**Canon 529**). The superiors of laical organizations (brotherhoods), exempt or non-exempt, have no ecclesiastical jurisdiction. They can at

most propose to the bishop the priests whom they wish to have for the administration of the sacraments to the brothers and for religious instruction or preaching.

The Code does not give any precise regulations as to the relation between the chaplain of laical religious institutes and the superior (superioress) of the respective house or institution. He has not parochial rights over the institution, unless the local Ordinary gives these to him. In any case, he is the appointed custodian of the Blessed Sacrament, and has the right and duty to perform the liturgical functions in the chapel, and to see that the laws of the sacred liturgy are properly observed. Leitner [54] remarks that in general his position is that of a rector of a church (non-parochial) spoken of in Canons 479–486 (cfr. above, nn. 360–363). He may not interfere in the management of the institution, the exercises of the religious community, *tc.* As the hours of divine service and the kind of divine service may have to be varied at times to fit the work of the institution, the chaplain must accede to all reasonable requests in this matter.

Manifestation of Conscience

409. All religious superiors are strictly forbidden to induce their subjects in any manner to manifest to them their state of conscience. The subjects, however, are not forbidden to manifest of their own free will and choice their conscience to the superiors. On the contrary, it is proper that the subjects should approach their superiors with filial confidence, and if the superiors are priests, reveal to them any doubts and anxieties of their conscience (**Canon 530**). The decree ''Quemadmodum'' of the Sacred Congregation of Bishops and Regulars, December 17, 1890, strictly forbade the superiors of all laical religious communities to insist on the manifestation of conscience. The Code goes further and forbids it in each and every religious community, and forbids this practice in reference to all persons subject to the religious superiors, novices or professed, postulants or other persons living in the community. Indirectly, the Code teaches that doubts and anxieties

---

[54] *Handbuch des kath. Kirchenrechts*, III (*Ordensrecht*), 342.

of conscience be manifested to priests only when a subject
seeks advice.[55]

410. Not only the religious organization itself, but also its
provinces and individual houses, are capable of acquiring and
possessing temporal goods, together with fixed revenues and
endowments, unless such capacity is excluded or restricted by
their rule and constitutions (**Canon 531**). Canon 1497 rules
that goods which belong to a legal ecclesiastical person or
body, are ecclesiastical goods. Therefore, Canons 1495–1551,
on ecclesiastical goods, apply also to the goods and property of
the religious communities. The Council of Trent [56] ruled: "The
Holy Synod permits that henceforth real property may be
possessed by all monasteries and houses, both of men and
women, and of mendicants, even those who were forbidden
by their constitutions to possess it, or who had not received
permission to that effect by apostolic privilege, with the exception of the houses of the brethren of St. Francis called
Capuchins, and those called Minor Observants." Since the
union of the various families by Pope Leo XIII in 1897, the
latter are called Friars Minor. In these Orders the Holy See
holds the title to the goods and property.

411. In the United States and in other countries where the
legal personality of ecclesiastical legal persons is not recognized, the religious communities must consult the laws of their
respective countries as to the manner of safeguarding their
property rights. In the United States the property is usually
held by corporations. The only instance where the law recognizes the Roman Catholic Church as a legal person is in the
case of the insular possessions which, after the Spanish-Amer-
ican War, came to the United States by the Treaty of Paris.
For further particulars as to the civil laws in reference to
church property, cfr. below, Canons 1499 sqq., on the Acquisition of Ecclesiastical Goods.

[55] Sacred Congregation of Bishops and Regulars, *Acta S. Sedis*, XXIII,
505; *Ecclesiastical Review*, VI, 232.
[56] Sessio XXV, cap. 3, *De Regul.*

412. The goods of the organization, its provinces and individual houses, shall be administered according to the constitutions of each religious organization. Expenditures and legal acts of ordinary administration can be validly performed not only by the superior, but also within the limits of their office by the officials designated for this purpose by the constitutions (**Canon 532**).

INVESTMENTS OF MONEY

413. In the investment of money, the particular constitutions are to be followed, as stated in Canon 532, but the consent of the local Ordinary must be obtained in the following cases:

(1) The superioress of nuns (Sisters with solemn vows) and of diocesan congregations needs this consent for every investment of money; if the monastery of nuns is subject to a regular superior, his consent is also required;

(2) The superioress in a congregation of papal law, if the money to be invested is the dowry of professed sisters (cfr. Canon 549);

(3) The superior, or superioress, of a house of any religious congregation, if funds or property has been donated or bequeathed to the religious house for the purpose of divine worship, or for works of charity to be carried on in the same place (**Canon 533, § 1, nn. 1–3**). Therefore, if property or money has been given for these purposes, but the donor has left it to the discretion of the superiors to use it for those purposes in any place they choose, the consent of the bishop is not required;

(4) Any religious, even of an exempt Order, if the money was given to a parish or mission, or to the religious for the benefit of a parish or mission (**Canon 533, § 1, n. 4**).

These rules apply not only to the first investment but also to any change of the investment (**Canon 533, § 2**).

ALIENATION OF GOODS AND PROPERTY OF RELIGIOUS

414. When there is question of disposing of objects of value or of goods exceeding in value the sum of thirty thousand francs (about six thousand dollars), or of contracting debts and assuming liabilities above the said sum, the contract is invalid

unless the *beneplacitum* of the Holy See has been first obtained. For smaller amounts the written permission of the superior authorized by the constitutions is necessary and sufficient, provided that it is given with the consent of his council manifested by secret ballot. In the case of nuns (Sisters with solemn vows) or diocesan congregations, the written consent of the local Ordinary is required; if the monastery of nuns is under the jurisdiction of a regular superior, his consent also is required. The congregations of brothers or sisters of papal law manage their financial affairs independently of the bishop; they are, of course, bound by this Canon to obtain the *beneplacitum* of the Holy See.

In the petition for consent to contract debts or assume obligations, must be stated the amount of the debts or obligations already resting on the religious organization, or the province, or the house for which respectively permission is asked: otherwise the obtained permission is null and void (**Canon 534**).

415. In estimating the value of goods or property to be disposed of, and thus ascertaining whether it reaches a value that requires the *beneplacitum* of the Holy See, the opinion of conscientious experts is to be consulted. If they estimate it as not over thirty thousand francs in value, the permission of the Holy See is not required, though at an auction it may sell at over thirty thousand francs.[57]

416. Canon 2347 decrees penalties for those who violate the laws of Canon 534, the most serious of which is the excommunication *nemini reservata* incurred *ipso facto* by those who with full knowledge of the law neglect to get the *beneplacitum* of the Holy See, or otherwise participate in the illegal transaction.

What Religious Communities Must Make Financial Report to the Local Ordinary?

417. (1) In all monasteries of nuns (Sisters with solemn vows), even exempt ones, the superioress shall once a year (or more frequently if the constitutions so demand) make a report to the local Ordinary of her administration, and also to the regular superior, if the house is subject to him. If the Ordinary

---

[57] Committee for Auth. Interp. of the Code, Nov. 24, 1920; cfr. App. III, 66, c. For new Instruction on alienation, see Vol. II, App. III, 66, h.

does not approve of this report, he may employ proper means to remedy the defect of administration, and may even remove, if the case demands it, the *œconomus* and other administrators. If the house is subject to the regular superior, the bishop shall admonish the superior to remedy the matter: if the latter neglects to act, the bishop himself has the right to proceed.

(2) In other religious organizations of women an account is to be given to the local Ordinary of the administration of goods which constitute the dowry of the Sisters. This must be done at the visitation of the local Ordinary, or more frequently if the bishop thinks it necessary.

(3) In diocesan congregations the local Ordinary has the right to inquire into the financial standing of the houses in his diocese.

(4) In all orders and congregations the local Ordinary has the right to demand an account of the goods and property administered by the religious, if such goods and property were given for Divine worship or charitable purposes to be applied in the diocese, as stated in Canon 533 (**Canon 535**).[57a]

From this Canon it follows that the religious Orders of men and all congregations both of men and women under papal law manage their own financial affairs and the property belonging to the community according to their constitutions without being obliged to make a report to the bishop of the diocese (except of course regarding the dowries, etc.).

418. According to the new faculties of the bishops in the United States, Canada and South America, the bishop may grant permission for the alienation of ecclesiastical goods up to $10,000 for the United States and Canada, and 15,000 pesos for South America. He may use the faculty only when there is no time to refer to the Holy See, and he must at once inform the Holy See of the permission he has granted. It is very likely that he can make use of the faculty for the benefit of the religious, for it is given in very general terms and a declaration of the Sacred Congregation of the Propaganda, January 15, 1903, had allowed the use of the faculty for alienation in favor of religious organizations of women.

419. Authors do not agree as to what constitutes an *object of value* which cannot be alienated without permission of the Holy See (cfr. Canon 534). A decision of 1840 declared that

[57a] Concerning financial account to bishop, cfr. App. III, 27, b.

objects valued at about two hundred and fifty francs (about $50) were *res pretiosæ*. All agree that this value is much too low for present conditions. As to the thirty thousand francs, authors discuss whether the gold standard is to be taken so that the value of the franc may not vary continually. It is evident that a fluctuating franc would cause great confusion. Wherefore it is reasonable to suppose that the gold standard is meant when the Canons speak of francs or lire.

Contracts Made by Religious

420. If a legal body (the religious organization as such, or a province, or a house) has contracted debts and assumed liabilities, even with the permission of the superiors, the respective body (not the superior whose permission was required) is liable for their satisfaction.

If a regular (member of an order) has made a contract with the permission of the superiors, the community whose superior gave the permission is liable for the contract. If a religious with simple vows has made a contract, he himself is liable, unless he transacted the business of the religious organization with the permission of the superior.

If a religious made a contract without any permission of his superiors, he is personally liable and the religious organization, or the province, or the house, cannot be held for it.

In any case, the principle holds that there is always a right of action against him into whose possession something has come through the contract (**Canon 536,** §§ 1–4). Whatever profit or gain either the religious or the other contracting party has made by the illegal contract, that profit or gain the injured party can reclaim when the contract is repudiated or rescinded.

421. The religious superiors shall beware of permitting the contracting of debts unless it is certain that from the usual revenues the interest on the debt can be paid, and that in not too long a time the debt can be wiped out by legitimate payments (**Canon 536,** § 5). The laws of this Canon apply also to religious women, for according to Canon 490 the terms, "religiosus, religiosi," apply to women unless the contrary is evident from the text of the law or from its subject matter. Canon 1538 seems to indicate that the payment of the debts should be taken care of by a sinking fund, that is by the setting aside of a certain amount of money each year for the purpose. The sooner part of the debt is paid off, the less interest is there to be paid.

422. The rules of the Code on responsibility for contracts follows the principles of natural justice. The religious community is not bound by the contracts of an individual religious, if it has not made this religious its agent. The fact that he is a member of the order or congregation, gives him no right to bind the organization by contract, except for necessaries when the individual is absent from the religious house and cannot reach his superior. There is an implied agency in this case. A religious in solemn vows cannot make a valid contract in his own name. A religious in simple vows can contract in his own name, since the Canon Law does not incapacitate him from holding title to temporal goods. However, if he contracts without authorization from the competent superior, he is personally liable for his contracts. If a solemnly professed religious makes a contract without authority from the competent superior, the contract is null and void. In the ecclesiastical court, that contract cannot be pleaded. Natural justice requires that, if it is still possible, the religious return what he got through the illegal dealing, and that both parties are put into the same condition as before the contract. In the civil law the religious is held personally to the contract, unless it is proved that he was authorized agent of the community. As our civil law does not recognize the rules of Canon Law as to the solemn vow of poverty, complications might arise, unless, in the abdication of all he possessed before his solemn profession, this cession was made in a manner valid in law.

423. If an individual religious has made a contract as duly authorized agent of the order, congregation, province, or house, the respective legal body is liable on the contract, provided the religious acted within the scope of his authority. If he clearly exceeded his authority, he binds himself personally, but the organization, province, or house is not bound. Persons who deal with agents are bound in civil law to investigate their authority, and cannot hold the principal in the contract responsible, if the agent actually exceeded his authority.

If, in the exercise of his office and while acting within the scope of his authority, a religious injures others, the house, province or organization whose official he is becomes liable for the damage. This holds good both in the civil law of the United States and in the ecclesiastical law. For the latter there is the decision of the special committee of the Sacred Congregation of the Religious, August 18, 1914.[58] In Canon 1529, the Code adopts the laws of the respective countries on the matter of contracts in all the business dealings of the Church. The civil law on contracts is an extensive subject, and cannot be discussed in a few notes, but we shall give the most important principles of that law when we come to Title **XXIX** On Contracts in the Third Book of the Code.

Donations Made by Religious

424. Donations from the goods of a house, province or religious organization are not permitted, except as alms or for other just cause, and with the permission of the superior and in accordance with the constitutions (**Canon 537**).

Since a donation means the transfer of goods to another without any benefit to the donor, it is evident that the donor must have a free and absolute ownership in the goods of which he wishes to dispose by donation. Though the legal ecclesiastical persons have the title to ecclesiastical goods, still this ownership is not an absolute and unconditional ownership. It is rather of the nature of a trusteeship in our civil law—namely, the ecclesiastical person holds title to the ecclesiastical property for the purposes of religion, charity, and the other usually accepted purposes of the Church. Therefore, the supreme authority of the Church also watches over the administration of all ecclesiastical property, and determines the extent of the power which individual ecclesiastical persons and organizations have over church property. The Church allows, and in some instances commands, the giving of alms by the administrators of ecclesiastical property. It further allows the giving away of goods for a just cause—which is explained in Canon 1535 under the head of remuneration, piety and Christian charity. Furthermore, the constitutions of all religious organizations have, as a rule, detailed regulations on this matter.

[58] Sacred Congregation of Religious, August, 18, 1914; *Acta Ap. Sedis*, VII, 104.

425. If a superior makes donations against the law of the Church, he has violated his trust and his donation is invalid. The donee is bound in conscience to return what he has thus received. The same may be said of an individual religious who without proper permission makes donations, unless it is a case where the superior cannot be reached at the time, and he has sufficient reason to presume the consent of the superior.

TITLE XI

OF ADMISSION INTO A RELIGIOUS ORGANIZATION

426. Any Catholic who is free from legal impediments, has the right intention, and is capable of bearing the burdens of the religious life, can be admitted into a religious organization (**Canon 538**).

The right which the Code gives to every Catholic under the above conditions entails an obligation for the religious organization to which a candidate applies to receive him or her. If a candidate possesses the proper qualifications for the respective community, and is able and willing to comply with the conditions for admission as they are determined by the Constitutions of the community, it is morally wrong to refuse admission. Practically, redress against an unreasonable refusal is difficult to obtain, because the superiors of the religious organization have the right to judge whether or not the candidate has the requisite qualifications, and moreover it would be unwise to insist on being received into a community under those circumstances. Canon 2352 punishes all persons with excommunication *nemini reservata* and incurred *ipso facto* who force a man or a woman to enter a religious organization, or force them to take vows in the community. In connection with the liberty guaranteed by the Code in the matter of consecrating one's life to the service of God in a religious community, it will be of interest for the reader to consult the older commentators on the history of the parental power to determine the future state of life of their children.

CHAPTER I

OF THE POSTULATE

427. All women in religious organizations with perpetual vows, and the lay-brothers (*conversi*) in communities of men, must pass fully six months as postulants before they can be admitted to the novitiate. In religious organizations with temporary vows, their constitutions are to be observed in regard to the necessity and the length of time of the postulate. The major superior may prolong the time of the postulate, but not for longer than another six months (**Canon 539**).

The postulate is not prescribed under pain of invalidity of the novitiate. Canon Law took notice of the postulate only in recent times, for formerly it was left to the discretion of the religious organization. The *Normæ* first insisted on a postulate for religious Congregations approved after the publication of the *Normæ*. By Decree of the Sacred Congregation of the Religious, January 1, 1911,[59] Pius X demanded two years of postulate for lay brothers in those religious orders in which the lay brothers take solemn vows under pain of the invalidity of the profession. A period of six months of postulate was prescribed for nuns with solemn vows and papal enclosure, by decree of August 15, 1912.[60] The Code modifies these decrees.

428. Though the present law requires only six months for lay-brothers and women in organizations with perpetual vows, the great majority of commentators (Chelodi, Vermeersch, etc.) do not believe that the Code forbids the orders and congregations to require a longer postulate. They hold that the wording of the Code does not absolutely insist on six months, but demands that as a *minimum,* so that a particular statute requiring a longer postulate cannot be said to be *contra,* but rather *præter legem.* However, the wording of Canon 539 suggests that the postulate should not be prolonged over one year. It is significant that Canon 555 provides specifically for a longer novitiate than the regular one year, if such longer novitiate is stipulated in the constitutions, and that Canon 571 positively forbids the prolongation of such novitiate beyond a further six months. Here,

[59] *Acta Ap. Sedis,* III, 29.
[60] *Acta Ap. Sedis,* IV, 565.

and in other instances where a period of probation is appointed (cfr. Canons 574, 634, 641), the Code sets definite limits to such period. Is the postulate the sole exception? Natural justice obviously requires that a period of probation should not be unnecessarily prolonged. As the postulate is not necessary for the validity of the profession, and is intended merely to furnish the postulant with an initial taste of the religious life to test his vocation and the Superiors with an opportunity of judging whether he gives evidence of dispositions which entitle him to the real test (the novitiate), Canon 537 should probably be interpreted as fixing not only the *minimum,* but also the *maximum* period proper for this purpose.[61]

429. The term *conversi* is not defined by the Code. In ancient times the *conversi* did not have the same obligations as the professed religious; in more recent times the term *conversi* became synonymous with *fratres laici,* and distinguished the lay brothers from the clerics of a religious community. Chelodi states that, from the accepted terminology of today, those religious come under the term of *conversi* who are destined for manual labor in the community.[62] In this general acceptation of the term *conversi,* it would find application to all religious organizations of men which have lay brothers destined for manual labor—not only those communities which have also priests, the clerical religious communities, but also laical communities, where all or nearly all the members remain laymen.

430. The postulate must be spent either in the house of novitiate or another house of the organization in which the religious discipline is accurately observed according to the constitutions, and the postulants should be placed under the special direction of a religious of tried virtue. The postulants shall wear plain clothing, which must be different from that of the novices. In monasteries of nuns the postulants are held to the law of enclosure during their postulate (**Canon 540**). Before they begin the novitiate, the postulants shall make a retreat for at least eight complete days and, according to the judgment of the confessor, a general confession of their entire past life (**Canon 541**).

The Code does not state the age at which postulants may

---

61 For the contrary opinion, cfr. Chelodi, ''Jus de Personis,'' 408, n. 264.
62 *Ibid., in nota* 5.

be received. Commentators generally concede that they may be received as postulants before they have the canonical age for the novitiate, provided they shall have attained the canonical age at the end of the postulate.

CHAPTER II

OF THE NOVITIATE

ARTICLE I.—OF THE CONDITIONS FOR ADMISSION

431. Besides the regulations given in Canons 539–541 and others imposed by the constitutions of the various religious organizations, the following shall be observed:

Admission into the novitiate is *invalid* in the case of:

(1) Persons who have lapsed from the Catholic faith into a non-Catholic sect;

(2) Persons who have not attained the required age—viz., their fifteenth year, according to Canon 555;

(3) Persons compelled to enter the religious organization by grave fear, or by deceit, or by force, or who are admitted by a superior thus constrained;

(4) Married persons for the duration of the marriage;

(5) Persons who are or have been professed members of another religious organization;

(6) Persons subject to penalty for grave crimes of which they have been, or may be accused;

(7) Either residential or titular bishops, even though they have only been designated by the Roman Pontiff, and have not yet been consecrated;

(8) Clerics who, by the law of the Holy See, are bound by oath to serve their diocese or mission, for such time as the obligation of the oath lasts (**Canon 542**, § 1).

432. The admission of the following is illicit, but valid:

(1) Clerics in major orders whose admission is unknown to their bishop, or is opposed by him because their leaving the diocese would result in grave detriment of souls, which cannot at all be averted by other arrangements;

(2) Those who have debts to pay and cannot settle the obligations;

(3) Persons who are under the obligation of giving an account (e.g., for positions of trust), or who are implicated

in other secular affairs, which might involve the religious organization in lawsuits and other annoyances;

(4) Children whose parents (i.e., father, mother, grandfather, grandmother) are in great want and in need of help from the children, and parents whose work is needed for the maintenance and education of their children;

(5) Candidates for the priesthood in the religious community who suffer from irregularity or any other canonical impediment;

(6) Catholics of an Oriental Rite into religious organizations of the Latin Rite without the written permission from the Sacred Congregation for the Oriental Church[63] (**Canon 542, § 2**).

These requisites for valid and licit admission to a religious organization bind all religious orders and congregations. That the individual organizations may prescribe more severe conditions for admission besides those laid down by the Code, is apparent from the opening words of Canon 542.

433. The Code does not forbid the reception into the community of converts from non-Catholic sects, but only of Catholics who have been guilty of apostasy from the faith and of joining a non-Catholic sect.[63a] As to the required age, fifteen completed years are demanded by the Code for all candidates without distinction. Before the Code a more advanced age was required for lay brothers in religious orders. The Constitutions of the various religious organizations may demand a more advanced age, and they may also fix the age limit beyond which the superiors may not admit an applicant. The Code does not set an age limit.

434. The liberty and free-will of the person entering the novitiate is so essential that one forced by a third party through fear, violence or deceit, does not make a valid novitiate, and consequently no valid profession. The novitiate is likewise invalid if the superior who has the right to admit persons to the religious community was constrained by fear, force, or deceit to receive an applicant. The interference with liberty must be grave to make the novitiate invalid. The gravity of the force, or fear, or deceit is naturally relative, some characters being more easily influenced than others. Canon 2352

63 Concerning Orientals, cfr. App. III, 24, c.

63a Cfr. App. III, 24, b.

punishes with excommunication *nemini reservata* and incurred *ipso facto* all persons who force any man or woman to enter a religious organization. To protect further the free-will of women, the local Ordinary or his delegate must question them individually before the beginning of the novitiate and also before the taking of temporary, and of perpetual vows (cfr. Canon 552).

435. In reference to married persons, the majority of commentators on the Code do not admit that a person who has a right to perpetual separation from bed and board (e.g., by reason of the adultery of the other party) is free to enter a religious community: others—for instance, Leitner [64] and Schäfer [65]— hold that he is free. The wording of the Code, "conjux durante matrimonio," seems to disbar married persons as long as the marriage bond is not dissolved. The provisions of the former Canon Law, which allowed married persons under certain conditions to be received into a religious community, are no longer in force.

436. Persons who have taken the vows (either temporary or perpetual) of a religious organization, cannot validly be received into any novitiate. Even if the vows have ceased or been dispensed with, such a person cannot again become a religious without the dispensation of the Holy See. The transition from one religious organization to another, or from one independent monastery to another, needs the permission of the Holy See, according to Canon 632. Commentators generally hold that readmission into the same organization after vows have been once taken is also invalid.

437. The secular clerics are, as a general rule, free to enter a religious community. Also clerics who were ordained under the title of service of the diocese, and who had to take the oath to serve the diocese perpetually (cfr. Canon 981), are free to enter religious life. That oath is taken for the purpose of acquiring the necessary title of promotion to major orders. The cleric who joins a religious community merely exchanges the former title of ordination for another title. The fact that the diocesan seminary incurred expenses in the maintenance of the cleric during his years of study does not deprive him of the

---

[64] Leitner, "Handbuch des kath. Kirchenr.," III, 372.
[65] Schäfer. "Ordensrecht," 152.

right to enter a religious community, as is evident from a decision of the Sacred Congregation of the Council, February 26, 1695. Those clerics only are barred from entering a religious community who in certain seminaries and missionary colleges by ordinance of the Holy See take an oath to serve the diocese or the missions for a period of time, and who are thus barred for their pledged period of service. Furthermore, those ordained under the title of the missions in places subject to the Sacred Congregation of the Propaganda, may not enter a religious community without permission of the Holy See.[66]

438. Among those who cannot be *licitly* admitted to the novitiate, the Code mentions in the first place clerics in major orders. It states that such cannot licitly leave their diocese to join a religious community, if the bishop objects to their departure because the diocese has not enough priests to attend to the spiritual wants of the people. The bishop is, however, obliged to give his permission as soon as he can get other priests to replace those who desire to enter the religious life.

439. The denial of licit admission to persons who have debts to pay, accounts to render, parents to support, or children to educate, is the same as in the former Canon Law. The refusal to receive young men for the priesthood in a religious community if they suffer from an irregularity or other impediment of ordination, is also the same as before. As to illegitimacy, Canon 984 states that solemn religious profession removes that irregularity, wherefore illegitimate sons may be received into religious organizations with solemn vows, unless their constitutions forbid the admission of such applicants.[67]

Right of Admitting Candidates

440. The right of admitting candidates to the novitiate and to subsequent profession, either temporary or perpetual, is vested in the major superiors after they have taken the vote of the council or of the chapter, according as the particular constitutions of each order or congregation prescribe (**Canon 543**).

The right of accepting candidates for the novitiate and for profession is given by the Code to the major superiors and

---

[66] Vermeersch-Creusen, "Epitome Jur. Can.," I, 237.
[67] Führich, "De Religiosis," 123, n. 75; Schäfer, "Ordensrecht," 157.

council (or chapter) of the respective religious organizations. The religious orders and the congregations of papal law had this right before the promulgation of the Code: now all religious bodies, including the diocesan congregations, possess it. The law of the Constitution "Conditæ," December 8, 1900, which gave to the bishop of the diocese the right to admit candidates to the novitiate in diocesan congregations, is modified by Canon 543.

The Code demands that the superior shall consult either the council or the chapter in the admission of candidates. The constitutions may determine whether the council of the major superior or the chapter is to vote on the candidates for the novitiate and for the profession. Very likely the community of the house of novitiate is here meant by the term "chapter." As the Code does not determine whether the vote is to be decisive or merely consultive in the voting for admission to the novitiate, the particular constitutions may rule whether the vote is to be decisive or only consultive. However, in virtue of Canon 575, the vote of the council or the chapter is decisive in the admission to the first vows after the novitiate, and merely consultive for the subsequent perpetual profession of either simple or solemn vows.

CERTIFICATES AND TESTIMONIALS OF CANDIDATES

441. In every religious organization all aspirants must, before they are admitted to the novitiate, submit certificates of baptism and confirmation.

In religious bodies of men the applicants must, moreover, get testimonial letters from the Ordinary of their birthplace and also from all other Ordinaries in whose dioceses they have stayed for more than one practically continuous year after the completion of their fourteenth year. Every contrary privilege exempting from this obligation is hereby revoked.

Candidates who have attended a seminary or college, or have been postulants or novices of another religious organization, must also produce testimonials from the rector of the seminary or college (issued after consultation with the Ordinary), or, in case of postulants or novices, from the major religious superior.

Candidates who are clerics require, besides the testimony of ordination, testimonial letters from all Ordinaries in whose dioceses they have lived after their ordination for over one morally continuous year and the testimonials of the rector of the seminary.

A professed religious who, by permission of the Holy See, joins another religious organization, needs only the testimonials of the major superior of the religious body to which he first belonged.

In addition to these testimonials required by law, the major superiors who have the right to receive applicants into the community, can demand of them such other testimonials as seem to them necessary or useful for the purpose in view.

Women should be received only after accurate investigation as to their character and disposition: if they have been in a college, or in the postulate or novitiate of another Sisterhood, the testimonials of the directress of the school or of the major religious superioress are required, as in the case of men (**Canon 544**).

442. Care must be taken that proof of the reception of baptism is obtained before an applicant is admitted into the novitiate. The Code also demands reception of confirmation before the novitiate. Circumstances may arise in which it is impossible to get the certificates at all or only after much delay. The law has in mind only the ordinary and usual circumstances. In unusual circumstances the general principles applicable to the observance of laws *de licitis et illicitis* apply.

443. Some commentators hold that the testimonials of the Ordinary are not required if the boy or young man stayed in the diocese for the purpose of the preliminary education in a school of a religious organization—a kind of junior seminary, in which are received only boys who intend to enter the community after the completion of the course of studies at that seminary. They base their opinion on an answer given to the Christian Brothers, July 28, 1918.[68] The answer is sufficiently general to entitle other religious to follow it.

444. Testimonial letters are to be given by the rector of a *collegium*, in which young men or young ladies have lived: apparently, the length of time (a school year or less) makes

68 Schäfer, "Ordensrecht," 161; Vermeersch, "Periodica." IX, 6.

no difference; if they were accepted as students and actually took up residence in the school, the testimonials are required, no matter how soon they left or were dismissed. However, commentators are not agreed on the understanding of the term, *collegium*. Vermeersch understands that term to mean only those houses of study in which the young men or young ladies receive their education in the hope of embracing the clerical or religious state,[69] and Schäfer approves of that acceptation.[70] Leitner [71] takes *collegium* in the sense of a higher school of learning under ecclesiastical management, which interpretation seems to be more correct in view of the decree of Sept. 7, 1909, of the Sacred Congregation of the Religious, which uses the term *collegia* in connection with, not only ecclesiastical and religious, but also laical institutes of learning.[72] The reason why commentators do not take the term *collegium* to cover also the laical institutes of learning is because many, if not most, of these are in the hands of non-Catholics who cannot effectively be forced to obey the law of the Church, and because the required consultation with the Ordinary seems to indicate that these colleges are such as fall under his jurisdiction or supervision.

445. Men who join a religious community must have testimonials from the bishop of their birthplace and from every bishop in whose diocese they stayed continually for over a year after completing their fourteenth year. Canon 90 (cfr. above, n. 67) defines the meaning of *locus originis* (place of origin or birthplace). In deciding what constitutes an interruption in the year of stay in a diocese, some commentators follow the rule of the Code for the complete interruption of the year of novitiate—namely, an absence from the diocese of over thirty days during the year.

MANNER OF GIVING TESTIMONIALS

446. Persons who are obliged by the law to issue the testimonials shall do so within three months from the time that they were asked for. They must be given, not to the aspirants

69 Vermeersch, ''Periodica,'' IX, 7.
70 Schäfer, ''Ordensrecht,'' 161.
71 Leitner, ''Handbuch,'' III, 365.
72 Sacred Congregation of Religious, Sept. 7, 1909, and April 5, 1910; *Acta Ap. Sedis*, II, 231.

themselves, but to the religious superiors, must be issued free of charge, and enclosed under seal. In the case of aspirants who have been in a seminary or college, or in the postulate or novitiate of another religious organization, they shall be given under oath by the superior.

If the persons from whom the testimonials are requested, believe there are serious reasons why they cannot answer the request, they shall within the stipulated three months explain these reasons to the Holy See.

If they answer that the applicant is not sufficiently known to them, the religious superior shall replace the testimonials by other accurate investigation and trustworthy reports. If those who are to give the testimonials do not answer at all, the superior who asked for them shall inform the Holy See about his failure to receive an answer (**Canon 545**, §§ 1–3).[72a]

447. As the result of careful investigation and also of secret information the Ordinaries and others are gravely bound in conscience to make a true report in their testimonial letters regarding the origin, character, talents, life, reputation, state of life, and studies of the candidate. Furthermore, whether the candidate is accused of crime, or rests under a censure, irregularity or other canonical impediment; whether his own family needs his help, and, in the case of candidates who have been in a seminary or college or in the postulate or novitiate of another religious body, whether they left of their own volition or for what reason they were dismissed (**Canon 545**, § 4). All persons who receive the above-mentioned information are strictly bound to observe secrecy as to the knowledge they have obtained and the persons who furnished the information (**Canon 546**).

Religious superiors who receive a candidate against the rules of Canon 542 (which deals with the qualifications for valid and licit admission to religious life), or against the law of Canon 544 (requiring the testimonials), or against the law of Canon 571 (forbidding the admission to profession of an unworthy novice), are to be punished according to the gravity of their guilt, even by removal from their office (cfr. Canon 2411).

[72a] Concerning refusal to give testimonials, cfr. App. III, 24, d.

DOWRY OF RELIGIOUS WOMEN

448. In monasteries of women with solemn vows the postulant must bring with her the dowry required by the constitutions or determined by legitimate custom. The dowry shall be given to the monastery before the reception of the habit, or at least its donation shall be assured in legal form recognized by the civil law.

In Sisterhoods with simple vows, the particular constitutions must be followed with regard to the dowry.

The prescribed dowry cannot be remitted, either in whole or in part, without an indult of the Holy See, if there is question of an organization of papal law, or without the permission of the local Ordinary, if there is question of a diocesan congregation (**Canon 547**).

It is evident from this Canon that the Code does not insist so much on the dowry in Sisterhoods with simple vows, because these Sisterhoods, as a rule, engage in active work which makes them self-supporting. If, however, the constitutions demand a dowry, it cannot be remitted without a dispensation of the Holy See or the Ordinary, as the case may be.

449. The dowry is acquired irrevocably by the monastery or religious congregation at the death of the religious, even though she has taken temporary vows only (**Canon 548**). If a Sister dies before the end of the novitiate, the dowry does not become the property of the religious community, but must be returned to the heirs—or, in the case of a will, to the legatees mentioned in the will. The profession allowed to a novice in danger of death before the expiration of the novitiate does not entitle the religious community to the dowry.

450. After the first profession of a religious, her dowry is to be placed by the superioress, acting with her council, in a safe, lawful and fruitful investment. The superioress must obtain the consent of the local Ordinary for this investment, and, in the case of a monastery of nuns subject to the jurisdiction of a regular superior, the consent of both bishop and superior. It is absolutely forbidden to expend the dowry in any way before the death of a Sister, even for the building of a convent or the payment of debts (**Canon 549**). If, in violation of Canon 549, the superioress expends the dowries

of Sisters, Canon 2412 decrees that she is to be punished by the local Ordinary according to the gravity of her guilt, even with removal from office.

All the dowries are to be carefully administered at the monastery or house of the habitual residence of the Mother General or Provincial. The local Ordinaries shall specially watch over the conservation of the dowries of the religious women, and demand an exact account of them particularly at the time of the visitation (**Canon 550**).

451. When a professed Sister, either in solemn or simple vows, leaves the Sisterhood for any reason, her dowry must be returned to her in its entirety, without the interests which have already matured, and have therefore become the legitimately acquired property of the Sisterhood. If a professed Sister, by indult of the Holy See, transfers to another religious organization, the new community has the right to the income from the dowry during the novitiate, subject however to Canon 570, which declares that no compensation may be claimed for the maintenance of novices, unless the constitutions or an explicit contract authorize a claim for food and clothing.[73] After the Sister has made her profession in the new community, the dowry itself belongs to the new Sisterhood. If a nun (Sister in community that has solemn vows) changes from one monastery to another of the same Order, the second monastery has the right to the dowry from the day of the transfer (**Canon 551**). The matter of transition from one religious body to another, or from one independent monastery to another, is regulated by Canons 632–636.

452. At least two months before the reception of the candidates into the novitiate in communities of women, both exempt and non-exempt, the superioress must inform the local Ordinary of the fact. The same must be done also before the profession of temporary vows, and again before the profession of perpetual vows, either simple or solemn.

The local Ordinary—or, in case of his being absent or impeded, a priest delegated by him—shall at least thirty days before the reception or profession conduct gratuitously a care-

---

[73] Blat, ''Commentarium,'' II, 534; Vermeersch-Creusen, ''Epitome,'' I, n. 554; Cocchi, ''Commentarium,'' IV, n. 67; Bastien, ''Directoire Canonique,'' n. 105.

ful examination (without entering the cloister) to determine whether the candidate has been forced or deceived, and whether she knows and understands the step she is about to take. If her free will and pious intention are clearly ascertained, then the aspirant can be admitted to the novitiate or the novice to the profession (**Canon 552**).

Canon 2412 rules that the local Ordinary shall punish, even with deposition from office, any superioress who has neglected to inform him of the approaching reception or profession, as demanded by Canon 552.

The immemorial custom of charging a fee for the examination (the so-called *exploratio voluntatis*) conducted by the bishop or his delegate as demanded by Canon 552, was condemned by the Sacred Congregation of the Religious.[74]

ARTICLE II.—OF THE EDUCATION OF THE NOVICES

453. The novitiate begins with the reception of the habit, or in such other manner as is prescribed by the Constitutions (**Canon 553**). Some religious organizations have no habit distinct from the clerical garb (the cassock), and thus no investing with the habit. The constitutions must indicate in what manner the novitiate begins.

454. A house of novitiate is to be erected according to the constitutions. Religious organizations of papal law require the permission of the Holy See for the erection of the novitiate. If an organization is divided into provinces, several houses of novitiate cannot be designated in the same province except for a grave reason and with the special indult of the Holy See. (If the organization is not yet divided into provinces, the Code does not forbid several houses of novitiate.) The superiors must place in the house of novitiate and studies only such religious as will give a good example of religious discipline (**Canon 554**). Note that according to Canon 497 the *beneplacitum* of the Holy See is required for the establishing of a religious house of any community, diocesan or of papal law, in districts subject to the Sacred Congregation of the Propaganda.

[74] Sacred Congregation of Religious, March 20, 1922; cfr. App. III, 24, e.

Conditions for a Valid Novitiate

455. Besides the conditions required for a valid novitiate by Canon 542, § 1, the following points are demanded under pain of invalidity:

(1) At the time of reception into the novitiate the candidate must have completed at least his fifteenth year;

(2) The novice must make the novitiate for one continuous and complete year;

(3) He must spend that year in the house of novitiate.

If the constitutions prescribe a longer period for the novitiate, this is not required for the validity of the profession, unless the constitutions explicitly demand it under pain of invalidity (**Canon 555**).

456. A candidate is fully fifteen years of age on the day following the fifteenth birthday, according to the rule of Canon 34, n. 3. The year of novitiate is reckoned by the same rule so that the year is not complete until after midnight of the anniversary day of the reception into the novitiate. In leap years, as Vermeersch-Creusen remarks, it is immaterial whether a novice is received into the novitiate on February 28 or 29, for he cannot make his profession until March 1 of the following year; and, if a novice is received on (e.g.) January 28 of a leap year, he cannot make profession until January 29 of the following year.[75] As the year is to be taken according to the calendar, the leap year prolongs the novitiate for an additional day.

457. In orders and congregations whose statutes prescribe two years' novitiate, the first year is the canonical year. If the constitutions permit a novice in the second year to be sent out of the house of novitiate to do some work, this should be done only in exceptional cases for the purpose of completing his training, where the means to that end are not adequate at the house of novitiate. For example, novices may not be sent out as teachers to fill a need of professed religious teachers. The novices must spend the last two months before profession

---

[75] "Epitome Jur. Can.," I, 252. The Committee for the Auth. Interpr. of the Code declared, Nov. 12, 1922, that the year of novitiate is to be computed according to Canon 34, n. 3; cfr. App. III, 24, f.

in the novitiate, and be relieved from all work that interferes with their preparation for profession.[76]

Interruption of the Novitiate

458. The novitiate is interrupted and must be made over again: (1) if the novice after dismissal by the superior has actually left the house; (2) if without permission of the superior he has deserted the house with the intention not to return; or (3) if for any reason—even with the permission of the superior—he has remained outside the house of novitiate for over thirty days, consecutive or otherwise, even though with the intention of returning.

If a novice has remained outside the house of novitiate for over fifteen days, but not over thirty days (consecutive or otherwise), either with the permission of the superior or through force of circumstances (e.g., fire, flood, sudden illness), and continued under the obedience of the superior, it is necessary and sufficient for the validity of the novitiate to supply the days spent outside the novitiate. If the entire period of absence from the novitiate does not amount to over fifteen days, the superior may prescribe that those days are supplied, but this is not necessary for validity of the novitiate.

The superiors shall not give permission to a novice to remain outside the novitiate, except for a just and serious reason. If the novice is transferred by his superiors from one house of novitiate to another of the same religious organization, the novitiate is not interrupted (**Canon 556**).

459. A day is a space of twenty-four consecutive hours reckoned from midnight (cfr. Canon 32). Absence of the novice for part of the day, even on many successive days, does not count in this connexion. According to the definition of the term "day" given by the Code, a novice is not absent for a day if he is out of the house of the novitiate for a part of one day and part of the following day—e.g., if he goes away on Sunday morning and returns Monday before midnight—for, although he has been away for more than twenty-four hours, these hours do not make a day according to the definition of the Code. Wherefore, Vermeersch-Creusen concludes

[76] Instruction of the Sacred Congregation of Religious, Nov. 3, 1921; cfr. App. III, 24, a. New declaration on two years' novitiate, cfr. App. III, 24, k.

that a novice who left the house Monday morning and returns Saturday evening, has been absent only four days.[77]

460. A novice who is dismissed by the competent superior and has actually left the house (for no matter how short a time), has broken the novitiate, and, if the superior admits him again even the same day on which the novice left, he must make a full year of novitiate from this readmission. As the Code does not distinguish between a justified dismissal and an unjust one, commentators do not distinguish in this case between just and unjust dismissal.

If a novice runs away—that is to say, departs without permission of the superior and with the intention not to return —recent commentators generally hold that the novitiate is broken at the very moment at which the novice leaves the novitiate cloister, provided his intention not to return can be proved in the external forum by his words, actions, or other circumstances. Commentators on the old Canon Law discussed the question of interruption of the novitiate by a novice who of his own accord leaves the novitiate with the intention of not returning, and whether a novice who soon afterwards regrets his step and is readmitted must make the novitiate over again from the beginning. Schmalzgrüber says that the question is disputed among doctors of Canon Law: some hold that, if the novice returns within a few days, the *modicum intervallum pro nihilo reputatur;* others that the shortest absence from the house of novitiate is sufficient to break the novitiate, if the novice left with the intention not to return.[78] Appeltern quotes a secretary of the Sacred Congregation of the Council as having stated, in 1772, that it is the more common and more accepted opinion that the year of novitiate is considered interrupted, if the novice either with or without the habit has gone out of the house of novitiate with the deliberate intention of abandoning the community, though he should afterwards regret his step and return immediately.[79]

77 Vermeersch-Creusen, ''Epitome Jur. Can.,'' I, 252. Chelodi, ''Jus de Personis,'' 415, footnote 3, thinks it makes five days, counting each twenty-four hours during the absence.

78 Schmalzgrüber, ''Jus Eccl.,'' VII, 27, n. 69.

79 Appeltern, ''Comp. Jur. Regul.,'' 57.

Habit of the Novices

461. During the entire year of the novitiate the novices shall wear the habit prescribed by the constitutions, unless the peculiar circumstances of a place demand otherwise (**Canon 557**).

The Council of Trent (Session XXV, Chapter XV, *De Ref. Regul. et Monial.*), which demanded a year's novitiate under pain of the invalidity of the profession, speaks of the year of novitiate "from the taking of the habit." As we saw above (Canon 553), the Code states that the novitiate begins with the reception of the habit or in such other manner as is prescribed by the constitutions, because not all religious communities have a special habit. In any case, the wearing of the habit is not required for validity.

Novitiate Made for One Class is Invalid for Other Class

462. In those religious organizations in which there are two classes of members, the novitiate made for one class is not valid for the other class (**Canon 558**).

This Canon is of importance since the validity of the novitiate and profession is concerned. Many of the religious orders have two classes of members—those destined for the priesthood and those destined for manual labor as lay brothers. Also many of the laical religious congregations of men as well as of women have two classes of members—those destined for teaching, nursing, or other professional work, and those destined for labor in the household. The constitutions of the various religious bodies must be consulted to determine whether there are two distinct classes of members recognized in the order or congregation. If the constitutions are not sufficiently explicit on the distinction of classes, and the novices are all considered of the same class and only after the novitiate the superiors put some of the newly professed to study and others to the common labors of the household, Canon 558 does not apply.[80] To apply a law, especially one which has an invalidating effect, the case must be certain to fall under that law beyond a reasonable doubt.

[80] Vermeersch-Creusen, "Epitome," I, 253.

Appointment and Duties of Master of Novices

463. A master of novices is to be appointed for the training of the novices. He shall be at least thirty-five years old, ten years professed (reckoned from his first profession), and conspicuous for prudence, charity, piety and religious observance; in clerical religious organizations, he must be a priest.

If on account of the large number of novices, or for another just cause, it seems advisable to have an assistant master of novices, he shall be under the immediate authority of the master in all matters concerning the management of the novitiate. The assistant master should be at least thirty years of age and fully five years professed (reckoned from his first profession), and possess the other necessary and proper qualifications for this office. Both the master and his assistant must be relieved from all offices and duties which might interfere with the guidance and training of the novices (**Canon 559**).

464. The master of novices and his assistant shall be elected according to the constitutions of each organization: if these fix any term of office, they shall not be removed from office during such term except for a just and grave reason, and may be re-elected (**Canon 560**).

465. The guidance and education of the novices belong exclusively to the master of novices: all others are forbidden to interfere under any pretext, except those superiors to whom the constitutions give such authority and the Visitors. In matters pertaining to the discipline of the entire community at the house of novitiate, master and novices alike are subject to the local superior. The novices are subject to the authority of the master and the superiors of the religious organization, and are bound to obey them (**Canon 561**).

The master of novices is under a grave obligation to exercise the utmost diligence in instructing the novices in the zealous practice of the religious life, according to the constitutions and the regulations of Canon 565 (**Canon 562**). During the year of novitiate the master shall make a report of the conduct of the individual novices to the Chapter or to the major superior, according to the regulations of the respective constitutions (**Canon 563**).

466. Canon 559 wants the master and assistant master of

novices relieved of all offices and duties which interfere with the proper training of the novices. Commentators, therefore, discuss whether a master (or mistress) of novices may be a member of the council of the general or provincial, and whether he may be local superior. The Code forbids the holding of offices only in so far as they may interfere with the duties of the office of the master of novices. The *Normæ* forbade the master of novices to be a member of the council, but they are not a law properly so called, and, unless the constitutions forbid the master to be elected a member of the council, the two offices are not incompatible. The office of local superior is considered by commentators to belong to those offices which interfere with the duties of the master towards the novices.

Separation of Novices and Special Instruction

467. In so far as possible, the novitiate must be separated from that part of the house where the professed live, and, without a special reason and the permission of the superior or the master, the novices shall have no communication with the professed, nor the professed with the novices. The novices for the lay-brotherhood (lay-sisterhood) shall be assigned a separate place (**Canon 564**). In commenting on Canon 558, we saw that, where the constitutions recognize two classes of religious, the novitiate made for one class is not valid for the other class. As the future duties of the different classes differ, their training in the novitiate must naturally differ to some extent. The Code wants the living quarters of the two classes of novices to be separate. Further details may be ordained by the constitutions.

468. The purpose of the year of novitiate under the guidance of the master must be the formation of the novices' character by the study of the rule and constitutions, by pious meditations and assiduous prayer, by instructions in all matters pertaining to the vows and the cultivation of virtue, and by pious exercises conducive to the complete eradication of faulty habits, the control of the passions and the acquisition of virtues. The candidates for lay-brothers (or lay-sisters) must, moreover, be thoroughly instructed in Christian doctrine, for which purpose a special instruction shall be given to them at least once a week.

If the novice is a priest, he shall not be appointed to preach, or to hear confessions, or to attend to outside offices or functions of the religious organization during the year of his novitiate. The novices shall not engage in intensive studies of literature, sciences or arts. The lay-brother novices may within the house of novitiate attend to the duties and work done by lay brothers—not, however, as principal brothers in charge of the offices, shops, etc., and only in so far as such work does not interfere with the exercises prescribed for them in the novitiate (**Canon 565**).

As is apparent from the foregoing Canon, the Code does not forbid all study during the novitiate, but the studies must not be so extensive that the special training in the religious life is made impossible or is assigned a secondary place. While commentators generally admit that the decree of the Sacred Congregation of the Religious on studies in the novitiate of religious organizations of men (August 10, 1910) has no longer the force of law, it may nevertheless serve as an indication of the amount of study which may be assigned to the novices.[81]

Confessors and Confession of Novices

469. According to the rules of Canons 520–527, the confessor of the novices in communities of women is to be the same as the one appointed for the professed Sisters (**Canon 566**, § 1). The novices have in this matter the same rights as the Code gives to the professed Sisters (cfr. above, nn. 401–406).

470. In communities of men, the following regulations shall be observed, without prejudice to Canon 519:

(1) One or more ordinary confessors shall be appointed according to the number of novices. The master of novices and his assistant are forbidden by Canon 891 to hear the confessions of their novices unless in an exceptional case a novice, for a grave and urgent reason, requests of his own free choice that they hear his confession;

(2) In clerical religious communities, the ordinary confessors must be residents of the house of novitiate. In laical religious communities the confessors must come to the house of novitiate frequently to hear the confessions of the novices;

(3) Besides the ordinary confessors, several other confes-

[81] *Acta Ap. Sedis,* II, 730.

sors should be appointed to whom the novices may have free access in particular cases without the master showing any displeasure;

(4) At least four times a year, the novices shall have an extraordinary confessor whom all novices must approach to receive his blessing, even if perhaps they do not want to confess to him (**Canon 566,** § 2).

Rights and Privileges of Novices

471. The novices enjoy all the privileges and spiritual favors granted to the respective organization; if they die as novices, they have a right to the suffrages prescribed for professed members. The novices shall not be promoted to orders during the novitiate (**Canon 567**).

Canon 614 rules that the novices enjoy the privileges of clerics contained in Canons 119–123. With reference to the suffrages for deceased novices, the question was proposed to the Holy See whether the novices are to have the same suffrages, even though in the constitutions approved by the Holy See a distinction is made between suffrages for professed and for novices. The Holy See answered that in the revision of the Constitutions the same suffrages are to be conceded to all members without distinction.[82]

472. Even before the termination of the novitiate, profession is granted to novices in danger of death in all orders, congregations and religious societies without vows, by Decree of the Sacred Congregation of the Religious, Dec. 30, 1922.[83] A Decree of September 10, 1912, permitted novices in danger of death to make profession that they might have the consolation of dying as professed members of the community. Now, the Holy See again allows this profession under the following conditions: (1) The novices must have begun the novitiate canonically; (2) the superior of the house of novitiate, the acting superior, the major superiors, or a person delegated by them, may receive the profession; (3) the formula of profession shall be the same as the one in ordinary use at the end of novitiate, and the vows or promises shall be

[82] Comm. for the Auth. Interp. of the Code, Oct. 16, 1919; cfr. App. III, 24, g.
[83] Cfr. App. III, 24, h.

taken without a fixed term and without expression of perpetuity; (4) the novice making this profession shall be entitled to all the spiritual benefits and suffrages of professed members of the respective community, and a plenary indulgence in the form of a Jubilee indulgence is mercifully granted to him; (5) the profession has absolutely no other effect than the one mentioned in the preceding number, wherefore, if the novice survives, he has the same standing as any other novice. He can leave the community, and may be dismissed like any other novice. If, at the end of the novitiate, he is accepted by the community, he must make profession like other novices. It may be noted that, in Sisterhoods, the dowry does not become the property of the organization because of this profession in danger of death.

Laws as to the Temporal Goods of Novices

473. If, during the novitiate, a novice renounces in any way his right to benefices or goods, or assumes any obligation concerning them, the renunciation or obligation is not only illicit but automatically invalid (**Canon 568**). As to benefices held by a cleric who enters the novitiate, Canon 584 provides that parochial benefices are lost to him one year after any profession, and other benefices three years afterwards. The Church does not allow a novice to dispose of his temporal goods and rights for the apparent reason that he may need them if he leaves or is dismissed. There is danger that a novice who has disposed of his goods and then finds that he has no vocation for religious life, is deterred from leaving the community because he has lost his goods.

474. Before the profession of simple vows, either temporary or perpetual, the novice must cede the administration of his temporal goods for the whole time that he shall be bound by the simple vows to a person of his choice, and shall also dispose of their use and revenue at pleasure, unless the constitutions rule otherwise in reference to the use and revenue of the goods of a novice.

If this cession and disposition have been omitted because the novice had no goods, and he afterwards obtained goods; or if the cession and disposition were made, but additional

goods came to the novice under any title, the cession and disposition may be freely made or repeated by the now professed
member, notwithstanding his simple profession.

Novices in congregations (organizations with simple vows)
may, before taking temporary vows, freely dispose by last will
of goods which they actually possess, and such as may perchance come to them in future (**Canon 569**).

The three paragraphs of Canon 569 order the novices to
arrange their worldly affairs before their profession, for, after
profession, they should not be troubled with these affairs,
unless this is absolutely necessary because of the new acquisition of property (e.g., by wills and bequests). The religious
order or congregation has no right to the goods which the
novices have; wherefore also the Code wants the novices to
dispose freely of the administration and the revenue and use
of their goods. We saw before that the novices cannot give
away their goods, but must keep what they have (cfr. n. 473).
Further laws on the goods of the professed are given in Canons
580–584. We shall there see that in all religious communities
with simple vows the professed members must keep the goods
and property they had, and cannot divest themselves of them.
As a religious organization of simple vows has no right of
inheritance to the goods of the members who die in the community, these religious should, towards the end of their novitiate, make their last will designating the persons to whom
they desire their goods and property to go after their death.

475. In religious organizations with solemn vows the novices
must make the arrangements about their temporal goods, as
required by Canon 569, for the time of the temporal vows.
Before solemn profession they must give away whatever they
possess to whom they please. From the moment of solemn
profession, all goods which come to the solemnly professed
revert to the religious order—or the Holy See, as the case
may be (cfr. Canon 582)—because the solemnly professed religious becomes incapacitated by the law of the Church from
owning any temporal goods personally.

In reference to Canon 569 a question arose as to the interpretation of the passage: "novitius . . . debet bonorum suorum
administrationem cedere cui maluerit et, nisi constitutiones
aliud ferant, de eorumdem usu, et usufructu libere disponere."

The Holy See declared that the constitutions approved before the promulgation of the Code are to remain in force, though they deprive the novice of the free disposal in reference to the use and usufruct of his goods.[84]

476. No compensation may be claimed for the expenditures of keeping a postulant or novice, except what the constitutions perhaps demand for food and clothing, or what was agreed upon for these purposes by explicit contract at the beginning of the postulate or novitiate. Whatever the applicant brought along, and has not actually consumed by use, must be returned to him if he does not make profession but returns to the world (**Canon 570**).

477. The novice is free to leave the religious organization, and the superiors or the Chapter, according to the constitutions, may dismiss the novice for any just cause without obligation on the part of the superiors or the Chapter to inform the novice of the reason for the dismissal. When the year of novitiate is completed, the novice, if judged qualified, shall be admitted to profession: if judged otherwise, he must be dismissed. If there is doubt as to his fitness for profession, the major superiors may prolong the time of the novitiate for not more than six months. Before taking vows the novice shall make a retreat for at least eight full days (**Canon 571**).

The reasons for dismissal should be carefully noted in some record, for they are of importance if the dismissed novice wants to join another religious community or to enter a seminary, or if the novice should complain to the Holy See of unjust dismissal. Superiors who admit an unfit novice to profession in contravention of the law of Canon 571, are to be punished according to the gravity of their guilt, even with deposition from office (cfr. Canon 2411).

CHAPTER III

OF RELIGIOUS PROFESSION

478. For the validity of any religious profession the following is required:

(1) The novice must have reached the age required by

[84] Committee for the Auth. Interp. of the Code, Oct. 16, 1919; cfr. App. III, 24, i.

Canon 573 (namely, at least sixteen years, for temporary profession) ;

(2) He must be admitted to profession by the legitimate superior—namely, him to whom the constitutions assign the right of admitting novices to profession;

(3) A valid novitiate must have preceded, according to the conditions of Canon 555;

(4) The profession must not be based on duress, fear or deceit;

(5) The profession must be explicit;

(6) The profession must be made in the hands of the superior authorized by the constitutions or his delegate.

For the validity of the profession of perpetual vows, whether simple or solemn, it is also required that the simple, temporary profession has preceded (according to Canon 574), and that the candidate has attained the required age of twenty-one years as stated in Canon 573 (**Canon 572**).

479. In the constitutions of some religious congregations of women under papal law, the formula of profession makes no mention of the Reverend Mother, but only of the bishop or his delegate. Wherefore, the question arises whether the bishop or his delegate is to be considered the legitimate superior for the reception of the profession, for Canon 572, n. 6, rules that the legitimate superior, as pointed out by the constitutions, must accept the profession. The Holy See answered that the bishop or his delegate is entitled to accept the vows as having a legitimate mandate by the constitutions.[85]

480. In reference to the profession of novices who are subject to *military service* according to the laws of their country, the Sacred Congregation of the Religious, July 15, 1919, ordered that the former regulations concerning these novices were to remain in force, though they are not embodied in the Code. Wherefore, novices who have not yet been exempted definitely from military service, are not to be admitted at the end of their novitiate to the three years of temporary vows, but only to vows lasting until they are called to the service. These vows cease on the day on which such a religious comes under military discipline, though he remains a member of the religious com-

[85] Committee for the Auth. Interp. of the Code, March 1, 1921; cfr. App. III, 25, a.

munity. He is, however, free to separate himself from the community by making declaration to that effect to the superior in writing or orally before witnesses. The question arose whether, in those communities where the temporary vows are taken for only one year at a time, the novice bound to military training may be allowed to take vows for a year.[86] The Sacred Congregation answered that he may take these vows, but they automatically cease on the day on which he becomes subject to military discipline.[87]

The Decree of the Sacred Congregation of the Religious, Jan. 1, 1911,[88] which is to continue in force, does not forbid the reception of novices who have not yet gone through their military training, but they may not be admitted to perpetual vows or to sacred orders before they have either finished their military training or have been definitely exempted from such service.

TEMPORARY AND PERPETUAL VOWS

481. All candidates for religious profession must have completed their sixteenth year if there is question of temporary vows, and their twenty-first year in the case of perpetual profession, whether simple or solemn (**Canon 573**). In every order of men or of women, and in every congregation which has perpetual vows, the novice must take temporary vows for three years, or for a longer period if he will not yet be twenty-one years of age after three years of temporary vows. These vows must be taken in the house of novitiate. If the constitutions demand yearly profession instead of the three years' vows, these constitutions are to be followed. The legitimate superior may prolong the period of temporary vows by making the religious again take temporary vows, but the prolongation may not extend for more than three years (**Canon 574**).

An exception to Canon 574 is contained in Canon 634 in the case of a perpetually professed religious who receives permission to join another religious organization. After the no-

---

[86] Sacred Congregation of Religious, July 15, 1919; cfr. App. III, 4, b.
[87] Sacred Congregation of Religious, Nov. 30, 1919; cfr. App. III, 25, c.
[88] Sacred Congregation of Religious, Jan. 1, 1911; *Acta Ap. Sedis,* III, 37.

vitiate in the new community, he is to take immediately perpetual vows, either simple or solemn, as the case may be. The Superior may indeed extend the period of probation, but not beyond an additional year.

The rule of Canon 574 that temporary vows must be taken in all religious orders, as well as in congregations, and that the persons who want to take perpetual vows, either solemn or simple, must have completed their twenty-first year, are new and important regulations. A former Decree of the Sacred Congregation of the Religious, which lost its force through the promulgation of the Code, ruled that the lay-brothers in religious orders could not begin the novitiate until they were twenty-one years of age, and that they had to be in simple vows for six years and be at least thirty years of age before they could be admitted to solemn vows.[89]

482. After the expiration of the time of temporary vows, the religious may either return to the world, or be dismissed (cfr. Canon 637) or make the perpetual profession, which is either simple or solemn according to the constitutions of the particular religious organization. If, before the expiration of the temporary vows, the religious is judged unworthy to take perpetual vows, he may be dismissed in the manner defined by Canon 647. The vote of the council or chapter for the admission of a novice to the first temporary vows is decisive, so that the superior admitting him against the vote of the majority acts invalidly; for the subsequent perpetual profession, both simple and solemn, the vote is merely consultive (**Canon 575**).

The Church wants the novices to be absolutely free to return to the world or to take vows, and she guarantees the same freedom to those who have taken temporary vows, so that they may leave if they wish as soon as the period of temporary vows expires. Canon 2352 punishes with excommunication, *nemini reservata* and incurred *ipso facto,* all persons who in any manner force a man or woman to take temporary or perpetual vows.

---

[89] Sacred Congregation of Religious, Jan. 1, 1911; *Acta Ap. Sedis,* III, 29. Cfr. also App. III, 3, b.

FORMALITIES OF THE PROFESSION

483. In the making of the profession the rite prescribed by the constitutions shall be observed. The record of the profession shall be signed by the religious who made profession and by at least the person before whom it was made. The written instrument shall be preserved in the archives of the organization. Moreover, in the case of solemn profession, the superior who received the profession shall inform the pastor of the place where the professed was baptized, as Canon 470 demands that his solemn profession is to be entered in the baptismal record of the respective person (**Canon 576**).

484. When the term of the temporary vows expires, there shall be no delay in the renewal of the vows. For a just cause the superiors may allow the *renewal of the temporary vows* to be somewhat anticipated, but not over one month (**Canon 577**). The text of the Canon plainly refers to cases where the temporary vows have to be repeated, either because in some organization the temporary vows are taken for only one year at a time, or because the religious after the three years of the temporary vows has not yet completed his twenty-first year, or because the superior hesitates to admit the religious to perpetual vows and wants to extend his probation. In any case, it seems quite certain from Canon 574 that fully three years of temporary vows must have elapsed before perpetual vows can be taken.

485. In some congregations the vows are taken under the condition "for as long as I shall live in the congregation." These vows cease either on the voluntary departure of the professed or on his dismissal. The Holy See has declared that in such congregations the first temporary vows need not be taken for three years.[90]

RIGHTS AND DUTIES OF TEMPORARILY PROFESSED RELIGIOUS

486. The rights and duties of religious who, in accordance with Canon 574, have taken temporary vows, are defined and qualified as follows:

(1) They enjoy the same indulgences, privileges and spir-

[90] Committee for the Auth. Interp. of the Code, March 1, 1921; cfr. App. III, 25, d.

itual favors as the religious in perpetual simple or in solemn vows, and, if they die in temporary vows, they have the right to the same suffrages as the other professed members;

(2) They are bound to observe the rule and constitutions, but, if the organization has the obligation of the choir, they are not held to the private recitation of the Divine office, unless they are in sacred orders, or the constitutions explicitly impose the private recitation;

(3) They have neither an active nor passive vote, unless the constitutions explicitly state otherwise. However, the time prescribed for obtaining active and passive vote is counted from the first profession, if the constitutions determine nothing on this point (**Canon 578**).

The last named rule of Canon 578 is of importance to determine the right to take part in elections and to be elected to offices in the religious organization. Through the temporary profession the religious becomes subject to the *potestas dominativa* of the superiors of the organization, and in exempt clerical organizations he becomes subject also to the *jurisdictio ecclesiastica* of the superiors. In virtue of Canon 1315, any vows which he has taken (private or devotional vows are meant) before the religious profession are by the first profession suspended for as long a time as the person remains in the religious community. Because of the *potestas dominativa,* the superiors can, according to Canon 1312, annul the private vows of the temporarily professed subjects, and of course of other professed members.

Attention may be drawn here to Canon 766 which forbids novices and professed members of any religious community to take the office of sponsor in baptism or confirmation, unless in a case of necessity the local or the higher superior permits it. The temporarily professed as well as those in perpetual vows cannot be members of any secular Third Order, and, if they belong to it before they make profession, the membership is suspended and revives in case the religious is freed from his vows and returns to the world (cfr. Canon 704). Furthermore, Canon 542 rules that persons who have taken vows in any religious community cannot be received again into a religious community without the permission of the Holy See, though the vows have ceased or have been dissolved by dispensation.

487. The simple profession, both temporary and perpetual, renders actions against the vows illicit, but not invalid, unless invalidity is decreed by special law. (In the Society of Jesus, for example, the profession in reference to the simple vow of chastity renders an attempted marriage invalid.) Solemn profession renders contrary actions invalid, if they are of such a nature that they can be annulled by the Church (**Canon 579**).

In Canon 579 the Code briefly indicates the distinction between simple and solemn religious vows. In their essence the vows are the same, whether simple or solemn, but the Canon Law introduces a distinction between them by adding to the solemn vows effects which are not given to the simple vows by the Church.

LEGAL STATUS OF SIMPLY PROFESSED RELIGIOUS WITH REGARD TO TEMPORAL GOODS

488. Every simply professed religious, whether in temporary or in perpetual vows, retains the ownership of his goods and the capacity to acquire other goods (within the limits of Canon 569), unless the constitutions provide otherwise. Whatever the religious after his profession acquires by work, or what is given to him in consideration of his being a religious, he acquires for the community (**Canon 580, §§ 1–2**).[90a]

489. The arrangements regarding the cession and disposition of his goods, which Canon 569 orders the novice to make before his profession, cannot be afterwards changed at will by the professed, unless the constitutions allow this, but a change may be made with the permission of the supreme head of the religious organization: in orders of nuns, the permission of the local Ordinary is required, and, if the monastery is subject to the regulars, also the permission of the regular superior must be obtained. The permission can be given only when there is no question of making a change in favor of the religious organization to which the professed belongs, at least not one which involves a notable part of the property. If the religious should leave the organization, this cession and disposition of his goods is cancelled by that very fact, and he regains the rights he had before making such arrangements (**Canon 580, § 3**).

With the exception of religious communities of women in

[90a] Concerning military pensions and payments, cfr. App. III, 25, e.

solemn vows, the supreme superior of the orders and congregations may permit the change of the administrator and of the persons who were given the use and usufruct of the goods of the individual religious by the first arrangement before profession. To avoid all suspicion that the community seeks to get hold of the goods or property, the Code rules that, when such changes are made, they must not be made in favor of the religious community, at least not with respect to a notable part of the goods. One third—according to others one fourth —would be a notable part, and the administration, use or usufruct of such a portion should not be given to the community when the change is made.

LEGAL STATUS OF SOLEMNLY PROFESSED RELIGIOUS WITH REGARD TO TEMPORAL GOODS

490. The simply professed religious cannot validly renounce the right of ownership of his goods until sixty days before solemn profession, when, conditionally on his future solemn profession, he must renounce all goods which he actually has in favor of a person or persons of his choice. Special indults given by the Holy See to organizations with solemn vows, allowing their members to retain title to their property, are to remain in force. When solemn profession has been made, the formalities of the civil law necessary to make the renunciation of the goods of the professed valid in the civil courts should be immediately complied with (**Canon 581**).

491. After solemn profession, saving special indults of the Holy See, all goods which may in any way accrue to the individual religious revert either (1) to the order, or province, or house, according to the constitutions, if the Order is capable of holding title to property; or (2) to the Holy See, if the Order is incapacitated by the special law of the Church from possessing (i.e., holding legal title to) property (**Canon 582**).[90b] The Council of Trent (Sessio XXV, cap. iii, *de Regul. et Monial.*) ruled that all monasteries and houses, both of men and women, may henceforth possess real property, with the exception of the houses of the Franciscan Friars, the Capuchins and those called Minor Observants.

In connection with the renunciation of all goods and pos-

[90b] Concerning military pensions and payments, cfr. App. III, 25, e.

sessions by those who are about to make solemn profession, commentators discuss the question whether they may dispose not only of those goods which they actually own and possess, but also of goods which will come to them in the future. In the former law it was generally considered to come within the rights of the person about to make solemn profession to determine to whom the goods should go which he was to get in future but to which he had a *jus certum*. In reference to other goods which he had only some hope of getting, or which might accidentally come to him, the Sacred Congregation of Bishops and Regulars had decreed that recourse is to be had to that Congregation in each individual case. Under the law of the Code it is certain that the person about to make solemn profession can dispose only of goods which he actually has. It may, however, be justly said that, if a person has a *jus certum*—or a vested right, as it would be called in our civil law—he actually has a right which has money value, and the *Commentarium pro Religiosis* (I, 79) and several other commentators of the Code are correct in saying that the person has a right to dispose of a vested right. Under the laws that are fairly generally followed in the States of the American Union, children have no vested right in the goods and property of the parents, but at most a hope that the parents will give them a share in their goods by last will. There is a right of inheritance of the children in case of intestacy of the father, but whether that right will ever give them anything depends on a contingency which may never happen—that is, the death of their father without a will. It may be noted that the Council of Trent (Sessio XXV, cap. xvi, *de Regul. et Monial.*) demanded that the renunciation be made with the permission of the bishop of the diocese where the monastery was located. The Code abolishes this part of the law.

RENUNCIATION FORBIDDEN IN COMMUNITIES WITH SIMPLE VOWS

492. Simply professed religious in religious congregations are not permitted: (1) to give away or make donation of their goods; (2) to change the last will which the Code (cfr. Canon 569) wants them to make at the end of the novitiate before they take the first temporary vows, unless they have received the permission of the Holy See. If the matter is urgent and

there is no time for recourse to the Holy See, the major superior may give permission, or, if he cannot be reached in time, the local superior (**Canon 583**).

The regulations regarding the last will and testament are obligatory in all congregations—i.e., organizations which have simple vows, including diocesan congregations. The last will is to be made by the novices before the first vows (cfr. Canon 569). The Code does not state what is to be done in case the novice did not make a last will. It seems that after the taking of the first vows the last will cannot be made without permission of the Holy See, because Canon 583 requires this permission even for a change of the last will. Even minors must make their last will, although this is invalid in civil law: later, when they come of age, the will must be legalized.[91]

PROFESSION AND LOSS OF BENEFICES AND PROPER DIOCESE

493. After one year from the making of any religious profession, all parochial benefices which the religious possessed become vacant; other benefices become vacant after three years of profession (**Canon 584**). Ecclesiastical offices which the cleric held before he became a religious, are lost by tacit renunciation as soon as he makes profession (cfr. Canon 188). If a priest who was pastor of a parish enters a religious community, the bishop must keep the parish open for one year after the first profession. Other benefices must be left open until three years after the date of the first profession. In the United States, parishes are practically the only benefices.

494. On taking perpetual vows, whether simple or solemn, a religious automatically loses his own proper diocese which he had as a secular (**Canon 585**). The same rule is repeated in Canon 115 which states that by religious profession one is excardinated from his own diocese in the manner stated in Canon 585. Now, in the exempt religious organizations, the major superior issues the dimissorial letters for the ordination of his subjects. In non-exempt communities the superior cannot issue dimissorials, unless a special indult has been obtained, for non-exempt religious follow the law for seculars in the matter of ordination (cfr. Canons 964 and 956). The non-

[91] Vermeersch-Creusen, ''Epitome,'' I, 260, n. 569.

exempt religious are to be ordained by the bishop of their domicile: they need not take the oath to stay permanently in the diocese, for they are already incardinated in their own religious organization, in which case Canon 956 states that the oath is not required. The religious has his domicile in the place where, by the order of his superiors, he is stationed as a member of the religious family of a certain house. The bishop of the place where such house is located ordains as *episcopus proprius,* and, if he wishes, he may issue dimissorial letters to another bishop to ordain these religious.[92]

MANNER OF RECTIFYING INVALID PROFESSIONS

495. A religious profession which is invalidated by some external impediment does not become valid by subsequent acts: it is necessary either to obtain a *sanatio* from the Holy See, or to make the profession over again, after the religious has discovered the nullity of his profession, and the impediment has been removed.

If the profession was invalid merely through lack of internal consent, it is validated by giving consent, provided the consent on the part of the religious organization has not been revoked.

If there is grave question of the validity of the religious profession, and the religious refuses either to ask for a *sanatio ad cautelam* from the Holy See or to renew the profession *ad cautelam,* the matter shall be laid before the Holy See (**Canon 586**).

If it is certain that the profession was invalid, the professed is not at liberty to leave nor can the superior give him permission to leave, for the Code states that, when there are grave reasons against the validity of the profession, the case must go to the Holy See if the professed does not want to stay. The formalities of the canonical process to establish proof of the invalidity were fixed by the Council of Trent (Sessio XXV, cap. xix, *De Regul. et Monial.*) and the Constitution "Si datam" of Pope Benedict XIV, March 7, 1748. The Code does not renew these laws, nor does it state any formalities of the process, but it orders the case to be referred to the Holy See.

If the profession of a religious in minor orders is invalid

[92] "Commentarium pro Religiosis," II, 299 (On the domicile and ordination of non-exempt religious).

because he practiced deceit, and the profession is declared null and void, he shall be reduced to the laical state; if he is in major orders, he remains *ipso facto* suspended until the Holy See shall have made other provision in his case (cfr. Canon 2387).

If a profession was invalid on account of an invalidating impediment then existing, and if such impediment later on ceases or is abolished by a change of the law, the profession is not *ipso facto* validated, but must be treated in the manner described above in Canon 586.

TITLE XII

OF STUDIES IN CLERICAL RELIGIOUS ORGANIZATIONS

496. Every clerical religious organization shall have houses of study approved by the General Chapter or by the superiors, and, according to Canon 554, those religious only shall be placed in the houses of study who are exemplary in the observance of the religious life. In the houses of study a perfect community life must be observed, as otherwise the students cannot be promoted to orders.

If an organization or a province cannot have properly equipped houses of study, or if it has them but the superiors find it difficult to send the students there, the religious students may be sent to a well equipped house of studies of another province or another religious organization, to the episcopal seminary, or to a Catholic university.

Religious who are sent to a distant place for study, are not allowed to board in private houses, but must live either in some house of their own organization or, if that is impossible, in the house of another religious community of men, or in a seminary or other ecclesiastical institution in charge of priests and approved by the ecclesiastical authority (**Canon 587**).

According to Canon 606, the superiors cannot permit their subjects to live outside a house of their own organization for more than six months without the permission of the Holy See, except for the purpose of study.

497. During the entire course of studies, the religious shall be under the special care of a prefect or master, who shall

instruct and guide them in their religious life. The prefect or master must have the same qualifications as are required in the master of novices by Canon 559. The superiors shall see that the regulations of Canon 595 for all religious are most perfectly observed in the house of studies (**Canon 588**).

498. After proper instruction in the lower studies, the religious shall engage in the study of philosophy for *at least two years,* and in theology for *at least four years,* following the teaching of St. Thomas in accordance with Canon 1366 and the instructions of the Apostolic See. During the term of studies no duties shall be imposed on the professors and students which may interfere in any way with their study or classes. The supreme superior, and in particular cases also other superiors, may exempt professors and students from some of the community exercises and even from the choir (especially the Nocturnal Hours), whenever they judge it necessary for the sake of the studies (**Canon 589**).

499. For at least five years after the completion of their studies, religious priests shall be examined annually by learned Fathers on the various branches of theology, the matter for the examinations being designated a reasonable interval beforehand. Priests who teach theology, canon law, or scholastic philosophy, are exempted from the examinations, and the major superiors may exempt others for grave reasons (**Canon 590**).

500. In every large community (*domus formata*) must be held at least once monthly a discussion on moral or liturgical cases, to which may be added, at the discretion of the superior, a sermon on dogmatic and kindred subjects. All professed clerics living in the respective community who are students of theology, or who have finished their studies, and the priests of the community must assist at these conferences, unless the constitutions rule otherwise (**Canon 591**). In some religious organizations the constitutions ordain that priests only shall take part in the conferences.

501. Regarding clerics who study at secular universities, a Decree of the Sacred Congregation of Seminaries and Universities [93] instructs bishops and religious superiors to send only priests who, they feel certain, will be an honor to the Church. It also declares that these priests, if newly ordained, are bound

[93] April 20, 1918; *Acta Ap. Sedis,* X, 237.

to submit to the annual examinations, and that their graduation from the university does not change the obedience they owe to their ecclesiastical superior.

OF THE DUTIES AND PRIVILEGES OF RELIGIOUS

CHAPTER I

OF THE DUTIES OF RELIGIOUS

502. All the religious are bound by the common obligations of the clergy outlined in Canons 124–142, unless the contrary is clear from the context or the nature of the law (**Canon 592**).

503. All religious, both superiors and subjects, must not only faithfully keep the vows which they have taken, but must also live according to the rules and constitutions proper to the individual organizations, and in this manner strive for religious perfection (**Canon 593**). In connection with this Canon the obligations of the vows should be studied. We do not deem it necessary to discuss these obligations since all canonists and moralists treat of the usual three religious vows of obedience, poverty and chastity. Besides, the obligation of the vow of poverty in many of its details depends on the constitutions of each organization. Another obligation mentioned in Canon 593 is the duty to observe the rules and constitutions. Moralists speak of the obligation of every religious to strive after the perfection of his state of life, and they declare it an additional obligation distinct from the duty of keeping the vows and observing the rule or constitutions. The Code merely states that they are bound to observe the vows and the rules and constitutions, and thus strive after religious perfection. It is similar to the obligation of the Christian to strive after Christian perfection by observing the commandments of God and the obligations he owes to his Church, his country and his fellow-men. Priests who are called upon to hear the confessions of religious should peruse the *tractatus de religiosis* in moral theology from time to time so as to keep in touch with the obligations of religious.

504. In every organization the community life shall be followed faithfully by all, even in those things pertaining to food,

clothing and furniture. Whatever is acquired by the religious, including the superiors, must be added to the property of the house, province, or organization, in accordance with Canons 580 and 582: any money, deeds of property and other valuable papers must be deposited in the common treasury. The furniture of the religious must be in harmony with the poverty they have vowed in their profession (**Canon 594**).

505. In connection with this Canon commentators discuss the question whether the *peculium* is lawful in religious communities. The *peculium* means a small amount of goods, money, or of money value, left to the free disposition of the religious. The Code wants all moneys and valuable papers, etc., to be kept in the common treasury from which the superiors entrusted with the administration are to furnish the necessaries for all subjects. This arrangement is an important safeguard of the common life and of the proper observance of the vow of poverty. There are no further explicit statements in the Code on this matter, wherefore the former laws on the subject must be consulted. The Council of Trent [94] has practically the same regulations as the Code, and the Council merely summed up the former laws on the vow of poverty. The conclusions of canonists from the various laws on the *peculium* are, that both the independent and the dependent *peculium* are forbidden by the law of the Church. The terms, independent and dependent, mean that the subject has the *peculium* either independently of the superior or with his consent and under his control. The first is directly against the vow of poverty and is subversive of the common life. The second is not necessarily opposed to the vow of poverty, but the superiors are forbidden by the Council of Trent to give such permission. In communities into which the dependent *peculium* has been introduced by ancient custom, the continuation of the custom may be tolerated, because the Code allows immemorial and centenary customs against the laws of the Code, unless such customs are explicitly rejected by the laws. There is no such clause in Canon 594.

In reference to pensions, bonuses, or other payments made to religious who served in the late European war, the Sacred Congregation of the Religious published a detailed instruction,[95]

---

[94] Sessio XXV, cap. ii, *De Regul. et Monial.*
[95] March 16, 1922; cfr. App. III, 25, e.

discussing whether money thus paid became the property of the religious organization or the personal property of the religious. The principal points decided were: (1) solemnly professed religious have no personal claim to the money, which belongs to their order; (2) simply professed religious whose vows did not cease with the entrance into the army, have no personal claim, and their pay belongs to the religious organization; (3) if their vows ceased with their entrance into the military service, the money belongs to the religious personally.

506. In reference to the literary manuscripts of religious, there was some doubt as to whether they are included under the vow of poverty, since many canonists held that they were, not a *res temporalis*, but rather a *fructus mentis*, and therefore not under the vow. However, the Holy See has declared [96] that they are a product of labor, and, under the general principle that the religious organization has a right to the products of the labor of its professed members, the manuscripts are the property of the religious organization. The Holy See has also declared that the religious has no right to publish the manuscript without the permission of the religious superior, and may not give it to a publisher to publish it with the *Imprimatur* of the local Ordinary, if his religious superior has denied permission to publish the same.[97]

Obligations Regarding Religious Exercises, Confession, Wearing of the Religious Garb

507. The superiors shall see that all religious: (1) make a retreat each year; (2) are present at the daily Mass, and make the meditation and other spiritual exercises prescribed by the rule and constitutions; (3) make their confession at least once a week.

The superiors shall promote frequent and daily Holy Communion; frequent and even daily Holy Communion must be freely allowed to religious who are properly disposed. If, however, a religious has since the last confession given grave scandal to the community, or has committed an external mortal

[96] Sacred Congregation of Religious, July 13, 1913; *Acta Ap. Sedis,* V, 366.

[97] Sacred Congregation of Religious, June 15, 1911; *Acta Ap. Sedis,* III, 270.

sin, the superior can forbid that religious to go to Holy Communion until he (or she) has gone again to confession. If any religious organization, whether of simple or solemn vows, has certain days for Holy Communion prescribed in the rule or constitutions, such regulations shall have merely directive force (**Canon 595**).

508. All religious shall wear the habit proper to their organization in the house as well as outside, unless in the judgment of the major superior—or in the case of necessity, of the local superior—there is a grave reason to make an exception (**Canon 596**). In Canon 592, the Code stated that all religious are bound by the common obligations of clerics: consequently, if their own constitutions do not prescribe a habit proper to the organization, the religious are bound to wear the garb of the secular clergy. In the United States and in other countries where the Catholics are scattered among a large non-Catholic population, particular laws provide that priests and religious shall not wear the cassock or the religious habit in public. For the United States, the Third Plenary Council of Baltimore prescribes the manner in which the secular clergy and the religious men should be clothed when they go out.[98] The important principle is that they should be known by their clothes as priests or religious, for, while the cassock or the habit might be ridiculed instead of influencing respect for religion, the ministers of any religion, Catholic or non-Catholic, are highly respected by the vast majority of the people of the United States. The Sisters who have the care of the sick in hospitals are, as a rule, obliged by the rules of the medical profession to be dressed in white when on duty as nurses. This is sufficient reason to dispense with the wearing of the proper religious habit for the time the Sisters are on duty, and there is no necessity for making them wear the white dress over their habits, which becomes a great hardship in the hot and sultry climate of summer.

The Law of Enclosure

509. The papal enclosure must be observed in all houses of religious men and women with solemn vows, even in the small houses or residences (the *domus non formatæ*). Under the law

[98] C. Baltimorense Plen. III, n. 77.

of enclosure falls the whole house inhabited by the religious, with the gardens and groves or orchards reserved exclusively to the religious. The church with the adjoining sacristy, the hospice for strangers, and the parlors (which should, in so far as possible, be near the door of the house), are excepted from the enclosure.

The places subject to the law of enclosure shall be indicated by public notices. The major superior or the General Chapter (as the constitutions may determine), and in case of nuns with solemn vows the bishop, shall have the right and duty to fix accurately the limits of the enclosure, and also to change them for legitimate reasons (**Canon 597**).[98a]

510. Within the enclosure of the houses of men in solemn vows, the admission of women of any age, nobility or state is forbidden under any pretext. Exception from this law is made for the wives of the highest actual rulers of states and their lady attendants (**Canon 598**).

If a house of men in solemn vows has attached to it a school or college for its own students (boys who are educated there to prepare them for entrance into the novitiate), or conducts other institutions proper to the order, at least a separate part of the building should be reserved, if possible, for the exclusive occupation of the religious, and this part should be subject to the enclosure. Even to the places outside the enclosure, which are set apart for extern or intern students or for other purposes of the order, women shall not be admitted except for a good reason and with the permission of the superior (**Canon 599**).

Enclosure of Nuns

511. No person of whatever sex, age, family, or condition of life may be admitted within the enclosure of nuns (Sisters with solemn vows) without the permission of the Holy See. The only exceptions granted are as follows:

(1) The local Ordinary, or the regular superior, or another Visitor delegated by them, may at the time of visitation enter the enclosure for the purpose of inspection only, and on condition that he is accompanied by at least one cleric or religious of mature age;

(2) The confessor, or the priest who takes his place, may

[98a] Concerning certain communities of women, cfr. App. III, 26, a.

with due precautions enter the enclosure to administer the Sacraments to the sick or to assist the dying;

(3) The highest actual ruler of the state with his wife and escort, may enter the enclosure, and also Cardinals;

(4) The Mother Superior may, with previous habitual permission of the local Ordinary and the observance of due precautions, admit within the enclosure doctors, surgeons and others whose help is needed. If necessity urges, and there is no time to ask the approval of the bishop for the admittance of the aforesaid persons, the permission is presumed by law (**Canon 600**).

The Code states that the actual rulers of states with their wives and proper escorts may enter the enclosure of the monasteries of men as well as those of nuns. Commentators discuss whether the term "rulers" refers to monarchs only, or also to presidents of states which have a republican form of government. While some commentators restrict that privilege to monarchs, many extend it to all who hold the highest governmental power in a state. That latter view is supported by the wording of the Code "qui supremum actu tenent populorum principatum." In the United States the President of the entire federation of States and the governors of the individual states come under the head of those "qui supremum principatum tenent." Each state of the American Union has its own legal existence as a state, and has its own government independent of every other state and of the federal government: the individual states have ceded certain rights to the federal governments, but they retain their sovereignty. Wherefore, the governor of a state holds sovereign power in the state. The privilege granted by the Code lasts only as long as the head of the state holds the highest governmental office. The supreme heads of states and their wives enjoy this privilege, not only in their own, but also in foreign countries, for the Code does not restrict it, and the former Canon Law had no such restriction in the case of kings and queens and other monarchs. Some commentators holds that the privilege is granted but to Catholic heads of states and Catholic wives, but the Code does not mention any such restriction.

512. Commentators discuss the question whether women may be allowed to enter the enclosure of monasteries of men in

religious processions held through the cloister, garden, etc. Pope Pius V had granted such a concession to the Carthusians of the Monastery of Monte Vergine, and it seems that this privilege was afterwards extended to all regulars. In his Constitution "Ubi gratiæ," Pope Gregory XIII revoked the concession and several Decrees of the Sacred Congregation of Rites—notably those of Sept. 30, 1628, and June 11, 1629—plainly state that the concession of Pope Pius V has been revoked. The Code forbids all women to enter the enclosure, with the exception of the wives of actual heads of states.

513. If nuns with papal enclosure desire to have a school attached to their convent, special arrangements must be made with the Holy See, for the nuns are not permitted to leave the enclosure for the sake of teaching and they are forbidden to admit even girls or women within the enclosure.

CANONICAL PENALTIES FOR THE VIOLATION OF THE ENCLOSURE

514. In virtue of Canon 2342, women who violate the enclosure of male regulars, and superiors or others, who introduce or admit within the enclosure females of any age whatsoever, incur *ipso facto* excommunication, reserved *simpliciter* to the Holy See. Furthermore, the religious who introduce or admit them, shall be deprived of their office, if they hold any, and of the active and passive vote. It is to be noted that the Code forbids the admission or introduction into the enclosure of "females of any age whatsoever," which phrase seems to be used by the Code to end the controversy as to the admission of infant girls. If the women who enter the enclosure are unaware of the penalty of excommunication, or that entrance is forbidden, or that the place which they enter is within the enclosure, they do not incur the excommunication, provided their ignorance is not *crassa* or *supina*. Girls under the age of puberty, though perhaps guilty of grievous sin, and women of unsound mind, do not incur the excommunication according to the general principles of the Code in the matter of penalties. The same excuse from the penalty holds good where a woman enters the enclosure constrained by grave fear, or by violence, or through necessity.

515. The excommunication falls on all, superiors and all others whoever they may be, religious or seculars, members of

the monastery or strangers, who admit or introduce women into the enclosure. The Code, therefore, punishes both the women who unlawfully enter the enclosure and those who coöperate with them to effect their entrance. While the exact meaning of "admit" and "introduce" is not so clear as to decide with certainty all cases of coöperation, it may be stated with good reason that all those who are in collusion with the woman, those who render indispensable aid to her committing the crime, those without whose help or advice the crime would not be committed, and those who command or commission the woman to violate the law of enclosure, incur the excommunication. The one who commands (*mandans*) the commission of a crime, is in law considered the principal author of the crime. The others who assist secondarily, are not held liable for the full guilt of the crime in which they participate, if it would have been committed anyhow without their help, or if they only made the commission of the crime easier. He who withdraws his coöperation in the crime before his action has taken effect, is free from punishment, though the other party could not be dissuaded from committing the crime (cfr. Canon 2209 on Coöperation). Those who coöperate negatively by neglecting their duty of preventing a woman from entering the enclosure do not incur the excommunication, as is evident from Canon 2231, unless the circumstances are such that the neglect to stop the woman is equivalent to commission of the crime by mutual agreement.

516. As to the violation of the enclosure of nuns, Canon 2342, n. 1, rules that the following incur *ipso facto* excommunication reserved *simpliciter* to the Holy See: Persons of whatever class, condition or sex, who violate the enclosure of nuns, by entering into their monasteries without lawful permission; likewise those who introduce or admit them. If they are clerics, they are furthermore to be suspended for a time to be determined by the Ordinary according to the gravity of their guilt.

The conditions as to introducing or admitting persons are the same as those discussed under the violation of the enclosure of the monasteries of men. As to the persons forbidden under excommunication to enter the nun's enclosure, the law forbids all persons of either sex to enter, whereas in monasteries of men only persons of the opposite sex are forbidden admission. Under the former law, of the Constitution "Apostolicæ Sedis" of Pope

Pius IX, children under the age of puberty, who had attained the use of reason, were also subject to the excommunication, if with knowledge of the censure they entered the enclosure of nuns. As the Code in Canon 2342 does not add "cujuscunque ætatis," it is held by commentators that children under the age of puberty do not incur the excommunication, nor the persons who admit them into the nun's enclosure; but Canon 600 certainly forbids their admittance.[99]

EXTENT OF THE ENCLOSURE OBLIGATION IN THE CASE OF NUNS

517. After her profession, no nun may, under any pretext whatsoever, leave the monastery even for a short time without a special indult of the Holy See, except in the case of imminent danger of death or some other very serious evil. If time permits, this danger must be recognized as such in writing by the local Ordinary (**Canon 601**). This obligation also binds nuns who have taken temporary vows previous to the solemn vows, and novices and postulants as long as they remain members of the community. As to postulants, the Holy See has declared that without its permission they may not leave convents subject to papal enclosure to visit their parents or friends or for some other reason.[100] In virtue of Canon 2342, n. 3, nuns who leave the enclosure unlawfully in violation of Canon 601, incur *ipso facto* excommunication reserved *simpliciter* to the Holy See. Some commentators had held that the temporarily professed, the novices and the postulants in the monasteries of nuns are also subject to this censure. This opinion, however, seems to be contrary to the wording of Canon 2342 which inflicts the penalty, and which says that "moniales" incur the penalty. It is a general principle of canon law that, in penalties, the terms must be interpreted in their strict legal meaning. Now, Canon 488, n. 7, which explains the meaning of the term "moniales" in the Code, states that it means religious women who have taken solemn vows.[101]

The Holy See has declared that the nuns who formerly had

[99] Vermeersch-Creusen, "Epitome," I, 301, n. 613.

[100] Sacred Congregation of Religious, Nov. 7, 1916; *Acta Ap. Sedis*, VIII, 446.

[101] The "Commentarium pro Religiosis," IV, 140-145, holds that the nuns who are in temporary vows, prior to the taking of solemn vows, fall under this excommunication.

solemn vows but whose vows have been reduced to simple vows by the authority of the Supreme Pontiff, have no papal enclosure.[102]

518. Access to a monastery of nuns to converse with them was strictly forbidden to all persons, laymen and clerics, bishops and prelates, except when the latter were on official duty. Parents and sons or daughters whose mother had become a nun, were allowed to visit once a week on any day except holydays of obligation, Sundays, Advent, Lent, Fridays, Saturdays and Vigils. Otherwise the written permission of the local Ordinary had to be obtained to speak to a nun. As the Code contains no law forbidding access, nor does it either explicitly or implicitly retain the old law, the latter is to be considered abrogated.

519. The enclosure of the monastery of nuns should be protected on every side in such a manner as to prevent, as far as possible, those within from seeing or being seen by persons outside (**Canon 602**). There are many decrees of the Sacred Congregation of Bishops and Regulars on the proper construction of a monastery of nuns to secure for them absolute privacy and guard them against the distractions of the world and possible danger to their virtue. As the local Ordinary is commissioned by the Code (Canon 603) to watch over the observance of the law of enclosure, it is his duty to see to the proper location and construction of monasteries of nuns. The Holy See desires that there be a suitable garden properly enclosed for the necessary recreation of the nuns.

The enclosure of nuns, even those subject to regulars, is under the vigilance of the local Ordinary who can correct and coerce, even with penalties and censures, all delinquents, not excepting men of religious orders. The custody of the enclosure subject to regulars is confided also to the regular superior who can likewise inflict punishments on the nuns or his other subjects for any delinquencies in this regard (**Canon 603**). The bishop has the exclusive right to determine the limits of the nuns' enclosure (Canon 597); he alone gives permission for persons to enter the enclosure (Canon 600); and decides the cases of necessity in which nuns may leave the enclosure (Canon 601).

[102] Comm. for the Auth. Interp. of the Code, March 1, 1921; cfr. App. III, 26, a.

In other matters touching the enclosure the bishop and the regular superior, if the monastery is subject to the latter, have equal powers to enforce the law of enclosure, but the regular superior's power is naturally confined to his subjects, the community of nuns and religious men subject to him as their superior. Summary of all details of the law on the enclosure of nuns is given in a recent instruction.[103]

ENCLOSURE OF COMMUNITIES IN SIMPLE VOWS

520. In the houses of religious Congregations, whether under papal or diocesan law, the law of enclosure must also be observed, so that no one of the other sex may be admitted excepting those mentioned in Canons 598 and 600, and others whom the superiors, for just and reasonable motives, consider may be admitted. The precept of Canon 599 applies also to houses of religious congregations, whether of men or women. In special circumstances and for grave reasons, the bishop may —except in the case of an exempt clerical institute—safeguard the enclosure by censures; however, he must be always vigilant in having the enclosure duly observed and in correcting any abuses that may arise in this respect (**Canon 604**).

In general, the various communities of men and of women in simple vows should conform themselves to the rules of enclosure for communities in solemn vows. Persons to whom the Code gives the right or privilege of entering the enclosure of the solemnly professed religious, have the same right or privilege in reference to the enclosure of the simply professed religious. A great difference between the two enclosures consists in this, that the superior or superioress of the house of simply professed can give permission to persons to enter the enclosure. The constitutions of the individual congregations may have more detailed rules on admission of persons, especially of those of the opposite sex. As the Sisters of a community of simple vows may be permitted by the local superioress to go out of the house for any reasonable cause, the parlor in the houses of these Sisterhoods need not be separated from the Sisters' parlor by an iron grill, as is prescribed in the houses of Sisters with solemn vows. The same difference exists

[103] Instruction of Sacred Congregation of Religious, Feb. 6, 1924; cfr. App. III, 21, f, 3.

in the church or chapel, for, in the Sisterhoods with solemn vows, the choir where the Sisters attend Holy Mass must be within the enclosure and separated from the church or chapel by an iron grating with only a small window at which the nuns receive Holy Communion. The Sisterhoods with simple vows do not need this separation since they are allowed to enter the church or chapel, though they should occupy a place separate from the people.

521. All those who have the custody of the enclosure shall carefully see that, during the visits of outsiders, the discipline is not relaxed nor the religious spirit weakened by useless conversation (**Canon 605**). Religious superiors must take care that the laws of their constitutions are faithfully observed regarding the egress of subjects from the cloister and their receiving visits from or visiting outsiders. It is not lawful for superiors—without prejudice to Canons 621–624, on going out in quest of alms—to permit their subjects to remain outside the house of their own institute, except for a just and grave cause and for as brief a period as possible in accordance with the constitutions: for an absence of more than six months, except for the purpose of studies, the permission of the Holy See is always required (**Canon 606**). The superioresses and the local Ordinaries shall vigilantly see that the religious, except in a case of necessity, do not go out singly from the house (**Canon 607**).

The Code puts down only a few general principles on the matter of the egress of religious from their houses: the constitutions are to regulate the particulars. Commentators discuss the question of the absence of a religious without the permission of the superior or superioress. There are a few authors who hold that going out without permission is in itself a mortal sin, and a short absence may—just like the *parvitas materiæ* in other sins—make it only a venial sin. In any case, the majority of canonists who discuss the question seem agreed that the mere going out without permission is neither flight nor apostasy, and, if he stays out only a short time, the religious is not guilty of mortal sin. The commentators, however, do not agree on what constitutes a short time. Whether a space of twenty-four hours is to be called a notable length of time, is not certain. When authors speak about going out at night without permission, they usually attribute the gravity of the violation of the law of this Canon to the scandal that people would take at seeing a religious outside at such an hour. However, it is difficult to see how people can tell whether one is out with permission and on necessary business, or whether one is out unlawfully and for the purpose of enjoyment, or perhaps sinful motives. There seems to be no doubt that frequent going out without permission and staying away all day and perhaps even at night, is a grave disturbance of religious discipline. Particular statutes can, of course, fix penalties for going out without permission, but they cannot make something a grave matter which is not such of its nature, unless particular circumstances make this matter unusually important. The law against fugitives and apostates is contained in Canons 644 and 645.

DUTIES OF THE SACRED MINISTRY AND DIVINE WORSHIP

522. The superiors shall see that, without prejudice to religious discipline, the religious subjects designated by them cheerfully discharge the sacred ministry, whether in their own churches, or in those of others, or in public oratories, especially in the dioceses in which they live, when their assistance is required by the local Ordinary or by the pastors for the spiritual needs of the faithful. Reciprocally, the local Ordinary and the pastors shall willingly use the services of the religious, especially of those resident in the diocese, for the sacred ministry and particularly for the administration of the sacrament of penance (**Canon 608**).

If the church attached to the residence of the religious community is also parochial, all the pertinent regulations of Canon 415 are to be observed (**Canon 609, § 1**). That Canon speaks of the relations between the cathedral or collegiate Chapter and the pastor of the cathedral or collegiate church. The religious community has the rights over the church which that Canon attributes to the cathedral or collegiate Chapter, while the religious appointed to the care of souls has the rights attributed by that same Canon to the pastor.

523. A church of religious women, whether with solemn or simple vows, cannot be made parochial (**Canon 609, § 2**). Canon 712 provides that, in the churches or oratories of re-

ligious women, the local Ordinary may permit the erection of associations for women only, or of pious unions whose object is purely spiritual, and whose members enjoy the communication of spiritual favors only. The evident purpose of the law is to minimize the Sisters' intercourse with the laity, with the consequent distraction and possible disturbance of religious discipline and recollection.

524. The superiors must see that the celebration of the divine services in their own churches be not a hindrance to the catechetical instruction or the preaching of the Gospel given in the parochial church; it pertains to the local Ordinary to judge whether or not this hindrance exists (**Canon 609,** § 3).

In the United States the clerical religious communities have, as a rule, a parish attached to their monasteries and residences. In such cases, they have Masses for the people, the same sermons and instructions as the bishop orders for all other parishes of the diocese, and thus there can be no question of conflict of their services with those in another parish church. If the people of their own choice prefer to go to the services in the parish of the religious, they are doing what they have a right to do. However, a certain difficulty arises inasmuch as, in many dioceses, the main source of revenue is derived from the collections taken up during the Masses and other services on Sundays and holydays of obligation: if many of the parishioners stay away from their own parish and go to another parish, their own parish loses a considerable amount of revenue. To overcome this difficulty, some dioceses have adopted the assessment system, whereby the heads of families and self-supporting single men and women are taxed to contribute a certain sum each month to their own parish.

If the religious have no parish attached to their house, they may have Holy Mass and other services in their churches or chapels, and admit the people who come to assist at these services, but Canon 609 gives the Ordinary the right to judge whether or not the services at those churches or chapels conflict with catechetical instructions and the explanation of the Gospel at the parish church. If the bishop thinks that they conflict, he has a right to demand that the religious arrange their services at hours that avoid conflict. If the religious refuse to accede to the orders of the bishop, because they believe that their services are unnecessarily interfered with, nothing remains but to put the matter before the Sacred Congregation of the Religious; meanwhile, the religious must comply with the orders of the bishop. Canon 1171 states that the Ordinary can for a just reason fix the hours of the sacred services in the churches and chapels consecrated or blessed for divine worship, but, when there is question of churches of an exempt religious organization, he cannot fix the hours for the services; [104] nevertheless, the right given to the bishop in Canon 609, is again cited in Canon 1171 to modify the exemption of the exempt religious communities. While the bishop cannot positively order that they hold services at certain hours, he can stop them from having services at those hours which in his judgment interfere with the preaching of the Gospel and the catechetical instructions at the parish church.

OBLIGATION OF RECITING THE DIVINE OFFICE IN CHOIR

525. In religious organizations of men or women, in which exists the obligation of the choir, the Divine Office must be recited daily in common, conformably to the constitutions, in every house with at least four religious who are bound to choir, and who are not at the time lawfully impeded: if the constitutions so prescribe, even less than four are obliged to recite the Office in choir. The Mass corresponding to the Office of the day, according to the rubrics, must also be celebrated daily in the communities of men, and, where possible, even in the communities of women. In these organizations, whether of men or women, the solemnly professed members who have been absent from choir must recite the canonical hours privately, except the lay brothers and lay sisters (**Canon 610**).

The Code does not state which of the religious organizations are obliged to the recitation of the divine office in choir, but, from the latter part of Canon 610, it can be inferred that the Code supposes this obligation to exist only in communities of men or of women with solemn vows. However, the law does not state that all religious communities of solemn vows have the obligation of choir; this fact must be learned from the particular laws of the individual organizations. Before the

---

[104] Sacred Congregation of Bishops and Regulars, March 14, 1879; *Acta S. Sedis*, XI, 603-613.

promulgation of the Code, the opinion that the obligation did not bind the small houses or residences was regarded as probable, since strictly speaking they were not religious communities. The Code, however, puts large and small houses on the same level, and there is no serious doubt today that the small houses are equally bound to recite the Divine Office if a sufficient number of men bound to choir duty are able to attend choir. The obligation rests on the community as a body, not on the individual religious, but as the simply professed religious clerics (that is, those destined for the priesthood) are members of the community, they share this obligation of the community equally with the solemnly professed.

526. There is some discussion among commentators on the Code as to whether Canon 610 means that all religious (even the various communities of simple vows), whose constitutions prescribe an office, either the *Officium parvum B.V. M.* or the ordinary canonical hours of the Roman Breviary, are bound under grave obligation. The majority incline to what seems to be the opinion better supported in law—namely, that the Code does not ordain anything new in Canon 610, but merely repeats the former law. Besides, the last words of that Canon (In these organizations, whether of men or women, the solemnly professed members . . .), indicate sufficiently that the Canon merely refers to the old law in which as a general rule (with a few exceptions such as the Society of Jesus and the Visitation Nuns) the religious communities with solemn vows had the obligation of the choir. The Holy See has declared that Canon 610 imposes the obligation of the Conventual Mass also on all religious houses of communities of women with simple vows, whose constitutions approved by the Holy See impose the obligation of the choir.[105]

Correspondence of Religious

527. All religious, whether men or women, are at liberty to send letters, free from all inspection, to the Holy See and its Legate in the country, to their Cardinal Protector, to their own major superiors, to the superior of their house when he is absent, to the local Ordinary to whom they are subject, and, in case of nuns subject to the jurisdiction of regulars, to the

[105] Committee for the Auth. Interp. of Code, May 20, 1923; cfr. App. III, 26, b.

major superiors of the Order; from all these persons the religious, men or women, may also receive letters which nobody else has the right to open (**Canon 611**).

The constitutions of the various religious organizations usually have very definite regulations as to the writing and receiving of letters. The Code does not state that the superiors have the right to read the letters sent out or received by the subjects, but it supposes such a right in Canon 611. The sacrifice of this right of privacy is one of the many sacrifices which a religious organization demands of those who desire to become members of the community. The *Normæ* according to which the Holy See wants the constitutions of new congregations to be drawn up, provided explicitly that letters sent or received must pass through the hands of the local superior, who shall use his (or her) privilege of reading them with prudence and charity and under the seal of secrecy. The last words "under the seal of secrecy" are of importance, as the natural law imposes that obligation on the superiors in the exercise of the right which the constitutions give them. Canon 611 enumerates the exceptions to the right of the superiors to inspect the correspondence of their subjects. Letters to confessors and spiritual advisers are not mentioned as excepted from the right of inspection. The law does not seem to contemplate that such communications should be made in writing.

The Code mentions another exception to the right of inspection of the correspondence of religious: Canon 2025, dealing with the process of Beatification and Canonization, states that the letters of religious who were well acquainted with the servant of God are to be sent either directly to the *Promoter Fidei* or the local Ordinary, or given to their confessor for transmission.

OBLIGATION OF RELIGIOUS IN REFERENCE TO ORDERS OF THE BISHOP ON PUBLIC WORSHIP

528. Besides the law of Canon 1345, if the local Ordinary prescribes from a public motive the ringing of the bells, certain prayers or sacred solemnities, all religious, even the exempt, must obey, without prejudice to the constitutions and privileges of each organization (**Canon 612**).

Canon 1345 states that on Sundays and holydays of obligation the Church desires that a short instruction either on the Gospel or on some part of Christian doctrine should be given in all churches and public oratories during the Masses which the people attend. If the local Ordinary has prescribed this to be done, and has given timely directions on the point, all priests are bound by this order of the bishop, even the religious in their own churches notwithstanding their privilege of exemption.

The bishop may for a public cause order certain prayers to be said and functions to be held throughout the diocese, or throughout a certain city, county, etc. This general order of the bishop binds even the religious communities, exempt and non-exempt, to conduct such services in their churches and public oratories. The Council of Trent (Sessio XXV, cap. xiii, *De Regular. et Monial.*) ruled that all exempted persons—secular as well as regular clerics, and even monks—on being summoned to public processions shall attend; those only are excepted who always live in strict enclosure. The Code states that it must be a public cause for which these special services are ordered, and it can be inferred from the wording of Canon 612 that the order of the bishop must be general, not for a church of the religious in particular. The prayers prescribed by the bishop at Mass (e.g., the *oratio imperata*) must be said by all religious who say Mass in the diocese. If some religious organization has special concessions from the Holy See by which they are exempted from the obligations which Canon 612 imposes, these concessions remain in force.

CHAPTER II

OF PRIVILEGES

529. Every religious organization enjoys those privileges only which are contained in the Code, or have been directly conceded to it by the Apostolic See, every communication of privileges being henceforth excluded. The privileges which a regular Order enjoys, belong also to the nuns of the same Order, in so far as they are capable of enjoying them (**Canon 613**).

There is no difficulty about the privileges which have been

granted directly to the individual religious organizations. The archives of the headquarters of the respective religious bodies and other sources can be consulted to know what privileges have been granted to them by the Holy See. The general principles on privileges are contained in Canons 63–79 (cfr. above, nn. 46–48).

In reference to the communication of privileges, there is a controversy among commentators of the Code as to whether Canon 613 revokes those privileges which a religious organization had through the communication of privileges. That the privileges acquired by communication are revoked is held by Führich, Leitner, Blat, Chelodi; that they remain in force is held by Fanfani, Brandys, Augustine, Vermeersch-Creusen, Larraona (in the "Commentarium pro Religiosis"), Schäfer, Prümmer. It does not seem likely that the Code revokes the privileges obtained by communication by those words "Every religious organization enjoys those privileges only which are contained in the Code, etc." For those privileges are acquired rights, and in many instances these rights were granted in remuneration for the work that the religious Orders had done for the Church by heroic sacrifices. According to Canon 71 the privileges contained in the Code are revoked by a general law; other privileges are governed by Canon 60 which states that no rescripts are revoked by a contrary law, unless the law states otherwise. Again, Canon 4 rules that acquired rights and privileges which have been granted heretofore by the Apostolic See, and are still in use, remain unimpaired, unless they are explicitly revoked by the Canons of the Code. Now, Canon 613 contains no explicit revocation of the privileges acquired in the past by communication, but only an explicit prohibition of the acquisition of privileges by communication in future (see Volume II, App. III, 27).

ALL RELIGIOUS HAVE THE PRIVILEGES OF CLERICS

530. Religious, even lay religious, and novices, enjoy the privileges of clerics enumerated in Canons 119–123 (**Canon 614**). These privileges (cfr. above, nn. 91–94) are deemed necessary by the Church for the dignity of the clerical and the religious state, just as the common obligations of clerics

are considered necessary for the honor and dignity of the religious. Wherefore, Canon 592 stated that the religious are bound by these obligations in so far as they are applicable to the religious.

The Privilege of Exemption of Regulars

531. Regulars, both men and women (including the novices), except those nuns who are not subject to regular superiors, are exempt together with their houses and churches from the jurisdiction of the local Ordinary with the exception of the cases expressed in law (**Canon 615**).

Regulars unlawfully absent from their house, even under the pretext of having recourse to their superiors, do not enjoy the privilege of exemption. Regulars who have committed a crime outside their house, and are not punished by their superior after he had been informed of the fact, may be punished by the local Ordinary even though they may have legitimately left their house and have returned to it (**Canon 616**).

If abuses have crept into the houses and churches of regulars or of other exempt religious, and after a warning the superior neglects to provide a remedy, the local Ordinary is bound to refer the matter immediately to the Apostolic See. A small house (*domus non formata*) remains under the special vigilance of the local Ordinary, who, if abuses arise which are a source of scandal to the faithful, can himself deal provisionally with them (**Canon 617**).

A brief sketch of the history of the exemption is given by Wernz,[106] extending from the first concession of this kind to the monastery of Bobbio by Pope Honorius I to its full development at the accession of Boniface VIII. The restrictions imposed on exemption by the latter Pope, the renewed extension of it by Pope Sixtus IV, and the limitations of that indult by the Fifth Lateran Council and especially by the Council of Trent, indicate what an agitated history the exemption of regulars has had. As the religious orders wanted freedom of action in developing their organization and in carrying on the work proper to their order, they naturally preferred to deal with one central authority, the Holy See, rather than

---

[106] "Jus Decretalium," III, nn. 701-702.

with many minor authorities. On the other hand, the bishops complained that their rights as supreme heads of the diocese were unduly curtailed when the Holy See gave the religious orders independent rights in their dioceses. As is usual in human affairs, there was fault on both sides, the bishops exaggerating the interference with their rights and the regulars making at times unfair use of their privilege of exemption.

Though the exemption has met with much opposition, the Church has not abolished it, but has by prudent restrictions made it a practical working system by which both the honor due to the bishop as the head of the diocese is upheld, and the life and activity of the religious Orders is protected from embarrassing interference. Speaking of the exemption, Pope Gregory XVI says that its utility is proved not only by ecclesiastical sanctions and the long experience of many centuries, but by the very hatred of it on the part of heretics and unbelievers.[107] On Dec. 23, 1900, when some laws were being enacted against the regulars in France on the pretence that the exemption of the religious encroached on the jurisdiction of the bishops and impaired the right of the secular clergy, Pope Leo XIII defended the exemption in a letter to the Archbishop of Paris, and said that the objection cannot be sustained: to assert that the bishops and the secular clergy are favorable to laws which are injurious to the religious, is an insult to the bishops and clergy which they cannot but resent with all the energy of their priestly souls.[108]

532. In many affairs the Code makes the regulars dependent on the local Ordinary. We will not here enumerate the various Canons as the respective rights of the bishop and the regulars can be ascertained by looking up our commentary on the various Canons. The restriction of the exemption must be explicitly stated in the Code, for the Code rules that the regulars are exempt *præterquam in casibus a jure expressis* (cfr. Canon 615).

Canon 616 states in which case the local Ordinary may punish a religious who has committed a crime outside the religious house. It must be remembered also that Canon 619 rules: In all cases in which the religious are subject to the local Ordinary, they can be punished by him also with penalties.

---

[107] Appeltern, ''Compendium præl. jur. regul.,'' 464, qu. 546.
[108] *Acta S. Sedis*, XXXIII, 361.

If abuses exist in the houses and churches of exempt religious, the bishop shall first warn the superiors to correct the wrong, and, if they are negligent, the bishop is commanded by Canon 617 to refer the matter to the Holy See. The small houses (*domus non formatæ*) in which there are less than six professed religious—four of whom must be priests, if it is a clerical organization—are not under the jurisdiction but the special surveillance of the local Ordinary (Canon 617). If scandalous conditions which are an offense to the people prevail in these small houses, the bishop can take steps to stop the scandal for the time. His action, however, is not definitive, for the Code says he can "interim providere." The matter must finally be settled either by the religious superior or by the Holy See.[109]

Autonomy of Religious Congregations of Papal Law

533. Organizations with simple vows do not enjoy the privilege of exemption, unless it has been specially conceded to them. As regards organizations approved by the Holy See (*juris pontificii*), the local Ordinary may not:

(1) make any change in the constitutions or inquire into the temporal administration, without prejudice to rights of the bishop specified in Canons 533–535;

(2) interfere in the internal government and discipline, except in the cases stipulated in law. Nevertheless, in regard to lay institutes, the local Ordinary can and must inquire whether the discipline is maintained conformably to the constitutions, whether sound doctrine and good morals have suffered in any way, whether there have been breaches of the law of enclosure, whether the reception of the sacraments is regular and frequent; and, if superiors having been duly warned of the existence of grave abuses have failed to remedy them, the Ordinary himself shall interfere; if the matter is something of unusual importance which will not suffer delay, the Ordinary shall decide immediately, but he must report his decision to the Holy See (**Canon 618**).

The internal government of the religious congregations approved by the Holy See is reserved to the superiors of the organization. The papal approval of a congregation begins,

---

109 Bondini, "De privilegio Exemptionis," 68.

as a rule, with the *decretum laudis* by which they pass under papal law. In Canon 618, the Code has practically the same regulations as the Constitution "Conditæ" of Pope Leo XIII, December 8, 1900. The internal government has reference to the reception of candidates, admission to the vows, dismissal, appointment of members to offices and duties, placing them in the various houses, Chapters and elections, administration of the goods and property of the organization. In lay congregations, brotherhoods and sisterhoods, the local Ordinary has the right and duty to hold the canonical visitation at least every five years, and inquire about the religious discipline, as is stated in Canon 512.

Episcopal Jurisdiction over Religious may be Enforced by Canonical Penalties

534. In all matters in which religious are subject to the local Ordinary he may coerce them even by penalties (**Canon 619**).

The general principle stated in Canon 2220 is that he who has the power to make laws or to impose a precept, has also the power to attach penalties to his law or precept. In the case of religious congregations of papal law and of the exempt religious organizations, the local Ordinary has jurisdiction over them in many matters pointed out by the Code, and in all those cases he can enforce obedience to his authority by penalties. By the law of the Holy See, certain religious orders cannot be punished by the bishop with censures, though he may inflict other penalties in those matters in which the law gives him jurisdiction over the exempt religious. This exemption from censures, if given directly to an Order, certainly remains under the new Code; if it was given by communication of the privileges of another order, the same controversy spoken of under Canon 613 recurs (cfr. n. 529).

Participation of the Religious in Indults Published by the Local Ordinary

535. By an indult lawfully granted by the local Ordinary dispensing from the obligation of the common law, that obligation ceases likewise for all religious living in the diocese, with-

out prejudice to the vows and particular constitutions of their own institute (**Canon 620**).

In reference to dispensations from fast and abstinence which the bishop gives to the people of his diocese in virtue of the powers received from the Holy See, the Holy Office had declared (Dec. 20, 1871, and Jan. 20, 1892) that the religious may participate in the dispensation of the fast and abstinence prescribed by the common law. The Code makes the concession general to extend to all obligations of the common law, if the bishop legitimately grants an indult dispensing from any of them. If the religious vows of some Order or congregation or their constitutions also impose the same obligation as the common law, and the bishop dispenses the people of his diocese, the obligation arising from the vows or the constitutions remains, unless the legitimate religious superior dispenses them. A religious violating such an obligation does not sin against the common law of the Church, for its obligation is taken away by the indult of the bishop, but he offends against the particular law of his organization.

Before the promulgation of the Code it was a disputed question among canonists whether the bishop could make use of the papal faculties of dispensation in favor of the exempt religious. Some authors called it a *communis sententia* that the bishop could do so. However, the matter was very much in dispute except as to particular points which had been settled by declarations of the Holy See (e.g., the above question about fast and abstinence). While the Code does not explicitly settle the question, it seems that the wording of the Code in Canon 620 is so general as to include all indults or dispensations from the common law that the bishop can give; for the Code does not restrict it to common indults given to all the people of the diocese but simply states: "an indult granted by the local Ordinary from the obligation of the common law."

COLLECTING OF ALMS BY RELIGIOUS

536. Regulars who by virtue of their institute bear the name of and are Mendicants, may, with the sole permission of their superiors, collect alms in the diocese in which their religious house is established; outside the diocese, however, they need

the written permission of the Ordinary of the place where they desire to seek alms. The local Ordinaries, especially those of the adjoining dioceses, shall not without grave and urgent reasons refuse or revoke this permission, if the religious house cannot possibly subsist on the alms collected only in the diocese in which it is situated (**Canon 621**).

The Holy See declared that only the Mendicant Orders, strictly so-called, are meant by Canon 621, and not those who in a wider sense are Mendicants (e.g., the Dominicans). The privilege to ask for alms is not restricted to begging for things necessary for life, but extends also to the building, decorating, etc., of the churches of the religious.[110] To enjoy the right granted to the Mendicants by law, they must personally do the begging, as the Decree of the Sacred Congregation of the Religious, Nov. 21, 1908, explicitly states.[111] In a Decree of the Sacred Congregation of Bishops and Regulars, March 27, 1896, it is stated that nothing prevents a superioress—without asking permission of the bishop—from accepting alms freely offered anywhere, or from asking any good and charitable persons by letter to help the houses and institutions over which she presides, as long as the legitimate superior has not for reasonable cause forbidden this manner of getting financial aid.[112] It is generally held by authors that the begging to which the laws of the Church apply means going from house to house or any other way of publicly soliciting the aid of a number of people. Approaching a few individuals is not contemplated, as may be seen from the various Decrees dealing with this matter.

The collection of alms in the form of "drives," seems to come under the laws of the Church on the begging of alms. Often these collections are made, not by the religious themselves, but by laymen who canvass their assigned districts. Now, Canon 1503 rules that, besides the laws of Canons 621–624, individual clerics and laymen are forbidden to collect alms for any charitable or ecclesiastical institution or purpose without the written permission of either the Apostolic See or their proper Ordinary and the Ordinary of the place where the collection is made.

[110] Comm. for Auth. Interp. of the Code, Oct. 16, 1919; cfr. App. III, 27, a.
[111] *Acta Ap. Sedis*, I, 153.
[112] *Acta S. Sedis*, XXVIII, 555.

537. The Code continues: All other religious of congregations of papal law are forbidden to seek alms without a special privilege of the Holy See, and those who may have obtained this privilege require besides the written permission of the local Ordinary, unless it be expressly stated otherwise in the privilege.

Religious of diocesan congregations cannot in any way seek alms without the written permission of the Ordinary of the place in which their house is located, as well as the Ordinary of the place in which they wish to collect.

Local Ordinaries shall not give to the religious mentioned in the two preceding paragraphs of this Canon the permission to seek alms, especially in places where there are convents of regulars, Mendicants by name and in fact, until they have satisfied themselves as to the real needs of the house or pious institution and the impossibility of its obtaining help in any other way. If it is possible to provide for these needs by seeking alms within the place, district or diocese in which these religious live, the Ordinaries shall not grant them any broader scope.

Without an authentic and recent rescript of the Sacred Congregation for the Eastern Church, the Ordinaries of the Latin Rite must not permit any Oriental of whatever order or dignity to collect money in their territory, nor may they send any of their subjects to Oriental dioceses for a similar purpose (**Canon 622**).

538. The superiors must not entrust the collection of alms to any others than professed subjects of mature age and character, especially in the case of women religious; those who are still engaged in studies must never be sent out to seek alms (**Canon 623**). In reference to the method to be followed and the discipline to be observed by those who go begging, the religious of both sexes must obey the instructions which have been issued by the Holy See on this matter (**Canon 624**). The principal Decrees referred to in Canon 624 are those of March 27, 1896, and Nov. 21, 1908, which we have already cited in the discussion on Canon 621.

The Decree of 1896 was for religious congregations of simple vows. Besides the permissions spoken of by the Code, this Decree states that the bishop who is requested for permission should not grant the same unless he is convinced that the house or institute of the Sisters is in need, and that the collecting cannot be done through others to be appointed by the bishop. The permission should be given only when the bishop finds that there is real necessity for it; if they can get sufficient help in their own diocese, the bishop of another should not give permission to collect in his diocese. The permission is to be given gratis and in writing. The superioress should always send two Sisters of ripened age and tried virtue. They should lodge in a Sisters' convent, or, if that cannot be done, with some woman of excellent character. They must not be out of the house during the night or after sunset. Religious men who are sent collecting should lodge with some religious institution of men, or in the houses of the clergy, or with some respectable Catholic layman. All religious who are collecting alms must not be away from their religious house more than one month, if collecting in their own diocese, or two months, if collecting in other dioceses. Before they are sent out again, they must have spent one or two months respectively in the religious community. The collections made for the benefit of the missions of the Holy Land entrusted to the Franciscans are exempt from the regulations of the Decree of Nov. 21, 1908, and other Decrees of the Holy See, whether these collections are made by the Friars themselves or by trustworthy men; they may be made anywhere according to the rules and customs thus far laudably observed.[113]

Privileges of Abbots

539. The regular abbots in charge (*de regimine*) of an abbey must within three months after they have been legitimately elected receive the blessing from the bishop of the diocese in which the abbey is located. After the reception of the blessing they have the power to confer the first tonsure and minor orders according to the rules of Canon 964, n. 1, and they enjoy also the privileges mentioned in Canon 325, with the exception of the purple skull-cap (**Canon 625**).

Canon 964 rules that the abbot in charge of an abbey, though without a territory *nullius,* may confer tonsure and minor orders

[113] Sacred Congregation of Religious, Oct. 1, 1909; *Acta Ap. Sedis,* II, 729.

provided he is a priest, has received the abbatial blessing, and ordains men who are his subjects at least by the profession of simple vows; otherwise, the ordination is null and void, unless the abbot has episcopal consecration. In virtue of Canon 325 and Canon 625 the abbot has the right to hold pontifical functions in his church with throne and canopy and the use of the pontifical insignia. He may wear the pectoral cross and the ring with the gem even outside his church. All abbots, even those who are not elected to that office for life, must receive the abbatial blessing as contained in the *Pontificale Romanum*, for the Code makes no distinction. By Brief of Pope Benedict XV, June 19, 1921, the abbots of the Order of St. Benedict receive the favor that all bishops have once and for all time the general papal mandate to impart that blessing to the abbots; if the bishop of the diocese where the monastery is located is absent, or impeded, or gives permission, the blessing may be received from any bishop.[114]

CHAPTER III

OF THE OBLIGATIONS AND PRIVILEGES OF RELIGIOUS PRO-
MOTED TO AN ECCLESIASTICAL DIGNITY OR IN
CHARGE OF PARISHES

540. A religious cannot without the authority of the Holy See be promoted to dignities, offices or benefices which are incompatible with the religious state. A religious legitimately elected to such offices by a body of voters cannot assent to the election without the permission of his superior. If the religious is bound by vow not to accept dignities, a special dispensation from the Roman Pontiff is required (**Canon 626**).

The Code refers to dignities and offices outside the religious organization. Generally speaking, dignities and offices outside the religious community are incompatible with the religious life, as they prevent the religious from following the religious discipline which he is bound to observe by his vows and the rule or constitutions of his community. The permission of the Holy See is required for the acceptance of dignities and offices which compel the religious to live outside the religious house, for we saw under Canon 606 that the religious superiors cannot allow their subjects to live outside the houses of their own Order or

114 *Acta Ap. Sedis*, XIII, 416.

congregation for more than six months, except for the purpose of study. With the permission of his superior, the religious may accept other offices which are compatible with the religious life—for instance, that of *censor librorum,* synodal examiner, diocesan consultor, etc. A religious cannot hold the office of vicar-general except in dioceses entrusted to his Order or Congregation (cfr. Canon 367).

541. A religious who is raised to the Cardinalate or to the episcopate (whether the bishopric be residential or titular), remains a religious: he continues to enjoy the privileges of his organization; he is bound by the vows and the other obligations of his profession, except as provided in Canon 628 and with respect to those things which, according to his own prudent judgment, are not compatible with his dignity; but he is exempt from the authority of his superiors, and by his vow of obedience owes obedience only to the Roman Pontiff (**Canon 627**).

The possession of property by religious who have been raised to the dignity of the episcopate or another dignity outside their own organizations, is governed by the following regulations:

(1) If by their profession they renounced the ownership of property, they have the use, usufruct and administration of the goods which now accrue to them: the proprietorship of goods acquired by a residential bishop, vicar Apostolic, or prefect Apostolic, belongs to the diocese, vicariate or prefecture; the proprietorship of goods acquired by others goes either to the religious organization or to the Holy See (as provided by Canon 582), but Cardinals have the right to dispose freely of the revenues derived from their benefices—even by last will (Canon 239, § 1, 19), except in the case of sacred furnishings which have been consecrated permanently to the divine worship (cfr. Canon 1298);

(2) If by their profession they did not renounce the ownership of property, they regain the use, usufruct and administration of whatever goods they owned, and those which they acquire after their promotion are acquired for themselves with full right;

(3) In both cases they must dispose of those goods which they do not acquire in consideration of their own persons according to the will of the donors (**Canon 628**).

We saw before that the Church rules that, by the solemn vow of poverty, a religious becomes incapacitated from holding title to any temporal property, real or personal. Men who have made solemn profession and are promoted to the episcopate or other dignity outside their own Order, are governed in the matter of temporal goods by the first paragraph of Canon 628. Men who take simple vows do not, as a rule, lose the right to the property which they had, and they retain the capacity to acquire additional property in their own name, even while they remain in the religious community. If these men are promoted to the episcopal or other dignity outside their own organization, they have full title and control of the property they had before profession and also of that acquired after their promotion. The rule of the third paragraph of Canon 628 is quite evident, for whatever the bishop or dignitary does not get personally but is offered to him for the purpose of religion or charity, cannot become his own personal property, but becomes church property to be administered by the bishop in harmony with the will and intention of the donors.

542. When a religious abdicates the cardinalate or episcopate, or has finished the office (or work) committed to him by the Holy See, he is bound to return to his religious organization. Such a cardinal or bishop on returning to his community has the right to choose any house of his organization for his residence, but he has neither an active nor passive vote (**Canon 629**).

Commentators discuss the question whether the religious who are cardinals and bishops, vicars or prefects Apostolic, etc., can have active or passive vote while they are outside the religious organization. On the one hand, they remain religious, as Canon 627 states, and there is no express prohibition in the Code against their voting; on the other hand, it seems illogical to say that they can have this power while they are outside the organization, when the Code states that those who return to the community cannot have active or passive vote.[115]

A RELIGIOUS AS PASTOR

543. The religious who is in charge of a parish with the title of either pastor or "vicar," remains bound to the observance of the vows and constitutions in so far as their observance is

[115] Vermeersch-Creusen, "Epitome," I, 316, n. 231.

consistent with the performance of the duties of his office. Wherefore, in those things which pertain to the religious discipline, he is subject to the religious superior, and the latter alone (to the exclusion of the local Ordinary) has the right to inquire into his observance of the religious life and, if needs be, to discipline him.

The goods which accrue to the pastor in consideration of the parish which he governs, are acquired for the parish; other goods are acquired in the same manner as other religious.

Notwithstanding his vow of poverty, the pastor is allowed to accept, collect, and administer alms offered in any manner for the benefit of the parishioners, or for the Catholic schools, or for pious institutes connected with the parish. He may also, according to his prudent judgment, spend those alms in accordance with the intention of the donors, subject always to the right of his superior to supervise his actions. The right to collect, accept, keep, and administer alms for the building, conservation, repair and decoration of the parish church, is vested in the superiors, if the church is owned by the religious community; otherwise in the local Ordinary (**Canon 630**).

In the last sentence of this Canon there is a difficulty which is wellnigh impossible to solve under the conditions in which parishes in the United States get their revenue. The Code wants some of those revenues to be in the hands of the pastor and other revenues to be in the hands of the superior of the community to which the church belongs. In the United States all offerings from whatever source constitute the only income of the parish, and that income is used for all parish purposes —ordinary running expenditures, payment of debts, repair, decoration, etc., of the parish church, and payment of salaries to the pastor, assistants, sexton, School Sisters, etc. The Code in Canon 630 is absolutely consistent, for Canon 609 rules that, where the religious church is at the same time a parish church, the relation between the religious community and the pastor shall be the same as that between the Cathedral or Collegiate Chapter and the pastor at the cathedral or collegiate church, as defined by Canon 415. Now in this Canon 415 the rules occur as to the finances to be partly managed by the pastor who "may collect alms for the benefit of the parishioners, receive those offered directly or indirectly, and administer and distribute them according to the will of the donors''; and to the Cathedral or Collegiate Chapter it belongs ''to take care of the church and to administer its goods together with pious bequests.'' Vermeersch-Creusen does not offer a solution to the question of the respective rights of the pastor and the religious superior under the American conditions when he says that the law defines rights but does not forbid delegation of power to the pastor by the religious superior or the local Ordinary.[116] It seems to us that the Code does not offer a solution of this particular problem, which is not surprising because the common law cannot possibly cover all questions which depend on local conditions.

544. The religious pastor or ''vicar'' is subject to the visitation, correction and entire immediate jurisdiction of the local Ordinary, just as the secular pastors, excepting only with regard to the observance of religious discipline; the bishop has this power over a religious pastor, though he exercises the ministry in the house or place where the major religious superiors have their ordinary residence.

If the local Ordinary finds that the pastor has been neglectful in his office, he can issue appropriate orders, and inflict just penalties on him. Nevertheless, the faculties of the Ordinary in this matter do not deprive the religious superior of his power over the religious pastor, but he has a ''cumulative'' right with the Ordinary to proceed against the pastor with this proviso, that if the religious superior and the Ordinary differ in their decisions, those of the Ordinary must prevail (**Canon 631,** §§ 1–2).

545. The removal of the religious pastor or vicar from the parish shall be governed by the law of Canon 454, the administration of the temporal goods of the parish by Canons 533, § 1, n. 4, and 535, n. 4 (**Canon 631,** § 3).[116a] According to Canon 454, § 5, the bishop and the superior have equal rights to remove the pastor, and neither has to give the reason to the other. Canon 533, § 1, n. 4, states that for the investment of moneys given to the parish or mission, or to the religious for the sake of the parish or mission, the previous consent of the local Ordinary is required by all religious, even those of a regular Order. Canon 535, n. 4, rules that the Ordinary of

---

[116] Vermeersch-Creusen, ''Epitome,'' I, 317, n. 632.
[116a] Concerning financial account to bishop, cfr. App. III, 27, b.

the diocese has the right to demand an account of the administration of lands and legacies given to the religious house for the purpose of divine worship or charity to be carried on in that very place.

TITLE XIV

OF TRANSITION TO ANOTHER ORGANIZATION

546. Without authorization from the Apostolic See, a religious cannot transfer to another religious organization (even to a stricter one), or from one independent monastery to another (**Canon 632**).[117]

A religious who transfers to another religious organization must make a novitiate. During the novitiate, the vows remain intact, but the rights and particular obligations of the former institute are suspended, and he is bound to obey the superiors of the new organization and also the master of novices, in virtue likewise of the vow of obedience. If he does not make profession in the new organization, he must return to the former one, unless the term of his vows has meanwhile expired. A religious who transfers to another monastery of the same order does not make either a new novitiate or a new profession (**Canon 633**).

The law of the Code on the matter of transition to another religious organization changes the former Canon Law, and provides one uniform rule for transition from each and every religious organization. Formerly one had to consider whether the religious order to which the transition was to be made was severer or easier in its religious discipline. The transition to a severer order could be made with the consent of the competent superior of one's own order, and if he refused without cause or gave a reason that was evidently inadequate, the religious might nevertheless go provided he was certain of being received.[117a] Many Orders, however, had obtained the privilege that their subjects could not transfer to another Order without the leave of the superior or the permission of the Holy See. The Council of Trent (Sessio XXV, cap. xix, *De regul. et*

[117] Transition absolutely reserved to Holy See, cfr. App. III, 28, c.
[117a] *Decretales Greg. IX*, C. 18, *De Regular.*, etc., lib. III, tit. 31; Sacred Congregation of the Council, Sept. 21, 1624, in Richter, ''Can. et Decr. C. Trid.,'' 432.

monial.) forbade the transition to a less severe Order. For the transition from one congregation with simple vows to another congregation with simple vows there was no provision in the common law.

547. The Holy See has declared that a professed religious who obtains permission to join another religious organization shall not wear the habit of his own organization during the novitiate, but that of the organization in which he makes the novitiate.[118] The term "alia religio" in the law of transition means a religious organization distinct from and independent of other religious bodies in its own supreme government. Orders and congregations which in the course of time have become divided into several organizations independent of each other, form as many distinct religious organizations between which transition from one to another is not possible without permission of the Apostolic See.

548. If a religious who has made profession of solemn or of simple perpetual vows joins another organization with solemn or simple perpetual vows, he must at the end of the novitiate either be admitted to solemn or simple perpetual vows (the temporary profession spoken of in Canon 574 being omitted), or return to the former organization; the superior, however, has the right to prolong the period of probation for not more than one year after the completion of the novitiate (**Canon 634**).

The case mentioned in Canon 634 is the only one in which perpetual vows, either solemn or simple, are taken immediately after the novitiate. The vote of the Chapter—the Chapter of the community of the house of novitiate is meant—on the admission to perpetual vows of the religious spoken of in Canon 634, is decisive so that he cannot validly be admitted to profession without a favorable vote of the majority.[119]

549. Religious who transfer to another monastery of the same order, lose from the day of transition—those who pass to another organization, from the moment of the new profession—all the rights and are freed from the obligations of the former religious organization or monastery, and assume the

---

[118] Sacred Congregation of Religious, May 14, 1923; cfr. App. III, 28, a.

[119] Comm. for the Auth. Interp. of the Code, July 14, 1922; cfr. App. III, 28, b.

rights and duties of the new organization or monastery (**Canon 635,** n. 1).

The former organization or monastery retains those goods the ownership of which it has already acquired by reason of the religious [i.e., according to Canon 580, § 2, whatever a religious after his first vows acquires by his work or is given to him as a religious, becomes the property of the organization or monastery. In the case of solemnly professed religious Canon 582 must likewise be considered to determine the rights of the former organization or monastery.] In reference to the dowry and the accrued interest and other personal goods which a religious might have, Canon 551 is to be followed.

Finally, the new organization has the right to just compensation for the time of novitiate if, according to Canon 570, it is entitled to it either by the constitutions or by express stipulation (**Canon 635,** n. 2).

550. The solemnity of the vows of one who according to the foregoing Canons lawfully makes profession of simple vows in a religious Congregation, is by that very fact extinguished, unless the Apostolic indult allowing a solemnly professed religious to transfer to an organization with simple vows explicitly rules otherwise (**Canon 636**).

TITLE XV

OF EGRESS FROM A RELIGIOUS ORGANIZATION

551. Under this title the Code speaks of the right of the person who has made temporary vows to leave the community at the expiration of the term for which such vows were taken, and of the right of the community to refuse him under certain conditions permission to take further vows. The Code also treats of the permission which a religious may obtain by indult of the Holy See to live outside the religious community either temporarily (*exclaustratio*) or permanently (*sæcularizatio*). The case of a religious who claims that his religious profession was invalid, and that therefore he has a right to leave, is not treated here, since this matter was already disposed of by the Code under Canon 586.

552. Religious who have made temporary vows may freely leave the organization, after the term of the vows has expired.

Likewise, the organization may, for just and reasonable causes, refuse to allow the religious to renew the temporary vows or to make profession of perpetual vows; however, it cannot do so because of the ill-health* of the religious, unless it be clearly proven that the religious had fraudulently concealed or hidden such illness before the profession (**Canon 637**).

Since a religious cannot be dismissed after the expiration of the first temporary vows for reason of illness—even when it is evident that such illness already existed before the taking of the first vows, except wilful deceit can be proved—it is very important that the religious organization take all possible precautions to ascertain the state of health of the candidates before they are admitted to the first vows.

TEMPORARY PERMISSION TO LIVE OUTSIDE THE COMMUNITY

553. The indult for remaining outside the cloister—either temporarily (i.e., the indult of *exclaustratio*) or permanently (i.e., the indult of *sæcularizatio*)—can be granted by the Apostolic See only in the case of organizations under papal law; in diocesan religious organizations, such indults may be granted also by the local Ordinary (**Canon 638**).

Religious who have obtained from the Apostolic See the indult of *exclaustratio,* remain bound by the vows and all the other obligations of their profession compatible with their state of temporary separation. However, they may not wear the exterior form of the habit of their community; they lose the active and passive vote for the duration of the indult, but enjoy the purely spiritual privileges of their religious organization; they also become subject to the local Ordinary of the place where they stay by reason of their vow of obedience, in place of the superiors of their own organization (**Canon 639**). By Declaration of the Committee for the Authentic Interpretation of the Code, the local Ordinary in granting the indult may allow the temporarily secularized religious to wear the habit for special reasons.[120]

554. The Code states that the religious who obtains an indult to live temporarily outside his organization must keep the religious vows and other obligations in so far as they can be reasonably kept in his life outside the monastery. The law

[120] Nov. 12, 1922; cfr. App. III, 29, c.

does not state any particulars about the vow of poverty, but, since he remains a religious, it seems that whatever he acquires by his work becomes the property of the religious organization. Since he has to provide for his own living, it seems that he has the use and administration of the goods he acquires. The reason for which he obtained the indult may also entitle him to further rights over those goods—as, for instance, when an indult was obtained to support a needy father or mother.

The question whether the religious organization has any obligation to support the religious who is temporarily separated from the organization is answered in the negative by Brandys and Vermeersch-Creusen, but it seems that the organization is obliged to come to his aid if he does not have the necessary means for a decent living, because he still remains a member of the organization. Since, however, the organization at the profession of the religious binds itself implicitly only to support the religious in the manner in which this obligation is usually understood—namely, after the manner in which its members living in the community are supported— it seems the organization has a right to insist that he return to the community, if he claims the rights of a member of the community.

At the expiration of the Apostolic indult, either because the motive reason for which the indult was granted has ceased or the time for which it was granted has expired, the religious is obliged to return and the community is obliged to receive him. He may also return at any time before the indult expires. Supposing that he returns before the indult expires, and after a short time changes his mind and wants again to make use of the indult and leave the community, can he do so, or was the indult cancelled by his voluntary return? There is nothing definite in law on this point. The religious organization, however, should protect itself against his fickleness by admitting him only on condition of a written renunciation of the indult to be forwarded to the Holy See.

INDULT OF SECULARIZATION

555. When a religious, having obtained the indult of secularization, leaves the organization: (1) he is cut off from his organization, must lay aside the external form of the habit of

the organization, and is on the same footing as secular priests with regard to the Mass, Divine Office, and the use and administration of the sacraments; (2) he is relieved of his vows, but, if he is in sacred orders, the obligations attached to major orders remain; he is not obliged to recite the Divine Office, where such obligation arose by virtue of the religious profession, nor is he bound by any other rules and constitutions of his former organization.

If by Apostolic indult he is again received into the organization, he must make a new novitiate and profession, and his place among the professed members is to be reckoned from the day of his new profession (**Canon 640**).

The indult of secularization separates the religious completely from his religious organization, and wipes out all the effects of the religious profession in so far as the obligations of the vows and of the rule and constitutions are concerned. In this aspect the law is new, for under the former Canon Law the vows were not *ipso facto* dissolved. The secularization of the Code dissolves all religious vows, both simple and solemn. The secularization does not take effect until the religious who asked for and obtained it, accepts it and leaves the organization. Before he leaves, he still has a chance to decline the indult, even though the Superior General has already issued the decree for the execution of the indult, according to Canon 56 of the Code. In its declaration on this point, the Sacred Congregation of Religious states that, if the superiors have grave objections to the refusal of the religious to accept the indult and do not want him to remain in the community, they should refer the matter to the Sacred Congregation of the Religious.[121] The Committee for the Authentic Interpretation of the Code declared [122] that the regulations of Canon 640 regarding the effects of the secularization apply to all who obtained an indult of secularization, whether from the Apostolic See or from the local Ordinary.

556. With reference to the refusal to accept the secularization, the question arises whether, if the religious first accepts it, he may afterwards, before he has left the religious house, refuse to take the indult. Nothing definite can be said on this

---

[121] August 1, 1922; cfr. App. III, 29, a.
[122] November 12, 1922; cfr. App. III, 29, b.

question, but it seems that according to the opening words of Canon 640—''when a professed religious, having obtained the indult of secularization, leaves the organization''—the final step which separates him from the organization consists not merely in the acceptance of the indult, but in the acting on the indult, namely, his leaving the organization.[123] Vermeersch [124] touches on this question, saying that the acceptance once made completes the legal act, and it is no longer in the power of one party to escape the effects of the act. He suggests, however, that it might be in harmony with the intention of the above declaration of the Sacred Congregation if, by the mutual consent of both superior and the subject, the act of acceptance be considered as not made.

Secularized Religious Who Are in Major Orders

557. If a religious in major orders did not lose his diocese (as determined by Canon 585), and returns to the world either at the expiration of his temporary vows or by indult of secularization, he must go to his own diocese, and his proper Ordinary is bound to receive him. If he lost his proper diocese, he cannot exercise his major orders outside the religious organization until he has found a bishop who is willing to receive him, or until the Holy See has made other provision for him.

The bishop may receive the secularized religious either unconditionally or for a three years' probation. If he receives him unconditionally, the religious becomes forthwith incardinated in that diocese; in the other case the bishop can prolong the time of probation, not however for longer than another term of three years. When the second term of three years has expired, the religious becomes *ipso facto* incardinated, unless he has been dismissed before the end of the term (**Canon 641**).

Canon 585 states that by the profession of perpetual vows, either simple or solemn, the professed loses the proper diocese he had in the world. He is therefore cut off completely from his former diocese, and the former proper Ordinary has no obligations towards such a secularized religious. If a young man was in minor orders before he entered a religious organization, and did not lose his diocese by perpetual profession but

---

[123] Maroto, ''Commentarium pro Religiosis,'' IV, 99-106.
[124] *Periodica*, XI, 151.

got secularized during the three years of temporary vows, he remains a cleric of the diocese to which he belonged before he joined the religious community. If he was promoted to minor orders in the community during his temporary vows, and then obtains a secularization, must his proper bishop receive him as a cleric? It seems the bishop must receive him, for the religious has not yet lost his proper diocese. Since, however, the bishop has a right to judge who is or is not a fit subject for the priesthood in his diocese, the bishop can make use of the power which Canon 211 gives him—namely, for a just reason he may reduce a cleric in minor orders to the lay state. Leitner [125] seems to hold that one can infer from Canons 640, n. 1, and 669, that the secularization itself effects the reduction of a cleric in minor orders to the lay state. However, Canon 640, n. 1, does not speak of clerics, but of all secularized religious, men and women; Canon 669 speaks of the dismissal of *perpetually* professed religious who are in minor orders, and is therefore not to the point in the case of a man in temporary vows.

558. The condition of secularized clerics in major orders is very explicitly defined in the Code. This new law changes the former law on the condition of secularized men in major orders to some extent, though in substance it is about the same as the Decree "Auctis admodum" of November 4, 1892, which forbade the secularized religious in major orders to leave his community until he had found a bishop who was willing to receive him. If he left before getting a bishop, he fell *ipso facto* into suspension from orders. By the Code he is not forbidden to leave to look for a bishop, but, before he gets a bishop, he may not exercise his major orders while he is away from the religious organization, unless he obtains permission from the Holy See to exercise the orders in the meantime.

559. Every professed religious who has returned to the world, though he may exercise sacred orders after the manner defined in the preceding Canon 641, is forbidden without a new and special indult of the Holy See:

(1) To hold any benefice in minor or major basilicas and in cathedral churches;

(2) To hold any professorship or office in the major and minor seminaries or colleges in which clerics are educated, and

[125] *Handbuch des kath. Kirchenr.*, III, 454.

also in universities and institutions which enjoy the papal privilege to confer academic degrees;

(3) To hold any office or position in the Curia of the bishops, or in religious houses of either men or women, even in the case of diocesan congregations (**Canon 642,** § 1).

These rules apply also to those who have taken temporary vows or the oath of perseverance, or who have made certain special promises according to the constitutions of their organizations, and have been dispensed from them, if they have been bound by them for fully six years (**Canon 642,** § 2).

The Holy See has declared (Nov. 24, 1920; *Acta Ap. Sedis,* XII, 575) that Canon 642 also affects religious who, before the promulgation of the Code, had obtained permission from the Holy See to stay outside their religious organization. Canon 642, § 1, seems to refer to the perpetually professed, as may be deduced from the Decree of the Sacred Congregation of the Religious, June 15, 1909.[126] In reference to those organizations which have no perpetual vows but only temporary ones, or an oath of perseverance, or certain promises to stay in the organization, Canon 642, § 2, provides that, if the members have been fully six years under such a profession and then get a dispensation, the men are barred from the secular benefices, offices or positions mentioned in this Canon. This paragraph of Canon 642 is taken almost *verbatim* from a Decree of the Sacred Congregation of the Religious, April 5, 1910.[127]

EFFECTS OF SECULARIZATION, DISMISSAL, AND VOLUNTARY DEPARTURE ON THE HOLDING OF TEMPORAL GOODS

560. Religious who leave their organization either on the expiration of the term of temporary vows or in virtue of an indult of secularization, or who have been dismissed from the organization, cannot demand any compensation for services rendered by them to the organization (**Canon 643,** § 1).

If, however, a woman was received without a dowry and she cannot provide for herself out of her own goods, the organization must give her out of charity that which is required for the safe and proper return to her home, and provide her for a certain period—to be fixed by mutual agreement, or

126 *Acta Ap. Sedis,* I, 523. Cfr. also App. III, 5, a.
127 *Acta Ap. Sedis,* II, 232.

in case of disagreement by the local Ordinary—with the means for a decent livelihood in accordance with natural equity (**Canon 643, § 2**).

The Code speaks of women who were received without a dowry, and who have no other goods or property to support them until they can earn their livelihood. If they brought a dowry, that must be returned to them (as was stated in Canon 551), and the Code supposes that the dowry is sufficiently large to furnish them maintenance until they find suitable employment. Equity and charity may oblige the organization to assist even women who have a dowry, if it be so small as to keep them only for a few days. An organization of men may likewise be obliged by equity and charity to render the men who leave or are dismissed some assistance until they can find employment. It is not a matter of justice, for those who entered a religious organization knew that they entered to give their services freely for the sake of the religious motive which, if they were sincere, they had when they asked to be received; if they were not sincere, they practised fraud on the community.[128]

ILLEGAL DEPARTURE FROM THE RELIGIOUS ORGANIZATION

561. Any religious who has made profession of perpetual vows, either simple or solemn, and unlawfully leaves the religious house with the intention of not returning, or who, having left the house legitimately, does not return because he intends to withdraw himself from religious obedience, is called an apostate from the religious life (*apostata a religione*). The culpable intention of disowning religious obedience is legally presumed, if within one month the religious has neither returned nor manifested to his superior his intention of returning.

A "fugitive" is one who leaves the religious house without the permission of his superior, but with the intention of returning to the religious organization (**Canon 644**).

If the intention not to return can be proved in the external forum from other circumstances, there is no need of the pre-

[128] Sacred Congregation of Religious, March 2, 1924, rules that the return of a small dowry to a woman does not relieve the Sisterhood from all further responsibility, but it must furnish her with further relief in addition to returning the dowry, cfr. App. III, 29, d.

sumption of law, and the apostate can be declared guilty of the crime as soon as proof has been furnished of his intention to apostatize from the religious life. Greater caution is necessary in judging the circumstances when the religious has left the house with the permission of the superior. Even the presumption of law that he stayed away with the intention to apostatize when he is still absent thirty days after the date on which he should have returned, can be refuted by proof to the contrary.

The Code is severer than the old law in this, that it regards apostasy from organizations with simple vows in the same light as apostasy from those with solemn vows, while in the former Canon Law the apostasy from religious life (*a religione*) occurred only in the case of solemnly professed religious. If a religious in temporary vows, or one who has made the promise of perserverance in organizations which have no vows, illegally leaves the organization with the intention not to return, he is not an apostate, and does not incur the penalties of the common law against apostasy.

562. The definition of a fugitive in the Code has a broader application than that of apostates. The Code states that any religious who deserts the house without permission of the superior but with the intention to return, is a fugitive. It seems, therefore, that all professed religious are comprehended, whether the vows are temporary or perpetual, simple or solemn. Merely leaving the house for a short time without permission, does not make a religious a fugitive. Some commentators hold that, if a religious stays out over twenty-four hours, he becomes a fugitive; some hold that he is to be called a fugitive only after two or three days' illegal absence. Much depends on the constitutions of each religious body, since the common law does not determine the length of time required to make one a fugitive. The Constitutions of the Friars Minor regard a religious as a fugitive, if he is illegitimately absent from the house over one natural day, whether he leaves the house without permission, or, being away with permission, absents himself for over a day longer than the appointed period.

563. Neither the apostate nor the fugitive is relieved of the obligations of his rule and vows, and both must return without delay to their organization. The superiors must seek them with solicitude, and receive them if they return animated

by sincere repentance. The local Ordinary—and, if the monastery be exempt, also the regular superior—shall exercise due circumspection in effecting the return of apostate or fugitive nuns (**Canon 645**).

The penalties decreed by the Code against apostates and fugitives are contained in Canons 2385–2386.

TITLE XVI

OF THE DISMISSAL OF RELIGIOUS

564. The following religious are *ipso facto* considered as lawfully dismissed:

(1) Religious who publicly apostatize from the Catholic faith;

(2) A religious who has run away with a person of the opposite sex (*cum viro aut cum muliere*);

(3) Religious who attempt or contract marriage, even the so-called civil marriage.

In these cases it suffices that the major superior with his Chapter or council makes a declaration of the fact in the manner prescribed by the constitutions. He must take care to preserve in the records of the house the collected evidence of the fact (**Canon 646**).

The Code in Canon 646 speaks of religious generally. This Canon, therefore, applies to all professed religious, whether their vows are temporary or perpetual, simple or solemn. If the religious fled accompanied by a child under twelve or fourteen years respectively (according to the sex), the case does not come under this Canon, for the person of the opposite sex must be of the age of puberty to come under the term "mulier" or "vir." If the person of the opposite sex accompanying the fugitive religious is a blood relation in the direct line, or in the first degree of the collateral line, it is reasonable to assume, as Leitner holds,[129] that the case does not fall under Canon 646, since travelling with such persons does not ordinarily show evil intention or purpose.

[129] *Handbuch des kath. Kirchenr.*, III, 462. See recent declaration on Canon 646 (App. III, 30, e).

CHAPTER I

OF THE DISMISSAL OF RELIGIOUS IN TEMPORARY VOWS

565. In orders and in congregations of papal law, the professed religious with temporary vows can be dismissed by the supreme head of the organization, or the abbot of an independent monastery, with the consent of their respective councils to be expressed by secret vote. In monasteries of nuns, the local Ordinary—or, if the house is subject to the regulars, the regular superior—can dismiss the nun, after the superioress of the monastery with her council have in writing attested the reasons for dismissal. In diocesan congregations, the Ordinary of the place where the house is located has the right to dismiss the Sister, but he shall not make use of his right without the knowledge nor against the reasonable objection of the superioresses (**Canon 647, § 1**).

566. The aforesaid persons are gravely bound in conscience not to exercise the right of dismissal except under the following conditions:

(1) The reasons for dismissal must be grave;

(2) These reasons may be either on the part of the religious organization [e.g., inability of the subject to serve the purposes of the community] or on the part of the religious [e.g., loss of vocation]. The lack of the religious spirit which is a source of scandal to others is a sufficient reason for dismissal, if repeated admonition together with a salutary penance has produced no effect. Poor health is no reason, unless it is known with certainty that it was fraudulently concealed or disguised before profession; [129a]

(3) The reason for dismissal must be known with certainty to the superior who decrees the dismissal, but a formal canonical trial to establish the reason is not necessary. The religious, however, must be informed of the reason for the dismissal, and an ample opportunity given to answer the charges: this answer must be faithfully submitted to the superior who has the right of dismissal;

(4) The religious has the right to appeal to the Holy See against the decree of dismissal, and, pending the appeal, the dismissal has no juridical effects;

[129a] On dismissal and supervening insanity, cfr. App. III, 30, d.

(5) In reference to the dismissal of religious women Canon 643, § 2, must be observed, which states that, if a woman has been received without a dowry and has no means of her own, she must be furnished with the necessary means to reach her home in safety and to enable her to live for a while until she can take care of herself (**Canon 647, § 2**).

With reference to the appeal of the religious against the decree of dismissal, the question arose as to the *length of time* that is open to the religious for the appeal after he gets the decree of dismissal. The Sacred Congregation of the Religious declared that the right of recourse must be exercised *within ten days* from the time when the religious has been informed of the decree of dismissal. The Sacred Congregation further states that the religious can make this recourse either by letter addressed to the Sacred Congregation, or through him who communicated to the religious the decree of dismissal. To prove that recourse was taken, it suffices to draw up an authentic document, or to have the testimony of at least two trustworthy men.

In reckoning the ten days within which the recourse is to be made, the first day is not counted (Canon 34, n. 3). According to Canon 35, if the religious does not know of his right of recourse, or if he is not able to act, the recourse remains open to him even after the lapse of the ten days, and the ten days begin to run only from the day on which he obtained knowledge and was able to act. When the superior informs the dismissed religious of the decree of dismissal, it is advisable that he should also tell him of his right of recourse and of the interval within which it must be exercised.

Pending the recourse, the dismissed religious is still to be considered a religious; he is bound to perform the same duties and enjoys the same rights as other religious, just as before the dismissal. He has, therefore, the right and duty to live in the religious house, and must remain under the obedience of the superior.[130]

567. A religious who has been dismissed according to Canon 647 is *ipso facto* absolved from all the religious vows; a cleric in major orders, however, is subject to the obligation of those

[130] Sacred Congregation of Religions, July 20, 1923; cfr. App. III, 30, a.

orders and to the other regulations of Canons 641–642. A cleric in minor orders is by the very dismissal reduced to the state of the laity (**Canon 648**).

Canon 641 refers to secularized religious in major orders, and the Code here applies the same rules to religious in major orders who are dismissed during their temporary vows. To them also Canon 642 applies, which enumerates certain benefices and positions which a secularized cleric is forbidden to hold.

CHAPTER II

OF THE DISMISSAL OF RELIGIOUS WITH PERPETUAL VOWS IN NON-EXEMPT CLERICAL AND IN ALL LAICAL ORGANIZATIONS

568. In non-exempt clerical and in all laical organizations of men, a religious with perpetual vows cannot be dismissed unless he has previously committed three offenses and been twice admonished without result, in accordance with the rules of Canons 656–662 (**Canon 649**).

When such a threefold offense has been committed and the prescribed warnings have been made without producing the amendment of the religious, the supreme head of the organization with his council, considering all the circumstances of the case, shall deliberate whether there is cause for dismissal (**Canon 650, § 1**).

If the majority of the votes are in favor of dismissal:

(1) In *diocesan congregations* the entire matter is to be referred to the Ordinary of the place in which the religious house of the professed religious is located, and he has the right to decide the matter according to his prudent judgment following the rules of Canon 647;

(2) In an *organization of papal law* the supreme head of the organization issues the decree of dismissal, but in order to have effect it must be confirmed by the Holy See (**Canon 650, § 2**).

The religious has a right to defend himself freely, and his defense must be faithfully entered in the acts of the proceeding (**Canon 650, § 3**).

Dismissal of Religious Women

569. For the dismissal of religious women with perpetual vows, either simple or solemn, serious external causes are required together with incorrigibility (which means that, after attempts to correct the Sister have been made unsuccessfully, the superioress judges that there is no further hope of amendment). The rule of Canon 650 that the dismissed religious must be given a chance to defend herself and that this defense must be included in the acts of the case, holds good also in the dismissal of religious women (**Canon 651**).

In the case of *diocesan congregations,* it is the duty of the Ordinary of the diocese in which the house of the respective professed sister is located to inquire into the reasons for dismissal and to issue the decree of dismissal (**Canon 652, § 1**).

In the case of *sisterhoods with solemn vows,* the local Ordinary shall forward all acts and documents to the Sacred Congregation together with his vote on the case, and also that of the regular superior if the monastery is subject to the regulars (**Canon 652, § 2**).

In the case of *other organizations of women under papal law,* the Mother-General (i.e., the highest superioress, by whatever name she may be called) of the organization shall refer the entire matter of dismissal with all acts and documents to the Sacred Congregation. In this as in the preceding case, the Sacred Congregation will then decide what action is to be taken, but the law of Canon 643, § 2, must be observed in case of dismissal (**Canon 652, § 3**). Canon 643, § 2, declares that a Sister who was received without a dowry and has no means of her own, must be provided with the necessary means to reach her home in safety and to keep her for some time until she can support herself.

Dismissal in Case of Great Scandal or Danger of Very Great Harm to the Community

570. In the case of grave external scandal or of very serious imminent injury to the community, a religious may be dismissed immediately and deprived of his habit by the major superior with the consent of his council. If there be danger in **delay**

and time does not permit recourse to the major superior, he may be dismissed even by the local superior with the consent of his council and of the local Ordinary: in this case, the Ordinary or the major superior, if he be present, must without delay submit the matter to the judgment of the Holy See (**Canon 653**).

This Canon provides in general for emergencies which might happen, and in which the regular proceedings of dismissal are too slow to avoid serious disaster. Canon 646 stated the three cases in which the religious is by the very commission of the crime dismissed from the religious organization. Canon 653 provides protection to the religious community in unusually serious emergencies. Lest haste and excitement cause injustice to the offending religious, the Code provides sufficient safeguards in the proceedings against him.

CHAPTER III

OF THE CANONICAL TRIAL FOR THE DISMISSAL OF RELIGIOUS WITH PERPETUAL SOLEMN OR SIMPLE VOWS IN EXEMPT CLERICAL ORGANIZATIONS

571. A male religious who has taken solemn or simple perpetual vows in a clerical exempt organization shall not be dismissed except by the process of a canonical trial: all contrary privileges are revoked, and the cases mentioned in Canons 646 and 668 are the only exceptions to the rule of this Canon (**Canon 654**). These exceptions are the three crimes of public apostasy, running away with a woman, and marriage or an attempt to marry. Canon 646 rules that every religious who is guilty of one of these offenses is to be considered *ipso facto* legitimately dismissed. The case of Canon 668 is the same as that considered under Canon 653, namely, unusual emergencies involving great scandal or very grave and imminent danger to the religious community.

The power to issue the sentence of dismissal is vested in the supreme head of the organization or monastic Congregation, with his council or chapter: this must consist of at least four religious, and, if that many are not at hand, the president with the consent of the others who constitute together with him the collegiate tribunal, must elect other religious to complete the tribunal. The president with the consent of the other judges shall nominate a *promotor justitiæ* (or prosecutor), in accordance with the regulations of Canon 1589, § 2, which rules that in the tribunal of religious the prosecutor must be a member of the same religious organization (**Canon 655**).

572. A canonical trial may be initiated only under the following conditions: (1) grave external offenses must have been committed either against the common law or the special law for religious; (2) the admonitions must have been given; (3) there must be a failure to amend (**Canon 656**).

The offenses must be at least three in number and of the same species, or, if of different species, they must be such that, taken together, they manifest perversity of will and obstinacy in sin. One continued offense which is made virtually threefold by the admonitions, is also sufficient (**Canon 657**).

The three offenses must be grave. By an offense the Code in Canon 2195 understands an external and morally imputable violation of a law to which at least an indeterminate canonical sanction is attached. Though the violation of a law appears grave on its face, there are many reasons why grave guilt may be absent in a given case. Canons 2199–2209 which deal with the imputability and the causes which either aggravate or diminish it, are of great importance in determining the gravity of guilt in a violation of a law. Before it is certain that the three offenses spoken of here in connexion with the canonical trial are gravely sinful, the prosecutor cannot begin the process, as is evident from the opening words of Canon 656.

The Admonitions and Failure of Amendment

573. To justify an admonition, it is necessary that the offense be notorious, or that it be manifest either from the extrajudicial confession of the culprit or from other sufficient proofs furnished by previous investigation. In making the investigation, the rules of Canons 1939 sqq. are to be observed, *congrua congruis referendo* (**Canon 658**). The Latin phrase means that, where these Canons speak of the local Ordinary, they are to be applied to the immediate major superior of the religious organization; where the Canons speak of delegating one of the synodal judges to make the investigation, the religious superior delegates a religious of his organization.

The admonition must be given by the immediate major superior personally or by another acting on his mandate, but the superior must not give the mandate until he has obtained information on the facts, according to the terms of the preceding Canon 658; the mandate given for the first admonition holds good also for the second (**Canon 659**).

There must be two admonitions, one for each of the first two offenses; in the case of continued or permanent offenses, an interval of at least three whole days must elapse between the first and second admonitions (**Canon 660**).

The superior shall add to the admonitions appropriate exhortations and corrections, and impose in addition penances and other penal remedies calculated to effect the amendment of the culprit and the reparation of the scandal. The superior is also bound to remove the culprit from the occasions of relapse, even to the extent of transferring him, if necessary, to another house where the vigilance will be easier and the occasion of offending more remote. To each admonition must be added the threat of expulsion (**Canon 661**).

The religious is considered not to have amended if, after the second admonition, he commits a new offense, or perseveres in the old one; after the last admonition, at least six days must elapse before further steps may be taken (**Canon 662**).

THE CANONICAL TRIAL

574. After the admonitions and corrections have proved unavailing, the immediate major superior shall carefully collect all the acts and documents and send them to the supreme head of the organization. The supreme superior shall give the documents to the prosecutor who must examine them and submit his conclusions (**Canon 663**).

The prosecutor has the right to institute such further investigations as he shall think proper. If he concludes that the accusation should be made against the culprit, the canonical trial must be begun, and conducted according to the rules of the Canons of the First Part of the Fourth Book, *congrua congruis referendo*. During the trial it must be shown that the offenses were committed, that the two admonitions were given, and that the culprit failed to amend (**Canon 664**).

After careful consideration of the charges of the prosecutor and the defense of the accused, the tribunal may pronounce the sentence of dismissal, if they judge that the commission of the offenses, the giving of the admonitions, and the failure of amendment have been sufficiently proved (**Canon 665**).

The sentence cannot be executed unless it is confirmed by the Sacred Congregation, to which the president of the tribunal shall forward as soon as possible the sentence and all the acts of the process (**Canon 666**).

For distant countries and also in ordinary cases, the supreme superior may, with the consent of his council or chapter, delegate the power of dismissal to trustworthy and prudent religious: these must be at least three in number, and are bound to proceed according to the foregoing Canons 663–666 (**Canon 667**).

575. In the case of grave external scandal or very great and imminent harm to the community (as stated in Canon 653), the religious may be immediately dismissed by the major superior; if there is danger in delay, and there is no time to have recourse to the major superior, he may be dismissed also by the local superior with the consent of his council. The religious who is dismissed must at once take off the religious habit. After the dismissal of the religious the trial must be begun immediately, if it had not been started, and must be conducted according to the foregoing Canons (**Canon 668**)

CHAPTER IV

OF DISMISSED RELIGIOUS WHO HAVE TAKEN PERPETUAL VOWS

576. The religious who has taken perpetual vows remains bound by his vows after dismissal from the organization, unless the constitutions of the organization or Apostolic indults declare otherwise. If the cleric is in minor orders, he is by the very dismissal reduced to the state of a layman (**Canon 669**).

A cleric in major orders who has committed one of the three offenses mentioned in Canon 646 (to which *ipso facto* dismissal from the religious organization is attached), or who has been dismissed for an offense which is punished by the common law with loss of good repute (*infamia juris*), or with deposition or degradation, is forbidden ever to wear the clerical garb (**Canon 670**).

577. If a cleric in major orders has been dismissed for offenses less serious than those mentioned in the preceding Canon 670, the following rules obtain:

(1) He remains *ipso facto* suspended until he obtains absolution from the Holy See;

(2) The Sacred Congregation may, if it deems it proper, command the dismissed religious to stay in a specified diocese wearing the garb of the secular clergy, after the reasons for his dismissal have been communicated to the Ordinary;

(3) If the dismissed cleric does not obey the orders of the Sacred Congregation, referred to in n. 2, the religious organization has no obligations towards the dismissed, and he is thereby deprived of the right to wear the clerical garb;

(4) The Ordinary of the diocese assigned to the dismissed religious for his residence shall send him to a house of penance, or commit him to the care and vigilance of a pious and prudent priest. If the religious does not obey, the religious organization has no responsibility towards him, and he forfeits the right to wear the clerical garb;

(5) If the dismissed religious obeys the orders of the Sacred Congregation and of the Ordinary, and has no other means of providing for himself, the religious organization to which he belonged shall in the spirit of charity furnish him with the necessary maintenance through the Ordinary of the diocese where the dismissed religious stays;

(6) If the dismissed religious does not lead a life worthy of a cleric, the Ordinary may after one year, or even sooner, deprive him of the maintenance charitably furnished by the religious organization, order him out of the house where he was to stay for probation, and deprive him of the right to wear the ecclesiastical garb. The Ordinary shall at once send a report of his action both to the Sacred Congregation and to the religious organization which dismissed him;

(7) If, however, the dismissed religious behaves so well during the time of probation that he can justly be considered truly amended, the Ordinary shall endorse his petition to the Holy See for absolution from the censure of suspension, and, after

he has obtained the absolution, shall, with due precautions and limitations, allow him in his diocese to say Holy Mass, and also, if he sees fit, to discharge other functions of the sacred ministry by which he may properly support himself. In this case the religious organization may discontinue the charitable assistance. In the case of a deacon or sub-deacon, the matter should be referred to the Holy See (**Canon 671**).

A dismissed religious whose vows have not been dissolved is bound to return to the cloister. If he has for three years given signs of complete amendment, the religious organization is bound to receive him: however, if either on the part of the organization or on the part of the religious there are serious objections against the return, the matter shall be submitted to the judgment of the Holy See (**Canon 672, § 1**).

If his vows have been dissolved or have ceased, and the dismissed religious has found a bishop who is willing to receive him, he shall remain under the jurisdiction and special vigilance of the bishop, the regulations of Canon 642 (about the benefices and offices which a secularized religious may not hold) being duly observed. If the dismissed religious does not find a bishop who is willing to receive him, the matter shall be referred to the Holy See (**Canon 672, § 2**).

TITLE XVII

OF SOCIETIES OF MEN OR WOMEN LEADING A COMMUNITY LIFE WITHOUT VOWS

578. A society of men or women who lead a community life after the manner of religious under the government of superiors and according to approved constitutions, but without the three usual vows of religious life, is not a religious organization properly so called, nor are its members religious in the strict sense of the term. Such a society is either clerical or laical, of papal law or of diocesan law, as defined by Canon 488, nn. 3 and 4 (**Canon 673**).

There are many such societies in the Church. If they are approved by the Holy See, they come under papal law; if they are approved only by a bishop, they are organizations of diocesan law. Such a society may also have the privilege of exemption, as, for instance, the *Pia Societas Missionum*.

579. The erection and suppression of such societies and of their provinces and houses are governed by the laws laid down for religious congregations (**Canon 674**). Their government is determined by their individual constitutions, but they must follow the laws of the Canons 499–530 in reference to their superiors and chapters and their confessors and chaplains (**Canon 675**).

Such societies and their provinces and houses are capable of acquiring and possessing temporal goods. The administration of goods and property is governed by Canons 532–537. Whatever the members of the society acquire in consideration of the society, belongs to the society; the members may retain, acquire and administer other goods according to the constitutions (**Canon 676**).

In the admission of candidates the constitutions of the society shall be observed, subject to the laws of Canon 542 on the valid and licit admission of candidates (**Canon 677**). In all matters concerning the arrangement of studies and the reception of orders, the members of the society are bound by the same laws as the secular clergy, subject to any special regulations which the Holy See may have made for the society (**Canon 678**).

Besides the special obligations imposed by their own constitutions, the members of the society are bound by the common obligations of clerics, unless the nature of the law, or its context, shows that the law is not intended for members of a society. They are also bound by the obligations of religious as specified in Canons 595–612, unless their constitutions rule otherwise. They shall observe the enclosure according to their constitutions, under the supervision of the local Ordinary (**Canon 679**).

The members of the society, both clerics and lay members, enjoy the privileges of clerics as specified in Canons 119–123, and other privileges given directly to the society, but they do not have the privileges of religious unless these are granted to them by special indult (**Canon 680**).

580. Besides the proper constitutions of each individual society, the laws of Canons 632–635 and 645 shall with due

distinction (*congrua congruis referendo*) be observed regarding the transition of members to another society or to another religious organization, and the departure of members from the society, even though it be one of papal law. In the dismissal of members, the laws of Canons 646–672 shall be observed (**Canon 681**). The Committee for the Authentic Interpretation of the Code has declared [131] that, if the bond which links the members with the society is temporary, the laws on the dismissal of temporarily professed religious are to be followed; if the bond is perpetual, the laws for the dismissal of religious with perpetual vows are to be followed.

By declaration of the Committee for the Authentic Interpretation of the Code,[132] the following Canons apply to Societies without vows: Canon 2386, on penalties for fugitives; Canon 2387, on penalties for those whose profession was declared invalid on account of fraud; Canon 2389, on serious violations of the common life; Canon 2410, on penalties for unlawfully sending a subject for ordination to another diocese, if the society has the privilege of giving dimissorial letters; Canon 2411, on penalties for superiors who receive candidates without the qualifications demanded by Canon 542 or without the testimonials demanded by Canon 544; Canon 2413, on penalties for superiors who interfere with the canonical visitation of their subjects.

PART III

OF THE LAITY

581. The laity has the right to receive from the clergy the spiritual goods and especially the necessary means of salvation, according to the rules of ecclesiastical discipline (**Canon 682**).

Laymen are not allowed to wear the clerical garb, with the exception of: (1) seminarians and the other candidates aspiring to orders referred to in Canon 972, and (2) laymen legitimately employed in the service of the church (e.g., sextons), while they are within the church building, or outside

[131] March 1, 1921; cfr. App. III, 30, b.
[132] June 3, 1918; cfr. App. III, 30, c.

when they take part in some ecclesiastical service (**Canon 683**). Canon 972 refers to seminarians who, by special permission of the bishop, are permitted to live outside the seminary under the supervision of a priest appointed for that purpose.

TITLE XVIII

OF ASSOCIATIONS OF THE FAITHFUL IN GENERAL

582. The faithful deserve praise when they join associations which have been erected, or at least recommended, by the Church. They should beware of associations which are secret, condemned, seditious or suspected, and of those which strive to withdraw themselves from the legitimate supervision of the Church (**Canon 684**).

In the following Canons the Code treats exclusively of associations which are strictly ecclesiastical, and which are, therefore, subject to the jurisdiction of the Church in all their actions as an ecclesiastical organization. Other societies of Catholic laymen or women organized for the purpose of Christian charity are private affairs of Catholics, just as societies of a literary, artistic or social character. Consequently, such societies are not subject to the ecclesiastical authorities, except in so far as the Church, in her capacity of the divinely appointed authority and guardian of the faith and morals of her subjects, has always a claim on their obedience. The whole question of the difference between ecclesiastical societies and other societies of Catholic laymen or women was discussed in the *Acta Apostolicæ Sedis* in connexion with the case of the St. Vincent de Paul Society in the Diocese of Corrientes in Argentina.[133]

Associations distinct from the religious organizations and societies spoken of in Canons 487–681, may be erected by the Church either to promote a more perfect Christian life among her members, or for the undertaking of works of piety and charity, or for the advancement of the public cult (**Canon 685**).

[133] Sacred Congregation of the Council, Nov. 13, 1920; cfr. App. III, 31, a.

ERECTION OF AN ASSOCIATION

583. No society is recognized in the Church unless it has been either erected by the competent ecclesiastical authority, or at least approved by it. The right to erect or approve associations is vested in the Roman Pontiff, and also in the local Ordinary except in the case of those associations the erection of which is by Apostolic privilege reserved to others. Even though it can be proved that a papal privilege was granted, the written consent of the local Ordinary is always required for the validity of the erection, unless it is stated otherwise in the privilege: however, the consent of the Ordinary granted for the erection of a religious house applies also to the erection in that same house—or in the church attached to it—of an association which is not constituted after the nature of an organic body and is proper to the respective religious organization (**Canon 686**, §§ 1–3).

584. The vicar-general in virtue of a mere general mandate, or the vicar-capitular, cannot erect associations or give consent for their erection or aggregation. The letters of erection given by persons who in virtue of an Apostolic privilege have the right to erect an association must be given gratis, excepting only a tax for covering the necessary expenses (**Canon 686**, §§ 4–5).

The phrase, "constituted after the manner of an organic body," occurs frequently in the decrees of the Sacred Congregation of Indulgences dealing with confraternities. It is not easy to render the precise meaning of the phrase. In general, it means an association which has a more complete organization than the *Uniones Piæ* and *Pia Opera* have. Some of the characteristics of associations constituted after the manner of an organic body are given in an Instruction of the Sacred Congregation of Indulgences and Sacred Relics:[134] they usually have regulations for the reception of members with certain solemnities and sacred rites (as for instance, petition and presentation of the new member), a period of probation or novitiate, or at least a ceremony of investing with a habit, scapular, or cincture which necessitates the presence of the one to be received. This explains the difference to some extent, but it is difficult to

[134] Nov. 26, 1880; *Acta S. Sedis*, XIII, 266.

get an exact notion of what is meant by organic body. It seems that it means societies which are organized somewhat after the manner of religious organizations, with officers, rules, and meetings in which the business of the association is transacted. From some of the decrees on confraternities and societies it seems that the same association may be established in a church either after the manner of an organic body or merely after the manner of a pious union.

585. The associations of the faithful acquire the right of a legal person in the Church only when they have obtained from the legitimate ecclesiastical superior a formal decree of erection, as stated in Canon 100 (**Canon 687**). An association shall not assume a title or name which savors of levity or unbecoming novelty, or which gives expression to a form of devotion not approved by the Holy See (**Canon 688**).

586. Every association shall have its statutes examined and approved by either the Holy See or the local Ordinary. Statutes which have not been confirmed by the Apostolic See, are subject at all times to modification and correction by the local Ordinary (**Canon 689**).

All associations—even those erected by the Apostolic See, unless an association has a special privilege—are under the jurisdiction and vigilance of the local Ordinary, who has the right and duty to visit them in accordance with the rules of the Sacred Canons. However, in the case of associations which have been erected by exempt religious in their own churches in virtue of an apostolic privilege, the local Ordinary's right of visitation does not extend to the internal discipline or spiritual direction of the association (**Canon 690**).

RIGHTS OF ASSOCIATIONS

587. Unless the contrary is expressly stated, a legitimately erected association may possess and administer temporal goods under the authority of the local Ordinary, to whom it must render a financial statement at least once a year, as provided by Canon 1525. The association cannot hold property by the authority of the pastor in whose parish it is erected, unless the Ordinary himself has ruled otherwise. If so provided by the rules of its statutes, the association may receive offerings

and spend them for the pious purposes of the association itself, subject always to the intentions of the persons who made the offerings.

No association may collect alms unless either the statutes permit or necessity requires it: the consent of the local Ordinary is also necessary, and the manner which he prescribes for collecting the alms must be observed. If the association desires to collect alms outside the diocese, the written permission of each bishop in whose diocese it wishes to collect is required. The association shall give to the local Ordinary an exact account also of the offerings and alms and how they have been spent (**Canon 691**).

Admission and Expulsion of Members

588. To participate in the rights, privileges, indulgences and other spiritual favors of an association, it is necessary and suffices that a person be validly received into the association according to the proper statutes of the association, and that he has not been legally deprived of membership (**Canon 692**).

Non-Catholics, members of a condemned sect, persons publicly known to be under an ecclesiastical censure, and in general any public sinners, cannot be validly received into an association (**Canon 693, § 1**).

589. The same person may be enrolled in several associations, subject to the law of Canon 705, which states that nobody can belong at the same time to two Third Orders. Absent persons shall not be enrolled in associations which are constituted after the manner of an organic body; those present cannot be received except with their knowledge and of their own will. Religious may be received into associations, except Third Orders (cfr. Canon 704), unless, in the judgment of the superiors, the laws of the association are incompatible with the observance of the rule and constitutions (**Canon 693, §§ 2–4**).

590. The reception shall be performed according to the rules of law and the statutes of each association. In order that there may be a record of the reception, the names shall be entered in the roll-book of the association; indeed, this entry is required for validity of membership, if the association

has been erected as a legal person (**Canon 694**). A Decree of the Sacred Congregation of Indulgences, July 16, 1887, already decided that the reception into a confraternity strictly so called required the entering of the names of the members in the roll-book of the confraternity. The physical work of entering the names need not necessarily be done by the one who received the members, but he may commission another to do that work.

On the occasion of the reception into an association, no payment shall be demanded either directly or indirectly, except the fee which the legitimately approved statutes prescribe, or which the Ordinary of the diocese has sanctioned explicitly on account of special circumstances (**Canon 695**).

591. No legitimately enrolled member of a society shall be dismissed from the association except for a good reason and in accordance with the statutes. Catholics who have fallen into one of the categories mentioned in Canon 693, § 1 (namely, those who have joined a condemned sect, incurred a censure by public offense, or otherwise became public sinners), shall after previous admonition and with the observance of the proper statutes be deprived of membership; the right of recourse to the Ordinary remains to them. The local Ordinary shall have the right to dismiss members of any association, though there be nothing explicitly stated in the statutes about this right of the Ordinary; the religious superior may dismiss members of associations which are by virtue of an Apostolic indult erected by the religious (**Canon 696**).

GOVERNMENT OF ASSOCIATIONS

592. Legitimately erected associations have the right, after the manner laid down in their statutes and in the Canons, to hold meetings, to issue particular regulations respecting the association itself, and to elect administrators of goods, officers and assistants, subject to the jurisdiction and rights of the local Ordinary as defined by Canon 715. In reference to the convocation of meetings and the elections, the rules of the common law as contained in Canons 161–182 must be followed and also the statutes of the association in so far as they are not contrary to the common law (**Canon 697**).

593. Unless an Apostolic privilege explicitly states the con-

trary, the nomination of the moderator and the chaplain of associations which are either erected or approved by the Ordinary or by the Apostolic See, and also of associations erected by religious in virtue of an Apostolic privilege outside their own churches, rests with the local Ordinary. In associations, however, erected by the religious in their own churches the consent of the local Ordinary is required only if the superior appoints a moderator and chaplain from among the secular clergy (**Canon 698, § 1**).

The moderator and the chaplain can during the term of their office bless the habit or insignia, scapulars, etc., of the association, and invest the new members with them. In reference to sermons preached before the association, the precepts of Canons 1337–1342 shall be observed. The moderator and chaplain may be removed from office for a just cause by those who appointed them and by their successors or superiors. The same priest may be moderator and chaplain (**Canon 698, §§ 2–4**).

594. For serious reasons the local Ordinary may suppress not only those associations which were erected by himself or his predecessors, but also associations erected with the consent of the local Ordinary by religious in virtue of an Apostolic indult. Recourse to the Holy See is open to the association against the bishop's decree. Associations, however, which have been erected by the Apostolic See itself, may be suppressed only by the Holy See (**Canon 699**).

TITLE XIX

OF ASSOCIATIONS OF THE FAITHFUL IN PARTICULAR

595. There are three distinct kinds of associations of the faithful in the Church: Third Orders Secular, Confraternities, and Pious Unions (**Canon 700**). The order of precedence among the various associations of lay people is as follows: (1) Third Orders; (2) Archconfraternities; (3) Confraternities; (4) Primary Pious Unions; (5) Other Pious Unions. The Confraternity of the Blessed Sacrament precedes other archconfraternities in processions with the Blessed Sacrament. However, associations have the right of precedence only when the

members in a body, under their own cross or banner and vested with the habit or insignia of the association, take part in an ecclesiastical function (**Canon 701**).

CHAPTER I

OF THIRD ORDERS SECULAR

596. Secular tertiaries are those persons who strive to attain Christian perfection in the world under the guidance and according to the spirit of some Order, in a manner compatible with the secular life and according to the rules approved for them by the Apostolic See. If a Third Order Secular is divided into several associations, each legitimately established branch is called a Sodality of Tertiaries (**Canon 702**).

597. No religious organization can add to itself a Third Order, but the privilege granted to some Orders remains. Even though an Order has an Apostolic indult to erect a Third Order, the religious superiors, while they may indeed receive individual persons into the Third Order, cannot validly erect a sodality of tertiaries in any church without the consent of the local Ordinary, as is stated in Canon 686, § 3. Furthermore, they cannot allow the sodalities of tertiaries erected by them to wear their special garb in public sacred functions without the special permission of the local Ordinary (**Canon 703**).

598. Persons who have taken either perpetual or temporary vows in some religious organization cannot at the same time belong to any Third Order, even though they had been received into the Third Order before they embraced religious life. When such a person is freed from the vows and returns to the world, the former membership revives (**Canon 704**).

Without an Apostolic indult, no sodality of tertiaries can receive tertiaries of another Third Order, if they intend to remain in the former Third Order. Individual tertiaries may for a just reason transfer from one Third Order to another, and also from one sodality to another of the same Third Order (**Canon 705**).

With reference to the three Orders of St. Francis, of which each has a Third Order Secular, the Holy See has declared that the novices as well as the professed members may, if they find it more convenient, transfer from one Third Order of St. Francis to another Third Order under the jurisdiction of another Order of St. Francis. Likewise, a secular priest who has been empowered by the Superior General of one of the three Orders of St. Francis to be director of a sodality of the Third Order and to receive members, may when transferred to another parish, where the Third Order has been established by another of the three Orders, assume the directorship without new faculties, but he must inform the Visitor of that Third Order branch of his change to the parish, and transact the business of the Third Order with this Visitor.[135] A similar interchange between the Third Orders established by the two Carmelite Orders, Calced and Discalced, has been granted by the Holy See.[136]

599. The tertiaries may, but are not obliged to, take part in a body in public processions, funerals and other ecclesiastical functions. If, however, they are present, they must march under their own cross, wearing the insignia of the Order (**Canon 706**).

CHAPTER II

OF CONFRATERNITIES AND PIOUS UNIONS

600. Associations of the faithful erected for the practice of some work of piety or charity come under the name of *pious unions;* if they are established after the manner of an organic body, they are called *sodalities.* Sodalities which have also for their purpose the furtherance of public worship, are called *confraternities* (**Canon 707**).

Confraternities can be established only by a formal decree of erection. For the erection of pious unions the approval of the Ordinary suffices, and, when this approval has been granted, these pious unions, though they are not legal persons, are capable of obtaining spiritual favors and especially indulgences (**Canon 708**).

---

135 March 4, 1903; *Acta S. Sedis*, XXXV, 637.
136 January 16, 1912; *Acta Ap. Sedis*, IV, 143.

601. The members of a confraternity cannot officially assist in sacred functions unless they wear the habit or insignia of the confraternity. Women may be enrolled in the confraternities only to gain the indulgences and spiritual favors granted to the confraternity (**Canon 709**). From a declaration of the Sacred Congregation of Rites,[137] it seems that, in places where it is not the custom to wear the special garb of the Third Order or the confraternity, it suffices if the members wear the insignia of the Third Order or the confraternity without the habit (or *sacco*), but the Sacred Congregation desires that they should wear the habit.

602. The names or titles of confraternities and pious unions are to be taken from the attributes of God, from the mysteries of the Christian religion, from the feasts of our Lord or of the Blessed Virgin, from the Saints, or from the pious work of the society (**Canon 710**). There should not be several confraternities or pious unions of the same title and institute in the same place, unless the law or special regulations allow an exception. In the case of large cities it is left to the judgment of the local Ordinary to decide what distance should intervene between confraternities or pious unions of the same kind. The Holy See desires that the Ordinary establish in every parish church the Confraternities of the Blessed Sacrament and of Christian Doctrine, which, when legally erected, obtain automatically affiliation with the corresponding archconfraternities erected at Rome by the Cardinal Vicar of the City (**Canon 711**).[137a]

603. Confraternities or pious unions should be erected only in churches and public or semi-public oratories. They should not be established in a cathedral or collegiate church without the consent of the Chapter. In churches and oratories of religious women the local Ordinary may allow only the erection of an association of women, or of a pious union, which only meets for the recitation of certain prayers and has merely communication of spiritual favors (**Canon 712**). A decree of the Sacred Congregation of Bishops and Regulars [138] declared that the prohibition refers to the establishing of confraternities strictly so called in the chapels of religious women; other pious

---

[137] November 10, 1905; *Acta S. Sedis*, XXXVIII, 295.

[137a] No strict duty to establish Confraternity of Blessed Sacrament, cfr. App. III, 31, b.

[138] January 18, 1907; *Acta S. Sedis*, XL, 141.

associations of women may be established in these chapels, and the establishing of associations which comprise both men and women is left to the prudent judgment of the Ordinary.

604. The religious can and must give to the confraternities and pious unions erected by them all those spiritual favors— and those only—which are specifically and particularly called communicable in the faculties obtained by the religious from the Holy See. In the act of erection these graces should be made known to each confraternity or pious union, and Canon 919 must be observed. The confraternities erected by the religious cannot use a proper garb or insignia in public processions and other sacred functions without the special permission of the local Ordinary (**Canon 713**).

Canon 919 prescribes that even in the churches of regulars indulgences cannot be published without consulting the local Ordinary, if they have not been promulgated at Rome; the pamphlets or leaflets containing the indulgences cannot be published without the permission of the local Ordinary, and in some cases without the permission of the Holy See.

A Confraternity shall not abandon nor change its proper habit or insignia without permission of the local Ordinary (**Canon 714**).

Meetings and Sacred Functions of Confraternities

605. The local Ordinary has the right to preside, either in person or by his delegate, at the meetings of confraternities even in the churches and oratories of regulars, but without a vote; he has the right to confirm the election of worthy and capable officers and assistants, to reject or remove unworthy or incapable ones, and to correct and approve the statutes or other regulations, unless they were approved by the Apostolic See. If a confraternity wishes to hold extraordinary meetings, it shall advise the local Ordinary or his delegate in due time, otherwise the Ordinary has the right to prevent the meeting or to annul its decrees (**Canon 715**).

606. If the confraternities and pious unions have a church of their own, they have the right, with due observance of the laws, to hold non-parochial functions independently of the pastor, provided they do not impair the parochial ministry in the parish church. The same is to be observed also in the case

where a parish is erected in the church of a confraternity. If there is doubt whether the functions of the confraternity or pious union impair the parochial ministry, the right to decide and to prescribe practical rules to be followed is vested in the local Ordinary (**Canon 716**). If they are erected in a church which is not their own, the confraternities and pious unions can hold their proper ecclesiastical functions only in the chapel or at the altar where they are erected, subject to the rule laid down in Canon 716 and their respective statutes. The property of a confraternity or pious union erected in a church which is not its own, or where the church is its own but serves at the same time as a parish church, must be kept separate from the goods of the church or the community (**Canon 717**).

Canons 716–717 speak of churches owned by confraternities. In the United States these societies usually have no church or chapel of their own but are erected in the parish churches. The pastor or other priest who is the director of the confraternity conducts their meetings and special services, and there is no conflict between the services of the parish and those of the confraternity. In countries where the confraternities have their own church or chapel conflict may arise between the services of the parish and those of the confraternity. The rule of the Code about keeping a separate account of the goods of a confraternity, e.g., fees of members or donations made to the confraternity, applies also in the United States, and, as far as we know, the accounts of the confraternities are always kept separate from the parish funds.

607. The confraternities are obliged to take part in a body with their own insignia and under their own banner in the usual processions and others ordered by the local Ordinary, unless the Ordinary has ruled otherwise (**Canon 718**).

With the consent of the local Ordinary, a confraternity or pious union may be transferred from one place to another, unless such a transfer is forbidden by law or by the statutes approved by the Holy See. Whenever there is question of transferring a confraternity or a pious union reserved to some religious organization, the consent of the superior must be sought (**Canon 719**).

CHAPTER III

OF ARCHCONFRATERNITIES AND PRIMARY UNIONS

608. Sodalities which possess the right to aggregate or affiliate to themselves other associations of the same kind, are called *archconfraternities* (or *archsodalities*), and pious unions which have this right are called *primary* unions, congregations, or societies (**Canon 720**). Without an Apostolic indult, no association can validly affiliate or aggregate other associations. An archconfraternity or a primary union can affiliate to itself only those confraternities or pious unions which have the same title and the same purpose, unless an Apostolic indult grants broader powers (**Canon 721**).

609. By the aggregation are communicated all indulgences, privileges and other communicable spiritual favors which have been granted to the affiliating body directly and specifically by the Holy See, or which shall in future be granted in this manner, unless a restriction is made in the Apostolic indult. The affiliating association does not acquire any right over the other by the communication of indulgences and spiritual favors (**Canon 722**).

610. For the validity of the aggregation the following conditions are required:

(1) The association which is to be affiliated must already have been canonically erected and must not have been affiliated to any other archconfraternity or primary union;

(2) The aggregation, or affiliation, must be done with the written consent of the local Ordinary together with his testimonial letter;

(3) The indulgences, privileges and other spiritual favors which are communicated by the aggregation must be enumerated in a list inspected by the Ordinary of the place in which the archconfraternity is located, which list is to be delivered to the aggregated society;

(4) The aggregation is to be done in the form prescribed by the statutes and is to be perpetual;

(5) The letters of aggregation are to be given entirely free of charge, and absolutely no payment—even if voluntarily

offered—may be accepted, with the exception of the necessary expenses (**Canon 723**).

611. An archconfraternity or a primary union can be transferred from one place to another only by the Apostolic See (**Canon 724**). The title of *archsodality,* or *archconfraternity,* or *primary union,* even as a mere honorary title, can be given to an association by nobody but the Apostolic See (**Canon 725**).

Note: Many of the confraternities and associations spoken of in the preceding Canons have a scapular of cloth, usually made of wool, with which the members are invested, and which they are to wear in order to gain the indulgences of the association. The Holy See allows the wearing of a scapular medal in place of the scapular after one has been properly invested with the regular scapular. The medal is to show on one side the figure of Jesus with the Sacred Heart, and on the reverse side the image of the Blessed Virgin Mary. The medal may be blessed by any priest who has the faculty to receive persons into the association. One medal suffices for several scapulars, but it must receive one separate blessing for each scapular it is to replace. The blessing is given by making the sign of the cross over the medal (Holy Office, December 16, 1910; *Acta Ap. Sedis,* III, 22). It is permitted to bless scapular medals at missions and other religious gatherings even if the priest blessing them does not actually see all the medals. Moreover, a number of medals may be blessed for a certain scapular or scapulars, and given to people even before they are enrolled in the scapular, but they can gain the indulgences by the use of them only after enrollment (Holy Office, June 5, 1913; *Acta Ap. Sedis,* V, 303). New scapular medals, used to replace old ones, must be blessed by a priest having the faculty to enroll in the scapular (Holy Office, May 11, 1916; *Acta Ap. Sedis,* VIII, 175). Scapular medals are not allowed as a substitute for the Third Order scapular of St. Francis or any other Third Order. By the rule of Pope Leo XIII for the Third Order of St. Francis, the Superiors and Visitors have the right to commute the habit (*i.e.,* the large scapular) to something else, and therefore to a scapular medal (S. C. of Religious, March 25, 1922; *Acta Ap. Sedis,* XIV, 353). Orientals may use the scapular medal and may even be invested with it instead of the cloth scapular (Sacred Congregation for the Oriental Church, March 25, 1935; *Acta Ap. Sedis,* XXVII, 145).

THE THIRD BOOK
OF THINGS

612. The things spoken of in this book are so many means for attaining the purpose of the Church: some of these are spiritual, others are temporal, and others mixed (**Canon 726**).

The title of the third book "Of Things" is to receive a very general interpretation, just as the title of the second book of the Code was "Of Persons" generally. The third book is divided into six parts in which are treated all things which serve the Church to attain the ends which God has assigned her and for which she was established. Thus we have: (1) the Sacraments and Sacramentals; (2) Sacred Places, to which are added the Canons on Sacred Seasons; (3) Divine Worship; (4) the *Magisterium Ecclesiasticum,* Preaching, Seminaries, Schools, Books, Profession of Faith; (5) Benefices and Other Non-Collegiate Institutes; (6) Temporal Goods of the Church.

SIMONY

613. Before the Code treats of ecclesiastical things, it speaks of simony, which consists in the will and intention to buy or sell for a temporal price things which are spiritual. This crime against the reverence due to spiritual things is well expressed in the words of St. Peter: "Keep thy money to thyself, to perish with thee: because thou hast thought that the *gift of God* may be *purchased with money*" (Acts, viii. 20). Canonists and moralists generally treat of simony and its various forms. The Code very briefly sums up the principal points on simony, and then refers to the penalties against simony stated in other Canons (cfr. Canon 729).

The deliberate will to buy or sell for a temporal price things intrinsically spiritual (e.g., the Sacraments, ecclesiastical jurisdiction, consecration, indulgences, etc.), or to buy or sell a temporal thing annexed to a spiritual thing in such a way that the temporal thing cannot exist independently (e.g., an ecclesiastical benefice, etc.), or to make the spiritual thing even the partial object of a contract (e.g., the consecration in the sale of a consecrated chalice), is *simony forbidden by the Divine Law* (**Canon 727,** § 1).

To give temporal things annexed to spirituals for other temporal things annexed to spirituals, or spirituals for spirituals, or even temporal things for temporal things, if it is forbidden by the Church on account of danger of irreverence to spiritual things, is *simony of ecclesiastical law* (**Canon 727,** § 2).

When there is question of simony, the terms "buying and selling," "exchange," etc., are to be interpreted in a broad sense as applying to any agreement, though it has not taken effect, and as comprehending also *tacit* agreements in which the simoniacal intent is not expressly manifested, but may be deduced from the circumstances (**Canon 728**).

614. The Code defines simony as a deliberate will or intention to buy or sell spiritual things for a temporal price. The evil will or intention must of course find overt expression, for only as an external act does it become a crime in the eyes of the Church; merely internal acts cannot be reached by ecclesiastical penalties according to the old axiom: *De internis non judicat prætor.* The terms, *emendi vel vendendi,* imply a necessary element in the crime of simony, namely, that it must be a bilateral agreement to constitute simony. It need not be strictly a contract of buying and selling; any bilateral agreement between the parties suffices to constitute simony, as may be deduced from Canon 728. Thus, a tacit agreement of the two parties is simony; also an agreement in which the simoniacal intention is not explicitly manifested, but can be gathered from the circumstances; finally, an agreement which did not take effect, because neither party acted on the agreement.

615. The temporal price which one offers to pay may be anything which has temporal value. Usually three kinds of things which can serve as a price are indicated by commentators: (1) the *munus a manu,* a gift handed over, such as money or any movable or immovable goods; (2) the *munus ab obsequio,* an offering made in the form of service, which can be rendered in various ways; (3) the *munus a lingua,* when praise, flattery,

intercession, etc., are offered as the price for some spiritual good one expects to receive from another. In order to constitute simony, it is necessary that the temporal thing is offered as a price for the spiritual good; if the temporal thing is offered only after the manner of an alms on the occasion of receiving something spiritual, it is not simony (as is stated in Canon 730), unless the Church has forbidden such offering explicitly.

The *spiritual things* which are given in exchange for something temporal are distinguished by the Code into things *intrinsically* spiritual and spiritual things *annexed* to things temporal. Canon 727 gives examples of both kinds of spirituals. Here many distinctions occur according to the various kinds of spiritual goods, which may be found in any of the standard works on canon law or moral theology.

616. With regard to the distinction between simony of *divine law* and of *ecclesiastical law,* Canon 727 states that it is simony of divine law if a temporal price is offered for things either intrinsically spiritual or for temporal things which have become spiritual by the annexation of something spiritual to the temporal thing, provided that the annexation is such that the temporal thing cannot exist without the spiritual, or that, while the temporal value of the thing to which something spiritual has been annexed does indeed remain (e.g., a consecrated chalice still keeps its value as a utensil of more or less precious metal or skillful workmanship), the spiritual is made at least the partial object of the sale by an increase in the price demanded.

Simony by *ecclesiastical law* is described in Canon 727, § 2. In this kind of simony there is no question of giving something temporal for something spiritual, but rather of the exchange of goods of the same nature: spiritual goods for spirituals, temporal goods annexed to spirituals for other temporal goods annexed to spirituals, and temporal goods for temporal goods (e.g., one piece of church property for another piece). These transactions constitute simony of ecclesiastical law only in cases where the Church has forbidden them on account of the danger of irreverence to things spiritual.

617. The division of simony into *mental, contractual* (conventional), and *confidential,* explains the various forms in which the agreement can be made between the interested parties to give and take something temporal as a price for something

spiritual. *Purely mental* simony, as we explained before, is not considered by the law of the Church, which can deal only with overt acts when there is a question of enforcing such laws in the external forum. But the circumstances of a transaction may be of such a nature that the simoniacal intention can be construed from the facts, and this constructive simony can be punished by the ecclesiastical courts. *Contractual* or conventional simony is committed by a bilateral contract, explicit or implied; if the contract has not yet been executed on either side, it is purely contractual; if the agreement has been carried out by one of the contracting parties, it is called *simonia conventionalis mixta* (or partially executed contractual simony); if the agreement has been executed by both parties, it is called *realis* (or simony by fully executed agreement). *Confidential* simony appears only in the matter of ecclesiastical benefices, and consists in this, that one person procures for another an ecclesiastical benefice (by election, presentation, collation, resignation) with the confidential understanding, either explicit or implied, that he who gets the benefice obliges himself to resign the benefice afterwards in favor of him who procured the benefice, or in favor of a person chosen by this individual; or with the understanding that the incumbent of the benefice shall pay a pension out of the benefice to him who procured it or to a person of his choice. The commentators of the former Canon Law distinguish the various forms in which confidential simony can be committed. Some of the commentators of the Code hold that confidential simony is not considered by the Code. The name "confidential simony" does not appear in the Code, but the underlying principle is retained there, as can be deduced from Canons 1441, 1488 and especially Canon 1486.

JURIDICAL CONSEQUENCES OF THE CRIME OF SIMONY

618. While the penalties of law remain, the simoniacal contract is null and void; and, if simony is committed in connection with benefices, offices or dignities, the subsequent conferment is likewise void, even though the simony was committed by a third person and without the knowledge of the person who obtained the benefice, office, etc., provided it was not done fraudulently to render the appointment of the other invalid or

done against his protest. Wherefore (1) before any sentence of the judge (*ante quamlibet judicis sententiam*), the thing given and accepted simoniacally must be returned—if such restitution is possible and can be done without irreverence to the spiritual thing—and the benefice, office or dignity must be vacated; (2) the person who through simony obtained the benefice, office, etc., does not become the owner of the income: if he received the income in good faith, it is left to the prudent judgment of the judge or the Ordinary to condone the income thus received, either in whole or in part (**Canon 729**).

619. Note that what the Code states here about the effect of obtaining a benefice, office or dignity by simony, is not a penalty, but merely a condition for the valid or invalid acquisition of a benefice, etc. Wherefore, the Code also states that the two parties guilty of simony cannot gain any advantage from their invalid act: one must restore the illegally gotten temporal goods, and the other must give up the benefice *ante quamlibet judicis sententiam,* for there is no need of a judgment when there is question of restoring ill-gotten goods. The Code states plainly that the man who obtained a benefice, office or dignity through simony, cannot become the owner of the resulting income: he must therefore give up the benefice, though neither bishop nor court know about the simony. If it was merely a matter of penalty for a crime, it is certain from the law of the Code that, pending the declaratory sentence of the court, nobody need execute even a penalty *latæ sententiæ* against himself, if he cannot submit himself to the penalty without infamy (cfr. Canon 2232). The incapacity to obtain a benefice, office or dignity through simony, and the consequent obligation to restore the price and to give up the benefice, refer to both kinds of simony—that of divine and that of ecclesiastical law—because the Code speaks generally of a simoniacal contract in reference to benefices, offices and dignities.

The penalties against simony are stated in two Canons, 2371 and 2392 of the Fifth Book of the Code, which deals exclusively with the matter of ecclesiastical punishments for offenses against the laws of God and ecclesiastical laws.

620. An exception from the rule of Canon 729 is made in favor of the election of the Supreme Pontiff: to remove all pretext of attacking the validity of the election of the Roman

Pontiff, this election, though obtained through simony, is declared valid by the Constitution "Vacante Sede Apostolica" of Pope Pius X, December 25, 1904 (cap. VI, 79).

621. There are several other Canons which refer to simony. Canon 185 states that a resignation of an ecclesiastical office, if induced by simony, is invalid. Canon 1441 condemns as simoniacal any deductions, compensations and other payments which a cleric is expected to make from the fruits at the time when an ecclesiastical benefice is conferred on him, if such payments go to the one who confers the benefice, or to the patron or to others. Peaceful possession of an ecclesiastical benefice for three years, though the title to it was invalid, is lawful prescription (according to Canon 1446), except when simony was committed in obtaining the benefice. Canon 1465 rules that the presentation to an ecclesiastical benefice and the subsequent conferring of it is invalid, if simony was committed in the presentation. Offenses committed in the matter of Mass stipends, though not called simony by the Code, are nevertheless punished as offenses against religion, as can be seen from Canon 2324 which commands the Ordinary to punish—even with suspension and excommunication—clerics and lay persons who violate Canons 827, 828 and 840.

622. The Code continues: There is no simony when the temporal thing is given, not for the spiritual, but merely on the same occasion for a just reason acknowledged by law or legitimate custom. Furthermore, it is no simony when a temporal thing is given for a temporal thing which has something spiritual annexed to it (e.g., a consecrated chalice), provided the price is not raised on account of the annexed spiritual (**Canon 730**).

The Code here states that the offerings of the faithful received by the ministers on the occasion of the administration of the Sacraments and other ecclesiastical functions are received by a just title—namely, the right of the ministers to proper maintenance. It is not merely as alms that the ministers accept what is offered to them, for they have a right to support just as any man who works for another is entitled to his pay. St. Paul (I Cor., ix. 7–14) explains this point sufficiently. Abuse must of course be avoided—all the more so as any abuse on the part of the ministers of religion does harm to the faith.

Wherefore, the Code in various Canons which speak of the matter of stole fees, Mass stipends and other offerings, insists that the rights of the priest be well defined so that he may know what he can demand, and may have no excuse for greed.

623. It is not simony, Canon 730 states, to buy or sell things which have something spiritual annexed to them, as in the example of a chalice which has been consecrated. Canonists draw a distinction in the annexation of the spiritual to the temporal: one annexation is called *concomitanter* (further distinguished into *concomitanter intrinsece* and *extrinsece*), which implies that a certain act or work may be considered at the same time spiritual and physical (or temporal). In every spiritual work there is necessarily a physical element, the work or exertion to do the spiritual act; such work is intrinsically connected with the spiritual, and cannot be separated from it. Compensation for such work is allowed by law or custom, and the extent of the allowance fixed by it under the title of the minister's maintenance. Beyond this fixed stipend nothing can be charged for such work. To a spiritual act there may be accidentally attached a greater amount of work than what is intrinsically required to do the act: for instance, religious services may be demanded by someone to be performed under circumstances which require long travelling, or, in the case of Holy Mass, fasting to a very late hour, etc. That work is called extrinsically annexed to the spiritual act. It is evident that the minister is entitled to compensation for such work; in many instances, however, compensation is fixed by diocesan law for such cases.

The annexation which is called *antecedenter* implies that the object which has been blessed or consecrated had its value prior to its blessing or consecration. These objects can be sold even after the consecration or blessing for what they are worth in themselves, but their price must not be raised in the least because they are blessed objects. In the case of objects to which indulgences are attached, the Code in Canon 924 rules that the indulgences are lost when beads and other indulgenced objects are sold. The sale is not forbidden, but in order to remove all occasion for raising the price on account of the indulgences attached, the law states that the indulgences are lost to the objects by the very sale.

The annexation which is called *consequenter* means that the temporal thing is the effect of the spiritual thing—e.g., the income attached to an ecclesiastical office or benefice—so that the temporal thing does not exist at all without the spiritual. The sale of such a thing is called simony by divine law in Canon 727, § 1.

PART I

OF THE SACRAMENTS

624. As all the Sacraments instituted by Christ our Lord are the principal means of sanctification and salvation, the greatest care and reverence should be employed in their suitable and proper administration and reception. It is forbidden to administer the Sacraments of the Church to heretics or schismatics, even though they err in good faith and ask for them, unless they have first renounced their errors and been reconciled with the Church (**Canon 731**).

The last sentence of this is of far-reaching importance, and there is a great deal of controversy over the precise meaning of its ruling. In the first place, all canonists and moralists agree that those who are heretics or schismatics and know that they are wrong, cannot be given the Sacraments of the Church unless they renounce their errors and are reconciled with the Church. Numerous decrees of the Holy Office put this point beyond controversy.

The controversy turns about those Christians who are separated from the Church in good faith. It is evident that the Church cannot, as a rule, allow the administration of the Sacraments to non-Catholics. She would thereby prove false to her trust and deny her very principles. The Church governed by the successor of St. Peter is the only one Church authorized by Christ to teach the way of salvation and to distribute the means of salvation—the Sacraments. The doors of the Church are open to all who are willing to live as the Church teaches, and those who will enter are entitled to all that the Church by Christ's commission can give them. But, with regard to those who stay outside in spite of the standing invitation, what business has the Church to minister to them the blessings which Christ commissioned her to give to His flock?

625. Is there no exception to the rule forbidding the administration of the Sacraments to baptized non-Catholics who are in good faith? In the case of those who are in good health, the prohibition is absolute; no dispute on this point is possible in view of the repeated explicit declarations of the Holy Office.[1]

If they are in danger of death, it seems that the general rule stated in the Code may suffer an exception. The fact that the Code does not explicitly mention an exception to the rule, is not necessarily an argument against the possibility of an exception, for in very many laws of the Code no exception is stated, and yet, by a reasonable *epikeia,* exceptions are legitimate in a number of cases where unusual circumstances make the application of the law obnoxious. From a decision of the Holy Office [2] it is certain that the Church permits the administration of the Sacraments to heretics and schismatics provided that they are in good faith and have given at least a probable sign of that good faith, and provided scandal is avoided. In reference to those who have become unconscious, a declaration of the Holy Office [3] recently stated that conditional absolution and Extreme Unction may be given if one can judge from the circumstances that the schismatic has at least implicitly rejected his errors; scandal to Catholics present should be prevented by the declaration of the priest that the Church supposes that the person in his last moments of consciousness desired to return to the unity of the faith. One may, therefore, conclude that the Code does not state a new prohibition in Canon 731, and that the Canonists and moralists who wrote on this question before the Code may be followed.

626. The question is full of difficulties which seem to be beyond solution; it is very questionable whether the administration of the Sacraments of Penance and Extreme Unction (the two Sacraments about which there is question in the case of non-Catholics in danger of death), does avail anything in many cases. The principal difficulty centers in the intention

[1] August 28, 1669; *Collect. de P. F.,* I, n. 185.
[2] July 20, 1898; *Collect. de P. F.,* II, n. 2012.
[3] May 26, 1916; *Eccl. Review,* LXVII, 450, where the question of giving the Sacraments to Protestants is ably discussed.

necessary for the valid reception of the Sacraments. As most Protestants do not believe in the Sacraments of Penance and Extreme Unction, their case is not one of a mere lack of faith, but of positive rejection of the Catholic teaching on these Sacraments. How, even when coupled with a general sorrow for their sins, a general will and intention to do all that God requires of them is a sufficient intention to receive the Sacraments is difficult to understand since the very foundation of an intention is lacking. Their frame of mind resolves itself at most into this, that they would want to receive these Sacraments if they knew that they were Sacraments, and if they knew that God wanted them to receive them. As actually they do not know or do not believe, it is difficult to understand how they can have a will or intention concerning something which they do not know or believe. There does not seem to be possible even an implied intention. The question is briefly summed up by Capello,[4] Vermeersch-Creusen [5] and Sabetti.[6]

A Decree of the Holy Office [7] reads as follows: "Whether approval may be given to the custom introduced in a certain hospital whereby dying heretics and schismatics are absolved conditionally on account of the presumed good faith of many who have been raised in heresy or schism, even though there has been no previous act by which they could be considered at least implicitly reconciled to the Catholic Church, and nothing has been said to them about reconciliation either because this was impossible, or because the priest does not want to disturb the conscience of the dying non-Catholic?" The answer was: "The custom in question is to be condemned in the form in which it is explained. The intention of the Sacred Congregation is to inform the Patriarch of Jerusalem that, whenever the dying heretic or schismatic has given some sign on which one can base a reasonable presumption that he adheres to the Holy Catholic Church, the priests may follow the rules laid down by recognized authors."

627. The Sacraments of Baptism, Confirmation and Orders which imprint a character cannot be received a second time. If, however, there is a prudent doubt whether they have been

4 Capello, "De Sacr., I, 53-54.
5 Vermeersch-Creusen, "Epitome Jur. Can.," II, 9.
6 Sabetti, "Theol. Moral." (Ed. 1919), 712, n. 753.
7 January 13, 1864; Collect. de Prop. Fide, I, n. 1246.

conferred at all, or whether they were validly conferred, they may be conditionally repeated (**Canon 732**).

The point raised in this Canon confronts the priest mostly in the reception of converts from the various non-Catholic denominations. It is the question whether he should rebaptize conditionally, or whether he should consider the non-Catholic baptism valid. There are numerous decrees of the Holy Office which insist that a careful investigation be made before the priest rebaptize conditionally. If the investigation of the particular baptism, and of the manner in which it was conferred, does not give such certainty as one naturally desires in a matter involving the gravest consequence, baptism may be conferred conditionally. What constitutes a *prudent doubt,* is impossible to define satisfactorily by one universal formula. It depends not only on the various facts and circumstances, but also on the mental condition of the investigator, whether the doubt is reasonable and such as to justify conditional rebaptizing. The Holy See has issued repeated warnings against excessive haste in forming a general conclusion as to the invalidity of baptisms conferred by non-Catholic denominations. In a lengthy Instruction of the Holy Office on this matter, dated January 24, 1877, the Holy See would not admit that one could consider invalid all the baptisms conferred by Methodist ministers, but demands investigation in each individual case.[8]

628. In the celebration, administration and reception of the Sacraments, the liturgical rites and ceremonies prescribed in the rituals approved by the Church must be accurately observed. Each one shall follow the rite to which he belongs, except in the cases mentioned in Canons 851 and 866 (**Canon 733**).

The principal liturgical books of the Latin Rite are the *Pontificale Romanum,* the *Cæremoniale Episcoporum,* the Roman Missal and the Roman Ritual, in which the approved rites and ceremonies for the liturgy of the Sacraments are contained. Since there is nothing of greater importance in human life than the divine worship rendered by the Church through its ministers, the law naturally insists on the faithful and devout execution of the rules and regulations of the liturgical books. There are a few Latin rites which differ somewhat from the Roman Rite—the Milanese or Ambrosian, the Mozarabic, and the rite

8 *Collectanea S. Cong. de Prop. Fide,* II, n. 1465.

followed by some of the Religious Orders (e.g., the Order of St. Dominic or Friars Preachers). Other Latin rites have disappeared. The Oriental rites, of which there are many, differ from the Latin Rite not only in the ceremonies and prayers, but also in language. Every priest must observe the rite to which he belongs. For the administration and reception of Holy Communion consecrated according to another rite, cfr. Canons 851 and 866.[9]

HOLY OILS USED IN SOME OF THE SACRAMENTS

629. The holy oils required in the administration of several of the Sacraments must have been blessed by the bishop on the Holy Thursday immediately preceding, and the oils blessed previously are not to be used except in a case of necessity. If there is danger of the holy oils giving out, more olive oil which has not been blessed may be added even repeatedly, but always in a quantity less than the holy oils (**Canon 734**).

If the pastor could not get the new holy oils in time for the blessing of the baptismal font on Holy Saturday, he shall omit the ceremony of the mixing of the holy oils with the water and pour them in when he gets them; if, however, he has to baptize some one, he shall use the old oils for the blessing of the baptismal font.[10] If the pastor has to confer baptism before he can get the new holy oils, the anointings prescribed in baptism shall not be omitted, but made with the old oils.[11]

As a rule, a sufficient quantity of the various oils should be blessed by the bishop to satisfy the whole diocese for the entire year. It is not lawful to bless only a small quantity of the oils and immediately increase the quantity by adding unblessed oil before the oils are distributed among the priests of the diocese.[12]

630. The pastor must obtain the holy oils from his own Ordinary, and keep them under lock and key in a safe and becoming place in the church. Only under pressure of necessity

[9] On Sundays and holydays of obligation Holy Mass may be heard in the church of any Catholic rite (Canon 1249). The Sacrament of Penance may be received from a duly approved priest of any rite (Canon 905).

[10] Sacred Congregation of Rites, Jan. 31, 1896; *Acta S. Sedis*, XXVIII, 504.

[11] Sacred Congregation of Rites, Sept. 23, 1837, Sept. 19, 1859; *Decr. Auth. S. R. C.*, nn. 2773, 3092.

[12] Sacred Congregation of Rites, Jan. 28, 1910; *Acta Ap. Sedis*, II, 118.

or other reasonable cause may he keep them in his house, and in such a case he needs also the permission of the Ordinary (**Canon 735**).

There are several decrees of the Sacred Congregation of Rites which rule that mere convenience is no valid reason for keeping the holy oils in the pastor's residence, even where the parochial residence does not adjoin the church.[13]

No Fee to be Charged for Administration of the Sacraments

631. Regardless of the reason or the occasion, the minister shall not either directly or indirectly exact or ask for any remuneration for administering the Sacraments, except the offerings spoken of in Canon 1507 (**Canon 736**).

The tax covering the expenses in the issuing of dispensations in marriage is to be fixed by the local Ordinary (Canon 1056). The tax of the funeral offerings (Canon 1234) and the amount of the Mass stipends (Canon 831) are likewise fixed by each bishop for his diocese. Other offerings are to be determined by the bishops of each ecclesiastical province, subject to the approval of the Holy See (Canon 1507). Offerings voluntarily made by the people may, of course, be accepted by the ministers, unless the law explicitly forbids it. We have such a prohibition for the United States by the Second Council of Baltimore which forbids the priests to receive even voluntary offerings in the administration of the Sacrament of Penance, even Mass stipends.[14]

TITLE I

OF BAPTISM

632. Baptism—the door and foundation of all other Sacraments, the Sacrament which, if we are to attain salvation, must be either actually received or at least desired—is given validly only by ablution with truly natural water and the pronouncing of the prescribed form of words. Baptism administered with the observance of all the rites and ceremonies

---

[13] Dec. 16, 1826, *Decr. Auth.*, n. 2650; Aug. 31, 1872, *Decr. Auth.*, n. 3276; Nov. 15, 1890, *Decr. Auth.*, n. 3739; June 23, 1892, *Decr. Auth.*, n. 3779.
[14] *Decreta Conc. Plen. Baltimoren.*, II, n. 289.

prescribed in the ritual is called *solemn;* otherwise it is called not solemn, or *private* (**Canon 737**).

Nothing further is stated in the Code about the *matter* and *form* of Baptism, because these subjects belong to the domain of dogmatic and moral theology. Numerous questions have in the course of centuries been proposed to the Holy See about the water as the valid *materia* of the Sacrament and also about the form of words. All these questions are fully treated in the standard moral theologies, and need not be repeated in a commentary on the Code.

CHAPTER I

OF THE MINISTER OF BAPTISM

633. The *ordinary* minister of Solemn Baptism is the priest. Its administration, however, is reserved to the pastor or another priest acting with the permission of the pastor or of the local Ordinary, which permission is legitimately presumed in a case of necessity. Even a *peregrinus* (i.e., a person who is at the time outside the parish where he has his domicile or quasi-domicile) should receive Solemn Baptism from his proper pastor in his own parish, if this can be easily done and without delay; otherwise, any pastor may within his territory solemnly baptize a *peregrinus* (**Canon 738**).

The right to confer Solemn Baptism is reserved to the pastor within the territory of his parish. Outside his territory he has no right to baptize even his own subjects. Who comes under the name of pastor in canon law, is stated in Canon 451. Infants and all children of Catholic parents under the age of twenty-one have the same domicile or quasi-domicile as their parents, but a minor after the age of infancy can acquire a quasi-domicile of his own, and consequently a parish of his own (cfr. Canons 93–94). If a *peregrinus* cannot be baptized easily and without delay in his own parish by his own pastor, the pastor of the parish where such a person—or the parents, if there is question of an infant—actually stays, has the right to baptize. Therefore, the offering made at the baptism is also his. If a priest, in baptizing a person, acts for the pastor and in his parish, and either with his permission or (in a case of necessity) with his presumed permission, the stole fee or offering belongs to the pastor (Canon 463), and it likewise belongs to the pastor if another priest unlawfully baptized his subject—for instance, when parish churches are near to each other, and the pastor of one parish baptizes the subject of a neighboring pastor. In all cases where the proper pastor was entitled to the offering, the priest who performed the baptism must in justice make restitution. If, however, a priest baptizes in a case of necessity (as he is authorized to baptize by Canon 738), he seems to be entitled to some remuneration, inasmuch as necessity makes him the pastor's agent in the matter.

No priest is allowed, without due permission, to baptize solemnly even a resident of his own parish in the territory of another pastor (**Canon 739**). As we saw above, the pastor's rights in reference to baptism are limited to the territory of his parish so that he cannot go into another parish to baptize without permission a child of one of his parishioners who is staying temporarily outside his parish.

Where parishes or quasi-parishes are not yet established, the particular statutes and accepted customs must be consulted in order to determine what priest, besides the Ordinary, has the right to baptize, either in the entire territory or in some particular district (**Canon 740**).

634. The deacon is the extraordinary minister of Solemn Baptism. He shall not, however, use his power without the permission of either the local Ordinary or the pastor, which may be given for a just reason; when necessity urges, that permission is legitimately presumed (**Canon 741**). The *Pontificale Romanum*, in the address of the bishop to the candidates for deaconship says: "Diaconum enim opportet . . . baptizare." Before the promulgation of the Code, the exercise of this right was so very much restricted that the common opinion of canonists held that the deacon who gave Solemn Baptism without having obtained permission incurred irregularity. From Canon 985 which enumerates the irregularities, it is certain that the deacon does not incur irregularity by conferring Solemn Baptism without permission. The case of necessity in which the deacon can give Solemn Baptism with presumed permission, need not be an extreme case of necessity, but rather a common or ordinary case where Baptism could not be deferred without serious inconvenience or difficulty.[15] It must be, however, a far more

15 Noldin, "Theol. Moral." (13th ed.), III, 75, n. 64.

serious reason than a priest needs with the presumed permission
of the proper pastor to baptize. The deacon may not bless the
baptismal water or the salt, as was declared by the Sacred
Congregation of Rites, February 10, 1888.[16]

PRIVATE BAPTISM

635. Private Baptism, as spoken of in Canon **759**, may
be given by any one who uses the proper matter and form
and has the right intention. In so far as possible, two witnesses,
or at least one, should be present, by whom the conferring of
Baptism can be proved. A priest who happens to be present,
shall be preferred to a deacon; a deacon to a subdeacon; a
cleric to a lay person, and a man to a woman, unless decency
demand that a woman be preferred, or the woman is more
conversant with the form and manner of baptizing. The father
or mother are not allowed to baptize their own child except
in danger of death when there is no one else at hand who can
baptize (**Canon 742**).

Private Baptism may be given when the person to be baptized is in danger of death; also when baptism with all the
ceremonies cannot take place without considerable delay and
there is danger of death without baptism. Thus, the Holy
Office [17] declared that a midwife may baptize in such a case,
even though the child is presently well and strong; also that
Private Baptism may be administered when the infant cannot
without danger be brought to the church on account of the
distance, stormy weather or other serious reasons.[18] As the
priest is the ordinary minister of Baptism, he is to be called
even for Private Baptism if time permits. An heretical or
schismatic minister may not be called even in a case of danger
of death to baptize, unless there is nobody else who knows how
to baptize and is willing to do so.[19] A Catholic lay person is
to be preferred to a priest who is suspended, personally interdicted, or excommunicated when these censures have been imposed by declaratory or condemnatory sentence of the ecclesiastical court, for Canon 2261 desires that the people do not

16 *Decreta Auth.*, S. R. C., n. 3684.
17 January 11, 1899; *Collect. S. C. de P. F.*, II, n. 2033.
18 Sacred Congregation of the Prop., Jan. 21, 1789; *Collect.*, I, n. 598.
19 Holy Office, July 5, 1853; *Collect. S. C. Prop. Fide*, I, n. 1095.

request them to administer the Sacraments if there is anyone else at hand who can do so.[20]

636. The pastor should take care that the faithful, especially midwives, doctors and surgeons, learn how to baptize properly in a case of necessity (**Canon 743**). In the United States licensed nurses are frequently employed to attend women in childbirth, wherefore it is of importance that at the nurses' training schools which are established at many Catholic hospitals some instruction be given on the manner of baptizing. This instruction indeed cannot be neglected without a serious violation of the law of Canon 743. Here the responsibility to comply with the law of the Church lies as much with the authorities who are in charge of the hospital, as with the pastor in whose parish a Catholic hospital is located. A prudent pastor will also find ways and means to get into touch with the non-Catholic doctors, nurses and midwives in his parish. The law of Canon 743 certainly obliges him to do what is reasonably within his power to impart the necessary information to these professional persons who are his parishioners.

BAPTISM OF ADULTS

637. The baptism of adults, where it can be conveniently done, should be referred to the local Ordinary, so that, if he so desires, he himself or his delegate may baptize more solemnly (**Canon 744**). This Canon recalls the discipline of the Church in the early centuries when all baptisms were reserved to the bishop of the diocese. The Code does not strictly command that the baptism of adults be referred to the bishop, but only emphasizes the right of the Ordinary to baptize if he wishes.

CHAPTER II

OF THE SUBJECT OF BAPTISM

638. The subject capable of Baptism is *omnis et solus homo viator* (that is, every living human being, and such alone), who has not yet been baptized. In connexion with Baptism, the term *parvulus* or *infans* means (according to Canon 88) one

20 Blat, ''Comm. Jur. Can.,'' III, 30.

who has not yet the use of reason, and persons insane from infancy are regarded as equivalent to *parvuli,* no matter what age they may be. The term *adults* here implies those who have the use of reason: for admission to Baptism, it is sufficient if these of their own free will ask individually for it (**Canon 745**).

Canon 89 states that persons who have not reached their majority are subject to the authority of their parents or guardians in the exercise of their rights, except in those matters in which the law exempts them from the paternal power. Canon 745 is an example of such an exception; a minor has a right to receive Baptism when he understands what Baptism is, and his conscience tells him that he should receive it though his parents object. This is not merely a right given the minor by ecclesiastical law; he has this right by divine law, for in affairs that concern the salvation of his soul he has his own individual duties and rights in the exercise of which no human power may interfere. Practically, a case of that kind offers great difficulty if the parents are absolutely opposed to his receiving Baptism, or, if already baptized in the non-Catholic sect, to his reception into the Church. If the child is not of age, he cannot leave home against the will of the parents, and the civil law would force him to return to his parents' home if he went away and the parents insist on his return. In that case there would be great danger of the loss of faith. If the Church does not allow the priest to baptize an infant unless there is some guarantee of the Catholic education of the child, it may be argued in the case of the minor who stands in such precarious circumstances that he should rather not be baptized until he has a chance to live according to the Catholic faith. Besides, it is not certain that the delay of Baptism, even for a long time, is a serious matter, since St. Thomas and other theologians hold the opinion that it is not *per se* a mortal sin to delay baptism until danger of death unless the reason on account of which it is deferred is gravely sinful.[21]

---

[21] *Suppl.*, q. 6, art. 5; St. Bonaventure (*Sent.*, lib. IV, dist. IV, pars II, art. 1, q. 1). When time and place offer opportunity for Baptism and its reception is neglected, the neglect is a mortal sin.

UNUSUAL CASES OF INFANT BAPTISM

639. An infant shall not be baptized while still enclosed in the mother's womb as long as there is probable hope that it can be baptized when born. If the infant puts forth the head, it may be baptized on the head in case of imminent danger of death, and Baptism shall not afterwards be repeated conditionally if the child lives. Should any other limb emerge, the infant may be baptized on that limb conditionally, if the danger of death is imminent, but if the infant is born alive it must be baptized again conditionally. If the mother dies in pregnancy, and the *fetus*, when extracted by those whose duty it is to do this, shows sure signs of life, it shall be baptized absolutely; conditional baptism is given if life is doubtful. If the *fetus* was baptized in the mother's womb, it shall, when born, be baptized again conditionally (**Canon 746**).

The Church did not want to decide the disputed question whether a child can be validly baptized in the mother's womb, wherefore the Code gives a practical solution of the difficulty by insisting on a conditional repetition of the Baptism of an infant baptized in the mother's womb. Even if one admits that the child in the mother's womb can be considered as a "homo viator," that is to say, as having a distinct body and soul, a human individual existing in this world and only dependent on the mother as a necessary condition for the uterine stage of life, still in nearly every case the very fact whether the water of baptism properly touched the child does remain doubtful. Another doubtful baptism remains unsolved in the Code namely, whether Baptism conferred on any part of the human body other than the head is a valid Baptism.[22] Theologians disagree whether baptism conferred by the pouring of water on a hand or foot, arm or leg, is a valid baptism. If the water is poured on the shoulders or the breast, St. Thomas and many theologians with him hold that the Baptism is undoubtedly valid. Pope Benedict XIV, St. Thomas, and many others discuss the question, but no satisfactory reason is given why

[22] To guard against danger of infection in baptisms attempted in the mother's womb, the Holy Office, Aug. 21, 1901, allowed the water to be mixed in the proportion of one to a thousand parts with bichloride of mercury.

the baptism on one part of the body is not as good as baptism on another. Though St. Thomas says that the soul does manifest itself in its entirety in the head more than in any other part of the body, he does not seem to consider it a very cogent reason, for he adds that, for this reason, "it seems to some that . . . baptism is to be conferred again after the birth." [23]

640. The Code gives directions that, in case of death of a woman in pregnancy, the *fetus* should be extracted by those whose duty it is, and baptized either absolutely or conditionally as life is certain or doubtful. The priest has at most the duty to urge the relatives and the surgeon to perform the operation as soon after death is ascertained as the law of the respective state permits. It is said that the medical profession in Europe considers it part of medical ethics to perform the operation if the family does not object, and there is hope of extracting the *fetus* alive. In the United States also men of high standing in the medical profession favor the operation after the death of the pregnant mother when there is hope of extracting the *fetus* alive.[24]

Care should be taken that every *fetus* born prematurely, no matter at what stage of pregnancy, be baptized: the baptism shall be absolute, if it is certain that the *fetus* is alive, and conditional, if life is doubtful (**Canon 747**). Some diocesan statutes insist that the pastor in his instructions to the bridal couple and in instructions to doctors, nurses and midwives shall remind them of the obligation to secure the baptism of a *fetus* in case of miscarriage. The manuals of pastoral medicine indicate the manner in which an abortive *fetus* may be baptized.

641. Monstrous and unusual forms of the *fetus* should always be baptized, at least conditionally; when there is doubt whether the *fetus* is one being or several, one should be baptized absolutely and the others conditionally (**Canon 748**).

The last few Canons were taken from the Roman Ritual on Baptism, and the Canon about the misformed *fetus* is likewise taken from that source. Here the Code corrects the Ritual, which distinguished between "monstra" that have a human form and those which do not have that form. It is generally ad-

---

[23] Benedict XIV, "De Synodo Diœcesana," lib. VII, c. 5, nn. 7-10; St. Thomas, "Summa," P. III, t. III, q. 68, art. 11.

[24] *Am. Eccles. Review*, II, 358, "Cæsarean Operation *post Mortem Matris*."

mitted today that a woman can give birth to no other than a human being, however deformed that infant may be, even to the extent of resembling an animal rather than a human being. If the thing born is nothing but a mass of flesh and membrane without any definite shape, it will be very doubtful whether there is any life at all; if life is doubtful it should be baptized conditionally.

INFANTS ABANDONED BY THE PARENTS

642. Infants who have been abandoned and found shall be baptized conditionally, if after careful investigation there is no certainty about their Baptism (**Canon 749**).

Parents who abandon their infants by leaving them in the street or hallways so that someone may find them and care for them, lose their right to the child. There would thus be no objection to baptizing such infants if those who are willing to care for the child give assurance that the child will be raised in the Catholic faith. Though there is not much probability that the abandoned infant was baptized, since as a rule the infant is abandoned soon after birth, the uncertainty necessitates a conditional conferring of Baptism. Investigation in such cases is usually fruitless, for the mother who thus treats her infant knows that the authorities of the city or town would punish her severely, and therefore takes good care that all marks of identification are obliterated.

BAPTISM OF INFANTS OF NON-CATHOLIC PARENTS

643. An infant of unbaptized parents can be lawfully baptized, even despite the objection of the parents, if the danger of death of the infant is such that it may be prudently judged the child will die before it comes to the use of reason.

Provided there is guarantee for the Catholic bringing up of the child, an infant may be licitly baptized even though there is no danger of death: (1) if the parents or guardians, or at least one of them, consent; (2) if there are no parents (i.e., father or mother, grandfather or grandmother) or guardians, or if they lost the right to the custody of the child, or cannot in any way exercise that right (**Canon 750**).

Pope Benedict XIV, in his Constitution "Postremo Mense,"

February 28, 1747, states that by the law of nature children are under the care of their parents as long as they cannot provide for themselves, and therefore it would be as great a breach of natural justice to baptize infants against the will of the parents as to baptize an adult against his own will.[25] In the same Constitution he states that in danger of death the infant may be baptized, and shows that this had been decided previously by the Sacred Congregation of the Holy Office. It is evident that, when the infant is in danger of death, his right to baptism which he gets through the Redemption of Christ is superior to the right of the parents over the child, for he is then in extreme spiritual need in which all inferior rights must give way. When children come to the use of reason, they are able to help themselves in the affairs of their soul, and, as we saw before, in the affairs of one's soul one becomes independent of the paternal power, having the duty to obey God rather than men, if God's grace calls one to His Church.

644. In reference to the baptism of an infant whose parents belong to an heretical or schismatic sect, or have become apostates from the Church, or have lapsed into heresy or schism, the regulations laid down in the preceding Canon are to be followed (**Canon 751**).

Here the Church for practical reasons does not insist on the right she has to force all baptized persons to obey her laws. As the Church has no physical means of enforcing her laws against those who refuse to obey her or to recognize the power she has received from Christ, it would not be prudent to allow the baptism of their infants in the Catholic Church when there is no hope that the children will be raised as Catholics.

The Code wants some guarantee of the future Catholic education of the children before it allows the baptism in the Catholic Church of the children of unbaptized parents, of heretical or schismatic parents, or of Catholic parents who have lapsed from the faith. The parents or guardians, or at least one of them, must consent to the baptism of the child, and give assurance that the child will be brought up in the Catholic faith. Just what amount of certainty there must be of the future Catholic education of the child whose parents

---

[25] *Benedicti XIV Opera Omnia*, XVI, 171-172. This constitution is reprinted in Gasparri, "Fontes Cod. Juris Can.," II, 62.

are non-Catholics, but ask that the child be baptized by a Catholic priest, cannot be determined by one absolute rule, because much depends on the circumstances of the case. In answering cases of this kind, the various decrees of the Holy Office speak of a "probabilis spes," or a "rationabilis spes Catholicæ educationis." When the child of non-Catholic parents is presented for baptism by Catholic sponsors, but there appears no hope that the child will be raised in the Catholic faith, the Holy Office, Nov. 29, 1764, forbade baptism.[26] On the other hand, the Sacred Congregation of the Propaganda, January 31, 1796, ruled that, even though the parents were indifferent Catholics or otherwise of such a character as to hold out little hope that the child would be brought up in the practice of the Catholic faith, the infant should nevertheless be baptized by the priest. It seems that the hope of conversion of such Catholics was the reason why the Sacred Congregation was in favor of baptism.[27]

Baptism of Adults

645. An adult shall not be baptized except with his own knowledge and consent and after due instruction. He is, moreover, to be admonished to repent of his sins. In danger of death, if he cannot be more thoroughly instructed in the principal mysteries of faith, it suffices for the conferring of baptism that he manifest in some way his assent to these mysteries, and promise solemnly that he will keep the commandments of the Christian religion. If he cannot even ask for baptism, but has either before or in his present condition given some probable manifestation of an intention of receiving it, he should be baptized conditionally. If afterwards he gets well, and there remains doubt as to the validity of the Baptism, he shall be baptized again conditionally (**Canon 752**).

In an Instruction of August 3, 1860, the Holy Office teaches that in an adult faith and sorrow for sin are required for the licit reception of the Sacrament of Baptism, but the intention to receive the Sacrament is required for validity.[28] Ordinarily the instruction in the principal points of faith must precede the

---

26 *Collectanea de Prop. Fide*, I, n. 457.
27 *Collectanea de Prop. Fide*, I, n. 625.
28 *Collectanea de Prop. Fide*, I, n. 1198.

baptism of adults, and they must show that they believe and want to be baptized before the priest is allowed to give them baptism. In case of illness, if there is no time for a full instruction, the principal points of faith and the requirements of a Christian life must be briefly proposed to the sick persons, and if they manifest their belief in the truths proposed to them and seriously promise to live according to the Christian faith in the case of recovery, their petition for baptism may be granted.

646. In extreme cases where neither instruction nor a manifestation of the intention to receive baptism on the part of the sick person is possible, the Code allows conditional baptism on the basis of a probable intention. In his Constitution ''Postremo Mense,'' Pope Benedict XIV teaches that there must be some positive sign of the intention to receive baptism, and that it is not sufficient for validity to be neither for nor against the reception. He furthermore holds that if one has had the intention to receive Baptism and has not retracted it, the intention perseveres: thus, in case of sudden loss of consciousness or other illness which makes it impossible for him to manifest his mind, a person might be baptized on the supposition that his intention perseveres.[29] If the signs of an intention to receive baptism remain doubtful, and the person is in such a condition that he cannot manifest his mind, the baptism is to be conferred conditionally. If the intention is certain, but there is some doubt as to the faith and the sorrow for sin and danger of death is imminent, Baptism is to be conferred absolutely, because these are conditions for licit reception only: such was the declaration made by the Holy Office on September 18, 1850, and again on August 3, 1860.[30] If an infidel has joined a Protestant sect and has obtained some knowledge of the Blessed Trinity, Incarnation and Redemption, but does not know or understand the difference between the Catholic Church and the other Christian Churches, and if he is in danger of death and cannot be taught the difference between the Churches either because his death is imminent or because by a short instruction which might be possible nothing could be accomplished except to upset his mind, he may be left in good faith and baptized by the priest, if he wants to receive baptism. This decision is contained in

[29] *Opera Omnia Benedicti XIV*, XVI, 184-185, nn. 46 and 48.
[30] *Collectanea de Prop. Fide*, I, nn. 1050 and 1198.

an Instruction of the Holy Office, January 27, 1892, which added
that, if the person has been invalidly baptized in the Protestant
Church, he shall be baptized absolutely, and if the Protestant
baptism is doubtful, he shall be baptized conditionally.[31]

647. The Code desires that the priest who baptizes an adult
be fasting, and that the adult baptized be also fasting, if he
is in good health. Unless grave and urgent reasons prevent
it, the baptized adult should immediately after Baptism assist
at Holy Mass and receive Holy Communion (**Canon 753**)

The words of this Canon are taken from the Roman Ritual.
The Code recalls the ancient discipline of the Church according
to which adults were, as a rule, baptized on the eve of Easter
and Pentecost, and immediately after Baptism, at midnight,
Holy Mass was celebrated at which the newly baptized were
solemnly introduced to the assembled congregation, and were
for the first time permitted to assist at the entire Mass and
receive Holy Communion with the faithful. The Code prescribes in words indicating a grave obligation that soon (*statim*)
after Baptism the adult assist at Holy Mass and receive Holy
Communion. According to Vermeersch-Creusen,[32] the adverb
used in the Code (*statim*) is taken in law to mean within at least
two or three days. There seems to be no objection to baptizing
the adult in the afternoon or evening, as is usually done in the
United States, and arranging that the baptized person go to
Holy Mass and Communion the next day or at least within a
few days. The reception of converts from the various Christian
Churches is regulated by the Decree of the Holy Office, July 20,
1859, which decree is embodied in the Baltimore Ritual.

Baptism of Mentally Defective Persons

648. Insane and frenzied persons shall not be baptized unless
they have been such from birth, or became afflicted before they
had obtained the use of reason, in which case they should be
baptized like infants. If they have lucid intervals, they should
be baptized during such a moment if they manifest a desire
for baptism. They should also be baptized in imminent danger
of death, if, before they became insane, they showed a desire for
baptism. Those suffering from lethargy or phrenesis shall be

31 *Collectanea de Prop. Fide*, II, n. 1780.
32 *Epitome Juris Can.*, II, 20, n. 39.

baptized only while they are conscious and desirous of baptism; if the danger of death is imminent and they have shown a desire for baptism before they lost control of their minds, they should be baptized (**Canon 754**).

It is evident that those unfortunate persons who have never had the use of reason and whose insanity is as far as human knowledge can ascertain permanent, are to be regarded as infants. If one can reasonably foresee that they will never have the use of reason, they may be baptized even against the will of their parents, just as one may baptize an infant against their will when such an infant is sick beyond hope of recovery. The Holy See has warned missionaries to be prudent in baptizing sick infants or permanently insane persons against the will of the parents so as not to arouse hatred and persecution against the Church.[33]

With regard to persons who have had the use of reason, the same rules apply as to the baptism of adults in general. As we saw in Canon 752, in the case of adults whom one finds unconscious and in danger of death, the Church demands that they have given at least some probable sign of an intention to receive Baptism.

CHAPTER III

OF THE RITES AND CEREMONIES OF BAPTISM

649. Baptism shall be given solemnly, except in the cases spoken of in Canon 759. The local Ordinary may for a grave reason allow the use of the ceremonies prescribed in the baptism of infants for the baptism of adults (**Canon 755**).

Solemn Baptism means baptism with all the ceremonies of the Ritual. The exceptions to the rule that Solemn Baptism is to be ordinarily given are contained in Canon 759, and refer to baptism in danger of death and the baptism of converts to the Church who are baptized conditionally. The Ritual has two distinct sets of ceremonies—one form for the baptism of infants and another long and complicated form for the baptism of adults. Formerly the bishops got permission to allow the use of the ceremonies of infant baptism in baptizing adults by applying to the Holy See for the faculty. The Second Council

---

[33] *Collectanea de Prop. Fide,* I, nn. 522, 534.

of Baltimore (n. 243) asked for that faculty for all the bishops of the United States for ten or twenty years, but the Holy See did not grant the general faculty, saying that the individual bishops should apply for it. Now the Code grants the bishops this faculty to be made use of for grave and reasonable cause.

LATIN AND ORIENTAL RITE OF BAPTISM

650. The child must be baptized in the rite to which the parents belong. If one of the parents belong to the Latin Rite and the other to an Oriental Rite, the child shall be baptized in the rite to which the father belongs, unless a contrary ruling has been made by special law. If only one of the parents is a Catholic, the child shall be baptized in the rite of the Catholic party (**Canon 756**).

The laws of the Code are, as a rule, published for the Latin Rite exclusively, but in those matters where rites come necessarily into contact (as in the case of baptism of children whose parents belong to different rites), the Code had to take cognizance of the circumstances and determine rules for both rites. The general rule is that the child is to be baptized in the rite to which its parents belong. If a priest of the parents' rite is not at hand or cannot be reached without difficulty, the baptism need not be delayed, for the parents can take the infant to a priest of another rite, as Canon 98 states. That Canon likewise rules that such a baptism does not make the child a subject of the other rite, but it belongs to the rite of the parents. The Committee for the Authentic Interpretation of the Code confirms this interpretation of Canon 98.[34] The case is liable to happen quite frequently here in the United States where the Oriental Catholics are scattered all over the country and have but comparatively few priests to attend to them. As they cannot be said to belong to any parish of the Latin Rite, they are free to go to any parish to have their children baptized when they cannot have them baptized by a priest of their own rite.

The Code also provides for the case where one of the parents belongs to the Latin and the other to an Oriental rite. Ordi-

[34] October 16, 1919; cfr. App. III, 32, a.

narily the child is to be baptized in the rite of the father, unless the special laws of that rite approved by the Holy See provide otherwise.

SOLEMN BAPTISM AND BAPTISMAL WATER

651. In Solemn Baptism water blessed specially for this purpose shall be used. If the water in the baptismal font is so diminished that it does not suffice, other common water may be added in smaller quantity than the remaining blessed water, and this may be done repeatedly. If the baptismal water has become putrid, or has escaped from the font, or is lacking for any other reason, the pastor should have the font well cleaned, then put fresh water into it and bless it with the form prescribed in the liturgical books of his own rite (**Canon 757**).

The Church insists that in all churches which have a baptismal font the baptismal water be blessed both on the vigil of Easter and on the vigil of Pentecost, and only recently the Holy See declared that the custom of blessing the baptismal water only once a year on the vigil of Pentecost may not be continued.[35] If it becomes necessary to bless the baptismal water outside of the vigils of Easter and Pentecost, the Roman Ritual has a formula of blessing provided for such cases. In 1830 the Sacred Congregation of the Propaganda gave permission to the priests of the United States for twenty years to use a very short formula for blessing baptismal water outside of the vigils of Easter and Pentecost.[36] Sabetti-Barrett states that this formula may still be used.[37] However, after careful investigation, we have not been able to find a record of the renewal of this faculty.

652. Though Baptism may be conferred validly in any of the three ways: infusion, immersion, aspersion, nevertheless the first method or the second or a mixture of the two, whichever may be more widely in use, shall be retained, according to the approved rituals of the various dioceses (**Canon 758**).

The Roman Ritual is used very extensively in the churches of the Latin Rite, but it was not made obligatory for all dioceses of the Latin Rite. When the Roman Ritual was compiled

---

[35] Sacred Congregation of the Council, June 10, 1922; cfr. App. III, 32, b.

[36] *Collectanea de Prop. Fide*, I, n. 820

[37] Sabetti-Barrett, ''Theol. Moral.'' (ed. 1919), 573, q. 2.

and published by authority of Pope Paul V, June 17, 1614, the document of promulgation reprinted at the beginning of the Roman Ritual did not make allowance for the continuation of contrary ancient customs, as the Bull of Publication of the Roman Missal does. Nevertheless, diocesan rituals varying in their ceremonies from the Roman have been approved by the Holy See. For this reason the Code, in Canon 758, speaks of "probati diversarum Ecclesiarum rituales libri." The Sacred Congregation of Rites has declared that the local Ordinary can compel all pastors and priests of his diocese to follow the Roman Ritual notwithstanding any contrary custom, even of time immemorial.[38]

PRIVATE BAPTISM

653. In danger of death Private Baptism may be given. If it is administered by a person who is neither a priest nor a deacon, only that should be done which is necessary for the validity of baptism. If a priest or a deacon baptizes, and time permits, he should perform the ceremonies which follow baptism.

Except in danger of death, the local Ordinary may permit Private Baptism only in the case of adult converts from heresy who are baptized conditionally. The ceremonies which for any reason have been omitted in the conferring of baptism, shall be supplied as soon as possible in church, except in the case of conditional baptism of converts from heretical sects (**Canon 759**).[38a]

If baptism is repeated conditionally, the ceremonies should be supplied if they were omitted in the first baptism, saving the exception of the foregoing Canon in reference to conditional baptism of converts from heretical sects. If the ceremonies were employed in the first baptism, one is at liberty to repeat them or not (**Canon 760**).

Here the bishop is empowered to allow Private Baptism in the conditional baptism of converts from the various Christian sects. If one finds that the convert was never validly baptized, baptism must be given absolutely, and the formula for the baptism of adults used. For a grave reason the bishop can give permission to use the formula of Infant Baptism, as we

[38] *Decr. Authentica S. R. C.*, n. 3276.   [38a] Cfr. App. III, 32, f.

saw in Canon 755. Whether Solemn Baptism can be conferred in private houses, and how far the bishop may permit this is stated in Canon 776. In the Second Council of Baltimore (n. 244), the Fathers of the Council applied for the permission to allow the priests in the United States to confer conditional baptism on converts privately and without ceremonies, merely using holy water and the form of baptism. At that time the Holy See answered that it did not think it expedient to grant the request. It may be noted that in Private Baptism, either given in danger of death or to converts from non-Catholic churches with the permission of the bishop (conditional baptism), the use of baptismal water is not of obligation, but, if a priest or deacon baptizes and he has baptismal water at hand, it is proper to use it. Otherwise holy water should be used, if possible, in preference to common water.[39]

CHRISTIAN NAME TO BE GIVEN IN BAPTISM

654. The pastors shall endeavor to see that the person baptized receives a Christian name; if they cannot accomplish this, they shall add to the name given by the parents the name of some saint, and enter both names in the baptismal record (**Canon 761**).

The custom of assuming the name of a saint at Baptism cannot be traced back to the first few centuries of the Church. In fact, Tertullian, in his book on "Idolatry," says that a person does not necessarily honor Saturn or Mars, if he should be called by these names. In the First Œcumenical Council of Nicæa the names of the bishops who signed the acts of the Council include many purely heathen names, as Nestor, Telemachus, Æneas, Athenodorus, Artemidorus, etc. In the fourth century the tendency appears to have been to assume names from the Old Testament or those of the Apostles and early martyrs. St. John Chrysostom and St. Ambrose urge the Christians of their time to adopt the beautiful practice of giving their children the name of one of the holy martyrs. This practice has long since become well established, and one finds it rather strange to meet with a case where the parents do not want to give their child a Christian name. In such a case the

[39] Holy Office, June 20, 1883; *Collectanea de Prop. Fide*, II, n. 1598.

pastor is to add a Christian name of his own choice and enter it in the baptismal record, together with the name selected by the parents.

The Roman Ritual further directs the pastors to see to it that the names given in Baptism are not obscene, fabulous, ridiculous, or the names of heathen deities or impious heathen men.

CHAPTER IV

OF SPONSORS

655. According to the most ancient custom of the Church, nobody shall be baptized solemnly unless he has, whenever possible, a sponsor. Even in Private Baptism a sponsor should be procured, if it is easily possible; if there was no sponsor in the Private Baptism, one should be procured in the supplying of the ceremonies, but in such a case he does not contract any spiritual relationship (**Canon 762**).

Sponsors at Baptism are mentioned as early as the second century of the Christian era. Tertullian refers to sponsors of children and their serious obligation to see that the children grow up as true Christians. Some authors think that Tertullian has reference to the sponsors of orphan children, for as late as the time of St. Augustine the parents seem to have taken the place of sponsors, as may be gathered from the Saint's words that the parents answer the questions at Baptism for their children. Cæsarius of Arles (d. 542) speaks of sponsors of adults who are to give the converts before and after baptism a good example of Christian life, and encourage them by word and deed in the practice of virtue.

When baptism is repeated conditionally, the same sponsor shall, if possible, be employed as at the first baptism; except in this case, there is no need of a sponsor in conditional baptism. In the conditional repetition of baptism neither the sponsor of the first nor the sponsor at the second baptism contracts spiritual relationship, unless the same sponsor was secured on both occasions (**Canon 763**). There shall be but one sponsor, who may be either of the same or of different sex from the person to be baptized; two sponsors at most, one man and one woman, shall be employed (**Canon 764**).

Because the spiritual relationship contracted in baptism

by the sponsor constitutes a diriment impediment of marriage (according to Canon 1079), it was important that the Code settled the question concerning the sponsor at a doubtful baptism. The ruling of the Code is precise. If baptism was doubtful so that one feels justified in conferring it again conditionally, neither the sponsor at the first nor the sponsor at the second baptism contracts the spiritual relationship. If the same sponsor acts as such at both baptisms, he contracts the spiritual relationship.

656. In Private Baptism the former law did not demand a sponsor, but the Code prescribes that a sponsor should be present, if it is easy to have one, which indicates that the law does not impose a grave obligation. Under the former Canon Law there was a controversy as to whether the sponsor in Private Baptism contracted the spiritual relationship, and the Sacred Congregation of the Council, March 5, 1678, after long discussion of the question, decided that by the law of the Council of Trent, which rules that spiritual relationship is contracted in Baptism, the sponsor contracts that relationship also in Private Baptism.[40] Some theologians after that decision questioned the competency of the Sacred Congregation to give such a decision without special authorization of the Supreme Pontiff, calling it a declaration which extended the law of the Council beyond its original meaning. However, it is evident from the wording of the decision that the Sacred Congregation intended nothing else than to interpret officially the law of the Council of Trent, which it has full power to do. Even since the appearance of the Code, the same controversy—if it still deserves the name after the decision of 1678—persists. Some commentators of the Code hold that Canon 768 does away with all controversy in this matter. However, Canon 768 is no more than a repetition of the law of the Council of Trent, with the only difference of a limitation of the relationship to a smaller number of persons. The declaration of 1678, however, does settle the question so that a sponsor at a valid Private Baptism does contract the spiritual relationship. The argument of the contrary opinion has found so few supporters that Cardinal Gasparri calls the opinion *practice certa* in favor of the contracting of the relationship.

40 Gasparri, ''De Matrimonio,'' I, 595.

657. The Code is very careful to state the rule as to the sponsor in a doubtful baptism, exempting him from relationship and consequent marriage impediment. Nothing is stated about the minister in a doubtful baptism, whether he contracts the spiritual relationship. The sound principle seems to be that a doubtful fact (*dubium facti*) does not make the law doubtful or deprive it of its force. Only a *dubium juris* has the effect of making the law itself doubtful. Wherefore, Canon 15 states that the laws in a *dubium juris* do not oblige, while they do oblige in a *dubium facti*, but that same Canon gives the Ordinary power to dispense from the law in a *dubium facti*, if it is one of those cases in which the Roman Pontiff usually grants a dispensation.

658. The lawful number of sponsors is limited to two, which is the same law as that of the Council of Trent. If more than two are designated and admitted, it is illicit, but all the persons are valid sponsors, for Canon 764 which limits the number of sponsors to two does not carry an invalidating clause against an act contrary to this rule. According to Canon 11, such a clause would be necessary to exclude the possibility of more than two sponsors.

REQUISITES FOR VALID SPONSORSHIP

659. In order that a person may act *validly* as sponsor, the following rules apply:

(1) He must be baptized, have attained the use of reason and have the intention of discharging that office;

(2) He must not belong to an heretical or schismatic sect, nor have been excommunicated by a condemnatory or declaratory sentence, nor suffer from infamy of law, nor be excluded from legal acts, nor (if a cleric) have been deposed or degraded from the clerical rank;

(3) The father or mother or spouse of the person to be baptized cannot be sponsor;

(4) He must be designated either by the person to be baptized or by the parents or guardians, or in their default by the minister of baptism;

(5) The sponsor must, either in person or through proxy,[40a] physically hold or touch the one baptized, or receive him im-

[40a] Concerning sponsorship by proxy, cfr. App. III, 32, c.

mediately after baptism from the sacred font or from the hands of the minister (**Canon 765**).

To act as sponsor, the person must be baptized. Baptism outside the Catholic Church is no obstacle if the sponsor now belongs to the Catholic Church, and is not under an excommunication pronounced by the ecclesiastical court, or under any of the other disabilities mentioned under n. 2. The crimes to which infamy of law is attached are specified in various Canons of the Code. It can be incurred only in the cases specifically enumerated in the Code.[41] Furthermore, the infamy of law and the exclusion from legal acts in question must have been inflicted by the ecclesiastical court. The disability to act as sponsor is not incurred *ipso facto* by the crimes to which the law attaches an *ipso facto infamia juris* or *ipso facto* exclusion from legal acts, as is to be inferred from the following Canon 766.

The intention to undertake the office of sponsor is of course necessary so that it is not sufficient if the adult to be baptized or the parents or guardians of an infant request some one to be sponsor, but the person requested must manifest his consent and appear either in person or through a proxy appointed by him to assist at the Baptism and physically touch the person baptized, as declared in the Code.[42]

660. Protestants or schismatics cannot be sponsors, and, if the priest cannot prevent the intervention of non-Catholics, the Holy Office demands that the priest inform the non-Catholic that he cannot be a sponsor properly so called, but can assist at most as a witness.[43] The Holy Office has declared that, if suitable sponsors are not available, it is preferable to have none at all, rather than admit a person belonging to an heretical sect.[44] The Holy See has declared that, even where one of the parents was a Catholic and the other a non-Catholic and they were married outside the Church, a Protestant sponsor should not be admitted in the baptism of their child.[45]

661. The choice of the sponsor rests with the person who is to receive baptism, if that person has the use of reason. In

[41] Canons 2293, 2320, 2328, 2343, 2351, 2356, 2357.
[42] Holy Office, Sept. 15, 1869; *Collectanea de Prop. Fide*, II, n. 1347.
[43] *Collectanea de Prop. Fide*, I, n. 447.
[44] *Collectanea de Prop. Fide*, II, n. 1831.
[45] Holy Office, June 27, 1900, *Acta S. Sedis*, XXXIII, 372.

the case of an infant, the choice rests with the parents; if the parents are dead or have for any reason lost the custody of their child, the right rests with the guardian. If neither the parents nor the guardian appoint a sponsor, the minister of Baptism shall appoint one. The Holy Office, Sept. 15, 1869, declared that the ceremonies of baptism shall not be omitted for want of a sponsor, and if the case really happens that nobody can be present but the parents, they are to take the part of the sponsor, without however becoming thereby sponsors. If the parents or the guardian appoint a sponsor who by the law of the Code cannot validly or licitly act as such, the minister of baptism is obliged to reject him, and, if the parents or the guardian refuse to appoint another, the minister of baptism must appoint a sponsor. A person who without a proper designation assumes to act as sponsor, does not become a sponsor, for, as stated in Canon 765, n. 4, the designation is one of the requisites for validity of sponsorship.

662. If the appointed sponsor cannot or does not wish to attend at the baptism in person, he may appoint a representative (proxy) to take his place. The Code does not lay down any restrictions as to the persons who may be appointed as proxies. Therefore, the only requisite is that he is capable of accepting the mandate and performing the material acts in the place of the sponsor. Though it is not becoming to appoint as proxies non-Catholics, excommunicated persons or others whom the Code excludes from sponsorship, still the Code does not forbid it. The name of the proxy is not entered into the baptismal record, but the name of the sponsor represented by the proxy.

663. The physical contact of the sponsor with the one baptized in the act of baptizing or immediately afterwards is necessary for valid sponsorship. It is not necessary, however, that the sponsor hold the infant: a nurse or a maid may hold the child, the sponsors placing one hand on the child during the pouring on of the water, for the Decree of the Sacred Congregation of the Propaganda states that the sponsor is considered to hold the child, "if he by physical contact with the child identifies himself with the one who holds the child." [46]

[46] January 21, 1856; *Collectanea de Prop. Fide,* I, n. 1119.

REQUISITES FOR LICIT SPONSORSHIP

664. For licit admission as sponsor, the following conditions must be observed:

(1) The sponsor must be fourteen years of age, unless for a just reason the minister admits younger persons;

(2) The sponsor must not be under excommunication, nor excluded from legal acts, nor suffer from infamy of law for reason of a notorious crime, even though no sentence was pronounced against him, nor must he be under an interdict, or otherwise a public criminal, or disgraced by infamy of fact;

(3) The sponsor must know the rudiments of the faith;

(4) The sponsor must not be a novice or professed member in any religious organization, unless there is nobody else to be had and the permission is granted by at least the local superior;

(5) The sponsor must not be a cleric in sacred orders, unless he has the explicit permission of his proper Ordinary (**Canon 766**).

In case of doubt whether one can validly or licitly be admitted as sponsor, the pastor shall, if time permits, consult the Ordinary (**Canon 767**).

Canon 2197, n. 3, declares that an offense is notorious by notoriety of fact if it is publicly known and committed under such circumstances that it cannot be concealed by any artifice nor excused by any extenuating circumstances admitted in law. In general, the Code in Canon 766, n. 2, excludes from sponsorship persons who are guilty of a grave public offense which in the common estimation of respectable Catholic men makes them so unworthy of the office of sponsor that their admission would cause scandal. The Holy See ruled that Freemasons who are publicly known as such cannot be admitted as sponsors.[47] The same holds good of Catholics who belong to any other forbidden society, and are notoriously known as members; likewise Catholics whose life is unchristian and scandalous. Ojetti quotes a declaration of the Sacred Penitentiary, December 10, 1860, to the effect that Catholics who are notoriously known to be under ecclesiastical censure may be admitted as sponsors when they cannot be kept away without great harm. This has to be limited to those whose censure has not been inflicted by

---

[47] Holy Office, July 5, 1878; *Collectanea de Prop. Fide*, II, n. 1495.

the ecclesiastical court (by declaratory or condemnatory sentence), for the latter are declared by the Code entirely incapable of acting as sponsors.[48]

665. The Code does not state whether the minister of baptism may be simultaneously sponsor for the person he baptizes. When the question was proposed to the Holy See in reference to Confirmation, the Sacred Congregation of Rites answered that, if the bishop wanted to be sponsor, he should appoint a proxy.[49] The same may perhaps be said concerning the minister of Baptism. A cleric in major orders, however, needs the permission of his Ordinary to be sponsor (for liceity).

SPIRITUAL RELATIONSHIP OF THE SPONSORS

666. The minister of baptism and the sponsor contract spiritual relationship from baptism with the person baptized only (**Canon 768**).

As the Sacrament of Baptism is truly a spiritual regeneration, the idea of a spiritual fatherhood between the minister of baptism and the person baptized can be traced back to the very times of the Apostles. St. Paul calls Timothy, Titus and Onesimus his sons. Expressions like this: "by the Gospel I have begotten you," also occur.[50] It was, therefore, quite a natural conclusion to which the various local councils of the early Church came, when they declared that there was a sacred bond or relationship between the baptized and those who were instrumental in bringing about his regeneration. The spiritual relationship being considered more sacred than the natural bond of blood, a practice developed in the Church forbidding the marriage of persons between whom spiritual relationship existed. In the beginning there was no general law for the whole Church in this matter, but the various local councils passed decisions on the matter of the spiritual relationship and on marriage between spiritually related persons.

On October 30, 530, Emperor Justinian forbade in one of his laws marriage between the sponsors and the person baptized. Canonists hold that he merely enforced in the civil forum a custom which had already become a law in the Church. In

---

48 Ojetti, "Synopsis Rer. Moral et Jur. Pont.," I, 367.
49 June 14, 1873; *Decr. Auth. S. R. C.*, n. 3305.
50 Cfr. II Tim., ii. 1; Titus, i. 4; Philem., 10; I Cor., iv. 15.

692, the Concilium Trullanum adopted the Justinian law in its Canons, and extended the prohibition of marriage to marriage between the sponsor and the mother of the person baptized. In the Western Church similar prohibitions of marriage for reason of the spiritual relationship were passed, for example, in the Roman Council in the year 721.[51]

The spiritual relationship and the prohibition of marriage were extended more and more so that many controversies arose as to the validity of marriage. The Council of Trent limited the spiritual relationship and prohibition of marriage by defining that the relationship existed only as follows: between the minister of baptism and the person baptized and his parents; between the sponsor and the person baptized and his parents.[52] The Code limits still further the spiritual relationship, stating that it is contracted by the minister of Baptism and the sponsor with the person baptized only, and not with his parents.

DUTIES OF THE SPONSORS

667. In virtue of the office which they have accepted, it is the duty of the sponsors to take a lasting interest in their spiritual child, and to take good care that he leads a truly Christian life, as in the solemn ceremony they have pledged that he would do (**Canon 769**).

The obligation of the sponsors is truly a moral duty, and it obliges the sponsors to act, as the Holy Office declared,[53] in case the parents are negligent in the spiritual education of the child. In Canon 1335, the Code repeats that the sponsors have the duty to see to it that their godchild is instructed in Christian doctrine. The duty of the sponsors does not cease when their godchild comes of age, for the Code explicitly states that they must take an interest in his spiritual welfare "perpetuo" (i.e., forever, a lasting interest), and that they must take care that during his *whole life* he lives up to the principles of the Catholic faith.

---

51 Wernz-Vidal, "Jus Canonicum," V, n. 390.
52 Sess. XXIV, cap. 2, *De Reform. Matr.*
53 Dec. 9, 1745; *Collectanea de Prop. Fide*, I, n. 355. Cfr. App. III, 5. c, 1.

CHAPTER V

OF THE TIME AND PLACE OF BAPTISM

668. Infants shall be baptized as soon as possible. Pastors and preachers shall often remind the faithful of this grave obligation (**Canon 770**).

The Council of Trent rules: "If anyone says that little children, for that they have not actual faith (*actum credendi*), are not, after having received baptism, to be reckoned among the faithful; and that, for this cause, they are to be rebaptized when they have attained to years of discretion; or that it is better that the baptism of such be omitted, rather than that, while not believing by their own act, they should be baptized in the faith alone of the Church; let him be anathema."[54]

The meaning of "quamprimum" (as soon as possible) cannot be determined with absolute exactness. In fact, the law did not want to specify the exact number of days, as it could easily have done, for circumstances are so varied that a narrow law in this matter is not desirable, at least as a general law. The individual bishops who know the conditions in their diocese, the facility or the difficulty of reaching the parish church, climate, roads, etc., can make particular regulations. It is considered to be within the power of the bishop to demand that the baptism be conferred within eight days after birth, making due allowance for circumstances where that regulation would impose undue hardship. In an Instruction of the Sacred Congregation of the Propaganda, July 31, 1902, to the missionaries among the Nestorians, it states that baptism shall be conferred on the infants at least within eight days after birth, and if necessary Private Baptism should be given rather than wait longer for Solemn Baptism.[55]

669. If there is no particular law limiting the time and no special danger of death from the condition of the child or other circumstances, one may hold with Noldin[56] and Vermeersch-Creusen[57] that one cannot delay Baptism over a month without sinning gravely against the law. If circumstances are such—

---

54 Sessio VI, Canon 13, *De Bapt.*
55 *Collectanea de Prop. Fide*, II, n. 2149.
56 *Theol. Moral.*, III, 78, n. 66.
57 *Epitome Jur. Can.*, II, 25, n. 52.

and they certainly exist in the scattered districts of the United States—that the priest cannot be had within a month, some lay person should be asked by the parents to baptize the child, rather than delay the baptism. The Sacred Congregation of the Propaganda approved an Instruction given to the catechists and other well-instructed Catholics to baptize any of the infants of the Christians, though they are in good health, if the priest is absent or it is difficult to go to him.[58] We saw that the Instruction to the missionaries among the Nestorians insisted that baptism should be conferred within eight days, and that, when necessary, the infants should be baptized privately rather than delay baptism and expose the infants to the danger of dying without it.

670. Private Baptism may, in case of necessity, be given at any time and in any place (**Canon 771**). Solemn Baptism may be given on any day. However, in accordance to the most ancient rite of the Church, it is a becoming practice to baptize adults on the vigils of Easter and Pentecost, especially in metropolitan and cathedral churches, if it can be done conveniently (**Canon 772**). The proper place for the administration of Solemn Baptism is the baptistry in a church or public oratory (**Canon 773**).

Up to about the ninth century, Solemn Baptism in churches of the Latin Rite was given only on the vigils of Easter and Pentecost. In the Oriental Rite and in the dioceses of Northern Africa, the Epiphany was added to the baptismal days. In Spain they began to baptize also on the feasts of the Apostles and martyrs, but the Roman Pontiffs objected to that practice. As the number of baptisms of adults got fewer, the practice of baptizing on the two vigils only ceased of itself. Pope Simplicius (d. 483) is said to have appointed several priests at Rome who had to be ready any day and any hour of the day to baptize infants.[59] Very likely baptism of infants in danger of death is meant. When there was even a slight danger, the infants were baptized immediately at the time when Solemn Baptism was still limited to the two days. A certain Bishop Fidus in Africa had, in 253, contended that it was not lawful to baptize infants before the eighth day because in the Old Testament circumcision was to be given only on the eighth day

---

[58] Jan. 16, 1804; *Collectanea de Prop. Fide*, I, n. 674.
[59] Binterim, ''Denkwürdigk.,'' I, part I, 61.

after birth. St. Cyprian[60] writes to him: "Nobody in our council agreed with what you thought should be done; on the contrary, we all have held that to no human being born into this life should mercy and grace be denied."

The Code states that the church or a public oratory is the proper place for the conferring of Solemn Baptism. The question was proposed to the Sacred Congregation of Rites whether the custom that prevailed at the cathedral of a certain archdiocese of conferring Solemn Baptism in the *sacristy* could be continued. The Sacred Congregation answered that the custom cannot be continued unless there is reasonable cause approved by the archbishop.[61]

CHURCHES WHICH MUST HAVE BAPTISMAL FONT

671. Every parish church shall have a baptismal font; all contrary statutes, privileges and customs interfering with that right of parish churches are disapproved and recalled. If other churches have acquired the right to baptize *cumulatively,* such cumulative right continues. The local Ordinary can for the convenience of the people allow or demand that baptismal fonts be placed also in another church or public oratory within the limits of a parish (**Canon 774**).

In former times it often happened that, when a new parish was created by the division of a larger parish, the right to baptize was reserved to the original parish, and the new parish was not allowed to have a baptismal font. Such reservations were recognized in the former law. The Code, however, changes this regulation, and rules that every parish church has a right to have a baptismal font and to baptize its own parishioners. The Committee for the Authentic Interpretation of the Code has declared that the churches which had the exclusive right to confer all the baptisms in a certain town or city or district, shall henceforth have only a cumulative right simultaneously with the parish churches of that town, city or district. They may, therefore, baptize people from any of those parishes where in former times they had the exclusive right of baptizing, but each parish has the right to baptize its own

---

[60] *Epist. lix Cypriani ad Fidum Episc.*
[61] March 14, 1861; *Decr. Auth. S. R. C.,* n. 3104.

subjects if they come to it. If the church which has the right to perform any baptisms of a city or town, baptizes persons who belong to another parish by reason of domicile, it must as soon as possible inform the proper pastor of the conferring of baptism, as is prescribed by Canon 778.[62]

If a parish has a very extensive territory so that it is very inconvenient for people of a certain district of that parish to take the infants to the parish church for baptism, and if there is another non-parochial church or chapel which is more convenient for the people, the bishop can allow or even command that the church or chapel have a baptismal font and baptize the people of that district.

672. If the person to be baptized cannot go to or be brought to the parish church or another church that has the right to baptize without great inconvenience or danger, on account of the distance or other circumstances, Solemn Baptism can and should be given by the pastor in the nearest church or public oratory within the parish, even though there is no baptismal font in that church or oratory (**Canon 775**).

The case contemplated in this Canon is not very common in the United States, where the churches and chapels are not so plentiful as they are in some countries in Europe. In some sections of the United States extensive districts have to be covered by the pastor. Wherefore, baptism at the house of the faithful, spoken of in the next Canon, becomes necessary more frequently than in European countries. Some American dioceses contain more, others nearly as much territory as all Italy, and are served by a mere handful of priests. A few illustrations will suffice: Diocese of Salt Lake, 157,000 square miles with 27 priests; Tucson, 133,000 square miles with 62 priests; Cheyenne, 101,000 square miles with 26 priests; Baker City, 68,000 square miles with 27 priests. These figures are taken from the 1923 Catholic Directory; for the square miles we took the round thousands. The number of priests includes secular priests and religious working in those immense territories. Italy with its islands has about 124,000 square miles.

62 Cfr. App. III, 32, d.

Solemn Baptism in Private Houses

673. Solemn Baptism cannot be given in private houses except under the following circumstances:

(1) If the persons to be baptized are the sons or nephews of the highest actual ruler of a country, or have the right of succession to the throne, whenever they properly ask for it;

(2) If the local Ordinary with prudent and conscientious judgment should allow it in some extraordinary case where there is a just and reasonable cause.

In these cases Baptism must be given in the private chapel of the house, or at least in a decent place, and baptismal water is to be used (**Canon 776**).

The phrase, ''qui supremum populorum principatum tenent,'' does not necessarily mean kings or emperors; in plain words, the phrase means nothing but the head of a state. The same phrase occurs in Canon 600, n. 3, and 598, in reference to the privilege of entering the cloister of religious houses with papal enclosure. As was said in commenting on those Canons, there is no reason why a president of a republic or a governor of one of the States of the American Union should not be included under this general phrase of the Code. They are certainly heads of the state, and the title borne by the head of a state makes no difference. If it did, the Code could have easily said so.

The Second Council of Baltimore, n. 237, insisted that all baptisms should, in so far as possible, be conferred in the church. In places where the people live at a great distance from the church, or when on account of bad weather, the condition of the roads, the poverty of the people, it was very difficult for the people to take the infants to church, the Council gave the priests in charge of the parishes and missions general permission to baptize the infants in private houses with all the ceremonies. That general permission must be considered abolished by the Code, for a particular law which is contrary to the Code has been annulled by the promulgation of the Code. The reasons, however, which moved the Council to give that general permission still exist, and the individual bishop knowing the condition of his diocese and finding it necessary to provide for the scattered districts should request the Holy See for faculties to allow Solemn Baptism in private houses under certain conditions. Without a special Indult he cannot do so, for the Holy See has declared (July 22, 1925; cfr. App. III, 32, f) that he can only decide in each individual case whether there are sufficient reasons to give Solemn Baptism in a private house.

CHAPTER VI

OF THE RECORD AND PROOF OF BAPTISM

674. The pastor shall carefully and without delay enter in the baptismal records the names of the persons baptized, the minister, the parents and sponsors, the date and place of the baptism.

In the baptism of illegitimate children the name of the mother is to be entered, if her motherhood is publicly known, or if she of her own accord asks in writing or before two witnesses that such entry be made. Also the name of the father is to be entered, provided he himself demands it of his own accord in writing or before two witnesses, or if he is known to be the father from some public and authentic document. In other cases the baptism is to be recorded as of a child of unknown father or of unknown parents (**Canon 777**).

The pastor has the obligation of recording the baptisms in the manner pointed out in the Code, no matter who baptizes a subject of the parish. The actual entries may be committed by the pastor to trustworthy persons in accordance with the general principle that one is considered to do an act oneself, if one does it through another. However, as the registration of the baptism is to be a public and official record, it should be authenticated by the pastor's signature, just as very many important documents are authenticated by the signature of the person who issues the document. In Canon Law the pastor's records of baptisms, marriages and deaths are recognized as public records and as full proof of the facts affirmed in such records (cfr. Canons 1813 and 1816). In the civil law the parochial records —for example, the record of baptism—have no official standing. The baptismal record is admissible in evidence under the rule which admits entries made in the regular course of one's business. In so far as the civil law is concerned, it is safer for the baptizing priest to make the record or at least sign it. If the baptizing priest is still alive and within the jurisdiction of the court when the question of baptism comes up in the civil court, the written entry would not be admitted, and the priest himself would have to testify, if within the jurisdiction of the court. He may use the entry in the baptismal record to refresh his memory.

675. Canon 470 rules that the baptismal register should also contain the records of confirmation, marriage, subdeaconship, and solemn religious profession.   At the end of the Roman Ritual, just before the Appendix, there are several pages of directions as to how the record should be made in each parochial register. When some of the popular baptismal and matrimonial registers are examined in the light of these regulations of the Ritual, it would appear that these books are very incomplete and inadequate for the proper satisfaction of the regulations.

676. Great caution must be taken not to make any corrections in the record, such as striking out words, misspelling and writing over again: all such alterations mar the record and make it worthless to prove anything in law, if made in a point which may become important. That they lose their value as documents is indicated in Canon 1818, which states that such documents are left to the mercy of the judge to attach whatever value he thinks proper to them.

677. The recording of the baptism of illegitimate children requires great caution. The names of the mother and the father may be entered only under the conditions laid down in Canon 777. Special caution is necessary in baptizing a child whose parents are married lawfully in the eyes of the civil law, but invalidly in the eyes of the Church. The priest may not make a note to the effect that the child is illegitimate, but he may note that the parents were married only before a non-Catholic minister or a civil magistrate. This is stating a fact for which nobody can accuse the pastor of libel. As there is less chance that the fatherhood of an illegitimate child is publicly known, the Code rules that the father's name cannot be entered, unless he himself declares in writing or before two witnesses that he is the father of the child, or unless his fatherhood is known from a public and authentic document—for instance, if the court has pronounced a man to be the father, and charged him with the maintenance of the child.[62a]

678. If baptism was not given by the proper pastor, or in

[62a] Concerning baptism of illegitimates, cfr. App. III, 32. e.

his presence, the minister shall as soon as possible inform the pastor of the domicile of the person baptized about the baptism (**Canon 778**).

This Canon refers especially to those cases where Private Baptism was conferred in danger of death, and to cases where the mother was absent from her home when she gave birth to a child and the child was baptized in the strange place because it could not be taken to the parish of the parents without unduly delaying the baptism. In these and similar cases in which baptism had to be conferred outside the proper parish church, the record is to be sent to the proper pastor. If the place where a child of another parish was baptized has a baptismal font, and therefore a baptismal record, the baptism is of course to be entered there, but an annotation is to be made that the child belongs to another parish, and a copy of the record is to be sent to the proper pastor.

PROOF OF BAPTISM

679. Unless the rights of a third party are prejudiced thereby, one witness who is absolutely trustworthy, or the oath of the baptized party himself, if he was baptized at adult age, suffices for the proof of baptism (**Canon 779**).

If the baptismal record has been properly made, it is full legal proof of baptism according to Canon 1813. If, however, for any reason no record can be had, baptism must be proved by witnesses. The general principle is expressed in Canon 1791 that the deposition of one witness does not constitute full proof, unless he is a qualified witness who gives testimony concerning acts done in his official capacity. But, when there is question merely of getting the testimony of baptism as it is required before Confirmation, First Holy Communion, ordination, marriage, where the rights of third parties are not concerned, the testimony of one absolutely reliable witness who testifies out of his own personal knowledge is sufficient. In all other cases where the rights of third parties are affected by the proof of baptism—for instance, in a marriage case in which the validity of the marriage is attacked on account of the baptism—one witness does not fully prove baptism or non-baptism. The same is to be said where rights of inheritance depend on the proof of baptism, for in such cases the rights of one person affect the rights of others.

When there is question as to whether baptism should be conferred again, the Holy Office declared that the testimony of one trustworthy witness suffices to establish the fact of baptism, and the Sacrament may not be repeated conditionally where one such witness testifies that baptism has been properly conferred.[63]

TITLE II

OF CONFIRMATION

680. The Sacrament of Confirmation is to be conferred by the imposition of the hand, by the anointing of the forehead with holy chrism, and by the words prescribed in the pontifical books approved by the Church (**Canon 780**).

The chrism to be used in the Sacrament of Confirmation must be blessed by a bishop, even though a priest, by law or special indult, confers this Sacrament. The anointing shall not be done with any instrument, but by the hand of the minister properly imposed on the head of the person to be confirmed (**Canon 781**).

The Holy Office has declared that the first imposition of hands over all *confirmandi* in general during the recitation of the oration ''Omnipotens'' is not necessary for validity, and that Confirmation need not be repeated if some of the candidates came after this imposition of hands.[64] The same Sacred Congregation ordered a conditional repetition of Confirmation in certain cases in which a schismatic priest had made use of an instrument in performing the anointing.[65]

Tertullian and St. Cyprian speak of the ''imposition of hands by which the Holy Ghost is conferred.'' Rufinus, who lived toward the end of the fourth century, calls the confirmation a ''signaculum chrismatis.'' Pope Innocent I (401–417) writes to Bishop Decentius of Gubbio that, in baptism, the priests are not allowed to sign the forehead of those baptized with the same

---

[63] March 18, 1896; *Collectanea de P. F.*, II, n. 1923.
[64] April 17, 1872; *Collectanea de P. F.*, II, n. 1383.
[65] January 14, 1885; *Collectanea de P. F.*, II, n. 1630.

oil which is allowed to bishops only when they confer the Holy Spirit.

681. Priests who by law or by special indult have the faculty to give Confirmation must use the holy chrism blessed by a bishop. In his work "De Synodo Diœcesana," Pope Benedict XIV discusses the question whether the Supreme Pontiff can delegate a priest to bless the holy chrism, and states that, while the more common opinion holds that the Pope cannot delegate a priest, there are authors who hold that he can. Thus, Wadding (*Annales Minorum*) relates that Pope Eugene IV gave to Father Fabian of Bachia the faculty to bless the chrism when he went to the missions in India. Pope Benedict XIV doubts as to whether this and another instance of delegation related by authors are genuine, and evades expressing an opinion by saying that in any case there is no necessity for such a faculty, because the missionaries who are far away from every bishop can always get the chrism blessed by a bishop, and if necessary use it longer than a year.[66] Noldin states that there is hardly any doubt that on January 28, 1444, Pope Eugene IV gave to the Provincial of the Franciscans in Bosnia the faculty to bless the holy chrism.[67]

CHAPTER I

OF THE MINISTER OF CONFIRMATION

682. The ordinary minister of Confirmation is the bishop only. The extraordinary minister is a priest who, either by the common law or by special indult of the Apostolic See, has received the faculty to confirm. The following have this faculty by law: Cardinals (Canon 239, § 1, n. 23), abbots and prelates *nullius*, vicars and prefects Apostolic. With the exception of the Cardinals, these clergy cannot validly make use of the faculty except within the limits of their respective territory, and during their term of office only.

Unless the indult explicitly provides otherwise, a priest of the Latin Rite, who has this power by virtue of an indult, can confer Confirmation validly on Catholics of his Rite only. It is not lawful for priests of the Oriental Rite who have the faculty or privilege to give Confirmation together with Baptism to the

[66] *De Synodo Diœcesana*, lib. VII, c. 8, nn. 1–2.
[67] *Theol. Moral.*, III, 101, n. 86.

infants of their own Rite, to confirm infants of the Latin Rite (**Canon 782**).

Commentators discuss the question whether a bishop could delegate priests to give Confirmation, if the Holy See had not deprived them of the power. The authorities are divided, but there seems to be no convincing reason for denying this power to the bishop. Otherwise one cannot explain how the Oriental priests could give confirmation, for it seems that they did so by commission of their bishops. At present it is generally said that the Oriental priests confirm by delegation of the Supreme Pontiff, but they went on confirming many centuries before the Holy See said anything about the matter. In the same chapter cited above, Pope Benedict XIV weighs the reasons on both sides, and seems to incline to the opinion which denies the power of the bishops to delegate priests.

683. The Code in Canon 782 specifies the extent of the faculty which certain priests have by law, and which others may get by special indult. As the power is a delegated power, they have only what is granted to them, and they are bound to respect the limitations of the faculty. Concerning the Oriental priests who have the right to give Confirmation to infants of their own Rite, the Code does not state whether they give Confirmation invalidly, if they confirm infants of the Latin Rite. Under the general principle of the Code that no law has an invalidating effect unless the law explicitly or equivalently states that an act is invalid or a person is incapacitated from acting validly (cfr. Canon 11), the Confirmation should be considered valid. In various Decrees of the Holy See it has been strictly commanded that, before confirming, priests who confirm by indult of the Holy See must declare to the persons present that they confirm by Apostolic Indult. The Sacred Congregation of the Propaganda has declared that the Confirmation is valid, though the priest has omitted to make the declaration.[68]

Persons who have by law the power to confirm cannot delegate that power to a priest, for, as we saw above, the Code does not grant bishops the faculty to delegate a priest to give Confirmation, and besides there is no question here of delegating jurisdiction but rather a power of orders. No power of orders delegated to a person or annexed to an office can be committed

[68] Sept. 11, 1841; *Collectanea de P. F.*, I, n. 940.

to another, unless this is expressly permitted by law or by indult (Canon 210). When necessary, the Holy See grants bishops and others (vicars and prefects Apostolic) the faculty to delegate a priest for the conferring of Confirmation.[69]

684. Vicars and prefects Apostolic are ordered by Canon 309 to appoint at the very beginning of their term of office a pro-vicar or pro-prefect, who *ipso facto* takes charge of the district in case of the death, exile, captivity, or total disability of the vicar or prefect. The pro-vicar or pro-prefect has then all the ordinary and delegated faculties of the vicar or prefect (cfr. Canon 310), and the ordinary powers of the vicars and prefects Apostolic (cfr. Canon 294) include the power to confirm. It seems, therefore, that the pro-vicar and the pro-prefect obtain by the Code the right to confirm in the case of a vacancy of the vicariate or prefecture, or the inability of the vicar or prefect, as described in Canon 429. The former law did not give this power to the pro-vicars and pro-prefects, as is evident from a Decree of the Sacred Congregation of the Propaganda, September 12, 1821.[70]

685. Within his diocese the bishop can lawfully confirm even strangers, unless an explicit prohibition of their own bishop forbids it. In the diocese of another bishop, a bishop must have at least the reasonably presumed permission of the local Ordinary, except when he confirms his own subjects privately and without crozier and mitre (**Canon 783**).

It is generally admitted that a bishop confirms validly all persons capable of receiving this Sacrament, though they are not his subjects and he is outside the territory of his diocese. For the licit administration, the bishop is bound by the regulations of Canon 783. After outlining the ceremonies of the solemn administration of Confirmation by the bishop, the Roman *Pontificale* states that the less solemn administration may take place on any day and at any hour or place. In the less solemn administration the bishop wears only the white stole over the rochet and the plain mitre. While he may confirm his own subjects privately in any diocese, the solemn administration with crozier and mitre is forbidden him outside his own territory under the general law that a bishop may not make

[69] Holy Office, March 4, 1903; *Collectanea de P. F.*, II, n. 2161.
[70] *Collectanea de P. F.*, I, n. 766.

use of the pontifical insignia of crozier and mitre in the diocese of another Ordinary without the latter's permission (cfr. Canon 337).[71]

686. A priest who has a local Apostolic privilege to confirm, may also confirm strangers in the territory of his jurisdiction, unless the Ordinaries of these strangers have explicitly forbidden it (**Canon 784**). Abbot and prelates *nullius,* vicars and prefects Apostolic, have a local faculty to confirm in virtue of Canon 782. Whether other priests who by particular indult get the power to confirm have a personal or local indult must be learned from the wording of the indult itself.

Obligation of the Minister to Confirm

687. The bishop is bound to administer Confirmation to his subjects who legitimately and reasonably ask for it, especially at the time of his visitation of the diocese.

A priest who by Apostolic privilege has the power to confirm is bound by the same obligation with respect to those people in whose favor this faculty was given to him.

An Ordinary who is prevented by a legitimate reason from giving Confirmation, or an Ordinary who has no faculty to confirm, must see that, at least every five years if possible, this Sacrament is administered among his subjects. If he is gravely negligent in administering Confirmation to his subjects, either in person or through another, Canon 274, n. 4, is to be observed (**Canon 785**). Canon 274, n. 4, demands that the archbishops refer to the Holy See the abuses existing in the dioceses of their suffragan bishops.

Canon 343 demands that the bishop shall visit at least part of his diocese annually, so as to cover the entire diocese at least every five years.

Chapter II

OF THE SUBJECT OF CONFIRMATION

688. Persons who have not been baptized, cannot be validly confirmed. To receive Confirmation licitly and with fruit, the recipients must be in the state of grace, and, if they have the use of reason, they must be sufficiently instructed (**Canon 786**).

[71] Holy Office, February 12, 1851; *Collectanea de P. F.,* I, n. 1057.

Though this Sacrament is not an absolutely necessary means of salvation, none may neglect to receive it when occasion offers. The pastors shall see that the faithful receive Confirmation at the proper time (**Canon 787**).

In the Rubrics on Confirmation the Roman *Pontificale* states that adult candidates for Confirmation should go to Confession before receiving this Sacrament, or at least have contrition for all mortal sins into which they may have fallen.

The Code does not settle the controversy whether there is a grave obligation to receive Confirmation when an opportunity presents itself. The theologians are divided, and there is no authoritative decision on the question. The Constitution of Pope Benedict XIV, "Etsi Pastoralis," deals with a special problem of the Greek-Italian population in Southern Italy. Speaking there of persons who have been confirmed by Greek priests, he states that these priests have no power to give Confirmation, and that those who have been confirmed "are to be admonished by the local Ordinaries that they are guilty of mortal sin, if, when they can receive Confirmation, they refuse and neglect it." On the other hand, he says that, if scandal would arise from an attempt to force them to get confirmed again, they should not be forced, because this Sacrament is not so necessary that without it one could not be saved.[72] Here there is question of an ecclesiastical precept in a particular case, and the Pope does not speak of the general question of the obligation to receive Confirmation. The Sacred Congregation of the Propaganda seems to have held that there is a grave obligation to receive Confirmation, for, in an Instruction to the priests who have by indult the power to confer Confirmation, it says that the priests should instruct the people that, when there is an opportunity to receive it, Confirmation cannot be refused (*respui*) and neglected without committing mortal sin.[73] However, this Instruction is not a general law, and the controversy remains undecided.

689. Although, in the Latin Church, Confirmation is usually deferred until about the seventh year of age, it may nevertheless be conferred before this age, if the infant is in danger of

---

[72] *Benedicti XIV Opera Omnia*, I, 201; Gasparri, "Fontes Cod. Juris Can.," I, 734.

[73] May 4, 1774; *Collectanea de P. F.*, I, n. 503.

death, or if the minister in any other case thinks it expedient
for good and weighty reasons (**Canon 788**). If there are several to be confirmed, all should be present at the first imposition of hands, and should not leave until the Confirmation
rite is completed (**Canon 789**). We saw in the discussion on
Canon 780 that the first imposition of hands is not essential to
the validity of the Sacrament; it is, however the duty of the
pastor to see that all who are to receive Confirmation are
present at the beginning of the ceremonies, and that they do
not leave until after the last blessing given by the minister
of Confirmation.[74]

CHAPTER III

OF THE TIME AND PLACE OF CONFIRMATION

690. Confirmation may be administered at any time, but it
is most befitting to administer it during the week of Pentecost
(**Canon 790**). The proper place for the administration of Confirmation is a church; nevertheless, for a cause which the minister considers just and reasonable, he may confer this Sacrament in any becoming place (**Canon 791**). The bishop has the
right to administer Confirmation also in exempt places within
the confines of the territory of his diocese (**Canon 792**).

Priests who by Apostolic indult have the faculty to confirm
may not wear any pontifical insignia, but merely the alb and
stole, unless they enjoy the additional privilege of the *pontifi-
calia*.[75] For the solemn administration by the Ordinary, cfr.
above, n. 685.

CHAPTER IV

OF THE SPONSORS

691. In accordance with a most ancient custom of the
Church, a sponsor should be procured at Confirmation also, if
one can be had (**Canon 793**). The sponsor should stand for

[74] The custom of some places of delaying Confirmation until the children
are twelve or fourteen years of age is not approved by the Church, as is evident
from a Decree of the Sacred Congregation of the Council, Nov. 19, 1854
(*Collect. de P. F.*, I, n. 1105), and from a letter of Pope Leo XIII to the
Bishop of Marseilles, June 22, 1897 (*Collect. de P. F.*, II, n. 1973).
[75] Sacred Congregation of the Propaganda, April 23, 1774; *Collectanea
de P. F.*, I, n. 502.

one or two only, although the minister may for a just reason allow him to stand for more. No candidate for Confirmation shall have more than one sponsor (**Canon 794**).

Following the opinion of St. Alphonsus and many other theologians, the Holy Office declared the obligation of having a sponsor at Confirmation as a grave obligation, and would not grant a bishop a general faculty to dispense with sponsors, although the bishop had informed the Sacred Congregation that he found it very difficult to obtain sponsors, and that the churches were very small.[76]

The practice of having a few sponsors for a large number of candidates is not approved of by the Holy See, and violates the rubrics of the Roman *Pontificale,* which rules that one sponsor shall not present more than one or at most two, unless necessity forces the bishop to deviate from this rule. The Second Council of Baltimore (No. 253) insists very strongly that the rubric of Roman *Pontificale* (which is the same as the law of the Code) shall be observed, and, only when it is entirely impossible to comply with the law, may the bishop allow two women to act as sponsors for all the girls and two men as sponsors for all the boys. In a letter to the Bishop of Burlington, in the United States, the Holy Office takes occasion to remind the bishop that the provision of the Council of Baltimore is meant only for cases of necessity.[77]

Requisites for Valid Sponsorship

692. In order that one may *validly* be sponsor, the following conditions are required:

(1) The sponsor must have received Confirmation, have attained the use of reason, and have the intention of performing the office of sponsorship;

(2) The sponsor may not be a member of an heretical or schismatic sect, nor be declared liable to any of the penalties spoken of in Canon 765, n. 2, by a declaratory or condemnatory sentence;

(3) The sponsor may not be the father or mother of, or married to the candidate;

---

[76] Holy Office, Sept. 5, 1877; *Collectanea de P. F.,* II, n. 1480.
[77] November. 26. 1873; *Collectanea de P. F.,* II, n. 1408.

(4) The sponsor must have been designated by the candidate, or by his parents or guardians, or, in their default or refusal to appoint a sponsor, by the pastor;

(5) The sponsor must physically touch the candidate in the very act of the Confirmation, this action being performed personally or by proxy (**Canon 795**).

The requisites for valid sponsorship in Confirmation are practically the same as those required, in Canon 765, for valid sponsorship in Baptism (cfr. above, n. 659).

REQUISITES FOR LICIT SPONSORSHIP

693. In order that one may licitly be admitted to the sponsorship, the following conditions must be observed:

(1) The sponsor at Confirmation should not be the same person who acted as sponsor in Baptism, unless for a reasonable cause the minister of Confirmation thinks it proper to allow an exception to this rule, or unless Confirmation is legitimately given immediately after Baptism;

(2) The sponsor must be of the same sex as the candidate, unless in particular cases the minister for a reasonable cause thinks it proper to allow an exception;

(3) The prohibitions of Canon 766 in reference to persons who may not be lawfully admitted to sponsorship in Baptism shall apply also to sponsorship in Confirmation (**Canon 796**, cfr. above, n. 664).

SPIRITUAL RELATIONSHIP OF SPONSOR

694. From valid Confirmation arises a spiritual relationship between the person confirmed and the sponsor, by which the sponsor is bound to take a permanent interest in the person confirmed and to care for his Christian education (**Canon 797**).

The spiritual relationship contracted in Confirmation is no longer a diriment impediment of marriage, because Canon 1079 mentions only the spiritual relationship contracted in Baptism as constituting an impediment to marriage.[78]

The sponsor, however, has a true obligation to take a lasting interest in the spiritual welfare of the person whom he

---

[78] For the impediments resulting from Confirmation under the former Canon Law. cfr. *Conc. Trid.*, Sessio XXIV, cap. 2, *De Matrimonio.*

presented for Confirmation, and, if that person is not yet fully instructed in Christian doctrine (as is the case with most children who are confirmed), the sponsor is obliged to do what is reasonably within his power to see that the child shall receive a complete Christian education, if his parents or his guardian do not attend to this important duty. Commentators discuss whether this obligation binds the sponsor under grave or venial sin. The wording of the Code seems to express a grave obligation. The terms in which the obligation of the sponsor in Confirmation is expressed, are as strong as the words of Canon 769, which speak of the obligation of the sponsor in Baptism. In his commentary on the Code, Cappello [79] says that authors generally hold that the sponsor in Confirmation does not contract the obligation to see to the Christian instruction of the person confirmed. However, for centuries past the Roman *Pontificale* has had these words: "After the Confirmation, the bishop shall announce to the sponsors that they shall instruct their [spiritual] children in good morals, that they avoid evil and do good, and they shall teach them the Creed, the Our Father and Hail Mary, because they are bound to do this."

CHAPTER V

OF THE RECORDS AND PROOF OF CONFIRMATION

695. The pastor shall enter in a book kept specially for this purpose the names of the minister of Confirmation, of the persons confirmed, of the parents and the sponsors, also the date and place of Confirmation, besides making note of the Confirmation in the baptismal record, as demanded by Canon 470, § 2 (**Canon 798**).[79a]

If the proper pastor of the person confirmed was not present, the minister of Confirmation shall either personally or through another inform the pastor as soon as possible of the conferring of the Sacrament (**Canon 799**).

For the proof of Confirmation, when nobody else's rights are affected, it suffices to have one absolutely trustworthy witness, or the oath of the person himself who received Confirmation, unless he was confirmed in infancy (**Canon 800**).

Though the Confirmation register is not so important as the

---

[79] *De Sacramentis*, I, 156, n. 217.   [79a] Cfr. App. III, 33.

baptismal, it is nevertheless highly advisable that the records be kept accurately. Great inconvenience might be caused by the failure to keep the records, since a certificate of Confirmation may be needed by those who are to be ordained (cfr. Canon 974), or who want to join any religious organization (cfr. Canon 544).

As a rule, every candidate is to be confirmed in his own parish, for Canon 1330 supposes this by saying that the pastor shall prepare the children of his parish for the Sacrament of Penance and Confirmation. Candidates are not forbidden, however, to go to another parish to receive Confirmation. The Code puts the duty of informing the proper pastor of those confirmed outside their own parish on the officiating bishop, if the pastor of these persons was not present at the Confirmation.

As to the proof of Confirmation, the Code has the same identical words as Canon 779 on the proof of Baptism, merely substituting for the word "Baptism" the word "Confirmation" (cfr. above, n. 679).

TITLE III

OF THE BLESSED EUCHARIST

696. In the Blessed Eucharist, Christ Himself, our Lord, is contained, offered, and received under the species of bread and wine (**Canon 801**).

In this opening Canon on the greatest of all Sacraments the Code puts the dogmatic foundation by way of introduction to the two chapters in which it treats of the Holy Eucharist, first as a Sacrifice and secondly as a Sacrament. The goodness of Christ in giving Himself to us in the Blessed Eucharist is the marvel of all creation—the tree of life to those who believe in Christ and the stumbling block to those who do not submit their hearts and minds to God. Happily the well-attested history of Christian antiquity is so intimately interwoven with the worship of Christ in the Holy Eucharist that it is impossible to separate this Sacrament from the very life of the Early Church. This great work of God done by means of very common elements is in harmony with His other great works, for all through nature, as the observations of scientists prove, the most marvellous results of nature come from the **tiniest germs** or cells.

CHAPTER I

OF THE HOLY SACRIFICE OF THE MASS

ARTICLE I.—THE CELEBRANT

697. Priests only have the power to offer the Sacrifice of the Mass (**Canon 802**). This point of Catholic teaching is so well attested in the earliest history of the Church that its truth cannot be impugned. Tertullian tells us that there were heretics in his time who had men who were "priests today and tomorrow laymen; for also to laymen they commit priestly functions." [80] With a few exceptions, the great bulk of Christians of the early centuries, Catholics and sectarians alike, always considered it an institution of Christ that only bishops and priests validly ordained had the power to do what Christ had done at the Last Supper. The penalty for the violation of this Canon is given in Canon 2322.

CONCELEBRATION

698. Several priests may not concelebrate, except in the Ordination Mass of priests and in the Consecration Mass of bishops, as described in the Roman *Pontificale* (**Canon 803**).

The concelebration consists in this, that several priests say Holy Mass together at the same altar reading all the prayers and the words of consecration in unison, the bishop (or one of the priests) leading as the principal celebrant. This manner of saying Holy Mass was the ordinary way in which the Holy Sacrifice was offered in the early days of the Church and it continued for many centuries. At present concelebration is quite common in the Oriental Churches, both schismatic and Uniate. The Acts of the Council of Mount Lebanon (1736) give detailed instruction with reference to concelebration in the Maronite Rite. In the Church of the Latin Rite we have references to the concelebration of the priests of the principal churches in Rome with the Pope in the liturgical works,[81] and also from Pope Innocent III.[82] In the early days of the Church only one Mass

---

[80] *De Præscrip. Hæretic.*, cap. xli.
[81] *Ordo Romanus*, I, n. 48.
[82] *De Altaris Mysterio*, IV, xxv.

was celebrated in each cathedral or parochial church. When the number of Christians increased, it was impossible for all to attend the one Mass. It was then that the Church ordered the celebration of additional Masses. In a letter of Pope Leo I to Bishop Dioscurus of Alexandria, we read that on more solemn days, when there is a great multitude of people coming to church, Holy Mass should be repeated as often as a new congregation fills the church.[83]

ADMISSION OF STRANGE PRIESTS TO SAY MASS

699. A priest who desires to say Holy Mass in a church other than that to which he is attached must show authentic and still valid letters of recommendation (commonly called "Celebret") to the priest in charge of the church. A secular priest must obtain these letters from his Ordinary, a religious priest from his superior, and a priest of an Oriental Rite from the Sacred Congregation of the Oriental Church. A priest who has a proper "Celebret" shall be admitted to say Mass, unless it is known that in the meantime he has done something for reason of which he must be kept from saying Holy Mass.

If the priest has no "Celebret," but the rector of the church knows well that he is a priest in good standing, he may be allowed to say Mass. If, however, he is unknown to the rector, he may nevertheless be permitted to say Mass once or twice, provided he wears the ecclesiastical garb, does not receive any remuneration under any title from that church for the celebration of Mass, and enters his name, office and diocese in a book to be specially kept for that purpose.

The special regulations made by the local Ordinary on this matter, in so far as they are not contrary to the regulations laid down in this Canon, must be observed by all—even by the exempt religious, unless there is question of allowing religious to say Mass in a church of their own organization (**Canon 804**).

700. The Council of Chalcedon (451) ruled that no strange cleric or lector should be permitted to minister outside his own town without letters of recommendation from his own bishop.[84] Pope Innocent III issued the same prohibition, but said that the priest who did not have his letters of recommendation might

---

[83] *Decretum Gratiani,* c. 51, D. I *De Consecratione.*
[84] *Decr. Gratiani,* c. 7, D. 71.

be admitted to say Mass if he desired to do so out of devotion: he might not, however, say Mass before the people, but privately.[85] The Council of Trent again made the rule absolute—as the Council of Chalcedon had it—that no priest should be permitted to celebrate Mass and administer the Sacraments without letters of recommendation from his own bishop.[86] The Code mitigates the rule to some extent in favor of travelling priests. If, however, they have no letters of recommendation and do not wear clerical clothes, they should not be admitted. In the United States priests do not wear the cassock on the street, but the Roman collar and black suit are the recognized clerical attire. The duty of an unknown priest to register in a record kept for that purpose is introduced by the Code.

701. Speaking of priests who come from other countries to collect money for religious purposes without any authorization, the Council of Baltimore [87] rules that such priests are not to be permitted to say Holy Mass—not even once, unless they have received permission from the local Ordinary. This rule, as the Council states, is necessary in the United States to protect the people against impostors.

The letters of recommendation are, as a rule, given for a definite length of time. After the lapse of the time specified, they become invalid. Priests of Oriental Rites need letters of recommendation from the Sacred Congregation for the Oriental Church. Very likely those letters are required only when they want to say Mass in a church of the Latin Rite. For churches of their own Rite the letters of their own Ordinary should suffice.[88] The Ruthenian Rite in the United States has its own bishop, who can issue letters of recommendation to the priests subject to him.

702. With reference to priests from Europe and all countries about the Mediterranean Sea who desire to go to America or the Philippine Islands for an indefinite length of time or for ever, the Sacred Consistorial Congregation has issued special laws as to the manner in which the letters of recommendation shall be issued, and for the correspondence between the bishop in Europe and the bishop of those dioceses into which they wish

---

85 *Decretales Greg. IX*, c. 3 *De Clericis Peregrinis*, lib. I, tit. 22.
86 Sessio XXIII, cap. 16, *De Reform*.
87 *Concil. Balt. III*, n. 295.
88 Augustine, ''Commentary on Canon Law,'' IV, 129.

to go. For the Italian priests the Sacred Congregation reserves to itself the right to issue these letters; for Spain and Portugal the Papal Legates of these countries have the right to issue the letters. Letters not conforming to these laws are invalid.[89]

OBLIGATION TO SAY MASS

703. All priests are bound by obligation to say Holy Mass several times a year. The bishop or religious superior, however, shall see that their priests say Holy Mass at least on all Sundays and other feasts of obligation (**Canon 805**).

Many prominent theologians maintained that the priest had no obligation by divine law to say Holy Mass. Even Suarez, who is sometimes numbered among those who affirm the obligation, says that it seemed to him very doubtful, so that he who follows the negative opinion could be excused from mortal sin. The controversy is summed up by Gasparri, who quotes a decision of the Sacred Congregation of the Council to the effect that the priest who without a just cause does not say Holy Mass three or four times a year commits a mortal sin, and may be punished by the bishop.[90] The Code does not settle the controversy, for it does not state that the priest is bound to say Holy Mass by divine law or by reason of the priesthood, but simply passes an ecclesiastical ordinance obliging the priest to say Holy Mass several times a year (i.e., two or three times).

ONE MASS A DAY

704. With the exception of Christmas and All Souls' Day, on which every priest may say three Holy Masses, the priest is forbidden to say more than one Mass a day, unless he has an Apostolic indult or permission from the local Ordinary. The local Ordinary cannot grant this permission except in cases in which, according to his prudent judgment, a considerable number of the faithful would otherwise have to miss Mass on a day of obligation owing to the lack of priests. The Ordinary has no power to permit a priest to say more than two Masses on the same day (**Canon 806**).

[89] December 30, 1918; *Acta Ap. Sedis*, XI, 41.
[90] Gasparri, "De Eucharistia," I, 291–294.

In the first centuries of the Church Holy Mass was not said every day. After the custom of saying daily Mass had developed, it soon became a frequent practice for priests to celebrate Mass several times a day. It is related of St. Gregory of Tours that he said Holy Mass seven times a day. Pope Leo III (d. 816) said Holy Mass from seven to nine times a day; St. Ulrich, Bishop of Augsburg (d. 973), three times a day. Unfortunately, it was not always devotion which prompted the priests to say Mass repeatedly the same day; the desire for a larger number of stipends was at times the motive, as may be concluded from the prohibition of Pope Alexander II (1061–1073), who forbade the celebration of more than one Mass a day except when it became necessary to say a Mass for a deceased person besides the Mass of the day.[91] Pope Innocent III (1198–1216) ruled that a priest may say only one Mass a day except on Christmas and in a case of necessity.[92]

705. The custom of saying three Masses on Christmas is very ancient. Pope Gregory the Great (590–604) mentions the custom in one of his homilies, of which part is read in Matins on Christmas Day by those who use the Roman Breviary.

On All Souls' Day three Masses were allowed to be read by every priest in Spain and Portugal and their colonies by the Constitution "Quod Expensis" of Pope Benedict XIV, August 27, 1748.[93] By the Constitution "Incruentum" of August 10, 1915, Pope Benedict XV, extended this privilege to all the priests of the Catholic world.[94] One Mass may be said for any intention and a stipend may be taken, another is to be applied for all the faithful departed, the third is to be applied according to the intention of the Holy Father. By Decree of October 15, 1915, the Sacred Congregation of the Council forbade absolutely the acceptance of any remuneration under any consideration for the second or third Masses on All Souls' Day. Since Canon 824 allows the priest, whenever he says a second or third Mass on the same day, to receive a remuneration for his services, though he may not take a stipend for the application of the Mass, the Cardinal Prefect of the Committee for the Authentic

[91] Decr. Gratiani, c. 53, D. I De Consecrat.
[92] Decretales Greg. IX, c. 3, De Celebr. Missar., III, tit. 41.
[93] Opera Omnia Bened. XIV, XVI, 420.
[94] Acta Ap. Sedis, VII, 401. Concerning Indult of priest to say always Votive Mass and the three Masses on Christmas and All Souls', cfr. App. III, 34, g.

Interpretation of the Code declared that the Decree of 1915 is to be considered abolished by the Code.[95] The Sacred Congregation of Rites ordained that the first Mass is to be said as in the Missal "In die Commemorationis Omnium Fidelium Defunctorum," the second as "In Anniversario" (special orations being appointed), and the third as in the "Missa Quotidiana" (also with special orations).[96] Finally, the Sacred Congregation of Rites ruled that the Mass and Office of All Souls' Day is to be considered as a Feast of the First Class of the Universal Church, so that all particular feasts must give way to it. If November 2 is a Sunday, the Commemoration of All the Faithful Departed shall be held on November 3.[97] If All Souls' Day is transferred to November 3, the Holy Office, December 14, 1916, declared that the *toties quoties* plenary indulgence is also transferred: by this Decree it reverses that of the Sacred Congregation of Indulgences, November 20, 1907, which had ruled the contrary.[98] If a funeral occurs on All Souls' Day, the body may be brought to church and Mass said for the deceased, but the Mass formula shall be one of the three appointed for the day by the Sacred Congregation of Rites and to the oration of the Mass the oration for the deceased shall be added under one conclusion.[99]

706. In the above-quoted Canon 806, the Code gives the bishop the right to allow a priest to say two Masses on Sundays and holydays of obligation, if there are not sufficient priests and a considerable number (*notabilis pars*) of the faithful would have otherwise to go without Mass. Formerly the bishops in missionary countries usually got the faculty to allow bination. It seems, however, that there was no need of such a faculty for bination on Sundays and holydays of obligation if it would be otherwise impossible for people to hear Mass. The law of the Decretals quoted above did not forbid bination in case of necessity.

What is a *notabilis pars fidelium,* or how many people must desire Mass to justify a priest in binating? The Sacred Congregation discusses the question in a long Instruction on bina-

---

[95] Cfr. App. III, 3, c.
[96] August 11, 1915; *Acta Ap. Sedis,* VII, 422.
[97] February 28, 1917; *Acta Ap. Sedis,* IX, 186.
[98] *Acta Ap. Sedis,* IX, 179.
[99] Sacred Congregation of Rites, January 10, 1919; *Acta Ap. Sedis,* XI, 143.

tion, May 24, 1870, citing various former Decrees on the matter, and it concludes that the matter is left to the prudent judgment of the bishop, no precise number of people being fixed. The governing principle is that the Holy See wishes that all the faithful should have an opportunity of fulfilling easily the obligation of hearing Mass.[100] Authors generally declare that, if about twenty persons would otherwise have to miss Mass, the priest may binate.

Preparation of Priest for Mass

707. A priest who is conscious of the fact that there is a mortal sin on his soul shall not dare to say Mass without previous confession, however contrite he may esteem himself to be. If such a priest has no opportunity to approach a confessor, and necessity demands that he say Mass, he shall make an act of perfect contrition and celebrate, but he must go to confession as soon as he can (**Canon 807**).

According to the Council of Trent,[101] ecclesiastical custom declares that the words of St. Paul, "Let a man prove himself" (I Cor., xi. 28), are to be understood of the confession of persons conscious of mortal sin who desire to approach the Holy Table. Canon 11 of the Canons on the Holy Eucharist in the same Session of the Council punishes with *ipso facto* excommunication all who presume to teach, preach, stubbornly assert, or defend the contrary in a public debate. This censure has ceased, since it is not to be found in the Code. The term "quamprimum" (as soon as possible) is usually interpreted by canonists to mean within three days. If, however, the priest is under the necessity of celebrating Mass again the next day, and he can without great difficulty find a confessor before he says Mass again, he is bound to do so. For a further explanation of difficulties which may occur in complying with this law of the Church, we refer the reader to the moralists who discuss these cases. Referring to lay persons receiving Holy Communion when they are conscious of a mortal sin, Canon 856 uses practically the same words as Canon 807, except that in the former Canon the phrase "quamprimum confiteatur" is missing.

[100] *Collectanea de P. F.*, II, n. 1352.
[101] Sessio XIII, cap. 7, *De SS. Euchar.*

708. Canonists have discussed the case in which the only sin on the conscience of the priest who wanted to say Mass was a reserved case. They have disputed whether in such a case a priest was obliged to confess to a priest who had no faculty to absolve from that sin. Since the promulgation of the Code the case is not practical, except in the rare cases where a censure has been inflicted *ab homine*—that is to say, by a particular order of the ecclesiastical authority. In all papal cases of reserved censures any confessor can absolve, if it is difficult for the penitent to wait until the faculty to absolve him can be obtained. Recourse by letter through the confessor within one month must be made to the Sacred Penitentiary or to the bishop or another superior who has the faculty to absolve (cfr. Canon 2254). Canon 900 gives every confessor the right to absolve from the bishop's reserved cases, when the confessor judges that the faculty to absolve cannot be obtained except with great inconvenience to the penitent.

709. The priest may not say Mass unless he has kept the natural fast from midnight (**Canon 808**).

The custom of saying Holy Mass and of receiving Holy Communion fasting, is very ancient in the Church. Pope Benedict XIV discusses the question in his work, "De Synodo Diœcesana," and states that some authors hold that the Apostles introduced the fast.[102] The passage from St. Paul, I Cor., xi. 21, often cited in this connection, does not prove anything: some commentators of the Epistle hold that he speaks of a meal before the Eucharistic celebration, while others believe he refers to a meal which took place after the divine worship. Some who hold that he speaks of a meal before the celebration of Holy Mass, maintain that by the words, "the rest I will set in order when I come," he meant to forbid the meal before the celebration of Holy Mass. Cardinal Gasparri believes that in the earliest times there was no law demanding the fast from midnight.[103] It is evident that, apart from a miracle, the practices of the Early Church could not become immediately uniform throughout the Christian communities spread over many and distant countries. The Council of Hippo (in 393) insisted on the Eucharistic fast, and allowed only on Holy Thursday the

---

102 *De Synodo Diœcesana*, lib. VI, cap. viii, n. 10.
103 *De Eucharistia*, I, 304, n. 426.

meal (*agape*) before Holy Mass in commemoration of the Last Supper. In his answer to Januarius, St. Augustine says that it has pleased the Holy Ghost that, in honor of such a great Sacrament, the mouth of the Christian should not receive any other food before receiving the Body of the Lord, and that for this reason that custom is observed throughout the world. He holds that the fast was instituted by the Apostles.[104]

710. Recently the Holy See has published a Decree which is a remarkable departure from the severity with which the Church has insisted on the Eucharistic fast for the priest. Even when Pius X allowed persons who had been sick for a month to receive Holy Communion once or twice a month without fasting,[105] no concession was given to priests to say Mass without keeping the fast. In missionary countries, indeed, a relaxation of the law had at times been granted. Now the Holy See declares that it is willing to grant permission to priests to take liquid food (excluding intoxicants), whenever they have to say two Masses, or a Mass at a very late hour, on Sundays and holydays of obligation, and cannot keep the fast without great difficulty or injury to their health. The Holy See is willing to give habitual faculties to the bishop to grant this dispensation in dioceses where it is needed frequently. In emergencies, when there is no time to have recourse to the Holy See, the bishops may even now, without the faculty, grant that dispensation.[106] Priests who get the dispensation from the Eucharistic fast may take the ablution during the first Mass.[107]

Persons for Whom Holy Mass May be Said

711. The priest is free to apply Holy Mass for any living person and also for the poor souls in purgatory, subject however to the rules of Canon 2262, § 2, n. 2 (**Canon 809**). This Canon allows Mass to be privately applied, if scandal is avoided, for an excommunicated person; but when he is an *excommunicatus vitandus*, Mass may be said for his conversion only.

Mass may be applied either for the repose of the souls in

---

[104] *Decr. Gratiani*, can. 54, D. 2 *De Consecr.*
[105] Sacred Congregation of the Council, Dec. 7, 1906; *Acta S. Sedis,* XXXIX, 603.
[106] Cfr. App. III, 34, a.
[107] Cfr. App. III, 34, b.

purgatory or for the intention of the living. In both classes
of intentions there are difficulties. Regarding the application
for the deceased, the Holy See has declared that Mass may not
be said for those who have died in manifest heresy, though the
Mass intention is known only to the priest and the person who
offers the stipend.[108] If, by the phrase "manifest heresy," the
Sacred Congregation meant "culpable heresy," the question of
saying Mass for those in good faith remains open. The Code
allows private or secret application of Mass for the *excommunicati tolerati,* which include the members of heretical and schismatic sects. That the Code speaks of the application of Mass
for the living excommunicated persons, is evident from the next
phrase of Canon 2262: "if they are *excommunicati vitandi,*
Mass may be said for their conversion only" (i.e., not for other
intentions of theirs). In Canon 1240, the Code enumerates those
persons to whom ecclesiastical burial is to be denied, and, in
Canon 1241, it forbids any funeral Mass for such persons, also
the anniversary Mass, and any other public funeral services or
divine offices. It does not mention the secret or private application of Mass for these persons. The Code, therefore, does not
answer the question whether Mass may be said privately for the
repose of the soul of a baptized non-Catholic or a schismatic.
Noldin [109] holds that Mass may be secretly applied for them,
but he argues from Canon 2262, which speaks of the living only.
In the edition of 1914, Noldin discusses the question, and quotes
Aichner, Lehmkuhl and Genicot in support of the opinion that
Mass may be said privately for deceased heretics and schismatics when they gave probable signs of good faith and of the
state of grace. He himself does not favor that opinion. Writing
before the Code, Cardinal Gasparri [110] discusses whether a stipend may be taken and Mass applied, if Mass is requested for
persons who died in infidelity, heresy, excommunication, or manifest sin. He answers that the priest should say that he can
apply Mass for all the faithful departed with the intention of
helping the soul for whom Mass is requested, if it be pleasing
to God. It is evident that this is no answer to the difficulty.
The question is of practical importance and a uniform mode

---

[108] Holy Office, April 7, 1875; *Collectanea de P. F.,* II, **n. 1440.**
[109] *Theol. Moral.,* III (13th ed., 1920), n. 176.
[110] *De Eucharistia,* I, n. 489.

of action is desirable lest people wonder how one priest can be so *liberal* and another so *narrow*. Though we know that many Protestants are such merely because they happened to be born of Protestant parents (not from any spirit of opposition to the Catholic Church), still the fact remains that they are in the enemy camp just like the alien enemy during the war. The Catholic Church cannot recognize them as members of the Church without sacrifice of principle. Wherefore it is unreasonable to request a priest to say Mass for a deceased non-Catholic, whether a private person or an official of a state or nation. The Mass is essentially an official religious act of the Church, and thus can never be a merely private act of the priest. In reference to the saying of Mass for deceased non-Catholic princes and other official personages, there is the declaration of Pope Gregory XVI that the ancient and the new discipline of the Church forbid us to honor with Catholic religious rites persons who have died in external and notorious profession of heresy.[111]

712. Mass may not be said for deceased unbaptized persons,[112] nor for Catholics who die in apostasy, excommunication or in a publicly known state of sin, unless they have given a sign of repentance: the very nature of these cases excludes application of Holy Mass for them.[113] For unbaptized persons who died suddenly while they were taking a course of instruction to become Catholics, Mass may be said according to the ancient practice of the Church. In his sermon on the death of Emperor Valentinian, a catechumen, St. Ambrose asks that Masses be said for the repose of his soul.

713. With regard to the celebration of Mass for the living, it may be applied for the lawful intentions of both a spiritual and a temporal nature at the request of Catholics as well as of non-Catholics, baptized and unbaptized. For excommunicated persons, including heretics and schismatics, the Code (Canon 2262) allows the priest the private application of Mass, if no scandal is given and if the persons are *excommunicati tolerati;* for the *excommunicati vitandi* Holy Mass may be said only for the intention of obtaining their conversion. Canon 2258 states that those persons only are *excommunicati vitandi*

---

111 *Epist. ad Ep. Augustan.,* Febr. 16, 1842; Gasparri, ''Fontes Cod. Jur. Can.,'' II, 793.

112 Sacred Congregation P. F., Sept. 12, 1645; *Collectanea,* I, n. 114.

113 Gasparri, ''De SS. Euchar.,'' I, nn. 483, 485.

who are by name excommunicated by the Holy See, whose excommunication is made public, and who in the Decree itself are declared to be *vitandi*. Persons who lay violent hands on the person of the Roman Pontiff are by that very crime *excommunicati vitandi*. With regard to the application of Mass for the intention of unbaptized persons, the Holy Office has declared it permissible, provided no scandal is given, and it be certain that their intention is not superstitious or otherwise sinful.[114]

PREPARATION OF PRIEST AND VESTING FOR MASS

714. The priest should not fail to prepare his soul by pious prayers for the oblation of the Eucharistic Sacrifice, or upon its conclusion to give thanks to God for so great a boon (**Canon 810**). The moralists discuss the duty of preparation and thanksgiving. The Code merely mentions that duty supposing it to be known from other sources. Due respect for God and a right appreciation of His gifts will prompt priests to do what the Code exhorts them to do.

The priest who is to say Mass should wear the cassock and the sacred vestments prescribed by the rubrics of his rite. He must not wear skull-cap and ring, unless he be a Cardinal, bishop, or abbot who has received the abbatial blessing, or unless he has an Apostolic indult which allows him the use of skull-cap and ring in the celebration of Holy Mass (**Canon 811**). All these matters are a repetition of the laws and regulations taken from the liturgical books of the Church, and are merely mentioned by the Code, as it were incidentally. Canon 2 of the Code stated that the Code does not, as a rule, treat of the rites and ceremonies of the sacred liturgy, and that the former laws of the liturgy remain in force, unless the Code explicitly modifies some of them.[114a]

ASSISTANT PRIEST AND SERVER AT HOLY MASS

715. Except the bishop and other prelates having the use of the pontificals, no priest is allowed to have an assistant priest for the sole reason of honor and solemnity (**Canon 812).** While the Sacred Congregation of Rites has repeatedly forbidden

114 July 12, 1865; *Collectanea*, I, n. 1274.
114a Concerning Gothic vestments, cfr. App. III, 34, c.

priests who have not obtained the privilege of the **pontificals** to have an assistant priest in the celebration of Holy Mass, the same Congregation has stated that the presence of an assistant priest at the first Solemn Mass of a newly ordained priest may be tolerated.[115]

716. The priest should not say Mass unless he has a server who serves and answers him. The server at Mass should not be a woman, unless no male server can be had, and unless the woman stays at a distance to answer the prayers and does not in any way approach the altar (**Canon 813**).[115a] The law concerning the server is not new. By the Quinquennial Faculties the bishops in the United States had permission to say Holy Mass without a server, and usually the bishops communicated the faculties to the priests. Now that these faculties are revoked, the question of saying Mass without a server has attracted attention. The Code has nothing new on the matter, but merely repeats the former law. One must therefore go to the commentators on the former law to ascertain the obligation imposed by that law. The law requiring a server is contained in the Decretals of Pope Gregory IX,[116] and the rubrics of the Roman Missal repeat the same law. It seems that all moralists and canonists of note are agreed that the obligation is grave in itself. When it is difficult to get a boy or a man, it is permissible for a cause that is reasonable, but not necessarily grave, to say Mass with a woman answering the priest. St. Alphonsus held that it was a venial sin to say Mass with a woman answering the prayers. The Code demands a *justa causa* to allow a woman to take the place of the server. Augustine [117] thinks that the custom of saying Mass without a server which had become quite general in the United States under the Quinquennial Faculties, would make it permissible to say Mass without a server, if otherwise Mass could not be said and some frequent communicants would be disappointed. However, the Sacred Congregation does not easily tolerate customs contrary to the rubrics, and it seems that the custom based on the former faculties was, in many instances, rather an abuse of the faculties, for they read that the priest could say Holy Mass without a

[115] Sacred Congregation of Rites, Dec. 1, 1882; *Decr. Auth. S. R. C.,* n. 3564.

[115a] When altar boy should ring bell in Mass, cfr. App. III, 34, f.

[116] C. 6, *De Filiis Presbyt. ord. vel non,* lib. I, tit. 17.

[117] Augustine, ''Commentary,'' IV, 151.

server, "si necessitas urgeat." It may be more difficult now to break off the habit and to get boys or adult men to serve Holy Mass on weekdays, because for many years, under the pretext of the former faculties, little or no effort was made to train servers. There is no doubt, however, that the law obliges the priest to make a far greater effort to get a server at Mass than has been made when the former faculty was in vogue. The *Linzer Quartalschrift* takes the same view in discussing this question, and asserts that with a reasonable effort a server could be had even in country parishes.[118] The *Ecclesiastical Review* [119] is more lenient in its view on the necessity of a server, but the fact remains that insufficient efforts have been made to procure servers because of a mistaken interpretation of the former faculty.[119a]

ARTICLE II.—OF THE RITES AND CEREMONIES OF HOLY MASS

717. The Holy Sacrifice of the Mass must be offered up in the form of bread and wine, a very small quantity of water being mixed with the latter (**Canon 814**). The bread must be made of pure wheaten flour, and it must be recently baked so that there is no danger of corruption. The wine must be the natural juice of the grape vine and uncorrupted (**Canon 815**).

That pure wheaten bread and pure grape wine are essential to the Sacrifice of the Mass, is and has always been the teaching of the Church. The altar breads must be recently baked to avoid all danger of disintegration. The Code does not define the term "recenter confectus," but there is a declaration of the Sacred Congregation of Rites to the effect that hosts which have been baked three months ago cannot be used.[120] There is also a recent Decree of the Sacred Congregation of the Sacraments which prohibits the custom of using hosts which are two or three months old, saying that the law of the Roman Ritual and of the Code shall be observed, which law requires that the hosts used for Mass and the Communion of the faithful be *recently* baked. The Decree does not further specify what is means by "recently baked," but quotes Canon 1272 which rules that the priests shall faithfully observe the instructions which the local Ordinary has given with reference to using fresh hosts

118 LXXII (1919), 242.   119 LXVIII (1923), 294.
119a People answering priest and reciting aloud some parts of Mass, cfr. App. III, 34, e.
120 Dec. 16, 1826; *Decr. Auth. S. R. C.*, n. 2650; cfr. App. III, 34, d.

so that all danger of the corruption of the altar breads may be avoided.[121]

As to the wheaten flour, the Holy Office allowed some missionaries in India who had difficulty in getting such flour to make their own by crushing the grain, soaking it in water for several hours, and then pressing it: from the white matter which resulted from the pressing, they were to make the altar breads by pouring it on hot irons.[122] In places where it was very difficult to get pure wine, the Holy Office allowed the missionaries to make altar wine out of dried grapes or raisins, a certain number of pounds of raisins being crushed and mixed with as many pounds of water and after having been standing for from six to at most ten hours, the water not absorbed was drained off and the rest of the mixture pressed. The Sacred Congregation added the proviso that the liquid thus obtained from its color and taste must prove to be real wine.[123]

718. In the celebration of Mass the priest must, according to his own rite, use either unleavened or leavened bread, wherever he celebrates (**Canon 816**). Most of the Oriental Rites use leavened bread. Before the Code, it was disputed whether a Latin priest travelling in places where there are only churches of an Oriental Rite, or an Oriental priest travelling through places where there are only Latin churches, should follow his own rite as to the altar bread or should follow the rite of the church where he says Mass. Cardinal Gasparri, who discussed the question,[124] held that from the various Papal Constitutions dealing with this matter one would conclude that the priest is to follow his own rite wherever he celebrates Mass. The Code, which follows the opinion of Gasparri, settles the controversy. Whether a Latin priest may in case of necessity use common (fermented) wheat bread, is discussed by the moralists. They hold quite unanimously that a priest of the Latin Rite may not say Mass with fermented bread, even for the sake of giving the Holy Viaticum. They are not very consistent, for many of them hold that a Latin priest when travelling where there are only churches of an Oriental Rite, may use the fermented bread

---

[121] Dec. 7, 1918; *Acta Ap. Sedis*, XI, 8.
[122] June 23, 1852; *Collectanea de P. F.*, I, n. 1076.
[123] July 22, 1706; *Collectanea de P. F.*, I, n. 270. Cfr. Lehmkuhl, "Theol. Moral.," II (ed. 1898), 86.
[124] *De SS. Eucharistia*, II, n. 805.

of the Orientals. However, there is no doubt that the obligation is grave for the priest to use the altar bread prescribed by his respective rite.

719. Even in a case of extreme necessity, it is forbidden to consecrate one species without the other, or both outside of Holy Mass (**Canon 817**).

The celebrant must observe the rubrics of his liturgical books accurately and devoutly, and beware of adding other ceremonies and prayers of his own choice. All contrary customs by which other ceremonies and prayers are introduced into the Rite of the Mass, are disapproved (**Canon 818**). Mass must be celebrated in the liturgical language proper to each priest's own rite, as approved by the Church (**Canon 819**).

ARTICLE III.—OF THE TIME AND PLACE OF HOLY MASS

720. Mass may be said on all days except those which are excluded by the priest's own Rite (**Canon 820**). Mass shall not be begun earlier than one hour before dawn (*aurora*), nor later than one hour after midday. On Christmas Day only the conventual or parochial Mass may be begun at midnight, but no other Mass without an Apostolic indult. In all religious or pious houses having an oratory with the faculty of reserving the Blessed Sacrament there habitually, one priest may say at midnight on Christmas three Masses according to the liturgy of the day, or only one: this Mass will satisfy the obligation of hearing Mass for all who assist at it, and Holy Communion may be given to those who wish to receive (**Canon 821**).

The celebration of Midnight Mass on Christmas Day in parochial churches is very ancient. The churches of cathedral and collegiate Chapters and of religious communities with solemn vows were regarded as equivalent to parochial churches with respect to the community attached to these churches. The general concession of the Christmas Midnight Mass to religious communities with simple vows and to other ecclesiastical institutes having a chapel where the Blessed Sacrament is habitually reserved, is quite recent (August 1, 1907).[125] In the former law it was forbidden to give Holy Communion at the Midnight Mass in those churches which by the common law had the right to have the Midnight Mass (viz., parochial and conventual

125 *Acta Ap. Sedis*, I, 146.

churches). There is a question whether the Code changes the former law and allows the distribution of Holy Communion at the Christmas Midnight Mass. It seems that the Code allows it, for Canon 867 rules generally that Holy Communion may be given at those hours at which Holy Mass may be said.

A private decision was given to a bishop in the Philippine Islands in 1920, allowing the giving of Holy Communion in parochial and conventual churches. A recent general decision declares that Holy Communion may be given unless the local Ordinary forbids it in a particular case for just reasons. Local Ordinaries have the right and duty to guard public worship against anything unbecoming.[126]

The Code, like the former law, allows only one Mass at midnight in parochial and conventual churches; without an Apostolic Indult no other priest can say Mass before the dawn of day, nor can the priest who said the Midnight Mass say a second or third Mass. The exception to this law, in Canon 821, in favor of religious houses and charitable institutions (*piæ domus*), does not apply to the churches of religious which serve as a place of worship for the faithful generally. If, however, the religious do not have a Midnight Mass for the public but only for their own community, the religious community enjoys the privilege regarding the three Masses and Holy Communion.[127]

ALTAR AND PLACE FOR MASS

721. Mass must be said on a consecrated altar, and in a church or oratory consecrated or blessed according to law. In the case of private and semi-public oratories, Canon 1196 is to be observed. The privilege of the *portable altar* is conceded either by law or by an indult obtainable only from the Holy See. The privilege of the portable altar is to be understood in such a sense that it bestows the faculty to say Mass on a consecrated altar-stone anywhere in a decent and respectable place, but not at sea. The local Ordinary—or, in the case of an exempt religious house, the major superior—can give permission for a just and reasonable cause to celebrate Mass outside a church or

---

[126] See latest decision which is more explicit, App. III, 36, f.
[127] Vermeersch, "Periodica," IV, 312; Augustine, "Commentary," IV, 168.

oratory on a consecrated altar-stone in a decent place, but never in a bedroom.[128] This permission can be given only in an extraordinary case and in individual cases (*per modum actus*), not habitually (**Canon 822**).

The altar-stone, and a church or oratory blessed or consecrated for Divine worship, have since ancient times been required for the celebration of Mass.[128a] It is likewise an ancient law that the Holy See only can allow the celebration of Mass in oratories which are strictly private (i.e., those in the houses of lay persons or individual ecclesiastics). Canon 1192 gives the Ordinary the right to erect semi-public oratories in colleges and other schools, military stations, prisons, hospitals, asylums, etc., and to allow there the celebration of Mass and the holding of other ecclesiastical functions. Canon 1194 rules that in private oratories the bishop may allow Mass on some extraordinary occasion and in individual cases only, but not habitually. In virtue of Canons 239 and 349, Cardinals and bishops, including titular bishops, have the privilege of the portable altar, which entitles them to say Mass, not only in their own residence, but wherever they may stay, and to allow another Mass to be said in their presence: by the same Canons they have the right to say Mass at sea. The seven Prothonotaries Apostolic *de numero participantium* were given the privilege of the portable altar by the *Motu Proprio* of Pope Pius X, February 21, 1905.[129] Vicars and prefects Apostolic who are not consecrated bishops have by Canon 308 the privileges of the Prothonotaries *de numero participantium*, but their privileges are by the same Canon restricted to their term of office and the territory of their jurisdiction.

722. Mass may not be said in the churches of heretics or schismatics, even though they were in the past properly consecrated or blessed. If there is no altar of the priest's own rite, he may say Mass on a consecrated altar of another Catholic rite—not, however, on the Greek *antimensia*. No one is allowed to celebrate Mass on papal altars without an Apostolic Indult (**Canon 823**).

In some instances the Holy See has permitted Catholics to

---

[128] Concerning Mass in private houses, cfr. App. III, 34, h and j.

[128a] The Sacred Congregation of the Sacraments declared, July 26, 1924, that political gatherings and profane celebrations are not good reasons why the bishop may permit Holy Mass to be said outside the usual places of divine worship. Cfr. App. III, 34, i.

[129] *Acta S. Sedis*, XXXVII, 491.

have Mass in the same church as is used by Protestants, for in many districts in Europe Catholic churches were taken by the Protestants at the time of the Reformation, and it was not always possible for the few Catholics scattered among a Protestant population to build their own churches. The custom of saying Mass on an altar made of stone—or at least on a small stone which holds the chalice and paten—originated soon after the centuries of the Roman persecutions. The Oriental Rites have, as a rule, only one consecrated altar of stone in each church.[130] In the consecration of churches the Orientals bless the *antimensia:* these are pieces of cloth about as large as our corporals, decorated with inscriptions and imprinted with holy images, and with relics sewed up in them. On these the Oriental priests may say Mass. The priests of the Latin Rite are not allowed to use these *antimensia,* but they may use a consecrated altar of an Oriental Rite, if they cannot go to a Latin church. Papal altars are found in churches which have received from the Holy See the title of a *basilica.* As a rule, one altar in such churches is declared a papal altar in the document conferring the title.

ARTICLE IV.—OF MASS ALMS OR STIPENDS

723. According to an established and approved custom of the Church, any priest who says and applies Mass may accept an alms or stipend. Whenever he says Mass several times on the same day, and has to apply one Mass from a title of justice, he cannot receive another stipend, excepting some compensation for an extrinsic reason. On Christmas, however, he may receive a stipend also for the second and third Masses (**Canon 824**).

The Code sums up the former legislation on Mass stipends. The history of the Mass stipend is treated by many of the canonists of the former law.[131] Bishops and pastors who on Sundays and holydays of obligation, including the abolished holydays, are obliged to apply Mass for the people, may not take a stipend if they say a second Mass on some Sunday or holyday of obligation, with the sole exception of Christmas Day. The extrinsic title referred to by the Code means the

---

[130] Gasparri, "De SS. Eucharistia," I. n. 290.
[131] Gasparri, "De SS. Eucharistia," I, n. 535. Concerning Indults to take stipend for bination Masses, cfr. App. III, 35, a.

labor or work for which compensation may be received. Thus, if a priest who has said one Mass on Sunday, is requested to say another Mass in some church, he is entitled to compensation for his services. On All Souls' Day three Masses may be said, but a stipend may be taken for one Mass only.[132]

724. It is never lawful:

(1) To apply Mass for the intention of one who may offer a stipend in the future, but who has not yet asked for the Mass, and then to accept the stipend offered later for the Mass applied before the request was made;

(2) To accept a stipend for a Mass which was due and applied for another title;

(3) To receive two stipends for the application of one and the same Mass;

(4) To receive one stipend for the mere fact of saying the Mass, and another for the application of the same Mass, unless it is certain that one stipend was given for the saying of Holy Mass exclusively without the application (**Canon 825**).

The various abuses here condemned have been censured by the Church long before the promulgation of the Code. In n. 4, the term stipend is not used in its technical meaning, but rather in its general sense of compensation for work or services rendered, for a stipend in its proper sense is given for the application of Holy Mass.[132a]

Various Kinds of Stipends

725. *Manual* stipends are those which the faithful offer to the priest either out of their own devotion, or from an obligation, even a perpetual one imposed by a testator on his heirs.

Ad instar manualium are stipends of foundation Masses which cannot be said in the proper church or by those who, according to the terms of the foundations, should say them, and which are therefore either by law or by Indult of the Holy See given to other priests to say.

Foundation stipends are those which are received from a fund set apart for foundation Masses (**Canon 826**).

The classification of Mass stipends is of importance for the understanding of the various Canons which use the terms,

[132] See above, n. 705; cfr. also App. III, 3, c.
[132a] Stipend belongs to priest who says the Mass, cfr. App. III, 35, b.

stipendia manualia, ad instar manualium, or *fundata.* Pious foundations are defined by Canon 1544; Canons 1546 and 1550 discuss what churches can accept such foundations.

ABUSES TO BE AVOIDED

726. All negotiation or trading of any kind in connection with Mass stipends must be absolutely avoided (**Canon 827**). So many Masses must be said and applied as Mass stipends (even though they are small) were offered and accepted (**Canon 828**).[133] If the Mass stipends once accepted are lost, though through no fault of him who has the duty to say tne Masses, the obligation to say them does not cease (**Canon 829**). If a person has offered a certain sum of money for Masses without stating how many Masses he wants said, the number must be reckoned according to the ordinary stipends customary in the place where the giver of them lived, unless circumstances are such that it may be legitimately presumed that the donor's intention was different (**Canon 830**).

These Canons all deal with fidelity in the handling of Mass stipends. In the first place, the law strictly forbids any kind of negotiation and trading in connection with Mass stipends. As the Code does not define in what this trading and negotiation consists, this information must be sought in former Decrees, especially the Decree "Ut debita" of the Sacred Congregation of the Council, May 11, 1904. On this matter Noldin [133a] and other moralists may be consulted. Canon 828 demands that a Mass must be said for each stipend accepted, and it is strictly forbidden to say one Mass for several stipends. Canon 2324 gives the penalties for priests guilty of forbidden negotiation with Mass stipends.

727. By the precept of the Code (Canon 829), and by the general principle of *res perit domino,* the priest who is under obligation to say Masses for the stipends he has actually received (i.e., had in his possession), is obliged to say the Masses even though the stipends were stolen from him or lost in any other manner. Gasparri and other commentators of the former Canon Law held that, if the stipends in the possession of the priest were lost without his fault, he was not bound to say the Masses. Evi-

[133] Concerning combination of several intentions, cfr. App. III, 35, c.
[133a] Noldin, "Theol. Moral.," III (ed. 1920), n. 186.

dently they did not consider the priest as the owner of the stipends before the Masses were said, but merely as a bailee.[134] The question of the loss of stipends by lay persons under obligation to forward them to a priest is not decided by the Code. If one lay person who wants Masses said should give stipends to another lay person to take them to the priest, and the bearer should lose the stipends, his liability depends on the question whether and how far he has been negligent. The amount of care he owes to the owner of the stipends, depends to a great extent on the fact whether his services were gratuitous or paid for. In entirely accidental loss, the owner must bear the loss according to the principle, *res perit domino*. The question of the loss of stipends sent by one priest to another is mentioned in Canon 839.

728. Canon 830 rules that, when a certain sum of money is given for Masses without any further specification of the number of Masses, the number is ordinarily to be figured according to the usual stipend introduced either by custom or by the law of the bishop in the diocese where the person making the offering lived. The question arises whether one may say High Masses as well as Low Masses for that sum of money. It seems that High Masses may be said as well as Low Masses. The Code certainly does not demand Low Masses, but merely wants that number of Masses to which the person is entitled by the stipend fixed in his diocese. There is a fixed stipend for Low Masses and for High Masses. One may argue that it is the intention of the donor to have as many Masses as he can possibly get for the amount he offers: if there is some expression in the gift or bequest which justifies such an interpretation of his intention, Low Masses only should be said, but, if there is no indication of that intention of the donor, it seems a gratuitous assumption to maintain that Low Masses only can be said—all the more so, if, as is the case in many churches, most of the Masses said are High Masses. Besides, in many cases the donor intends to bestow a benefit on the priest by a legacy of Masses. If only Low Masses can be said, the priest would not benefit by the bequest in many instances, as he has already a sufficient number of such Masses on hand. We refer mainly to bequests of Masses, for when the donor is living he usually manifests his will, or, if he does not, it is easy to inquire what his intention is.

[134] Gasparri, ''De SS. Eucharistia,'' I, n. 588.

Right of the Local Ordinary to Fix Amount of Mass Stipends

729. The local Ordinary has the right to fix by decree the amount of the manual stipends in his diocese, which should, in so far as possible, be done in a diocesan synod; the priest is not permitted to demand a larger stipend than has been fixed by the law of the bishop. Where there is no law of the bishop fixing the stipend, the custom of the diocese shall be followed. All religious, even the exempt, are obliged to observe the law of the local Ordinary, or the custom of the diocese, concerning the manual stipend (**Canon 831**). A priest may accept a larger stipend for the application of Mass, if voluntarily offered; and, unless the Ordinary has forbidden it, he may accept a smaller stipend (**Canon 832**).

The Council of Trent [135] commanded the bishops to prohibit all abuses in the matter of Mass stipends. That the exempt religious organizations are bound by the law of the bishop on Mass stipends, was declared by the Sacred Congregation of the Council on January 15, 1639.[136] The same Congregation declared on January 16, 1649, that the bishop cannot forbid the acceptance of a larger stipend freely offered, and in another declaration of July 16, 1689, said that the bishop could under penalties forbid priests to take a smaller stipend than that fixed by the bishop's law. In connexion with this decision Gasparri remarks that the bishop cannot forbid a priest to say Mass for someone without taking a stipend.[137] The Code allows the saying of Mass for a smaller stipend, unless the Ordinary forbids it.

Obligation Arising from Acceptance of Stipend

730. It is presumed that the donor of the stipend only requests the application of Mass; if, however, he has explicitly stipulated certain circumstances for its celebration, the priest who accepts the stipend must fulfill these conditions (**Canon 833**).

The priest is free to accept or refuse the stipend, but, if he accepts it, he is bound by the stipulations made by the giver of

---

[135] Sessio XXII, *Decretum de Observandis et Evitandis in Celebratione Missæ.*

[136] Gasparri, ''De SS. Euchar.,'' I, n. 558.

[137] ''De SS. Euchar.,'' I, n. 556.

the stipend, unless he persuades the giver to waive them. Generally speaking, priests in the United States are not troubled much with stipulations except in regard to the time of saying the Mass, with which the next Canon deals.

731. Concerning the *time* when Mass is to be said for a stipend, the following rules must be observed:

(1) If the time was specified by the giver of the stipend, Mass must absolutely be said at the specified time;

(2) If the giver of a manual stipend did not explicitly specify the time, then (a) Masses ordered for an urgent cause must be said as soon as possible, and in sufficient time to fulfill the purpose (e.g., a Mass for the success of a dangerous operation must be said before the operation takes place); (b) in all other cases Mass must be said within a short time, varying according to the number of Masses requested by one and the same person;

(3) If the giver of the stipend expressly left the time of saying the Masses to the judgment of the priest, he may say them at whatever time he prefers, subject to the precept of Canon 835 (**Canon 834**).

If the giver of the stipend wants Mass to be said on a fixed date, and the intention is not so urgent that a delay frustrates the intention, the delay without his consent is wrong, but, if the delay is a month or less, it is probably not a mortal sin.[138] If a Mass is requested for a certain day and the intention is not known, the Mass cannot be delayed without danger of frustrating the intention. In ordinary cases when Mass stipends are offered but no special time specified, the Church demands that the Masses be said within a short time. The Code does not state what is meant by "modicum tempus," but the Decree "*Ut debita*," May 11, 1904, ruled that the time is one month for one Mass, six months for one hundred Masses. A Decree of July 17, 1755, stated that the phrase "modicum tempus" in the Decrees on Mass stipends meant one month.[139] If several persons offer the priest a Mass stipend on the same day, all these Masses have to be said within a month, for the Decree "Ut debita" refers only to the case where the same persons offer a large number of stipends at one time. This decision was given by the Sacred

---

[138] Gasparri, "De SS. Euchar.," I, n. 591.
[139] *Opera Omnia Bened. XIV, Inst. Eccl.* 56, n. 14, vol. X.

Congregation of the Council on February 27, 1905.[140] Both the old law and the more recent Decree "Ut debita," therefore, demand that the Mass be said within a month: the Code confirms the old law by using the same phrase "modicum tempus." Lehmkuhl writes that, if the Mass is deferred notably over two months without the consent of the giver of the stipend, authors commonly hold that it is a mortal sin.[141] The law being so severe, it is advisable that the priest to whom Mass stipends are offered for intentions which are not urgent request the people to leave the time of the fulfillment of the obligation to the priest; that this is permissible, can be deduced from the last paragraph of Canon 834.

732. Nobody is allowed to receive more stipends for Masses to be said by himself than he can satisfy within one year (**Canon 835**).

The words "to be said by himself" indicate that the Church does not allow a priest to accumulate a great number of stipends for his own use with the consequent danger of not saying them within the prescribed time, even if the giver of the stipends offers them expressly with the provision that the priest may say the Masses at any future time. The law does not forbid a priest to accept more stipends than he himself can satisfy; on the contrary, a great deal of good can be done if the priests in the places where there are many Catholics and where many stipends are offered to them, accept the stipends and send them to the priests in the missions and the poor parishes in districts which have very few Catholics.

TRANSFER OF STIPENDS TO OTHER PRIESTS

733. In churches where, on account of the special devotion of the faithful, stipends for Masses are offered in such a number that it is impossible to say all of them in those churches within the required time, the faithful should be notified by notices posted in a public and conspicuous place that the Masses requested will be said either in that church when possible or elsewhere (**Canon 836**). There is a special reason for this rule of the Code. For, while as a rule it is a matter of indifference

---

[140] *Acta S. Sedis*, XXXVII, 525; "Ut debita," XXXVI, 672.
[141] *Theol. Moral.*, II (ed. 1898), n. 199.

to the people where the Masses are said, the church may be a special place of grace—one of the sacred shrines where God bestows special favors—and therefore the intention of the people who offer Mass stipends there is naturally that the Masses should be said in that church.

734. A priest who has stipends for Masses which must be said by others, shall distribute them as soon as possible, subject to the precept of Canon 841 which rules that, if one year has elapsed from the time of their reception, the stipends must be surrendered to the Ordinary. Unless the contrary is certain for other reasons, the time for the saying of the Masses which are transferred to others begins on the day when they are received by the priest who is to celebrate them (**Canon 837**). It is important that all Mass stipends be distributed without unnecessary delay, since the obligation of the priest to whom the stipends are transferred begins only from the day of their receipt.

735. Persons who have a number of manual stipends which they are at liberty to give to others, may distribute them among priests of their own choice, provided they know for certain that the latter are absolutely trustworthy, or are recommended by the testimony of their own Ordinaries (**Canon 838**). Persons who have received stipends from the faithful or in any other way (for instance, an heir who by last will has the obligation to have a number of Masses said for the testator), is bound by this obligation until he has received notice that the stipends were received, and that the priest in question has assumed the obligation of saying those Masses (**Canon 839**).

Stipends for Masses which need not be said in a certain place, may thus be forwarded to any priest whom one knows, either from personal knowledge or from other reliable sources, to be absolutely trustworthy. If one knows nothing about the priest, but he has genuine letters of recommendation from his own Ordinary, one may transfer stipends to him. The question arose whether the Ordinary can forbid his priests to send stipends to priests of other dioceses without his consent. The Sacred Congregation of the Council declared on February 19, 1921, that the bishop cannot forbid the sending of manual stipends to priests of other dioceses, but he can forbid it in reference to stipends of foundation Masses, stipends *ad instar manualium* and stipends given *intuitu causœ piœ,* because all these stipends adhere to the places, and he has control over the sacred places and ecclesiastical institutes of his diocese. In discussing this question the Sacred Congregation lays down the general principle that, whenever the common law explicitly and undoubtedly permits anything, the bishop cannot forbid it unless the law clearly gives him that power.[142] Formerly the person who transferred Mass stipends to a priest was not freed from his obligation until he had been notified that the Masses were said. The Code simplifies matters by ending the obligation of the first party as soon as he receives notice that the other priest has received them and assumed the obligation of saying the Masses.

736. The sending of stipends to priests of the various Oriental Rites is regulated by special laws. The Code does not repeat these laws, but under the general rule of the Code (Canon 1) that the Code legislates for the Church of the Latin Rite and only incidentally speaks of matters pertaining to the Oriental Church, it is quite certain that the laws with reference to sending stipends to priests of the Oriental Rites in the Orient are still in force. The Decree of the Sacred Congregation of the Propaganda, July 15, 1908, briefly sums up the regulations in this matter. Mass stipends may not be forwarded to lay people in the Orient to distribute the stipends among the priests, nor may they be sent directly to priests of Oriental Rites, nor to the superiors of Oriental religious congregations, nor to Oriental prelates who are merely titular bishops or patriarchal vicars. However, Mass stipends may be sent directly to Oriental bishops in charge of dioceses to distribute among their own priests. Lest one bishop get too many stipends and the Masses be unduly delayed, the Oriental bishops shall inform the Apostolic Delegate of their respective district of the number of Mass stipends received. One may also send the stipends to the Sacred Congregation of the Propaganda or to the Apostolic Delegates in the Orient, indicating to what priests one wants the Masses to be given.[143]

737. A person who transmits manual stipends to others is bound to send the entire stipends received, and cannot retain part of them (even of the excess) unless the giver explicitly permits the retention of a part of the stipends, or unless it is certain that

---

[142] Cfr. App. III, 3, d.
[143] *Acta S. Sedis,* XLI, 640.

the excess above the ordinary stipend as fixed by the law of the diocese was given as a personal gift (*intuitu personæ*).[144]

In Mass stipends *ad instar manualium,* unless the will of the founder rules otherwise, the excess over the ordinary stipend may legitimately be retained, and it suffices to give merely the ordinary stipend of the diocese where the Masses are to be said, if the larger stipend takes the place of a partial endowment of the benefice or charitable foundation (**Canon 840**).

If a priest does not himself say the Masses for the stipends he has accepted, he cannot make any profit from the stipends— for instance, by having the Masses said in places where the stipend is smaller and sending only the usual stipend of that place and retaining the rest. It is also forbidden to make any profit from the stipends by taking advantage of the difference of the exchange between the currency one receives and the currency of the country to which one sends the Masses.[144a] The expenses incurred in forwarding the Mass stipends need not be borne by the sender, but may be deducted from the stipends.[145]

738. Stipends *ad instar manualium* are, according to Canon 826, stipends of foundation Masses established in some church or ecclesiastical institute. If these Masses cannot be said in the place where they are founded and have, therefore, to be transferred to other priests, the full foundation stipend (which is, as a rule, larger than the usual stipend) need not be given to the priest to whom the Masses are transferred, but only the ordinary stipend of the diocese where the Masses are transferred to, provided the larger stipend of the foundation Masses forms a part of the endowment of a benefice or of a charitable foundation (*causa pia*). In Europe there are many churches in which the salary of the priests is partly made up of the income from a sum of money bequeathed or donated for foundation Masses. In such cases the income of the foundation goes to the holder of the benefice as part of his salary with the obligation of saying a certain number of Masses for the founder. If the holder of the benefice cannot say the Masses, he is not to be deprived of his salary, and he is obliged only to give the ordinary stipend to the priest to whom the

[144] Concerning transfer of entire stipend, cfr. App. III, 35, d.
[144a] Sacred Congregation of the Council, November 21, 1898; *Acta S. Sedis,* XXXI, 623.
[145] Sacred Congregation of the Council, Febr. 25, 1905; *Acta S. Sedis,* XXXVIII, 15.

Masses are transferred. Canon 2324 demands that the Ordinary punish with ecclesiastical penalties all persons who violate the law of Canon 840.

Mass Stipends Not to be Held Over One Year

739. Each and every administrator of charitable foundations (*causæ piæ*), and all other persons (whether clerics or laymen) who are under any obligation to have Masses said for stipends, must at the end of a year transmit to their respective Ordinaries —and according to the manner which these may specify—those Mass stipends which have not yet been satisfied. This time is to be understood in such a way that the obligation of forwarding stipends *ad instar manualium* (from foundation Masses) to the Ordinary begins with the end of the year during which they should have been said; for manual stipends, one year from the day on which they were received, unless the givers of the stipends allowed a longer period for the saying of the Masses (**Canon 841**).

Canon 834 rules that, when the giver of the stipend explicitly leaves the time of saying the Masses to the convenience of the priest, he is not bound by the rule which requires the saying of Masses within a short time, but he is bound by the law of Canon 835 which forbids a priest to accept so many Masses to be said by himself that he cannot say them within a year. Unless the giver of a large number of stipends allows the priest to keep them over a year (*salva diversa offerentium voluntate*), the priest must transmit them to his Ordinary after a year from the reception of the stipends has elapsed. Likewise, laymen who perhaps as heirs, or for any other reason, have the obligation to have a certain number of Masses said each year, must at the end of the year during which the Masses were to be said give the stipends to the local Ordinary, if they have not yet attended to the obligation of having the Masses said.

740. The right and duty to see that the obligation of the Mass stipends is satisfied in secular churches pertain to the local Ordinary; in churches of the religious, to their superiors (**Canon 842**). Whenever the Code uses the term "Ordinary," the major superiors of exempt religious organizations are included in that term. The term "local Ordinary" excludes the religious superiors. In the matter of Mass stipends the non-

exempt religious communities were in the former Canon Law subject to the supervision of the bishop of the diocese just like the secular clergy. In Canon 842, the Code gives the superiors of non-exempt religious organizations control over the manual stipends of Masses to be said in their own churches. As to the exempt religious organizations, the exclusive right of the major superiors over the Mass stipends had been upheld in a case decided May 11, 1904, by the Sacred Congregation of Bishops and Regulars.[146] Canons 1546 and 1550 declare who has the control of foundation Masses.

RECORD OF MASS STIPENDS

741. The rectors of churches and other pious places, both of seculars and religious, in which stipends for Masses are usually received, shall have a special book in which they shall accurately enter the number of Masses, the intention, the amount of the stipend and the celebration of the Masses for which they have received stipends. The Ordinaries are bound by obligation to inspect these books at least once a year, either in person or through others (**Canon 843**).

These rules apply to manual stipends, for Canons 1544–1551 have special rules about foundation Masses. The Ordinaries who are obliged to inspect the Mass intention book are the bishop of the diocese (for all secular churches and institutes and for the houses of non-exempt religious organizations) and the major superiors of exempt religious communities (for the churches and houses of their organization). Although Canon 842 states that, in churches of religious (meaning both exempt and non-exempt), the superiors have the duty to watch over the faithful fulfillment of the obligations arising from Mass stipends, in non-exempt religious organizations the bishop of the diocese has by Canon 843 the right and duty to inspect the Mass intention book. Under the term "Ordinarii" in Canon 843, Fanfani[147] seems to include the religious superiors of non-exempt organizations. However, Canon 198 defines the term "Ordinarii" as including the major superiors of exempt or-

---

[146] *Acta S. Sedis*, XXXVI, 718. Regular prelates come under the name of Ordinaries in the matter of Mass stipends; Sacred Congregation of the Council, Febr. 27, 1905; *Acta S. Sedis*, XXXVII, 526.
[147] *De Jure Religiosorum*, n. 259.

ganizations only. Augustine [148] agrees with Fanfani for the reason that otherwise Canon 842 would be meaningless. That reason does not hold against the explicit definition of the term "Ordinary" in the Code. Canons 842 and 843 do not contradict each other. Canon 842 gives all religious superiors the right and duty to watch over the obligations arising from Mass stipends, and Canon 843 gives the Ordinary the right to inspect the Mass intention book at least once a year. That additional safeguard for the fulfillment of the obligations in non-exempt religious organizations cannot be called a contradiction.

742. Local Ordinaries and religious superiors, who entrust Masses to their subjects or to others, shall also mark down in a book at once in the proper order the Masses they have accepted together with the offerings made, and shall do their utmost to have them said as soon as possible. Moreover, every priest, whether secular or religious, must make an accurate note of the Mass intentions which they have received and those which they have satisfied (**Canon 844**).

The necessity of keeping a record of the Mass stipends and intentions is evident when a person handles a large number of them. The Code goes further, and insists that every individual priest who receives stipends must keep a record of the same. This law is new in the Code. There is no doubt, however, that before the promulgation of the Code the bishop had a right to inquire whether his priests had complied with the obligations arising from the Mass stipends which they had received. This law of the Code, requiring each priest to keep a record of the Masses he has received and of the number which have been said and which remain unsaid, is important, for otherwise nobody would know how many Masses remain to be said if the priest dies suddenly. In religious communities the superior of the house keeps the record for all the priests of the house, and the individual priests have, of course, the duty to give the Mass stipends which they receive to the superior promptly so that they may be entered in the record.

[148] *Commentary*, IV, 211.

CHAPTER II

OF THE HOLY EUCHARIST AS A SACRAMENT

ARTICLE I.—OF THE MINISTER OF HOLY COMMUNION

743. The priest alone is the *ordinary* minister of Holy Communion. The deacon is the *extraordinary* minister, but he must have the permission of the local Ordinary or of the pastor, which may be given for a grave reason, and may be legitimately presumed in case of necessity (**Canon 845**).

The Council of Trent states: "As to the reception of the Sacrament [Holy Eucharist], it was always the custom in the Church of God that laymen should receive Communion from priests, but that priests when celebrating should communicate themselves; which custom, as derived from an Apostolic tradition, ought with justice and reason to be retained." [149] In the ordination rite of the Roman Pontifical the deacons are called "comministri et cooperatores Corporis et Sanguinis Domini." In ancient times, when the faithful received Holy Communion under both species, it was the office of the deacon to minister the chalice with the Precious Blood. After the Latin Church discontinued giving Holy Communion under both species, the deacon was allowed to administer Holy Communion in urgent cases and only with the permission of the priest. The Code modifies the former law in this matter to the extent that it does not demand a necessity, but rather a grave reason. However, if one consults the commentators of the former Canon Law, it appears that in practice they interpreted this necessity in the sense of a grave reason. They thus held that, if the priest were very much occupied on some feast day and there was a deacon at hand, the pastor could allow him to distribute Holy Communion.[150]

744. Every priest may distribute Holy Communion during his Mass, and, if he celebrates privately, also immediately before or after Mass, subject to the precept of Canon 869. Outside Holy Mass any priest may also administer Holy Communion, and, if he is not a priest stationed at that church but an outsider, he enjoys this faculty on the basis of the at least presumed permission of the rector of the church (**Canon 846**).

---

[149] Sessio XIII, *De SS. Euch.*, cap. 8.
[150] Gasparri, "De SS. Euch.," II, n. 1079.

The Code states that the priest may distribute Holy Communion not only during Mass, after he himself has received the Sacred Host and the Precious Blood, but also immediately before or after the Mass, if this be private (Low). Holy Communion may not be given immediately before or after a Solemn High, a High, or a Conventual Mass, as was declared by the Sacred Congregation of Rites, January 19, 1906.[151] Canon 869 rules that Holy Communion may be distributed in every place where the celebration of Holy Mass is allowed—even in a private oratory, unless the local Ordinary has for just reasons forbidden it in particular cases. In private oratories the former law forbade the administration of Holy Communion, but the Code allows it. A strange priest naturally should not enter a church and give Holy Communion to people without at least the presumed permission of the priest in charge of the church. If a priest is admitted to say Holy Mass in a church, he has the implied permission to give Holy Communion.

745. Holy Communion should be brought to the sick publicly, unless good reasons make the private ministration advisable (**Canon 847**).[151a] The right and duty to carry Holy Communion publicly to the sick within a parish, even to non-parishioners, is vested in the pastor. Other priests may do so only in a case of necessity, or with at least the presumed permission of the pastor of the parish or of the Ordinary (**Canon 848**). Any priest may bring Holy Communion privately to the sick with at least the presumed permission of the priest to whom the custody of the Blessed Sacrament is entrusted. When Holy Communion is administered privately to the sick, the reverence and respect due to so great a Sacrament should be zealously safeguarded by observance of the regulations laid down by the Holy See (**Canon 849**).

These Canons have reference to the devotional Holy Communions of the sick. Canon 850 speaks of the Holy Viaticum. The Church desires that Holy Communion should be publicly taken to the sick in their homes, but the law does not absolutely insist on the public administration, allowing the private administration for just and reasonable cause. In countries like the United States where the Catholics are scattered among a non-Catholic population, the local Councils usually prescribe the

[151] *Decreta Auth. S. R. C.*, n. 4177.
[151a] Concerning private ministration to the sick, cfr. App. III, 36, e.

manner of private administration of Holy Communion to the sick.[152]   Only the public carrying of the Blessed Sacrament to the sick is reserved to the pastor within the limits of his parish. The priest carrying the Blessed Sacrament secretly should, if possible, be accompanied by at least one layman; he should wear the stole under his coat, and, in the room of the sick or in the prison cell, he should if possible put on cassock, surplice and stole.   The Sacred Congregation of Rites demands that cassock, surplice and stole be put on in the house or in the room of the sick, if there is no danger to the priest from enemies of the faith, and if danger of death is not imminent.[153]

746. In accordance with the law of Canon 848, the administration of the Holy Viaticum, whether public or private, is vested in the pastor within the limits of his parish, except in the cases stated in Canons 397, n. 3, and Canon 514 (**Canon 850**).

The pastor has the right to administer the Holy Viaticum within the limits of his parish to his parishioners and to strangers who are actually staying in his parish.   He has no right to give the Viaticum to one of his parishioners who actually stays outside his parish—for instance, in some hospital, in the house of a friend, etc.   To do so, he needs the permission of the pastor of the place where his parishioner actually stays. The permission may be presumed if one has positive reasons to know that the pastor of the other parish does not object. Canon 397, n. 3, has reference to the last Sacraments received by the bishop of the diocese.   The dignitaries and Canons, in the order of precedence, have the right to give the last Sacraments to the bishop.   Canon 514 speaks of the administration of the last Sacraments to the religious (cfr. above, n. 391).

HOLY COMMUNION MUST BE GIVEN ACCORDING TO THE RITE OF THE MINISTERING PRIEST

747. The priest shall give Holy Communion either in unleavened or leavened bread, according to the rules of his rite. In case of urgent necessity, when there is no priest of another

---

[152] *Conc. Balt. Plen.* II, n. 264.

[153] *Decreta Auth. S. R. C.*, Febr. 4, 1871, n. 3234.   The bishop may permit private administration of Holy Communion to the sick if there are many sick persons in the parish, or if one wishes to receive frequently (Sacred Congregation of the Sacraments, Dec. 23, 1912; *Acta Ap. Sedis*, IV, 725).

rite at hand, a priest of an Oriental Rite, who uses leavened bread, may give Holy Communion in unleavened form, and a Latin or an Oriental priest who uses unleavened bread may give Holy Communion in leavened bread. Each one, however, shall observe the ceremonies of his own rite in the manner of giving Holy Communion (**Canon 851**).

The Code does not settle the question whether a priest of the Latin Rite, who cannot get any altar bread as prescribed by his rite, could say Holy Mass with the leavened bread for the purpose of giving the Holy Viaticum to a dying person, if otherwise the latter would probably die before Holy Communion could be given to him. Canon 851 does not touch on this question, as it speaks only of administering Holy Communion. As the precept to receive the Holy Viaticum is a divine law, and the regulation regarding the altar-bread is an ecclesiastical law, it seems that in such a case a Latin or an Oriental priest can say Holy Mass with any kind of valid altar-bread. This reason, however, is not altogether conclusive, since one might argue that, while the person is obliged by the divine law to receive the Holy Viaticum in danger of death, this obligation ceases when the ordinary manner of complying with it is not possible.

748. It is not easy to define what is meant by the phrase ''in case of urgent necessity'' (*ubi vero necessitas urgeat*) in Canon 851. How grave must the necessity be to entitle a Latin priest to take the Blessed Sacrament in the form of leavened bread—and a Greek priest to take the Blessed Sacrament from a church of the Latin Rite—to give Holy Communion? The question is not answered by Canon 866, which gives all Catholics the right to receive Holy Communion in any Catholic Rite at any time except as the Holy Viaticum, which must if possible be received in one's own rite. Nor is any solution offered by the Constitution of Pope Pius X, September 14, 1912,[154] which granted permission to all Catholics, both of the Latin and the Oriental Rites, to receive Holy Communion according to any rite. Some commentators—e.g., Blat,[155] Vermeersch,[156] and Augustine [157]—seem to confuse the privilege of the people to

---

[154] *Acta Ap. Sedis*, IV, 609.
[155] *Commentarium*, lib. III, Pars I, p. 179.
[156] *Theol. Moral.*, III, n. 422.
[157] *Commentary*, IV, 222.

receive Holy Communion in any rite with the question of the circumstances under which a priest may give the Blessed Sacrament consecrated in a rite differing from his own in the use of fermented or unfermented bread. The mere fact that a person would otherwise have to miss an ordinary devotional Communion, is certainly not sufficient to entitle the priest to administer the Blessed Sacrament consecrated according to another rite. That much is certain from Canon 851. On the other hand, the "necessity" of receiving Holy Communion need not be so extreme as the danger of death, but the circumstances must be such that it is very important for the person to receive that day—e.g., if he would not again have an opportunity to receive for a long time, or if he was about to start on a dangerous journey, or other such extraordinary circumstances.

749. Holy Communion is to be given only under the species of bread (**Canon 852**). This is the rule for priests of the Latin Rite, and it does not apply to priests of the Oriental Rites, for the Code itself states (Canon 1) that its laws are for the Church of the Latin Rite, not for the Oriental Rites. For many centuries the Church of the Latin Rite, as well as the Oriental Rites, gave Holy Communion under both species. As late as the time of St. Thomas Aquinas, Holy Communion under one species had not yet become the general practice, for he explains and defends the custom of *some churches* of not offering the people the Precious Blood, but only the Host.[158] The Council of Trent passed the general law mentioned here in the Code.

ARTICLE II.—OF THE RECIPIENT OF HOLY COMMUNION

750. Every baptized person, who is not barred by law, may and must be admitted to Holy Communion (**Canon 853**). Catholics may be barred from receiving Holy Communion either by the divine or the ecclesiastical law. Non-Catholics are not considered in this Canon, for, in the very first Canon on the Sacraments, the Code has laid down the rule that it is forbidden to administer the Sacraments of the Church to heretics or schismatics, though they err in good faith, unless they have first rejected their errors and been reconciled to the Church (cfr. Canon 731). It seems that the divine law requires

---

158 *Summa Theol.*, p. III, qu. 80, art. 12, *Utrum liceat sumere Corpus Christi sine Sanguine.*

nothing further for the reception of Holy Communion than a valid baptism and the state of grace, and in persons who have (or have had) the use of reason, the intention to receive the Sacrament. The ecclesiastical law has added prohibitions not contained in the divine law, because the Church has the obligation to see that due reverence and respect are paid to our Lord in the Blessed Sacrament, and may therefore pass regulations which in her judgment are conducive to that end. The following Canons contain such regulations.

COMMUNION OF CHILDREN

751. Children who by reason of their age have not yet a knowledge of and desire for this Sacrament, should not be given Holy Communion. In case of danger of death Holy Communion may and must be given to children, if they are able to distinguish the Holy Eucharist from ordinary bread and reverently adore it. Except in case of danger of death, a fuller knowledge of Christian doctrine and a more careful preparation are justly demanded: the children must, in so far as their capacity allows, be acquainted with at least the mysteries of faith which are necessary as absolute means of salvation, and they must approach Holy Communion with such devotion as can be expected from young children (**Canon 854,** §§ 1–3).[159]

The decision as to the sufficient disposition of children for first Holy Communion shall rest with the confessor of the children and their parents, or those who take the place of the parents. It is the duty of the pastor to see that the children do not approach Holy Communion before they have come to the use of reason or without sufficient disposition: wherefore, he has the right to examine the children, if he thinks it proper. It is the further duty of the pastor to see that children who have attained the years of discretion and are sufficiently disposed shall be as soon as possible strengthened by the Divine Food (**Canon 854,** §§ 4–5).

The Council of Trent [159a] has authoritatively defined that, before they attain the use of reason, children are under no necessity of receiving Holy Communion. At the same time, the Council declares that it does not condemn the custom which

---

[159] Concerning use of reason, cfr. App. III, 36, a.
[159a] Sessio XXI, can. IV, cap. 4, *Doctrina de Communione sub Utraque Specie et Parvulorum.*

existed in ancient times of giving Holy Communion to infants.
In the Latin Rite that custom had died out long before the
Council of Trent, but in the Oriental Church it still exists in
some places. When the Holy Office was requested to suppress
the custom practised by the Copts in Egypt of giving the Holy
Eucharist to infants after Baptism under the species of wine,
the Sacred Congregation, on June 16, 1761, answered that nothing was to be changed.[160] According to the Code (Canon 88),
children are assumed to attain the use of reason on the completion of their seventh year, but this is merely a presumption
of law, which does not hold if facts show that a child has attained discretion before that age. The reverse is likewise true,
when facts show that a child of seven years of age has not
yet come to the use of reason.

752. Though the First Communion of children is not a function reserved to the pastor, he ordinarily takes charge of this
matter. If the confessor and the parents claim that the child
has sufficient knowledge to be admitted to first Holy Communion,
the pastor has the right to test this claim. Besides, the Code
obliges the pastor to instruct children who have come to the
use of reason so that their first Holy Communion may not be
unduly delayed. Most of the points of Canon 854 are taken
from the Decree of the Sacred Congregation of the Sacraments
on the First Communion of children.[161]

UNWORTHY PERSONS NOT TO BE ADMITTED TO HOLY COMMUNION

753. Catholics who are publicly known to be unworthy (for
example, those who have been excommunicated or interdicted,
or who are manifestly of ill repute) must be refused Holy
Communion until their repentance and amendment has been
established, and satisfaction has been made for the public scandal
which they have given. Occult sinners, who secretly ask for
Holy Communion, shall be refused by the minister if he knows
that they have not amended; if, however, they seek Communion
publicly and the priest cannot pass them by without scandal,
he shall not refuse them (**Canon 855**).[161a]

These rules are a restatement of the former law. It may

---

[160] Gasparri, ''De SS. Euch.,'' II, n. 1122.
[161] August 8, 1910; *Acta Ap. Sedis*, II, 577.
[161a] Concerning public sinners, cfr. App. III, 36, c.

be difficult in some cases to judge when a person is to be regarded as a public sinner. No general rule covering all cases can be given for distinguishing a public sinner from an occult one, and the circumstances of every individual case must be considered. The case of an occult sinner asking for Holy Communion publicly or secretly, is fully discussed by the moralists.

754. Nobody who is conscious of having a mortal sin on his soul shall go to Holy Communion before making a sacramental confession, no matter how contrite he may believe himself to be. If necessity urges the reception of Holy Communion, and there is no opportunity to go to confession, an act of perfect contrition shall be made before receiving Communion (**Canon 856**).

This law is taken from the Council of Trent.[162] The Council states that the words of St. Paul to the Corinthians, "Let a man prove himself," [163] are by ecclesiastical usage understood to refer to the confession of mortal sins before receiving Holy Communion (cfr. n. 707).

Holy Communion to be Received Only Once Daily and Only by Persons Fasting from Midnight

755. None may receive Holy Communion a second time on the same day, except in the contingencies mentioned in Canon 858, § 1 (**Canon 857**). Those who have not kept the natural fast from midnight are not allowed to receive Communion, except in danger of death or unless it should become necessary to consume the Blessed Sacrament to safeguard it against irreverence (**Canon 858, § 1**). The sick who have been confined to bed for a month without certain hope of speedy recovery, may, with the advice of the confessor, receive Holy Communion once or twice a week though they have taken medicine or liquid food (**Canon 858, § 2**).

It was formerly a disputed question among theologians whether a person, who had received Holy Communion in the ordinary way and later in the same day was in danger of death, was permitted to receive again.[164] The Code states that

162 Sessio XIII, cap. VII, *De SS. Euchar.*
163 I Cor., xi, 28.
164 Gasparri, "De SS. Euch.," II, n. 1152.

he may receive again, and, while it does not affirm there is any obligation, it again touches on this question in Canon 864, and says explicitly that Holy Communion in such a case is highly advisable.

756. The law of the natural fast before Holy Communion was introduced by a very ancient custom of the Church (cfr. n. 709). Dispensation from the Eucharistic fast is reserved to the Holy See. The Sacred Congregation of the Sacraments is entrusted with the general authority to grant dispensations to receive Holy Communion without fasting: the Sacred Congregation of the Religious has authority to grant this dispensation to religious, both men and women.[165] For the celebration of Holy Mass without fasting the Sacred Congregation of the Holy Office has exclusive power of dispensation (cfr. Canon 247).

757. To persons who have been sick in bed for a month without certainty that they will shortly (that is, within a few days) be able to keep the Eucharistic fast, the Code grants permission to receive Holy Communion, though they are forced to take medicine or some liquid food before they can receive. This they may do with the advice of the confessor once or twice a week. The first general concession of this kind was issued by Pius X through the Sacred Congregation of the Council, December 7, 1906.[166] It allowed Holy Communion only once or twice a month, if the sick were in their own private houses; once or twice a week, if they were laid up in a religious house, hospital, or other place where the Blessed Sacrament is habitually kept. A Declaration of the Sacred Congregation of the Council, March 25, 1907, ruled that the term ''decumbunt'' of the original Decree meant not only people whom sickness confined to bed, but also other persons afflicted by a serious illness who cannot stay in bed, or who can get out of bed for several hours a day, provided the physician judges that they cannot keep the fast.[167] There is hardly any doubt that this Declaration was an extension of the original Decree, for the term ''decumbunt'' undoubtedly means being confined to bed. That the Sacred Congregation had doubts whether it was giving a mere declaration of the former Decree or an extension is indi-

[165] Committee for Auth. Interp. of the Code, Dec. 7, 1922; *Acta Ap. Sedis*, XV, 39.
[166] *Acta S. Sedis*, XXXIX, 603; also in *Acta Ap. Sedis*, II, 898.
[167] *Acta S. Sedis*, XL, 344.

cated by the phrase of the Decree: "facto verbo cum Sanctissimo ad cautelam."

The question arises whether this Declaration of March 25, 1907, applies also to the Code, for the Code uses the same term as the Decree of December 7, 1906: "Infirmi qui jam a mense decumbunt." The former Decree and its Declaration have been superseded by the Code and are not law any longer, nor does the Code repeat the former decree in its entirety, but makes several important changes. Very many authors maintain that the former concession still holds good, but it seems that the extension of the term "decumbunt" cannot be applied to the Code. If a dispensation from the Eucharistic fast is necessary for persons who are sick and not confined to bed, and their sickness is according to the judgment of the physician such that they cannot without danger keep the fast, application for a dispensation may be made to the Apostolic Delegate, who has the faculty to dispense.[168]

758. The Code does not specify that it must be impossible or very difficult for the sick person to keep the Eucharistic fast. From this some commentators [169] conclude that the sick persons who have been laid up for a month, have the privilege of receiving Holy Communion without keeping the fast, even though they can keep it without danger to their health. Such an interpretation of the dispensation given by the law of Canon 858 does not seem to be reasonable. In Canon 84, the Code rules that a dispensation from an ecclesiastical law shall not be granted without just and reasonable cause proportioned to the gravity of the law which is dispensed with. It is not probable that the legislator himself intends to violate this general rule.

PRECEPT OF THE EASTER COMMUNION

759. From the time that he attains the use of reason, each and every Catholic is bound to receive Holy Communion at least once a year at Easter, unless for some reasonable cause his pastor or confessor has advised him to abstain for some time. The Easter Communion is to be received between Palm Sunday and

[168] "Faculties of Nuntios, Internuntios and Apostolic Delegates," chap. IV, n. 42; see copy of faculties in Vermeersch-Creusen, "Epitome," I, 359, n. 715.

[169] Cappello, "De Sacramentis," I, 374; Vermeersch-Creusen, "Epitome," II, 71, n. 124.

Low Sunday. The local Ordinaries, however, have the right to extend this period for all their subjects—if they think it necessary on account of the conditions of the places and people—from the fourth Sunday in Lent to Trinity Sunday, but no further. The faithful are to be urged to satisfy their Easter duty in their own parish church, and those who receive in another church shall take care to inform their own pastor of the fulfillment of their duty. If for any reason one has not made his Easter duty within the prescribed time, he is still bound by this precept (**Canon 859**).

The obligation of the Easter duty for children below the age of puberty rests principally on those who are responsible for the children, namely, their parents, guardians, confessor, teachers and pastor (**Canon 860**).

The precept of receiving Holy Communion is not satisfied by a sacrilegious Communion (**Canon 861**).

760. It is generally admitted that the faithful are obliged by the commandment of Christ to receive Holy Communion during their life. "Except you eat the Flesh of the Son of man and drink His Blood, you shall not have life in you" (John, vi. 54). In the first centuries of the Church it was the common practice for all the faithful who assisted at Mass to receive Holy Communion. Later we find laws to the effect that the faithful must receive at least at Easter, Christmas and Pentecost—e.g., in the Councils of Agatha (506) and Tours (813).[170] The law of the Easter Communion was passed in the Fourth Lateran Council,[171] and was confirmed by the Council of Trent.[172]

The obligation of the Easter Communion binds all Catholics who have come to the years of discretion, and Canon Law presumes discretion at the age of seven years. If a child's mind is sufficiently developed earlier to acquire sufficient knowledge of the Blessed Sacrament, the obligation begins immediately.[173] The question has been raised whether the use of reason demanded in the law must be such that a child is capable of committing a mortal sin. That question was pro-

---

[170] *Decretum Gratiani*, Can. 19, D. 2, *De consecr.; Can. 13, D. 2, consecr.*
[171] *Decret. Greg.* IX, c. 12, *De pœnit. et remission.*, lib. V, tit. 38.
[172] Sessio XIII, can. IX, *De Eucharistia.*
[173] Committee for Auth. Interp. of the Code, Jan. 3, 1918; cfr. App. III, 36, b.

posed to the Holy See by the Bishop of Norcia, but the Committee for the Authentic Interpretation of the Code gave an answer which evaded the issue, and simply said that the use of reason required for receiving Holy Communion is sufficiently specified in Canon 854, §§ 2–3, and for Confession in Canon 906.[174] The Code wants children to be instructed as soon as possible in the fundamental principles of the faith, in the knowledge of Christ's teaching on the Blessed Sacrament, and in reverence and devotion to His sacramental presence. The question whether they can commit mortal sin, has nothing to do with a sufficient knowledge of the Blessed Sacrament. That is very likely the reason why the Committee simply referred to the respective Canons on Holy Communion and Confession. The obligation of children under the age of puberty rests mainly on those who have them in their charge.

761. According to the former Canon Law, the time for fulfilling the Easter duty ran from Palm Sunday to Low Sunday, but the Code adds the faculty of the bishops to extend the time from the Fourth Sunday in Lent to Trinity Sunday. In the United States the Easter season has by special concession been prolonged from the First Sunday in Lent to Trinity Sunday, as the Second Council of Baltimore states. This indult remains after the promulgation of the Code under the general principle of Canon 4.[175]

The Code states that the "proprius sacerdos" may in a particular case allow a person to make his Easter duty outside the Easter season. According to the Decree of the Fourth Lateran Council, this "proper priest" is the pastor; later on, the confessor was also understood to be included under the term of "proper priest" in the law on the Easter Communion.[176] In the former Canon Law the Easter Communion had to be made in one's own parish church. The Code does not demand this but advises it, and, if one does not receive Holy Communion during the Easter season in his own parish, he should inform his own pastor that he has made his Easter duty.

The Code adds that one does not satisfy the precept of the Easter Communion by a sacrilegious Communion. There

174 Feb. 24, 1920; *Arch. für kath. Kirchr.*, CI, 68.
175 *Conc. Balt. II*, n. 257.
176 Gasparri, "De SS. Euch.," II, n. 1156.

seemed to be no need of such declaration, because it is repugnant to good sense that such a Communion should count for a fulfillment of the law. As, however, some theologians held that a sacrilegious Communion did satisfy the law of the Church, the Holy Office on March 2, 1679, condemned this opinion expressly.[177]

HOLY COMMUNION OF THE CLERGY ON HOLY THURSDAY

762. It is proper that on Holy Thursday all clerics, including priests who do not say Mass that day, shall receive the Body of Christ in the Solemn or Conventual Mass (**Canon 862**).

As the liturgical laws of the Church are not affected by the Code unless it explicitly corrects them (cfr. Canon 2), the clergy attached to cathedral churches are obliged by the law of the *Cæremoniale Episcoporum* to receive Holy Communion at the Solemn Mass on Holy Thursday. Various Decrees of the Sacred Congregation of Rites urge the law of the *Cæremoniale Episcoporum*.[178] At other churches no strict obligation is imposed on the clergy to receive Holy Communion by the laws of the liturgy, or by the Code.

FREQUENT AND DAILY COMMUNION

763. The faithful shall be encouraged to receive Holy Communion frequently, and even daily, according to the regulations given in the Decrees of the Apostolic See, and those who assist at Mass should be urged to receive not only spiritually but sacramentally our Lord in the Blessed Eucharist with the proper dispositions (**Canon 863**).

This Canon of the Code on frequent and daily Holy Communion refers to the former Decrees of the Holy See on the subject. Foremost among these is the Decree of the Sacred Congregation of the Council, December 20, 1905.[179] That Decree speaks at length on frequent and daily Communion, and quotes other Decrees of the Holy See in which the Supreme Authority of the Church condemns the erroneous opinions of theologians, who either held that daily Communion was necessary by divine

---

[177] Denziger, ''Enchiridion,'' 354, n. 1205.
[178] Sept. 27, 1716, Sept. 19, 1654; *Decr. Auth. S. R. C.*, nn. 2240 and 970.
[179] *Acta S. Sedis*, XXXVIII, 400–406.

law, or demanded an almost superhuman sanctity before they would allow a person to receive frequently or daily. Finally, the Decree gives very definite rules to the confessor, saying that nobody is to be forbidden to receive daily who comes in the state of grace and with the proper intention of getting help and grace from our Lord to lead a Christian life and to combat successfully his sins and faults.

Holy Communion in Danger of Death

764. In danger of death, from whatever cause it may proceed, the faithful are bound by precept to receive Holy Communion. Though they may have received Holy Communion the same day, they should be strongly advised to receive again if in the course of the day they are in danger of death. While the danger of death lasts, they may, according to the prudent judgment of the confessor, receive the Holy Viaticum repeatedly on different days (**Canon 864**).

The Code does not state whether that precept is of ecclesiastical or of divine law. Theologians commonly teach that it is of divine law. Gasparri [180] reconciles the prohibitions of some of the early Councils to administer Holy Communion even on the death bed to certain sinners with the general teaching of theologians that there is a divine precept to receive Holy Communion in danger of death, by saying that these were not general Councils of the Church, and that the commandment of Christ is conditional, namely, that one is to receive provided the Church allows him to receive.

Canon 858 stated that the Eucharistic fast does not oblige those who receive in danger of death. Some moralists have distinguished between those persons who incur danger of death from internal causes, and those incurring danger of death from other causes (e.g., battle, a dangerous operation, capital punishment). The law draws no distinctions, wherefore no distinctions should be made. If one has received the Holy Viaticum and hangs between life and death for some days, one may and is advised by the Code to receive every day while the danger lasts. These Communions are given like the Viaticum, and there is no obligation to keep the fast.

[180] *De SS. Euch.*, II, n. 1149.

The administration of the Holy Viaticum to the sick should not be deferred too long, and those who have the care of souls shall diligently see that sick persons receive the Viaticum while fully conscious (**Canon 865**).   The right and duty to administer the Holy Viaticum is by law reserved to the pastors, and to those held equivalent to pastors in Canon Law.   The Code obliges all who have the care of souls to attend faithfully to the dying, because at that time they need the priest more than at any other time in life.   The assistant priests in parishes, who by order of the pastor attend to the sick, have the responsibility for the cases committed to them.

Holy Communion and the Various Rites

765. All the faithful of any Rite are given permission to receive for devotion's sake the Blessed Sacrament consecrated in any Rite.   All should be urged, however, to receive the Easter Communion in their own Rite.   The Holy Viaticum should be received in one's own Rite, but in case of necessity it is lawful to receive it in any Rite (**Canon 866**).

The first general concession to receive Holy Communion, outside the case of necessity, in another Rite was given by the Decree of the Sacred Congregation of the Propaganda on August 18, 1893, for places where there was no church or no priest of one's own Rite.   On Dec. 4, 1894, Pope Leo XIII extended this permission to cases where, on account of the great distance of their church, it was very inconvenient for the people to receive in their own Rite.   On September 14, 1912, Pope Pius X granted permission without any restriction except as to the Easter duty.   Canon 866 is taken from the Constitution of Pope Pius X with this difference that the Code allows the reception of the Easter Communion in another Rite, while the Constitution demanded that the Easter Communion be received in one's own Rite.[181]   The faithful are, therefore, at liberty to receive Holy Communion in any Rite—the Catholics of Oriental Rites in Latin churches and Latin Catholics in the churches of Oriental Rites.   The Viaticum alone is excepted from the general concession.   Canon 851 rules that, in the administration of Holy Communion by the priest,

---

[181] Sacred Congregation of the Prop. (*Acta S. Sedis*, XXVII, 441); Pope Leo XIII (*Acta S. Sedis*, XXVII, 257–264); Pope Pius X (*Acta Ap. Sedis*, IV, 609–617).

the priest must give Communion consecrated in his own Rite, except in case of necessity.

ARTICLE III.—OF THE TIME AND PLACE FOR THE DISTRIBUTION OF HOLY COMMUNION

766. Holy Communion may be distributed every day. On Good Friday, however, it may be given only in the form of the Holy Viaticum to the sick. On Holy Saturday Communion cannot be given to the people except in the Mass of the day, or immediately after Mass is finished.

Holy Communion is to be given only during those hours when the celebration of Mass is allowed, unless there is good reason to give it at other times. The Holy Viaticum, however, may be given any hour of the day or night (**Canon 867**).

The regulations about the last two days of Holy Week are taken from the liturgical laws, and the Code does not change them. The former regulation that in non-parochial churches, especially in the churches of regulars, Holy Communion was not to be distributed on Easter Sunday, has been revoked by the Decree of the Sacred Congregation of the Council, November 28, 1912.[182]

The ordinary and usual time for the distribution of Holy Communion are the hours when the celebration of Mass is permitted. From this rule of the Canon it seems to follow that, whenever Mass is said, Holy Communion may also be given, whether it be Christmas night or any other time when Holy Mass is legitimately celebrated. For the administration of Holy Communion outside of Mass and outside the hours of Mass, whether at night or in the afternoon, a reasonable cause suffices.

767. The celebrating priest is not allowed to give Holy Communion during the Mass to people who are so far away that he has to go out of sight of the altar (**Canon 868**). This rule of the Code recurs constantly in various Decrees of the Sacred Congregation of Rites. The question became practical in hospitals and other ecclesiastical institutes where some of the inmates of these places might be sick in rooms and wards near the chapel where Mass was said. As the continuity of the Mass must not be broken except in case of necessity, the Church does not want the celebrant to go out of sight of the altar. Ordi-

---

[182] *Acta Ap. Sedis*, IV, 726.

narily there is no reason for thus interrupting the ceremonies of the Mass, as Holy Communion may be given to the sick a few minutes later after the Mass.

768. Holy Communion may be given in any place where Mass is allowed to be said, even in a private oratory, unless the local Ordinary should for good reasons have forbidden it in particular cases (**Canon 869**).[183] The Church wants to encourage the reception of Holy Communion, for the Council of Trent said that it indeed desired that all who assist at Mass should also receive Holy Communion.[183a] In the former law it was not allowed to distribute Holy Communion in private oratories to all who were present at the Mass, but at most to the persons mentioned in the indult granting the private oratory, as was declared by the Sacred Congregation of Rites, Feb. 10, 1906,[184] but on May 8, 1907, Pope Pius X declared that thenceforth the indult of the private oratory included permission to give Holy Communion to all present at Mass.[185]

TITLE IV

OF PENANCE

769. In the Sacrament of Penance, by judicial absolution given by a legitimate minister, forgiveness of sins committed after Baptism is bestowed on the faithful who are properly disposed (**Canon 870**).

This is a restatement of the dogmatic teaching of the Church that the power exercised by the minister in the Sacrament of Penance is a judicial act. Christ first delegated the Apostles and their successors to exercise a power which no man could ever claim save by commission from God, and whosoever claims to have the power of forgiving sins must be able to show that he has been properly commissioned by the Church. The Council of Trent states: "If anyone asserts that the sacramental absolution of the priest is not a judicial act, but a mere ministry of pronouncing and declaring that the sins are forgiven to the penitent if only he believes that he is absolved, let him be

---

183 Concerning reception of Holy Communion outside the place of Mass, cfr. App. III, 36, d.

183a Sessio XXII, cap. 6, *De Sacrificio Missæ*.

184 *Acta S. Sedis*, XL, 173.

185 *Acta S. Sedis*, XL, 589.

anathema.'' [186] The Code says that the Sacrament of Penance deals with sins committed after Baptism, for it is evident that the sins committed before Baptism are forgiven in Baptism, and if they are not forgiven because a person did not receive Baptism worthily, such sins do not come under the jurisdiction of the Church because they were committed at a time when the person was not a subject of the Church. As to the legitimate minister, the following Canons deal with that subject explicitly.

CHAPTER I

OF THE MINISTER OF PENANCE

770. Priests alone are the ministers of this Sacrament (**Canon 871**). The Council of Trent has defined the teaching of the Church on the minister of the Sacrament of Penance in the following terms: ''If anyone says that the priests are not the only ministers of absolution, but that to each of the faithful it has been said, 'Whatsoever you shall bind on earth shall be bound also in heaven, and whatsoever you shall loose on earth shall be loosed also in heaven' (Matt., xviii. 18), and 'Whose sins you shall forgive, they are forgiven them, and whose sins you shall retain, they are retained' (John, xx. 23), let him be anathema.'' [187] Against those who interpreted the words of Christ, ''Receive ye the Holy Ghost, whose sins, etc.,'' in such a sense that only persons who have the Holy Ghost can forgive sins, the Council of Trent declared: ''If anyone says that the priests who are in mortal sin do not have the power of binding and loosing, let him be anathema.'' [188]

771. For the valid absolution of sins, the minister requires, besides the power of Orders, either ordinary or delegated power of jurisdiction over the penitent (**Canon 872**).

The term ''jurisdiction'' is used in a twofold sense in Canon Law, as the power of government and as judicial power. Derived from the Latin words, *jus* and *dicere*, the term means literally ''to give a decision as judge,'' or ''to act as a judge.'' In its wider sense, jurisdiction is used to denote the legislative, executive and judicial powers. Every independent organiza-

[186] Sessio XIV, can. 9, *De Sanctissimo Pœnitentiœ Sacramento.*
[187] Sessio XIV, can. 10, *De Sanctissimo Pœnitentiœ Sacramento.*
[188] *Ibid.*

tion or society of men inherently possesses this threefold power; if it lacks one or other of these powers, it is not truly independent of all other organizations of men. The organization which is called the Catholic Church is singular in its nature, since (unlike other societies, states, etc.) it owes its very existence, not to any development by men, but to the act of Christ exclusively. In fact, its very nature and purpose exclude all possibility of its being formed by the combined will and effort of men, for no man or combination of men has any right to claim power over the human soul: as this is God's exclusive province, He alone can commission that power to others.

The power of Orders (*potestas ordinis*) is essentially distinct from the power of jurisdiction. The power of Orders is conferred by the sacred rites of ordination; the power of jurisdiction by commission of the competent authority. The power of Orders once validly conferred by the ordination rites inheres permanently in the person consecrated to the sacred ministry; the power of jurisdiction commissioned today can be taken away tomorrow.

772. The Code speaks of a twofold power of jurisdiction, ordinary and delegated. Ordinary jurisdiction is that which is by law attached to an office, so that by the legitimate conferring of the office jurisdiction also is conferred; delegated power is that which is committed to a cleric by a superior who possesses ordinary jurisdiction, and who is not forbidden by law to delegate the powers of his office. In Canon 108, the Code states that the power of jurisdiction is by divine ordinance given to the Supreme Pontiff and the subordinate episcopate.

The granting of absolution from sins is, as we saw, an exercise of jurisdiction. The soul is called to trial, and, if found properly disposed to merit pardon, it receives forgiveness of the sins and crimes of which it was found guilty. The Code repeats the constant teaching of the Church that, for the administration of the Sacrament of Penance, jurisdiction alone is not sufficient, but that one must also have the sacerdotal Order. Neither one nor the other power alone is sufficient for a valid absolution.

PERSONS WHO POSSESS ORDINARY JURISDICTION

773. Besides the Roman Pontiff, the Cardinals of the Roman Church possess ordinary jurisdiction for the hearing of confessions for the whole Church. The local Ordinaries have ordinary jurisdiction in their respective territories, and pastors and other priests holding the place of pastors have ordinary jurisdiction in their respective domains. The canon penitentiary of cathedral and collegiate churches has ordinary jurisdiction for the hearing of confessions in the diocese, and has power to absolve also from the episcopal reserved sins and censures, as conceded by Canon 401. The superiors of exempt religious organizations have ordinary jurisdiction over their subjects, according to their respective Constitutions (**Canon 873,** §§ 1–2).

774. The ordinary jurisdiction for the administration of the Sacrament of Penance ceases with the loss of the office to which that jurisdiction is attached (cfr. Canon 183, on the loss of office), and after a declaratory or condemnatory sentence inflicting excommunication, suspension from office, or interdict has been passed by a competent ecclesiastical court (**Canon 873,** § 3).

775. This faculty of the Cardinals is enumerated among their privileges in Canon 239, § 1, n. 1, and n. 2 grants them the further faculty of choosing for themselves and the members of their household any priest as confessor, and, if that priest has no jurisdiction to hear confessions, he gets it automatically by the law. This faculty is considered a personal privilege, and cannot be delegated. Canon 349 grants to all bishops, residential and titular, the privilege of choosing for themselves and their household any priest as confessor, who, if he has not jurisdiction, gets it by law. Canon 401 states explicitly that the canon penitentiary in cathedral and collegiate churches cannot delegate other priests to hear confessions. As to the pastors, the question was submitted to the Holy See whether they could delegate other priests to hear confessions in their parishes. The Committee for the Authentic Interpretation of the Code answered that the pastors and others who are held equivalent to them in the Code, cannot delegate other priests for the hearing of confessions.[189] Local Ordinaries, and pastors or priests

---

[189] Cfr. App. III, 37, a.

held equivalent to pastors, can hear the confessions of their own subjects even outside their respective territory.[190]

DELEGATED JURISDICTION FOR THE HEARING OF CONFESSIONS

776. The Ordinary of the place where confessions are to be heard grants delegated jurisdiction to secular priests as well as to religious (even of an exempt organization) to hear the confessions of all seculars and religious. The religious priests, however, should not make use of the jurisdiction without at least the presumed permission of their superiors. If, however, they do hear the confessions of religious without the permission of their superior, and the religious come to confession for the peace of their conscience, the absolution is nevertheless valid, as stated in Canon 519 (**Canon 874, § 1**).

The local Ordinary shall not grant habitual faculties for the hearing of confessions to religious priests who have not been presented by their own superior. Moreover, the Ordinary should not without a grave reason refuse jurisdiction to those priests whom the religious superior presents, although he has the right, according to Canon 877, to test their fitness (**Canon 874, § 2**).

This Canon of the Code disregards the distinction of the former law between the approval and the jurisdiction in the matter of the delegation of priests for confessions. The question of approval as distinct from jurisdiction arose in the Council of Trent. Up to that time the superiors of exempt religious organizations had the right to give the faculties to hear confessions to priests of their Orders, and thereby gave them power to hear the confessions of seculars in any diocese. The Council of Trent wanted to limit that power of the regulars, and decreed [191] that all priests, including the regulars, needed the approval of the bishop of the diocese to hear the confessions of seculars. The Code goes one step further by stating that the local Ordinary grants delegated jurisdiction for the confessions not only of seculars and non-exempt religious but of all re-

---

[190] In virtue of his office the pastor has no general jurisdiction for the hearing of confessions in the diocese, but only in his parish. His own parishioners he can hear in any place. The former law was the same on this subject. Practically, priests who are made pastors have long before obtained general faculties for the hearing of confessions in the diocese.

[191] Sessio XXIII, cap. 15, *De Reform.*

ligious. That the jurisdiction delegated by the bishop should extend even to the confessions of exempt religious, had been decreed by the Holy See a few years before the promulgation of the Code. The contrary privileges of some religious organizations that their subjects could not be absolved except by a priest approved by the superior for the confessions of the religious, were revoked by that Decree.[192] The Code does not repeat the revocation of those privileges, but takes this revocation for granted when it states that the bishop gives jurisdiction for the hearing of confessions of all persons, secular and religious. Since the privileges were revoked in 1913, there was no need of mentioning them.

777. In exempt clerical organizations of religious the proper superior also (that is, besides the bishop) can give delegated jurisdiction to hear the confessions of the professed, the novices and those who board in the religious house, as specified in Canon 514. The Constitutions of the respective organization must determine who has the power to delegate. The same jurisdiction may be given by the superior also to secular priests and to priests of another religious organization. In laical exempt organizations the superior proposes the confessor, who, however, must obtain jurisdiction from the Ordinary of the diocese where the religious house is located (**Canon 875**).

The Code leaves to the exempt religious organizations, if they are clerical communities, the right which they had before the promulgation of the Code to give jurisdiction to their own priests and to any other priests to hear the confessions of the subjects of the organization. The exemption, however, does not extend so far that the subjects of the religious organization can be absolved only by the jurisdiction of the superiors of the exempt religious; the local Ordinary as well as the religious superiors can give jurisdiction to absolve the exempt religious.

JURISDICTION FOR CONFESSIONS OF RELIGIOUS WOMEN

778. Both secular and religious priests, of whatever rank or office, need special jurisdiction for the valid and licit hearing of the confessions of any religious women and their novices, and every contrary particular law or privilege is revoked. The only

[192] Sacred Congregation of Religious, Aug. 5, 1913; *Acta Ap. Sedis,* V, 431.

exceptions to this law are: (1) the faculties of all Cardinals to hear confessions of religious women in any diocese, as stated in Canon 239, § 1, n. 1; (2) the liberty granted to all religious women to confess to any approved confessor of the diocese in any church, or public or semi-public oratory, as stated in Canon 522; (3) the privilege of religious women when seriously ill, though not in danger of death, to call for any approved confessor of the diocese and to confess to him as often as they desire during the illness, as stated in Canon 523 (**Canon 876, § 1**). This special jurisdiction is, in accordance with Canon 525, conferred by the Ordinary of the diocese where the convent of the religious women is located (**Canon 876, § 2**).

Special approval is required for the ordinary, extraordinary, and special confessors of houses of religious women spoken of in Canon 521. The Sisters cannot call a priest to the convent to go to confession to him, nor can a priest go to a convent to hear confessions unless he has the special approval, except in case of serious illness. Otherwise, Canon 876 and Canon 521 would be superfluous. A doubtful case is that in which a priest who has the common faculties of the diocese visits a convent of Sisters, and one or more Sisters ask him to hear their confessions. It is very generally admitted by authors that Canon 522 includes also the chapel in the convent of the Sister who wants to take advantage of Canon 522. It thus seems to be a proper application of Canon 522, if a Sister avails herself of this occasion to go to confession. If a priest was asked to come to the convent, and then learns that he was called because a Sister wants to go to confession, it does not seem that he has faculty to hear the confession. On other points, cfr. commentary on Canon 522.[193]

EXAMINATION OF PRIESTS BEFORE APPROVAL AS CONFESSORS

779. The local Ordinary as well as the religious superiors shall grant jurisdiction or permission to hear confessions only to priests who have been found qualified by examination, unless the theological knowledge of the priest is well known from other sources.

If, after the concession of jurisdiction or permission to hear

---

[193] Cfr. *Linzer Quartalschrift,* LXXVI, 109; Creusen in *Nouvelle Revue Theologique* (1922), 381.

confessions, the bishop or the religious superior has a justified doubt as to whether a priest who has been approved by him is still qualified, he should oblige him to undergo a new examination concerning his knowledge, even though there he is a pastor or a canon penitentiary (**Canon 877**).

Under ordinary circumstances the Code demands that jurisdiction for the hearing of confessions be granted only after a satisfactory examination. Since the bishop is the only authority in the diocese who can grant jurisdiction for the hearing of confessions of seculars and non-exempt religious, he has the right and duty to subject all priests who ask for this jurisdiction to an examination. There is nothing in the Code which forbids the bishop to accept the testimony of the religious superior that the priests of the community presented for the faculties of the diocese have passed a satisfactory examination before the board of examiners of the religious organization. There is no necessity for a twofold examination for the same purpose. However, if the bishop deems it advisable to insist on his right to examine all priests who desire the faculties of the diocese, he may do so.

780. Canon 877 gives the bishop and the religious superior full authority to insist on a new examination of a priest approved for confession, if they have good reasons for doubting whether he has the necessary knowledge. The Canon gives power to the bishop to demand this examination even in the case of priests who have ordinary jurisdiction for confessions, such as the pastor and the canon penitentiary. This settles the controversy under the former Canon Law whether a bishop could recall for examination a priest of an exempt religious organization, who had been unconditionally approved after previous examination. Here only this one reason—want of knowledge—is spoken of. Canon 880 speaks of other reasons why the jurisdiction may be revoked.

LIMITATION OF DELEGATED JURISDICTION FOR CONFESSION

781. Delegated jurisdiction or permission to hear confessions may be conceded with certain defined limitations. The local Ordinary and the religious superior, however, must beware of limiting the jurisdiction or permission excessively without reasonable cause (**Canon 878**).

Inasmuch as the jurisdiction of the priest is a delegated power, the extent of the power he receives depends on the delegating authority. The Code warns against unreasonable restrictions, but it does not abrogate the power of the bishop or superior to make unreasonable restrictions, which bind the priest, nevertheless. Those powers which the Code gives to every confessor are the only powers which the bishop or the superior cannot restrict—for instance, the power given to pastors by Canon 900 (and to missionaries by Canon 899) to absolve from episcopal reserved cases under certain circumstances, and the faculty to absolve from Papal reserved cases under the circumstances mentioned in Canon 2254.

MANNER OF GRANTING DELEGATED JURISDICTION

782. For the valid hearing of confessions, it is necessary that jurisdiction shall have been explicitly granted either in writing or orally. For the granting of jurisdiction no charge or tax may be demanded (**Canon 879**).

Explicit conferring of jurisdiction in writing or by word of mouth is required for the validity of delegated jurisdiction for the hearing of confessions. Tacit, presumed, interpretative, or any other kind of delegation which cannot be called explicit, is not considered valid. The terms *tacit* and *implied* delegation must not be confused, for they are not synonymous as Fr. Augustine seems to think.[194] An implied delegation is one in which the jurisdiction for the hearing of confessions is granted by the explicit grant of another faculty or favor, which includes the faculty to hear confessions. Thus, if a pastor has received from his bishop the faculty to call priests to help him with his work or to call missionaries to give a mission, and to communicate to them the faculties of the diocese, it is reasonable to say that if he calls a priest and asks him to go to one of the mission chapels attached to his parish, or calls missionaries to give a mission, he grants thereby—without saying anything further about the faculty to hear confessions—the jurisdiction for the hearing of confessions as it is plainly implied in the commission he gives them.[195] In the tacit delegation there is no positive

194 *Commentary*, IV, 277.
195 Blat, "Commentarium," III, Pars I, 225.

act by which delegation is given, but only non-resistance to its assumption by another.

REVOCATION AND SUSPENSION OF JURISDICTION

783. The local Ordinary or the religious superior shall not recall or suspend the jurisdiction or permission for the hearing of confessions without a grave cause. The Ordinary may for grave reasons forbid even a pastor or a penitentiary the exercise of the office of confessor, but they have the right of recourse to the Apostolic See *in devolutivo* (*scil.*, in the meantime they are obliged to obey the injunction of the bishop). The bishop, however, is not allowed, without consulting the Holy See, to deprive all confessors of a religious house of jurisdiction simultaneously, if it is a *domus formata*—viz., one in which there are six or more professed members, of whom four at least must be priests (**Canon 880**).

What constitutes a grave reason is not defined by the Code, but is left to the judgment of the bishop and the religious superior. The Code does not restrict the right to recall or to forbid the exercise of jurisdiction to reasons connected with the hearing of confessions. Serious misconduct of the priest in any matter suffices to entitle the bishop or the superior to recall or suspend the jurisdiction. The authority who grants the delegated jurisdiction can recall it, and the revocation is valid, though illicit, if done without grave reason. The religious superior cannot recall the jurisdiction which his subject has received from the bishop, for he cannot take away what he has not given, but he can forbid the licit exercise of it. The jurisdiction to hear the confessions of the subjects of the religious superior of exempt communities comes from the superior, and that jurisdiction he can take away. If, however, the religious priest has received jurisdiction also from the bishop, and this jurisdiction according to Canon 874 extends over all seculars and religious making their confession in the territory of that bishop's diocese, the recall of the faculties given by the religious superior cannot invalidate the faculties given by the bishop, but only makes their use illicit.

The bishop has the right to forbid even pastors and penitentiaries who have ordinary jurisdiction the licit exercise of their jurisdiction, but, since they have jurisdiction for the hearing of confessions in virtue of the offices they hold, it follows that, in so far as validity is concerned, they retain their jurisdiction as long as they hold their offices.

784. The revocation of delegated jurisdiction leaves the priest without power to hear confessions validly. If the bishop suspends a priest from the hearing of confessions, it is a debated question whether such a suspension makes the exercise of that power null and void. Some commentators [196] argue from Canon 2284 that the mere suspension by a precept of the bishop makes the hearing of confessions illicit, but does not make it invalid. It seems, however, that Canon 2284 is not applicable to suspensions issued by the bishop in the form of an injunction or command to cease hearing confessions, for this Canon speaks of incurring a censure of suspension. Everything, therefore, depends on the wording of the prohibition as showing the intention of the bishop. If it is not clear from the wording of the prohibition whether the bishop intends to take away the faculties altogether for the time being, they remain but their exercise becomes illicit.

785. The last section of Canon 880 about taking away the faculties of all the confessors of religious houses specified in the Code is taken from the Constitution "Superna" of Pope Clement X, June 21, 1670, with this difference that the Constitution had reference to monasteries of exempt religious only, whereas the Code applies it to all clerical religious organizations.[197] The Code merely forbids the bishop to do so without consulting the Holy See; if he nevertheless takes away the faculties, his action is valid.

EXTENT OF JURISDICTION

786. All priests, seculars and religious, approved for the hearing of confessions in some place, whether vested with ordinary or delegated jurisdiction, can validly and licitly absolve also *vagi* and strangers coming from another diocese or parish, and furthermore all Catholics of any Oriental Rite. Priests with ordinary jurisdiction for confession can absolve their own subjects anywhere in the world (**Canon 881**).

[196] Blat, "Commentarium," III, Pars I, 227.
[197] Gasparri, "Fontes Cod. Jur. Can.," I, 472.

In the former Canon Law there was a good deal of controversy about the absolution of persons who went to confession outside their own diocese and of persons who have no proper diocese (called *vagi* in law). The former law did not clearly express how jurisdiction over them could be exercised. The Code removes all uncertainty in this matter. The concession of jurisdiction over Catholics of Oriental Rites is not new. There are several Decrees of the Sacred Congregation of the Propaganda [198] forbidding the bishops of Oriental Rites to prevent their subjects from going to confession to priests of the Latin Rite. Canon 905 states as a general principle that any member of the faithful may make his confession to a lawfully approved confessor of a Rite other than his own. That applies to Catholics of the Latin Rite as well as to Catholics of the various Oriental Rites. The principle repeated by the Code that one who has ordinary jurisdiction for confession may absolve his subjects anywhere in the world has long been recognized in Canon Law. Canon 873 enumerated the persons who have ordinary jurisdiction.

Power to Absolve Persons in Danger of Death

787. In danger of death all priests, though not approved for confessions, can validly and licitly absolve any penitent from any sins and censures, although reserved and notorious, even if an approved priest is present. Canons 884 and 2252, however, remain unimpaired (**Canon 882**).

The rule of the Code here stated is the same as in the former law. St. Thomas Aquinas discusses this question, and comes to the same conclusion as is given in this Canon of the Code.[199] The Council of Trent [200] says, "Lest any may perish on this account [lack of jurisdiction of the priest over reserved cases], it has always been very piously observed in the said Church of God that there be no reservation at the point of death, and that therefore all priests may absolve all penitents whatsoever from every kind of sins and censures whatever." The Code does not specify imminent death, but merely danger of death. It does

---

[198] June 2, 1835; Dec. 11, 1838; April, 30, 1862; *Collectanea de Prop. Fide*, I, nn. 839, 879, 1228.

[199] *Suppl.*, q. VIII, art. 6.

[200] Sessio XIV, cap. 7, *De Sanctissimo Pœnitentiæ Sacramento.*

not matter from what source the danger of death arises—sickness, wounds, impending serious operation, call of a soldier to war, etc.[201]

Canon 884 refers to the absolution of one's accomplice in a sin of impurity: if the priest hears the confession of his accomplice and absolves him or her from that sin without necessity, the absolution given in danger of death is valid but illicit. Canon 2252 refers to absolution in danger of death from censures inflicted *ab homine* (that is, by precept of the superior or by sentence of an ecclesiastical court) and from censures reserved to the Holy See *specialissimo modo*: if the person recovers, recourse must be had to the authority who inflicted the censure *ab homine,* or to the Holy See or a person delegated by the Holy See when there is question of censures reserved *specialissimo modo.*[201a]

Hearing Confessions on the Ocean

788. On an ocean trip, all priests may hear confessions on the boat during the time of the voyage and absolve the faithful who travel with them (even though the boat may pass through districts subject to various Ordinaries or stop for a while in some port), provided they have been properly approved for confessions either by the bishop of their own diocese, or by the bishop of the port where they take the boat, or by the Ordinary of any of the ports at which the boat calls. Whenever the boat stops at a port during the voyage, such a priest may hear confessions and absolve not only the people who for any reason enter the boat, but also, if the priest goes ashore for a while, persons who request him to hear their confessions, and he may absolve them even from sins reserved to the local Ordinary (**Canon 883**).

A declaration of the Committee for the Authentic Interpretation of the Code has decided that, if the boat stops in some port and the priest goes ashore, he can hear confessions on land of all who want to confess to him, even though the boat stops for two or three full days. The priest may hear confessions for the same length of time, when he changes boats in some port and has to wait for the connecting boat. In both cases, he

[201] Sacred Penitentiary, May 29, 1915, about soldiers drafted during a war; *Acta Ap. Sedis,* VII, 282.

[201a] Absolution is limited to internal forum, cfr. App. III, 37, b.

cannot hear confessions beyond three days, if the local **Ordinary** can easily be reached.[202]

As the ocean beyond the three-mile limit does not constitute the territory of any particular country, it was impossible from general principles to determine what bishop had a right to give faculties to hear confessions on the ocean. It seems that the Holy See alone could grant that faculty. On March 17, 1869, the Holy Office ruled that the Ordinary of the place from which the boat started could give the faculty for confessions, which was to last until the boat reached a port subject to another Ordinary. By Decree of the same Congregation of April 9, 1900, the faculties of the Ordinary of the starting place were extended for the entire trip, even though the boat stopped for a while in places subject to other local Ordinaries. Finally, on August 23, 1905, the Holy Office ruled that the approval received from one's own proper local Ordinary, or from the Ordinary of the port from which the boat started, or from a local Ordinary of any intermediate port at which the boat called, was sufficient. This concession was further extended by Decree of the Holy Office of December 13, 1906, to the effect that the priest could hear confessions also on land in ports where the boat stopped a while, but that this permission was restricted to places where there was either no priest at all or one only, and where it was not easy to reach the local Ordinary to obtain faculties from him. The Code goes still further and drops the two restrictions of the Decree of December 13, 1906.

ABSOLUTION OF THE PRIEST'S ACCOMPLICE IN SINS OF IMPURITY

789. The absolution of the priest's accomplice in a sin of impurity is invalid except when that person is in danger of death. Even in danger of death, the priest absolves illicitly unless another priest cannot be had, or the calling of another priest under the circumstances would implicitly reveal the sin of the priest with the person now in danger of death, as is ruled by the Apostolic Constitutions, especially by that of Pope Benedict XIV, "Sacramentum Pœnitentiæ," June 1, 1741 (**Canon 884**).

The Church fears that a priest whose faith is weakening

[202] Cfr. App. III, 37, c. Religious Superiors cannot give faculties for confessions on ocean (App. III, 37, c, second paragraph).

and who no longer struggles with all his might against the common enemy of mankind, carnal lust, may abuse the priesthood which gives him influence over others, and, instead of helping a soul in its struggle against sin, drive it deeper into sin under the pretext that he can absolve the person who consents to sin with him. For this reason the Church has deprived the priest of all power over the sin of his accomplice in a sin of impurity with the exception of the extreme cases of danger of death under circumstances where either no other priest is at hand to absolve the dying person, or where another priest cannot be summoned without betraying the sin of the priest. It is understood here that there is question of a case in which the accomplice has not yet confessed that sin to and been absolved by another priest.

790. The priest who attempts to absolve his accomplice from a sin of impurity incurs excommunication reserved in a most special manner to the Holy See. He incurs this excommunication even when he absolves his accomplice in danger of death, if there was no necessity for his ministration, though the absolution given in danger of death is valid. There is no need of discussing this case at length since the law in this matter has not been changed by the Code, and all text-books of moral theology explain the law in reference to the forbidden absolution of an accomplice in sins of impurity (cfr. Canon 2367 and the Constitution of Pope Benedict XIV, "Sacramentum Poenitentiae," published in the appendix of the Code).[203]

Rules to Be Observed in Hearing Confessions

791. Though the prayers attached by the Church to the formula of absolution are not necessary for the validity of the absolution, nevertheless they should not be omitted except for a good reason (**Canon 885**). The Code does not state what words are absolutely necessary for the validity of the absolution. From the nature of the Sacrament it is evident that the words must indicate that the priest absolves the penitent from his sins. The words by which this is signified are not determined by Christ. The Church has prescribed the form: "**Ego** te absolvo a peccatis tuis, in nomine Patris, etc." Though

[203] De Smet, "De Absolutione Complicis et Sollicitatione" (2nd ed., 1921).

other words expressing the same idea suffice for validity, the priest is under grave obligation to use the form of words prescribed by the Church.

792. If the confessor has no reason to doubt the proper dispositions of the penitent who asks for absolution, he may neither deny nor defer absolution (**Canon 886**). Since the penitent has a right to receive the Sacrament when he is properly disposed, it follows that injustice is done him by the priest who refuses his request for absolution. Though the priest may think that a delay of absolution would be of greater benefit to the penitent, he may not for that reason delay absolution without the free consent of the penitent.

793. The confessor shall impose a salutary and proper penance in proportion to the number and gravity of the sins confessed and accommodated to the condition of the penitent, which penance the penitent must accept with a willing heart and perform personally (**Canon 887**). Prudence and discretion are necessary in imposing the penance. In many cases it is not possible to impose a penance in proportion to the number and gravity of the sins confessed on account of the condition of the penitent. Persons who are not accustomed to prolonged prayer may be easily discouraged by penances of long and frequent prayers. To preserve some proportion between the sins confessed and the penance imposed, it may be necessary to direct the penitent to offer his work and daily hardships to God for that intention and also his daily prayers and his Sunday Mass.

794. The priest must remember that in hearing confessions he acts the part of both judge and physician, and that he has been appointed by God a minister of both the divine justice and the divine mercy to safeguard the honor of God and promote the salvation of souls. The priest must absolutely guard against inquiring into the name of an accomplice in sins confessed, against detaining penitents with inquisitive and useless questions (especially concerning the sixth commandment), and especially against imprudently questioning young people about things of which they are ignorant (**Canon 888**).

These are important directions laid down by the authority of the Church for the guidance of the confessor. They are not new rules, for all authors of moral theology have explained the duties of the confessor in the same sense as this Canon does, but, by embodying these rules in her Code of Law, the Church removes all possible doubt as to whether the confessor is obliged to be guided by these principles.

THE SEAL OF CONFESSION

795. The sacramental seal is inviolable, and the confessor must therefore carefully beware of betraying a penitent by words or signs, or in any other way, for any reason whatsoever. The obligation of keeping the sacramental seal also binds the interpreter and all others to whom the knowledge of the confession has in any way come (**Canon 889**).

The confessor is absolutely forbidden to use the knowledge derived from confession to the disadvantage of the penitent, even when there is no danger of revelation. The actual superiors, as well as confessors who are afterwards made superiors, cannot make any use whatever of the knowledge of sins gained in the confessional for the purpose of the external government (**Canon 890**).

These are the ancient rules of the Church on the secrecy to which the priest is bound concerning the sins confessed to him in Sacramental Confession. In the case of all other secrets committed by one person to another, there may be reasons which excuse the revelation of what was entrusted to one's confidence. In the case of confession, however, the Church does not admit excuses of any kind, and binds the priest to secrecy, though it may entail the sacrifice of his life, his honor, or anything else that is most dear to him. Canon 2369 imposes the penalties for confessors who directly or indirectly violate the seal of confession.

796. A recent Instruction of the Holy Office to the local Ordinaries and religious superiors insists on the duty of the confessors to avoid all talk about what they have heard in Confession, whether it be in public sermons and instructions or in private conversation. There has been some discussion of the legal value of this Instruction of the Holy Office, since it was given before the Code, and has not been embodied in the Code or referred to by the Code. However, that Instruction certainly has all the force of law, because the Holy Office indicates that

it is not making a new law, but rather explaining the full import of the divine law, which binds the confessor to absolute secrecy as to what he has heard in Sacramental Confession. It is always offensive to Catholics to hear a priest say that someone told this or that in confession. When a missionary, a teacher of religion, or a professor of moral theology wishes to teach the proper confession of sins, it is unnecessary and highly improper to tell how somebody confessed a certain sin or crime, for that somebody may be present, and, if he is not there, others will fear lest this missionary, teacher, or professor may one day speak similarly of their confessions. To make a jest of the confession of some sin or ugly story heard in confession, does not speak well for the faith and reverence of the priest for the Sacrament of Divine Mercy. *Sapienti pauca!* [204]

797. The master of novices and his assistant, and the superior of a seminary or college, shall not hear the sacramental confessions of their alumni, who live with them in the same house, except in particular cases where an alumnus for a grave and urgent reason may of his own accord request it (**Canon 891**). The constitutions of some of the religious organizations ruled that the novices had to confess to the master of novices. Such a regulation is directly opposed to Canon 891, and must be disregarded, if it has not yet been eliminated in obedience to the Code. The Church is anxious to remove every possibility that the priest may use, even unconsciously, the knowledge gained in confession for the external government of the person who has made the confession.

798. Pastors and others who have the care of souls in virtue of their office, are bound by a grave obligation of justice to hear, either in person or through others, the confessions of the faithful in their charge whenever they reasonably ask to be heard. In case of urgent necessity, all confessors are bound by the obligation of Christian charity to hear the confessions of the faithful, and in danger of death all priests have the same obligation (**Canon 892**).

Since the duty to confess is distasteful and requires the spirit of sacrifice, the pastor and all other priests entrusted with the care of souls must be generous and kind, and anxious to

---

[204] Text of the Instruction of the Holy Office, June 9, 1915, cfr. excellent commentary in *Linzer Quartalschrift*, LXXV (1922), 198.

encourage the Christian people to fulfill this disagreeable duty. Every parish usually has appointed hours when confessions are heard, but that cannot and must not mean that at all other times the door to the Sacrament of Penance is barred. One shudders to think of the consequences, if the minister of Christ should block the way that leads to his Divine Master.

CHAPTER II

OF THE RESERVATION OF SINS

799. Those who have the *ordinary* power to grant the faculties for the hearing of confessions or to inflict censures, can also reserve some cases to their own tribunal and thus limit the power of absolution of their inferiors. Though the vicar-capitular [205] and the vicar-general have ordinary jurisdiction, the former cannot reserve cases, and the vicar-general can do so only by special mandate of his bishop. This restriction of jurisdiction is called the *reservation* of cases. In reference to the reservation of censures, the precepts of Canons 2246 and 2247 must be observed (**Canon 893**).

When we remember that the Sacrament of Penance has the nature of a tribunal or court, it is not difficult to grasp the principle of reservation or limitation of jurisdiction. In the civil and criminal procedure of every country, there are courts of restricted and courts of general jurisdiction. In a similar manner, the confessor who is appointed judge over the crimes in their spiritual aspect, may have a restricted or a general jurisdiction according to the amount of power assigned him by the superior who makes him a judge. The Council of Trent devotes a whole chapter to the teaching on the reservation of cases, and deduces the notion of reservation from the nature of the Sacrament of Penance, as explained above. Wherefore, the Council states that the Pope, by reason of his universal jurisdiction over the Church, can restrict the power of absolution of bishops and reserve cases to his own tribunal, and that the Ordinaries can restrict the power of all priests who hear confessions in the territory within their jurisdiction. The Council punishes with excommunication all who deny that the sacramental abso-

---

[205] In the United States and other countries which have no cathedral chapters, the diocesan administrator takes the place of the vicar-capitular.

lution is a judicial act, and also those who deny the power of the bishops to restrict the power of the priest.[206]

800. The Code states that all superiors who have the ordinary power to grant faculties for the hearing of confessions can reserve cases. This includes also the superiors of exempt religious organizations, as is stated in Canon 896.

801. Canon 2246 states the general rules on reservation of censures. Censures should not easily be reserved except for sins which have a special malice and against which it is necessary to use all available means to provide for the maintenance of ecclesiastical discipline and the morality of the faithful. It further rules that, if a person did not incur the censure because of an excuse admitted in law (e.g., ignorance), the sin is not reserved. The ecclesiastical superior could reserve both the censure and the sin (that is, make it a twofold reservation), but he must state that clearly, otherwise the sin is not reserved when one escapes the censure by an excuse admitted in law.

802. Offenses to which neither the particular law of a diocese or country nor the common law attaches a censure, cannot be punished with a censure except after a warning to repent or to desist from crime. In a law which states that the person is to be excommunicated, suspended, etc., for certain offenses, the law itself is considered sufficient warning. If the bishop or religious superior issues a command or prohibition under threat of censure, this threat is considered a sufficient warning and the breaking of the command or prohibition entitles the authorities to inflict the censure without further warning.

803. Canon 2247 rules that when a censure is reserved to the Holy See, the Ordinary cannot attach another censure reserved to himself for the same offence. Furthermore, censures of a particular territory do not have any force outside the boundaries of that territory, even though the one who incurred the censure went purposely outside the territory to obtain absolution. This holds good only for censures and reservations inflicted by law or statute.

A censure called *ab homine* cannot be taken away by any confessor except by the authority of the superior who inflicted it. What are censures *ab homine?* They are censures inflicted by a particular command or injunction given to an individual

[206] Sessio XIV, cap. 7, *De Sanctissimo Pœnitentiæ Sacramento*, can. 11.

person. Also censures inflicted by a condemnatory sentence of the ecclesiastical court are censures *ab homine*. For instance, a diocesan statute has a suspension *ferendæ sententiæ* for a certain offense: a priest commits the offense, the bishop hears of it, investigates and finds that the fact is true, and punishes the priest with suspension. Before the declaration it was a suspension *a jure* (by law), but after the condemnation it becomes a censure *ab homine* (cfr. Canon 2217).

804. Finally, Canon 2247 rules that if a confessor ignorant of the reservation of a censure absolved a penitent from censure and sin, the absolution from the censure is valid, provided it is not a censure *ab homine,* or a censure reserved to the Holy See *specialissimo modo.*

Reserved Case of False Denunciation

805. The only sin which, as sin, is reserved to the Holy See is the false accusation by which an innocent priest is accused of the crime of solicitation before ecclesiastical judges (**Canon 894**).

The crime of false denunciation of a priest accusing him of having solicited a penitent to sins of impurity on the occasion of or in connection with his confession, is punished by Canon 2363 with *ipso facto* excommunication reserved to the Holy See *speciali modo*. Now, Canon 894 makes it also a reserved sin, so that the sin is reserved to the Holy See, even though the person did not incur the censure on account of ignorance or some other excuse admitted in law. Since the life of a priest can be so easily ruined by either a demented or an unscrupulous person, the Church wants every case of solicitation in confession reserved to the highest authority. Besides, in a case of false accusation, the Holy See is best qualified to undo the injury which has been done to the priest.

The crime of solicitation is certainly a horrible abuse of the priestly office and a sacrilege which throws doubt on the very faith of the priest. If a confessor has a penitent who claims to have been solicited by another priest in connection with confession, the priest must carefully question the person, and it is advisable not to decide at once but have the person come again for crossexamination to make certain that the penitent is absolutely truthful. If the case is certain, the priest is bound to tell the penitent of the duty to denounce the priest to the bishop.

Any penitent who does not obey, incurs excommunication not reserved, but cannot be absolved until after the obligation of denouncing the priest has been satisfied, or a faithful promise given that the denunciation will be made. The priest who solicited a penitent to a sin of impurity in connection with confession does not fall into any censure *ipso facto*, but Canon 2368 prescribes the penalties which are to be imposed, and which he cannot escape, if the penitent obeys the law of the Church and denounces the priest. For the rest, the approved authors on moral theology explain this case at length and the Code has not changed the former legislation in this matter.

Diocesan Reserved Cases

806. The local Ordinaries shall reserve sins only after discussing the matter in a diocesan synod, or outside the synod with the Cathedral Chapter and some of the more prudent and experienced priests exercising the care of souls in his diocese, so that thereby the real necessity or utility of the reservation may be ascertained (**Canon 895**).

In the United States and other countries having no Cathedral Chapters the diocesan consultors take the place of the Chapter. The exchange of ideas on any subject is helpful, and in the important matter of the reservation of sins it may be considered necessary if the reservation is to attain its real purpose. That purpose is not to demonstrate the superior power of the bishop, nor to penalize the confessors who usually have to bear the burden of it, but rather to suppress some sin or vice which on account of its peculiarly dangerous nature or its frequency threatens to undermine Christian morality or ecclesiastical authority in matters of faith and discipline. Experience proves that in not a few cases the reservations do not have the desired effect, but rather discourage weak souls and keep them away from confession if they cannot get absolution immediately. Moralists are fairly agreed that delay of absolution should but rarely be resorted to by the confessor as a means of correction on account of the danger that the penitents may never come back. This danger is also found in the reservation of sins, wherefore the Code warns earnestly in Canon 897 that the reservations should be few and well considered.

Reservation of Cases in Exempt Religious Organizations

807. In exempt religious organizations the only person who can reserve cases of his subjects is the Superior General, and in monastic Orders the abbot of an autonomous monastery, with their respective councils. Canons 518 and 519 must be observed (**Canon 896**).

Canon 518 rules that in all houses of clerical religious organizations several confessors must be appointed, and in exempt religious communities those confessors shall be given the power to absolve also from cases reserved in the religious organization. If the superior appoints confessors, but does not give them the power to absolve from cases reserved in the organization, they do not have the power, for the Code does not give it but orders the superior to give the power. Canon 519 grants to all religious, even of exempt organizations, the right to go to confession "for the peace of their conscience" to any confessor approved by the Ordinary of the place where the confession is made, and this confessor may validly and licitly absolve the religious even from any sin and censure reserved in the religious organization.

Pope Clement VIII, May 26, 1593, had restricted the power of reservation of the superiors of religious Orders to eleven cases enumerated in his Constitution "Sanctissimus Dominus." Some commentators on the Code hold that this Constitution is not revoked by the Code.[207] The Code, however, grants power to reserve three or four only of the more grievous external crimes (cfr. Canon 897) when the superior with his council deems this necessary or useful, while the Constitution granted the power of reservation for eleven specific cases without otherwise limiting the number reserved.

Reserved Cases Must Be Few in Number

808. The reserved cases must be few in number (namely, three or at most four), and they shall be only the more grievous and hideous external crimes specifically defined. The reservation, however, shall not remain in force any longer than necessary for the extirpation of some inveterate public vice or for the restoration of perhaps collapsed Christian discipline (**Canon 897**).

[207] Schäfer, "Ordensrecht," 109; Prümmer, "Manuale Jur. Can." (3rd ed.), n. 189.

By Decree of January 6, 1601, the Sacred Congregation of Bishops and Regulars warned the Ordinaries that the number of reserved cases must be very small, and the Code is more definite in allowing at most four. The Code also describes the character of the sins to be reserved, and demands that the reservation be abolished as soon as its purpose is accomplished.

PAPAL CASES NOT TO BE RESERVED BY INFERIOR AUTHORITIES

809. All inferior authorities must absolutely abstain from reserving sins which are already reserved to the Holy See by reason of a censure, and as a rule also from reserving those sins to which a censure is attached by law, though such censure is not reserved to anyone (**Canon 898**).

If a reserved censure is attached to a sin, the sin is reserved only by reason of the censure, and, if the censure was not incurred, the sin is not reserved. It seems that some bishops wanted to interfere in Papal cases by reserving to themselves the sin, if perchance the penitent had not incurred the censure through ignorance of the penalty or some other excuse admitted in law. Thus, for instance, they desired to make joining the Freemasons a reserved sin, if the penitent had not incurred the Papal censure through some legal excuse. The Code strictly forbids inferior authorities to meddle in Papal cases. There is some difficulty in deciding whether the bishop may reserve the sin in the six excommunications which by the Code are reserved to the local Ordinary. It seems rather repugnant from the very nature of the case that the bishop can reserve to himself a case from which he cannot absolve unless the Holy See has given him power. Besides, the illogical conclusion would follow that a priest who has received power to absolve (e.g., abortion) from the Holy See, can absolve if the penitent has incurred the excommunication, but cannot absolve when the excommunication was not incurred, because the bishop has made it a diocesan reserved case. Some doubt remains because the Code says that the inferior authorities may by no means reserve sins which are already reserved *to* the Holy See by reason of the censure. If the Canon read "reserved *by* the Holy See," there would be no doubt.[208]

[208] Noldin, "Theol. Moral.," III, n. 359. Cfr. also Decree of the Holy Office, July 13, 1916 (*Acta Ap. Sedis*, VIII, 313), from which the several Canons on diocesan reservations are largely taken.

ENFORCEMENT OF DIOCESAN RESERVED CASES AND FACULTIES TO
ABSOLVE FROM THE SAME

810. Once they have reserved some cases which seemed to them necessary or useful, the local Ordinaries shall see that these reservations come to the knowledge of the people, and they shall not too freely grant faculties to absolve from the reserved cases.

The power to absolve from the diocesan reserved cases is granted by law to the Canon Penitentiary, as stated in Canon 401, and it shall be habitually given at least to the vicars forane (or deans), especially in districts far away from the episcopal city, with the additional power to subdelegate confessors of their respective districts, if and when these have recourse to them in some specific and more urgent case.

By the law itself the pastors, and others who come under the name of pastors in law, have the faculty to absolve from the diocesan reserved cases (no matter in what manner the Ordinary has reserved them to himself) during the entire time in which the Easter duty can be fulfilled, and all missionaries during the time that a mission is held for the people (**Canon 899**).

The reservations, as said before, are usually as much of a burden to the confessor as to the people, but, if they are few and really necessary to fight against some pernicious vice, the confessor must be willing to bear the burden. Usually the confessor has to write for faculties to absolve the persons, and not unfrequently the persons never return. Their good-will often hangs by the tiniest thread, and is easily broken by the slightest test.

811. The Canon Penitentiary has faculties to absolve from all sins and censures reserved to the bishop, in virtue of Canon 401. It is not altogether certain whether this power includes the cases reserved to the Ordinary by the Code, but, as Blat says, where the Code does not distinguish we should not distinguish.[209] It seems that the law gives the Canon Penitentiary the same power as the bishop has in the sacramental forum.

812. The faculties given by law to the pastors during the paschal season and to the missionaries during missions do not include the power to absolve from the Papal cases reserved by

---

[209] *Commentarium,* 370, lib. II, *de Personis.*

law to the Ordinaries, for the Code gives them power to absolve from diocesan reserved cases, and the Papal cases reserved to the Ordinaries are not diocesan reserved cases. It is desirable, however, that the bishop grant them power to absolve from these cases, for the paschal season and the missions are times of special grace, and the work of the pastor and the missionaries should be facilitated as much as possible. If the bishop extends the time for the Easter duty from the First Sunday in Lent to Trinity Sunday (as he can do according to the privilege granted to the bishops of the United States), the faculties of the pastors extend over this entire period. As to missions, in which may be included retreats, it is a question whether other priests who help the missionaries to hear confessions also have the faculties given by the Code to missionaries. It seems that the spirit and intention of the law includes these priests because they are actually doing missionery work.

Circumstances in Which Reservations Cease

813. Every reservation [210] ceases: (1) when sick persons who cannot leave the house, or persons prior to their marriage, go to confession; (2) whenever the legitimate superior has refused the faculty to absolve asked for in an individual case, or in cases wherein the confessor prudently judges that the faculty to absolve cannot be asked from the legitimate superior without great inconvenience to the penitent, or without danger of violation of the sacramental seal; (3) if the penitent goes to confession outside the diocese where the case is reserved, even though he does so for the sole purpose of obtaining absolution (**Canon 900**).

Canon 900 has reference to diocesan reserved sins only and the one Papal case (cfr. Canon 894). Canon 2254 makes liberal concessions to every confessor for the absolution of all censures in more urgent cases.

814. The great inconvenience to which the penitent is exposed by the delaying of absolution until the priest has written to the bishop and obtained the faculty to absolve, may be caused by various circumstances of which the confessor has to judge whether they really seriously inconvenience the penitent so that he may absolve him from the reserved sins.[210a]

[210] "Every reservation" refers to reserved sins only, cfr. App. III, 38, b.

[210a] Noldin, "Theol. Moral.," III, n. 364.

815. A person who has committed a reserved sin and who goes to confession in another diocese, does not escape the reservation, if that same sin is reserved also in the diocese where he goes to confession. In the matter of confession strangers are treated by law like the residents, for Canon 881 states that priests who have jurisdiction to hear confession in some place (parish or diocese) can also absolve strangers. The Committee for the Authentic Interpretation of the Code has declared that strangers are bound by the diocesan reservations of the place in which they stay.[211] This is an authoritative interpretation of Canon 893: it refers to the reservation of sins, for, with regard to the reservation of censures mentioned at the end of the same Canon, it states that Canons 2246 and 2247 are to be applied. According to Canon 2226 those persons only incur the penalty attached to the breaking of a law who are subject to that law. Now, the strangers are not, as a rule, subject to the diocesan laws of the strange diocese, therefore they are not subject to the censures attached to those laws. The answer of the Committee, therefore, cannot be applied to diocesan censures (cfr. Canon 14, § 1, n. 2).

CHAPTER III

OF THE SUBJECT OF PENANCE

816. A person who has committed mortal sins after Baptism which have not yet been directly pardoned by the power of the keys of the Church is obliged to confess all such sins of which he is conscious after careful examination of conscience, and he must besides explain in confession those circumstances which change the species of sins (**Canon 901**).

Men who believed in Christ, but not in the absolute authority of the Catholic Church over spiritual matters, have made many attempts to show that the obligation to confess mortal sins is a mere church regulation, and not a law of Christ. Without entering deeply into this question which belongs primarily to the domain of dogmatic theology and apologetics, we may state that the early history and practice of the Christian faith is perhaps the most convincing of the arguments for the Divine institution of confession. Time and again these argu-

211 Cfr. App. III, 38, a.

ments from history have been fully discussed by able theologians in various countries and languages. The question of forgiveness of sins was brought to the attention of the Church soon after she began to set out on her mission of teaching all nations. Apostasies and other scandalous misconduct occurred which made it early imperative to define the conditions under which such Christians might obtain pardon.

For this reason we find very explicit teaching on this subject in the writings of the early Fathers of the Church and in the early synods. They insist that not only must public sins and scandals be confessed to the bishop or the priest authorized by him, but also sins which were secret. As the person who is ashamed to manifest a secret malady to the physician must die, so the Christian who is ashamed to uncover the secret wounds of his soul must endure spiritual death. In such and similar comparisons the early Fathers of the Church express the necessity of the confession of sins to obtain pardon from God.

817. However, there are many difficulties especially with reference to the minister of the Sacrament of Penance. It took a considerable length of time before all dogmatic questions connected with any of the big principles of our faith were clarified and well defined. While the main principle in the Sacrament of Penance, the authority of the Church to forgive sins by the power delegated to her by Christ, was well established from the very beginning, many questions arising out of this principle were not settled at once. The man who acknowledges the teaching authority of the Church and believes that she is guided in her final pronouncements on questions of faith and morality by God's infallible guidance has a secure foundation.

818. The expression "power of the keys," used here by the Code, is familiar to the student of patrology. It is an ancient and very common term to designate the power which Christ delegated to St. Peter and the other Apostles to grant in His name forgiveness of sins to properly disposed Christians. As sin bars the soul from the beatific vision of God, absolution opens, as it were, the gates to the eternal home of our Heavenly Father.

That mortal sin separates the soul from union with God is indicated sufficiently by Christ when He speaks of keeping the commandments, and declares that those only who know and observe them love God truly and are in turn loved by God. The Code states that only mortal sins committed after Baptism are matter for confession, because by Baptism the sins of an adult are wiped out. It is possible that Baptism was received without even an imperfect sorrow for sins committed, and consequently the soul could not receive the grace and friendship of God, but the person will receive that sanctifying grace as soon as he supplies what was wanting—the necessary disposition. The sins before Baptism do not fall under the jurisdiction of the Church, which extends to Christians only.

819. Not only must all mortal sins committed after Baptism be confessed, but also those circumstances which change the character of the sins. If the Church is empowered by Christ to judge whether sins should or should not be forgiven, the confessor must be informed of the exact standing of the conscience of the penitent in all serious matters. A Christian who has the proper reverence and love of God has a fine spiritual instinct by which he keenly feels any offence he has given to God, and he also knows the difference between the malice of the various kinds of sins against the same commandment or the same virtue. He may not know all the minute distinctions made by moralists, but the big and important circumstances do not escape his attention.

Why does the Code say "mortal sins which have not yet been directly remitted"? Because a person may have obtained forgiveness of sin without direct application of the power of absolution by the Church. Thus, a person making his confession may through forgetfulness or some disturbance of the mind omit to mention some mortal sin. His confession is good and the absolution will free him from all sin, but in reference to the sin not confessed there is no direct remission or absolution. Again, in danger of death or some other emergency where it is necessary to absolve a person though he has no chance to make a complete confession, and in any other cases wherein there was no direct submission of the sin to the judgment of the Church and no direct absolution, the obligation to submit that sin remains, the Divine precept being suspended for the present.

SINS WHICH MAY BUT NEED NOT BE CONFESSED

820. Mortal sins committed after Baptism and already properly confessed and directly absolved, and venial sins committed after Baptism, are sufficient but not necessary matter for the Sacrament of Penance (**Canon 902**).

In the preceding Canon the rule was given to determine what sins must necessarily be confessed. The present Canon speaks of the so-called *materia libera*—sins which may but need not be confessed.

As to mortal sins confessed and absolved, and as to all venial sins, one is free to make them a matter for confession or not, as one pleases. There is no doubt that we may again and again ask the Divine Mercy for pardon of past sins, and pray to hear the Divine assurance "thy sins are forgiven thee," thus making so many manifestations of our sorrow for having displeased God and injured our own souls. Not knowing whether all the effects of our sins have been wiped out completely, we may well pray continually for the forgiveness of our sins.

CONFESSION THROUGH AN INTERPRETER

821. Persons who cannot confess in any other way may, if they so desire, confess through an interpreter, provided abuse and scandal are avoided and the interpreter understands that he is bound by the seal of confession (**Canon 903**).

It is a general principle that one's obligations are to be fulfilled by the use of the ordinary means, so that fulfillment is not considered possible whenever one cannot comply with a duty imposed by law without adopting extraordinary means. In cases, therefore, where persons want absolution from their sins and cannot easily reach a confessor who understands their language, they can get the benefit of absolution though they cannot make a complete confession. The obligation of confessing their sins is suspended, until they have occasion to confess to a priest who understands their language. It is entirely optional with such penitents to confess through an interpreter, but the Code warns against any abuse that might come from such a manner of confessing. The case will rarely occur that a penitent wants to make use of this extraordinary means of making his confession. The Code makes it clear that there is never an obligation to confess in this manner. The penitent can by other external acts show good disposition and sorrow for sin which would be sufficient under the circumstances to secure him absolution. In countries like the United States, where often there are in one and the same place people from all parts of the world, it happens quite frequently that Catholics cannot easily go to a priest who understands their language. They are not for this reason to be deprived of the Sacrament of Penance, but, when they have an opportunity to confess to a priest who understands them, they must confess all the mortal sins which they have not yet declared to a confessor who understood their language. The Sacred Congregation of the Propaganda forbids the vicars and prefects Apostolic in the missions to approve a priest for the hearing of confessions unless he understands the language of the respective mission district.[212] The same Sacred Congregation also decreed that the Ordinary of the mission district cannot forbid the people to make their confession through an interpreter, if they of their own free will want to confess in that manner and could not otherwise make a complete confession.[213]

Obligation of Denouncing the Solicitation of a Priest

822. According to the laws of former Apostolic Constitutions and especially the Constitution of Pope Benedict XIV, "Sacramentum Pœnitentiæ," June 1, 1741, the penitent is obliged to denounce to the local Ordinary or to the Sacred Congregation of the Holy Office, within one month, a priest who is guilty of the crime of solicitation in confession. The confessor is obliged under grave obligation of conscience to inform the penitent of this duty (**Canon 904**).

The Code does not enact a new law in this matter, but embodies the former laws of the Holy See on solicitation and especially the above-mentioned Constitution of Pope Benedict XIV. We need not discuss here at length the questions in reference to solicitation because all text-books of moral theology deal with this matter.[214] One very important point in the

---

212 March 17, 1760; *Collectanea de P. F.*, I, n. 427.
213 September 6, 1630; *Collectanea de P. F.*, I, n. 61.
214 Cfr. De Smet's excellent treatise, "De Absolutione Complicis et Sollicitatione" (Bruges, 1921).

matter of solicitation is the decision of the confessor whether he should in a given case oblige his penitent to make the denunciation (cfr. above n. 805).

Confession to a Priest of a Different Rite

823. All the faithful may confess their sins to any legitimately approved priest of another Rite, if they so desire (**Canon 905**). All that is required is that the priest has received jurisdiction for the hearing of confessions in the place where the confession is made. The priest approved by a local Ordinary of an Oriental Rite may hear the confessions of all Catholics, no matter to what Rite they belong, and a priest approved for confession by a local Ordinary of the Latin Rite may likewise hear the confessions of any Catholics. This was explicitly stated in the Decree regulating the relation of the Greek-Ruthenian Catholics to the Catholics of the Latin Rite in the United States. That Decree also reminded the priests that the priest of the Latin Rite cannot absolve the Greek-Ruthenians from the episcopal reserved cases of the bishop of the Greek-Ruthenian Rite, and the Greek-Ruthenian confessors cannot absolve a Catholic of the Latin Rite from the episcopal reserved cases of the bishop of the Latin Rite. The permission of the respective bishop is necessary to absolve from the reserved cases.[215] There are several Decrees in the official collection of the Propaganda which insist on the liberty of the people to confess to any approved priest of the Church without distinction of Rite.[216]

Precept of Annual Confession

824. All Catholics of either sex who have reached the years of discretion (that is to say, the use of reason), are obliged to confess all their sins accurately once a year (**Canon 906**). A person who makes a sacrilegious or intentionally invalid confession does not satisfy the precept of confessing his sins (**Canon 907**).

---

[215] Sacred Congregation of the Prop., August 17, 1914, art. 22; *Acta Ap. Sedis*, VI, 462.

[216] June 2, 1835; December 11, 1838, and other Decrees quoted in that of 1838; *Collectanea de P. F.*, I, nn. 839, 879.

The commandment to confess mortal sins committed after Baptism to obtain forgiveness is a divine law; the time for the confession of such sins is a law of the Church. It was always understood in the Church that he who approaches the Divine Banquet must come clothed with the nuptial garment (sanctifying grace), but before the Fourth Lateran Council (1215) there was no general law of the Church demanding confession within a specified period of time. The "Admonitio Synodalis" of the Roman *Pontificale*, which is said to date from about the tenth century, demands that the priests admonish the people on Ash Wednesday to go to confession, and that they exhort the people to receive Holy Communion on the feasts of Christmas, Easter, and Pentecost, and above all not to omit Communion on Easter Sunday.

The Canon demanding confession once a year must be understood of the confession of mortal sins, so that the precept does not bind those who with the grace of God have not committed a mortal sin. For one Canon of the Code cannot contradict another, and, as we saw, Canon 902 stated that the confession of venial sins is entirely optional. The Fourth Lateran Council from which the Code takes this law is interpreted by the Council of Trent to the effect that the obligation of the Divine law to confess one's sins was determined by that Council to be complied with at least once a year. Now, by the Divine law, mortal sins only have to be confessed.[217]

825. The Code does not specify when the space of one year begins, neither did the Fourth Lateran Council. It is generally understood to mean the common designation of a year from January to January. Some authors hold that it means from Easter to Easter; others within a year after the commission of a mortal sin. Practically, the people who go to confession and Holy Communion during the time set for the Easter duty fulfill both obligations of annual confession and Easter Communion.[218] Regarding the confession of children who have attained the use of reason, cfr. above, n. 760.

[217] Sessio XIV, *De Sanctissimo Pœnitentiæ Sacramento,* cap. 5.
[218] Lehmkuhl, "Theol. Moral.," I (ed., 1898), n. 1204.

CHAPTER IV

OF THE PLACE WHERE CONFESSIONS ARE TO BE HEARD

826. The proper place for sacramental confession is a church or a public or semi-public oratory (**Canon 908**). The confessional for hearing the confessions of women shall always be placed in an open and conspicuous place, and as a rule in a church or a public or semi-public oratory appointed for women. The confessional must be so constructed that between the penitent and the confessor there is an irremovable grating with small holes (**Canon 909**). The confessions of women shall not be heard outside the confessional, except in case of illness or other real necessity, and under the precautions prescribed by the local Ordinary. The confessions of men may be heard even in private houses (**Canon 910**).

The Roman Ritual says: "He shall hear confessions in church, not in private houses, except for a reasonable cause; and, if such cause exists, he shall endeavor to hear the confession in a respectable and open place." The Code is more specific, demanding greater precaution against possible abuse in the hearing of confessions of women. It demands a case of illness or other true necessity to hear the confessions of women outside the usual confessional in churches and chapels. In emergencies and in circumstances which make an exception from the general rule necessary (as is the case in the pastorizing of the many scattered districts in the United States where there is neither church nor chapel), good sense and a deep reverence for the Sacrament of Mercy will guide the priest to come as near to the spirit of the law as is possible under the circumstances. During a retreat it is sometimes necessary to erect additional movable confessionals in the convents of Sisters, and, if there is no room in the chapel, they have to be put up elsewhere. Where it is not merely a matter of emergency but done regularly, the local Ordinary should be consulted, since he has the supervision of these matters and can approve other places besides churches and chapels as proper places for the hearing of the confessions of women. The Holy See was asked whether men's confessions must also be heard in the usual confessionals in churches and chapels. The Committee for the Authentic Interpretation of the Code answered that ordinarily their confessions should be heard in those places, but the permission of Canon 910 that men may be heard also in private houses stands.[219]

827. A question about the place of confession was raised in connection with Canon 522, which gives religious women the right to go to confession to any approved priest in any church or public or semi-public oratory. Must the confession necessarily be made in those places so that confession outside of these places is invalid? The Committee answered that the confession is licit and valid, provided it is made in a church or a public or semi-public oratory, or in a place legitimately appointed for the hearing of the confessions of women.[220] Schäfer holds that this decision does not make the validity of the confession depend on the place.[221] This opinion might be debated, since the answer seems rather to make the place a condition for licit and valid confession. Still, the Decree of February 3, 1913, which allowed the nuns and sisters to make their confession to any approved priest in any church or public or semi-public oratory, if they were outside their own convent, was explained by the Sacred Congregation of the Religious, July 3, 1916, in an answer to the Bishop of Linz as meaning that the place of confession was not required for validity, and that it was not forbidden to make the confession in any other decent place.[222] In any case, nobody holds that, in the case of the confessions of lay women, the place of confession affects the validity.

Chapter V

OF INDULGENCES

Article I.—OF THE CONCESSION OF INDULGENCES

828. All the faithful should hold in high esteem indulgences or the remission of the temporal penalty due before God for .sins which have already been blotted out as to their guilt. These indulgences are granted by ecclesiastical authority from the treasury of the Church to living members by way of absolution, and to the deceased by way of suffrage (**Canon 911**).

In the preceding Canons the Code treated of the Sacrament

[219] Cfr. App. III, 39.
[220] Controversy about place of confession settled by latest decision, cfr. App. III, 21, g, 2.
[221] *Ordensrecht*, 117.
[222] Leitner, ''Handbuch des kath. Kirchenr.,'' III, 336.

of Penance, which has for its object the pardon of the guilt contracted by sin. The treatise on indulgences follows logically after the Sacrament of Penance, for the indulgences complete the work of pardon and wipe out the last effects of sin, namely, the temporary punishment regularly due for every infringement of God's laws.

In the first place, the Church admonishes us to hold the indulgences in high esteem. That we may appreciate their value, the Church tells us what is meant by an indulgence. Since the time of Luther there has been and there still is a great deal of misunderstanding among non-Catholics of the teaching of the Church on indulgences. The Code explains very well what an indulgence means. There are several elements in that definition: (1) it is a remission not of the guilt of sin, but of the temporary penalty due to sin after its guilt has been pardoned by absolution in the Sacrament of Penance; (2) this remission of the penalty is granted by that authority which was given to the Church by Christ to reconcile sinful men with God, and this reconciliation would not be complete without the power also to remit the penalties due to sin; (3) the indulgences are derived from what is here called the treasury of the Church, that is to say, from the merits which Christ and the Saints offered to God the Father in satisfaction for the sins of mankind; (4) the indulgences are applied to the souls of the living members of the Church in the manner of a direct dischargal or remission of the penalty; (5) to the deceased the indulgences are applied by the way of suffrage or prayer of the Church that God may be pleased to apply them to the souls in purgatory. As the souls of the deceased are no longer subject to the authority of the Church, she cannot directly and immediately pardon them, but, inasmuch as the Church in her official capacity represents Christ, her prayer has efficacy.

The words of the Saviour to the Holy Apostles: "As the Father sent me, so I send you," give us an understanding of the great mission of the Church. Christ says plainly that the Church is to take His place with the same authority and power with which He Himself had been sent by His Heavenly Father. All the powers of Christ, all the fruit of His work of redemption, are in the hands of the Apostles and their successors, for these are to carry on the work of salvation of souls as Christ had done while He stayed on earth. The Church, therefore, possesses a great and unlimited power to be exercised for the benefit of the souls of men, and this power is hampered by nothing save the unwillingness of a soul to receive its benefits. Sin and all effects of sin can be blotted out by the Church, if only the sinful soul is properly disposed.[223]

PERSONS HAVING POWER TO GRANT INDULGENCES

829. Besides the Roman Pontiff, to whom Christ our Lord has committed the disbursement of the whole spiritual treasury of the Church, those persons only to whom the power is expressly given by law can grant indulgences by ordinary power (**Canon 912**).

Christ built His Church on St. Peter, whom He commissioned to be the head of the organization which was to carry on the work begun by Him. In St. Peter, therefore, was centered all the power that Christ gave the Church for the salvation of the souls of men. All spiritual power in the Church must come through St. Peter and his successors in the office first committed to St. Peter. The Head of the Church controls and directs all that is done in the name and by the power of Christ. Whether there is question of indulgences or of any other exercise of spiritual power in the name of Christ, all this must of necessity be subject to the Head of the Church, if it is admitted that Christ wanted an orderly and organized continuation of His work on earth.

830. Persons inferior to the Roman Pontiff cannot: (1) give to others the faculty of granting indulgences, unless this power has been expressly granted to them by the Apostolic See; (2) grant indulgences applicable to the souls in purgatory; (3) attach further indulgences to an object, or pious work, or society, to which the Holy See or another authority has already attached indulgences, unless new conditions for gaining the additional indulgences are prescribed (**Canon 913**).

The matter of indulgences has its own special rules, and one cannot always follow the general principles of law which gov-

---

[223] For the history of indulgences, the literature on the subject, and actually existing indulgences and the conditions for gaining them, consult Beringer-Steinen, "Die Ablässe, ihr Wesen und Gebrauch" (15th ed., Paderborn, 1921–1922).

ern in other matters. The very first point of this Canon which declares that inferior authorities cannot delegate their power to grant indulgences, is an application of the clause of Canon 199, "nisi aliud expresse jure caveatur" (cfr. n. 151).

THE PAPAL BLESSING

831. The Papal Blessing with a plenary indulgence may be given according to the prescribed formula by bishops in their respective dioceses twice a year—once on Easter Sunday and again on another solemn feast to be designated by the bishop; the blessing may be given, even though the bishop does not say the Mass himself, but only assists at it. Abbots and prelates *nullius*, vicars and prefects Apostolic, though they are not consecrated bishops, may give the Papal Blessing on one of the solemn feasts of the year only (**Canon 914**).

Regulars who have the privilege of giving the Papal Blessing are obliged not only to give it with the prescribed formula, but are restricted also in the use of the privilege to their own churches and those of the nuns and tertiaries legitimately aggregated to their Order. They may not give the Papal Blessing on the same day and in the same place where the bishop gives it (**Canon 915**).

The Papal Blessing spoken of in Canon 914 is to be given with the formula prescribed by Pope Clement XIII in 1762, which is to be found in the *Pontificale Romanum*. Regulars who have obtained the privilege of giving the Papal Blessing must use the other formula, which is published in the Roman Ritual (chapter XXXII, under the title of "Pontificia Benedictio").

Another Papal Blessing is mentioned in Canon 468, which may be given to persons in danger of death by the pastor or any priest who assists the dying. The formula to be used was prescribed by Pope Benedict XIV; it is inserted in the Roman Ritual, following the chapter *De Visitatione et Cura Ægrotorum,* and also in the Baltimore Ritual under the title of "Last Blessing."

832. The Papal Blessing is distinct from the "General Absolution," which also carries with it a plenary indulgence. Regulars who have received the privilege to grant this absolution on

certain days of the year must use the formula prescribed by Pope Leo XIII, July 7, 1882, and given in the Roman Ritual under the head of "Benedictiones Novissimæ." There are two formulas, one for the Secular Third Order and another for the religious community. With reference to the members of the Secular Third Order, Pope Pius X granted the religious superiors permission to delegate in their own churches a priest of their Order to impart the general absolution, though this priest has not been approved for the hearing of confessions.[224] Another concession in favor of the members of the Secular Third Order is the permission to any priest approved for confession to give the Papal Blessing as well as the General Absolution, if the priest in charge of the Third Order should for any reason be absent when the members are assembled to receive the Papal Blessing or the General Absolution on the appointed days.[225] Some Secular Third Orders (e.g., Franciscan, Carmelite) have received the privilege that the General Absolution may be given to them privately by the confessor after Sacramental Confession, if they cannot attend the meeting of the Third Order in which the General Absolution is given to all. The confessor may use the following short formula: "Auctoritate a Summis Pontificibus mihi concessa plenariam omnium peccatorum tuorum indulgentiam tibi impertior. In nomine Patris et Filii et Spiritus Sancti. Amen."[226]

PRIVILEGED ALTARS

833. Bishops, abbots or prelates *nullius*, vicars and prefects Apostolic and major superiors of exempt clerical communities of religious have the power to designate and declare one altar as daily and perpetually privileged in the cathedral, or in the church of an abbey, or in collegiate, conventual, parochial and quasi-parochial churches (provided there is no other privileged altar in the church). They cannot declare an altar privileged in public or semi-public oratories, unless they are united to or subsidiaries of parochial churches (**Canon 916**).

The term "privileged altar" means that, by virtue of the concession of the Church, a plenary indulgence can be gained

---

[224] May 28, 1914; *Acta Ap. Sedis*, VI, 347.
[225] December 15, 1910; *Acta Ap. Sedis*, III, 22.
[226] Mocchegiani, "Collectio Indulg.," nn. 1584–1585.

for a soul in purgatory by saying Holy Mass at such an altar for one of the departed. In order to gain the indulgence it is necessary that the Mass be applied to one soul for which the Mass is offered up, and, if it is said for several souls, the indulgence must be applied for one of these souls in particular. The former condition that the Holy Mass must be said in black vestments, when permitted by the rubrics, or that in a Mass of a feria or vigil an oration for the dead must be added, is no longer necessary for the purpose of gaining the plenary indulgence of the privileged altar.[227]

Canon 916 is very explicit as to the churches in which the ecclesiastical superiors can declare one altar privileged. If by special concession there was already a privileged altar in one of those churches, the superior cannot declare another altar privileged. The chapels which are built within a parish to relieve the congestion of the main parish church, or the mission chapels in outlying districts, come within the privilege of this Canon as subsidiary chapels or chapels united to a parish church. The major religious superior of exempt communities may declare an altar privileged in the churches at which a religious community resides, not in other churches and chapels entrusted to their care, for the Code says in "ecclesiis conventualibus," and the term "conventualis" or "conventus," of the former Canon Law seems to be the same as the term "domus formata" in the Code. The Sacred Congregation of Indulgences has declared that the concession of the privileged altar to a religious Order or Congregation applies only to the churches connected with their monasteries, not to other churches and chapels entrusted to the care of the Order or Congregation.[228]

834. On All Souls' Day all Masses have the same privilege as though they were said at a privileged altar. All the altars of a church are privileged during the days on which the Forty Hours' Devotion is conducted (**Canon 917**). To indicate that an altar is privileged, no other inscription shall be put on the altar than "privileged altar," with the addition "perpetual," "temporary," "daily," or otherwise, according to the wording

---

[227] Holy Office, February 20, 1913; *Acta Ap. Sedis*, V, 122.
[228] Blat, "Commentar.," III, pars I, 304; Mocchegiani, "De Altaribus Priv.," 19; *Rescripta Authentica*, Aug. 3, 1748, n. 174.

of the concession. A larger stipend may not be demanded on account of the privilege for Masses which are said at a privileged altar (**Canon 918**).

In connection with the privileged altar attention may be drawn to the fact that the priests who join the Sodality "A Transitu S. Josephi" have, among other faculties, the faculty of the privileged altar whenever they say Mass for the dying. Priests who make the Heroic Act of Charity have by Decree of the Sacred Congregation of Indulgences, September 10, 1852, the personal concession of the daily privileged altar.[229]

PUBLICATION OF NEW INDULGENCES

835. New indulgences which have not been promulgated at Rome, including those granted to churches of regulars, shall not be published without first consulting the local Ordinary. In publishing books, pamphlets, etc., in which concessions of indulgences for various prayers or good works are enumerated, the law of Canon 1388 is to be observed (**Canon 919**).

The publication of indulgences which were never granted by the authority of the Church but were pure inventions, resulted in grave abuses in the past. Lest such recur in the future, any person claiming to have received an indulgence for a church or for the public generally may not publish such an indulgence before he has given satisfactory proof of its concession to the bishop of the diocese where the indulgence is to be made public, and has received permission to publish it. If, however, the concession of an indulgence has been published by the Holy See (e.g., in the *Acta Apostolicæ Sedis*), nothing further is required to entitle one to make the indulgence known to the people. To prevent the publication of false indulgences in books, pamphlets, or any kind of a printed publication, the Code demands, in Canon 1388, that they be submitted to the approval of the bishop before publication. Any one of three bishops may give permission: either the bishop where the author of the publication is domiciled, or the bishop of the place where it is printed, or the bishop of the place where the publisher has his place of business.

836. Persons who have obtained from the Supreme Pontiff

---

[229] *Rescripta Authentica Sacr. Congr. Indulg.*, n. 392.

the concession of an indulgence for the benefit of all the faithful are obliged, under pain of nullity of the favor received, to submit to the Sacred Penitentiary a copy of that concession (**Canon 920**).

Up to the Fourth Lateran Council (1215), there was no restriction of the power of the bishops to grant indulgences. That Council restricted their power to one year's indulgence at the consecration of a church, and to forty days on other occasions, and their power could be exercised only within their own diocese. By the Constitution of Pope Clement IX, July 6, 1669, the Sacred Congregation of Indulgences and Relics was given jurisdiction over the matter of indulgences. In the reorganization of the Roman Curia under Pope Pius X, the Holy Office was put in charge of the matter of indulgences,[230] but the Code in Canon 258 entrusts this matter to the Sacred Penitentiary.

By *Motu Proprio* of April 7, 1910,[231] Pope Pius X demanded that all indulgences both general and particular which did not exclusively concern the persons who had obtained a particular indulgence had to be submitted to the Holy Office for authentication. Also faculties granted to any priest of whatever dignity or grade to bless sacred objects and annex indulgences and privileges for the benefit of any person had to be submitted. All the above indulgences were to have force only after being authenticated by the Holy Office. If they were not submitted and authenticated within six months from the publication of this Decree, they were forfeited. All persons who after this *Motu Proprio* obtain any such indulgences, must under pain of nullity exhibit a copy of the concession to the Holy Office for inspection and ratification. By *Motu Proprio* of September 16, 1915,[232] Pope Benedict XV declared that the document of concession has to be exhibited to the Sacred Congregation only in the case of indulgences conceded to all the faithful. Neither particular indulgences, no matter how extensive, nor faculties given to priests to bless religious articles and attach indulgences and privileges to them have to be submitted to the Sacred Congregation. The Code substantially confirms the *Motu Proprio* of Pope

---

[230] *Const. Sapienti Consilio,* June 29, 1908; *Acta Ap. Sedis,* I, 7.
[231] *Acta Ap. Sedis,* II, 225.
[232] *Acta Ap. Sedis,* VII, 457.

Benedict XV in Canon 920. Instead of the original document of concession, the Code allows authenticated copies of the concession to be submitted for approval.

INDULGENCES ATTACHED TO CERTAIN FEASTS

837. A plenary indulgence granted for feasts of our Lord, or for feasts of the Blessed Virgin Mary, is understood to have been granted for feasts only which are contained in the universal calendar of the Church. A plenary or a partial indulgence granted for the feasts of the Holy Apostles is to be understood as granted for the day of their death only. A plenary indulgence granted either daily and perpetually, or for a limited time, to those who visit some church or public oratory, is to be understood in such a manner that it can be gained any day but once a year only by each individual, unless the contrary is explicitly stated in the document of concession (**Canon 921**). The rules of this Canon are almost entirely taken from a Decree of the Sacred Congregation of Indulgences and Relics, September 18, 1862.[233]

TRANSFER OF FEASTS AND INDULGENCES

838. Indulgences attached to feasts, pious exercises, novenas, or seven or three days' devotions, held before or after a feast or during its octave, are to be considered transferred to the day to which the feasts are legitimately changed, if it is a perpetual transfer of a feast which has Office and Mass but no external solemnity and celebration, or if it is either a temporary or perpetual transfer of the solemnity and external celebration of a feast (**Canon 922**).

Solemnity and external celebration do not mean the same as a holyday of obligation, but rather refers to the solemn functions and special prayers which the people are accustomed to observe on these days. If the solemnity and external celebration of a feast is held on its proper day but the Mass and Office only are transferred to another day, the indulgence is not transferred. In the United States the Feasts of Corpus Christi and Sts. Peter and Paul are, in so far as their solemnity and external celebration are concerned, observed on the Sunday following these feasts. The indulgences attached to these feasts are

233 *Decreta Authentica*, n. 392.

therefore transferred. The solemnity and external celebration of the Feast of the Holy Rosary, which now has a fixed day in the calendar, is kept on the first Sunday in October, wherefore the indulgences are transferred to that day.[234] The Holy See was asked whether the indulgences are lost or remained attached to the day, if a feast is temporarily transferred and such feast has no external celebration and solemnity. The Sacred Penitentiary answered that the indulgences are not lost, but remain attached to the day, and that this is also true if the feast has to be transferred on account of falling on Good Friday. The indulgences remain for Good Friday in the case.[235] By Declaration of the Holy Office [236] the *toties quoties* plenary indulgence granted for All Souls' Day is transferred with the Office and Mass, if November 2 happens to be a Sunday.

TIME FOR VISITS TO A CHURCH ON INDULGENCED DAYS

839. To gain an indulgence attached to a certain day under condition of visiting a church or oratory, it suffices to make the visit from noon of the preceding day to midnight of the day itself (**Canon 923**).

Formerly the time for the visits used to be from the first vespers of the preceding day to sunset of the day itself. By concession of the Holy See the time was extended from noon of the preceding day to midnight of the feast itself, and the Decree granting the extension, which is here retained by the Code, explained that it includes the gaining of all indulgences attached to a certain day whether plenary or partial—those which can be gained once only and those that can be gained *toties quoties*.[237] The Sacred Congregation of Indulgences and Relics declared many years ago that the visits to a church can be made either before or after the other conditions for gaining the indulgence are complied with.[238]

[234] Sacred Congregation of Rites, October 28, 1913; *Acta Ap. Sedis*, V, 457.
[235] Cfr. App. III, 40, b.
[236] Dec. 14, 1916; *Acta Ap. Sedis*, IX, 179.
[237] Holy Office, January 26, 1911; *Acta Ap. Sedis*, III, 64.
[238] May 19, 1759; *Decreta Auth.*, n. 214.

Cessation of Indulgences Attached to Churches and Religious Articles

840. According to Canon 75, the indulgences attached to a church do not cease if the church is entirely destroyed but is rebuilt within fifty years on the same or nearly the same spot and under the same title. Indulgences attached to prayer beads and other objects cease only when the beads or objects are entirely destroyed or are sold (**Canon 924**).

As to the rebuilding of a church in the same or about the same place, the law of the Code is the same as the former law. The precise meaning of the words "fere eodem loco" was declared by the Holy See to be that the church is rebuilt on the same spot or at a short distance, for instance twenty or thirty paces (one Roman pace is a little less than five feet); and that it does not mean that a church may be rebuilt in the same town or the same parish without losing the indulgences.[239]

Blessed articles lose the indulgences when they are entirely destroyed.[239a] If the article breaks, as happens quite frequently with prayer beads, they may be repaired, and even the loss of a few beads does not destroy the identity of the object and the indulgences remain. If one buys a religious article and commits to the seller the task of having them blessed, and the buyer pays the price and the expenses for the sending after he has received the blessed articles, the indulgences are not lost. If, however, one foresees that on a certain occasion (e.g., at a large gathering of the faithful) many will want to get blessed articles, the seller may not get a large quantity of prayer beads, crucifixes, etc., blessed and then sell them for the regular price: otherwise, with the sale, the indulgences are lost.[240]

Finally the Code recognizes only two ways in which blessed articles lose the indulgences—total destruction and sale. The articles may, therefore, be donated to another; they may be used by another without losing the indulgences. As there were several decrees to the effect that the indulgences were lost if the religious articles were donated to others after having been used by the first owner, the Holy See was requested to declare

[239] March 29, 1886; *Acta S. Sedis*, XIX, 93.
[239a] Prayer beads of solid glass or crystal may be blessed with indulgences, cfr. App. III, 40, a. For faculties to bless articles, cfr. App. III, 40, b.
[240] July 10, 1896; *Acta S. Sedis*, XXIX, 320.

whether the Code by Canon 924 revoked those decrees, and the answer was that the contrary decrees are revoked and the indulgences are lost only by either total destruction or by sale.[241]

ATRICLE II.—OF THE GAINING OF INDULGENCES

841. In order that a person may be capable of gaining an indulgence for himself, it is necessary that he be baptized, free from excommunication, in the state of grace at least at the end of the good works prescribed, and that he be a subject of the authority granting the indulgence. To actually acquire indulgences which he is capable of gaining, the person must have at least the general intention to gain them, and he must perform the required good works at the appointed time and in the proper manner as prescribed by the wording of the concession (**Canon 925**).

When the Church grants an indulgence to a person who has performed the good works upon the fulfillment of which it was conditioned, she makes use of the power of jurisdiction over souls which Christ conferred upon the Church. Though that jurisdiction differs essentially from human power or authority over others, still it is analogous to it. As persons who have not been baptized are not considered subjects of the Church, the Church cannot exercise her power in their behalf. That limitation of her power comes from the very nature of her institution, for she has received power to be the spiritual guide and leader of those baptized in Christ. Baptized persons who have incurred the censure of excommunication are deprived of indulgences as well as of other spiritual favors which come through the medium of the Church (cfr. Canon 2262).

842. Another essential condition for the gaining of indulgences is the state of grace at the time when one performs the last of the good works prescribed for the gaining of an indulgence. Naturally a soul which is in mortal sin cannot get forgiveness of the temporal punishment due to sin while the guilt of mortal sin remains. The good deeds done in the state of mortal sin benefit a soul, inasmuch as these good works incline God to help it to regain the state of grace more speedily, but they cannot benefit the soul any further on account of the lack of union of the soul with God. It is a merciful concession

241 Cfr. App. III, 3, e.

on the part of the Church to grant a soul the benefit of an indulgence, though some of the good works required for gaining it were performed while the soul was in mortal sin.

The Code speaks of the state of grace as an essential condition for gaining an indulgence for oneself. It does not speak of the gaining of an indulgence for the poor souls in purgatory. The question is controverted, and remains *in statu quo*. The Sacred Congregation of Indulgences was petitioned for an answer on this point, but answered on August 20, 1822: *Dilata*. When the question was again proposed by a bishop, it answered, February 22, 1847, that approved authors should be consulted.[242] The authorities are divided, and therefore nothing certain can be said on this point. The argument in favor of the gaining of an indulgence for the poor souls by a person who is in mortal sin is chiefly based on the intrinsic effectiveness of the indulgences (*ex opere operato*) after the manner of the sacraments. But one would have to prove that the Church makes each of the faithful who intends to gain an indulgence for the poor souls her minister and representative in the performance of the good works. There does not seem to be any foundation for asserting that the Church gives a person that official capacity.

Finally, the Code states that the person who wishes to gain an indulgence must be a subject of the authority granting the indulgence. The reason is apparent, because the nature of an indulgence is an absolution or pardon, and nobody has a right to interfere with the subjects of another authority. Note, however, that Canon 927 allows travelers and the exempt religious to gain the indulgences granted by a bishop in whose diocese they actually stay, unless the bishop restricts it to the residents of the diocese.

The intention to gain an indulgence must, according to the Code, be at least a general intention, which is practically the same as the habitual intention spoken of by moralists. No more than a resolution or desire formed at some time in life to gain all possible indulgences is required, but the important point is the faithful performance of the good works prescribed at the time and in the manner in which they are prescribed.

242 Beringer, ''Die Ablässe,'' I, 109.

Failure to Gain Plenary Indulgence Does Not Entail Loss of Entire Indulgence

843. A plenary indulgence is understood to be granted in such a manner that, if one cannot fully gain it, he may nevertheless gain it partially according to his actual dispositions (**Canon 926**).

A plenary indulgence means the wiping out of all temporal punishment due to sins committed by a person. To gain such an indulgence, the soul must previously have obtained pardon of the guilt of all sins both mortal and venial, for otherwise a complete pardon of all temporary penalties is not possible. Now, it is by no means easy to be free from the guilt of every venial sin, because often there is an attachment to some venial sin, and this prevents true sorrow for such a sin and consequently the possibility of obtaining pardon from its guilt. Wherefore, it is difficult to gain a plenary indulgence. Our Holy Mother Church takes this difficulty into consideration and grants her children partial indulgences, if their souls are not so entirely free from sin as to be able to gain a plenary indulgence. Otherwise the faithful might be discouraged from doing the good works demanded for the plenary indulgence.

Indulgences Granted by Bishops

844. Indulgences granted by a bishop may be gained not only by his subjects, though they are actually outside his diocese, but also by strangers and *vagi* and all exempt persons who are actually staying in the diocese, unless the wording of the concession of the indulgence states otherwise (**Canon 927**).

This Canon supplements Canon 925, which laid down the general principle that, to gain an indulgence, the person must be a subject of the authority who grants the indulgence. This Canon is an exception to the general rule. The power of the bishops to grant indulgences, is very limited (cfr. Canons 349, n. 2, and 1166).

Repeated Gaining of Indulgences on the Same Day

845. Even though the prescribed good works are performed repeatedly, a plenary indulgence can be gained once a day only, unless the concession explicitly states otherwise. Partial indul-

gences may be gained repeatedly during the same day by the repetition of the same good work, unless the contrary is explicitly stated (**Canon 928**).

One may, however, gain several plenary indulgences by repeating the good works prescribed, if they are based on various distinct concessions. Thus, for instance, if on the same day several churches of a place happen to have a plenary indulgence for visiting them, or if the same church should have two plenary indulgences on the same day by reason of distinct concessions, the repeated visits and prayers for the intention of the Holy Father(besides the other conditions, which usually are Confession and Holy Communion) enable one to gain the various indulgences. The Sacred Congregation of Indulgences and Relics declared that, if a plenary indulgence is granted for the feast of a saint to all the churches of some religious Order or of a diocese, that indulgence may be gained once only in each church, but one can gain it in as many churches as one visits.[243] The same holds good if the churches of various religious Orders have the same indulgence on the same feast by concession of the Holy See.

846. As to some plenary indulgences, it is uncertain whether they can be gained repeatedly the same day. The indulgences attached to the Way of the Cross were until recently included in this category, but by Letter of the Sacred Penitentiary of October 20, 1931, the Holy See abolished all other indulgences granted for centuries and assigned specific plenary and partial indulgences for the practice of this devotion.[244] There also exists a doubt as to the repeated gaining of the plenary indulgence granted for the recitation of the Franciscan Crown of the Seven Joys of the Blessed Virgin to the members of the various Franciscan communities and the Secular Franciscan Tertiaries. It seems, however, that Pope Pius X admitted that it had been granted as a *toties quoties* plenary indulgence in the introduction to the concession of various indulgences to the faithful generally for the recitation of the Franciscan Crown.[245] Mocchegiani discusses the two indulgences at length.[246] The question of the

---

[243] September 13, 1905; *Acta S. Sedis*, XXXVIII, 351.
[244] For a list of these indulgences, see App. III, 40, h.
[245] Brief of Pope Pius X, Sept. 15, 1905; *Acta S. Sedis*, XXXVIII, 140.
[246] *Collectio Indulgentiarum*, on the Way of the Cross, 543–548; on the Crown of the Seven Joys, 323–325.

precise nature of the concession of some of the indulgences which were granted many centuries ago is difficult, because the original document of concession has either been lost or mislaid, and other documents or early references to the indulgences may not be explicit enough to determine the character of the original concession.

Special Concessions for Persons Living in Institutions

847. The faithful of either sex who for the purpose of Christian perfection, or studies and education, or health, live in common in houses which have been established with the consent of the Ordinaries, but which have no church or public chapel attached to the institute, may gain all indulgences for which the visit to a church or public chapel in general is required by visiting the chapel of their house in which they can by law satisfy the obligation of hearing Mass, provided they properly perform all the other good works enjoined. All persons who live in these houses for the purpose of serving the inmates share in this concession (**Canon 929**).

If the religious house or other institution has a church or public oratory attached, that church or oratory must be visited. Even if the parish church is quite close to such an institution but does not belong to it, the inmates of the institution can gain the indulgences in their own chapel. The chapel must be such that the obligation of hearing Mass can be satisfied there (Canon 1192; cfr. below, n. 1227).

The Code grants the concession of gaining the indulgences only when a visit to any church or public oratory is required. If the visitation of a specified church or oratory is demanded, the visit to the chapel of the institute will not suffice. Finally the concession is restricted to members of the community, school, hospital, sanatorium, seminary, etc., and the persons who live there to manage the institute or to serve the inmates of the same. Mere visitors and others staying there accidentally do not participate in the concession. Canon 929 is taken from a Decree of the Holy Office, January 14, 1910.[247]

[247] *Acta Ap. Sedis*, I, 210.

APPLICATION OF INDULGENCES TO OTHERS

848. Nobody who gains indulgences can apply them to other living persons. All indulgences granted by the Roman Pontiff may be applied to the poor souls in purgatory, unless the contrary is evident from the concession (**Canon 930**).

The rule of Canon 930 establishes the general principle that one person cannot gain indulgences for another living person. The Church could, of course, allow such application, and instances are quoted by some authors where the Church has done so, but the Church desires rather that those who can by their own efforts gain indulgences should exert themselves.[247a]

As the poor souls in purgatory can no longer gain these graces by their own effort, the Church not only allows but urges her living members to do good works to which indulgences are attached in favor of the faithful departed. Wherefore, by a general provision the Code also allows the application to the poor souls of all indulgences granted by the Roman Pontiff, which includes those granted by the Roman Curia.

CONFESSION AND HOLY COMMUNION AS CONDITIONS FOR INDULGENCES

849. If Confession is required for the gaining of any indulgence, that Confession can be made within eight days immediately preceding the day to which the indulgence is attached. Holy Communion may be received on the day previous to the day of the indulgence; both Confession and Holy Communion may also be made on any day within the octave (that is, the day itself and the seven subsequent days). In like manner, Confession and Holy Communion required for the gaining of indulgences attached to pious exercises conducted for three, seven, or more days, may be made also within eight days after the close of the exercises.

The faithful who, unless legitimately hindered, are in the habit of going to Confession at least twice a month, or who receive Holy Communion daily in the state of grace and with a good and devout intention (though they may abstain from receiving once or twice during the week), can gain all indulgences without actually going to Confession, when Confession

[247a] Concerning privileged altar for the dying, cfr. App. III, 40, c.

would otherwise be a necessary condition for the gaining of the indulgences. Indulgences granted for an ordinary or extraordinary Jubilee, or after the manner of a Jubilee indulgence, are excepted from this concession, and the Confession is a necessary requisite for the gaining of such indulgences (**Canon 931**).

By these concessions concerning Confession and Holy Communion, the Code has made it easier than ever to gain the plenary indulgences. Many working people cannot without great difficulty receive Holy Communion on weekdays, while they can comply with the other conditions (for instance, a visit to the church, participation in some devotion in the evening, etc.). Besides, in many parishes confessions are never heard on weekdays, except before the first Fridays and on Saturdays. The present concession gives two weeks' time for the Confession and nine days for the Holy Communion necessary to gain any of the indulgences for which the reception of the Sacraments is required. Those who go to Confession regularly twice a month and those who receive Holy Communion daily (or almost daily), do not have to go to Confession specially for the purpose of gaining the indulgences. The Jubilee indulgences follow special rules, and the requirements for gaining them are announced in the special papal document published on those occasions.

Obligatory Good Works and Indulgences

850. An indulgence cannot be gained by a good work which one is already bound to perform by reason of some law or precept, unless the document of concession explicitly states the contrary. However, the person who performs a good work enjoined on him as a penance in Sacramental Confession may, if such work is perchance enriched with indulgences, perform the penance and also gain the indulgences (**Canon 932**).

The Code settles a controversy, and clearly states that good works which one is obliged by law or precept to perform cannot at the same time count as a good work necessary for the gaining of indulgences. Thus, the assistance at one Holy Mass on Sunday cannot count as a visit to the church; the saying of the Divine Office by those who are obliged to it cannot count as prayer requisite for the gaining of an indulgence. In the former law a decision of the Sacred Congregation of Indulgences, May

29, 1841, had settled the question that obligatory prayers, like the Divine Office, did not count as prayer prescribed for the gaining of an indulgence.[248] As to other good works, the matter was not settled, though Pope Benedict XIV mentions the controversy in his Constitution "Inter Præteritos," § 53, and says that the truer opinion seems to be that a condition for the gaining of an indulgence cannot be satisfied by a good work which a person is bound to perform.[249]

RELIGIOUS ARTICLES OR PLACES TO WHICH VARIOUS INDULGENCES ARE ATTACHED

851. To one and the same object or place various indulgences may be attached under different titles. But by one and the same good work which is enriched with indulgences from various sources, the several indulgences cannot be gained, unless the good work required is Confession or Holy Communion, or unless the concession of the indulgences explicitly allows the cumulative gaining of the various indulgences by one and the same work (**Canon 933**).

As the Church desires that works of devotion or charity to which indulgences are attached should be performed frequently, she wants her children to repeat the good works to gain the various indulgences which might have been attached to the same kind of good works under different titles. Thus, one may bless the rosary beads with the various indulgences, Dominican, Crozier, Bridgettine, etc., if one has the faculty; but a person cannot by one and the same prayer on those beads gain at the same time all the various indulgences, unless by special concession of the Holy See some of them may be gained cumulatively. Pope Pius X granted the special favor that rosaries blessed with the Dominican and Crozier indulgences may serve to gain both indulgences at one and the same time by the same prayers (June 12, 1907, *Acta S. Sedis,* XL, 442).

PRAYER FOR THE INTENTION OF THE SUPREME PONTIFF

852. If prayer in general for the intentions of the Holy Father is prescribed for the gaining of an indulgence, mental

[248] *Decreta Authentica,* n. 291.
[249] December 3, 1749; *Opera Omnia Bened. XIV,* XVII, pars 1, 160; Gasparri, "Fontes Cod. Jur. Can.," II, 265.

prayer alone does not suffice. Unless a special prayer is assigned, it is left to the choice of the people what vocal prayers they wish to say.

If a special prayer is assigned, the indulgences can be gained by reciting the prayer in any language provided the exact translation of the same is attested by the declaration of either the Sacred Penitentiary or one of the Ordinaries of a locality where the language into which the prayer is translated is in common use. The indulgences, however, cease absolutely in case of any addition, omission or interpolation.[249a]

For the gaining of the indulgences it suffices to say the prayers alternately with a companion, or to follow the prayers mentally while they are recited by some one else (**Canon 934**).

The intentions of the Supreme Pontiff for which one is to pray are: the exaltation of the Church, propagation of the faith, ending of heresy and schism, conversion of sinners, peace and harmony among Christian rulers and nations, and other blessings for the welfare of Christianity. It suffices to have the general intention to pray for the intentions of the Pope or the Church. The Code does not specify the amount of prayer or the length of time that one is to pray for the intentions of the Church. The Holy See had been previously asked to decide whether five Our Fathers and Hail Marys were sufficient, but the Sacred Congregation of Indulgences answered that the prayers to be said were left to the choice of the faithful when no specified prayer is demanded.[250] The question was again proposed whether the opinion of some authors saying that one Our Father and Hail Mary is sufficient must be rejected, and the opinion of those who say five Our Fathers and Hail Marys or its equivalent are necessary, should be upheld. The Sacred Congregation of Indulgences answered that in reference to this point the Decree just quoted is a sufficient answer.[251] The Holy See evidently left it to the good will of the individual how long he wants to pray. However, in an Instruction of the Sacred Penitentiary, July 3, 1924, to Confessors in reference to the Jubilee Indulgences, the statement is made that "by the common opinion the recitation of five Our Fathers, Hail Marys and Glorias, suffices to comply with the condition to pray

---

[249a] For recent decision, see App. III, 40, p.

[250] May 23, 1841; *Collectanea de P. F.*, I, n. 922. See however App. III, 40, f.

[251] Sept. 13, 1888; *Collectanea de P. F.*, n. 1693.

for the intention of the Holy Father'' (*Acta Ap. Sedis*, XVI, 337).

853. Indulgenced prayers may be said in any language provided the translation is correct and authorized in the manner stated by the Code. The authorized versions must be followed faithfully by the person, who must recite the prayers without adding to, abbreviating or modifying them. As to the interpolation or insertion of the mysteries of the Holy Rosary after the first part of the Hail Mary, the Sacred Penitentiary, July 27, 1920,[252] stated that the practice could not be observed and propagated without losing the indulgences. The question was raised again on account of the widespread custom of thus saying the Rosary in Switzerland and in Germany, which custom had been approved in 1859 by Pope Pius IX for places where this custom had already become established. The Sacred Penitentiary, January 22, 1921, answered: (1) the general law of the Code does not revoke the indult of Pope Pius IX; (2) the Holy Father was to be requested for an extension of the same indult in favor of all persons in any place or country who are accustomed to recite the Holy Rosary in that manner (which extension Pope Benedict XV granted).[253]

854. The various approved Litanies must be chanted exactly as they stand in the approved formulas in order to gain the indulgences. Thus, it does not suffice if the choir sing two or three invocations without the ''ora pro nobis,'' and the people answer ''ora pro nobis'' once after every third invocation. This is a mutilation of the Litanies. The Sacred Penitentiary allows the choir to sing three of the invocations together with the responses, and the people answer by singing the fourth invocation and response.[254] There was a collection of indulgenced prayers, called ''The Raccolta,'' which was pronounced by Pope Leo XIII, May 24, 1886, as genuine and authentic. A translation into English was made by the Oratorian Fathers of England with the approval of the said Congregation. A new collection of indulgenced prayers and good works (Preces et Pia Opera) published in 1938 replaces ''The Raccolta.''

An exception from the rule that the indulgenced prayers

[252] *Acta Ap. Sedis*, XIII, 163.
[253] Cfr. App. III, 40, e. Concerning plenary indulgence for recitation of Rosary and Divine Office, cfr. App. III, 40, i, j and o.
[254] Cfr. App. III, 40, d.

may be said in any authorized translation is the Little Office of the Blessed Virgin, which must be said in Latin. The Sacred Congregation of Indulgences extended the indulgences to the *private* recitation of the Little Office in the vernacular.[255] When Cardinal Mercier requested that the indulgences be extended also to the recitation by religious communities of the Little Office in the vernacular, the Sacred Congregation stated that it is to be considered a private recitation, when the community recites the office within the enclosure, and, even if they recite it in a church or public oratory attached to the religious house, but the recitation is done while the doors are locked and the public is kept out, it is still a private recitation and the vernacular can be used without loss of the indulgences.[256]

FACULTY OF CONFESSOR TO COMMUTE PRESCRIBED GOOD WORKS

855. The good works prescribed for the gaining of indulgences may be changed by confessors to others for the benefit of people who for reason of a legitimate impediment cannot perform the prescribed works (**Canon 935**).

By Decree of the Sacred Congregation of Indulgences, September 18, 1862, Pope Pius IX granted confessors the faculty to commute the prescribed good works in favor of persons who were habitually infirm, and who could not leave the house on account of some permanent ailment. That decree speaks of the commutation of Holy Communion and the visit to a church or public oratory.[257] The Code is more general in its concession, not only regarding the good works demanded, and also as to the impediment, which need not be physical but may be a practical impossibility to do the prescribed works. The confessor may commute the required conditions, not only during, but also apart from Confession, for the Code does not restrict his faculty to the sacramental forum. It is understood that the confessor can commute the prescribed good works of those indulgences only which the person could have gained in the place where he lives, if he were not prevented by unusual circumstances or peculiar conditions which, while they last, make the fulfillment of the conditions either physically or morally impossible. That

---

[255] August 28, 1903; *Acta S. Sedis,* XXXVI, 185.
[256] December 18, 1906; *Acta S. Sedis,* XL, 187.
[257] *Decreta Authentica,* n. 393; also published in *Acta S. Sedis,* II, 538.

much seems to be certain both from the Decree of September 18, 1862, and also from a reasonable interpretation of Canon 935, for that Canon cannot mean that the confessor can enable the penitent to gain every indulgence that may be gained anywhere by simply imposing other good works.

How Mutes May Say Prayers for the Gaining of Indulgences

856. Mutes can gain the indulgences attached to *public* prayers if, praying in the same place together with the other people, they raise their hearts and minds to God. In the case of *private* prayers, it suffices that they say them mentally, or by the sign language, or merely read the prayers by sight (**Canon 936**).

The Code sums up former Decrees on this matter. A Decree of the Sacred Congregation of Indulgences, February 16, 1852, had granted the mutes the favor of gaining the indulgences which require a visit to a church and prayer for the intentions of the Holy Father by visiting the church devoutly and raising their hearts and minds to God. At the public prayers the same Decree said that their presence there with the other people and interior prayer was sufficient. As to private oral prayers, the confessor could commute them to other good works.[258] The last provision of the Decree of 1852 was retained by Decree of July 18, 1902, but it granted general permission to the mutes to say the prayers mentally or to read them with their eyes without any pronunciation, so that they need not apply to the confessor for a change of the prayers to other good works.[259]

TITLE V

OF EXTREME UNCTION

Matter and Form of the Sacrament

857. The Sacrament of Extreme Unction must be administered by the sacred anointings, with the use of the olive oil properly blessed and the words prescribed in the rituals approved by the Church (**Canon 937**).

Early formulas for the blessing of holy oils have been handed

---

[258] *Decreta Authentica*, n. 355; *Raccolta* (London, 1920), p. xiii.
[259] *Acta S. Sedis*, XXXV, 570.

down to us in the *Sacramentarium Gelasianum,* but the custom
of blessing oil is older than that document.[260] In a letter to
Bishop Decentius, Pope Innocent I (401–417) speaks of the oil
blessed by the bishop for the purpose of giving the Sacrament
to the sick. Catholic tradition teaches that the blessing of the
oil by the bishop is necessary for the validity of the Sacrament,
and it further teaches that the Supreme Pontiff can give the
power to a priest to bless the *oleum infirmorum.*[261] The Greek
priests have by a long-standing tradition the right to bless this
oil, and this right has been explicitly recognized in a Constitution of Pope Clement VIII, August 31, 1595.[262]

858. The form or words which are to accompany the anointing are not explicitly mentioned in the Code. We are referred
to the approved rituals of the Church. The Apostle St. James
in his reference to the Last Anointing does not mention any
definite form of prayer, but merely says that the presbyters are
to pray over the sick person. It is a well-known fact that there
has been a variety of forms used in the Church in the course
of the centuries. Not only does the Greek form differ from the
Latin of our present Roman Ritual, but even within the Latin
Church various forms were in use in various dioceses until the
Roman Ritual published in the sixteenth century was introduced
into most dioceses of the Latin Rite. The so-called indicative
forms like that of the Celtic Church (*Ungo te de oleo sanctificato
in nomine Trinitatis, ut salveris in sæcula sæculorum*)[263] remind
us of the controversy of theologians whether the deprecative
form is essential, or whether the indicative is admissible. Pope
Benedict XIV[264] with many theologians holds that the indicative
form is valid, but the obligation to use the deprecative form of
the Roman Ritual is strongly insisted upon by him.

[260] Binterim, ''Denkwürdigkeiten,'' VI, part III, 246.
[261] For further discussion cfr. Benedict XIV, ''De Synod. Diœc.,'' lib.
VIII, cap. 1, n. 4.
[262] Gasparri, ''Fontes Cod. Jur. Can.,'' I, 343.
[263] Warren, ''The Liturgy and Ritual of the Celtic Church,'' 168.
[264] *De Synod. Diœc.,* lib. VIII, cap. 2, **n. 3.**

CHAPTER I

OF THE MINISTER OF EXTREME UNCTION

859. This Sacrament can be validly administered only by a priest. Except in the cases mentioned in Canons 397, n. 3, and 514, the pastor of the parish in which the sick person stays is the ordinary minister. In case of necessity, or with the permission (at least reasonably presumed) of the pastor or of the local Ordinary, any other priest may administer this Sacrament (**Canon 938**).

Catholic tradition has always interpreted the words of St. James "presbyteros ecclesiæ" as ordained priests. The Council of Trent defines against the Lutherans that priests ordained by the bishop are the only ministers of Extreme Unction, not the elders or seniors of the laity.[265]

The pastor is the ordinary minister of the Sacrament within the territory of his parish. Canons 397 and 514 contain exceptions to this rule. Canon 397, n. 3, rules that the dignitaries and canons of the cathedral chapter, in the order of the rule of precedence, have the right and duty to administer the Last Sacraments to their bishop. Canon 514 rules that in all clerical religious communities the superior of the house has the right and duty to give the Last Rites to his religious subjects and the lay persons who stay permanently in his house. In the convents of Sisters with solemn vows the ordinary confessor administers the Last Rites. In other lay communities of religious the pastor is the ordinary minister, unless the bishop has appointed a chaplain with parochial rights over the religious house or institute. The Code insinuates that the right to administer Extreme Unction is not a personal right of jurisdiction but local. The pastor has the right to anoint all sick persons in his territory, no matter whose subjects they are. The exception as to the religious has to be understood of cases in which the religious stays in the religious house during his illness; if he is in a hospital or other place not subject to the religious superior, the pastor of the place or the chaplain, as the case may be, has the right to administer the Last Sacraments.[266]

860. The ordinary minister is obliged in justice to administer

[265] Sessio XIV, can. 4, *De Sacramento Extremæ Unctionis.*
[266] Blat, "Commentarium," III, pars I, 343.

the Sacrament either in person or through another priest, and in a case of necessity any priest is in charity bound to do so (**Canon 939**).

By accepting his office, the pastor implicitly agrees to perform the services attached to the office for which in return the Church gives him the income of the parochial benefice, or a fixed salary. Other priests have no obligation in law towards the people of a particular parish, except that regularly appointed assistants are obliged in law to assist the pastor in the duties of his office. For all priests there remains the common duty of Christian charity to assist those who stand in need of help. Inasmuch as spiritual distress is more serious than temporal, it is evident that the obligation to give spiritual assistance to people in danger of death falls on any priest who knows that there is nobody else at hand to help them. The duty to assist the dying is of course proportioned to the greater or lesser spiritual need of the individual and the facility or difficulty entailed in rendering assistance.

CHAPTER II

OF THE SUBJECT OF EXTREME UNCTION

861. Extreme Unction can be given only to a Catholic who, after having attained the use of reason, incurs a danger of death through sickness or old age. In the same illness this Sacrament cannot be repeated, unless the sick person rallied after the reception of the last anointing and his illness again becomes critical (**Canon 940**).

One of the direct purposes of Extreme Unction is the removal of the weakness of the soul induced by sin, commonly called the *reliquiæ peccatorum*. Therefore, a soul must have been capable of committing sin in order to receive Extreme Unction. Given this capability, one may justly presume that a human being has been guilty of at least venial sins in his life, and that therefore he is a fit subject for the reception of Extreme Unction. Children who have not attained the use of reason (ordinarily before the completed seventh year of age), and adults who have been insane from infancy, cannot receive Extreme Unction, because they have not sinned.

Danger of death from sickness or old age is another essential condition for receiving the Sacrament. The vital peril of a soldier marching into battle, or of a criminal awaiting execution, are not dangers of life caused by internal disorders of the human body. On the other hand, one may be anointed before a dangerous surgical operation, if that operation is to remove or cure a disorder of the body, which endangers life unless relieved by a successful operation. A person who attempts suicide and succeeds only in endangering his life by the wound or poison or other injury to the body, may be anointed if penitent.

862. The degree of danger of death is an element which is incapable of precise definition. It is, however, certain that the danger need not be imminent, nor the malady so serious that there is little or no hope of recovery. The ancient practice of the Church teaches that any ailment which may be fatal to the patient is sufficient ground for administering Extreme Unction, and one need not wait until the sickness takes a fatal turn. In several Rituals of the ninth and following centuries we read that the sick person should stand or kneel, or recite the Our Father and answer the questions addressed to him, all of which supposes that the sick person was not very close to death when anointed.

863. The second part of Canon 940 teaches that Extreme Unction can be given once only in the same sickness. In protracted diseases like tuberculosis, cancer, and similar disorders, the disease endangering life is there, and therefore the patient is entitled to Extreme Unction. Often it happens that the patient lives a long time before the disease finally takes him away. If the patient has rallied after the reception of Extreme Unction, and is again in danger of death, he may be again anointed. At times it is difficult to know whether one crisis passed and a new crisis arose, or whether it is the same lingering condition caused by the same disease. If in protracted diseases the patient recovered and felt considerably better for quite a while (about one month), moralists hold that the sick person may be anointed again. Pope Benedict XIV says that in a doubt whether the same danger continues or a new crisis has arisen, one should decide in favor of repetition of the Sacrament, since repetition in that case is more in conformity with the ancient practice of the Church.[267]

267 *De Synod. Diœc.*, lib. VIII, cap. 8, n. 4.

Conditional Extreme Unction

864. When one doubts whether the sick person has attained the use of reason, whether he is really in danger of death, or whether he is dead, Extreme Unction shall be given conditionally (**Canon 941**). This Sacrament is not to be administered to those who obstinately and impenitently persevere in open mortal sin; if this is doubtful, they may be anointed conditionally (**Canon 942**).

Here are four cases in which Extreme Unction is to be given conditionally: (1) in doubt about the use of reason; (2) in doubt about the reality of danger of death from an ailment; (3) in doubt about death itself having overtaken the person before the priest comes to anoint them; (4) in doubt about the proper disposition of the soul.

The fact that one has had the use of reason is presumed in every person after the completed seventh year of age, and that presumption holds unless there is proof to the contrary. With children under seven years of age and with mentally defective persons who have been thus afflicted from infancy, doubt may arise whether they have been capable of committing sin. The Sacrament is to be given conditionally in such cases.

If the priest doubts whether the patient is really in danger of death, the Code rules that conditional Extreme Unction is to be given. The priest usually has to be guided by the judgment of the attending physician. If he cannot find out what the physician thinks of the illness, and he regards it as dangerous, he does no wrong by anointing the patient unconditionally. If he has no idea at all of the nature of the illness and at the same time fears to go away without anointing the sick person, he should anoint him conditionally.

Doubt as to actual death may arise in those cases where the priest arrives shortly after the sick person has ceased to give any signs of life. The moment when the separation of the soul from the body takes place, is known to nobody, but it is generally held that some time intervenes between the last apparent signs of life and the actual separation of the soul from the body. In cases of previous illness and gradual weakening of the vitality, it is generally believed that the space of time between apparent death and actual dissolution is very short.

In cases of sudden collapse in accidents, strokes of apoplexy, and the like, some writers hold that even two hours after the last signs of life Extreme Unction may be given conditionally. The Roman Ritual directs that, in doubt as to the death of a person, the priest shall express the conditional anointing by the words: "Si vivis, per istam sanctam Unctionem, etc."

865. The rule of the Code that Extreme Unction is to be given conditionally in case it is doubtful whether a person who was in open mortal sin is repentant, seems at first sight to be opposed to the common teaching of theologians that a Sacrament should not be given conditionally but absolutely when there is doubt about the disposition of the soul of the recipient. However, some commentators explain those words of the Code as a lack of will and intention to receive the Sacrament, and, when interpreted in that sense, the Code agrees with the common teaching of theologians that, if there is doubt about the intention to receive the Sacrament, it can at most be administered conditionally. This acceptation of the words of Canon 942 seems reasonable. No adult who has or has had the use of reason, can receive any gift of God unless he is *willing* to receive it. Obstinate perseverance in open mortal sin excludes all will and intention to receive a Sacrament. If a person known to be in mortal sin is suddenly overtaken by illness which renders him unconscious so that he has no chance to show signs of repentance, the case stands somewhat different and falls under the next Canon.

Extreme Unction of Unconscious Persons

866. Sick persons who, while they were still conscious, asked for the Sacrament at least implicitly, or who very likely would have asked for it, may be anointed absolutely though they have lost consciousness or the use of reason (**Canon 943**).

Persons who ask for the Sacrament and subsequently lose consciousness certainly have the necessary intention to receive Extreme Unction. Proper disposition for the worthy reception of the Sacrament is likewise presumed in such cases, unless there is evidence to the contrary. If there is doubt about the worthiness of an unconscious person who, before becoming unconscious, called for the priest, Extreme Unction is to be given absolutely. The Church goes still further and admits an interpretative intention to receive Extreme Unction, for the Code states that to those also from whose life one can reasonably presume that they would have asked for the Sacrament if they had known or realized the approaching danger of death before they became unconscious, Extreme Unction is to be given unconditionally. These rules are based on a reasonable presumption in favor of the sick person. All presumption in law falls when in a particular case there is evidence to the contrary, and, if there are circumstances which clearly indicate a want of intention to receive the Sacrament, no priest may administer the Sacrament, because God does not force His grace on anyone who chooses to reject it.

Catholics who have regularly practised their religion, and who are suddenly overtaken by illness and rendered unconscious, may certainly be anointed unconditionally, for of them is true what the Code states that they would very likely ask for the Sacrament if they were able to ask for it. A difficulty arises when neglectful Catholics are suddenly overtaken by unconsciousness. In this case one must consider the character of the person. It may be that such a man or woman was not altogether opposed to conversion, but rather delayed it from day to day. In such a case, we believe the rule of Canon 942 applies that their intention to receive the Sacrament becomes doubtful, and therefore Extreme Unction may be given them conditionally. If the opposition of a neglectful Catholic to his spiritual duties was so pronounced that the priest has no reason at all for believing it likely that he would have asked for the Sacrament before he became unconscious, the priest may not give him Extreme Unction even conditionally.

OBLIGATION TO RECEIVE EXTREME UNCTION

867. Though this Sacrament is not in itself a necessary means of salvation, nobody may neglect it. Great care and solicitude must be used to have the sick persons receive Extreme Unction while they are still fully conscious (**Canon 944**).

The wording of this Canon carefully avoids a decision on the controversy among theologians concerning the obligation to receive Extreme Unction. Some theologians (including Peter

Lombard and St. Bonaventure) hold that there is a divine precept to receive Extreme Unction. Others (e.g., St. Thomas and Suarez) interpret the words of St. James (*inducat presbyteros ecclesiæ*) as an advice and exhortation to call the priest. The Council of Trent did not decide the controversy, but merely said: "Extreme Unction may not without sin be *contemned* by the faithful." [268] Canon 944 closely resembles the words of the Council of Trent. The question does not seem to be of practical importance, for one cannot imagine that a Catholic sound in mind and otherwise well disposed to receive the Sacrament of the dying would refuse to receive Extreme Unction, unless he is grossly ignorant or has a superstitious fear of the sacred anointing. It does happen that, on account of this superstitious fear, the priest in some cases cannot get the sick person to consent to the administration of Extreme Unction. Still, one cannot say that such a person despises or wilfully neglects the Sacrament; he is rather mentally affected and not altogether responsible for his refusal.

CHAPTER III

OF THE RITES AND CEREMONIES OF EXTREME UNCTION

868. The olive oil to be used in Extreme Unction must be blessed for that purpose by a bishop, or by a priest who has received the faculty for this blessing from the Apostolic See (**Canon 945**). The oil of the sick is to be kept by the pastor in a clean and properly ornamented place and in a receptacle of silver or white metal; he shall not keep it in his house except in the case provided for in Canon 735 (**Canon 946**).

It has been disputed whether the blessing of the olive oil by a bishop is so essential to the Extreme Unction that the Sacrament is invalid if administered with unblessed oil or with oil blessed by a priest who has no special faculty from the Holy See. A Declaration of the Holy Office sanctioned by Pope Paul V, January 13, 1611, condemns as rash and bordering on error (*propositionem esse temerariam et errori proximam*) the opinion that Extreme Unction can be validly conferred with oil not blessed by a bishop. Another Decree of the Holy Office approved by Pope Gregory XVI, September 14, 1842, states that a pastor

---

[268] Sessio XIV, cap. 3, *De Ministro Extr. Unct.*

cannot validly, even in a case of necessity, give Extreme Unction with oil not blessed by a bishop.[269]

The Code says that the oil must be specially blessed for the purpose of administering Extreme Unction. The Code does not state that this special blessing is required for validity, nor whether any of the holy oils blessed by a bishop may be valid *materia* in Extreme Unction. The question remains open and, therefore, if the priest has only the *oleum catechumenorum* or the *sanctum chrisma* at hand, he may annoint the sick conditionally in an urgent case, but if there is time, he must repeat, likewise conditionally, with the *oleum infirmorum*. For the blessing and preservation of the holy oils, cfr. above, nn. 629–630.

869. The anointings are to be performed with the words and in the order and manner prescribed in the rituals. In case of necessity, a single anointing of one of the senses (preferably on the forehead) with the prescribed shorter form suffices, but the obligation remains to supply the individual anointings when the danger ceases. The anointing of the loins is always to be omitted. The anointing of the feet may be omitted for any reasonable cause. Except in a case of grave necessity, the anointings are to be made by the hand of the priest without the use of any instrument (**Canon 947**).

There is an ancient disputed question among theologians whether the anointing of the five senses is essential to the Sacrament of Extreme Unction. In recent times the study of ancient rituals has revealed such a variety in the manner of anointing various parts of the body that today the great majority of theologians do not consider the anointing of the five senses essential. In the Greek Church the ritual now in use prescribes the anointing of the forehead, chin, hands and knees. In the ritual of the Latin Church the anointing of the eyes, ears, nose, mouth, hands, feet and loins is mentioned. The Code modifies the Ritual to some extent. The Church has never officially decided what anointing is absolutely essential. The theoretical question is not decided by the Church. The practical procedure in a case of necessity, which had been considered valid by some authors, was sanctioned by Decree of the Holy Office, April 26, 1906, which states that in a case of real necessity the following form (with one anointing) suffices: "Per istam sanctam unctio-

---

[269] Denziger, "Enchiridion," n. 1628; *Acta S. Sedis*, I, 41.

nem indulgeat tibi Dominus quidquid deliquisti. Amen."[270] The Code reaffirms that declaration. The question was submitted to the Holy Office whether the individual anointings which are to be given immediately after the anointing under the above form, should be given conditionally or absolutely. The Holy Office, March 9, 1917, answered that they are to be given absolutely.[271] The reason is evident, namely, the individual anointings are nothing but a continuation of the same sacred rite.

870. As the imposition of hands is not essential in Extreme Unction, it is not necessary for validity that the priest make the anointings with his own hand. The Roman Ritual, however, prescribes that the priest dip his thumb in the holy oil and make with it a sign of the cross while anointing the various parts of the body. In danger of infection from contact with the sick person—which danger must not be imaginary but real —or any other case of true necessity, the priest may anoint by means of a small brush or other instrument (for instance, a piece of cotton rolled tight).

TITLE VI

OF HOLY ORDERS

871. The Sacrament of Holy Orders by Christ's institution distinguishes in the Church the clergy from the laity for the government of the faithful and the ministry of divine worship (**Canon 948**).

In this first Canon on Orders the Code repeats a fundamental principle of Catholic faith, namely, that the distinction between the clergy and the laity is of divine origin. This is an essential constitutional element of that society which is known by the name of the Catholic Church. If Christ Himself established the system of government of the Church, no human power can change this essential feature of the organization of the Church without thereby attempting to destroy Christ's work. The governing and ministering body of the Church is to consist of men consecrated and set apart for that purpose. This governing body is further organized in various grades or degrees and

[270] *Acta S. Sedis*, XXXIX, 273.
[271] *Acta Ap. Sedis*, IX, 178.

unified in one common head, the Supreme Executive of the Church who is very appropriately called the Vicar or Representative of Christ.

The history of the Catholic Church from Apostolic times shows that the Christians were always firmly convinced of the divine institution of the governing body of the Church. Dissenters can be found in the early days of the Church as well as in later centuries, but they were a small minority, and their separation from the Church was not prompted by conscientious scruples that the Church was wrong in her belief in the divinely instituted organization. The motives for dissent and separation differed in various cases, but, even after the formation of the early sects, the separated churches kept up the selfsame organization by which an ordained clergy governed the body of separated Christians. In more recent times, mostly since the Protestant Reformation, sects were formed which denied the fundamental principle of the constitution of the Church that an ordained clergy is to govern the Church. The effects of the denial of this principle have been rather disastrous to those separated churches. It has served to create ever-increasing divisions and subdivisions into a great variety of independent denominations without a definite, well-defined creed and with antagonistic tendencies not only towards the Catholic Church but also towards all other separated groups of Christians.

The Sacramental Character of Holy Orders

872. In the following Canons, the term "major" or "sacred orders" implies the priesthood, diaconate and subdiaconate; the term "minor orders" implies the orders of acolyte, exorcist, lector and *ostiarius* (**Canon 949**). The Code does not here speak of the sacramental character of Holy Orders because that feature does not come within the scope of Canon Law but rather of dogmatic theology. It distinguishes between *major* or *sacred* Orders (under which term fall the priesthood, deaconship, subdeaconship), and *minor* Orders (those of the acolytes, exorcists, lectors and *ostiarii*, or porters).

There is only one Sacrament of Holy Orders which confers spiritual power over the Holy Eucharist and over the body of the faithful—over the real and the mystical Body of Christ, as theologians express it. There is an intimate union between the God-Man Christ and the faithful, for He is the Head of the body of the faithful, and the faithful are in the New Testament called members of the Body of Christ. The power conferred by Orders varies according to the degree to which that power is conferred in the various Orders.

HISTORICAL DEVELOPMENT OF THE VARIOUS ORDERS

873. The New Testament mentions bishops, priests and deacons frequently. There is a difficulty in deciding whether, in some of the passages of the New Testament, bishops or priests are spoken of, for at the time when those books were written no technical term existed for either of these offices; and that the Greek words *episcopus* (ἐπίσκοπος) and *presbyter* (πρεσβύτερος), strictly interpreted, are not in themselves sufficiently distinctive to denote bishops or priests exclusively, is commonly admitted by scholars of the ancient Greek language. Soon, however, these terms acquired a definite technical meaning. St. Ignatius of Antioch and St. Irenæus, disciples of the Apostles, teach very plainly that there were three degrees of sacred ministers, bishops, priests and deacons. St. Ignatius of Antioch calls the priests "the bishop's senate." St. Cyprian assures us that he did nothing without consulting the priests, and that especially before ordinations he sought the advice of the priests concerning the candidates.

Apart from some references to the priests in the writings of the early Fathers of the Church, we read very little of their activities in the first two hundred years after Christ, because the bishops themselves administered practically all the Sacraments. As the Church branched out from the cities and towns into the country districts, and Christian communities were formed at a distance from the episcopal residence, the work of the priests assumed greater proportions, and consequently we hear more of them in the history of the third and succeeding centuries.

The deacons are mentioned very frequently in the writings of the early bishops of the Church. They served at the altar, they distributed Holy Communion in the form of the Precious Blood, they received the offerings of the people during Holy

Mass, kept order in church during the services, and were the assistants of the bishop in his administrative duties.

874. The subdeaconship and the four minor orders are mentioned in a letter of Pope Cornelius to Bishop Fabius of Antioch about the year 250. There were at that time in the City of Rome, besides the bishop, forty-six priests, seven deacons, seven subdeacons, forty-two acolytes, and fifty-two exorcists, lectors and *ostiarii*. Subdeacons are mentioned at about the same time in Carthage in Africa by Bishop St. Cyprian. In the Oriental Church we find references to subdeacons by St. Athanasius, Bishop of Alexandria in Egypt, and also in the Council of Antioch (341), which gives to the *chorepiscopi* the power to ordain subdeacons. The document known under the name of the Apostolic Constitutions calls the subdeacons assistants of the deacons.

875. The four minor orders are, as we have just remarked, mentioned in the letter of Pope Cornelius. With the steady growth of the Church the duties of her ministers also increased, and the great reverence with which all matters pertaining to the sacred worship were regarded by the early Christians made them set apart even for inferior offices in the Church ministers publicly dedicated to God's service. The first of the four minor orders is that of *acolytes* (a Greek word meaning follower, disciple, or also servant). The acolytes assisted the deacon and subdeacon at the altar. The acolytes had more important functions in the early days of the Church than today. Thus, in the City of Rome, they were employed by the Pope to carry to the priests of the ancient parish churches of the city particles consecrated in the Pope's Mass as a sign of union between him and the priests who on Sunday had to say Mass in their own churches, and, therefore, could not attend the Papal Mass. In the Oriental Church the order of acolytes was not introduced.

876. The order of *exorcists* reminds us of the fact that, in the ancient heathen world, cases of diabolical possession and other forms of vexation by the evil spirits were frequent. We need only read the Gospel to learn how people suffered from the evil powers of the spirit world. The extraordinary powers which God gave to many of the early Christians (the so-called *charismata*), were evidently intended for the special needs of those times when the Christian faith had to fight against all the powers of heathenism to establish the reign of Christ over the souls of

men. Among these specially favored Christians there were many who had the power of expelling evil spirits from people tormented by them. When the Church was well established in the heathen world, these extraordinary powers ceased, but there were still many cases of diabolical possessions, and the Church ordained the exorcists for the purpose of combating the evil spirits whenever they showed their wicked influence over unfortunate human beings. In the Oriental Church the order of exorcists existed for some time, and is mentioned in the Synod of Laodicea, but later it disappeared.

877. The next minor order is that of *lectors,* or public readers of the Holy Bible in the assemblies of the Christians. After the orders of bishops, priests and deacons, this order is the oldest. The early Christian writer, Tertullian, mentions the lectors as ordained ministers together with the bishop, priest and deacon. In the writings of Bishop St. Cyprian also, the lector appears as an ordained minister. In the Oriental Church the office of the lector is mentioned in the Councils of Laodicea and Antioch. Later on, when the public reading of the Epistles and Gospels was done by subdeacons and deacons, boys were raised to the degree of lectors and formed into the *scholæ cantorum* to sing the liturgical parts of the Mass. We also find that some of the young lectors lived in the houses of the priests for the purpose of being educated by them for the priesthood.

878. Finally there is the order of *ostiarii* (or porters). It sounds very learned when the Protestant scholar Harnack looks to the *ædituus* (or porter) of the heathen temples as the inspiration for the *ostiarius* of the Christian Church. However, there is no need to suggest such an origin of this office, for it was very natural that the Christian churches should have someone to watch over the edifice used for divine worship, to keep the place closed when not in use, and to open it at the proper hour. The sacredness of the place would suggest that the porter be appointed to his charge by a sacred ceremony. In the thirteenth century the ringing of the church bell to call the people to the divine services was also made part of the duties of the *ostiarius*. In the Oriental Church the Synod of Laodicea speaks of a clerical porter, but this office was not retained by the Eastern Church.

879. The *tonsure* is not an order but a sacred ceremony by which young men are enlisted in the ranks of the clergy before

they receive any orders. In the ancient monasteries of Egypt and Syria, the shaving of the heads of the monks was quite common in the fourth century. The shaving or close cutting of the hair as a symbol of dedication to the divine service was known also in heathen times, at least in Egypt. That the monks of the East generally adopted some kind of tonsure, is well known. The first regulations in reference to the secular clergy prohibit them from letting their hair grow. In the Roman Catacombs we find pictures from the fifth century in which clerics have a tonsure. Several forms of the tonsure developed in the sixth century, the most popular being the *tonsura S. Petri* and the *tonsura S. Pauli*. The tonsure of St. Peter gained the greatest popularity in the Western Church. This tonsure consisted in shaving the entire head with the exception of a narrow wreath-like circle of hair around the head. It is still the tonsure of the Franciscans and other Friars. The large tonsure of St. Peter which the secular clergy received in ancient times dwindled down in the course of time to a very small circle shaved on the crown of the head, and this tonsure is still practised by the secular priests in Europe. In the Oriental Church the so-called tonsure of St. Paul was customary, and consisted in shaving the entire head or at least clipping the hair very short.

After the tonsure had become common among the secular clergy, it was given together with the minor orders. In the ninth century the giving of the tonsure appears as a separate ceremony. The fact that in the Middle Ages young children were frequently dedicated to the sacred ministry by their parents and entrusted to monasteries or churches for education for the clerical career, may, as some archæologists believe, have been the chief reason why the tonsure became a distinct ceremony. It was not proper to give to the young boys the minor orders the duties of which they were not yet able to fulfill, and the tonsure was given to signify that they were devoted to God's service. In the *Ordo Romanus vulgatus* is an oration entitled "Oratio ad puerum tondendum." Pope Innocent III says: "By the tonsure given according to the form of the Church the clerical status is conferred."

880. In the laws of the Code the words, "ordain," "order," "ordination," and "sacred ordination," imply besides the episcopal consecration the orders in Canon 949 (the three major and

the four minor orders) and also the first tonsure, unless the nature of the case or the context show that some particular order or orders are referred to (**Canon 950**).

CHAPTER I

OF THE MINISTER OF HOLY ORDERS

881. The bishop is the ordinary minister of sacred ordination. The extraordinary minister is that person who, though without the episcopal character, has received the power to confer some orders either by law or by special indult of the Apostolic See (**Canon 951**).

A validly consecrated bishop can validly confer all orders from the minor orders to the episcopate inclusively, though he be a heretic, schismatic, or deposed and degraded from the episcopal dignity, for he nevertheless retains the episcopal character in virtue of which he can validly ordain, provided he observes the essentials of the form of ordination and has the intention to do what the Church does in performing the sacred ordination rites. For this reason the ordinations performed by the schismatic (*Orthodox*) bishops of the Greek Church, by the Jansenist bishops in Holland, and by the Old Catholics in Germany and Switzerland are considered valid.

The doctrine maintaining the validity of ordinations performed by heretical and schismatic bishops is generally held by the Church. There have been instances in history where individual authorities did not adhere to this principle, but ordained again men who had received orders from heretical or schismatic bishops. The first instance of re-ordination of this kind is said to have taken place when John Scholasticus, Patriarch of Constantinople (564-578), ordered that a number of clerics who returned from heresy be deposed from the sacred orders received in heresy and be re-ordained in the same orders. There are also some Canons of the Council of Nicæa (325) and the Synod of Constantinople (381) which seem to declare null and void the orders conferred by heretics, but they are explained by most canonists to the effect that the canonical and juridical consequences of such orders were not admitted by the Church, and that a certain rite of reconciliation had to take place before the men ordained by heretics were permitted to exercise the functions of their orders.

The Extraordinary Minister of Ordination

882. The Code states that some orders may be conferred by a cleric who is not a consecrated bishop, and that this extraordinary power is granted either by the law of the Church or by special indult of the Apostolic See. In the present legislation of the Church Cardinals, abbots, vicars and prefects Apostolic have the power to confer the tonsure and minor orders only. It is supposed that these men are not consecrated bishops but have only the order of the priesthood. Before the Council of Trent many abbots had the power by special privilege to give also subdeaconship.

883. Whether priests have ever received from the Holy See the power to confer deaconship and the priesthood, and whether such a power can be given to a priest by the Supreme Pontiff, is an interesting question. It seems that, by the Constitution "Exposcit" of April 9, 1489, Pope Innocent VIII gave the Abbot of the Cistercians at Citeaux and four other abbots of the same Order the power to ordain deacons. Much has been written for and against the genuineness of this concession. A number of the older prominent authors affirm the privilege. Cardinal Gasparri found the document in the Vatican archives, but he states that there was no mention in it of the privilege to confer deaconship.[272]

Recently it has been asserted that in 1401 Pope Boniface IX granted to the Abbot of St. Osyth, in England, and to his successors forever, the power to confer on the professed subjects of his abbey all the orders from the minor orders to the priesthood, inclusively. In his commentary on the Code,[273] Dr. Martin Leitner relates that the English scholar, Egerton Beck, sent him copies of two documents of Pope Boniface IX—one of February 1, 1401, granting the above-mentioned privilege, and another of February 6, 1404, revoking it. His conclusion is that there is no pronouncement of the Church either in the Council of Trent or in any other dogmatic document by which it has been decreed

[272] Pohle, "Lehrbuch der Dogmatik," III, 639; Gasparri, "De Sacra Ordinatione," II, n. 798.

[273] *Handbuch des kath. Kirchenr.*, II, 117. For further information, cfr. App. III, 41, a.

that the Supreme Pontiff does not possess the power to delegate to a priest the faculty to ordain deacons or priests. Strange as this opinion may seem, it finds its counterpart in the opinion of many theologians of the Middle Ages, who held that the minor orders conferred the Sacrament of Orders, and yet they did not call in question the power of the Supreme Pontiff to delegate priests to confer these orders.

ORDINATIONS RESERVED TO THE ROMAN PONTIFF

884. It is not lawful for anyone to raise a man who has been ordained by the Roman Pontiff to higher orders without faculty from the Apostolic See (**Canon 952**).

In deference to the Holy Father, the Code rules that, if His Holiness has given some orders to a man, no inferior authority shall confer on such a man further orders without permission of the Supreme Pontiff. It rarely happens that the Holy Father himself ordains anyone, for the ordinations at Rome are conferred by the Cardinal Vicar of Rome who executes all diocesan affairs in the name of the Supreme Pontiff. The rule of Canon 952 dates from the time of Pope Innocent III. The cleric ordained by the Roman Pontiff has precedence among clerics of the same rank and order, as ruled by Canon 106, n. 3.

885. The episcopal consecration is reserved to the Roman Pontiff in such a manner that no bishop is allowed to confer episcopal consecration on anyone unless he has first ascertained that there is a Papal mandate to that effect (**Canon 953**).

In the eighth *Ordo Romanus* we read that, when a candidate had been elected by the clergy and the people of the city to fill a vacant episcopal see, the clergy accompanied the bishop-elect to Rome, and presented a written petition to the Supreme Pontiff to consecrate him. The Pontiff had the bishop-elect conducted to the archdeacon, whose duty it was to ask the candidate whether he was guilty of one of the four capital crimes (*adulterium, sodomia, bestialitas, violatio virginis Deo consecratæ*). He had to assert his innocence by oath on the book of the Holy Gospels and the relics of St. Peter. The following day the Pope assembled the bishops and priests who were in the city of Rome, together with the priests and the people who had accompanied the bishop-elect to the Eternal City. One of the priests of the city for which the new bishop was to be consecrated had to answer the Holy Father a series of questions concerning the candidate, among which were these: what orders the candidate had already received; whether he was from the diocese for which he had been elected bishop; if he belonged to another diocese, whether he had dimissorial letters; whether he had been married; what were the reasons for electing him; had simony been committed in the election. Finally, the Supreme Pontiff asked for the decree or acts of the election, and ordered them to be read. The bishop-elect was then presented to the Holy Father, who asked him the same questions as he had addressed to the priest. The Pope later questioned the bishop-elect as to what books of the Holy Scriptures were read in his church, and finally whether he knew the canons. The candidate's answer to the last question was: "Teach us, Lord." Whereupon the Holy Father recited some of the ecclesiastical laws concerning ordination, and told him that he would receive a copy of a collection of canons. The examination closed with the admonition of the Pope to the candidate to keep the fast on the day previous to his consecration.

886. It is beyond the scope of this commentary to attempt to give even a brief outline of the history of the election of bishops, because there have been many changes in the manner of election in the course of centuries, and even in the same century different forms of election have prevailed in the various countries. Generally speaking, the bishops of the ecclesiastical province had the principal part in the election, but the priests and the people of the diocese had also a voice in the election; this was the system in the Church for many centuries. The metropolitan or archbishop of the province had the right of confirming the election and of consecrating the new bishop with the assistance of two bishops of the same province.

In the twelfth century the right of electing the bishop had passed into the hands of the Cathedral Chapters in many countries of Europe. In the thirteenth century we frequently find that the Supreme Pontiff reserved to himself the right to choose the bishops for vacant dioceses. At about the same time the Roman Pontiffs reserved to themselves the right of confirmation of the election by the Cathedral Chapters and the consecration of the new bishop. The Code in Canon 329 states that the Supreme Pontiff has the right freely to nominate bishops, but it does not abolish the rights of election, nomination or presentation of bishops, where such rights have been recognized by the Church before the Code was promulgated. In the United States all bishops are nominated by the Supreme Pontiff, but in many other countries one of the other systems is in vogue. In all cases the Holy See reserves to itself the canonical institution and consecration of bishops. No bishop can be consecrated or take possession of the diocese without authorization by the Supreme Head of the Church.

887. The consecrating bishop must employ two other bishops to assist him in the consecration, unless the Apostolic See has given a dispensation in this matter (**Canon 954**).

It is generally admitted that one bishop suffices for the valid consecration of a bishop. The custom of having three bishops officiate at the consecration of a bishop originated in the early centuries of the Church. The Apostolic Constitutions prescribe that three (or at least two) bishops shall perform the consecration of a bishop. The Œcumenical Council of Nicæa (325) passed the law that all the bishops of the respective ecclesiastical province, or at least three, shall be present at the election and consecration of a bishop. Exceptions to this law were made at times by the Supreme Pontiff. Thus we read that Pope Gregory the Great allowed St. Augustine, Bishop of Canterbury in England, to consecrate bishops without the assistance of any other bishops.[274] In 1562, Pope Pius IV granted permission that in the East Indies one bishop with the assistance of two dignitaries or Canons might consecrate a bishop.

CANDIDATES TO BE ORDAINED BY THEIR OWN BISHOP

888. Everyone shall be ordained by his own proper bishop or with legitimate dimissorial letters received from him. The proper bishop shall himself ordain his own subjects, unless prevented from doing so for some good reason. He cannot, however, lawfully ordain a subject of an Oriental Rite without an Apostolic indult (**Canon 955**).

It is evident that the personal qualifications of the candidates for ordination, their responsibility to a bishop as their superior, and their proper maintenance after ordination, are of the great-

---

[274] Pohle, "Lehrbuch der Dogmatik," III, 636.

est importance for the dignity of the clerical state. Nobody is better qualified to pass judgment on these important points than the bishop in whose diocese the candidate is domiciled. While the law of the Church under proper safeguards does allow men a choice of the field of work in the sacred ministry, the general rule is that the bishop ordain his own subjects for the ministry in his diocese. If one diocese has more vocations than are necessary for the ministry of the diocese, and other sparsely settled dioceses need men for the ministry, arrangements can be made according to the rules of the Code for the transfer of clerics from one diocese to another.

889. The history of the Church shows that, as early as the end of the third century, there were laws forbidding bishops to ordain men who did not by right belong to their diocese. How did a person become a subject of a bishop for the purpose of ordination? Naturally, domicile or long-standing residence in a diocese appears among the first of the ways by which a man's diocese and bishop were determined. Baptism in a diocese is also mentioned in the early legislation as one of the ways in which one became a subject of the bishop of the place of baptism, but it does not seem certain that baptism alone sufficed.

In the time of Pope Boniface VIII birth in a diocese, or the acquisition of an ecclesiastical benefice, entitled the bishop to consider a man as his subject in the matter of ordination. A few more ways in which a bishop became competent to ordain a man were added (e.g., *familiaritas* and *incardinatio*), but domicile seems to have been the most important of all the ways by which a bishop became competent to ordain a man, and this title of domicile is the only one under which the Code allows a bishop to consider a man his subject in the matter of ordination, as will be seen in Canon 956.

The Code practically withdraws all jurisdiction in the matter of ordination from the bishops of the Latin Rite over subjects of Oriental Rites. At the present time there are many Orientals settled in the United States, and it may happen that a young man who grew up in an English-speaking parish hardly realizes that he belongs to an Oriental Rite. Still, the fact that the Orientals attend services regularly in a church of the Latin Rite, as many have to do because there are but few priests of the Oriental Rite in the United States, does not make them Catholics of the Latin Rite. Permission of the Holy See is required to change from the Oriental to the Latin Rite.

RULES DETERMINING THE PROPER BISHOP OF CANDIDATES FOR ORDINATION

890. In so far as the ordination of seculars is concerned, that bishop alone is the proper minister who is the Ordinary of the diocese in which the candidate for promotion to orders has his domicile and place of origin, or his domicile only. In the latter case, however, the candidate must declare upon oath his intention of remaining permanently in the diocese, unless he has been already incardinated in another diocese by first tonsure, or is destined for the service of another diocese as stated in Canon 969, or is a professed religious as stated in Canon 964, n. 4 (**Canon 956**). The reason for the last exception evidently is because the religious has the obligation to serve his community according to the commands of his superiors.

THE CANONICAL DOMICILE

891. It is necessary for the understanding of Canon 956 to recall the rules of the Code on the canonical domicile contained in Canons 92–95 (cfr. nn. 69–72). If both father and mother are dead, the legal guardian's domicile counts as the domicile of the minor ward. If no legal guardian was appointed for the minor children, the Code does not state whether they have any domicile at all during minority. Very likely such children cannot acquire a canonical domicile of their own until they are twenty-one years of age.[274a]

892. A few examples will illustrate who the proper bishop is in the various cases covered by Canon 956:

A man is born in diocese A and has his parental domicile in diocese A. The bishop of diocese A is the only one who can ordain the young man or allow another bishop to ordain him for diocese A.

A man is born in diocese A but has his parental domicile in diocese X. The bishop of diocese X is the only one who has the right to ordain the young man but the candidate before receiving tonsure has to take the oath that he intends to stay permanently in the diocese. If the parents of this man should afterwards establish their domicile in diocese Z before the young man is

[274a] About domicile and proper Ordinary, cfr. App. III, 41, c.

twenty-one years old, he does indeed acquire domicile in the diocese Z but, having already been incardinated by first tonsure in diocese X, the bishop of diocese X has the right to ordain the young man.

A man has his domicile in diocese A but in that diocese there are too many men who apply to the bishop to study for the priesthood. If the bishop should say that he has no vacancies in the diocese but that he would be willing to let the young man study in his seminary and in the course of time ordain him under the condition that he will arrange with another bishop to go into his diocese after ordination, we have a case contemplated in Canon 969, and referred to in Canon 956. The young man is ordained by his own proper bishop and becomes provisionally a member of the clergy of his proper bishop, but, in virtue of the previous agreement with his own bishop and with the bishop of another diocese, he is to be excardinated by the proper bishop and incardinated by the other bishop who had agreed to adopt him.

893. Finally, we have Canon 111, § 2, which states that by the reception of first tonsure the cleric is ascribed to or incardinated into the diocese for the service of which he has been promoted to the clerical state. What case is contemplated here? It is evident that only the bishop of domicile is authorized to raise a man to the clerical state, and by doing so he incorporates the young man into the clergy of his diocese. Is it possible under the law of the Code for the bishop of domicile to promote a layman to tonsure for the service of the diocese of another bishop so that by the fact of receiving tonsure the man is incardinated into the diocese of the other bishop without further letters of excardination and incardination? That seems to be the meaning of Canon 111, § 2, for unless it means that by previous agreement between the two bishops and the layman this manner of incardination by tonsure is possible, it is difficult to know what else could be meant by Canon 111. Besides, the formalities of excardination from the proper diocese and incardination into a strange diocese by letters of the respective bishops have reference to those who are already clerics and wish to change from their proper diocese to a strange diocese.

894. Some years previous to the promulgation of the Code, the Holy See issued a Decree by which the excardination and incardination of laymen could be made by letter of excardination

from the proper bishop of the layman and letter of incardination by the bishop of the strange diocese into which the layman desired to be received. This mode of transfer was sanctioned by the Holy See, because in many cases it was not easy for a young man to establish a domicile of his own in the diocese which he wished to choose as his field of labor. Under the laws of the Code it is made easier to establish a domicile, but even now it is difficult for a young man to have a domicile of his own, for he must be twenty-one years of age before he can have a domicile of his own different from that of his parents. The easier way under the Code to become incardinated into a strange diocese is the incardination by first tonsure spoken of in Canon 111. All that is required is that the proper bishop of the young man and the strange bishop agree that the young man is to get tonsure for the diocese of the strange bishop. The Committee for the Authentic Interpretation of the Code was asked whether the man who is ordained by his proper bishop for the service of another diocese becomes incardinated in the diocese for the service of which he is ordained, or whether he is incardinated in the diocese of his own proper bishop. The Committee answered: *Affirmative ad primam partem, negative ad secundam.* Therefore, he becomes incardinated in the diocese of the strange bishop by first tonsure.[275] It is evident that the agreement of the two bishops must be drawn up in writing so that there is proof of the transfer of the young man from his proper diocese to the strange diocese.

INCARDINATION INTO RELIGIOUS COMMUNITIES

895. In religious orders and congregations with perpetual vows the young man loses the proper diocese to which he previously belonged by domicile at the moment when he makes perpetual vows (cfr. Canon 585). In orders and congregations which have the privilege of exemption, the major superior of the religious organization authorizes the reception of tonsure and the various orders by issuing dimissorial letters to the candidates requesting the bishop of the diocese of the house of studies to ordain the men for the order or congregation. During the temporary vows the superior can issue dimissorial letters for tonsure and minor orders only, as Canon 964 rules. The Code does not

state whether the temporarily professed religious who receive tonsure belong, as clerics, to the diocese or to the religious community. On the one hand, the religious is not excardinated from the proper diocese which he had before entering religious life until he makes perpetual profession; on the other hand, he receives tonsure for the religious community and should become incardinated in it, just as a young man who receives tonsure for a strange diocese, after previous agreement of the two bishops, is incardinated in that strange diocese.

Ordination Rights of Ordinaries Who Are Not Bishops

896. Vicars and prefects Apostolic, and abbots and prelates *nullius* who have episcopal consecration, are regarded as equivalent to the bishops of dioceses in the matter of ordination (**Canon 957, § 1**).

If they are not consecrated bishops, they may nevertheless confer first tonsure and minor orders in the territory of their jurisdiction, but only during their term of office. They may thus ordain, not only their own secular subjects who are domiciled in their territory, but also others who have been presented to them by proper dimissorial letters of other local Ordinaries. Ordinations by the vicars and prefects Apostolic, abbots and prelates *nullius,* in excess of the powers given to them in this Canon are invalid (**Canon 957, § 2**).

The prelates mentioned in this Canon have ordinary jurisdiction over their territory just as a bishop has over his diocese. The only reason why they cannot ordain is because, as a rule, these prelates do not have episcopal orders. If they are titular bishops they have, of course, the same right and power to ordain as the bishops of regularly established dioceses.

Who Has Power to Issue Dimissorial Letters?

897. Dimissorial letters for seculars may be issued by the following persons during the time of their jurisdiction in the territory:

(1) The proper bishop after he has taken canonical possession of his diocese (cfr. Canon 334), though he has not yet been consecrated;

(2) The vicar-general by special mandate of his bishop;

(3) The vicar-capitular with the consent of the Cathedral Chapter after the episcopal see has been vacant for one year. Within the year he can give dimissorial letters to those only who must be ordained on account of a benefice which they have received or are to receive, or for reason of some certain office for which provision must be made without delay on account of the scarcity of clerics in the diocese. (In the United States and other countries which do not have cathedral chapters, the administrator of the diocese with the consent of the diocesan consultors has the same power as the vicar-capitular);

(4) Vicars and prefects Apostolic, abbots and prelates *nullius*, though they lack episcopal consecration, may issue dimissorials even for major orders.

The vicar-capitular (or diocesan administrator) shall not give dimissorial letters to those men who have been rejected by the bishop (**Canon 958**).

The superior who has the right to raise his subjects to the clerical rank should, as a rule, perform the ordination in person, as Canon 955 rules, but the same Canon allows him for a good reason to have the men ordained by another prelate. If he wants to send his men to another prelate for ordination, he must give the candidates dimissorial letters directing the candidate to present himself to the prelate mentioned in the letters, and the letters contain the request of the superior that the prelate give to the subject the order or orders specified in the dimissorials. The letters also contain a statement that the necessary preliminary requisites as to studies, character of the candidate, etc., have been investigated by the superior so that there is no canonical obstacle to his ordination.

898. The person who has the right to issue dimissorial letters for the reception of orders may confer these orders himself if he has the necessary power of orders (**Canon 959**).

The dimissorial letters shall not be issued until after all testimonial letters demanded by Canons 993–1000 have been received. If after the issuance of the dimissorial letters by the Ordinary new testimonials are required, according to the law of Canon 994, the ordaining bishop shall not ordain the candidate before he has received these letters. If the candidate has spent a sufficient length of time in the diocese of the ordaining bishop to contract an impediment (as determined by

Canon 994), the ordaining bishop shall himself directly obtain the testimonials (**Canon 960**).

The Code attaches great importance to the testimonials regarding the life and character of the young man who asks to be ordained. The proper bishop is held responsible for the men whom he ordains either in person or through another bishop. If, therefore, a bishop sends his candidates to another bishop with the request that he ordain the men for him, the law demands that the proper Ordinary himself attend to the investigations as to the character of the men, and all other requirements of law for valid and licit ordination. If through sickness or for other reasons six months or more elapsed since the issuance of the dimissorial letters, new testimonials testifying to the good conduct of the candidate during that time are required. If the candidate spent these six months or more in the diocese of the Ordinary to whom the dimissorial letters were addressed, that Ordinary himself must get the testimonials covering this space of time before he ordains the man.

To Whom May Dimissorial Letters be Addressed?

899. The dimissorial letters may be directed by the proper bishop, even by a suburbicarian Cardinal Bishop, to any bishop in communion with the Apostolic See. Without an Apostolic indult, however, the bishop cannot send a candidate to a bishop of a Rite different from that of the candidate (**Canon 961**).

The reference to the Cardinal Bishops in charge of one of the six suburbicarian bishoprics in the vicinity of Rome is made here to indicate that the former law is revoked, which law required the Cardinal Bishops to send their candidates for ordination to no other than the Cardinal Vicar of Rome, if they themselves did not perform the ordination of their own subjects. Thus Pope Alexander VII ordained by the Constitution "Apostolica Solicitudo," August 7, 1662.[276]

Any bishop who has received proper dimissorial letters may licitly ordain the subjects of another Ordinary, provided he has no reason to doubt the genuineness of the dimissorials, and provided the regulation of Canon 994 is duly observed (**Canon 962**).

900. The dimissorial letters may be limited or revoked, either by the Ordinary who issued them or by his successor in office,

[276] Gasparri, "Fontes Cod. Jur. Can.," I, 459.

but once they have been issued they do not become void by loss of office of the Ordinary who issued them (**Canon 963**).

The proper Ordinary who issues the dimissorial letters may attach conditions to the same, and the ordaining bishop is bound by these limitations. The Code is in harmony with the former law when it states that the dimissorial letters do not become void by the death or transfer of the Ordinary who issued them.

The law that nobody except the proper local Ordinary may licitly ordain a man is to be found in the Council of Nicæa (in 325), and has been insisted upon by many Decrees of the Supreme Pontiffs in the course of centuries, and the same law is retained by the Code. The Code also retains the penalty against those who ordain the subject of another Ordinary without dimissorials from the proper Ordinary of the candidate (cfr. Canon 2373, n. 1.).[276a] As was stated above, Canon 955 forbids a bishop of the Latin Rite to ordain Catholics of an Oriental Rite, though they are domiciled in his diocese, and are therefore his subjects in the matter of ordination. The penalty of Canon 2373 would not fall on a bishop who ordains his Oriental subject without permission of the Holy See, because the said Canon speaks of ordaining "alienum subditum."

Ordination of Religious

901. The following regulations shall be observed in reference to the ordination of religious:

(1) A regular abbot entrusted with the government of an abbey, though without a territory *nullius,* may confer first tonsure and minor orders under the following conditions: the candidates ordained must be his subjects by reason of at least simple profession, and the abbot must be a priest and have legitimately received the abbatial blessing. Beyond these limits all ordinations given by him are invalid, unless the abbot is a titular bishop, and every privilege to the contrary is revoked;

(2) Exempt religious cannot licitly be ordained by any bishop without the dimissorial letters of their proper major superior;

(3) The superiors can issue dimissorial letters to their subjects spoken of in Canon 574 (temporarily professed men) for first tonsure and minor orders only;

[276a] Concerning privilege to ordain without dimissorials, cfr. App. III, 41, b.

(4) The ordination of all other members of any religious organization is governed by the laws for seculars. Every indult granted to superiors to issue to the temporarily professed religious dimissorial letters for major orders is revoked (**Canon 964**).

The foregoing Canon states by whose authority the religious in the various orders and congregations are to be ordained. The old monastic orders have their autonomous abbeys, and the abbot in charge of an abbey may himself give tonsure and minor orders to his subjects, who have at least made profession of simple vows. The abbot must send his subjects who have made solemn profession and are to receive major orders to the bishop of the diocese where the abbey is located, issuing dimissorial letters to that effect. If the abbot is a titular bishop, he may, of course, himself confer major orders on his solemnly professed subjects. Regarding the abbatial blessing, cfr. Canons 322, 625 and 2402.

902. All religious orders and congregations which have the privilege of exemption have the right to issue dimissorial letters, and without these letters no bishop can licitly ordain exempt religious. The major superior of exempt religious is restricted by Canon 964 in reference to the ordination of those subjects who have not yet taken either simple or solemn perpetual vows; he may admit temporarily professed religious to the tonsure and minor orders, but the religious must have taken perpetual vows, before he can issue dimissorial letters for the reception of major orders. The ordinations of all other religious are regulated by the laws for secular candidates. Thus, if some non-exempt religious organizations have received the privilege to issue dimissorial letters to their subjects, these concessions remain except the privilege that the superior may issue dimissorial letters for major orders to religious in temporary vows.

The underlying reason why a man who has not taken perpetual vows may not be raised to major orders is that a *title* of ordination is required which would be difficult to procure in that case. Besides, by major orders the incardination into a diocese or a religious organization becomes permanent, and a religious does not lose his own diocese until he has taken perpetual vows (cfr. Canon 585). The tonsure and minor orders do not offer so much difficulty, for a religious in temporary vows who during these vows has received the tonsure and minor orders, or who had been thus promoted before he was received into the religious organization, is by dismissal reduced to the rank of a layman (cfr. Canon 648). Whatever the reason may be, the Code does not permit the exempt religious to be promoted to sacred orders by dimissorial letters of the major superior during the three years of temporary vows. Can they be promoted at all to major orders during the three years of temporary vows? It may happen that a student who enters the novitiate has nearly completed his theological course. Must he be kept waiting three years until he has taken final vows in an exempt religious organization? If he belongs to an exempt organization, it seems he cannot be promoted to major orders without permission of the Holy See, for on the one hand Canon 964 rules (in n. 2) that the exempt religious cannot licitly be ordained by any bishop without dimissorial letters of their major superior, and on the other hand forbids (in n. 3) the superior to issue dimissorial letters to temporarily professed subjects.

903. The ordination of non-exempt religious is governed by the law for seculars, and so is the ordination of novices in exempt communities and the ordination to major orders of the temporarily professed religious in any organization. Some commentators [277] hold that the major superiors of non-exempt religious bodies can give dimissorial letters to their temporarily professed subjects for tonsure and minor orders just as the exempt religious can. Whether that is the meaning of Canon 964, n. 3, is not certain, and, since the former law did not give that right to the non-exempt organizations, it seems that the opinion of the commentators denying that they have that right under the Code is preferable. Vermeersch-Creusen (*Epitome,* II, n. 241) maintains that the superiors of non-exempt religious cannot, without a special indult or privilege which is frequently conceded, give dimissorial letters to their subjects. He adds that these religious do not need the dimissorial letters, for the Ordinary of the place where the non-exempt religious have their domicile is their *episcopus proprius* for ordinations, and he can ordain them without dimissorial letters.

904. Who is the *episcopus proprius* of religious whose ordination is governed by the law for seculars? Before a religious has pronounced perpetual vows in a religious community, he

[277] Augustine, ''Commentary,'' IV, 437.

does not lose the proper diocese which he had in secular life, as may be deduced from Canon 585. Therefore, the bishop of the domicile which the religious had before he entered the community remains his proper bishop in the matter of ordination until he loses that diocese by taking perpetual vows. Unless the religious congregation has a special privilege in the matter of ordination, the bishop of domicile of the individual temporarily professed religious is the only one who has the right to ordain the temporarily professed religious, or to issue dimissorial letters to another bishop. As we saw before, temporarily professed religious may receive tonsure and minor orders but no major orders.

As to the *episcopus proprius* of perpetually professed religious whose ordination is governed by the law for seculars, the Code does not give very definite information, and it is thus difficult to point out who the *episcopus proprius* is in this case. The difficulty is accentuated by the fact that the Code states that by profession of perpetual vows one loses the proper diocese he had in secular life. If then he is to have some one *episcopus proprius* in the matter of ordination, he must acquire a domicile after taking perpetual vows. There are commentators who hold that a religious cannot have a canonical domicile, and that he does not need one.[278] That he can and must have one is apparent from Canon 964, which rules that the ordination of all other religious not excepted in this Canon is subject to the laws of ordination of seculars. It seems that a religious with perpetual vows does acquire a domicile in the religious house to which he is sent by his superiors as a member of the local community. Unless this is admitted, there is no way in which a perpetually professed religious in non-exempt communities can be ordained. This manner of acquiring a domicile on the part of the religious is upheld by P. C. Voltas, C. M. F.,[279] and Vermeersch.[280] In the former law reliable canonists like Schmalzgrüber held that a religious has a domicile in the place where the religious house is located, and to which a subject was sent by his superior to be there as *de familia*.[281]

---

[278] *Commentar. pro Religiosis*, V (1924), 167.
[279] *Commentar. pro Religiosis*, II, 307.
[280] *Periodica*, IX, 7.
[281] *Jus Eccl. Univers.*, lib. II, tit. 2, n. 14.

To What Bishop Must Religious be Sent for Ordination?

905. The bishop to whom the religious superior must address the dimissorial letters is the bishop of the diocese wherein is located the religious house to the family of which the *ordinandus* belongs (**Canon 965**). The superior may direct the dimissorial letters to another bishop only if the bishop of the diocese has given permission, or if he is of a different Rite from the *ordinandus,* or if he is absent, or if he does not have ordinations on the next following regular ordination days (as pointed out in Canon 1006), or finally if the diocese is vacant and the cleric in charge cannot ordain because he does not possess the episcopal character. In each of the above mentioned cases it is necessary that the ordaining bishop knows by an authentic statement of the episcopal curia that the superior is entitled to send his subjects to him (**Canon 966**).

The religious superiors are forbidden to send their subjects who are candidates for ordination to another religious house with a view to circumventing the bishop of the diocese, or to delay intentionally the issuing of the dimissorial letters until such a time as the bishop will either be absent or not have ordinations (**Canon 967**).

The three preceding Canons point out the bishop to whom the religious superior has to send his subjects for ordination. The bishop of the diocese where the young religious live (ordinarily, where the house of theological studies is) is to be honored and recognized by the religious superior as the bishop having by the law of the Church the right to ordain the students of the religious organization. This law of the Code is substantially taken from a Decree of the Sacred Congregation of the Council, March 15, 1596, promulgated by order of Pope Clement VIII.[282] Previously it had been disputed whether the religious superiors who had the right to issue dimissorial letters were entitled to send their subjects for ordination to any bishop of the same Rite. The Council of Trent had merely ruled that each one shall be ordained by his own proper bishop. The aforesaid Decree states that, according to the law of the Council of Trent, the religious superior must have his men ordained by the proper bishop, who is the bishop of the diocese wherein is located the

[282] Gasparri, "De Sacra Ord.," II, n. 919.

religious house in which the candidates are stationed as *de familia*. Like Pope Benedict XIV in his Constitution "Impositi," of February 27, 1747,[283] the law of the Code forbids the religious superior to change the candidates for ordination from one house to another for the purpose of depriving the bishop of the place where they were stationed of the right to ordain the men. Canon 2373, n. 4, punishes the bishop or prelate who ordains these men in violation of Canon 966 with suspension for one year from conferring orders, which suspension is incurred *ipso facto* and is reserved to the Holy See. Some religious organizations have the privilege to send their subjects for ordination to any Catholic bishop, and the Code does not revoke such privilege.

CHAPTER II

OF THE SUBJECT OF HOLY ORDERS

906. Sacred ordination can be validly received only by a baptized man. For the licit reception it is necessary that a man have the qualifications required by the laws of the sacred Canons, and that his proper Ordinary judge him thus qualified, and that he be free from any irregularity or other impediment. Men who suffer from irregularity or other impediment are forbidden to exercise the orders which they have received, though through no fault of their own they incurred an irregularity or impediment after the reception of the orders (**Canon 968**).

From Apostolic times the tradition of the Church has excluded women from becoming ordained ministers of the Church. The same practice obtained also in the Old Testament priesthood, which is the type of the Christian priesthood. Though God Himself at times gave very important rôles to women (e.g., Esther, Judith), they were excluded from the service of the altar. St. Paul's teaching in I Cor., xiv. 34, and I Tim., ii. 11, is absolutely opposed to the ministry of women in the Church. Several of the early Fathers of the Church (e.g., St. Irenæus, St. Epiphanius, St. Ambrose, St. Augustine) call it an heretical error to admit women to the office and dignity of the priesthood.[284] That an unbaptized man cannot be ordained, is abso-

---

[283] Gasparri, "Fontes Cod. Jur. Can.," II, 56.
[284] Gasparri, "De Sacra Ord.," I, n. 124.

lutely certain from the tradition of the Church, which has always taught that no other Sacrament can be received before Baptism.

907. Certain positive qualifications are required by law for ordination, and also freedom from certain defects of a physical or spiritual nature. These irregularities and impediments are enumerated in the Code in Canons 983–991. The proper Ordinary of the candidate is the judge in the matter of the requisite qualifications. The irregularities and impediments are not penalties, though some are incurred by the commission of crimes, but they are conditions imposed to safeguard the dignity of the ministry. For this reason the Code states that not only ordination but also the exercise of the orders actually received is forbidden, if, even without his own fault, the person incurs an irregularity or an impediment.

Bishop May Not Ordain More Men than He Can Usefully Employ in His Diocese

908. No secular is to be ordained unless his proper bishop judges him necessary or useful for the churches of his diocese. The bishop, however, is not forbidden to ordain a subject who is destined for the future service of another diocese: when the time for his transfer has arrived, the legal excardination from the diocese of the proper bishop and the incardination into the diocese of the strange bishop must take place (**Canon 969**).

Canon 969 supposes that the bishop educates the young men destined for service in other dioceses in his own seminary without a previous transfer of these men to other dioceses. When he ordains these men, they become members of the clergy of his diocese, but they have no right to look to their proper bishop for a position in his diocese, since, as is supposed in Canon 969, they agreed to enter some other diocese where there is need for priests. The Code does not state how one is to be destined for the future service of another diocese. It is evidently advisable that written agreements be drawn up to bind both the candidate and the strange bishop, otherwise the proper bishop can have no certainty that the men ordained for the future service of another diocese will get into another diocese. The transfer by excardination and incardination cannot be made until the candidate has received at least the tonsure. There is no provision made in the Code for the excardination and incardination of a layman.

Who Has the Right to Prohibit Reception of Orders?

909. The proper bishop or the major religious superior can deny his clerics for any canonical reason (even an occult one), and without canonical procedure, promotion (*ascensum*) to receive orders. The cleric has the right of recourse to the Holy See, and, in the case of a religious, also to the superior general, if the provincial has denied the promotion (**Canon 970**).

The Code supposes that a man has already received at least the tonsure for it speaks of clerics and of "ascent" to orders. The case of denying ordination to a man canonically qualified for the priesthood, is covered by the following Canon 971. To stop a cleric from receiving further orders, the bishop or the religious superior must have a canonical reason to justify his action. There must be lacking some requirement of the Code for the respective order, or some irregularity or impediment which perhaps had not been discovered before the candidate was admitted to tonsure. As it may happen that the candidate believes himself unjustly rejected (especially in the case of insufficient mental ability in the pursuit of studies, or of conduct and character), the Code rules that the secular candidate as well as the religious has a right of appeal to the Holy See. The religious candidate who has been denied orders by his provincial, has the choice of appealing directly to the Holy See or to the superior general of his organization. The constitutions of some of the religious organizations had a rule that their subjects were not allowed to have recourse to the Holy See, unless they had first subjected their grievance to the superior general, but direct recourse to the Holy See is open to the religious in virtue of Canon 970, unless the constitutions approved by the Holy See after the promulgation of the Code provide otherwise.

Freedom of Choice of the Clerical State

910. It is unlawful for anyone to force a man in any manner and for any reason into the clerical state, or to keep a man canonically qualified from entering the clerical state (**Canon 971**).

From the nature of the case it seems evident that nobody can have any right to force a man to enter the clerical ranks. There has been some discussion among canonists whether the bishop can oblige men to become priests in case he absolutely needs priests for his diocese, and the opinion that he can oblige them has had quite a few defenders.[285] That the bishop can force inferior clerics to receive the priesthood where the bishop thinks them necessary or useful for the service of his diocese, was stated in the old *Corpus Juris*.[286] The Code not only forbids the forcing of laymen into the clerical ranks, but also (in Canon 973) forbids bishops to force a cleric in inferior orders to receive higher orders; nor may he forbid these clerics who do not want promotion to further orders to exercise the orders received, unless they are stopped from the exercise of the orders by a canonical impediment or for other reason that the bishop judges to be grave. Under the old law, the bishop could deprive them of the right to exercise the orders received, if they did not accept the higher orders.

Canon 2352 punishes with *ipso facto* excommunication *nemini reservata* all persons (except only Cardinals) who in any manner force a man to enter the clerical state.

911. The Code declares it wrong to keep a man from the clerical state if he is canonically fit. That is a logical deduction from the Divine law. If, in contrast to the ministry of the Old Testament, Christ did not restrict the sacred ministry to any certain class of men, it follows that it should be open to any Catholic young man who is qualified for the clerical state, and is willing to devote his life to the service of God and the Church. We may not say, however, that every man has a strict right to ordination, as the bishop is free to choose whom he pleases from the qualified candidates, as the Holy See decided on the occasion of the controversy caused by Canon Lahitton's work on ''The Sacerdotal Vocation.'' [287] The Holy See approved also the further contention of Lahitton that the sacerdotal vocation does not necessarily consist in a certain internal aspiration of the candidate or in invitations of the Holy Ghost, but that nothing further is required in the candidate than that the bishop legiti-

---

285 Gasparri, ''De Sacra Ord.,'' I, n. 639.
286 *Decretum Gratiani*, cans. 3 & 4, Dist. 74.
287 Secretariate of State, July 15, 1912; *Acta Ap. Sedis*, IV, 485.

mately calls him, and that he has given proof of his proper qualifications and has the right intention in accepting the call of the bishop.[288] The possession of the proper qualifications with the bishop's call is sufficient presumption of the divine vocation.

Aspirants to the Priesthood Are to be Educated in Seminaries

912. Care must be taken that those who aspire to sacred orders are received into the seminary from tender age. All are bound to live in the seminary at least during the entire course of sacred theology, unless the Ordinary dispenses from this rule in particular cases and for grave reasons: for such dispensations he is responsible in conscience. Those who aspire to orders and lawfully live outside the seminary, shall be entrusted to a pious and capable priest who shall watch over them and train them to lead a life of piety (**Canon 972**).

This rule of the Code is in harmony with the Council of Trent which states: "Whereas the age of youth, unless it be rightly trained, is prone to follow after the pleasures of the world; and, unless it be formed from its tender years unto piety and religion before habits of vice have taken possession of the whole man, it never will perfectly and without the greatest and well-nigh special help of Almighty God persevere in ecclesiastical discipline; the Holy Synod ordains that all cathedral, metropolitan, and other churches greater than these shall be bound, each according to its means and the extent of the diocese, to maintain, to educate religiously, and to train in ecclesiastical discipline a certain number of youths of their city and diocese— or, if that number cannot be secured there, of that province— in a college to be chosen by the bishop for this purpose." [289]

Some educators claim that it is not good for a young man to be separated at too young an age from the world so that he may try his strength and learn to fight temptation. If he is guarded from temptation all the years of his youth and then, as a young priest, meets the temptations of the world for the first time, there is danger that the sudden change may prove

---

[288] Vermeersch, "Periodica," VI, 262.
[289] Sessio XXIII, cap. 18, *De Reform.* Translation of Canons and Decrees of the Council of Trent by Waterworth, 187.

dangerous to his untried strength. There is a good deal of fallacy in the reasoning of the men opposed to seminary training. In the first place, though we educate the boys and young men in the seminary, they are not so completely shut off from the world that they do not know what is going on in the world. The time of vacation, which in the United States is usually spent outside the seminary, gives the boy and the young man sufficient contact with the world to know its dangers and temptations— perhaps more than is good for them. But even if we kept our seminarians at school for the whole time, as seems to be the practice in many European seminaries, who can prove that they will be less qualified to withstand the temptations of the world than those young men who have been educated in worldly surroundings? Must one taste poison to know its deadly quality? Is there not enough of the worldly spirit drifting into our houses even with the doors shut? We may feel very secure in following the spiritual leadership of the Church; there is no more secure policy.

ARTICLE I.—OF THE REQUISITES IN THE SUBJECT OF HOLY ORDERS

913. First tonsure and orders shall be conferred on those only who have the intention of advancing to the priesthood, and who one may reasonably expect will be worthy priests. A cleric who refuses to receive higher orders cannot be forced by the bishop to do so, nor can the bishop forbid the cleric the exercise of the orders received unless he is under a canonical impediment or there is, in the judgment of the bishop, another serious reason. The bishop shall not confer major orders on any candidate unless he is certain from positive proofs that the candidate is canonically qualified; otherwise the bishop not only sins very grievously, but also exposes himself to the danger of coöperating in the sins of another (**Canon 973**).

In former times, no law obliged one who had received the tonsure or minor orders to advance to the priesthood, with the exception of the case referred to above in n. 910. He could stop at any of the orders, and serve the Church in them for his whole life. Even up to the time of the promulgation of the Code, there was no explicit law obliging clerics to advance to the priesthood, though it had become the common practice for all to advance, unless some impediment chanced to prevent the ascent to higher orders. The Council of Trent had already ruled that the bishop should receive into the seminary those boys only of whom one could reasonably foresee that they would persevere in service of God and the Church,[290] and it had also stated that, inasmuch as the minor orders are the entrance to higher orders, nobody should be admitted to these orders unless he seemed to be qualified to be raised in due time to higher orders.[291]

914. The Code demands that the candidate for Sacred Orders give *positive* proof of having the required qualifications. The Code here endorses the practically unanimous teaching of theologians that it does not suffice that there be nothing serious to be said against a candidate (a negative sort of qualification), but that the candidate has to give positive evidence of conduct, mental ability, and general fitness for sacred orders. Most writers thus hold that a candidate is not to be admitted to Sacred Orders if his fitness is doubtful, and the Code confirms this opinion by forbidding the bishop to confer Sacred Orders on anyone, unless he is morally certain that the candidate has the qualifications demanded by Canon Law.

Requisites for Licit Ordination

915. The following requisites are demanded for licit ordination:

(1) previous reception of Confirmation;

(2) moral character corresponding to the order a candidate is to receive;

(3) canonical age;

(4) due knowledge;

(5) reception of inferior orders;

(6) observance of the prescribed intervals between orders;

(7) canonical title, if major orders are in question.

In the case of episcopal consecration, the law of Canon 331 is to be observed (**Canon 974**).

The lack of Confirmation was considered an irregularity before the Code became law, now it is merely called a requisite for licit ordination.[292] The other requirements enumerated in

---

[290] Sessio XXIII, cap. 18, *De Reform.*
[291] Sessio XXIII, cap. 11, *De Reform.*
[292] Wernz, "Jus Decretal.," II, n. 119.

the preceding Canon are individually dealt with in succeeding Canons with the exception of the second requisite (character), which was sufficiently discussed in Canons 972 and 973.

Requisite Age for Major Orders

916. The subdeaconship is not to be conferred before the completion of the twenty-first, the deaconship not before the completion of the twenty-second, and the priesthood not before the completion of the twenty-fourth year (**Canon 975**).

The Council of Trent had ruled that nobody should be ordained subdeacon before the twenty-second year, deacon before the twenty-third, or priest before the twenty-fifth year.[293] It sufficed that these years had been commenced, not completed. In his Decretals,[294] Pope Clement V had demanded eighteen years for subdeaconship, twenty-two for deaconship, and twenty-five for the priesthood. The Council of Trent modified the law of the Decretals in reference to the age of subdeacon and deacon. In earlier times the age for subdeaconship had been twenty years, for deaconship twenty-five, and for the priesthood thirty years.[295] The dispensation from the requisite age for major orders is reserved to the Holy See under the general principle that an inferior authority cannot dispense with the law made by his superior.

917. The Code does not explicitly state the age at which tonsure and minor orders may be received, but Canon 976 requires that the candidate must have begun his theological studies before he can receive the tonsure. Thereby the Code changes the former law which required merely the use of reason for the reception of tonsure and minor orders. Though the Council of Trent [296] demanded that the boys know how to read and write before they may be given the tonsure, it did not explicitly change the law of Pope Boniface VIII which merely required that a child have passed the stage of infancy (seven years of age) before a bishop might grant him tonsure.[297] The *Pontificale Romanum* likewise has: "First tonsure and minor orders must

---

[293] Sessio XXIII, cap. 6, *De Reform.*
[294] *Clementinæ,* lib. I, tit. VI, *De ætate,* etc., cap. 3.
[295] *Decretum Gratiani,* Dist. 77, can. 4 (subdeacon), can. 5 (deacon), can. 7 (priest).
[296] Sessio XXIII, cap. 4, *De Reform.*
[297] *Liber Sextus,* cap. 4, *De Temporibus Ordinationum,* lib. I, tit. 9.

not be conferred before the completed seventh year of age.''
The Code puts the age much higher by demanding that a candidate for tonsure must have begun his course of theology.

COURSES OF STUDIES REQUIRED BEFORE THE VARIOUS ORDERS

918. Neither secular nor religious candidates are to be promoted to first tonsure before they have begun their theological course. Though the candidate has the age required by Canon 975, subdeaconship is not to be conferred until towards the end of the third year of theology, deaconship until after the commencement of the fourth year, and priesthood until after the first semester of the fourth year. The theological course must not have been pursued privately, but in schools destined for that purpose according to the plan of studies prescribed by Canon 1365 (**Canon 976**).[297a]

The laws concerning the requisite knowledge of candidates for the various orders have necessarily changed with the general educational standards in the various centuries. At present the law of the Church does not permit a young man who is studying for the priesthood to begin the course of theology until he has gone through the elementary course or the grammar grades, the high-school grades and the course of philosophy. Some latitude must of necessity be allowed in the studies preparatory to the philosophical and theological course, because the standards of education vary in different countries. Wherefore Canon 1364, speaking of the schools attended before the candidates begin the philosophical course, says that the studies must correspond with the general educational standards and the standing of the clergy in the respective countries where the candidates are to serve in the priesthood. The Code again insists that the course of theology at least may not be made privately, but in the seminary. Canon 972 gave the same rule and stated that the theologians must live in the seminary during the course of theology. In particular cases and for a grave reason, the Ordinary may allow a student to live outside the seminary, but that clause of Canon 972 refers only to boarding outside the seminary, not to the pursuit of the theological studies, which must be made in a school of theology and may not be made privately.

[297a] Interpretation of indult contrary to Canon 976, cfr. App. III, 41, d.

Prescribed Order and Intervals in Ordinations

919. The orders must be conferred in proper succession so that the omission of any is absolutely forbidden (**Canon 977**).

In the ordinations the intervals of time between the orders are to be observed, and during these intervals the clerics shall exercise the orders received according to the bishop's regulations.

The intervals between the first tonsure and the first minor order (ostiariate) and between the individual minor orders are left to the prudent judgment of the bishop. Unless the necessity or utility of the diocese in the bishop's judgment demands otherwise, there must be at least one year's interval between the last minor order and the subdeaconship, and at least three months between the subdeaconship and deaconship and between the deaconship and priesthood, and during these intervals all candidates should exercise the orders they hold.

Without special permission of the Roman Pontiff, minor orders and subdeaconship, or two major orders, cannot be conferred on a candidate on one and the same day, and all contrary custom is condemned. It is not even lawful to confer the tonsure and one of the minor orders, or all minor orders, on a candidate in one day (**Canon 978**, §§ 1–3).

With reference to the *ordinatio per saltum* (that is, the conferring of some higher order with the omission of the lower ones), St. Thomas Aquinas says: "In the primitive Church some men were ordained priests who had not first received the inferior orders; nevertheless, they could do all that the men in inferior orders could do because the inferior power [of orders] is comprehended in the superior power, as the senses are contained in the intellect, and the generalship in the kingship. Later on it was decreed by law of the Church that one should not receive a higher order who had not first humbled himself in lower offices."[298] There are several canons in the old *Corpus Juris* forbidding the *ordinatio per saltum*.[299] The Council of Trent, in various chapters of Session **XXIII** (notably chapter 13), insists on a gradual conferring of the orders. Canon 2374 punishes the candidate who maliciously had himself ordained *per saltum* (*ad ordines malitiose accesserit*) with *ipso facto* suspension from the order thus received.

[298] *Summa*, In 4, dist. 24, qu. 1, art. 2, qu. 5.
[299] Gasparri, "De Sacra Ord.," I, n. 495.

920. Referring to the intervals between orders, Pope Benedict XIV states that Bishop Osius proposed the law of intervals at the Council of Sardica, and that the Fathers of the Council approved of it, but desired to leave it to the judgment of the individual bishops. Popes Siricius, Cœlestine and Leo the Great decreed that candidates should remain two years in the lectorate and in the order of exorcists, five years in the order of acolytes and subdeacons, and another five years in deaconship.[300] The Council of Trent required that candidates for the tonsureship should at least understand Latin, that they should be raised gradually to the various orders with time to exercise each, and that one year after the last minor order they might be promoted to major orders; if the necessity or utility of the church demanded an exception from the rule, the bishop might use his judgment. Subdeacons should not be promoted to deaconship until a year after reception of subdeaconship. Two sacred orders might not be given to a candidate on the same day. A year's interval was to be observed between deaconship and priesthood.[301] The law of the Council of Trent on the intervals between orders was in force until the promulgation of the Code, which changes the former law in several points as is apparent from the text of Canon 978.

The rule that the bishop may not confer the tonsure and a minor order or all minor orders on a candidate on the same day, is in harmony with the former law of the Council of Trent. The Council, however, did not insist so strongly on the separation of tonsure from minor orders and of minor order from minor order, but left it to the judgment of the bishop. The Code gives the bishop no power to dispense with the rule that tonsure and a minor order, or all minor orders, may not be given to a man on the same day. The new form of faculties of the bishops does not contain the concession to dispense with this rule.

The Canonical Title

921. The canonical title for the secular clergy is the title of a benefice or, in default of a benefice, of a patrimony or pension. This title should be really secure for the whole life of the cleric

---

[300] *Institutio 18*, in *Opera Omnia Benedicti XIV*, X.
[301] Sessio XXIII, cap. 11, 13, 14, *De Reform.*

and truly sufficient for the proper maintenance of the cleric, according to the rules to be laid down by the Ordinaries in accordance with the needs and circumstances of the respective localities and times (**Canon 979**).

If the cleric in major orders should happen to lose his title, he must secure for himself another, unless his bishop judges that his proper maintenance is provided for in another way. Prelates who without an Apostolic indult have knowingly ordained or allowed the ordination of a subject to major orders without a canonical title, must assume for themselves and for their successors the obligation of furnishing the needy cleric with proper sustenance, until other provision is made for his suitable maintenance. If the bishop has ordained a candidate without a canonical title under an agreement that the one ordained shall not ask him for maintenance, such agreement is null and void (**Canon 980**).

If there is none of the titles of ordination, spoken of in Canon 979, this deficiency may be supplied by the title of "service of the diocese"—and in places subject to the Propaganda by the "title of the mission"—provided that the candidate shall promise under oath to serve the diocese (or the mission) forever, subject to the authority of the local Ordinary. The Ordinary must give to the priest who was promoted to major orders under the title of the service of the diocese or the mission a benefice or office or salary sufficient for his proper support (**Canon 981**).

To safeguard the dignity of the clerical state, the Church has from early times forbidden the so-called *absolute ordination* —that is, the ordination of a cleric who is not attached to a certain church or chapel or monastery, which he has to serve from his first assumption into the clerical ranks, and which is responsible for his support. Such a prohibition was passed by the Council of Chalcedon in 451.[302] It seems the ancient law was not strictly adhered to in the Middle Ages. In the Second Lateran Council (1179), Pope Alexander tried to stop the abuse of having men ordained deacons or priests who were not attached to any church, but wandered from place to place.[303] In 1198, Pope Innocent III extended the law of the canonical title to

---

[302] *Decretum Gratiani*, c. 1, Dist. 70.
[303] *Decretales Gregorii IX*, c. 4 *de præbendis*, lib. III, tit. 5.

subdeaconship,[304] but later ruled that clerics in minor orders who had sufficient goods of their own to maintain them might be promoted to major orders, though they had not yet obtained an ecclesiastical benefice.[305] Ordinations without a title must have become frequent again, for the Council of Trent rules: "Whereas it is unseemly that those who are enrolled in the divine ministry should beg or exercise any sordid trade to the disgrace of their order; and whereas it is well known that, in very many places and almost without any selection whatever, many persons are admitted to sacred orders who by various artifices and deceits pretend to have an ecclesiastical benefice or sufficient means for their support, this Holy Synod ordains that henceforth no secular cleric shall be promoted to sacred orders unless it be first legitimately ascertained that he is in the peaceful possession of an ecclesiastical benefice sufficient for his respectable livelihood." As to the title of patrimony, the Council recognizes it as a title of ordination to major orders, but it cautions the bishop to make certain that the patrimony or pension really exists, and that it is sufficient for a decent maintenance of the cleric.[306]

922. The Code admits the same two titles of benefice and of patrimony or pension. If a bishop ordains his subject to major orders or has him ordained by another without a canonical title, he and his successors have the obligation of furnishing the cleric with sufficient means for a respectable living until they provide for his maintenance in some other way. Besides, Canon 2373 punishes such a bishop with *ipso facto* suspension for a year from conferring orders.

Canon 981 creates another supplementary title of ordination, the title of "service of the diocese," and for missionary districts the "title of the mission." This title had already been approved for individual countries before the promulgation of the Code, but it is now approved by the common law. It is, nevertheless, only a supplementary title, the titles of benefice and patrimony or pension being the regular canonical titles. Candidates who are promoted to major orders under this supplementary title of service of the diocese (or of the mission) must before their

---

304 *Ibid.*, c. 16 *de præbendis*, lib. III, tit. 5.
305 *Ibid.*, c. 23 *de præbendis*, lib. III, tit. 5.
306 Sessio XXI, cap. 2, *De Reform.*

ordination take the oath to serve the diocese (or mission) permanently. In the United States secular candidates are usually ordained under the title of "service of the diocese," since benefices are hardly known. The irremovable pastorships in our country have all the requirements of an ecclesiastical benefice, but they are never conferred on a man who is just ordained, older and experienced men being promoted to such parishes. Ordinations under the title of patrimony or of pension are justified, in default of the title of benefice, if the candidate has sufficient goods of his own, or if he is entitled to a pension either from secular or ecclesiastical goods. The Code leaves it to the Ordinary to judge whether the goods or the pension are sufficient, and whether there is the necessary guarantee that the income is secure for the life of the candidate.

Title of Ordination for Religious

923. The canonical title for regulars is the solemn religious profession, which is called the "title of poverty." For religious with perpetual simple vows, the title of ordination is the title of *mensa communis,* or *congregationis,* or a similar one, according to their constitutions. All other religious are governed by the law for seculars also in reference to the title of ordination (**Canon 982**).

As early as the Council of Chalcedon (451), the monastery is mentioned as a title of ordination, for this Council forbids the ordination of a cleric unless he is permanently ascribed either to a church or a monastery. Neither the law of the Decretals nor the Council of Trent made any new regulations concerning the title of ordination of religious. In his Constitution "Romanus Pontifex" of October 14, 1568, Pope Pius V states that it had happened that certain men who lived after the manner of religious but had never made profession of religious vows, or had made such profession for a limited time only, and had afterwards left the religious house though they were ordained under the title of religious profession; he, therefore, forbids the ordination of those who are not professed for life.[307] Various religious organizations obtained the papal privilege to ordain to major orders men who had taken simple

307 Gasparri, "Fontes Cod. Jur. Can.," I, 229.

perpetual vows. Thus, the Society of Jesus by Constitution "Ex Sedis Apostolicæ" of Pope Gregory XIII, February 28, 1573; the Congregation of the Redemptorists by Constitution of Pope Leo XII, "Inter Religiosas," March 11, 1828; and others.[308] A Declaration of Pope Pius IX, January 20, 1860, ruled that, during the three years of simple profession previous to the taking of solemn vows, the religious could not be raised to major orders.[309] The Decree "Auctis admodum" of November 4, 1892, ruled that religious organizations with simple perpetual vows could not promote the men to major orders under the title of "mensa communis," or the title of the mission, unless the men had made profession of perpetual vows; in communities which deferred the profession of perpetual vows beyond three years, the men had to be at least three years in temporary vows.[310]

The Code recognizes for solemnly professed religious the ancient title of religious profession or title of poverty; for perpetually professed religious of simple vows the title of "mensa communis," "congregationis," or a similar title. All other religious in any religious order or congregation, in the matter of the canonical title, are subject to the law for seculars.

ARTICLE II.—OF IRREGULARITIES AND OTHER IMPEDIMENTS

924. No perpetual impediment which is called an irregularity, either from defect or from crime, is contracted unless it be one of those expressly enumerated in the following Canons (**Canon 983**). Irregularities are canonical impediments which permanently bar a man from entering the clerical state, or forbid the exercise of the orders already received. The former law as well as the Code have two distinct classes of irregularities, one arising from defect and the other from crime. The Code differs from the former law in this matter by adding to the irregularities also a list of mere impediments. No irregularity or impediment has the juridical nature of a penalty; they are impediments specifying negatively the qualifications the Church demands in her ministers for admission to the service of the altar. The positive requirements we have seen already. The

---

[308] Wernz, "Jus Decretal.," II, n. 92, p. 138, note 68.
[309] Vermeersch, "De Religiosis Inst.," II, 348.
[310] Vermeersch, op. cit., II, 435.

purpose of Canon 983 is to prevent all arbitrary exclusion of men from the ministry.

IRREGULARITIES FROM DEFECT

925. The following are irregular from defect:

(1) Illegitimates, whether the illegitimacy is public or occult, unless they have been made legitimate or have pronounced solemn religious vows;

(2) Bodily defective men who on account of debility cannot safely, or on account of deformity cannot becomingly engage in the ministry of the altar. To impede, however, the exercise of lawfully received orders, a greater defect is required, nor are actions which can be properly performed forbidden by a supervening defect;

(3) Individuals who are or have been epileptics, insane, or possessed by the devil. If, after the reception of orders, they become thus afflicted but later on are certainly rid of the affliction, the Ordinary may again allow his subjects the exercise of the orders which they had received;

(4) Bigamists, that is to say, men who contracted successively two or more valid marriages;

(5) Men who have incurred infamy of law;

(6) A judge who has pronounced a death sentence;

(7) Men who have undertaken the office of executioner and their voluntary and immediate assistants in the execution of the capital sentences (**Canon 984**).

The seven defects here specifically enumerated are the only defects that cause irregularity. In the former law the exact number of irregularities of this kind was not so well defined, nor were the precise facts which caused such irregularities. The present irregularities were all contained in the former law, and in some instances the old Canon Law helps us to understand the terms employed by the Code in describing them. A few words of explanation on each of the irregularities from defect will be helpful.

926. *Illegitimacy.*—Canon 1114 lays down the rule according to which children are to be judged legitimate.

Canon 1116 treats of the legitimation of children by subsequent marriage (cfr. below, n. 1150). Children who have been abandoned by their parents and of whose origin nothing is known need not be considered illegitimate, since illegitimacy must be certain—not merely suspected or probable—before anyone can be called irregular. Wernz remarks that at Rome and in many other dioceses a *dispensatio "ad cautelam"* is usually insisted upon when the candidate cannot with certainty prove legitimacy.[311]

In the early centuries there was no irregularity from illegitimacy, the candidates being judged on their personal qualifications. However, with the progress of civilization, certain new ideas develop, and, when the civil laws of the European nations in the Middle Ages branded illegitimate children with ignominy, the Church had to take account of the public opinion. In the Council of Poitiers (1087), sons of priests and others born of fornication were forbidden to be promoted to sacred orders, unless they either became monks or led a regular life in a canonical congregation. They might not be promoted to any prelacy. This rule became the general law of the Church by being incorporated in the official Decretals of Pope Gregory IX.[312]

927. *Bodily Defect.*—Following the example of the Old Law (Lev., xxi. 16), the Church has from early times excluded from the sacred ministry men whose bodily defects were such that they could not safely, or with becoming dignity, exercise the sacred functions. In the old *Corpus Juris* we find Decrees in reference to this subject from Pope Gelasius (494), Pope Gregory I, Alexander II, and from some local Councils, the sum total of which regulations was finally embodied in the official Decretals of Pope Gregory IX.[313] The Code does not enumerate the particular bodily defects, but gives the general principle by which the Ordinary must be guided in admitting or rejecting a candidate. The Ordinary must also in particular cases consult the decisions of the Sacred Congregation of the Council to ascertain whether a certain defect constitutes an irregularity. In doubtful cases, he may ordain the candidate or allow him to be ordained.[313a]

928. *Epilepsy, Insanity, Diabolical Possession.*—The reason for establishing these maladies as irregularities is obvious. If a man has been afflicted with any of these three maladies before

---

[311] *Jus Decretal.*, II, n. 132.

[312] *Decretales Gregorii IX*, cap. 1, lib. I, tit. 17.

[313] *Decretum Gratiani*, c. 1, D. 55; c. 10, D. 34; c. 10, D. 55; c. 3, D. 33; c. 1, C. VI, qu. 2. *Decretales Gregorii IX*, c. 4, *De clerc. ægr.*, lib. III, tit. 6.   [313a] Cfr. App. III, 41, e.

he received orders, the bishop cannot, according to the common opinion of canonists, ordain such a man though he seems at present free from the affliction. With reference to epilepsy contracted before puberty, Gasparri with other authors holds that the bishop can ordain such a one if he has been completely cured, and the cure is attested by reliable physicians.[314] If these afflictions befall a man after ordination, the Code allows the Ordinary to judge whether the cleric is freed from the affliction and to permit him to exercise the orders received.

929. *Bigamy.*—It must be noted that the Code does not use the term bigamy in its popular sense but in the technical meaning of Canon Law—namely two or more valid marriages contracted successively. St. Paul demands that those who are to be ordained deacons, priests, or bishops be married once only.[315] In the Greek Church the man who had married several times before Baptism was not considered irregular, while in the Latin Church the man who had married twice before his Baptism, or contracted one marriage before and one after Baptism, was considered irregular.[316] In 404, Pope Innocent I decreed the irregularity in the sense of the Latin Fathers. He was followed by Popes St. Leo I and St. Gregory I, and his law passed into the Decretals of Pope Gregory IX and thus became the universal law.[317] In the former law the irregularity from bigamy extended to other cases besides the one retained by the Code. The bigamy retained as irregularity by the Code was spoken of by former canonists as the *bigamia vera.* There was in the pre-Code law the *bigamia interpretativa,* which consisted of the following cases: if after a valid and consummated marriage a man attempts marriage with another woman and has sexual intercourse with her; if a man married a widow and consummated the marriage, after the widow had conjugal intercourse with the first husband; if a man married a woman and consummated the marriage, if that woman had sexual intercourse with another man before marriage; if the man had intercourse with his wife after she had committed adultery, or even if she had been forced to have intercourse by another man.

Furthermore, there was the *bigamia similitudinaria* which

314 Gasparri, ''De Sacra Ord.,'' I, n. 278.
315 I Tim., iii. 2, 12; Tit., i. 6.
316 Wernz, ''Jus. Decretal.,'' II, n. 120.
317 Cc. 4-5, *De Bigamis non ordinandis,* lib. I, tit. 21.

consisted in the attempt of a cleric in major orders or a solemnly professed religious to marry a woman; sexual intercourse with the invalidly married woman seems to have been essential to the irregularity. The Code retains this irregularity but places it under the irregularities arising from crime (cfr. Canon 985, n. 3).

Attention may be drawn to another difference between the bigamy of the former law and that of the Code. In the former law [318] a man did not incur the irregularity from *bigamia vera* (the one retained by the Code), unless he consummated both marriages, while the Code rules that it arises from two or more valid marriages consummated or not consummated.[319]

930. *Infamy of Law.*—The loss of good repute is twofold, either by law or by fact. *Regula Juris* 87 in the *Liber Sextus* of Pope Boniface VIII states: "Infamibus portæ non pateant dignitatum." The infamy of law is incurred only in those cases in which the Code attaches this penalty to the commission of an offence. The infamy of fact is defined in Canon 2293 as a loss of good reputation among good and serious-minded Catholics by reason of a crime committed or general bad character. The infamy of fact was numbered among the irregularities from crime in the former law, and the Code (Canon 987, n. 7) includes it among the simple impediments of ordination. The infamy of law is of itself a permanent impediment unless a dispensation from the Holy See is obtained; the infamy of fact lasts only as long as the bad reputation lasts. The Ordinary is to decide whether the infamy of fact has ceased.

The following crimes are punished with infamy of law either by the very commission of the crime (*ipso facto*), or by sentence of the ecclesiastical court when the Code commands the judge to impose that penalty:

(1) Formal adhesion to a non-Catholic sect on the part of any Catholic (*ipso facto*. Canon 2314, § 1, n. 3);

(2) Wilful desecration of consecrated hosts (*ipso facto*. Canon 2320);

(3) Dishonoring the bodies of the dead by theft or other crimes committed on the bodies or the graves of the deceased (*ipso facto*. Canon 2328);

---

[318] Blat, "Commentar.," III, *De Rebus*, pars I, p. 429.
[319] Gasparri, "De Sacra Ord.," I, n. 376.

(4) Personal violence committed against the Roman Pontiff, Cardinals, Papal Legates (*ipso facto.* Canon 2343, §§ 1–2);

(5) Duelling and officially witnessing the duel (*ipso facto.* Canon 2351);

(6) Attempting to contract a so-called civil marriage while one's lawful spouse is living (*ipso facto.* Canon 2356);

(7) Crimes of impurity with minors under sixteen years of age; also rape, sodomy, bawdry, incest. In these cases lay persons and clerics in minor orders incur infamy *ipso facto;* clerics in major orders are to be declared *infames,* suspended, and deprived of all offices, benefices, dignities (Canons 2357–2359).

931. *Judge Who Has Pronounced a Death Sentence.*—The sixth irregularity from defect is that incurred by a judge of a criminal court who has issued a death sentence against a criminal. The spirit of the sacred ministry is a spirit of mercy and forgiveness, wherefore the Church declares it improper to raise to the sacred ministry a person who has concurred in procuring the execution of a man, no matter how legitimate and guiltless such action may have been. From the earliest times of the Church men who had shed human blood, even apart from any guilt, were refused admission to the sacred ministry.[320]

In the former law it was generally held that all persons who participated in a criminal law suit of their own free will and contributed effectively to the conviction and the death sentence were irregular. There was some dispute as to the jury and the witnesses: Wernz held that the jury incurred the irregularity, while Gasparri demurred.[321] It seems that witnesses who were obliged to appear were generally held free from the irregularity. The Code limits the irregularity to the judge or judges who pronounce the death sentence.

932. *Executioner and His Assistants.*—The Code makes it clear that only those executioners are meant who of their own accord have sought this office. For instance, the words of the Code (*qui munus carnificis susceperint*) cannot be applied to the firing squad of soldiers who are commanded to shoot a person condemned to death by a court martial (as is done in time of war, riots and rebellions). The manner of execution (whether by

---

[320] Pope Innocent I (in 404), *Decretum Gratiani,* c. 1, D. 51; cfr. also in the same *Decretum,* cc. 4-8, D. 50; cc. 36-51, D. 51.

[321] Wernz, "Jus Decretal.," II, n. 123, note 193; Gasparri, "De Sacra Ord.," I, n. 454.

electrocution, hanging, decapitation) is of no consequence. As to the immediate and voluntary assistants, one would have to know the system of execution in each state to determine what helpers become irregular. The Code speaks of voluntary and immediate assistants. These men must, therefore, have asked for a position which obliges them to give immediate coöperation in the work of the execution. In every prison where the condemned men are kept guards are also employed, and some of these may be ordered to take the condemned man from his cell to the death chamber: they very likely do not come under the class of immediate and voluntary assistants of the executioner. Gasparri remarks that the irregularity is not contracted by the judge if, after he has pronounced the death sentence, the criminal is pardoned by the head of the state.[322] The reason is evident, for the irregularity is incurred only by reason of voluntary, immediate and effective coöperation in the application of the death penalty.

IRREGULARITIES FROM CRIME

933. The following are irregular from crime:

(1) Apostates from the faith, heretics, schismatics;

(2) Those who, except in a case of extreme necessity, permit themselves to be baptized in any manner by non-Catholics;

(3) Those who, while bound by a valid marriage bond, or by sacred orders, or by even simple and temporary religious vows, dare to attempt marriage or go through the civil formalities of marriage. Likewise, men who dare to attempt marriage with a woman bound by a valid marriage bond or by such religious vows;

(4) Men who have committed voluntary homicide or effectively procured abortion, and all their accomplices;

(5) Men who have mutilated themselves or others, or have attempted suicide;

(6) Clerics who practise the forbidden professions of medicine or surgery, if thereby the death of any person was caused;

(7) Men not ordained to major orders who perform an act of orders reserved to clerics in major orders. Also clerics who have major orders but have been forbidden to exercise these orders by a canonical penalty either personal, corrective or punitive, or local (**Canon 985**).

[322] Gasparri, ''De Sacra Ord.,'' I, n. 409.

These offences do not cause irregularity unless they are mortal sins, committed after Baptism (except in the case of Canon 985, n. 2), and unless they are external, whether public or occult (**Canon 986**).

Canons 985 and 986 are the only two Canons which deal with the crimes punished by irregularity. For the understanding of the nature of these offences it is necessary to resort to the former Canon Law and the recognized authorities on that law.

934. *Apostates, Heretics, Schismatics.*—Apostasy, heresy and schism are defined in Canon 1325. Heresy and schism are mentioned as irregularities by Pope Innocent I and Pope St. Leo the Great.[323] Apostasy from the Christian faith which, as the former commentators say, includes the crime of heresy and is even more serious than heresy, was likewise considered an irregularity.[324]

Contrary to the former law in which it seems that heretics did not incur irregularity unless they had been declared such by an ecclesiastical court or had joined an heretical sect,[325] the irregularity is now incurred though one does not join an heretical sect. From the definition of heresy given by the Code some commentators—e.g., Leitner[326] and Noldin[327]—hold that those sectarians and schismatics are not irregular, who have been born or raised from infancy in their sect, have never been convinced that the Catholic faith is the only true and authorized Church of Christ, and are thus in good faith. Vermeersch-Creusen[328] holds that they need a dispensation *ad cautelam* from the irregularity; Genicot[329] holds that the irregularity binds all persons belonging to an heretical or schismatic sect irrespective of good or bad faith, but that, if a Protestant or schismatic boy becomes a Catholic before his completed fourteenth year of age, his irregularity is doubtful.

It is difficult to decide which of these opinions is best founded on the Code. In his "Moral Theology," Vermeersch argues that heretics in good faith need a dispensation *ad cautelam* because of the presumption in the external forum that the adherents of

---

[323] Gasparri, "De Sacra Ord.," I, n. 461.
[324] Wernz, "Jus Decretal.," II, n. 141.
[325] Gasparri, "De Sacra Ord.," I, n. 466.
[326] *Handbuch des kath. Kirchenr.*, II, 163.
[327] *Theol. Moral.*, III, n. 491 (ed. 1920).
[328] *Epitome*, II, n. 257.
[329] *Institut. Theol. Moral.* (ed. 1921), II, n. 633.

heretical sects are formal heretics.[330]　Sole [331] and other commentators on the excommunication inflicted by Canon 2314 on persons guilty of heresy hold that it must be formal heresy. However, in the external forum the internal disposition can hardly be considered; otherwise the guilty person could always shield himself by asserting that he did not know his words or actions to be wrong, and it is difficult to prove or disprove anything about a person's mind or conscience.　Canon 2200 states: "When there is an external violation of the law, the evil will (*dolus*) is presumed in the external forum until the contrary is proved." It seems therefore that one must conclude from this Canon that men who profess openly a non-Catholic creed are formal heretics in the external forum, and are subject to the excommunication and also to the irregularity, unless they can prove to the bishop their good faith.　The life and character of a man and the circumstances under which he has lived may easily prove good faith in some cases.　Children of heretical parents, and also grandchildren in the paternal line, were irregular in the old law, if the parents still lived in heresy, or had died in heresy. The Code in Canon 987 makes it a simple impediment, and restricts it to the children of non-Catholics.

935. *Reception of Baptism from Non-Catholics.*—In the former Canon Law, this was called the irregularity from the abuse of Baptism.　Pope Felix III, in 487 or 488, decreed that any man baptized or rebaptized at any age elsewhere than in the Catholic Church shall not be admitted to the ecclesiastical ministry.[332] The Code supposes that a person is of an age that enables him to act independently in the matter of asking Baptism from non-Catholics, for it says, "who permitted themselves to be baptized." The *Decretum Gratiani* quotes the Third Council of Carthage (397), which ruled that children who were baptized by heretics in their infancy and later on became converts to the Catholic Church should not be excluded from the ministry of the altar, because it was not their own doing but the error of their parents.[333]　The Sacred Congregation of the Council decided, May 21, 1718, that a man who had been baptized by heretics when two years of age was not irregular.[334]

---

[330] *Theol. Moral.*, III, n. 705 (ed. 1923).
[331] *De Delictis et Pœnis*, n. 315.
[332] *Decretum Gratiani*, c. 10, C. I, qu. 7.　　　[333] *Ibid.* c. 3, C. I, qu. 4.
[334] *Canones et Decreta Conc. Trid.* (ed. Richter), 182.

936. *Attempting Certain Forbidden Marriages.*—The irregularity in its present form is an innovation introduced by the Code. Some of the cases covered by Canon 985, n. 3, were contained in the former law under the title of bigamy. The present irregularity covers four distinct classes of persons: (1) Married men who attempt a second marriage while their first lawful wife is living—a civil marriage suffices to cause the irregularity; (2) Clerics in major orders who attempt marriage (a civil ceremony suffices); (3) Men belonging to some religious organization in which they have taken either solemn, or simple, or temporary vows, who attempt, or actually contract, marriage while bound by those vows; (4) Men who attempt marriage either with a validly married woman, or with a woman bound by either solemn, or simple, or temporary vows in a religious community.

937. *Murder.*—There are many documents cited in the *Decretum Gratiani* (Dist. 50) which deal with the irregularity arising from homicide. The Decretals of Pope Gregory IX (lib. V, tit. 12, *De homicidio voluntario et casuali*) have many cases which illustrate the circumstances under which homicide is an irregularity. The Council of Trent rules: "He who intentionally kills his neighbor, by lying in wait for him, is to be taken away from the altar, because he has voluntarily committed a homicide; even though that crime have neither been proved by ordinary process of law nor be otherwise public, but is secret, such a one can never be promoted to sacred orders." [335]

Purely accidental killing of another, or killing in self-defence, is not voluntary homicide, and therefore does not cause irregularity, for the Code punishes only voluntary homicide with irregularity. There is some controversy over the *homicidium casuale-mixtum*, that is, unforeseen and unpremeditated homicide that results from the exercise of an unlawful act, or the exercise of a lawful act from which the homicide results because of gross carelessness in the exercise of that act. Some canonists hold that no distinction is to be made between an unlawful and a lawful act from which the homicide results, but rather that in both cases the neglect of proper care to avoid the killing of another is to be considered. If the neglect is gravely sinful, the killing is considered voluntary *in causa*. If due precaution was taken, or the neglect was not gravely sinful, the killing can in no wise be

[335] Sessio XIV, cap. 7, *De Reform.*

called voluntary and is therefore not punished with irregularity by the Code[336]

938. *Abortion.*—Abortion consists in the voluntary and criminal expulsion of a human *fœtus* during uterine gestation before the *fœtus* is viable. It is generally considered viable after six months of uterine gestation. Under certain circumstances delivery may be hastened after the child is viable. Again, in some cases a remedy given to save the life of the mother may cause the death or ejection of the *fœtus*. The irregularity or any other punishment of law against abortion punishes the intentional and direct attack on the life of the *fœtus*, when the act has for its set purpose the killing of the *fœtus*. While the borderland between voluntary criminal and accidental killing of the *fœtus* cannot be defined with mathematical accuracy, it would be useless to call unintentional any act which can have no other direct effect than the killing of the *fœtus*. The distinction drawn by commentators of the former law between an animate and an inanimate *fœtus* (i.e., with or without a human soul) seems to be immaterial in the Code, for it uses the term *fœtus humanus* which seems to be general enough to cover both the *fœtus animatus* and *inanimatus* (if indeed the latter exists at all in human embryology).

All accomplices in homicide and in the procuring of abortion are also made irregular by the Code. Canon 2209, §§ 1–5, enumerates the active accomplices, § 6 the negative accomplices, and § 7 the accessories after the fact (namely, persons who receive, relieve, comfort, or assist a criminal after the commission of a crime). Leitner [337] holds that the accomplices (*cooperantes*) should be interpreted in the light of the former law which declares irregular those who command, counsel or efficaciously consent, while the negative accomplices (that is, those who were bound to prevent the crime and did not do so) are not irregular. Vermeersch-Creusen [338] and Blat [339] hold the same opinion. Genicot holds that the opinion excusing the negative coöperators from irregularity is probable.[340] That opinion has in its favor the explicit rule of the former law,[341] and the fact that, strictly

[336] Wernz, "Jus Decretal.," II, n. 146; Leitner, "Handbuch des kath. Kirchenr.," II, 165.

[337] *Handbuch des kath. Kirchenr.*, II, 168.   [338] *Epitome*, II, n. 257.

[339] *Commentar.*, lib. III, 439.   [340] *Institut. Theol. Moral.*, II, n. 634.

[341] *Liber Sextus Bonifatii VIII*, c. 3, *De homicidio*, lib. V, tit. 4.

speaking, only active or positive accomplices in a crime can be called "cooperantes."

939. *Mutilation and Attempted Suicide.*—By mutilation is meant the cutting off or destruction of a limb or organ of the human body which has its own proper function. The irregularity is incurred both by mutilating one's own body and that of another. The former law speaks of mutilation in connection with homicide. Commentators generally hold that the mutilation does not cause irregularity *ex delicto,* unless the act is a mortal sin (cfr. Canon 986). Nevertheless, even when not a mortal sin, and perhaps fully justified (as in a case of necessity to save the rest of the body), the mutilation may cause an irregularity from bodily defect.

Suicide attempted deliberately and with full knowledge induces irregularity. Canon 2212 defines what is meant by an attempted crime, and Canon 2213 states when the attempted crime is not imputable. Acts of preparation alone (e.g., the purchase of poison, a gun and ammunition, even with the declared purpose of ending one's life) do not constitute an attempt; a further act tending proximately to the accomplishment of the crime is necessary to constitute attempted suicide.

Just what mutilation constitutes the irregularity is difficult to determine, for the canonists do not agree on what individual injuries constitute mutilation. The former Canon Law is very explicit in stating irregularity if a man has himself castrated, or castrates himself; whether one becomes irregular by having vasectomy performed on himself is not certain. Vermeersch-Creusen hold that the irregularity is more probable.[342] A person castrated in his infancy, or in adult age against his own will, or because of illness, is not irregular.[343]

940. *Practice of Medicine and Surgery by Clerics.*—This irregularity is discussed by commentators of the former law under the head of irregularity *ex defectu lenitatis.* The accidental killing of a person by the practice of medicine or surgery is made an irregularity by the Code on account of the violation of the prohibition to clerics to practise medicine or surgery. Both elements are essential to the irregularity—the forbidden practice and the causing of the death of a person in the course of such practice. If, therefore, a cleric has the permission from

[342] *Epitome,* II, n. 257.   [343] *Decretum Gratiani,* cc. 7, 8, 9, D. 55.

the Holy See to practise medicine or surgery, and in the course
of such practice he causes the death of a person without grave
neglect on his part, he does not become irregular. Again, if in
a case of necessity no physician or surgeon can be had and
immediate action is necessary to save a human life, a cleric who
attempts in such emergency to assist a person does not incur
irregularity, even if his act brought about the death of the
person, provided his action was not a reckless or foolish venture.

941. *Abuse of Sacred Orders.*—According to the former law
clerics and laymen who knowingly and rashly exercised in a
solemn and official manner the functions of an order which they
had not received (even of a minor order), were punished with irregularity. Also clerics exercising an order which they had indeed
received but which they were forbidden by a censure to exercise,
and clerics exercising their orders in a place which had been
nominatim placed under an interdict, incurred irregularity.[344]
In more recent times when the exercise of the functions of the
minor orders was by silent permission of the Church allowed
to laymen, irregularity was not incurred any longer by exercising these orders. The Decree of the Sacred Congregation of
the Council, May 25, 1893, had a partial irregularity against
clerics who were not yet ordained priests, and who were guilty
of conducting forbidden traffic with Mass stipends (suspension
from the orders received and incapacity for reception of further
orders). The Code recasts the law on irregularity in punishment for abuse of sacred orders as follows:

Irregular are: (1) clerics in minor orders or laymen who
exercise an act of orders reserved to clerics in major orders;
(2) priests, deacons, subdeacons who exercise an act of orders
reserved to clerics in major orders after they have been forbidden to do so by a canonical penalty, either personal, corrective or punitive, or local.

The exercise of an act of major orders by a layman or a
cleric in minor orders does not, according to many commentators,
cause irregularity unless it is exercised solemnly (that is, with
the distinctive insignia of the respective major order and in
a function which is exclusively one of major orders). This

---

[344] *Decretales Gregorii IX*, c. 1, *De clerico non ordinato ministrante*, lib.
V, tit. 28; cc. 1-3, *De clerico excommunicato, deposito vel interdicto minis-
trante*, lib. V, tit. 27. Cfr. also *Liber Sextus Bonifatii VIII*, cc. 18 & 20,
De sententia excomm., susp. et interdicti, lib. V, tit. 11.

opinion is held by Leitner,[345] Blat,[346] Vermeersch-Creusen,[347] Genicot,[348] and Noldin.[349] The opinion is based on the former law, from which the Code does not in this particular seem to differ—at least, no certain change can be deduced from Canon 985, n. 7. By Decree of the Sacred Congregation of Rites, March 14, 1906, clerics in tonsure or minor orders are permitted to act as subdeacons in Solemn High Mass, but may not wear the maniple, nor do certain acts there specified which are done by an ordained subdeacon.[350] No permission is granted to seminarians who do not have at least the tonsure to act as subdeacons without wearing the maniple, but, if they do so, they do not according to the above-stated opinion incur irregularity.

A cleric in major orders who is forbidden to exercise functions of his order by a canonical penalty in the form of either a censure or a so-called vindictive or punitive penalty, becomes irregular by the exercise of such function. The same irregularity is incurred by these men if they exercise functions reserved to major orders in a place that is under an interdict. The former law decreed the same punishment for such violation of these canonical penalties.

The canonical penalty has to be distinguished from a mere prohibition to exercise the sacred functions of major orders. Such a prohibition is not strictly speaking a penalty, because Canon 2222, § 2, states that mere prohibition to exercise the sacred ministry is not to be considered a penalty but rather one of the penal remedies and penances spoken of in Canons 2306–2313.

CONDITIONS NECESSARY TO INCUR IRREGULARITY ''EX DELICTO''

942. The offences which are punished with irregularity are thus punished only if the offence is a mortal sin committed after baptism (or in the act of baptism when one has oneself baptized by a non-Catholic), and the offence must be committed by an external grievously sinful act. It is not necessary that the external act be public, for an occult act suffices (cfr. Canon 986).

---

345 *Handbuch des kath. Kirchenr.*, II, 172.
346 *Commentarium*, III, 443.   347 *Epitome*, II, n. 257.
348 *Institut. Theol. Moral.*, II, n. 635.
349 *Theol. Moral.*, III, n. 497.   350 *Decreta Authentica.* n. 4181.

As baptism remits all sins, the irregularities cannot arise from crimes committed before baptism. If, however, the offence is such that it causes one of the defects spoken of in Canon 984 (irregularities from defect), such defect is not removed by baptism. With regard to the condition which stipulates that the offence must be grave to incur an irregularity *ex delicto,* it is generally admitted that the offence must be a mortal sin both in conscience and also in the exterior act. Wherefore, all circumstances which diminish culpability to such a degree as to prevent a mortal sin (e.g., ignorance, lack of attention or intention, fear or force) have the effect of preventing irregularity from crime. However, if the external violation of the law appears grievously sinful, Canon 2200 holds a man to be guilty unless he can establish his freedom from guilt—at least from grievous guilt—by proving that he was ignorant of the law, that he acted out of grave fear, etc.

Impediments to Ordination

943. Simply impeded from receiving orders are:

(1) Children of non-Catholics so long as the parents remain in their error;

(2) Married men;

(3) Men who hold an office or administration forbidden to clerics and of which they must give an account. The prohibition ceases when they have given up such office or administration, have rendered account of the same, and have thus become free to enter the clerical state;

(4) Slaves properly so called until they have been emancipated;

(5) Men liable for ordinary military service to which the civil law obliges them, until they have finished that service;

(6) Converts to the Church until they have been sufficiently tested according to the judgment of the Ordinary;

(7) Men who suffer from infamy of fact until they have regained their good reputation, according to the judgment of the Ordinary (**Canon 987**).

944. *Children of non-Catholics.*—Commentators on the former law discuss the question of the ordination of children of non-Catholics under the head of ''defectus famæ.'' There was

an irregularity in the former law for children of Protestant parents who either had died as Protestants, or were still living in heresy when the question of ordination came up. Even if the parents had become Catholics, but the grandfather was a Protestant who was either living at the time of ordination or had died as a Protestant, the candidate was irregular.[351] The irregularity is incurred by children born of mixed marriages, even though a dispensation for the marriage was granted by the Church. In the former law this was commonly held by canonists, and it is put beyond all doubt by the explicit declaration of the Committee for the Authentic Interpretation of the Code.[352]

The Code speaks of sons of non-Catholics generally, while the former law spoke of the irregularity of sons of heretics. Is the term "non-Catholics" to be interpreted as "heretics"? It seems that the commentators take the Code literally as meaning all those who have not been baptized in the Catholic Church or been converted to her. Vermeersch-Creusen restrict the impediment to sons of heretics.[353]

Does the impediment of ordination for sons of non-Catholics cease if the non-Catholic parent or parents have died as non-Catholics before the son is to be ordained? The Code says that the impediment lasts so long as the parents continue in their error. Leitner,[354] Genicot,[355] and Vermeersch-Creusen[356] hold that if the non-Catholic parents (or parent, if one only was a non-Catholic) are dead, the impediment ceases, though they died non-Catholics. Blat[357] and Noldin[358] hold that the impediment continues after the death of the non-Catholic parent or parents, arguing from the analogy of the irregularity of the old law for sons of heretics, which irregularity was declared by the Holy Office to affect also the sons of heretical parents who had died in heresy.[359] If the Code had retained the former law on irregularities, one would be bound (in virtue of Canon 6, n. 2) to follow the interpretation of the former law. The Code, however,

---

[351] Wernz, "Jus Decretal.," II, nn. 130, 139.
[352] Cfr. App. III, 41, f. Term "filii" of non-Catholics explained, cfr. App. III, 41, g.
[353] *Epitome*, II, n. 259.
[354] *Handbuch des kath. Kirchenr.*, II, 178.
[355] *Institut. Theol. Moral.*, II, n. 640.
[356] *Epitome*, II, n. 259.   [357] *Commentar.*, III, 446.
[358] *Theol. Moral.*, III, n. 498.
[359] December 4, 1890; *Collect. de Prop. Fide*, II, n. 1744.

has recast the whole law on irregularities and made important modifications in it. One of these changes is the irregularity of sons of heretics, which is reduced to a mere impediment and extended as an impediment to the sons of all non-Catholics. The opinion that the impediment ceases with the death of the parents is perhaps better supported by the wording of the Code (*quamdiu in suo errore permanent*), as the Code seems to speak of the living only. Besides, *in odiosis* the more benign opinion is to be followed when the case is doubtful. Raus [360] discusses the question at length, and comes to the conclusion that it is at least doubtful whether the impediment is incurred and that therefore, according to Canon 15, *leges in dubio juris non urgent*.[361]

945. *Married Men.*—In the former Canon Law, the irregularity *ex defectu libertatis* affected married men who, on account of the obligations of the marital state, are not free to receive major orders. This law is as old as the law of celibacy in the Latin Rite, and a sequence of it. The phrase ''men who have a wife,'' in which the Code formulates the impediment, needs some explanation. A man is freed from the impediment by the death of his wife, by a declaration of nullity of his marriage by a competent ecclesiastical court, by the dissolution of a non-consummated marriage by papal dispensation, or by solemn religious profession.[362]

Whether a man is free from the impediment if he has a canonical cause for permanent separation, or if his wife freely consents to his entering the clerical state, is not altogether certain. In the former law, the man who had a right to permanent separation because of the adultery of his wife was free to go into the ministry. Under the former law a wife could under the prescribed formalities and conditions give her consent to her husband's receiving major orders. The Decretals of Pope Gregory IX stated: ''No married man shall be promoted to sacred orders unless he be freed from his wife professing continency.'' [363] According to Canon 1130, the innocent party in case of adultery can separate forever from the guilty partner,

---

[360] *Linzer Quartalschrift*, LXXVI (1923), 122-127.
[361] Cfr. *Homiletic and Pastoral Review*, XXIII, 263, where we had expressed preference for the view that the impediment does not cease with the death of the non-Catholic parent.
[362] Wernz, ''Jus Decretal.,'' II, n. 127.
[363] C. 5, *De conversione conjugum*, lib. III. tit. 32.

either upon sentence of the judge or on his own initiative; the innocent party has the right to recall the guilty party to conjugal life, unless the guilty party has, with the consent of the innocent party, embraced a state contrary to marriage. Outside the case mentioned in Canon 1130, it seems that a married man cannot be raised to major orders during the life-time of his wife, for Canon 132 rules that, if a married man receives major orders without a dispensation of the Holy See, he is suspended from the exercise of the orders, though he received them in good faith.

946. *Offices and Duties Incompatible with the Clerical State.* —The law that men who are engaged in secular business, offices and positions of responsibility shall not be ordained unless they have first freed themselves from these ties so as to give themselves entirely to the sacred ministry, is very old. It is based on the words of St. Paul: "No man, being a soldier to God. entangleth himself with secular business: that he may please him to whom he hath engaged himself" (II Tim., ii. 4). Pope St. Leo the Great,[364] Pope St. Gregory the Great [365] and Pope Gelasius [366] passed ordinances against ordaining men engrossed in secular affairs and responsibilities. The Decretals of Pope Gregory IX [367] specify in greater detail the prohibition to ordain men involved in secular affairs.

Canons 137–142 point out the various secular offices and positions forbidden to the clergy. A man who desires to become a cleric must, therefore, first relinquish such offices and secular duties, and free himself from all liabilities attached to them.

947. *Slaves.*—It is a well-known fact that at the time of Christ a large proportion of the population of the then known world were held in slavery by their fellowmen. Gradually the influence of Christianity abolished slavery, and at the present time all nations which lay claim to full civilization forbid the practice of slavery. As there are, however, countries which still recognize slavery, the Code had to have some provision on this matter. The Church necessarily had to forbid the ordination of slaves. We thus find prohibitions from Pope Leo the Great (about 443) and from various Councils in the Collection of the

---

[364] *Decretum Gratiani,* c. 1, D. 54.
[365] *Decretum Gratiani,* c. 1, D. 53.   [366] *Decretum Gratiani,* c. 1, D. 55.
[367] CC. 1-4, *Ne clerici vel monachi sæcularibus negotiis se immisceant,* lib. III, tit. 50.

Decrees of Gratian.[368] The Decretals of Pope Gregory IX likewise forbid the ordination of slaves before they have obtained their liberty,[369] and this injunction is included in the Code.

948. *Men Liable for Ordinary Military Service.*—In many countries the law forces all ablebodied men of a certain age to undergo military training for a couple of years. In those countries the young men studying for the priesthood are not to be ordained until they have either been discharged as unfit for military service or have finished their term of service. Sometimes, at their first physical examination, the young men are not considered strong enough, and are ordered to present themselves again for examination a year or two later. The Committee for the Authentic Interpretation of the Code has declared that young men may not even be promoted to tonsure before they have either finished their military training or have been definitely declared unfit.[370] There are several Decrees concerning seminarians and religious serving in the army, which are of importance for those countries which have compulsory military training laws.[371]

949. *Converts.*—In conformity with the former law, the Code rules that men converted to Christ as adults shall not be taken into the ranks of the clergy immediately after their conversion. They should first prove that they are firm in the faith, and that their desire to consecrate their lives to the sacred ministry is not caused merely by a sudden impulse to make a great sacrifice in return for the grace of faith. Wherefore, the Code rules that the Ordinary is to judge whether the neophyte has been sufficiently tested in the faith. The term "neophyte" is to be understood of adult converts who have not been baptized previously in an heretical or schismatic sect, for members of

---

[368] CC. 1-9, D. 54.

[369] CC. 1-4, *De servis non ordinandis et eorum manumissione*, lib. I, tit. 18.

[370] Cfr. App. III, 41, h.

[371] On Religious and Military Service, cfr. Sacred Congregation of Religious, Jan. 1, 1911 (*Acta. Ap. Sedis*, III, 37). On clerics returning from the World War, cfr. Sacred Consist. Congregation, Oct. 25, 1918 (*ibid.*, X, 481). On irregularity of clerics in major orders going of their own accord from non-combatant service to the fighting forces, though they did not kill or mutilate anybody, cfr. Sacred Consist. Congregation, March 28, 1919 (*ibid.*, XI, 177). For Italy, concerning priests in military service, cfr. Sacred Consist. Congregation, June 16, 1916 (*ibid.*, VIII, 266). For Italy, concerning ordination of clerics in military service, cfr. Sacred Consist. Congregation, Jan. 2, 1917 (*ibid.*, IX, 15).

such sects fall under the irregularity *ex delicto* in Canon 985, n. 1. From the earliest times the law of the Church forbade the ordination of adult converts. The Council of Nicæa (325) forbade the ordination of neophytes to the priesthood and the episcopate, and the Council of Sardica (343) to the deaconship, priesthood and episcopate. By the common practice of the Church neophytes were refused admission even to the tonsure and minor orders. The canonists did not agree as to whether neophytes were permanently inhabilitated (so that, even after years of trial in the faith, they could not be admitted to the ranks of the clergy), or whether the impediment ceased when the bishop judged them sufficiently firm in the faith.[372] There were also special ordinances in the former law against the ordination of converts who had culpably delayed their baptism until they became dangerously ill and were baptized in danger of death. They are designated in the former law by the term of "clinici." [373]

The commentators on the former law discuss the question of the lack of Confirmation as an impediment to ordination. Wernz calls it an irregularity,[374] but Gasparri calls it a simple impediment.[375] In any case, the Council of Trent forbids the conferring of tonsure on those who have not yet received Confirmation.[376] The Code does not enumerate the lack of Confirmation either under the irregularities or under the impediments of ordination, but it demands (Canon 993) that all candidates for tonsure exhibit certificates of Baptism and Confirmation.

950. *Loss of Good Reputation.*—Canon Law distinguishes between the loss of good reputation incurred by law (*infamia juris*), which is of the nature of a canonical penalty attached to certain crimes specified in the Code, and the loss of good reputation by bad conduct generally (*infamia facti*). *Infamia juris* is an irregularity *ex defectu* (cfr. Canon 984, n. 5). *Infamia facti* is a simple impediment of ordination, and ceases when the bad reputation ceases; the Ordinary is to judge whether one has regained one's good reputation. *Infamia facti* is de-

---

372 Wernz, "Jus Decretal.," II, n. 118; Gasparri, "De Sacra Ord.," I, nn. 267-272; *Decretum Gratiani*, c. 1, D. 48; c. 10, D. 61; c. 5, D. 51.
373 *Decretum Gratiani*, c. unicum, D. 57.
374 Wernz, "Jus Decretal.," II, n. 119.
375 Gasparri, "De Sacra Ord.," I, nn. 479-481.
376 Sessio XXIII, cap. 4, *De Reform.*

scribed in Canon 2293 as the loss of good name in the minds of good and serious-minded Catholics through crime or bad morals. The loss may be caused by the commission of one public crime of a revolting nature or by general bad public conduct. The good reputation may be regained by sincere amendment or by removal to a place where the man is unknown, and where there is no danger that his former crime or bad life will become known. The bishop is the judge in this matter, and, if he faithfully adheres to the law which demands the testimonials on the life and conduct of the candidate for orders from his fourteenth year of age, it will not easily happen that an unworthy candidate is admitted. The commentators on the former Canon Law discuss *infamia facti* under the general heading of *Defectus famæ*.

IGNORANCE NO EXCUSE FROM IRREGULARITIES AND IMPEDIMENTS

951. Ignorance of irregularities which arise either from crime or from defect, and ignorance of impediments does not prevent one from incurring them (**Canon 988**).

Commentators on the former Canon Law were unanimous in teaching that ignorance was no excuse in the case of irregularities arising from defect, but they were divided on the question whether ignorance excused from the irregularities arising from crime.[377] The Code does not admit ignorance as an excuse even in the irregularities from crime and in the impediments to ordination. The Church makes freedom from the irregularities and impediments part of the necessary qualifications for ordination, and whenever a man lacks any of these (either through his own fault, by mere accident, or through the malice of others), he cannot be ordained. While ignorance of the irregularity attached to the commission of certain crimes is not admitted as an excuse from the irregularity, we have pointed out before that the irregularities from crime do not take effect unless they were grave external sins, either public or occult, committed after Baptism. The excuses that the law admits in determining whether a grave offence was committed in the external forum, may be applied to offences to which irregularity from crime is attached (cfr. above, n. 942).

377 Gasparri, "De Sacra Ord.," I, nn. 203-205.

MULTIPLICATION OF IRREGULARITIES AND IMPEDIMENTS

952. Irregularities and impediments are multiplied in so far as they arise from different causes. The repetition of one and the same cause does not multiply an irregularity, except in the case of that arising from voluntary homicide (**Canon 989**).

This rule is important in applications for dispensations from irregularities and impediments. One must know whether the candidate who needs a dispensation is under one or more irregularities or impediments. The application of the rule of the Code is fairly clear. The various defects and crimes and impediments and their causes are clearly stated in the Code. A few examples will illustrate the multiplication of irregularities: A Catholic who is guilty of heresy or apostasy and joins a non-Catholic sect, incurs two irregularities—one by the crime of heresy or apostasy and another from defect by reason of the *infamia juris* attached to the offence of joining an heretical sect. Again, a candidate may suffer from some bodily defect, and also from some mental defect, and thus be under a twofold irregularity from defect. The repetition of the same crime (with the exception of homicide) does not multiply the irregularity. Thus, one may have been guilty of lapsing into heresy repeatedly, still it is only one irregularity; a priest who was suspended, may have repeatedly said Mass, heard confessions, etc. (without the necessity admitted in law), and yet he incurs only one irregularity, for the cause of it is one and the same (the forbidden exercise of sacred orders). In the case of voluntary homicide—the killing of a human being after birth or before birth (abortion)—the Code follows the former law, and is more severe than in the case of irregularities caused by any other crime. Vermeersch-Creusen holds that the multiplication of the irregularity by repetition of the same cause applies only to homicide strictly so-called, and not to abortion, so that several abortions procured or coöperated in by the same man does not multiply the irregularity.[378] If we understand Blat correctly, he seems to hold that repeated crimes of abortion effect a multiplication of the irregularity.[379] Genicot[380] inclines to the latter opinion, and Leitner[381] likewise seems to hold abortion equivalent to

[378] *Epitome,* II, n. 255.   [379] *Commentar.,* lib. III, 452.
[380] *Institut. Theol. Moral.,* II, n. 631.
[381] *Handbuch des kath. Kirchenr.,* II, 148.

homicide in this connexion. The opinion which holds abortion equivalent to homicide seems preferable, because it is in harmony with the former law.[382]

DISPENSATION FROM IRREGULARITIES

953. Ordinaries, acting either in person or by delegate, may dispense their subjects from all irregularities arising from an occult crime, with the exception of the irregularity arising from Canon 985, n. 4 (voluntary homicide or abortion), and other crimes carried into a court of law. The same faculty is given to all confessors in occult cases of unusual urgency, when the Ordinary cannot be reached and there is imminent danger of grave harm or of infamy. This faculty, however, is granted only for the purpose of allowing the penitent to exercise licitly the orders already received (**Canon 990**).

The power of dispensation is given to all *Ordinaries*—that is, bishops of dioceses, vicars and prefects Apostolic, prelates *nullius,* and major religious superiors of exempt religious. The faculty here given by the Code is identical with the faculty granted by the Council of Trent to bishops, but the Code extends it to all Ordinaries.[383] The offence which causes the irregularity must be *occult*. An occult offence is accordingly a crime which is not public (Canon 2197, n. 4). Canon 2197, n. 1, defines a *public* offence as one which has already been divulged, or which one may prudently judge can and must easily become publicly known. That definition leaves open the controversy as what amount of publicity is required to make an offence public. It seems to be fairly certain from the opinion of canonists that, if an offence is known only to two or three persons, it can be considered occult. Also if five or six in a smaller town (or seven or eight in a larger town or city) know of the offence, it still can be considered occult. It is presumed that these persons have not spread the knowledge of the crime.[384]

The power of the Ordinaries does not extend to irregularities

---

[382] *Decretales Gregorii IX,* c. 20, *De Homicidio etc.,* lib. V, tit. 12.

[383] Sessio XXIV, cap. 6, *De Reform.*

[384] Gasparri, ''De Matrimonio,'' I, n. 260. Leitner (*Handbuch des kath. Kirchenr.*) applies to the term ''occult'' the meaning given by the Code to an occult marriage impediment. This narrow interpretation is unnecessary, for in the irregularities from crime the law as to occult and public crime is to be consulted.

caused by homicide or abortion, nor to irregularities caused by other crimes, if the prosecution of the culprit for these crimes has been begun in a secular or ecclesiastical court. In the ecclesiastical court the case is before the court as soon as the judge has legitimately cited the guilty party at the instance of the *Promotor Justitiæ*, who presented the indictment. In the secular court in the United States the criminal action is not before the court until the grand jury has returned the indictment.

954. Ordinaries of exempt religious can dispense their subjects from all irregularities in virtue of privileges granted either directly or by communication; in the case of voluntary homicide, the dispensation from the irregularity is valid in the internal forum only. Every year, on the Monday after the first Sunday in Lent, the local superiors of exempt religious can either in person or through confessors appointed by them dispense their subjects, including novices, from any irregularity contracted for any reason.[385]

Vermeersch-Creusen discuss the Decree of the Sacred Consistorial Congregation, March 28, 1919, which declared that clerics in major orders who during the World War left the noncombatant service of their own accord and joined the fighting forces need a dispensation from the Holy See to be entitled to exercise the sacred orders, even though they did not kill or mutilate anybody. The authors seem to be correct in the assertion that under the law of the Code these men are not irregular, and that therefore this Decree is a special regulation for that particular case.[386]

955. Confessors have the faculty to dispense from the same irregularities as the Ordinaries under the following conditions: (1) that the case is occult; (2) that it is urgent so that the irregular cleric cannot abstain from the exercise of the sacred functions without immediate danger of serious damage or loss of good reputation, and there is no time to have recourse to the Ordinary; (3) the dispensation can be given only for the licit exercise of the orders received. The confessor cannot, for instance, dispense a deacon so that he can receive the priesthood, but he can dispense a deacon under the above circumstances so that he may legitimately exercise the deacon's functions. The confessor's jurisdiction is necessarily restricted to the internal

[385] Vermeersch-Creusen, "Epitome," II, n. 261.   [386] *loc. cit.*

forum, but he may dispense not only in the act of sacramental confession but also outside of confession, for Canon 202 rules that, when power is conferred for the internal forum without restricting it to the sacramental forum, it can be used both in and outside confession.

By a privilege conceded to the Order of the Minimi by Pope Sixtus IV and confirmed by Pope Julius II, the confessors of that Order, and the confessors of other religious organizations who had by the communication of privileges obtained the same concession, can dispense with those irregularities from which the bishops can dispense.[387] By communication of privileges the confessors of the religious organizations who had that privilege before the Code, can at the time of missions and retreats dispense in sacramental confession from all occult irregularities. The original concession was given to the Passionist Fathers by Pope Pius VI, May 27, 1789.[388]

Application for Dispensation from Irregularities and Impediments

956. In the petition for a dispensation all irregularities and impediments must be indicated. If they are not all indicated, a general dispensation is valid for those omitted in good faith, with the exception of the irregularities reserved in Canon 990 (viz., voluntary homicide and crimes brought before a court), but not for those concealed in bad faith. In the case of the irregularity from voluntary homicide, the number of crimes must be also stated under pain of invalidity of the dispensation conceded. A general dispensation for the reception of orders is good also for major orders, and the person dispensed may obtain non-consistorial benefices—even those to which the care of souls is attached—but he cannot be made a Cardinal, a bishop, an abbot or prelate *nullius,* or a major superior in clerical exempt organizations of religious. A dispensation granted in the internal non-sacramental forum shall be given in writing, and a record of it should be kept in the secret records of the diocesan Curia (**Canon 991**).

A general dispensation, by which seems to be meant a dispensation from all irregularities, has the special effect that it

---

[387] Blat, ''Commentar.,'' III, 456.
[388] Lyszczarczyk, **O. F. M.,** ''Comp. Privileg. Regular.,'' 147.

covers also those irregularities which were omitted in the petition in good faith, with the exception of the irregularity from homicide and from crimes brought before a court.

Dispensation from irregularities incurred by priests through the commission of an offence to which irregularity is attached is granted by the Sacred Congregation of the Council. Dispensations from irregularities *ex defectu* are reserved to the Sacred Congregation of the Sacraments.[389] The Sacred Penitentiary is empowered to grant dispensation from irregularities arising from occult crimes.

CHAPTER III

OF THE THINGS WHICH SHOULD PRECEDE HOLY ORDERS

957. All candidates for ordination, both secular and religious, must either in person or through others manifest to their bishop (or to the representative of the bishop in this matter) at an opportune time their desire to be ordained (**Canon 992**).

The Council of Trent [390] had a similar provision prescribing that the candidates for major orders approach the bishop one month before ordination to petition him formally for admission to major orders. Canon 992 differs from the law of the Council of Trent in so far as it requires candidates for any orders to announce to the bishop their intention of receiving orders. That declaration may be made through others (e.g., the rector of the seminary).

TESTIMONIAL LETTERS

958. The candidates for ordination, both secular and religious (who in the matter of ordination are governed by the law for seculars), are to procure the following testimonials:

(1) Testimony of the last ordination or, if they are to receive the first tonsure, certificates of Baptism and Confirmation;

(2) Testimony of the completion of the required courses of studies, as they are demanded for the various orders by Canon 976;

(3) Testimonial of the rector of the seminary as to the good conduct of the candidates. If, in an exceptional case, a candi-

389 S. Consist Congr., Nov. 28, 1911; *Acta Ap. Sedis*, III, 658.
390 Sessio XXIII, cap. 5, *De Reform.*

date has been permitted to live outside the seminary and has (as Canon 972 demands) been placed under the spiritual direction of a priest designated by the bishop, testimonials of good conduct must be obtained from that priest;

(4) Testimonial letters of the Ordinaries of the dioceses in which the candidate has lived so long that he might have contracted a canonical impediment (cfr. below Canon 994) ;

(5) Testimonial letters of the major religious superior, if the candidate is a member of a religious organization (**Canon 993**).

Special Rules about Testimonials from Various Dioceses on Account of Temporary Residence

959. The time in which a candidate for ordination might have contracted a canonical impediment is, as a rule, three months for men in military service, and for others six months, after the age of puberty. The ordaining bishop, however, if he judges it advisable, may demand testimonials also for a shorter period of residence, and even for the time prior to puberty.

If the local Ordinary does not have sufficient information about the candidate, either from his own personal knowledge or from the testimony of others, and thus cannot testify that the candidate during the stay in his diocese contracted no canonical impediment; or if the candidate has lived in so many dioceses that it becomes impossible or too difficult to get all the testimonials, the Ordinary shall at least make the candidate state under oath whether or not he has contracted a canonical impediment.

If, after the testimonials were obtained and before his ordination, the candidate has again lived for three or six months respectively in the diocese from which testimonials were obtained, new testimonials of the local Ordinary are necessary (**Canon 994**).

The testimonials spoken of in the preceding Canon are, as a rule, necessary once only, before the reception of the tonsure, for usually the student after reception of the tonsure stays in the diocese of his proper bishop. If he has been in another diocese for six months, or three months in case of military service, he needs the testimonials before he is further promoted. The oath, required from a candidate who has lived in many dioceses, is called *juramentum suppletorium,* because it supplements the information obtained by inquiry.

TESTIMONIALS TO BE ISSUED BY RELIGIOUS SUPERIORS

960. In his dimissorial letters, the religious superior must testify not only that the candidates have made the religious profession and are members of the community of the religious house in the diocese where they are to be ordained, but also that they have completed the required courses of study and possess the other qualifications demanded by Canon Law. Having received these dimissorials, the bishop does not need any other testimonials (**Canon 995**).

The ordination of exempt religious has its own special rules in reference to the dimissorials and the testimonials. If a religious organization has neither the privilege of exemption nor special concessions concerning the ordination of its subjects, it is governed in the matter of ordination by the laws for seculars (cfr. above, n. 899). Canon 995 refers only to religious bodies which have the privilege to issue dimissorial letters (cfr. Canons 964–967, nn. 901–905).

Blat holds that the superiors of religious organizations which are subject to the law for seculars in the matter of ordination need not get testimonials for their candidates from the dioceses where they have stayed six months after puberty (three months, if in the military service) before they joined the religious community, but only from the dioceses in which they stayed six or more months after joining the community. His reason is that the testimonials had to be obtained before they entered, and need not be obtained again. However, the testimonials required by Canon 544 for all men who join a religious community are quite different from the testimonials for ordination required by Canon 994, as can be easily seen from the wording of the two Canons.[391]

EXAMINATION OF CANDIDATES BEFORE ORDINATION

961. All candidates, both secular and religious, must undergo a careful examination before ordination with reference to the order which they are to receive. Candidates for major orders must make the examination also in the respective courses of

391 *Commentar.,* lib. III, 466.

sacred theology which are required before reception of the various sacred orders. The bishops have the right to determine the method of the examination, to appoint the examiners and to prescribe the subjects of sacred theology in which the examination is to be made (**Canon 996**).

The Council of Trent [392] had substantially the same law about the examination of all candidates, secular and religious. The bishop may, if he pleases, have the religious candidates examined by a board of examiners from the religious community, in which case the board acts as delegate of the bishop. The Code continues:

This examination is to be conducted for both seculars and religious under the authority of the local Ordinary, who by law has the right to ordain or to issue dimissorials requesting another bishop to ordain his subjects. For a good reason this Ordinary may also commit the examination to the ordaining bishop, if the latter is willing to assume that burden (**Canon 997, § 1**).

The bishop who ordains non-subjects (either secular or religious) who are sent to him with legitimate dimissorials in which it is stated that the candidates have been duly examined as demanded by § 1 of this Canon, and have been judged qualified, may accept this attestation as sufficient, but he is not obliged to do so. If he in conscience believes that a candidate is not suitable, he should not promote him (**Canon 997, § 2**).

In the chapter cited above, the Council of Trent ruled that the candidates of religious orders had to be of the same age as required for secular candidates, and that they should not be ordained without a careful examination on the part of the bishop; all contrary privileges were revoked by the Council. On September 22, 1582, the Society of Jesus obtained from Pope Gregory XIII the privilege which exempts their clerics from examination by the bishop. This privilege was not extended to other religious organizations by the communication of privileges. Lehmkuhl [393] states that the privilege of some religious organizations to have their candidates ordained by any Catholic bishop has in more recent times been considered to grant exemption from the examination before the bishop. The Code has no provision

---

[392] Sessio XXIII, cap. 12, *De Reform.*
[393] *Theol. Moral.*, II, n. 601.

about this examination in the cases enumerated in Canon 966, wherein the religious superior is entitled to have his candidates ordained by other than the bishop of the diocese where the candidates are domiciled. Perhaps here can be applied what Lehmkuhl says about the privilege to send the men to any bishop for ordination. The bishop who is requested by the legitimate authorities (the proper Ordinary or religious superior) to ordain non-subjects, has always the right to examine the candidates, as is plain from Canon 997. If the proper Ordinary or the religious superior object to his doing so, their only resort is to send their subjects to another bishop.

Publication of Names of Candidates for Major Orders in Their Parish Church

962. The names of the men to be promoted to any major order, with the exception of religious who have taken either solemn or simple perpetual vows, shall be publicly announced in the respective parish church of each candidate. The Ordinary, however, may use his judgment in either dispensing with this publication, or ordering it to be made also in other churches besides the proper parish churches of the candidates, or substituting for the publication an announcement posted at the door of the parish church and left there for several days among which there must be at least one feast-day. The publication is to be made on a Sunday or a holyday of obligation in church and during Mass, or on another day and at another hour when there is a large gathering of the faithful in church. If the candidates have not been ordained within six months after the publication, it should be repeated, unless the Ordinary judges otherwise (**Canon 998**).

The Council of Trent demanded the publication of the names of the candidates for any major order in their respective parish churches,[394] but in many dioceses this law had in the course of time fallen into disuse. The proper parish of a candidate is, as a rule, the parish in which his parents have a domicile or quasi-domicile, for usually the young man has not been in a position to acquire a domicile of his own, and during the course of studies he certainly retains the domicile of his parents—or of his legal

---

[394] Sessio XXIII, cap. 5, *De Reform.*

guardian, if both father and mother died before he reached the age of majority. However, he may also have a parish of his own, for Canon 93 states that a minor, after the years of infancy, can acquire a quasi-domicile of his own, and a quasi-domicile suffices to acquire a proper parish. In any case, there is no difficulty here since the Ordinary can dispense with the publication of the names.

963. All the faithful are bound by obligation to make known to the Ordinary or to the pastor before the ordination any impediment to sacred orders of which they have knowledge (**Canon 999**). The bishop should order the pastor who makes the publication—and also other priests, if it seems expedient to him—to inquire from trustworthy persons about the life and character of the candidates of ordination, and to transmit to the chancery office a report of the publication and investigation. The same Ordinary shall not neglect, if it seems to him necessary or useful, to make further investigations even privately (**Canon 1000**).

Retreat before Ordination

964. Candidates for promotion to first tonsure and minor orders shall make the Spiritual Exercises for at least three full days; candidates for major orders for at least six full days. If the candidates are to receive several major orders within six months, the Ordinary may reduce the days of retreat before deaconship to not less than three full days. If, after the retreat, the ordination is for any reason delayed for more than six months, the retreat shall be repeated; otherwise, it is left to the judgment of the Ordinary whether or not the retreat is to be repeated.

The religious shall make the spiritual exercises in their own house, or in any other appointed by their superior. The secular candidates shall make the exercises in the seminary or in some other ecclesiastical or religious house designated by the bishop. The superior of the house where the retreat is made shall testify to the bishop that the candidates made the retreat. In case of candidates from religious communities, their proper major superior shall supply this testimony (**Canon 1001**).

For the first time in the history of ecclesiastical legislation, the Code imposes by a general law the duty of making a retreat before ordination. The practice of preparing in a special manner by spiritual exercises for the reception of the various orders (at least the major orders) is not new in the Church. In the City of Rome there was a law from the year 1662 that the candidates for major orders prepare themselves by a retreat, and that law was extended to all the dioceses of Italy in 1682. The Holy See urged the bishops of other nations to insist likewise on a retreat before the reception of the major orders, and, long before the present law of the Code was enacted, it had practically become a universal custom to make a retreat before the reception of major orders.[395]

CHAPTER IV

OF THE RITES AND CEREMONIES OF SACRED ORDINATION

965. In conferring any of the orders, the minister must observe accurately the proper rites as described in the *Pontificale Romanum* and other liturgical books approved by the Church, and it is not lawful for any reason to omit these rites or invert their order (**Canon 1002**).

In the course of centuries the sacred rites and ceremonies observed in the conferring of the various orders have grown from their original simple forms to the present elaborate functions, which have become fixed law in virtue of the official character of the *Pontificale Romanum,* wherein are contained all the prayers and ceremonies of ordination. In 1596 Pope Clement VIII published the official *Pontificale Romanum,* and commanded that it be used exclusively in the Church of the Latin Rite in the ordination ceremonies and in other sacred functions which it described. The Code insists that the sacred rites of the *Pontificale Romanum* be followed with absolute accuracy. This is of the greatest importance because the essential rites of the various orders are so entwined with other sacred ceremonies that it would be dangerous to omit ceremonies indiscriminately, and thus perhaps fail to employ even the essential ones necessary for validity of the orders.

966. The Mass of ordination or episcopal consecration must always be celebrated by the actual minister of the orders or consecration (**Canon 1003**).

The major orders and the episcopal consecration must be con-

[395] Gasparri, ''De Sacra Ord., II, nn. 762-768.

ferred during the Ordination Mass. This Mass must be said by the bishop who confers the orders or consecrates a bishop, and the Holy See has always refused to grant permission to have the Mass said by another celebrant, even when a bishop on account of old age or poor health was not able to say the Ordination Mass.[396]

Clerics of Oriental Rites Joining Latin Rite

967. If a man has received some orders according to an Oriental Rite and afterwards obtains an indult from the Holy See to receive higher orders in the Latin Rite, he must first receive those orders according to the Latin Rite which he has not received in the Oriental Rite (**Canon 1004**).

The orders of *ostiarius*, exorcist and acolyte are missing in the Oriental Rites. Canon 1004 thus rules that, if a candidate has received some orders in the Oriental Rite and then obtains permission to receive further orders in the Latin Rite, the orders which are not given in the Oriental Rite must be supplied first before the cleric can get any other orders in the Latin Rite. In the Constitution "Etsi Pastoralis" of May 26, 1742 (Sec. vii, n. 7), Pope Benedict XIV goes into detail in reference to such ordination. The text of the Constitution is easily accessible either in the *Collectanea de Propaganda Fide* [397] or in the new collection of Decrees edited by Cardinal Gasparri.[398]

At Ordination to Major Orders the Candidates Must Receive Holy Communion

968. All the candidates for major orders are bound to receive Holy Communion in the Ordination Mass itself (**Canon 1005**). This obligation is considered a serious one, since the Church makes it a part of the sacred rite of ordination. The rule whereby major orders are conferred only at Holy Mass and Holy Communion is received by the candidates in the Ordination Mass, is very ancient, as Pope Benedict XIV teaches.[399]

[396] Sacred Congregation of Rites; *Decreta Authentica*, nn. 1071, 2772.
[397] I, 118.
[398] *Fontes Cod. Juris Can.*, I, n. 328.
[399] *De Synodo Diœcesana*, lib. VIII, cap. 11, 5.

CHAPTER V

OF THE TIME AND PLACE OF SACRED ORDINATION

969. The episcopal consecration should be conferred during Holy Mass on Sundays or on feasts of the Holy Apostles. Major orders are to be conferred during Mass on the Ember Saturdays, the Saturday before Passion Sunday, and on Holy Saturday, but for a grave reason the bishop may have these ordinations also on any Sunday or holyday of obligation.[399a] First tonsure may be given on any day at any hour; the minor orders may be conferred on Sundays and feasts which are doubles, but in the forenoon only. The custom of holding ordinations on other days than those stated in this Canon is reprobated. These ordination days must be observed also when a bishop of the Latin Rite by Apostolic indult ordains a cleric of an Oriental Rite, and *vice versa* (**Canon 1006**).

In the beginning of the Church there were no rules about days of ordination, and the functions were held whenever necessary. Soon, however, it became the custom to have the ordinations on certain days of the year only—the Ember Saturdays. In 494, Pope Gelasius ruled that the ordination of priests and deacons should take place towards the evening of the Ember Saturday fast days and the Saturday before Passion Sunday.[400] Pope Alexander III added Holy Saturday as an ordination day for major orders.[401] The consecration of bishops was not performed on the Ember Saturdays, but rather on the Sundays of the year, and Pope Leo I writes to the bishops of the Province of Vienne that from ancient times the consecration of bishops was conferred on Sundays.[402] The *Ordo Romanus Vulgatus* adds the feasts of the Apostles as days of consecration of bishops.

The Ordination Mass was celebrated on the Ember Saturdays towards the evening during those centuries when the fast on these days was observed so strictly that it was not broken by the taking of any food or drink until the evening. As late as 1095 Pope Urban II ordained, in the Council of Clermont, that the fast should be protracted to the evening of Saturday and the Ordina-

---

[399a] For meaning of holyday of obligation, cfr. App. III, 41, o.

[400] *Decretum Gratiani*, c. 7, D. 75.

[401] *Decretales Gregorii IX*, c. 3, *De temporibus ordinationum, etc.*, lib. I, tit. 11.

[402] Migne, "Patrol. Lat.," LIV, 628.

tion Mass should be held late in the evening, or, if possible, in the early morning of the next day so that the ordinations may rather be held on Sunday. When the discipline of the strict fasting relaxed, Holy Mass began to be said earlier in the day, and finally the forenoon hours of the Ember Saturdays were considered the proper time for ordinations.

970. Whenever the ordination is to be repeated or some rite is to be supplied, either absolutely or conditionally, this may be done even outside the ordination days and secretly (**Canon 1007**).

Defects and errors committed in carrying out the ceremonial of ordination may necessitate either the repetition of the entire ordination rite or the supplying of the ceremonies omitted or performed defectively. As these errors and defects are to be corrected as soon as possible, the Code allows the ordination ceremonies to be held on any day, and the rule concerning ordination days is not binding in such cases.

Right of the Bishop to Hold Ordinations Restricted to His Diocese

971. Except in the case mentioned in Canon 239, §1, n. 15, a bishop may not without the permission of the local Ordinary confer outside his own diocese those orders which require in the ordination rite the use of the pontificals (**Canon 1008**).

This rule of the Code is very ancient. The organization of the Church into dioceses goes back substantially to the times of the Apostles. The orderly administration of the affairs of the Church in the various dioceses made it necessary that each bishop's authority should be confined to the territorial limits of his bishopric. Several of the early Councils, from 300 and afterwards, forbid bishops to ordain even their own subjects outside their own diocese, or to ordain subjects of another diocese in their own without leave of the proper bishop of the candidates.[403] The Council of Trent [404] strictly forbade bishops to exercise the pontificals in another diocese without explicit permission of the Ordinary, punishing the transgression of that law with *ipso facto* suspension from the exercise of episcopal functions, and suspending the men thus ordained from the exercise of their orders (cfr. Canons 2373, n. 1, and 2374).

[403] *Decretum Gratiani*, c. 2, C. IX, qu. 3; c. 8, C. IX, qu. 2.
[404] Sessio VI, cap. 5, *De Reform*.

According to Canon 337, the exercise of the pontificals means functions in which the *Pontificale* demands the use of mitre and crozier. Now, in the ordination rites of the minor orders, the bishop does not need mitre and crozier, wherefore he could confer on his subjects outside his diocese tonsure and minor orders. Cardinals have the privilege to make use of the pontificals in all churches in the world outside the city of Rome, and they can therefore also confer orders in any church, provided the candidates have proper dimissorials from their own Ordinaries. If a Cardinal wishes to hold pontifical functions in a cathedral church, the law demands that he previously notify the local Ordinary to that effect (cfr. Canon 239, § 1, n. 15).

PLACE WHERE ORDINATIONS ARE TO BE HELD

972. General ordinations are to be held publicly in the cathedral church, and the canons of the cathedral shall be called and they must attend. If the ordinations are held in another place of the diocese, the most prominent church should, in so far as possible, be chosen for the purpose, and the clergy of that place shall attend the ordination service. The bishop, however, is not forbidden to have particular ordinations for any just reason in other churches—even in the chapel of the bishop's residence, of the seminary, or of a religious house. First tonsure and minor orders may be conferred even in private oratories (**Canon 1009**).

The first two sentences of this Canon are taken almost verbatim from the Council of Trent.[405] In the United States the diocesan consultors take the place of the cathedral chapter. As the ordination of the clergy is the most important of all episcopal functions, and as his power to confer sacred orders establishes most clearly the superior rank of the bishop over the priests, the Church desires that the ordination service be made as solemn as possible. The term "general ordinations" has reference to the ordinations held on any of the six Saturdays pointed out by the Code as regular ordination days.[406] The former faculties of our bishops contained the permission to confer orders outside the regular ordination days. These are not repeated in the new formula, but they have practically become superfluous since the

---

[405] Sessio XXIII, cap. 8, *De Reform.*
[406] Augustine, "Commentary," IV, 546.

Code allows the bishops for a grave reason to hold ordinations on any Sunday or holyday of obligation.

CHAPTER VI

OF THE RECORDS AND CERTIFICATE OF SACRED ORDINATION

973. After the ordination the names of all candidates ordained and of the ordaining minister, together with the place and date of ordination, are to be entered in a special book which is to be carefully kept by the Curia of the diocese where the ordination takes place. All documents of each ordination are also to be carefully preserved. To every candidate ordained an authentic certificate of the order received shall be given. If the men were ordained by a strange bishop with dimissorial letters, the certificate of ordination shall be exhibited by these men to their own Ordinary for the purpose of having the ordination recorded in a special book to be kept in the archives (**Canon 1010**).

Furthermore, the Ordinary in the case of seculars, or the major superior in the case of religious ordained with the superior's dimissorials, shall send notice of the ordination of each subdeacon to the pastor of his place of baptism, in order that this ordination may be entered in the baptismal record, as Canon 470, § 2, demands (**Canon 1011**).

The diocese in which the ordinations take place must keep a record of them, even if the candidates are ordained for another diocese and by another bishop with the consent or at the request of the local Ordinary. Augustine [407] is of the opinion that the phrase "curia loci ordinationis" in Canon 1010 does not mean exclusively that the ordination is to be recorded in the diocesan chancery or office of records, but in the archives of any church where the ordination actually takes place. We do not think that the term "curia" can be applied to the office or archives of such churches.

If, for instance, the Archbishop of New York ordains together with his own subjects some candidates from the Diocese of Newark (with the dimissorials of the Bishop of Newark), the ordination of the Newark candidates is to be recorded not only in the diocesan archives of New York but also in those of Newark, for, after demanding that the ordinations be recorded in the

407 *Commentary*, IV, 549.

diocese where they take place, Canon 1010 immediately continues that candidates ordained by another bishop must show the certificate of their ordination to their own Ordinary to have the ordination recorded in the archives of their own diocese. If the Ordinary invites another bishop to his diocese to ordain his subjects, there is no need of a double entry. From this Canon one must conclude that the religious organizations which have the privilege to issue dimissorial letters to their subjects must keep a record of the ordinations of their subjects. The proper Ordinary to whom in this case the subjects are to present the certificate of ordination, is the major superior of the religious organization.

974. Canon 1011 refers to the new regulation introduced by Canon 470, § 2, that the ordination of subdeacons is to be recorded in the baptismal record of these men. Canon 1011 determines the person who has the obligation to forward the ordination record of the subdeacons to the pastor of the parish wherein they were baptized. The proper local Ordinary has that duty in the case of his own subdeacons, and the major religious superior in the case of those for whom he issued dimissorials for subdeaconship. In the case of religious who have not the privilege of issuing dimissorials, the bishop of the diocese where the religious candidates belong as *de familia* must forward the record.[408]

TITLE VII

OF MARRIAGE

975. Christ our Lord raised the actual marriage contract between baptized persons to the dignity of a sacrament. Wherefore, there can be no valid matrimonial contract between baptized persons which is not also necessarily a sacrament (**Canon 1012**).

The Church is very emphatic and clear in her definition of the very important relation between the contract and the sacrament in marriage. She teaches that Christ transformed the contract itself into the sacrament whenever Christians make such a contract, so that no valid matrimonial contract can exist without being at the same time a sacrament. This stand of the Church with reference to the marriage of Christians is absolutely logical,

---

[408] Blat, ''Commentar.,'' lib. III, p. 492.

if one believes at all that Christ sanctified the marital union by attaching divine grace to it. If Christ did actually make marriage a sacrament, He had to make the contract—or mutual agreement of the parties to give themselves to each other as husband and wife for the purposes of marriage—the instrument by which to convey the sacramental grace, for by the contract the marital relation is created.

The great mass of Christians separated from the Catholic Church do not admit the teaching of the Church as to the sacramental character of marriage. There is a reason for this attitude, for, if they admitted the teaching that marriage is a sacrament, they would have to admit the necessary and logical conclusion that the Church alone, to the exclusion of all secular powers, has jurisdiction over the marriage contract of Christians. If it is a sacred contract, an essentially religious act, the secular power has no authority over such a contract of Christians. It is not very probable that the modern governments of Christian nations will ever again admit that right of the Church.

The statement of Canon 1012 on the sacramental character of the Christian marriage does not properly belong to the domain of Canon Law, but is inserted here as an evidence of the right of the Church to legislate in the matter of marriage. The proof of the dogmatic truth contained in Canon 1012 must be left to dogmatic theology. The reader may be referred to Pope Leo XIII's Encyclical "Arcanum" on Christian Marriage.[409]

Purpose of Marriage and Its Essential Characteristics

976. The primary purpose of marriage is the procreation and education of children. The secondary purpose is to furnish mutual aid and a remedy for concupiscence. The essential characteristics of marriage are its unity and indissolubility, which obtain a special stability in Christian marriage by virtue of the sacrament (**Canon 1013**).

There can be no controversy over the primary object of marriage. The perpetuation of the human race is willed by the Creator, who from the creation of mankind appointed the means for this purpose. The secondary purpose of marriage is mutual assistance of the married couple, which is promoted by

[409] February 10, 1880; *Acta S. Sedis*, XII, 385.

the closest companionship and fusion of the two lives for one common purpose. This is the so-called *consortium,* which is also in civil law recognized as a valuable asset in married life. A further aspect of the secondary purpose of marriage is the allaying of sexual lust. The sexual impulses of nature are very powerful so that a man or woman of average will-power and self-control can only with the greatest struggle restrain the sexual tendency. Wherefore, God has provided for an orderly and regulated indulgence of the sexual appetites by marriage.

The distinction between the primary and secondary purpose of marriage is ordinarily of little importance, but there are marriages in which the primary purpose is not obtainable (e.g., if the parties are sterile, advanced in age, etc.). There have been men who asserted that it was against the dignity of marriage to speak of this secondary purpose of the marital union. However, St. Paul's teaching ought to command the respect of all Christians, and there can be no doubt that he approves of this purpose of marriage when he says: *Propter fornicationem autem unusquisque suam uxorem habeat;* and again: *Melius est enim nubere quam uri* (I Cor., vii. 2, 9).

977. The essential characteristics of marriage pointed out by the Code are its unity and indissolubility. The unity of marriage is opposed to polygamy, for since the coming of Christ there can be no other than monogamous marriage (cfr. works on dogmatic theology). The indissolubility of marriage means that marriage validly contracted and consummated cannot be dissolved except by the death of one of the parties. It is the so-called *matrimonium ratum et consummatum* which has this absolute indissolubility. The dissolution of the *matrimonium legitimum* (two unbaptized persons) by the Pauline Privilege and the dissolving of the marriage bond of the *matrimonium ratum* (non-consummated marriage of Christians) by dispensation of the Supreme Pontiff and by solemn religious profession, will be discussed under the Canons which deal with these cases (cfr. below, nn. 1151–1161).

PRESUMPTION OF LAW IN FAVOR OF VALIDITY OF MARRIAGE

978. Marriage enjoys the favor of the law. Wherefore, in case of doubt, the marriage is to be considered valid until the contrary is proved. In cases of the Pauline Privilege, however,

the presumption is not in favor of upholding the marriage bond, but rather in favor of its dissolution, as stated in Canon 1127 (**Canon 1014**).

If doubt arises as to the validity of a marriage contracted, the validity must be upheld until the contrary is proved. Sound public policy confirms this rule of the Code. No contract which exercises so important a rôle as marriage in the life of human society (and still more so in the lives of Christians), should be set aside unless it is absolutely necessary.

TERMINOLOGY IN MARRIAGE LAW

979. *Matrimonium ratum* is the name for the valid marriage of baptized persons before they have made use of the marriage rights. *Matrimonium ratum et consummatum* is a marriage of Christians which has been consummated by the conjugal act to which the marriage contract is of its nature directed, and by which the married parties become one flesh. If the parties have cohabited after the marriage contract, consummation of the marriage is presumed until the contrary is proved.

Matrimonium legitimum is a valid marriage contracted between unbaptized persons.

Matrimonium putativum is an invalid marriage in which at least one of the parties contracted marriage in good faith; it remains *putativum*, until both parties become certain of its invalidity (**Canon 1015**).

The terms mentioned in this Canon occur repeatedly throughout the marriage laws of the Code, and one has to refer to this terminology frequently. The Code states that the consummation of marriage is presumed when the parties have been living together after their marriage. The presumption of law has this effect that it puts the burden of proof on the one who denies what the law presumes to have taken place. Our civil marriage laws agree in this particular with the church law. Canons 1825–1828 give the rules governing presumptions in law. Commentators on the former Canon Law held that the *matrimonium putativum* was such only if the marriage was contracted in the proper legal form but made invalid by an occult impediment unknown to at least one of the contracting parties. It is probable that the marriage of a Catholic and a non-Catholic outside the

Church can be called a *matrimonium putativum*, if the non-Catholic was in good faith, because of the general wording of the Code and of former Decrees—e.g., that of the Holy Office, Sept. 16, 1824 (*Collect.*, n. 784).

Marriage of Baptized Persons According to the Divine and Canon Law

980. The marriage of baptized persons is governed not only by the Divine, but also by Canon Law. The civil power is competent only to legislate concerning mere civil effects of such marriages (**Canon 1016**).

The Church claims exclusive jurisdiction over the marriage contract and marital state of Christians in all matters that concern their validity and liceity. While the Church has no power to modify the divine law in reference to marriage, she is the God-appointed custodian and interpreter of that law. As the civil governments of today do not, as a rule, admit the right of the Church to regulate the marriage contract and marital state by her laws, and they legislate on marriage independently of the Church, there is thus a conflict between the two sets of laws. The Church cannot enforce her laws except in so far as the conscience of the members of the Church respects these laws. Indirectly, the Church can enforce the laws by excluding from membership those of her children who disregard the authority that Christ has given to her. Here the words of St. Peter apply: "If it be just in the sight of God to hear you rather than God, judge ye" (Acts, iv. 19).

981. Marriage between unbaptized persons is subject to the civil power, and in the case of these marriages the civil law has the right to determine the conditions of the validity as well as the liceity of these marriage contracts. However, the civil power is bound to respect the divine law on marriage, and all civil laws which contradict the divine law are necessarily null and void. According to some canonists, if one party is unbaptized and the other baptized, the marriage can be valid only if neither party is prevented from contracting a valid marriage by the respective laws that bind them, for the unbaptized party is subject to the disabilities established by the civil law, and the baptized party is subject to the disabilities enacted by the church law. The ecclesi-

astical law is very explicit in specifying whether a prohibition of marriage affects merely its licitness or its validity. In the civil law the distinction is often not drawn so clearly, and the wording of the law and the decisions of the courts and the expositors of the civil law have to be studied closely. In the United States we have the additional difficulty that each state of the Union has its own laws in the matter.

The statements made in the preceding paragraph have not been admitted by all theologians.[410] In the first place, the power of the civil government to pass laws affecting the validity of the marriage contract of unbaptized persons was once widely challenged by eminent theologians, but it seems to be very generally admitted today that the civil government has this power, though, as Cardinal Gasparri states, several modern authors hold the contrary.[411]

Secondly, the question whether the disabilities of the civil law affecting the unbaptized party render null and void a marriage with a Catholic properly dispensed from the disparity of cult, is much debated. Wernz states that, in granting dispensations from disparity of cult, the Holy See attributes no invalidating force to the impediments of civil law for either party.[412] The passage which he quotes from the Constitution "Singulari" of Pope Benedict XIV, February 9, 1749, does not definitely decide the question, as anyone can convince himself by reading the seventh paragraph in which this passage is found.[413] Gasparri [414] states that the question is debated, some regarding the marriage as valid and others declaring it invalid. He himself inclines to the opinion that in such a case the impediments of the civil law do not invalidate the marriage. It seems to us more logical to say that both parties must be free from disabilities to make a valid marriage contract, and it is not sufficiently proved that the Church obtains jurisdiction over the unbaptized party by the fact that one of her subjects is given permission to marry such an unbaptized person, for the question returns whether the Church in the case can otherwise give that permission.

---

[410] For summary of controversy, cfr. Wernz, "Jus Decretal.," IV, nn. 75–81.

[411] *De Matrimonio*, I, n. 290.   [412] *Jus Decretal.*, IV, n. 60.

[413] Gasparri, "Fontes Cod. Jur. Can.," I, n. 394.

[414] *De Matrimonio*, I, n. 306.

The Betrothal Contract

982. The promise of marriage, whether unilateral or bilateral (which latter alone constitutes a betrothal), is invalid both in the internal and external forum unless it is made in writing, signed by the parties and either by the pastor or local Ordinary or at least two witnesses. If one or both parties do not know how to write, or are unable to write, it is necessary for the validity of the contract of betrothal that the inability to write be noted in the written contract, and that an additional witness be employed who, together with the pastor or local Ordinary or the above-mentioned two witnesses, signs the contract.

Though the promise of marriage is valid, and there is no just reason to excuse the non-fulfillment of the promise, neither party has a right of action to force the other to contract the marriage. There is the right only to institute action for reparation of damages, if any have been incurred. (**Canon 1017**).

The law of Canon 1017 embodies Article 1 of the Decree "Ne Temere," which became law on April 19, 1908. Several difficulties concerning this article arose soon after the publication of the Decree, and were settled by various answers of the Sacred Congregation of the Council. The Code has embodied some of these decisions in the wording of Canon 1017.

In civil matters it is generally admitted that the legislature has the right to regulate contracts of its citizens and to determine under what conditions a contract shall create obligations and to what extent the parties shall be obligated. The Church claims the same power in matters of religion, because Christ gave her charge over that part of man's affairs. If one admits that the marriage is a sacred contract and therefore subject to regulation by the Church, one must also admit that the promise of marriage falls under the jurisdiction of the Church as a preliminary agreement to the marriage contract itself.

983. The Church does not attach to the promise of marriage any force unless it is made as the law requires, namely: (1) it must be in writing—that is, in written words which sufficiently express the promise of marriage, the form of words being optional; (2) it must have the signatures of the parties and of either a pastor or local Ordinary or of two witnesses; (3) if one or both parties do not know how to write or if through some

cause or other they cannot write (though they know how), the signature of an additional witness is necessary. This inability to sign the contract must necessarily be indicated in the contract; in the United States, such inability is, as a rule, indicated by the words "his + mark," the illiterate party making a cross and another party signing the name of the illiterate against it. In the engagement contract the inability to write may be expressed in any manner which sufficiently indicates that the party or parties are unable to sign in person and an additional witness must sign his name for the illiterate party (or parties) in the contract.

984. A pastor or local Ordinary who acts as official witness to the agreement need not be the proper pastor or bishop of either party; any pastor or local Ordinary may act as such, but they can act only within the boundaries of their respective parish or diocese. Neither pastor nor bishop can delegate another priest to act as official witness, as was declared by the Sacred Congregation of the Council, March 30, 1908.[415] No private witnesses are required when a pastor or local Ordinary acts as official witness, except in case of inability of one or both parties to place their signatures to the contract, when one private witness is required.

That all parties whose signatures are necessary to the validity of the contract must sign the paper in the presence of one another, was decided by Decree of the Sacred Congregation of the Council, July 27, 1908.[416]

Finally, the written contract to be valid should contain the day, month and year (and the place) when (and where) the contract was made, as was declared by the same Sacred Congregation, July 27, 1908.[417] These Declarations of the Sacred Congregation on the "Ne Temere" are to be considered authentic interpretations of the law of the Code, for according to Canon 6, n. 2, when a former law is embodied in the Code, it is to be interpreted by former declarations and the interpretations of approved authors.

As to the signatures of the parties, if one or both feign illiteracy or inability to sign, the Code does not state whether the

---

[415] *Acta S. Sedis*, XLI, 287. [416] *Acta S. Sedis*, XLI, 510.
[417] Date only is spoken of in the Decree; as to the place, authors disagree whether it is required for validity.

contract is valid. Very likely it is not, for one of the essential requisites—the signatures of the parties—is lacking, and the law does not allow the substitution of an additional witness in place of the party or parties except in case of real inability to sign in person.

The parties who wish to make an engagement contract do not need the assistance of a pastor or a bishop, but may employ two private witnesses. As the law does not lay down any special rules regarding the qualifications of these witnesses, it suffices that they are of sound mind and sufficient mental capacity to understand the nature of the contract, and that they actually know what they are doing.

A further question arises as to whether the parties can conclude the contract of betrothal by proxy. There seems to be no objection to this. Canon 1089 lays down the rules under which even the marriage contract may be made by proxy. It is a general principle that all contracts or other transactions which a person has a right to conclude, may be made by proxy unless the law insists on personal action.

985. The Code is very explicit in its statement that no promise of marriage which is not made in legal form entails any obligation whatsoever, either in conscience or in the courts of law. In some cases hardships may result from this rule of the Code, because persons ignorant of the law of the Church may be deceived by the oral promise of marriage of one who knows that such promise does not bind him. However, the Church has made this rule for the benefit of the public, and the hardships in individual cases are unavoidable. The civil law in many instances follows the same principle, and makes contracts either altogether void, or at least unenforceable, unless they are made in the manner and form prescribed. The law is supposed to be known by all who are under its jurisdiction, and those who do not actually know the law are expected to investigate the law before they act.

The law never favors fraud and misrepresentation, but in some instances it may not be possible to get redress, because the injured party has not taken the steps to entitle him to redress in law. As before God, there can be no doubt that fraud and deceit is sinful, and if therefore one party has deceitfully represented to another that he intends marriage and has injured the other party by his malice, he is before God answerable for such injury. That question is not discussed by the Code. But, though the Code does not grant one party the right to force the other through the courts to keep his promise of marriage, the Code does not deny but rather supposes that a grave obligation to marry arises from a valid engagement contract. Otherwise, the Code would not give it the attention which it does in Canon 1017. Before the Code became law, the Church recognized the right of the parties to enforce the marriage promise in the ecclesiastical court by penalties and censures against the party who unlawfully broke the promise. The danger of such proceedings was recognized by the Church, and in one case the Sacred Congregation of the Propaganda said that excommunication should be used very sparingly in such cases, and a woman should not be forced under penalty of excommunication to marry as she promised.[418] In another case the Sacred Congregation of the Council said that, though the engagement contract was proved to have been validly made, the woman should not be forced by excommunication, but should be admonished by the bishop to keep her promise.[419]

986. As the reasons for which one may lawfully break the engagement contract are not stated in the Code, one must look to the former law and the approved authors for the motives which are held to be legally sufficient to justify a party in breaking his promise. Such reasons are, for instance, fornication committed by the other party, promise of marriage to a third party, considerable delay beyond the time agreed for the marriage to take place, or unreasonably long delay even though no time was agreed on explicitly, knowledge of certain facts about the other party which would have prevented the making of the engagement. In fact, it may be safely given as a general rule that the obligation to execute the promise of marriage ceases, when circumstances have become such that the marriage will very probably not be a happy one. The party who has by his own fault created circumstances which make the execution of the engagement contract impossible or inadvisable, is bound to make restitution for any injury done to the other party.

---

418 November 22, 1790; *Collectanea de Prop. Fide*, I, n. 603.
419 *Canones et Decreta Conc. Trid.* (ed. Richter), 223, n. 18.

That the objection of the parents of one or both parties to the engagement contract, if just and reasonable, obliges the children to respect the will of their parents, is evident from the divine law. If the objection of the parents comes from personal or other unworthy motives, the children are free to make the engagement. If, however, the opposition of the parents or other members of the family is so bitter that it is very difficult for a party to contract marriage in the face of that opposition, the Holy See has in several cases declared that there is a sufficient reason for that party to break the engagement contract.[420]

987. Under the former law there arose a diriment impediment of marriage, from a valid engagement contract, called *publica honestas,* which impediment rendered invalid marriages of the engaged parties with persons related in the first degree of consanguinity to the other of the contracting parties. This impediment has been abolished by the Code. The Holy See has declared that the Code is not retroactive in its laws affecting engagements and marriage, but their validity is governed by the law existing at the time when they were contracted, or the time they will be contracted. Therefore, if the marriage takes place after the Code went into force, no attention is to be paid to the impediment of *publica honestas,* which existed previously. The Holy See has likewise declared that the party who breaks the engagement contract, cannot be stopped or delayed in marrying another party by a breach of promise suit. Finally, the Holy See declared that the suit for damages against unwarranted breaking of the engagement may be instituted before either the civil or the ecclesiastical court.[421]

988. A valid engagement can be contracted only by parties who can validly and licitly contract marriage. They must, therefore, be free from all impediments which render their marriage illicit or invalid. If an impediment is of a nature that it ceases in the course of time without a dispensation (e.g., the impediment of the age required for a valid marriage), the promise to marry when the impediment shall have ceased is usually valid. The Holy Office decided that the promise of marriage of children after they have reached the years of discretion, but before they are of marriageable age, is valid; but, if they were not yet

[420] *Canones et Decr. Conc. Trid.* (ed. Richter), 223, nn. 22–23.
[421] Cfr. App. III, 5, c, 2 and 42.

of the age of puberty, they may reject the agreement after they have reached the age of puberty.[422] Not every impediment that may cease in the course of time, gives the parties freedom to promise marriage. Thus, the impediment of the marriage bond ceases with the death of one of the married parties; yet, if a married person in view of the anticipated death of the partner were to promise marriage to a third party, it would be considered a criminal promise by the law of the Church.

May parties who are under an ecclesiastical impediment of marriage make a valid engagement contract under the condition of marrying after they shall have obtained a dispensation? Cardinal Gasparri [423] holds that, if it is an impediment in which the Holy See can and usually does grant a dispensation and there is a good reason for the dispensation, the engagement contract is valid. However, he admits that weighty authors are ranged against that opinion. The Holy See has declared that the promise of marriage between a Catholic and a heretic or schismatic is illicit and invalid, unless it is made after the dispensation has been obtained.[424]

989. The Code gives the right to sue for damages in case of unlawful breach of the promise of marriage, if the promise was validly made (that is, in writing and with the observance of the formalities required by the Code). Now, in the civil law in the States of our Union the mutual promise of marriage is valid when made orally. May a party sue for damages in the case of breach of promise of marriage, which is valid in civil law and invalid in Canon Law? We think that the party may sue. While it is certain that the Church claims and has exclusive jurisdiction over the contract of promise of marriage as well as over the marriage contract proper, it is not certain that the Church intends to annul absolutely the natural obligation of repairing the damages done by the wanton breach of one's word of honor. The agreement made without the formalities of Canon Law has at least the nature of a word of honor. Wherefore, it seems that, though the Church pronounces the informal promise of marriage as of no consequence as a contract, it does not destroy the voluntary act, and there seems

[422] February 15, 1779; *Collectanea de Prop. Fide*, I, n. 532.
[423] Gasparri, "De Matrimonio," I, nn. 63, 102–104.
[424] Holy Office, December 12, 1888; *Collectanea de Prop. Fide*, II, n. 1696.

to be sufficient natural injustice in breaking without reason the informal promise to entitle the injured party to have recourse to the civil law to get redress, if any damage was sustained. It is to be construed as fraud to make such informal promise and break it to the damage of another.

Pastor Must Instruct People on Marriage

990. The pastor shall not omit prudently to instruct the people on the Sacrament of Matrimony and its impediments (**Canon 1018**).

There is no doubt that one of the principal duties of a pastor is to instruct his parishioners in the teaching and practice of the Christian faith. The sacraments are the greatest aid to Christian life, for they supply the strength and power of God to frail human nature. It is evident that the right understanding of the religious principles applicable to Christian marriage is of vital importance, because the general morality of the people depends in a great measure on their attitude toward marriage. The devil and his agents are constantly busy in propagating sinful sexual knowledge and abominable principles regarding the marital state. Since error is so bold in proclaiming its tenets, the priest should not fail to expound the truth. He must carefully avoid coarseness in dealing with a subject, which is naturally delicate, though grand and beautiful if viewed with a mind that reverences and respects God's work through the marvellous forces of nature. The priest whose long course of education is supposed to have instilled in him not only sound knowledge but also good sense and judgment, will know how to frame his instructions on delicate matters to suit the audience before which he appears. Prudery, however, is not virtue, and the priest must attack vice in no uncertain terms when such vice threatens, as it does, to undermine the very foundations of Christian society. The marital state and the fulfillment of the duties of that state are not a private affair: the public has a vital interest in that state of life and the right conduct of married persons, for on the family hinge the hopes and the fears of the nation and of the Church. Pope Leo XIII was indefatigable in exhorting the bishops and priests to teach the sanctity of Christian marriage (cfr. his Encyclicals "Inscrutabili

Dei," April 21, 1878; "Quod Apostolici Muneris," December 28, 1878; and especially "Arcanum," February 10, 1880).[425]

CHAPTER I

OF THE THINGS TO BE DONE BEFORE MARRIAGE, ESPECIALLY THE PUBLICATION OF THE BANNS

991. Before marriage is contracted it must be certain that there are no obstacles to its valid and licit celebration. In danger of death, if other proofs are not available and there are no indications to the contrary, the sworn affirmation of the parties that they are baptized and that there is no impediment between them suffices (**Canon 1019**).

The Code urges the necessity of investigating whether the parties who manifest to the pastor their intention to marry are legally qualified to contract a valid and licit marriage. It is evident that this duty rests with the pastor, for elsewhere the Code states that the assistance at marriage as official witness is the right and duty of the pastor. The obligation to inquire about the impediments which may invalidate the marriage, is not merely a regulation of Canon Law, but also a duty imposed by the divine law, which obliges the pastor to prevent (in so far as is in his power) irreverence to the Sacrament of Matrimony.

In many instances it is not sufficient merely to question the parties: other information must also be secured, as specified in the succeeding Canons. However, in danger of death of one or both parties, the Code declares it sufficient if the parties declare under oath that they are baptized, and that they are not under any impediment of marriage, provided there are no reasons to suspect the truth of their testimony.

MANNER OF CONDUCTING THE INVESTIGATION

992. The pastor whom the law entitles to assist at the marriage shall at an opportune time prior to the marriage inquire diligently whether there is any impediment to the marriage. He shall also question both the man and the woman carefully and separately as to whether they are under any impediment, whether they freely consent to the marriage (especially the woman), and whether they are sufficiently instructed in Chris-

[425] *Acta S. Sedis,* X, 585; XI, 372; XII, 385.

tian doctrine, unless he knows from the qualifications of the parties that this last investigation is superfluous.[426] The local Ordinary has the right to prescribe special regulations for this examination of the parties by the pastor (**Canon 1020**).

On August 21, 1670, the Holy Office issued a detailed Instruction on the manner of conducting the investigation concerning the freedom of the parties from any impediments, and demanded strict compliance with these regulations by bishops and pastors.[426a] The Code does not reënact this law, but prescribes certain details and leaves the rest to the bishops to regulate. A Decree of the Sacred Congregation of the Sacraments, March 6, 1911, complains of the great carelessness of pastors in making the investigation concerning impediments, especially with reference to strangers who have come from other countries and about whom little is known.[427] Another Decree of the same Sacred Congregation, July 4, 1921,[428] again complains about the laxness of pastors in this matter and issues the following regulations:

(1) Ordinaries shall instruct their pastors that they must not marry people under any pretext or for the purpose of avoiding or terminating sinful relations, unless they have proof that the parties are free to contract marriage. Pastors must get the baptismal record of parties baptized in other parishes;

(2) The pastor who assists at a marriage must, in accordance with Canon 1103, § 2, send without delay a complete copy of the marriage record to the pastor where the parties were baptized;

(3) Any testimony required to prove that the parties are free to marry, and the notification of marriage sent to the pastors where the parties were baptized, are to be forwarded through the chancery office of the Ordinary of the priest who sends such attestations or notifications;

(4) Working people who have only recently come from another country are in many cases *vagi* according to law, and the Code (Canon 1032) rules that no pastor may marry *vagi* without previously consulting his Ordinary. If they are not *vagi*, but there remains some doubt as to whether they are free to marry, the Code (Canon 1031, § 1, n. 3) again demands that

---

[426] Concerning ignorance in Christian doctrine, cfr. App. III, 43, a.
[426a] See Decree in Gasparri, "De Matrimonio," II, 480.
[427] *Acta Ap. Sedis*, III, 102.   [428] *Acta Ap. Sedis*, XIII, 348.

the pastor consult his Ordinary, except only in cases of necessity (especially danger of death) ;

(5) If the pastor of the place of baptism receives the notification of a marriage of parties of whom he knows that one or both were already lawfully married to another party still living, he shall at once notify the pastor who has been deceived by the parties, and such notice shall be sent through the chancery office of the priest who sends the information;

(6) Ordinaries are obliged to guard the observance of these regulations and to punish transgressions, even with canonical penalties.

With reference to the knowledge of Christian doctrine, the question arose whether a pastor who finds either one or both of the parties grossly ignorant of the elementary principles of Christian doctrine, should delay the marriage until the parties are sufficiently instructed. The Committee for the Authentic Interpretation of the Code answered that the pastor should rather teach them the elementary points of the faith, and, if the parties refuse to come for instruction, assistance at the marriage should not be refused.[429]

If the pastor finds that one or both parties had, since April 19, 1908, been married outside the Church, got a divorce and now want to marry again, he must investigate the facts and especially whether the marriage was ever validated by the Church, but, before he marries them, he must consult the Ordinary of the diocese. The Committee declared on October 16, 1919,[430] that no trial of the case is required nor the intervention of the *defensor vinculi*.

993. Unless the parties were baptized in his own parish church, the pastor must get proof of the baptism of both parties, or of the Catholic party only in the case of a Catholic and an unbaptized person to be married with the dispensation from the impediment of disparity of cult. Catholics who have not yet received Confirmation should first receive that sacrament if they can do so without great inconvenience (**Canon 1021**).

The term "testimonium baptismi" in Canon 1021 does not necessarily mean "baptismal certificate," but proof of Baptism, no matter how the proof is furnished, as the derivation of *testi-*

---

[429] June 3, 1918; *Acta Ap. Sedis*, X, 345.
[430] *Acta Ap. Sedis*, XI, 479.

monium from *testari* shows. One trustworthy witness proves the reception of baptism outside of litigated cases (cfr. Canon 779). Capello [431] holds that the pastor must get the baptismal certificate, and that no other proof suffices where it is possible to get the certificate. He also insists that it be a certificate recently issued by the pastor so that it may carry the notice of the marriage of the party, if perchance that party was married before. The Code (Canon 470) demands that the marriage be marked in the baptismal record. Nevertheless, most commentators hold that the "testimonium baptismi" in Canon 1021 has its literal meaning (proof of baptism). We saw that the Holy See insists that the pastor get the necessary papers to prove the "free state" of the parties; what documents he must get, from whom, etc., is to be regulated by the local Ordinaries.

Proof of baptism must be obtained also for the baptism of the non-Catholic party in mixed marriages, as is evident from the purpose of the law. The investigation is also necessary so that the pastor may know what dispensation to apply for (mixed religion or disparity of cult). If nothing certain can be proved about the baptism so that it remains doubtful, or if the party is commonly considered baptized, valid baptism is to be assumed for the purpose of marriage (cfr. Canon 1070).

PUBLICATION OF THE BANNS

994. The pastor must announce publicly the names of the parties who are to be married (**Canon 1022**). The banns of marriage are to be published by the proper pastor of the parties. If a party has lived in any other place for six months after the age of puberty, the pastor should refer the matter to his Ordinary who may use his judgment whether the banns shall be announced in that place, or otherwise order the pastor to gather proofs and information in reference to the free state of the party. If there is any suspicion that an impediment has been contracted, the pastor shall refer the matter to his Ordinary, even though the party has been living less than six months in another place, and the Ordinary shall not permit the marriage until all suspicion is removed by a further investigation (**Canon 1023**).[431a]

[431] *De Sacramentis*, III, n. 149.
[431a] Ordinary may not infringe on rule of Canon 1023, cfr. App. III, 43, c.

The banns are to be published in church on three successive Sundays or other holydays of obligation, during Mass or other divine services which are largely attended by the people (**Canon 1024**). The local Ordinary may also substitute in his diocese another form of publishing the banns, by posting the names of the parties at the doors of the parish or another church for at least eight days, during which period two days of obligation (i.e., Sundays or feasts) must occur (**Canon 1025**).

The first general law requiring the publication of the banns was passed by the Fourth Lateran Council in 1215, which law was embodied in the official collection of Decrees of Pope Gregory IX.[432] The Council speaks of one publication of the names. The Council of Trent extended the law to a threefold publication, on three successive feast-days.[433] While retaining in substance the law of the Council of Trent, the Code adds that the proclamation may be made not only at Holy Mass but also at other services largely attended by the people, and that the local Ordinary may substitute for the publication the posting of the names at the church doors.

995. Before the pastor announces the banns, he must have made proper investigation as to the free state of the parties, as the Code supposes by the fact that it gives the rules about the investigation concerning impediments before it speaks of the publication of the banns. The publication of the banns is an additional precaution to prevent people who are legitimately married and have separated from deceiving the pastor, as the Council of Trent points out in the chapter "Tametsi," referred to above. The Holy See was asked whether the pastor may require the supplementary oath of the parties to ascertain their freedom from the bond of a former marriage or from other impediments, when it is very difficult to observe the law of Canon 1023, because the parties have lived in various and very distant places. The Committee for the Authentic Interpretation of the Code answered that, in such cases, the pastor is to refer the matter to his Ordinary, who may use his own judgment as to what proof is sufficient, and who may also demand the supplementary oath.[434]

The Code rules that the banns are to be published by the

---

[432] *Decretales Gregorii IX*, c. 3, *De clandestina Desponsatione*, lib. IV, tit. 3.
[433] Sessio XXIV, cap. 1, *De Reform. Matrimonii*.
[434] Cfr. App. III, 43, b.

proper pastor of the parties. As a Catholic acquires a proper parish and pastor either by domicile or quasi-domicile (cfr. above, Canon 94), each of the parties may have more than one proper pastor, and all proper pastors of the parties must publish the banns in their parish church. It seems that the pastor who assists at the marriage by reason of the fact that a party has stayed in his parish for one month need not announce the marriage in his parish church, if neither party has a domicile or quasi-domicile in his parish; but this pastor must see that the banns are published in the parish or parishes where the parties have a domicile or quasi-domicile. The reason is that the law does not suppose the parties to have contracted an impediment in so short a time, six months being as a rule required. If, however, the party who has been one month in the parish intends to stay there either permanently or for the greater part of the year, the marriage has to be announced there, because the party has acquired a domicile or quasi-domicile.

The proper pastor of *vagi* is the pastor in whose parish these persons actually stay. He should, therefore, under the general rule of Canon 1023 announce their marriage. However, Canon 1032 demands that the pastor refer such marriages to his Ordinary, who has the right to decide whether or not the publication is to be made.

996. The publication of the banns shall be omitted in marriages contracted with the dispensation from the impediment of either disparity of cult or mixed religion, unless the local Ordinary judges it advisable to allow the publication and all danger of scandal is removed, and provided the apostolic dispensation has been obtained before the publication of the banns, and no mention is made of the religion of the non-Catholic party (**Canon 1026**).

Answering the question whether the publication of the banns was permissible in mixed marriages and those between a Catholic and an unbaptized person, the Holy Office, June 4, 1874, declared that they may be made without mentioning the religion of the contracting parties, provided the dispensation had been previously granted for the marriage. The Sacred Congregation added, however, that it would be better, at least in some cases and circumstances, to dispense with the publication of the banns rather than arouse astonishment and scandal among the faithful.[435]   In the United States it has not been the custom to announce mixed marriages in the Catholic churches.   On March 5, 1830, Pope Pius VIII allowed the publication of the banns of mixed marriages in the ecclesiastical province of Cologne, Germany.[436]

997. All the faithful are obliged to report to either the pastor or the local Ordinary any impediments of which they have knowledge before the marriage takes place (**Canon 1027**).

The evident purpose of the law of the banns is to prevent persons from getting married illegally because of some impediment which may not be generally known in the place where the parties get married, and which they can easily hide from the pastor.   The publicity also helps to prevent married parties who broke away from their partners from deceiving others and attempting to marry again in a place where they are unknown. If the banns are properly published in the parishes where such a person has lived for a considerable length of time after childhood, it will not be easy for such a person to remain unsuspected. The people who know of an impediment to the marriage which is about to take place, must make the matter known to the pastor or the bishop of the diocese.   The matter being of great importance, the Church puts the obligation on the people of reporting the impediment.   The Statutes of the Archdiocese of Baltimore, published by Cardinal Gibbons in the Diocesan Synod of September 24, 1886, decreed that persons who after the proclamation of the banns neglect to reveal the impediment of which they have certain knowledge, shall be punished with excommunication.[437]

Dispensation from the Banns

998. The proper local Ordinary of the contracting parties can for a legitimate cause dispense with the banns, not only in his own diocese but also in a strange diocese where the parties may have lived for six months or longer after the age of puberty.   If the parties have several proper Ordinaries, that one has the right to dispense in whose diocese the marriage is to be contracted.   If the marriage is to be contracted outside the

---

[435] *Collectanea de Prop. Fide*, II, n. 1417.
[436] Linneborn, ''Grundriss des Eherechts,'' 87.
[437] *Synodus Diœcesana Baltimorensis Nona*, p. 51.

proper dioceses of the parties, any proper Ordinary can give the dispensation (**Canon 1028**).

The *proper* local Ordinary of the parties is the Ordinary of the diocese where a party has a domicile or a quasi-domicile (cfr. Canon 94). The parties may, therefore, have several proper Ordinaries, for they may be domiciled in different dioceses, and either party may have (besides a domicile) also a quasi-domicile in still another diocese. The Code makes plain what proper Ordinary has the right to give the dispensation. The bishop of the diocese where a party has stayed one month without acquiring a domicile or quasi-domicile, is not a proper Ordinary of the party, although a pastor may marry persons who have stayed one month in his parish.

FURTHER DETAILS ABOUT THE PROCLAMATION OF BANNS

999. If another pastor has instituted the investigation or published the banns, he must at once inform the pastor who is to assist at the marriage by authentic document of the outcome of such investigation or proclamation (**Canon 1029**). After the investigation and the publishing of the banns have been completed, the pastor shall not assist at the marriage unless he has received all the necessary documents, and has waited three days after the last publication of the banns, unless there is a reasonable cause for the earlier solemnization of the marriage. If the marriage is not contracted within six months after the announcements, the publication of the banns must be repeated, unless the local Ordinary decides otherwise (**Canon 1030**).

It does not suffice that the banns are published in the various parishes, but the pastor who is to assist at the marriage must be informed of the outcome of the proclamations by a written statement signed by the respective pastors who had the duty to announce the banns. Likewise, if the parties obtain permission to be married by a pastor of a parish to which neither party belongs, that pastor is to be informed of the result of the examination of the parties by the pastor who by law was entitled to witness the marriage. The pastor who witnesses the marriage is not allowed to do so until he has received the documents that may be required in the case.

The Code rules that, if the marriage is delayed more than

six months after the publication of the banns, they are to be repeated, unless the local Ordinary dispenses with the repetition. The Roman Ritual directed that, if the marriage did not take place within two months after the last announcement, the publications were to be repeated, unless the bishop thought otherwise. In this particular, therefore, the law of the Roman Ritual is modified.

Procedure When an Impediment Is Suspected or Discovered

1000. When a suspicion arises as to the existence of some impediment, the following rules are to be observed:

(1) The pastor shall investigate the matter more thoroughly, and ask at least two trustworthy witnesses to make a statement under oath, provided there is no question of an impediment the knowledge of which would disgrace the parties. If necessary, he may also question the parties under oath;

(2) He should make, or finish, the publication of the banns, if the doubt arose before he began or during the publication of the banns;

(3) He shall not assist at the marriage without consulting his Ordinary, if in his judgment the impediment still remains doubtful (**Canon 1031, § 1**).

When an impediment has been discovered with certainty, the following rules are to be observed:

(1) If the impediment is occult, and the publication of the banns has been started before the discovery, the pastor shall continue or finish the publication, and refer the matter to the local Ordinary or to the Holy See, keeping secret the names of the parties;

(2) If the impediment is public, and is detected before the publication of the banns was begun, the pastor shall not announce the banns until the impediment is removed, though he may know that a dispensation of the impediment has been obtained in the forum of conscience only. If the impediment is detected after the first or second publication of the banns, the pastor shall finish the publication and refer the matter to the Ordinary (**Canon 1031, § 2**).

Finally, if there is neither a certain nor a doubtful impediment, the pastor shall admit the parties to the solemnization of the marriage after the publication of the banns has been completed (**Canon 1031**, § 3).

In many cases the pastor has no difficulty, because he knows the parties and their families, and the examination of the parties is not attended with difficulties. But, if he does not know the parties, he has naturally to be more careful to get the necessary information. We saw before that the investigation concerning the impediments must be made before the publication of the banns. Canon 1031 gives detailed instruction as to what must be done when doubt arises as to some impediment. If that doubt arises before the publication of the banns, he must try to settle it before he begins the publication. If the doubt cannot be removed at once, the Code does not oblige the pastor to delay the publication, for it states that if the doubt arose before the commencement or the completion of the publication of the banns, he may publish them or finish the publication. In the case of a doubtful impediment, the pastor may not assist at the marriage without consulting his Ordinary.

1001. In the rules determining the course of action when an impediment is discovered with certainty, there is one point which perhaps needs some explanation. The Code states that, if the pastor knows that the parties obtained a dispensation from a public impediment in the internal forum, he must nevertheless act as though no dispensation had been obtained. The reason is that Canon Law ascribes no validity in the external forum to a dispensation granted in the internal forum only (cfr. Canon 202), except in the case of a dispensation from an occult impediment granted by the Sacred Penitentiary in the internal non-sacramental forum: then no new dispensation in the external forum is required when the impediment afterwards becomes public. In order that there may be proof of the dispensation, it is to be recorded in the secret archives of the diocese (cfr. Canon 1047). A public impediment is one which can be proved in the external forum (cfr. Canon 1037).

Generally speaking, an impediment which remains doubtful even after due investigation, does not deprive the parties of the right to get married. Nevertheless, we saw that the Code forbids the pastor to marry the parties in the face of a doubtful impediment without referring the case to the Ordinary. The general rule stated in Canon 15 is, that even invalidating and inhabilitating laws do not bind in a *dubium juris;* in a *dubium facti,* where the fact on which the existence of an impediment in a given case depends is doubtful, the same Canon 15 gives the Ordinary power to dispense, provided it be a case in which the Roman Pontiff usually dispenses. An exception to the rule in the *dubium facti* is stated in Canon 1076, which rules that marriage is never to be permitted, if there is doubt whether the parties are blood relations in some degree of the direct line, or in the first degree of the collateral line.

MARRIAGE OF VAGI

1002. The pastor shall not assist at the marriage of *vagi,* except in a case of necessity, without referring the matter to the local Ordinary, or to the priest delegated by him for that purpose, and obtaining permission to assist (**Canon 1032**).

Vagi are persons who have no domicile or quasi-domicile (cfr. Canon 91). Though the pastor of the place where such persons actually stay is their proper pastor, the law does not permit him, in so far as licit assistance is concerned, to assist at their marriage without the permission of the Ordinary. This rule is taken from the Council of Trent,[438] and is based, as the Council clearly states, on the danger that such people are often validly married, but have separated and gone to a strange place there to attempt another marriage. Wherefore, the Church wants these cases referred to the Ordinary or his delegate, so that special precautions may be taken. If only one of the parties has no domicile or quasi-domicile, the case must be referred to the Ordinary because Canon 1032 speaks of *vagi* generally, and because, whether one or both are *vagi,* in either case there is the danger spoken of in the Council of Trent. An Instruction of the Sacred Congregation of the Sacraments, July 4, 1921, forbids pastors to assist at the marriage of workingmen who have emigrated from their own country, and who either are *vagi* in the new country or, if not *vagi,* are so little known that frequently there is no complete assurance of their freedom from impediments. In both cases the Code demands that the marriage be referred to the Ordinary. The Decree admits the right of the pastor to assist at the marriage without consulting the

---

[438] Sessio XXIV, cap. 7, *De Reform. Matrimonii.*

Ordinary in case of necessity, or "rather the danger of death." [439] The Sacred Congregation seems to interpret the phrase of Canon 1032 "excepto casu necessitatis" in the sense of cases of danger of death. From Canon 1019 one can form the conclusion that, only in danger of death, may the pastor assist at a marriage when all doubt has not been removed concerning its validity and licitness; when there is time to refer the matter to the Ordinary, the pastor may not pass judgment on a doubtful impediment.

INSTRUCTION OF THE BRIDE AND GROOM

1003. The pastor shall not fail to instruct the parties to be married, according to the divers conditions of persons, regarding the sanctity of the Sacrament of Matrimony, the mutual marital obligations, and the duties of parents towards their offspring. He shall also earnestly admonish them to make a good confession and receive Holy Communion piously before marriage (**Canon 1033**).

The pastor shall earnestly warn children who are still minors not to contract marriage without the knowledge of their parents or against their reasonable objections. If these young people reject his advice, he shall not assist at their marriage before he has consulted the local Ordinary (**Canon 1034**).

The pastor has the duty of instructing the persons who are to get married, and should see that they receive the Sacrament of Matrimony not only validly but also licitly. Now the knowledge of the marital duties, the obligation towards the offspring, the sanctity of the marital state, are matters which those people are obliged to know who want to enter the married state. Plenty of knowledge of sexual life is propagated among the young people of today, but unfortunately it is very often not of the right kind. Both science and education either ignore altogether or contravene the principles of religion as taught by the Catholic Church. Yet neither science nor education has the power to give a young man and woman sufficient will-power and strength to control their passions either before or after marriage. Confession and Holy Communion before marriage are not strictly prescribed, but the pastor will do what is in his power to per-

[439] Cfr. App. III, 43, d.

suade the couple to prepare themselves thus for the grave responsibility they assume on entering the marital state.[440]

1004. Children who are not yet of age (which, in Canon Law, is twenty-one years for both sexes), do wrong if they contract marriage without the knowledge or against the reasonable objections of their parents. This is evident from Canon 1034, which commands the pastor not to assist at such a marriage, but to refer the case to the Ordinary. The bishop is to judge whether in a given case there are circumstances and reasons which justify the marriage. Though the marriage is primarily a personal affair of the couple, and the Church wants them to be free in their choice of a life-partner, the parents have nevertheless a legitimate interest in the affair. Besides, filial love and respect for father and mother should prompt the children not to ignore them in a matter of such importance.

Announcement of Marriage in American Civil Law

1005. The announcement of marriage, or banns, is practically unknown in the laws of the States of our Union. All states have some sort of a license provision, but in only one state (Wisconsin) is a marriage invalid unless a license for it has been issued actually or constructively, as prescribed by law. Only eight states require advance notice to be given before a license may be issued: in five of these (Maine, Massachusetts, New Hampshire, New Jersey, and Wisconsin), all applicants must give such notice; in the other three (Connecticut, Rhode Island, and Vermont), the requirement applies only to nonresidents. Five days is the period of advance notice prescribed except in the case of New Jersey, where it is forty-eight hours. In several of these states provision is made for an immediate issuance of the license on order of the court in the case of immigrants or in cases of emergency due to physical condition, etc. Only one state (Wisconsin) provides that the notice shall be posted. In but two of the eight states (Maine and Wisconsin) is there definite provision for the filing and hearing of objections. In two states a period of time must elapse after the issuance of the license before the marriage may be performed: In Delaware there must be a period of at least twenty-four

[440] Holy Office, May 9, 1821, urges the reception of the Sacraments (*Collect. de P. F.*, I, n. 758).

hours, or, if both parties are non-residents, of at least ninety-six hours; in New Jersey the interval is twenty-four hours for all applicants, except that in case of arrest on certain criminal charges the marriage may be performed immediately. In three states (Georgia, Maryland, and Ohio) a marriage license is not required for marriages preceded by the publication of banns.

Every state requires the consent of the parent, guardian, etc., either for the issuance of a certificate or for the marriage of females under certain specified ages, and all states except Georgia and Michigan have a corresponding requirement regarding males. The ages established vary considerably, but in most states the age for males is twenty-one, for females eighteen.[441]

CHAPTER II

OF IMPEDIMENTS IN GENERAL

1006. All persons may contract marriage unless forbidden by law (**Canon 1035**). An *impedient* impediment entails a grave prohibition to contract marriage, but it does not invalidate a marriage contracted despite such an impediment. A *diriment* impediment not only gravely forbids the marriage, but makes its celebration null and void. Though the impediment may be on the part of only one of the parties, the marriage is nevertheless either illicit or invalid (**Canon 1036**).

The term ''impediment'' in connection with marriage means, as the word itself suggests, an obstacle to the contract. This obstacle may be of such a nature that the marriage is valid, though the parties sin grievously against the law, or it may be of such a nature that the law incapacitates the parties from making a valid contract. The first class of impediments are called *impedient,* the second are called *diriment* impediments. These technical terms in Canon Law were first employed in the Decrees of Pope Alexander III.[442]

The rule that the marriage is either illicit or invalid, though only one of the parties is affected directly by an impedient or diriment impediment, is reasonable, because in a contract both

441 Cfr. Fred S. Hall and Elizabeth W. Brooke, ''American Marriage Law'' (Russell Sage Foundation, New York, 1919).
442 *Decretales Gregorii IX*, c. 4, *Qui clerici vel voventes matrimonium contrahere possunt,* lib. IV, tit. 6.

contracting parties must be legally qualified to make the contract. Some impediments (e.g., blood relationship, affinity, adoption, public decency, spiritual relationship) affect both parties equally; other impediments, like the vow of chastity (age, impotency, marriage bond, or sacred orders) affect one party only.

PUBLIC AND OCCULT IMPEDIMENTS

1007. An impediment is considered *public* if it is such that it can be proved in the external forum; otherwise it is *occult* (**Canon 1037**).

The distinction between public and occult impediments is very important, because in questions regarding the power of dispensation the extent of the power may depend on the fact whether the impediment is occult or public. As the Code defines public and occult impediments somewhat differently from the way in which these terms were explained by canonists who wrote before its promulgation, the explanations of the latter must be read with caution. They distinguished impediments into those public by their very nature and occult by their very nature; and again, into those public *de facto* (or actually) and occult *de facto*. If an impediment could not be proved in the external forum because no persons competent to testify knew of it (e.g., nobody except the parties, the confessor and one or two persons knew of it), they called it *omnino occultum*. If only a few persons knew of the impediment (e.g., five or six persons in a town, seven or eight in a city), they called it *simpliciter* occult, provided those persons were such that there was no danger of their making it public. Gasparri states that the Sacred Penitentiary has given a dispensation from an impediment which was known to seven or eight persons in a city of 9000 inhabitants, and which it thus considered occult.[443]

The former canonists had also another distinction—viz., between impediments that were *formaliter* and *materialiter* public or occult. That was applied mostly to impediments arising from crime. Some interpreted those terms as follows: if the crime was public and the person who committed it was also known, but the people did not know that an impediment arose from that crime, they still called it an occult impediment—i.e., *forma-*

---

[443] Gasparri, ''De Matrimon.,'' I, n. 260.

liter occult, though *materialiter* public. Others—for instance, Pope Benedict [444] and Gasparri [445]—did not accept this interpretation of the term "occult." The Code retains the distinction between *formaliter* and *materialiter* occult crime in Canon 2197, n. 4, but explains it in the sense that a crime is *materialiter* occult if the fact of the crime is unknown, and *formaliter* occult if its imputability is unknown (that is, when it is unknown that the act was criminally culpable). Thus, in the impediment of crime, the fact that the wife was killed may be known publicly, but it is not known that the husband was the criminal; the imputability to him is unknown. The same applies if the public believes that the killing done by the husband was done in self-defence, by accident, etc.

1008. The new concept of public and occult impediments in the Code cannot be brought into harmony with the teaching of the canonists who wrote before its promulgation. Perhaps, in reference to the faculties of the Sacred Penitentiary to dispense in occult impediments of marriage, the distinctions of the former canonists may still determine the competency of that Sacred Tribunal, as Leitner [446] argues with some probability. In all other respects the explicit definition of public and occult impediment in the Code has certainly to be followed. In Canon 1971, n. 2, the Code states that the *promotor justitiæ* has the right to challenge the validity of a marriage in the case of an impediment *public of its very nature*. This phrase does not occur in the teaching of the Code on the impediments of marriage, but it was common among canonists before the Code, and its insertion in Canon 1971 has been responsible for the fact that some commentators have to a certain extent returned to the old distinctions of occult and public impediments.

The Code states that an impediment is public, if it can be proved in the external forum. Proof can be furnished either by the testimony of witnesses or by documents. As to proof by witnesses, cfr. Canon 1791 (below, n. 1732). The parties concerning whose marriage the case is to be proved are not, as a rule, to be admitted as witnesses because of the interest they have in the case (cfr. Canon 1757, n. 1708). In some cases

---

[444] Instit. 87, 48; *Opera Omnia*, X, 380.
[445] *De Matrimon.*, I, n. 260.
[446] *Katholisches Eherecht*, 272.

(e.g., impotency and non-consummation of marriage), they are admitted to testify, but the law demands additional proof besides their statements (cfr. Canon 1975; below, n. 1881). Proof by document is admitted in all cases that come before the ecclesiastical court. Documents are classified into public and private (cfr. Canons 1812–1824; below, nn. 1744–1753).

AUTHORITY TO ESTABLISH MARRIAGE IMPEDIMENTS

1009. The Supreme Authority of the Church alone has the right to declare authentically in what cases the divine law forbids or annuls marriage. The same Supreme Authority has the exclusive right of constituting impedient or diriment impediments for baptized persons either by universal or particular law (**Canon 1038**).

The local Ordinaries may in individual cases forbid any one actually staying in their diocese, and their subjects also while they are outside the diocese, to marry if there is a just reason, but only temporarily for the duration of such reason. The Holy See alone can attach to its prohibition of marriage the pain of invalidity (**Canon 1039**).

The Roman Pontiff alone can abolish or modify the ecclesiastical impediments of marriage, both impedient and diriment; and likewise no one else can dispense from these laws except in so far as this power is conceded to him either in the common law or by special indult of the Holy See (**Canon 1040**). Customs which introduce a new impediment or are contrary to existing impediments are condemned (**Canon 1041**).

Though the Vicar of Christ cannot give a dispensation from the divine law, he is competent to the exclusion of all other authorities to determine what that law is and its sphere of application. His power, then, is limited only by what is with certainty fixed by the divine law. This is a tremendous power, but Christ chose to give it to humans when He said: "All power is given to me in heaven and on earth. Going therefore, teach ye all nations, etc." (Matt., xxviii. 18–19). And again: "As the Father sent me, I also send you" (John, xx. 21).

The Holy See desires strict uniformity in the matter of impediments of marriage, and, if any special arrangements are necessary for some country or district, the Holy See reserves such to its own authority.   Wherefore, the Supreme Authority takes away from the authorities of the dioceses, vicariates, prefectures, and every other regional division of the Church, all power to establish impediments of marriage.   At most, a local Ordinary may prohibit marriage to an individual temporarily —that is, as long as some special reason for the prohibition lasts.   Even if such a person marries in violation of the prohibition, his marriage is valid (supposing that there was no diriment impediment of the common law hindering his marriage), for the local Ordinaries have no power to forbid marriage under pain of invalidity.   In the early centuries of the Church the bishops had, according to the opinion of the majority of canonists, the right to establish impediments of marriage for their respective dioceses; some canonists, however, held that the bishops lacked this power by the divine law.   Cardinal Gasparri is of the opinion that the right of the bishops to establish impediments of marriage was not taken away from them by explicit decree of the Supreme Pontiff, but rather by the custom and practice of the Holy See which was made necessary to avoid confusion in this important matter.   There can be no doubt that great difficulties would arise if each diocese had its own list of impediments of marriage.[447]   For the same reason the law does not recognize customs contrary to the impediments established by law, or customs introducing new impediments.

IMPEDIMENTS OF MINOR AND MAJOR DEGREE

1010. Impediments are of minor or of major degree.   The following are of minor degree:

(1) Consanguinity in the third degree of the collateral line;

(2) Affinity in the second degree of the collateral line;

(3) Public decency in the second degree;

(4) Spiritual relationship;

(5) Crime of adultery with promise of marriage or attempted marriage even by mere civil marriage (**Canon 1042**, §§ 1–2).

All other impediments are of major degree (**Canon 1042**, § 3).

This division of the diriment impediments of marriage into two groups, of minor and major degree, is important in the matter of dispensation from the impediments, wherefore the reader will have to refer to this list repeatedly.

[447] *De Matrimonio*, I, n. 278.   Concerning impediments abolished by the Code, cfr. App. III, 5, c, 1–3.

Dispensation from Impediments in Danger of Death

1011. In urgent danger of death the local Ordinaries can, for the sake of relieving a person's conscience and of rendering the offspring legitimate (if there be any), dispense from the form of the marriage contract as well as from any and all impediments of ecclesiastical law, public and occult as well as multiple, with the exception of the impediments arising from the sacred priesthood and from affinity in the direct line, if the marriage has been consummated. This dispensation may be granted to their own subjects wherever they may stay at the time, and to all who actually are within the territory of their jurisdiction. Scandal must be avoided, and, in case of dispensation from disparity of cult or mixed religion, the prescribed promises must be made (**Canon 1043**).

In the same circumstances as mentioned in the preceding Canon, but only in cases in which the local Ordinary cannot be approached in time, the pastor as well as the priest who assists at the marriage according to Canon 1098, n. 2, and also the confessor (but the latter only for the internal forum and in the act of sacramental confession), have the same faculties as those given to local Ordinaries in Canon 1043 (**Canon 1044**).

The Church gives these very extensive powers of dispensation to the local Ordinaries and also to the priest when there is danger that a party may die before the priest can in the ordinary mode of communication (personal interview, letter, etc.) get the dispensation from the bishop: telephone and telegraph cannot be considered. The Papal Secretary of State has declared that the Supreme Pontiff orders that all applications for favors to the Roman Curia made by telephone or telegraph shall be ignored, and that he wants the bishops to do the same.[448] The Committee for the Authentic Interpretation of the Code has also condemned the use of telephone or telegraph in such cases.[449]

How imminent the danger of death must be in order to justify the use of these faculties, is not stated in the Code, nor is it not possible to define this danger more closely, for it is a matter which varies with every case. A reasonably prudent

---

[448] December 10, 1891; *Collect. de Prop. Fide,* **II,** n. 1775.
[449] Cfr. App. III, 44, a.

opinion as to the proximity of the danger of death is all that can be demanded under the circumstances. The danger of death need not necessarily come from an illness: a former concession similar to that in the Code restricted the use of the faculties to "ægroti in gravissimo mortis periculo constituti," [450] but the Code has no such restriction.

The faculties may be used even though the party on whose side alone the impediment lies (e.g., the vow of chastity, sacred orders, etc.) is not in danger of death, but rather the other party. In this sense the Holy Office explained the faculties given in the Decree of 1888.[451] But the case must be such that the words of the Code are verified, namely, to afford relief to the conscience of the dying person.[452] Neither is it necessary for the use of the faculties that the parties are living in concubinage, or in an invalid marriage: the Code makes no mention of such a restriction, and the Sacred Congregation of the Sacraments had already declared that the faculties of the Decree of 1888 could be used though the parties were not living together.[453]

The reason for the dispensation may be either to ease the conscience of the one in danger of death—no matter in what manner the marriage helps to afford relief, whether by protecting the reputation of the parties, providing support for a party seduced, removing a proximate occasion of sin, etc.—or to legitimatize the offspring born or conceived by sinful intercourse. If one of the parties is a non-Catholic, the dispensation cannot be granted unless the required promises are made by the Catholic and the non-Catholic, for, as Canon 1061 states, the Church does not dispense from the impediment of mixed religion, and the same applies to disparity of cult (cfr. Canon 1071), unless these promises are made and the one granting the dispensation is morally certain that they will be kept.

With reference to the legitimation of the offspring, it must be borne in mind that adulterous and sacrilegious offspring cannot be made legitimate even by this very extensive power granted in Canon 1043 (cfr. Canon 1051). All illegitimate offspring, except adulterous and sacrilegious, is made legitimate by a dispensation from a diriment impediment granted by ordinary

---

450 Holy Office, February 20, 1888; *Acta S. Sedis*, XX, 543.
451 July 1, 1891; *Collect. de Prop. Fide*, II, n. 1758.
452 S. R. Rota, "Decisiones," II, *Decisio* III, n. 8, p. 27.
453 August 16, 1909; *Acta Ap. Sedis*, I, 656.

power or by power delegated through a general indult. The same restriction about adulterous and sacrilegious offspring was made in the faculties granted by the Decree of 1888, as is stated in an answer of the Holy Office, July 8, 1903.[454]

1012. The priest who answers sick calls is, as a rule, the one who encounters cases where a marriage in danger of death is to be contracted. If he is the pastor, he has power to dispense from the impediments for both the internal and external forum, supposing that there is no time to get the dispensation from the bishop. But even if the priest is merely a confessor—that is, a priest who has the faculties of the diocese, but no power to witness marriages—he can in case of danger of death dispense from all the impediments from which the Ordinary by Canon 1043 can dispense, supposing that there is no time to get the dispensation from the Ordinary, but his dispensation can be given only in sacramental confession and for the internal forum (cfr. Canon 882). If the party lives, as the marriage is not considered valid in the external forum (cfr. Canon 202), the priest must have it thus validated. As the powers of the confessor are incomplete (because he cannot dispense with the impediments in the external forum), the question has been raised by commentators whether the confessor can act in the capacity of the priest mentioned in Canon 1098, n. 2 (a priest who neither is pastor nor has delegated faculties to witness marriages and who happens to be at hand for a marriage in danger of death or in a place where the priest in charge will not be there for a month). There are not many commentators who discuss this point, for the majority simply repeat what the Code says about the power of the confessor. Cappello,[455] Schäfer,[456] and Augustine [457] hold that the confessor may act in the capacity of the priest of Canon 1098, provided of course the condition is verified that the Ordinary or the pastor or a priest delegated to assist at the marriage cannot be reached without great inconvenience. The text of Canon 1098 embraces any other priest except the pastor or a priest delegated for assistance at marriage.

Another question arises as to what faculties are possessed in

---

[454] *Collect. de Prop. Fide*, **II**, n. 2171.
[455] *De Sacramentis*, III, n, 238.
[456] *Das Eherecht*, 83. [457] *Commentary*, V, 103.

danger of death by a priest who is not the pastor of the parish where the sick person stays, but is delegated to assist at marriages in the parish—a general delegation which may, and in many dioceses is given to the regularly appointed assistant priests. If such an assistant on a sick call meets with a case in which marriage should be contracted, can he dispense with the impediments of marriage? Vermeersch-Creusen [458] hold that he has no power unless the pastor (or the bishop) has delegated to him the faculties of Canon 1043. Cappello,[459] Chelodi,[460] Schäfer,[461] Cerato,[462] and Leitner [463] hold that he has power to dispense when the Ordinary cannot be reached without great difficulty, according to and in virtue of Canon 1098, n. 2. They point out that it would be abnormal and ridiculous to ascribe the faculties to any other priest and deny them to the regularly appointed assistant priest in this case. Some of the commentators say that, if it is not admitted that he has the power of dispensation in virtue of Canon 1098 (combined with Canon 1044), he has it at least under the general principle of Canon 200, which states that, if delegated power (here to assist at marriage) is given to a person, this delegation is considered to include all those powers without which the delegated power could not be exercised. This latter reason is extremely doubtful. If one gets delegation for a certain affair, one gets all necessary power to execute the delegated power, but one does not get power in an entirely different affair though that may be connected with the first affair.

1013. The power of dispensation in danger of death extends to all impediments of ecclesiastical law, except that of priesthood and affinity in the direct line, after the consummation of the marriage. According to Canon 97, affinity arises from a valid marriage either unconsummated or consummated. Only the affinity in the direct line after the consummation of the marriage which caused that affinity, is reserved in danger of death. Thus a man could not be dispensed to marry the daughter or granddaughter of his wife, who had children from a former marriage, if he had been validly married and had had conjugal intercourse with his wife. Generally speaking, the consumma-

[458] *Epitome,* II, n. 353, I, 2.
[459] *De Sacramentis,* III, n. 236.
[460] *Jus Matrimoniale,* n. 44.
[463] *Kath. Eherecht,* 336.
[461] *Das Eherecht,* 83.
[462] *Matrimonium,* n. 72.

tion of the marriage is presumed. If it is certain that the marriage was not consummated, the dispensation from the affinity in the direct line can be granted.

The power of dispensation given in Canon 1043 to the local Ordinaries is a so-called *potestas ordinaria* (i.e., given by law to any one who holds the office and title of local Ordinary). The local Ordinaries can delegate that power according to Canon 199. The power extends to all who in law are held equivalent to local Ordinaries (cfr. Canon 198). As to the pastor, the commentators do not agree whether it should be called a *potestas ordinaria* or *delegata*. It seems more correct to say that it is a power delegated by law rather than an ordinary power, because the office of the pastor is an office to which no jurisdiction in the external forum attaches. Practically, it does not make much difference because, according to Canon 199, the power of jurisdiction delegated by the Holy See can be subdelegated, either for one act or also habitually. Wherefore, if the power of the pastor to dispense from the impediments in the external forum is considered a delegated power, it loses nothing of its effectiveness because it can be subdelegated.

Dispensation from Impediments in "Casu Perplexo"

1014. The local Ordinaries can, under the conditions stated in Canon 1043, grant dispensation from all the impediments spoken of in that Canon, if the impediment is discovered only after everything has been prepared for the marriage and the ceremony cannot be delayed until dispensation from the Holy See can be obtained without probable danger of grave evil. This faculty holds good also for the convalidation of a marriage already contracted, if delay is dangerous and there is not sufficient time to have recourse to the Holy See. In the same circumstances all priests mentioned in Canon 1044 have the same faculties, but their power extends over occult cases only, and provided there is no time to recur to the local Ordinary, or recourse to the Ordinary can be had only with the danger of violating the secret (**Canon 1045**).[463a]

The unexpected discovery of an impediment at the last moment when everything had been prepared for the marriage was properly called a "perplexing case" by canonists and moralists

[463a] Concerning meaning of "occult cases," cfr. App. III, 45.

who wrote before the promulgation of the Code. The Code gives ample powers of dispensation to the bishop over all impediments, except the priesthood and the affinity in the direct line after consummation of marriage. The priests spoken of in Canon 1044 have the same power, when there is no time to have recourse to the bishop, or when the recourse endangers the seal of confession.

They can dispense from *all the impediments,* not from the form of marriage, for this is not an impediment properly so called and is specially mentioned in Canon 1043, before that Canon speaks of the impediments. Besides, in the case contemplated in Canon 1045, there would be no occasion and no reason to dispense from the form of marriage; the Canon rather supposes that the parties, witnesses and everything else are ready for the marriage.

As to the discovery of the impediment, the Holy See has declared [464] that the faculties can be used if the Ordinary or the pastor learns of the impediment at the time when everything is ready for the marriage, though it was known before to others. The declaration makes no distinction whether others who knew of the impediment withheld this knowledge from the pastor or Ordinary intentionally or in good faith.

The phrase, "when all things are ready for the marriage," is not explained in the Code. It is quite certain that it need not be restricted to such narrow limits as to mean merely the day of the marriage itself. If the impediment is discovered some days before the marriage, it may nevertheless be true that everything is ready for the marriage, which cannot be delayed without probable danger of grave harm. That harm may be either spiritual or temporal—anything that is considered a serious evil. It need not be certain that such harm will inevitably follow, for the Code speaks of a "probable danger." Here in the United States it would take several months to get a dispensation from the Holy See. Once the date is set for the marriage, and perhaps the banns published and invitations sent out, the marriage can usually not be delayed without great harm to the parties and their families (cfr. Canon 81).

1015. If a marriage has been invalidly contracted, the same faculties to dispense from all the impediments except the two

464 Cfr. App. III, 44, b.

mentioned in Canon 1043 are granted if delay of the validation of the marriage is dangerous, and there is not sufficient time to have recourse to the Holy See. Does that mean that the marriage must have been contracted *in facie ecclesiæ,* though invalidly on account of some diriment impediment? Or does it also mean marriages contracted outside the church, that is before a minister or civil magistrate? Probably the marriage outside the Church has a sufficient appearance of a marriage to come under the general phrase of the Code "pro validatione matrimonii jam contracti." Of the marriage of a heretic or an infidel with a Catholic, Wernz says that their marriage, contracted after the manner customary with infidels or heretics in a country, cannot be called a fornicatious ūnion, but rather that it has the appearance of a marriage.[465] A Decree of the Holy Office, July 6, 1898, allowed the bishop or the pastor to make use of the faculties of dispensation from impediments given by the Decree of 1888 for the benefit of an unbaptized person and a Catholic living in civil marriage.[466] In marriages of a non-Catholic and a Catholic outside the Church, there may be a *matrimonium putativum,* for one party (the non-Catholic) may be in good faith, believing his marriage before the minister or the civil magistrate to be a true marriage. With two Catholics contracting marriage outside the Church, it is more difficult to concede that their union has any resemblance of marriage, for it is called a *turpis* and *exitialis concubinatus.*[467] Nevertheless, there is at least the natural foundation of a marriage, the manifestation of mutual consent to live as husband and wife, and the Code gives this some consideration when it rules in Canon 1139 that any marriage entered into with the naturally sufficient consent of both parties, but which consent is inefficacious for reason of a diriment impediment of ecclesiastical law or for lack of the legitimate form, can be validated by a *sanatio in radice.*

1016. The last part of Canon 1045 states that the pastor, or other priest, or the confessor, has the same power to dispense from impediments when the impediment is detected only when all things are ready for the marriage, but their power is (1)

[465] *Jus Decretal.,* IV, n. 29; Augustine, "Commentary," V, 108.
[466] *Collect. de Prop. Fide,* II, n. 2007.
[467] *Instr. S. Pœnitentiariæ,* January 15, 1866; *Collect. de Prop. Fide,* I, n. 1280.

limited to occult cases, and (2) conditioned by the circumstance that the Ordinary cannot be reached in time or cannot be approached without danger of violating the secret.

The phrase "occult cases" has been the occasion of much controversy among commentators. It has been debated whether occult cases mean the same as occult impediments. There are so few occult impediments in the acceptation of that term by the Code that the faculty of the pastor and other priests and confessors would be of little practical value. Under this supposition, the people could not get the relief the Code desires to give them in the plight of the "casus perplexus," for in many cases the Ordinary could not be reached in time to save the people from suffering through the unexpected discovery of an impediment. Many commentators hold that, in this case of urgent necessity and when there is no time to have recourse to the local Ordinary, the pastor and other priests mentioned in Canon 1044 can dispense from impediments which are actually occult, though they could be proved in the external forum.[468] The term occult has been discussed under Canon 1037. Some commentators, including Schäfer,[469] Ayrinhac,[470] Augustine,[471] and Hillig,[472] hold that the "casus occulti" are the same as the "impedimenta occulta" of Canon 1037, and that therefore the pastor and other priests cannot dispense from impediments which can be proved in the external forum, even though they are actually occult.

Canon 1045 states that the pastor and other priests can dispense in occult cases provided the Ordinary cannot be reached in time, or that he cannot be approached without *danger of violating the secret*. This last phrase may not be taken as synonymous with "violating the seal of confession." The Code simply says violating the secret, and there are various kinds of secrets —natural, professional, and sacramental. Now as to the sacramental seal, there can be no doubt that its danger of violation excuses from having recourse to the Ordinary. If the recourse

---

[468] Cappello, "De Sacrm.," III, n. 236; Vermeersch-Creusen, "Epitome," II, n. 353; Leitner, "Kath. Eherecht," 335; Chelodi, "Jus Matrimoniale," n. 44; Cerato, "Matrimonium," n. 38; Petrovits, "New Church Law on Marriage," 97; De Smet, "De Sponsalibus et Matrimonio" (ed. 1923), n. 793.

[469] *Das Eherecht*, 85.   [470] *Marriage Legislation*, n. 70.
[471] *Commentary*, V, 109.
[472] *Archiv für kath. Kirchenr.*, CII (1922), 1.

can be had without danger by giving fictitious names, and supposing that time permits the recourse, a dispensation must be sought from the Ordinary. Canon 1755 exempts from testifying in the ecclesiastical court pastors and other priests, civil officials, physicians, midwives, lawyers, notaries and others who know of a secret affair by reason of their office in counselling, assisting, etc. When Canon 1045 speaks of the violation of the secret, it does not limit it to any one kind of secrets, but rules generally that the pastor and other priests can make use of the faculties if the asking of the dispensation from the bishop cannot be done without danger of violating the secret.

Recording of Dispensations Granted by Pastor or Other Priests in the Foregoing Cases

1017. The pastor or priest spoken of in Canon 1044 who has granted a dispensation for the external forum shall at once inform the local Ordinary of this fact, and the dispensation shall be recorded in the marriage record (**Canon 1046**).

As the local Ordinary has the supervision of all affairs of the external forum in the territory of his jurisdiction, the Code wants him informed of all that transpires in the external forum. The pastor or other priest who granted the dispensation for the external forum must also see that the marriage and the dispensation is entered in the marriage records of the parish where the marriage took place. This Canon does not speak of the dispensation granted by a confessor, for as confessor he can grant that dispensation for the internal forum only, and these dispensations are spoken of in the next Canon.

Dispensations Granted in the Internal Forum

1018. Unless the Rescript of the Sacred Penitentiary contains other directions, the dispensation conceded for the internal non-sacramental forum from an occult impediment shall be recorded in the secret archives of the Curia spoken of in Canon 379, and there is no need of another dispensation in the external forum, though the impediment afterwards becomes public. If the dispensation was granted for the internal sacramental forum only, a new dispensation is required when the impediment becomes public (**Canon 1047**).

The Sacred Penitentiary's jurisdiction is limited to matters of the internal forum, sacramental and non-sacramental (cfr. Canon 258). The Rescript itself must be inspected to find whether a dispensation is granted for the sacramental or the non-sacramental forum. If the Sacred Penitentiary gives power to dispense *in actu sacramentalis confessionis tantum,* it is evident that the priest can apply the dispensation in confession only. If that clause or an equivalent one is not contained in the Rescript, the dispensation can be applied outside of confession, and it should be thus applied, because the Code wants a dispensation granted by the Sacred Penitentiary for the internal non-sacramental forum to be recorded in the secret archives of the diocesan curia. If the impediment becomes public afterwards, there is no need of a dispensation for the external forum; if, however, the dispensation granted by the Sacred Penitentiary was given for the sacramental forum only, a new dispensation in the external forum must be obtained when the impediment becomes public. We saw before that jurisdiction for the internal forum only is not valid in the external forum (cfr. Canon 202). An exception from that rule is here made in favor of the dispensations granted by the Sacred Penitentiary in the internal non-sacramental forum. This rule concerning dispensations of the Sacred Penitentiary for the internal non-sacramental forum does not apply to the confessor who, in danger of death and in the urgent case when all things are ready for the marriage, can grant dispensations, for he can grant them in the sacramental forum only.

Here the question arises whether the Sacred Penitentiary can dispense from impediments which are in fact occult, but can be proved in the external forum and are therefore according to the terminology of Canon 1037 public impediments. It seems that the jurisdiction of the Sacred Penitentiary has not been modified by the Code, for its powers are not detailed in the Code (cfr. Canon 258). Wherefore, these powers must be learned from other sources, and Canon 243 says that the Sacred Congregations, Tribunals and Offices of the Holy See are governed by the general and particular norms which the Holy See may have given them. Now, in the "Normæ Peculiares" for the Sacred Penitentiary and other tribunals, the rules for the Sacred Penitentiary state that it is to act "praesertim ad normas Constitutionis, *In Apostolicæ*," of Pope Benedict XIV, April 13, 1744.[473] The extent of its powers seem, therefore, to be the same as before the Code.

PETITION FOR DISPENSATION SENT TO THE HOLY SEE

1019. If a petition for a dispensation has been sent to the Holy See, the local Ordinaries shall not in that case make use of their faculties, if they have any, except for a serious and urgent reason, as stated in Canon 204 (**Canon 1048**). In the latter case, they shall immediately inform the Holy See of the action taken by them in such an emergency (Canon 204).

The case contemplated in Canon 1048 should but rarely occur. The pastor or confessor who desires to obtain a dispensation from any impediment should, as a rule, address the petition to his own Ordinary, giving precise information as to the nature of the impediment and the reasons why a dispensation seems necessary or proper, and he should request the bishop to forward the petition to the Holy See if he himself has not the faculties to dispense with the impediment. In all applications for dispensations from public impediments the Holy See demands that the petitions be endorsed by the bishop. In the occult impediments where one cannot mention the names of the parties because of danger of defamation, one may directly apply to the Sacred Penitentiary, giving fictitious names of the parties (or party), but even in this case better results are obtained by forwarding the petition with the endorsement of the bishop, unless the case is such that even from the circumstances told in the petition the parties might be revealed to the Ordinary.

Once the petition to the Holy See has been mailed, the Ordinary is forbidden to make use of the faculties of dispensation in that same case, unless the matter becomes meanwhile very urgent. If so, he can dispense but he must report the fact to the Holy See. Supposing that the bishop has the faculty, his act of dispensation is valid (cfr. Canon 204), but it is illicit, except in urgent necessity, to make use of the faculties in a case which has been referred to the higher authority. The command of Canon 204 to the Ordinary to report at once to Rome

---

[473] *Normæ*, etc., cap. VIII, Sept. 29, 1908; *Acta Ap Sedis*, I, 102; Const. "In Apostolicæ," *Opera Omnia Bened. XIV*, XV. 363.

(*statim*) is usually explained to the effect that he must write within three days.

1020. The dispensation given in the sacramental forum cannot be recorded anywhere because of the seal of confession. The Sacred Penitentiary usually orders destruction of the document of dispensation. If the impediment becomes public, a new dispensation must be obtained to validate the marriage in the external forum. Gasparri speaks of a case where a marriage of two people living together is invalid for reason of an impediment which is public of its nature, but *de facto* occult. He says a dispensation can be obtained from the Sacred Penitentiary in the form "parocho pro utroque foro," in which form it is demanded that the granting of the dispensation and the record of the marriage be entered in the secret marriage record which is to be carefully guarded in the parochial archives.[474]

Interpretation of Delegated Power of Dispensation

1021. In marriages, whether already contracted or to be contracted, a person who has a general indult to dispense from some certain impediment can dispense from it even though the same impediment be multiple, unless the indult itself provides otherwise. A person who has a general indult to dispense from several impediments of various kinds, either diriment or impedient, can dispense from those impediments though they are public and occur in one and the same case (**Canon 1049**).

This Canon treats of the "cumulatio facultatum," which is now conceded by the Code together with a general indult to dispense from one or more impediments. Formerly, a person with an indult to dispense (e.g.), in certain degrees of both consanguinity and affinity, could not dispense if both affinity and consanguinity occurred in the same case.[475] Likewise, the faculty to dispense from a diriment impediment and an impedient impediment reserved to the Holy See (e.g., mixed religion, simple vow of perpetual chastity), could not be used where both kinds of impediments occurred in the same case.[476] A special indult to combine the various powers of dispensation in one and the same case was required.[477] If there was a public impediment

---

[474] *De Matrimonio*, I, n. 421.
[475] Holy Office, July 2, 1884; *Collect. de Prop. Fide*, II, n. 1622.
[476] Holy Office, Aug. 18, 1897; *Collect. de Prop. Fide*, II, n. 1979.
[477] Holy Office, May 18, 1869; *Collect. de Prop. Fide*, II, n. 1344.

and an occult one in the same case, and the bishop had faculties to dispense from both, a special indult of "cumulatio" was not needed.[478] Much less, Gasparri argues, was a special indult required to dispense from two occult impediments in the same case.[479] The only restriction in the use of faculties of a general indult is contained in the following Canon, which reads:

1022. If a person who has a general indult to dispense from one or more public impediments meets with a case in which there is also another impediment from which he has no power to dispense, he must apply to the Holy See for dispensation from all impediments in the case. If, however, the impediment or impediments from which he can dispense are discovered only after the dispensation has been obtained from the Holy See, he may make use of his faculty (**Canon 1050**).

In the first place, Canon 1050 forbids the use of the faculties in a case in which there are several *public* impediments, if for one of them the bishop or other inferior authority has no power to dispense. The Code does not speak of the case in which a public and an occult impediment concur. If both impediments are public, it does not matter that one is impedient and the other diriment; the rule of this Canon will apply.

Furthermore, Canon 1050 prohibits the use of faculties obtained by indult only; it does not speak of the use of those faculties which are given to Ordinary or priest by law.

Whether the Ordinary can *validly* dispense with one public impediment when in the same case he has to apply to the Holy See for another public impediment, is disputed. As the Code rules that in such a case the dispensation must be obtained from the Holy See for all public impediments in the case, it seems to deny indirectly the power of the inferior authority to make use of his indult. Besides, the former Canon Law made the use of the faculties invalid in such a case,[480] and therefore, according to Canon 6, n. 4, in a doubt whether the Code differs from the former law, one must adhere to the former law.

The phrase "comperiantur post impetratam a Sancta Sede dispensationem" is somewhat ambiguous. Does it mean "after the request for the dispensation has been mailed to the Holy

---

[478] Cong. P. F., March 31, 1872; *Collect. de Prop. Fide,* II, n. 1382.
[479] *De Matrimonio,* I, n. 470.
[480] Gasparri, "De Matrimonio," I. n. 469.

See," or "after the dispensation has been obtained from the Holy See"? Very likely it means that the impediment is discovered only after the dispensation has reached the Ordinary, in which case he need not apply again but use his indult to dispense from the newly discovered impediment though it be public. In this sense it is interpreted by a number of commentators.[481] There remains the inconvenience of delaying the marriage and asking for a new dispensation if the second public impediment is discovered after application for the first has been mailed to the Holy See. However, the new faculties given to the bishops of the United States contain far-reaching power of dispensation "for grave and urgent reason when there is danger in delay of the marriage and it cannot be deferred until dispensation is obtained from the Holy See" (cfr. Canon 81). These faculties do not include all the impediments of ecclesiastical law, but they do contain most of them.

DISPENSATION FROM IMPEDIMENTS AND LEGITIMATION OF OFFSPRING

1023. By a dispensation from a diriment impediment granted either by ordinary power or by power delegated through a general indult, the legitimation of the offspring, born or conceived, is *ipso facto* granted, with the exception of adulterous and sacrilegious offspring. If the dispensation is granted by power given by rescript in a particular case, the legitimation is not granted *ipso facto* (**Canon 1051**).

This Canon supplements Canon 1116 which provides for the legitimation of offspring conceived or born of parents who were not married, but who in law would have been capable of contracting a valid marriage at the time of conception, or pregnancy, or birth. Canon 1051 provides for the legitimation of children born of or conceived by a couple who were not capable of contracting a valid marriage for reason of some diriment impediment. When the impediment is removed in virtue of a general indult, or in virtue of faculties which the law attaches to some office (e.g., the faculties granted by the Code to local Ordinaries), the offspring is *ipso facto* made legitimate, with the exception

---

[481] Cerato, "Matrimonium," n. 43; De Smet, "De Spons. et Matr.," n. 783; Cappello, "De Sacram.," III, n. 249; Schäfer, "Das Eherecht," 96; Linneborn, "Grundriss des Eherechts," 141.

of children born or conceived in adulterous or sacrilegious intercourse.

The rescript in particular cases is an answer of the Holy
See to a petition for a dispensation in individual cases, and in
these petitions the request for the legitimation of offspring (if
there be any born or conceived) should be added, for, unless
the rescript explicitly grants the legitimation, the offspring is
not made legitimate by the dispensation from the impediment.
It is known that the offspring conceived or born of parents one
or both of whom were validly married, and who defiled the
sanctity of marriage by adultery, is called adulterous offspring.
If one or both parents were bound by solemn religious vows,
or if the man was in major orders, the offspring is called sacrilegious. The Holy See can, of course, render these children
legitimate, but authors familiar with the practice of the Roman
Curia state that this is rarely done.

Mistakes about Impediments in Application for Dispensation

1024. The dispensation from the impediment of consanguinity
or affinity given for some degree of the impediment is valid,
although in the petition or in the concession there is an error
concerning the degree, provided the degree actually existing is
inferior; it is likewise valid though another impediment of the
same species was concealed, provided the concealed impediment
is of equal or inferior degree to the impediment expressed
(**Canon 1052**).

This Canon deals exclusively with dispensations of impediments of *consanguinity* and *affinity*. Its provisions, therefore,
may not be applied to other impediments. Neither does it apply
to a case where one asks for a dispensation from consanguinity
and actually affinity exists, or together with consanguinity an
impediment of affinity.

The phrase "although there is an error" (literally "if an error crept in") indicates that the Code in this part of the Canon
speaks of a mistake made in good faith, either by the petitioner
or by the one who drew up the document of concession. In the
second part of the Canon 1052, "though another impediment
of the same species was concealed," the Code allows for mistakes

made either inadvertently or intentionally because the term
"reticitum" is general enough to include both ways of concealment.

Dispensation from the "Matrimonium Ratum non Consummatum."—Permission to Re-marry on Presumed Death of Consort

1025. The dispensation given by the Holy See from the
matrimonium ratum non consummatum, and the permission to
marry again on account of the presumed death of the former
husband or wife, always includes the dispensation from the
impediment of adultery committed with the promise of or attempt of marriage (if there is need of such a dispensation),
but not from the impediment mentioned in Canon 1075, nn. 2–3
(**Canon 1053**).

The Decree of the Sacred Congregation of the Sacraments,
June 3, 1912, made the concession in the two cases now embodied
in the Code.[482] The Decree spoke of the impediment of crime
arising from a civil marriage of the adulterers, while the Code
simply has "attempted marriage" and adds besides the case
where the impediment of crime arises not from attempted marriage but from the mutual promise of marriage of the adulterers.

The dispensation from the *matrimonium ratum non consummatum* can be given by the Holy See only, and it is usually
not delegated to others. The permission to marry again after
the presumed death of the husband or wife can be given also
by the bishop, but the Code states that the permission to marry
again given by the Holy See (not by the Ordinary) includes
the dispensation from the impediment of crime arising from
adultery and mutual promise of marriage, or attempted marriage.

An Instruction of the Holy Office of 1868 states that, if all
the cases of presumed death of a husband or wife are sent to
the Holy See, a long delay in answering them is unavoidable
—all the more so if the documents of the local Ordinaries do
not cover the points needed for information of the Holy See,
or are not drafted in the proper form. Wherefore, the Holy
Office issues this Instruction for the guidance of the local Ordi-

[482] *Acta Ap. Sedis,* IV, 403.

naries, and they should decide the cases accordingly. If, even with the help of this Instruction, the local Ordinaries cannot come to a definite decision in some case, they should refer the matter to the Holy See, forwarding all the acts in the case.[483]

Mistake and Fraud in Application for Dispensations

1026. A dispensation from an impediment of minor degree is not invalidated by either a positive lie or by concealing the truth, even though the only one motive reason advanced in the petition is false (**Canon 1054**).

This Canon is an exception to the general rule laid down in Canon 40 in reference to rescripts granted by ecclesiastical authorities, namely, that the favors are granted under condition that the petition is truthful. As the Code speaks in general terms without distinguishing whether the dispensation is granted by the Holy See or by an inferior authority, the exception in favor of the validity of the dispensation applies to all dispensations from impediments of lesser degree, no matter who grants the dispensation. The impediments of lesser degree are enumerated in Canon 1042.

Execution of Dispensations Granted by the Holy See

1027. Dispensations from public impediments committed by the Holy See to the Ordinary of the petitioners shall be executed by the Ordinary who gave letters of recommendation to the petitioners or who forwarded the petition to the Holy See, though at the time when the dispensation arrives the parties have left their former domicile or quasi-domicile in the diocese and have gone into another diocese with the intention not to return to the former diocese. However, the local Ordinary of the diocese where the parties desire to contract marriage is to be advised of the dispensation (**Canon 1055**).

This is a practical rule to obviate longer delay in the execution of dispensations. The Holy Office, February 20, 1888, had made the same regulation as this Canon of the Code.[484] Public impediments are spoken of, because the dispensations from occult impediments are not as a rule sent to the local Ordinaries but

---

[483] *Collectanea de Prop. Fide,* II, n. 1321.
[484] *Collectanea de Prop. Fide,* II, n. 1685.

either directly to the petitioners (with instruction to present it to a confessor approved by the local Ordinary) or to the confessor himself, delegating him to grant the dispensation. The Ordinary may delegate another to execute the dispensation committed to him, unless the rescripts expressly forbids this (cfr. Canons 57 and 199).

Fees for the Dispensations

1028. With the exception of a small charge for the necessary expenses of the chancery office in dispensations which are not issued *in forma pauperum,* the local Ordinaries and their officials cannot demand any gain on the occasion of the concession of a dispensation, unless the Holy See shall have explicitly given them this right. If they nevertheless exact such profit, they are bound to make restitution. All customs contrary to this Canon are condemned (**Canon 1056**).

Without permission of the Holy See the local Ordinaries may not publish a list of fees for marriage dispensations, as was stated in a recent case by the Sacred Congregation of the Council.[485] They are entitled to a compensation for the labor and expenses of the chancery office, but that can be only a very small amount for an individual dispensation. In the faculties given to the bishops of the United States by the Sacred Congregation of the Sacraments we find the statement (after the faculties to dispense with impediments of marriage) that the Ordinary, when granting these dispensations, shall see that the parties to be married make a fair offering to the Holy See according to their means.

Papal Indult to be Mentioned in Dispensations Granted by Delegated Power

1029. He who grants a dispensation in virtue of delegated powers received from the Apostolic See must make explicit mention of the papal indult when granting the dispensation (**Canon 1057**).

From ancient times the Holy See has insisted that dispensations granted in virtue of a papal indult shall be granted with the mentioning of such indult. However, unless the pain of

---

[485] Dec. 11, 1920; *Acta Ap. Sedis,* XIII, 350.

invalidity is attached to this command, the non-observance of this precept does not make the dispensation invalid. The present Canon does not attach the pain of invalidity to its precept.[486]

CHAPTER III

OF IMPEDIENT IMPEDIMENTS

1030. Marriage is forbidden to those who have made the simple vow of virginity, of perfect chastity, not to marry, to receive major orders, or to embrace the religious life. No simple vow invalidates marriage, unless invalidity has been decreed in certain instances by special precept of the Apostolic See (**Canon 1058**).

Simple vows may be either private or public. A vow is called public when it is accepted by the competent ecclesiastical superior (cfr. Canon 1308). A simple vow may be either perpetual or temporary, but even a temporary vow, if one of the five enumerated in Canon 1058, forbids marriage during the time for which it binds the person. If the vow is invalid, the impediment does not exist. If the vow is entirely secret and not at all manifested externally, it is doubtful whether it constitutes an impediment *in facie Ecclesiæ*, because it is a disputed question whether the Church can enforce her jurisdiction in reference to merely internal acts.[487] In a doubt of law, the law does not oblige. A person who has made a vow which is incompatible with the marital state, or who, if he married, would be exposed to the proximate danger of breaking his vow, is bound in conscience to abstain from marriage or get a dispensation for the internal forum.

1031. The vow of virginity has for its direct object bodily integrity. The vow is broken by a voluntary gravely sinful act of sexual intercourse or by pollution. In women the vow is broken by a gravely sinful act of unchastity by which the virginal integrity is lost. Once the vow is thus broken, its fulfillment is no longer possible and ceases to exist.[488]

1032. The vow of perfect chastity has for its direct object the abstaining from all sexual pleasure both internal and ex-

---

[486] Bened. XIV, *Epist.* "*Ad tuas,*" August 8, 1748; *Opera Omnia Bened. XIV*, XVI, 416.
[487] Cappello, "De Sacram.," III, n. 296.
[488] Gasparri, "De Matrim.," I, n. 480.

ternal, and from not only illicit, but also licit sexual pleasure in marriage. If one contracts marriage while bound by such a vow, the vow does not cease; the party cannot without sin ask for the debitum, but cannot deny this to the other party if he or she insists on his or her right. The only practical way out of the difficulty is for the party bound by such a vow to ask for a dispensation. Unless the dispensation clearly states that the vow is entirely remitted, it revives after the first marriage is dissolved. An unusual case of a vow of chastity made in the Anglican Church was decided by the Sacred Penitentiary. An Anglican had made the vows of chastity, poverty and obedience before an Anglican minister. Now, in case of conversion to the Catholic Church, it was asked whether the vow remained or ceased. The answer was that it remained, and that the person was obliged to keep it, if there had been a true intention to make a vow.[489] Cappello holds that it is doubtful whether such a vow of chastity would constitute a prohibiting impediment of marriage.[490] However, the principle of the Code is that all baptized persons are subject to the laws of the Church, and, as in this particular the Church has not made any exception, it seems the impediment of marriage does apply in the case.

1033. The vow not to marry or the vow of celibacy, as it is also called, has for its direct object the promise to abstain from the marriage contract. If one contracts marriage in violation of the vow, one sins against the vow by making the contract, but not in the exercise of the marriage rights. After the marriage bond is dissolved, the observance of the vow is again possible, and therefore the person cannot licitly marry a second time without a dispensation, according to the more common opinion of canonists.[491]

1034. The vow to receive Sacred Orders is, as a rule, violated by marriage, because in the Church of the Latin Rite celibacy is obligatory for men in major orders. Married men are not absolutely barred from Sacred Orders, but marriage is among the simple impediments of ordination, and therefore a dispensation would be required besides the consent of the wife and other formalities of law.

[489] November 29, 1842; *Collect. de Prop. Fide*, I, n. 959.
[490] *De Sacramentis*, III, n. 300.
[491] Wernz, "Jus Decretal.," IV, n. 566.

1035. As the vow to embrace the religious life is of course incompatible with marriage, marriage is forbidden as long as the vow lasts. By "the religious life" the Code means any approved religious organization. It may be truly said that both the vow to receive sacred orders and the vow to embrace religious life are temporary in their very nature. They oblige the one who made either of these vows to a reasonable effort to be admitted to sacred orders or to a religious community. If he does not succeed, the vow ceases since he has done what he was obliged under the vow to do.

No simple vow invalidates marriage, the Code states, unless the Holy See has ruled otherwise for some persons. For the Society of Jesus such a special rule has been made by Pope Gregory XIII to the effect that the simple vows in the Society invalidate marriage of the men bound by these vows.[492]

DISPENSATION FROM THE IMPEDIMENT OF THESE VOWS

1036. A dispensation is required before a person who has made one of these five vows, and is actually bound by them, may licitly contract marriage. Among the private vows two are reserved to the Holy See—namely, the vow of perfect and perpetual chastity and the vow to enter a religious order in which solemn vows are taken—provided these vows were made unconditionally by a person fully eighteen years of age (cfr. Canon 1309). From the private vows not reserved to the Holy See the local Ordinaries can, in virtue of Canon 1313, dispense their own subjects and strangers. The simple vows in religious orders and congregations of papal law can be dissolved by the Holy See only (cfr. Canon 638). The vows in diocesan religious congregations, either temporary or perpetual, can be dissolved by the local Ordinaries (cfr. Canon 638). Confessors cannot dispense with any private vows (much less with public vows), unless they have received special faculties for this purpose.

IMPEDIMENT OF LEGAL ADOPTION

1037. In those countries where the relationship arising from legal adoption makes marriage illicit according to the civil law, marriage is also illicit by Canon Law (**Canon 1059**).

[492] Gasparri, "Fontes Cod. Juris Can.," I, n. 153.

In the former Canon Law there was a diriment impediment of marriage arising from legal adoption, provided the civil law followed the Roman civil law in this matter. It seems that in former times the Roman Law was followed in very many matters by the nations of Europe and in their colonies, but in modern times they have broken away from it more and more. The changes in the laws of the nations made the impediment of legal adoption very uncertain, as can be seen from canonists who wrote before the Code.[493]

The Code simplified matters by breaking away from the old Roman civil law as a basis for the impediment of legal adoption, and accommodating itself to the laws of the respective nations. Where the laws of a nation make legal adoption a prohibiting impediment of marriage, the Canon Law adopts it as such, and where the civil law makes it a diriment impediment, the Code adopts it as a diriment impediment (cfr. Canon 1080). To know, therefore, whether there is an impediment of legal adoption and how far it extends, one must consult the civil law of the respective country.

1038. In the United States each state is autonomous, except in a certain limited number of matters which are under the jurisdiction of the Federal Government. The question of adoption is entirely under the jurisdiction of each individual state, and, while some states have laws in reference to adoption, no state recognizes any impediment of marriage, impedient or diriment, arising from legal adoption. Wherefore, the impediment of legal adoption does not exist in the United States.

A difficulty may arise from the fact that persons come to the United States from other countries where the impediment of legal adoption exists. If they have left their domicile and come here to stay, the laws of their former domicile cannot affect them any longer (cfr. Canon 95). If they have not given up their former domicile but come to stay here only temporarily, they still remain subject to the laws of their own country. In Canon Law, as well as in civil law, the general principle is recognized that contracts are governed by the laws of the place where the contract is made. There may be exceptions to this rule for special contracts, and here in the United States some states demand that the stranger be qualified to marry by the

493 Gasparri, "De Matrimonio," I, nn. 851–870.

laws of his own state, and that the residents of the state intending to remain residents may not marry in another state,
if their marriage in the home state would be illegal.

The reforms suggested by the Commissioners on Uniform
State Laws in reference to marriage contain the following proposed enactments: ''Be it enacted . . . that if any person
residing and intending to continue to reside in this state who is
disabled or prohibited from contracting marriage under the laws
of this state shall go into another state or country and there
contract a marriage prohibited and declared void by the laws
of this state, such marriage shall be null and void for all purposes in this state with the same effect as though such prohibited
marriage had been entered into in this state.

''No marriage shall be contracted in this state by a party
residing and intending to continue to reside in another state or
jurisdiction, if such marriage would be void if contracted in
such other state or jurisdiction, and every marriage celebrated
in this state in violation of this provision shall be null and void.''

This act has been adopted in Illinois, Louisiana, Massachusetts, Vermont, and Wisconsin. Fourteen states have passed
special laws known usually as ''marriage evasions acts.'' Most
of these provide that *all* marriages are void, if contracted by
residents of the state who intend to remain so and who go to
another state for the purpose of marriage, provided they would
be void in the parties' own states of residence. Sometimes,
however, the provision relates only to marriages for the evasion
of certain specified restrictions. Thus in Missouri it applies
only to bigamous marriages; in Maine to bigamy, incest, and
the marriage of mental defectives; in Mississippi only to incestuous and miscegenetic marriages; in Virginia to miscegenetic and
incestuous marriages; in West Virginia to these and also to
bigamous marriages, or the marriage of an insane or physically
incapable person or person under the age of consent. In nine
other states—Arizona, District of Columbia, Georgia, Illinois,
Indiana, Louisiana, Massachusetts, Vermont, and Wisconsin—
the provisions relating to evasion are general.[494] In the other
states the general principle of contracts is recognized in marriage—namely, if the contract is valid in the place where it is

[494] Hall and Brooke, ''American Marriage Laws'' (New York, Russell
Sage Foundation, 1919), 47.

made, it is valid everywhere; if invalid in the place where made, it is invalid everywhere, though some of the states modify that principle to some extent in marriage.[495]

IMPEDIMENT OF MIXED RELIGION

1039. The Church most solemnly and everywhere forbids marriages between a Catholic and a person enrolled in an heretical or schismatic sect. If there is danger of perversion for the Catholic party and the offspring, such marriage is forbidden also by the divine law (**Canon 1060**).

The Church does not dispense from the impediment of mixed religion except under the following conditions:

(1) there must be good and weighty reasons;

(2) the non-Catholic party must promise to avert all danger of perversion from the Catholic party and both parties must promise to have all the children baptized and raised in the Catholic faith;

(3) there must be moral certainty that the promises will be kept. The promises are, as a rule, to be made in writing (**Canon 1061**).

The Catholic party has the obligation to work prudently for the conversion of the non-Catholic (**Canon 1062**).

The prohibition of mixed marriages is already found in Canon XVI of the Synod of Elvira (306), which rules that, if heretics do not want to join the Catholic Church, no Catholic girl should be given them in marriage.[495a] Later, this prohibition recurs frequently in other early Councils of the Church. Experience proves that frequently the promises are not kept by the non-Catholic, so that the Catholic party is impeded in the practice of the faith and in baptizing and raising the children in the Catholic religion. Possibly, if the Catholic party was a man or woman of profound religious principles and thorough knowledge and appreciation of the greatness and sacredness of the gift of faith, the loss of souls to the Church would be considerably lessened.

The impediment of mixed marriage means that one party actually is a member of the Catholic Church, and that he (or she) wants to marry a baptized non-Catholic. The Code supposes that the Catholic party is still a practical Catholic, whose

[495] Case about civil prohibition of marriage, cfr. App. III, 44, c.
[495a] Hefele, "Konziliengeschichte," I, 162.

faith the Church wants to guard by the precautions of Canon 1061. There is no question here of baptized Catholics, who have fallen away from the Church. As to the non-Catholic party, the Code speaks of a person enrolled in an heretical or schismatic sect: generally baptism in a sect constitutes enrollment in that sect. The prohibition of the divine law may be present also in a marriage with an apostate Catholic because of the danger to the faith of the Catholic and the children. In this sense the Holy Office said that whenever, in the case of a marriage between a Catholic and a party who has thus fallen from the faith, he (or she) has joined a false religion or sect, the usual dispensation under the usual promises must be obtained. If there is question of a marriage between a Catholic and a person who has lost the faith, but did not join a false religion or heretical sect, the pastor is indeed bound to prevent the marriage if he possibly can, but, if he fears that by refusing to assist at the marriage grave scandal or harm should arise, the pastor shall refer the matter to his Ordinary. The Ordinary is empowered by the Sacred Congregation to permit the marriage provided that the Catholic education of the offspring is safeguarded and other similar conditions are complied with.[496] A further declaration of the Holy Office states that the answer given in the Decree of January 30, 1867, applies to all local Ordinaries.[497]

In reference to the baptism of the non-Catholic which frequently may be of doubtful validity, Canon 1070 states a general principle which is applicable here, namely, that, if a party at the time of marriage was generally considered baptized or his baptism was doubtful, it is to be considered a valid baptism so long as it has not been proved with certainty that the party was not baptized.

1040. The Code repeats the former law on the subject of the promises to be made by the parties with some modifications. The clause requiring also of the Catholic party to make the promise that the children will be baptized and raised in the Catholic faith is new. On the other hand, the promise which was formerly demanded of the Catholic party that he will prudently work for the conversion of the non-Catholic party is

---

[496] January 30, 1867; *Collect. de Prop. Fide,* II, n. 1300.
[497] January 11, 1899; *Collect. de Prop. Fide,* II, 1, in footnote.

dropped by the Code and put down in Canon 1062 as a moral obligation.[498]

Moral certainty that the promises will be kept is required by the Code before a dispensation from the impediment of mixed religion is granted. This is both hard to define and hard to obtain. It is usually the pastor who, in his application to the bishop for the dispensation, must vouch for the necessary conditions under which only the dispensation can be given. The Holy Office declared that the promise should be such that the agreement made furnishes a moral foundation for the truth of the execution so that the fulfillment of the promises can be prudently expected.[499] The judgment of the sincerity of the promises and the guarantee of their future fulfillment depends on the character of both the non-Catholic and the Catholic party. Sometimes, however, the non-Catholic party is willing to stand by what he or she has promised, but the non-Catholic father or mother interferes and sows the seed of discord and influences the son or daughter to break the promises. Experience teaches that, in many cases of mixed marriages, the Church is practically forced to grant the permission for such a marriage to avoid breaking the last weak thread that holds the Catholic party to the Church. Usually, by the time that the pastor is informed of the marriage, all arrangements have been made so that there is no possibility to prevent it. It is a difficult problem which can be solved only by teaching the Catholics themselves to appreciate their faith as they ought to.

1041. Are the promises a condition without which the dispensation cannot validly be granted? There seems to be no doubt of this, for, in the first place, the Code says that the Church does not dispense from the impediment except under the three conditions, viz., that there is a good and grave cause, that the promises are made, that there is moral certainty of their fulfillment. Furthermore, numerous documents of the Holy See in this matter call the promises a condition under which only the dispensation can be granted.[500] In a case where

---

[498] Holy Office, December 11, 1854; *Collect. de Prop. Fide,* I, n. 1055.

[499] June 30, 1842; *Collect. de Prop. Fide,* I, n. 951.

[500] Holy Office, Jan. 21, 1863 (*Collect.,* I, n. 1236) ; *Litt. Ap. Pii VIII,* March 25, 1830 (*Collect.,* I, n. 811) ; *Litt. Ap. Gregorii XVI,* April 30, 1841 (*Collect.,* I, n. 920) ; Holy Office, Dec. 11, 1850 (*Collect.* I, n. 1054) ; *Secret. Status jussu Pii IX,* November 15, 1858 (*Collect.,* I, n. 1169).

the mixed marriage had been contracted outside the Church and was invalid on account of the "Ne Temere" Decree, the Holy Office answered that the bishop could not allow the renewal of consent before the pastor, if the non-Catholic is willing to renew the consent but does not want to make the promises. He can only give the *sanatio in radice* if he has that papal faculty.[501]

Canon 2319 punishes with excommunication reserved to the Ordinary those who contract marriage with the explicit or implicit agreement that all or some of the children are to be educated outside the Catholic Church. Catholics who dare to contract a mixed marriage, though validly, without the Church's dispensation are *ipso facto* excluded from legal ecclesiastical actions and from the sacramentals until they have obtained a dispensation from the Ordinary (cfr. Canon 2375).

MARRIAGE CEREMONY OUTSIDE THE CHURCH

1042. Though the Church has granted the dispensation from the impediment of mixed religion, the parties are forbidden either before or after the Catholic wedding to approach either in person or by proxy a non-Catholic minister as minister of religion to give or renew the matrimonial consent. If the pastor knows for certain that the parties will violate, or have already violated this law, he shall not assist at their marriage except for very serious reasons until he shall have consulted the Ordinary and all danger of scandal has been removed. If the civil law demands it, the Church does not censure parties for appearing even before a non-Catholic minister who is acting merely as an official of the government, provided that their purpose is solely to comply with the civil law and to get civil recognition of their marriage (**Canon 1063**).

There would be reason to doubt the good faith of the non-Catholic's promises if he insisted on having the marriage ceremony performed by a non-Catholic minister as a religious ceremony. Note that the Code uses the widest possible term "non-Catholic minister." In the United States the laws of the various states of the Union do not demand a civil ceremony, and the Catholic priests as well as the ministers of the various religious denominations are entitled by the civil law to witness marriages. Wherefore, a Catholic in the United States does wrong if he

[501] December 22, 1916; *Acta Ap. Sedis*, IX, 13. Cfr. App. III, 3, **g.**

contracts marriage before a civil magistrate or a non-Catholic minister, because the Church allows this only where the law makes this necessary to have the marriage recognized by the State. For the sake of a public record of all marriages, the marriage license law in the United States requires the parties to take out a license and forbids all persons entitled to witness marriages to do so unless the parties have obtained a license. On the reverse side of the license paper, the officiating priest, minister, or magistrate enters the record of the marriage and returns the same to the bureau which issued the license.

Under Canon 1098 we may have cases also in the United States in which the parties would have to contract marriage before a civil magistrate or a minister to get their marriage recognized by the State—namely, in scattered districts where the priest does not visit the various stations or missions except a few times a year. For countries where the civil law is not satisfied by the church wedding, but insists on a civil marriage ceremony, the Holy See has issued instructions the gist of which is contained in Canon 1063.[502]

The reasons why the Church must oppose the celebration of marriage before the civil magistrate or the non-Catholic minister, are based on the principle of faith that Christian marriage is a sacrament. Wherefore, the Church and not the State has jurisdiction over the marriage of Christians. The sacramental character—the essentially religious nature of marriage—forbids a Catholic to contract marriage before a non-Catholic minister as a minister of religion, apart from any positive prohibition of the Church. But the Church has also forbidden such marriages, and has often repeated her prohibition. Canon 2319 punishes with excommunication incurred *ipso facto* and reserved to the Ordinary those who contract marriage before a non-Catholic minister in the manner forbidden in Canon 1063, namely, either prior or subsequent to the Catholic marriage ceremony before a non-Catholic minister acting as a representative of religion (cfr. below, Canon 2319).[503]

---

[502] Holy Office, February, 17, 1864; *Collect. de Prop. Fide,* I, n. 1247.

[503] On the prohibition to marry before a non-Catholic minister, and when it is lawful to approach him as official of the government, see some of the many citations in the notes of Card. Gasparri to this Canon notably, Holy Office, Febr. 17, 1864, and Dec. 12, 1888; *Collect. de Prop Fide,* nn. 1247, 1696.

Duty of Bishops and Pastors Concerning Mixed Marriages

1043. Ordinaries and other pastors of souls shall:

(1) Deter the faithful as far as they can from mixed marriages;

(2) If they cannot prevent them, they shall make every effort to see that these marriages are not contracted in violation of the laws of God and the Church;

(3) They shall see that those who have contracted a mixed marriage in their diocese or parish, or come from other places where they contracted such marriages, faithfully keep the promises which they made;

(4) When assisting at a mixed marriage, they shall observe the rule of Canon 1102, which forbids the use of sacred ceremonies at mixed marriages, and desires the priest merely to ask for and receive the marriage consent (**Canon 1064**).

Marriage of a Catholic with a Renegade

1044. The faithful shall likewise be discouraged from contracting marriage with those Catholics who have publicly given up the practice of the Catholic faith though they have not joined a non-Catholic sect, and with those who have joined societies condemned by the Church. The pastor shall not assist at such marriages without first consulting the Ordinary. After considering all the circumstances, the Ordinary may permit him to assist at such a marriage provided there is a grave and urgent reason, and the Ordinary believes that the Catholic education of all the children is sufficiently guaranteed, and that the danger of perversion of the Catholic party has been removed (**Canon 1065**).

The Holy Office ruled that, in marriages of Catholics with Freemasons who had been Catholics, the matter is to be referred to the Ordinary.[504] The marriage should not be allowed unless it is impossible to prevent it, and the faith of the Catholic party and the children must be safe. In reference to marriages with apostates from the Catholic faith, the Holy Office demanded that the pastor refer the matter to his bishop.[505] Though the

[504] August 21, 1861; *Collect. de Prop. Fide,* I, n. 1219; July 5, 1878; *Collect.,* II, n. 1495.
[505] January 30, 1867; *Collect.,* II, n. 1300.

formal promises of mixed marriages do not apply to cases where the apostate Catholic has not joined a non-Catholic sect, the Ordinary must get sufficient guarantee that the Catholic party will be free to practise the Catholic faith, and that all the children will be baptized and raised in the Catholic Church, for under these conditions only can the bishop allow the pastor to assist at the marriage.

Marriage with Unworthy Catholics

1045. If a public sinner, or a person publicly known to be under censure, refuses to go to confession or to be reconciled with the Church before the marriage, the pastor shall not assist at the marriage unless there is a grave and urgent reason. Concerning this reason, he shall consult the Ordinary if it is possible (**Canon 1066**).

If time permits, the pastor is not allowed to act in these cases without consulting the Ordinary, as was declared by the Sacred Penitentiary, Dec. 10, 1860.[506] Marriage in the Catholic Church cannot be permitted unless there is guarantee of the freedom of the Catholic to practise his religion and of the Catholic baptism and education of the children.

Chapter IV

OF THE DIRIMENT IMPEDIMENTS

1046. The term "diriment" impediments (from the Latin verb, *dirimere,* to destroy) indicates that the impediments of this class are of such a nature as to destroy or annul the marriage if attempted in spite of one of these impediments. Canonists usually classify them into impediments of the natural or divine law and of ecclesiastical law. The Supreme Authority of the Church only has the right to declare authentically in what cases the divine law forbids or annuls marriage (cfr. Canon 1038). The distinction between impediments of the divine and of ecclesiastical law is of importance in questions of dispensation from impediments, for the Church cannot dispense from an impediment of the divine law, but she can dispense from the impediments created by her own law. That distinction is likewise important in cases where an unbaptized party is concerned, for

506 *Collect. de Prop. Fide,* I, n. 1205.

unbaptized persons are not bound by the laws which are purely ecclesiastical regulations, while they are bound by the impediments of the divine law.

The diriment impediments enumerated in the Code are generally speaking the same as those in force before the Code was promulgated. Several important changes, however, have been made which will be pointed out in the discussion of the individual impediments.

1. THE IMPEDIMENT OF AGE

1047. A boy under sixteen years of age and a girl under fourteen cannot validly contract marriage. Though marriage is valid when these years are completed, the pastors of souls should dissuade young people from marriage at an earlier age than is commonly the custom in the respective countries (**Canon 1067**).

The former impediment of age has been modified by the Code. The old law had the age of fourteen for a boy, twelve for a girl. Besides, the age in the former Canon Law was not fixed peremptorily, for the marriage under these ages was considered valid if a boy or a girl was physically developed to such an extent that from their sexual intercourse procreation of offspring was possible (*nisi malitia suppleat ætatem*).[507] The Code goes beyond the requirements of the natural law, and demands the above-mentioned ages absolutely for validity.

1048. In the Common Law of England a boy of fourteen and a girl of twelve years of age can contract a valid marriage. In the United States the Common Law of England was generally adopted, but many rules of that law have been changed by statutes in the various states. "In seventeen states no marriageable ages have been fixed by statute. In nine of these— Florida, Maine, Maryland, Massachusetts, Missouri, Pennsylvania, Rhode Island, Tennessee, and Vermont—the common law marriageable ages of fourteen for males and twelve for females have been formally recognized, and without doubt those ages hold good also in Colorado, Idaho, and Mississippi. . . . In five states marriages below the marriageable age are declared to be void, and in fifteen states voidable only. The five states in the first group are Michigan, New Mexico, Ohio, Utah, and Virginia.

[507] *Decretal. Gregorii IX*, c. 9, *De Despons. impuberum*, lib. IV, tit. 2.

. . . In the states where marriageable ages have been established by statute, the most usual ages are eighteen for males and sixteen for females.'' [508]

2. The Impediment of Impotency

1049. Antecedent and perpetual impotency, either on the part of the man or the woman, whether known to the other party or not, and whether absolute or relative, annuls marriage by the very law of nature. If the impediment of impotency is doubtful, either as to fact or to law, marriage is not to be forbidden. Sterility neither invalidates nor makes marriage illicit (**Canon 1068**).

Impotency and sterility have not been defined authoritatively by the Church. It has been the unanimous opinion of canonists and moralists that natural impotency exists when the man and woman are not capable of having sexual intercourse from which *per se* procreation of offspring is possible. The necessary sexual organisms in both man and woman and the possibility of natural connection or sexual intercourse have always been considered essential for a valid marriage. We do not believe that the well-established doctrine has been upset by a decision like that in which the loss of the womb and both ovaries in a woman was said not to constitute impotency, and that the woman could contract a valid marriage. This and similar decisions are necessarily based on the particular facts in the case, and, if the Sacred Congregation was not convinced that the sexual organisms had been removed by the operation, the impotency would be doubtful and in a case of doubtful impotency the right to marry prevails.[509]

That authorities are much divided on this question, can be seen from Cappello,[510] who sums up the question in his commentary. The reasons given by those authors who say that the lack of the womb or both ovaries does not induce impotency, are not very convincing. Their main reason seems to be that the presence or absence of organisms which are hidden cannot determine the validity of the marriage; otherwise one could never know whether a marriage is going to be valid, unless the

[508] Hall and Brooke, ''American Marriage Laws,'' 33.
[509] July 23, 1890; *Collect. de Prop. Fide*, II, n. 1733.
[510] *De Sacramentis*, III, 396–409.

parties are subjected to a rigid bodily inspection before marriage. However, there should be no more difficulty in this case than in many other cases of marriage. The organisms are by presumption supposed to be there in any person that appears fairly normal. If later on it is discovered that the necessary organisms were not there, the presumption is destroyed, and the invalidity of the marriage appears. The same difficulty arises in relative impotency which will usually be discovered only after the marriage. The same again happens where a party was considered baptized, but actually never received baptism. When that fact is discovered, the presumption in favor of baptism is destroyed, and the invalidity of the marriage is established. Again, where marriage was contracted by a person who seemed to consent freely and yet was forced to consent, the marriage appears null and void when the fact of compulsion is discovered and proved.

Another source of great division of opinion is found in the consequences of vasectomy. Does it effect sterility only or impotency? It seems that whenever a man or woman through human interference is made incapable of having sexual intercourse which *per se* is apt to produce offspring, there is no marriage possible. If hidden defects of nature at times produce the same result, the presumption is in favor of the right to marriage, unless the defect is discovered, and is such that there is no doubt about impotency.[511]

3. The Impediment of the Existing Bond of Marriage

1050. A person who is bound by a previous marriage bond, though it be not a consummated marriage, cannot validly contract another marriage. The exception as to the Pauline Privilege remains. Though the first marriage be for any reason invalid or dissolved, it is not lawful to contract another marriage before there is legal and sure proof of the invalidity or the dissolution of the first marriage (**Canon 1069**).

An existing valid marriage bond is a diriment impediment to another marriage by the divine law. Marriages are dissolved:

[511] Cappello, ''De Sacrm.,'' III, 415–418; *American Eccl. Review*, XLII, 271, 346, 602; XLIII, 70, 310, 356; XLIV, 562, 583, 679, 684, 742; XLVI, 207, 219, 322; XLVIII, 553; Antonelli, ''De conceptu impotentiæ et sterilitatis relate ad matrim.'' (1901); Arendt, ''Circa controversam validitatem matrimonii feminæ excisæ'' (Rome, 1923).

(1) either by the death of one of the parties; (2) in two cases by the authority of the Church (the *matrimonium ratum non consummatum*, by law through solemn religious profession, and by dispensation of the Holy See) ; (3) marriages of unbaptized persons by the Pauline Privilege. These cases will be discussed under Canons 1119 and 1120–27.

1051. The person who has once been married and wants to marry again must prove his freedom from the first marriage bond. As this proof is usually furnished by the death certificate of the first husband or wife, Canon 1238 demands that the pastor after the funeral services shall mark down in the record of the deceased the name and age of the person, the names of the parents or surviving husband or wife, the date of death, the name of the priest who administered the Last Sacraments and what Sacraments were given, and the time and place of burial.

In those cases in which no direct proof of the death of the former husband or wife is available, the Holy See has given an Instruction how to proceed (published in the Appendix to the Third Council of Baltimore). The mere fact of the disappearance of the husband or wife without any trace of his or her whereabouts is not considered sufficient proof of death no matter how many years the party has not been heard from. The Church does not follow the rule of civil law in this matter. Usually five years' absence, with the presumption of death, is sufficient in civil law. The Church demands greater certainty than the civil law requires. The bishop is to weigh all the circumstances of the case, and, if he considers the circumstantial evidence sufficient to create a moral certainty of the death of the other party, he may give permission to the surviving party to marry again. If the bishop does not feel safe in giving the permission, he shall turn the case over to the Holy See, submitting to it what proofs he has been able to gather as to the presumed death of the party in question.[512]

---

[512] Sacred Congregation of the Sacraments, Nov. 18, 1920 (*Acta Ap. Sedis*, XIV, 96), gave permission to marry again in a case where a man had gone to South America and disappeared and was not heard from between 1905–1918. The Third Council of Baltimore, n. 124, has an *ipso facto* excommunication reserved to the Ordinary against persons who after a civil divorce attempt another marriage, which penalty by the wording of that paragraph applies only to persons validly married getting a civil divorce and attempting another marriage (cfr. App. III, 44, d).

4. Impediment of Disparity of Cult

1052. Marriage between a person baptized in the Catholic Church, or received into the Church from heresy or schism, and an unbaptized person is null and void. If a party at the time when marriage was contracted was commonly held to have been baptized, or if his baptism was doubtful, the validity of such a marriage must, according to Canon 1014, be upheld until it is proved with certainty that one party was and the other was not baptized (**Canon 1070**).

This Canon contains an important change of the former law on the impediment of disparity of cult. Formerly not only Catholics, but also baptized non-Catholics, were bound by this impediment and the marriages of non-Catholics with unbaptized persons were invalid in the eyes of the Church. Under the Code such marriages are valid, wherefore the date on which the Code became law, May 19, 1918, must be kept in mind in judging their validity or invalidity. Contrary to the common opinion of the commentators on the Code, Slater and a few other authors hold that the impediment of disparity of cult has not been abolished by the Code in favor of persons baptized outside the Catholic Church. The main argument is that Canon 1070 says nothing about the baptized non-Catholics, but simply states the affirmative side of the question who is bound by the impediment.[513] We believe that the statement of the Code that persons baptized in the Catholic Church and heretics or schismatics converted to the Church are subject to the impediment, should be sufficient proof that nobody else is held to it, for, if one class is expressly declared to be liable, the others are excluded as effectively as though the exclusion were stated. Besides, the opening Canon on impediments of marriage rules that all can contract marriage who are not prohibited by law (cfr. Canon 1035).

1053. The term "baptized in the Catholic Church" creates some difficulty, especially in cases of baptism administered by lay persons. In the first place, if the father and mother, or at least one of them, are Catholics and adhere to the Church, the infant baptized at the request of the Catholic party by a non-Catholic doctor or nurse in a case of emergency may still be

[513] *Amer. Eccl. Review*, LXI, 19–25.

considered baptized in the Catholic Church, for there is but one baptism, and whether the reception of that baptism means the joining of the Catholic Church or of some non-Catholic denomination depends on the will of the person who has the right and duty to care for the welfare of the infant. If neither parent adheres to the Catholic Church (i.e., if both are Protestants or apostate Catholics), but one of them consents to have the infant baptized by a Catholic priest, one must know whether some guarantee was given of the Catholic education of the child; if so, the child was by the will of the parent legitimately enrolled in the Catholic Church. If such guarantee was not given, no Catholic priest or layman had a right to baptize the child, and it was not legitimately enrolled in the Catholic Church, except in urgent danger of death (cfr. Canon 750). In the latter case (baptism in danger of death), it is not so certain whether the child should be called "baptized in the Catholic Church"; yet, inasmuch as the infant is legitimately baptized by a Catholic priest or layman, even against the will of its parents (cfr. Canon 750), it was legitimately enrolled in the Catholic Church.[514] The rule of Canon 1099, § 2, that infants of non-Catholics baptized in the Catholic Church but raised from infancy in heresy or without any religion are not bound to observe the Catholic form of marriage, cannot be applied to their freedom from the impediment of disparity of cult, because one exemption from the law does not prove another exemption.

1054. Doubtful baptism is considered valid in determining the existence or non-existence of the impediment of disparity of cult. However, this Canon merely gives a rule by which the validity or invalidity of a marriage already contracted is to be judged. In the former law also a doubtful baptism was considered valid when there was question of contracting a marriage. Thus, the Holy Office answered that the baptism of non-Catholics whose ritual met the requirements of valid baptism was to be considered valid. If doubt as to its validity persisted, it was to be considered a valid baptism *in ordine ad matrimonium*.[515] The same Congregation forbade the pastor to give conditional baptism to non-Catholics who wanted to remain members of their

---

[514] Cappello, "De Sacramentis," III, n. 412; Vermeersch-Creusen, "Epitome," II, n. 320; Petrovits, "New Church Law on Matrimony," n. 226; Vlaming, "Prælect. Jur. Matrim.," n. 289.
[515] November 17, 1830; *Collect. de Prop. Fide*, I, n. 821.

own sect.[516] The Code likewise forbids the administration of the sacraments to heretics or schismatics unless they join the Church (cfr. Canon 731). Now, if the baptism of the non-Catholic remains doubtful (as happens quite frequently here in the United States), should the pastor apply for dispensation from mixed religion or from disparity of cult *ad cautelam*?

The commentators differ,[517] but for practical reasons at least it is preferable to get a dispensation from disparity of cult *ad cautelam* in cases where after due investigation nothing certain can be learned about the baptism of the non-Catholic party. Otherwise the pastor may have the disagreeable duty later on of validating the marriage, for, if the presumption of the validity of the baptism proves later to have been false, the marriage is invalid (cfr. Canon 1070). The faculties given to the bishops of America seem to suggest that the dispensation from disparity of cult *ad cautelam* should be given in case of doubtful baptism, for Faculty No. I of the faculties of the Holy Office reads: "Dispensandi . . . super impedimento mixtæ religionis, et si casus ferat, etiam super disparitate cultus, ad cautelam."

CONDITIONS UNDER WHICH DISPENSATION FROM DISPARITY OF CULT CAN BE GIVEN

1055. The rules prescribed in Canons 1060–1064 for mixed marriages must be applied also to marriages where there is the impediment of disparity of cult (**Canon 1071**).

The Supreme Pontiff can validly grant a dispensation from this impediment without any reason, inasmuch as it is an ecclesiastical law, but those who dispense in virtue of delegated power cannot validly dispense without cause (cfr. Canon 84). Besides grave and urgent reasons, the Code insists on the guarantees, since Canon 1061 states that the Church does not dispense from the impediment of mixed religion unless the conditions therein specified are satisfied. Commentators disagree on the point whether the guarantees are strict conditions, so that a dispensation given without them is invalid.[518] In answer to the ques-

---

[516] April 3, 1878; Vlaming, "Prælec. Jur. Matr.," n. 295.

[517] Vlaming, "Prælec. Jur. Matr.," n. 294 bis; De Smet, "De Sponsal. et Matrim.," n. 588.

[518] That the promises are necessary for the validity of the dispensation, is held by: Vlaming, n. 218; De Smet, nn. 508, 591, 874, 504–506; Ayrinhac,

tion whether a dispensation from the impediment of disparity of cult granted by a person who has power delegated by the Holy See is valid, if the promises were not demanded, or if they were demanded but refused, the Holy Office declared that, as the case is exposed, the dispensation is invalid.[519] This answer seemed to settle the controversy at least to the extent that the promises are an indispensable condition for the valid exercise of the delegated faculties of dispensation from this impediment. However, authors who hold that in the law it is not certain that the promises are a *conditio sine qua non* for the granting of the dispensation, draw attention to the phrase "prout exponitur" in the above answer of the Holy Office. Nevertheless, from that answer it does follow that, if a bishop dispenses from disparity of cult in virtue of his delegated power without requiring the promises, or after refusal of the promises, such dispensation is invalid, for that was the case submitted to the Holy See.

1056. Another disputed question is whether the dispensation from disparity of cult is valid, if the promises are apparently made only to deceive pastor and bishop, while in the presence of other persons the same individual has stated that he will make no promises, and is not going to be dictated to by the Popish Church. Some writers, attaching all importance to the outward formalities, hold that, if the promises are made in the usual way so that neither pastor nor bishop suspect the fraud, the dispensation is valid because the bishop has acted entirely within the law, and therefore the validity of his dispensation should not be questioned.[520] However, the question is not whether the bishop has done right or wrong, but whether insincere and fraudulent promises satisfy the condition under which only the bishop can dispense. Are insincere promises real promises, and if they are not and can be proved (as in the supposed case) to have been made fraudulently, does it make any difference, in so far as validity of the dispensation is concerned, whether the bishop knows or does not know of the fraud? In rescripts which are made void through fraud, the authority granting the favor

n. 121; Chelodi, nn. 41, 81; Schäfer, 77, 126. The contrary: Petrovits, n. 255; Cappello, n. 310; Cerato, n. 35; Vermeersch-Creusen, "Epitome," II, n. 307. We refer to their commentaries on the Code (*s. v.*, Matrimony).

[519] June 21, 1912; *Acta Ap. Sedis*, IV, 443.
[520] *Irish Eccl. Record*, XVIII (1921), 411.

does not know—otherwise he would not grant it at all—that the petition is fraudulent, and yet the law rules that in all rescripts the favor is granted only on condition that the petition is truthful.

1057. In the former Canon Law the Holy Office declared that, in marriages of Catholics with unbaptized persons, the dispensation from disparity of cult given to the Catholic party is understood to include also dispensation from those impediments from which the unbaptized party is exempt, and that therefore the exemption of the unbaptized party is communicated to the baptized party.[521] It must be an impediment which would affect both parties if both were subjects of the Church (e.g., consanguinity, affinity). Chelodi quotes another declaration of the Holy Office from the magazine, *Ami du Clergé* (said to have been given April 23, 1913), which states that this implicit dispensation given with the disparity of cult takes effect, though the dispensation from disparity of cult is granted in virtue of delegated power and by a person who has no faculties to dispense with the other impediments.[522] Does this rule hold good after the promulgation of the Code? De Smet [523] and Leitner [524] are of the opinion that it is abolished, because the Code does not mention this implicit dispensation or communication of exemption, whichever one wishes to call it. Chelodi [525] and Cappello [526] hold that this manner of issuing the said dispensation belongs to the *stylus Curiæ,* and, so long as it is not known that the practice of the Roman Curia has been changed in this matter, the old rule obtains. We do not know whether such force can be attributed to the *stylus Curiæ.*

5. IMPEDIMENT OF MAJOR ORDERS

1058. Clerics in major orders cannot contract a valid marriage (**Canon 1072**).

There are several authors who deal at length with the historical development of this impediment.[527] The *Concilium*

---

521 September 16, 1824; *Acta S. Sedis,* XXV, 583.
522 *Jus Matrim.,* n. 81.
523 *De Sponsal. et Matrim.,* n. 593.
524 *Kath. Eherecht,* 187.
525 *Jus Matrim.,* n. 81.
526 *De Sacramentis,* III, n. 422.
527 Scharnagl, ''Das feierliche Gelübde als Ehehindernis'' (*Strassburger Theol. Studien,* IX, nos. 2–3, Freiburg, 1908); Funk, ''Zölibat und Pries-

Arausicanum (441) ruled that nobody who was married should be ordained deacon unless he had promised before ordination to keep chastity. The Second Council of Arles repeated the same law, which Gratian inserted in his "Decretum." [528] The latter Council demanded the vow of chastity from the candidates for the priesthood.[529] The Second Lateran Council (1139) forbade clerics in Sacred Orders to marry, and, if they had attempted marriage, they were to be separated from their wives, because such marriages contracted in violation of the ecclesiastical rule were not to be considered marriages. Pope Alexander III ruled that, if subdeacons or men in higher orders attempt marriage, they must be separated from their wives.[530] The Council of Trent declared that if anyone says that the clerics in Sacred Orders are able to contract marriage, and that such marriage is valid notwithstanding the ecclesiastical law, let him be anathema.[531]

In the Oriental Church the vow of continency was not admitted, and the clerics can marry while they are in minor orders and live in marriage in major orders, as Pope Innocent III states.[532] The *Concilium Trullanum* forbade subdeacons, deacons and priests to marry under pain of deposition. The Sacred Congregation of the Propaganda reminded the Orientals of this law of their Church.[533] In the Maronite Rite, however, the marriage impediment of Sacred Orders extends only to deaconship and higher orders, as is stated in their Synod of Mount Libanon (1736), which was approved by the Holy See *in forma specifica*.[534]

1059. The impediment of Sacred Orders is one of those impediments from which the Holy See does not dispense. If for very special reasons a dispensation is granted, it is done secretly. In danger of death, Canons 1043 and 1044 provide for dispensation of subdeacon and deacon, as we saw.[535]

Of the two cases of the former law in which the obligation

---

terehe im christlichen Altertum" (*Kirchengeschichtliche Abhandlungen*, I, Paderborn, 1897); Freisen, "Geschichte des kanonischen Eherechts" (2nd ed., Paderborn, 1893).

528 C. 7 D. 28.
529 *Decr. Gratiani*, c. 6 D. 28.
530 *Decretal. Gregorii IX*, c. 1, *De Cler. conj.*, lib. III, tit. 3.
531 Sessio XXIV, can. 9, *De Matrim. Sacramento*.
532 *Decretal. Gregorii IX*, c. 6, *De Cler. conj.*, lib. III, tit. 3.
533 May 24, 1858; *Collect. de Prop. Fide*, I, n. 1158.
534 Gasparri, "De Matrimonio," I, n. 681.
535 Gasparri, "De Matrimonio," I, nn. 677, 678.

of celibacy did not attach to Sacred Orders, the Code mentions
only one—namely, reception of major orders by one who was
forced by grave fear to take that step (cfr. Canon 214). The
case must be proved in the manner outlined in Canons 1993–
1998. The other case, major orders received in infancy, is not
mentioned by the Code for the reason, perhaps, that the case
is scarcely pertinent today. If such a case should come up, it
would very likely be decided on the same principles as Pope
Benedict XIV decided the case of some Copts who had been
ordained deacons in infancy; they were to decide whether they
wanted to stay in the sacred ministry when they became sixteen
years of age.[536]

Clerics in major orders who attempt marriage, even by a
mere civil ceremony, incur *ipso facto* excommunication reserved
simpliciter to the Holy See (cfr. Canon 2388). By law and
without any further declaration they lose any ecclesiastical office
which they hold (cfr. Canon 188, n. 5). Finally, they become
irregular *ex delicto* (cfr. Canon 985, n. 3).

6. IMPEDIMENT OF SOLEMN RELIGIOUS PROFESSION

1060. Religious who have taken solemn vows, or whose simple
vows have by the special law of the Holy See the power to annul
marriage, cannot contract a valid marriage (**Canon 1073**).

Pope Damasus I (366–384) calls an attempted marriage by
a virgin consecrated to God an adulterous union.[537] Pope Innocent I calls such a marriage an adultery and demands separation.
The Council of Chalcedon (451) excommunicates deaconesses,
virgins, and monks who attempt marriage, but it does not indicate whether the Council considered the marriage invalid.[538]
Other Popes and Councils express themselves in like manner,
but not until the Second Lateran Council (1139) was it declared explicitly that marriages attempted by monks are invalid.[539]
The Code restates the old law, and adds the exceptional provision as to the simple vows, if the Holy See has made such
special law for some religious organization (as is done by the

---

[536] Const. "Eo quamvis," May 5, 1745; *Opera Omnia Bened. XIV,*
I, 515.
[537] Scharnagl, "Das feierliche Gelübde als Ehehindernis," 42.
[538] *Decr. Gratiani,* c. 22, C. 27, qu. 1.
[539] *Decr. Gratiani,* c. 40, C. 27, qu. 1.

Const. "Ascendente Domino" of Pope Gregory XIII, May 25, 1584, for the Society of Jesus).[540] The simple religious vows do not annul marriage but constitute a grave prohibition of marriage—either temporarily, if the vows are temporary, or for life, if the vows are perpetual.

The dispensation from the solemn religious vow of chastity is reserved to the Holy See. By law the vow is dispensed when a religious in solemn vows obtains the indult of secularization (cfr. Canon 640, n. 2). Formerly the obligation of the vows remained when a solemnly professed religious got the indult of secularization. In danger of death the Ordinary, pastor, and other priests mentioned in Canon 1044 can dispense with the impediment of solemn religious profession (cfr. Canons 1043 and 1044).

The penalty of *ipso facto* excommunication reserved *simpliciter* to the Holy See strikes the religious in solemn vows who dares to attempt marriage, even by a mere civil ceremony (cfr. Canon 2388). In virtue of Canon 646 a professed religious who attempts marriage is thereby dismissed from the religious organization. Religious in either temporary or perpetual vows who attempt marriage become irregular *ex delicto* (cfr. Canon 985, n. 3).

7. Impediment of Abduction

1061. Between the man guilty of abduction and the woman whom he abducts with the purpose of marrying her there can be no marriage so long as the woman is in the power of the man who carried her off. If the abducted woman, after having been separated from the man and put in a safe and free place, consents to marry the man, the impediment ceases. As far as the nullity of the marriage is concerned, the forcible detention of the woman is held equivalent to abduction, namely, when the man for the purpose of marrying the woman detains her by force in the place of her residence or a place to which she came of her own free will (**Canon 1074**).

This impediment is frequently called the impediment of *rape,* but it seems preferable to call it abduction, since the term "rape" in the American criminal law has quite a different meaning from the Latin "raptus" in Canon 1074.

[540] Gasparri, "Fontes Cod. Jur. Can.," I, n. 153.

In the law of the Decretals the impediment of abduction was not distinct from that of force and fear.[541] The Council of Trent made abduction a separate impediment, and its words are almost identical with the first two sentences of Canon 1074.[542] The last sentence of Canon 1074 settles the case of an equivalent abduction, which had not been provided for by the Council, but had been debated by canonists.

Elopement may or may not constitute the impediment of abduction, according to the circumstances of the case. If the woman consents both to running away with the man and to the marriage, there is no impediment of abduction. If the man and woman previous to the elopement promised each other to marry, even though there was no formal engagement, the presumption is that the woman consented to the elopement and marriage.[543] If the woman consented to run away, not with the intention of marrying the man but for some other reason, and the man with whom she elopes intends marriage, there is the impediment of abduction, as was declared in a case decided by the Sacred Congregation of the Council, March 14, 1772.[544]

If a girl is not yet of age and she consents to elope for the purpose of marrying the man, there is no impediment of abduction, for the fact that the parent or guardian does not consent cannot, in Canon Law, make the marriage invalid.[545]

If a girl runs away with a man, who, while he intends marriage, persuades her to do so under other pretenses and then detains the girl to make her consent to the marriage, the impediment of abduction exists, for the girl must consent both to the running away and to the marriage to avoid the impediment of abduction. The last paragraph of Canon 1074 applies here.

As far as the impediment is concerned, it does not matter whether the man who is guilty of abduction acts in person or employs another to act for him, because the action of the agent is attributed to the principal in both the Canon Law and civil law. The decision in the *Causa Parisiensis* by the Sacred Congregation of the Council, June 25, 1864, illustrates this point.[546]

[541] Wernz, "Jus Decretal," IV, n. 275.
[542] Sessio XXIV, cap. 6, *De Reform. Matrimonii.*
[543] Gasparri, "De Matrimonio," I, nn. 631–633.
[544] Cappello, "De Sacramentis," III, n. 461.
[545] Cappello, "De Sacramentis," III, n. 463.
[546] Sacred Congregation of the Council, August 27, 1864; *Acta S. Sedis*, I, 15–24.

8. The Impediment of Crime

1062. The impediment of crime invalidates marriage with the accomplice of the crime in the following cases:

(1) If a married person at any time during the continuance of the same legitimate marriage commits adultery and enters into mutual promise of marriage with his accomplice in the adultery, or if they attempt marriage, even by a mere civil ceremony;

(2) If a married person during the time of his or her valid marriage commits adultery, and one of the adulterers kills the husband or wife of the adulterer;

(3) If a married person, without committing adultery, brings about the death of his or her partner in marriage by mutual coöperation, physical or moral, with a third party (**Canon 1075**).

The threefold impediment of crime as here described existed in Canon Law before the promulgation of the Code. Since the impediment of crime is an ecclesiastical impediment, it does not bind unbaptized persons. Wherefore, the Sacred Congregation of the Propaganda declared that, if both adulterers were unbaptized at the time of the commission of the crime, they do not contract the impediment, but, if one of the adulterers was a Christian, the impediment enters and makes marriage between them invalid.[547]

The term "adultery" is taken in the sense of complete sexual intercourse. Both adulterers must know at the time of the sexual intercourse that one party is bound by a valid marriage, as otherwise it would not be formal adultery as to both parties. The mutual promise of marriage may either precede or follow the adultery; it suffices that both adultery and mutual promise of marriage are offences against one and the same marriage, while the marriage bond lasts. If both adulterers are married, but pretend to be single, the double adultery and mutual promise of marriage would not create the impediment of crime if neither party knew that the other was married. If, of the two married adulterers, one party only knows that the other is married and they together with the adultery promise marriage to each other, the canonists commonly hold—with some demurring—that the

[547] August 23, 1852; *Collect. de Prop. Fide*, I, n. 1079.

impediment enters, because both adultery and promise of marriage are deliberate offences against at least one of the two marriages in question.

The mutual promise of marriage means that each party by some external signs or words promises and accepts the promise of the other, and that such mutual offer and acceptance is serious. The mutual promise of marriage must have reference to marriage after the death of the other partner in marriage. If, therefore, Gasparri says, the adulterers promise marriage to each other on condition that the married party shall get a civil divorce, the impediment would not exist.[548] Since this was the common opinion of canonists before the promulgation of the Code, and it does not appear from the wording of Canon 1075 that the law has been changed, the old interpretation of the law must be retained. This is done by most commentators of the Code; a few—e.g., Chelodi [549] and Cerato [550]—hold the contrary opinion.

1063. Adultery with attempted marriage (e.g., after a civil divorce) entails the impediment of crime. For the attempted marriage the civil ceremony suffices, and also clandestine marriage provided the expression of the marriage consent is such that it would by the law of nature suffice to effect a marriage between persons free to marry, as is apparent from a Decree of the Sacred Congregation of the Propaganda, January 14, 1844.[551] Even if the attempted marriage comes first and the adultery follows, the impediment is nevertheless contracted.

Regarding the case of adultery and the murder of the spouse by one of the adulterers, there is some controversy among canonists whether the impediment is incurred if the adultery follows only after one of the adulterers has already instituted the physical cause of death (e.g., administered the poison).[552] It does not matter whether the partner in marriage kills his own spouse, or whether the other adulterer accomplishes the murder, for the Code comprehends both cases when it says: "eorumque alter conjugicidium patravit." Petrovits, emphasizing the literal

---

[548] Gasparri, "De Matrimonio," I, n. 737.
[549] *Jus Matrimoniale*, n. 93.
[550] *Matrimonium*, n. 70.
[551] Quoted by Gasparri, "De Matrimonio," I, n. 738.
[552] Wernz, "Jus Decretal.," IV, n. 532; Cappello, "De Sacram.," III, n. 492; Vlaming, "Prælect. Jur. Matrim.," I, n. 322.

meaning of the term "conjugicidium," holds that the adulterer must kill his own spouse to incur the impediment.[553] The law of the Decretals [554] and the greater number of commentators of the Code hold that it is not necessary that the adulterer kill his own spouse.

The killing after commission of adultery must be done for the purpose of marriage with the other adulterer. The Code does not state this explicitly, but it appears so from the purpose of the impediment, and the law was interpreted in that sense by the Sacred Congregation of the Council in a case where a man who had committed adultery and later found his wife in adultery in rage struck and killed his wife. When he later wanted to marry the woman with whom he had committed adultery, it was decided that he had not incurred the impediment.[555]

1064. The third instance of the impediment of crime occurs in cases in which the killing of a spouse is done by mutual physical or moral coöperation with the person one intends to marry; whether adultery preceded is immaterial, for the Code has "etiam sine adulterio." Mere approval by the other party after the murder does not constitute coöperation. Even if a person has manifested satisfaction or joy over the plans to kill his spouse, it is not coöperation. To cause the impediment, there must be mutual coöperation in bringing about the death of the spouse —such a conspiracy, in fact, that either of the two may be said to have killed the spouse.

The Code does not state that the killing must be done with the intention of marrying the accomplice, but canonists commonly hold that such intention is essential to constitute the impediment, and it seems that the law of the Decretals justifies that opinion.[556] It suffices, however, that one of the conspirators intends marriage, for the purpose of the law is to discourage the killing of a spouse to open the way to a marriage. Some canonists, however, require that intention on the part of both conspirators.[557] The *Instructio Austriaca,* quoted by Vlaming,[558]

---

553 *The New Church Law on Matrimony,* nn. 308, 309.
554 *Decretal. Greg. IX,* c. 6, *De eo qui ducit, etc.,* lib. IV, tit. 7.
555 September 28, 1726; *Canones et Decreta C. Trid.* (ed. Richter), n. 108.
556 *Decretal. Greg. IX,* c. 1, *De conversione infdel.,* lib. III, tit. 33.
557 De Becker, "De Spons. et Matrim.," 180.
558 *Prælect. Jur. Matrim.,* I, n. 324.

explicitly states that the intention of marriage of one of the conspirators suffices to induce the impediment. As to the manifestation of this intention, many canonists hold that it must be made known to the accomplice in the crime to effect the impediment; others hold that its manifestation is not necessary.

Multiplication of the impediment by multiplying the causes which induce the impediment between two adulterers or conspirators is commonly admitted by canonists. Gasparri gives an illustration of a case in which the impediment is ninefold. A double case which may occur more frequently is the adultery and mutual promise of marriage and later on an attempted marriage.[559]

9. IMPEDIMENT OF CONSANGUINITY

1065. (1) In the direct line of consanguinity marriage is invalid between persons of all degrees ascending and descending, legitimate as well as natural ancestors or descendants.

(2) In the collateral line, marriage is invalid between blood relations to the third degree inclusively, in such a manner, however, that the impediment is multiplied only whenever the common *stipes* (stock or root) is multiplied.

(3) Marriage shall never be permitted if there is any doubt whether the parties are blood relations in any degree of the direct line, or in the first degree of the collateral line (**Canon 1076**).[559a]

In consanguinity the terms *stipes, linea, gradus,* are of importance. The *stipes* is the ancestor at the head of a line of descent. When the ancestor at the head of several lines of descent is removed beyond the three degrees or generations, there is no impediment of blood relationship between the descendants of the various lines.

The *linea* (or series of generations) is distinguished into the *direct* and the *collateral* lines. In the direct line of blood-relationship one person is generated by the other. Grandfather begets the father, the father begets the son, the son the grandson. The collateral lines originate from the children of a common ancestor, and thus run parallel to each other. We speak of collateral relationship between the descendants of the various lines, which issued from one common ancestor. As the various

---

[559] *De Matrimonio,* I, n. 740.   [559a] Cfr. App. III, 44, e.

lines proceed in their course, they may again branch off into side lines. If two individuals from two different branch lines stand at an equal distance (measured by the number of generations) from the common ancestor from whom the lines originated, they are said to be related in a certain degree in the *equal* collateral line; if one person is removed from the common ancestor by more generations in his line than the other person in another line, they are said to be related in an *unequal* line.

The *gradus* (or degree) means the distance of persons from the common ancestor. In the *direct line* there are as many degrees as there are generations—for instance, one between father and son, two between grandfather and grandson or granddaughter, and so on. They are easily calculated by counting the number of persons who descend from one another, omitting the *stipes* or stock of the line of descent. In the *collateral line* the Canon Law counts only the generations, each making one degree (just as in the direct line), and then compares the number of generations in one branch line with the number in the other. If both branch lines show, two, three, etc., generations they are related in the second, third, etc., degree. If one line of generation is longer than the other—e.g., three generations between one person concerned and the *stipes* and only two generations in the line of the other—the two persons are related in the third degree, according to the rule of Canon 96. Thus, brother and sister are related in the first degree of the collateral line; first cousins (the children of this brother and sister) in the second degree, and the children of two first cousins in the third degree.

1066. In calculating the degrees of the collateral lines, the old Roman Law and the modern law of many countries follow a principle different from that of Canon Law. They do not count merely the number of generations in the longer line, but compute as many degrees as there are generations in both lines. Thus, brother and sister are related in the second degree, uncle and niece are related in the third degree, two first cousins in the fourth degree, first cousin and second cousin in the fifth degree, two second cousins in the sixth degree, and so on. In the United States each state has its own laws concerning the prohibited degrees within which marriage is declared null and void. Most of the states rule that marriage between relations in the direct line of any degree are void; other states enumerate and specify the persons in the direct line between whom marriage cannot be contracted. In the collateral line marriage is declared void between brother and sister (whether of the whole or half blood), uncles and nieces, and aunts and nephews. As to cousins, the following states bar first cousins: Arizona, Arkansas, Illinois, Indiana, Kansas, Louisiana, Michigan, Missouri, North Dakota, Ohio, Oklahoma, Oregon, Pennsylvania, and Wyoming. Nebraska and Nevada have first cousins among the persons who cannot contract a valid marriage, but Nebraska limits it to first cousins "when of the whole blood," and Nevada forbids marriage between persons nearer of kin than "second cousins or cousins of the half blood." North Dakota and Oklahoma had simply "cousins," without limiting it to first cousins, but later amendments specified first cousins; South Dakota's statute has "cousins" without restriction.[560]

1067. In the Fourth Lateran Council Pope Innocent III reduced the impediments of consanguinity and affinity from the seventh degree to the fourth in the collateral line. That remained the law until the promulgation of the Code, which reduces consanguinity to the third degree and affinity to the second degree. The Code settles a controversy as to the extent of the impediment of consanguinity in the direct line by stating explicitly that it extends to all degrees of ancestors and descendants. There had been no explicit rule of Canon Law on the extent of the diriment impediment in the direct line, and some canonists held that the impediment extended to all degrees of the direct line either by the law of nature, or at least by Canon Law; others held that the law of nature does by no means make marriage null and void in the more remote degrees of descent, and they applied the law on the four degrees of the collateral line also to the direct line. The Code makes marriage invalid between direct descendants in any degree.

In the first degree of the collateral line the Church does not dispense, nor does she allow the marriage if there is doubt whether the parties are related either in the direct line or in the first degree of the collateral line. The underlying reason for the prohibition of the Church is very likely the controversy whether marriage between all persons related in the direct line,

[560] *Marriage and Divorce*, 1867–1906, Department of Commerce and Labor (Government Printing Office, Washington, 1909).

and in the first degree of the collateral line (that is to say, between brother and sister), is rendered invalid by the law of nature. As soon as in one line the person is removed two degrees from the common ancestor, while the person on the other side is removed one degree only, for instance niece and uncle, it is considered a relationship in the second degree.

MULTIPLE CONSANGUINITY

1068. The Code simplifies the matter of multiple consanguinity by admitting one reason only for multiplicity of blood relationship, namely, the multiplication of the common stock. The ways in which this multiple consanguinity may occur are: (1) if one has children from a marriage with a blood relation; (2) if one has children from marriage with two persons who are blood-relations (e.g., when a man after the death of his wife marries his wife's sister) ; (3) if several blood-relations have children from marriages with persons who are blood-relatives (e.g., two sons of one family marrying two daughters of another family) ; (4) a combination of two of the above cases may result in triple or quadruple consanguinity. The following tables, taken from Cappello's ''De Sacramentis,'' [561] illustrate the cases:

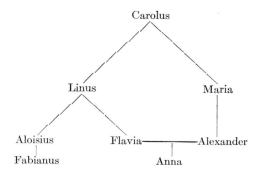

Fabianus and Anna are blood-relations in the second and third degrees from their common ancestors, Linus and Carolus.

[561] Cappello, ''De Sacramentis,'' III, n. 515; Chelodi, ''Jus Matrimoniale,'' n. 95; Vlaming, ''Prælect. Jur. Matrim.,'' I, n. 335; Vermeersch-Creusen, ''Epitome,'' II, n. 329.

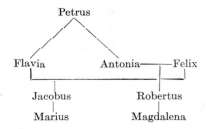

Marius and Magdalena are blood-relations in the second and third degrees from their common ancestors, Felix and Petrus.

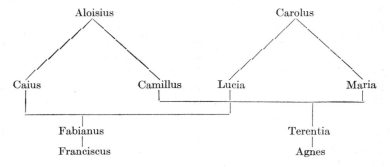

Franciscus and Agnes are blood-relations in the double third degree, Fabianus and Terentia in the double second degree from their common ancestors Aloisius and Carolus.

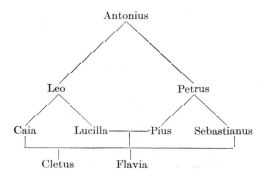

Cletus and Flavia are blood-relations in the double second degree from the common ancestors Leo and Petrus, and in the third degree from Antonius.

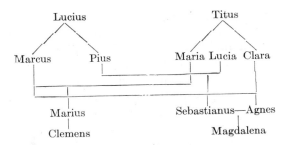

Clemens and Magdalena are blood-relations in the second degree through Marcus, and in the double third degree from Lucius and Titus.

10. IMPEDIMENT OF AFFINITY

1069. Affinity in the direct line invalidates marriage in any degree. In the collateral line marriage is invalid to the second degree inclusive between persons related by marriage. The impediment of affinity is multiplied: (1) whenever the consanguinity from which the affinity proceeds is multiplied; (2) by repeated successive marriages with blood-relations of the deceased spouse (**Canon 1077**).

Canon 97 changes the former Canon Law on affinity and rules that affinity arises from a valid marriage, either consummated or unconsummated. In the former law the foundation for the impediment of affinity was the sexual intercourse: in marriage consummated by sexual intercourse, the impediment of affinity extended to all degrees of the direct line and to the fourth inclusive in the collateral line; from sexual intercourse outside of marriage, the impediment of affinity extended to the second degree inclusive in the collateral line.

The history of the impediment of affinity is very complicated as can be seen from Wernz.[562] The impediment branched out to such an extent that the Fourth Lateran Council (1215) restricted the impediment to the fourth degree of the collateral line, and limited the concept of affinity to mean that the blood relatives of the woman with whom the man had sexual intercourse became *affines* to the man only, and the blood-relatives of the man to the woman only. The affinity to the fourth degree of the collateral line arising from illicit intercourse remained

[562] *Jus Decretal.*, IV, n. 429.

up to the Council of Trent, which restricted it to the second degree inclusive.[563] The Code abolishes the affinity from illicit intercourse, and limits the affinity from valid marriage to the second degree of the collateral line.

In affinity the husband only (not his parents, brothers, etc.) contracts relationship with the blood-relatives of his wife, and *vice versa* (cfr. Canon 97). The lines, direct or collateral, and the degrees are computed in the same manner as in consanguinity. Thus, the mother of a man's wife and the daughter of his wife from another marriage become the husband's *affines* in the direct line, and the Church does not allow marriage in any degree in the direct line of affinity; the aunts, sisters, and nieces of a man's wife become his *affines* in the collateral line in the same degree as they stand in blood-relationship to the wife. The same is true of the blood-relatives of the husband, who become the *affines* of his wife in the same line and degree as they are in blood-relationship to the husband.

1070. In former times there was much controversy among canonists as to whether the impediment of affinity in the direct line makes marriage between those thus related invalid by the law of nature.[564] Later on, however, the Holy Office declared that there was no doubt that the Roman Pontiff had the right to dispense with the affinity in the first degree of the direct line, even when such affinity arises from the consummation of a lawful marriage.[565] An Instruction of the Holy Office, September 16, 1824, states that the impediment of affinity, especially when arising from illicit intercourse, is not of the divine but merely of the ecclesiastical law, and does not bind an unbaptized person who contracts marriage with another unbaptized person. There was question here of the affinity in the first degree of the direct line. The Holy Office goes on to say that, if an unbaptized person has contracted this affinity and then becomes baptized and wishes to marry one who is an *affinis,* he is subject to the law, because the natural bond contracted in infidelity persists, and becomes an impediment when the infidel passes through baptism under the jurisdiction of the Church.[566]

[563] Sessio XXIV, cap. IV, *De Reform. Matrim.*
[564] Gasparri, ''De Matrimonio,'' I, n. 792.
[565] Sept. 4, 1743; quoted by Gasparri, ''De Matrim.,'' I, n. 792.
[566] *Collectanea de Prop. Fide,* I, n. 784; Holy Office, August 26, 1891; *Collect. de Prop. Fide,* II, n. 1766.

The Church, however, does not easily dispense from the impediment of affinity in the direct line, especially after the consummation of the marriage by which the bond between the husband and the wife's mother or daughter becomes more perfect (the same holds good with reference to the wife). Wherefore, even the Church does not give power to the bishop, pastor or priest to dispense, even in danger of death, from the impediment of affinity in the direct line when it arises from a consummated valid marriage (cfr. Canon 1043).

The impediment of affinity is multiplied: (1) whenever the consanguinity from which it proceeds is multiplied. Thus, if, after the death of her husband, a woman wants to marry one of his relatives who had a double blood-relationship to her husband, the impediment of affinity is double;[567] (2) if one successively marries blood-relations of one's deceased spouse. Thus, if, after the death of his first wife, a man marries her sister by dispensation and after the death of his second wife marries an aunt of the two sisters (his former wives), there is a double affinity. These two causes of affinity can be combined in a given case so that the affinity may become three and fourfold.

1071. In the civil law of the United States twenty-six states have no impediment of affinity. However, Alabama, Georgia, Iowa, Kentucky, Maine, Maryland, Massachusetts, Connecticut, Delaware, Michigan, Mississippi, New Hampshire, Oklahoma, Pennsylvania, Rhode Island, South Carolina, Tennessee, Texas, Vermont, Virginia, Washington, West Virginia, and District of Columbia, have degrees of affinity which annul marriage. Some states extend the impediment further than others. Thus, Alabama forbids the son to marry his stepmother and the widow of his uncle. The father may not marry the widow of his son. No man may marry the daughter of his wife, or the daughter of the son or daughter of his wife. Other states forbid marriage with a stepmother, stepdaughter, son's wife, grandson's wife, wife's mother and grandmother, son's son's wife and daughter's son's wife. Others add wife's daughter, wife's son's daughter, and wife's daughter's daughter.[568]

1072. The Code rules that affinity arises from valid mar-

---

[567] Vlaming, "Prælect. Jur. Matrimonialis," I, n. 350. See case on affinity in *Irish Eccl. Record* (Series V), XIII, 230–232.
[568] *Marriage and Divorce* (Department of Commerce and Labor, Washington, 1909).

riage, either *ratum* only or *ratum et consummatum* (cfr. Canon 97). The technical term *ratum* means a marriage of Christians, and, if it is to be interpreted thus in Canon 97, doubt arises whether the impediment is contracted by marriages of baptized persons with unbaptized ones. The same doubt arises in reference to marriages contracted by two unbaptized persons, of whom one later becomes a Christian. After the conversion of *one party,* does the marriage lay the foundation for the affinity? It is quite generally admitted that the impediment does arise when both unbaptized married persons receive baptism, for then their marriage becomes a *matrimonium ratum* (i.e., *baptizatorum*). Cappello,[569] De Smet,[570] and Leitner [571] hold that the baptism of one of the two married infidels does not suffice to make that marriage a foundation for the impediment of affinity, and they have the wording of the Code in their favor. Vlaming [572] and Chelodi [573] hold that the baptism of one, either before or after the marriage, suffices. The latter argue from the old Canon Law and from incongruities in the Code, but it is not certain whether *matrimonium ratum* may be thus interpreted.

11. IMPEDIMENT OF PUBLIC PROPRIETY

1073. The impediment of public propriety arises from an invalid marriage, either consummated or unconsummated, and from public or notorious concubinage. Marriage is invalidated in the first and second degree of the direct line between the man and the blood-relatives of the woman, and *vice versa* (**Canon 1078**).

The impediment of public propriety in the former Canon Law differs entirely from the law of the Code. In the old law the impediment arose from a valid engagement contract and from a marriage which had not been consummated (the *matrimonium ratum*). From a valid engagement the impediment extended to the first degree in both the direct and the collateral lines; from unconsummated marriage it extended to the fourth degree inclusive in both the direct and the collateral lines.[574]

The first source of the impediment of public propriety is

---

[569] *De Sacramentis,* III, n. 538. [570] *De Sponsal. et Matrim.,* n. 431.
[571] *Kath. Eherecht,* 159.
[572] *Prœlect. Jur. Matrim.,* I, n. 353. [573] *Jus Matrimoniale,* n. 99.
[574] Sessio XXIV, cap. 3, *De Reform. Matrimonii;* Pius V. Const. ''Ad Romanum,'' July 1, 1568. For recent decision, see Vol. II, App. III, 44, f.

an invalid marriage, and, as the Code does not distinguish between the causes of invalidity of such a marriage, we should not distinguish. Some canonists, however, basing their arguments on the former law, hold that a marriage rendered invalid for want of consent does not cause the impediment of public propriety. Since the Code changes entirely the former law on the impediment of public propriety, the arguments taken from the old law are beside the point.

Does the public propriety arise from a civil marriage, which, since the "Ne Temere" Decree, is invalid if one or both parties are Catholics? (The exceptional cases where no priest can be had for a month or more, and in danger of death, are discussed elsewhere.) Commentators on the Code disagree. Those who with Cappello [575] hold that the impediment does not arise from a mere civil marriage, argue that the civil marriage was not considered by the Church to have even the appearance of a true marriage, and that the Code does not refer to it under the terms of invalid marriage, but always calls it by its own name of "civil marriage" or "civil ceremony." However, no matter how sinful the marriage of a Catholic outside the Church may be, because of his criminal disregard for the authority of the Church and the dignity of the Sacrament of Matrimony, it cannot be classed as mere concubinage when there are present the essentials required by the natural law for marriage, and the Church recognizes this when in Canon 1139 she states: "Any marriage which has been contracted with the naturally sufficient consent of both parties even though this consent is juridically inefficacious because of some diriment impediment of the ecclesiastical law or the lack of the legitimate form, can be validated by the *sanatio in radice*, provided the consent endures."

1074. The second source of the impediment of public propriety is public or notorious concubinage. Concubinage denotes as a rule criminal cohabitation, but the constant living together of an unmarried male and female as husband and wife is not necessary: the keeping of a woman in a separate apartment or dwelling for immoral purposes and frequent sexual intercourse would be equivalent to concubinage. To cause the impediment, the concubinage must be either public or notorious (cfr. Canon 2197).

[575] *De Sacramentis*, III, n. 543. For recent decisions see Vol. II, App. III, 44, f.

The extent of the impediment of public propriety is well defined by the Code. It exists only between the man and the blood relations of the woman in the direct line in the first and second degree—viz., mother, grandmother, daughter (from another man), granddaughter—and between the woman and the father, grandfather, son (from another woman) and grandson of the man.

12. Impediment of Spiritual Relationship

1075. That spiritual relationship only which is mentioned in Canon 768 invalidates marriage (**Canon 1079**).

Canon 768 states that in baptism a spiritual relationship is contracted by the baptized person with the minister of baptism and the sponsors. The Roman Council (721) ruled: "If anyone marry his godmother, let him be anathema." Pope Nicholas in his answer to the Bulgarians states that, on account of the spiritual relationship of godfather to the godchild, there can be no valid marriage between them.[576] The spiritual relationship between a godfather and the parent of the godchild makes marriage invalid, according to the law of the Decretals.[577] The impediment was extended more and more. Pope Boniface VIII ruled that there could be no valid marriage between the person baptized and the godfather and his wife and children, and on the part of the sponsor and the one baptizing with the father or mother of the child. The same rule was applied to Confirmation.[578] In some countries the impediment was extended to the children of the sponsor and the children of the family for which the sponsor had acted. Finally, the Council of Trent restricted the cases of spiritual relationship as a diriment impediment of marriage between the sponsor and the godchild and his parents, and between the one baptizing and the child baptized and its parents. In Confirmation the impediment was not to extend beyond him who confirms, the person confirmed, his father and mother and the sponsor.[579]

The Code further restricts the impediment so that it is con-

[576] *Decr. Gratiani,* c. 1, C. XXX, qu. 3.
[577] *Decretales Greg. IX,* cc. 4 and 6, *De Cognatione Spirituali,* lib. IV, tit. 10.
[578] *Liber Sextus,* c. 1, *De Cognatione Spirituali,* lib. IV, tit. 3.
[579] Sessio XXIV, cap. 2, *De Reform. Matrim.*

tracted only by the minister of baptism and the sponsor or sponsors with the person baptized. There is no impediment between the parents and the minister or sponsor. The impediment from Confirmation is entirely abolished by the Code.

In discussing the conditional repetition of baptism, Canon 763 rules that spiritual relationship is not contracted by the sponsor of either the first or the second baptism, unless the same sponsor acted in both baptisms. As the Code does not give any rule about the spiritual relationship of the minister of baptism in conditional baptism, the commentators do not agree whether the ministers in both baptisms contract the spiritual relationship and impediment of marriage, or whether either of them does. However, since the Code rules that the minister of baptism does contract the spiritual relationship and it is merely a question of fact whether in a given case the baptism was validly conferred by that minister, one must conclude from Canon 15 that the spiritual relationship and impediment of marriage is contracted.[580]

1076. The Code rules that from baptism the minister and the sponsor (or sponsors) contract the spiritual relationship and impediment of marriage with the person baptized. Since the Code does not distinguish between solemn and private baptism, no distinction is to be made. Under the former Canon Law the authorities unanimously maintained the spiritual relationship of the minister of private baptism, but disagreed in reference to the sponsor in private baptism. The Sacred Congregation of the Council, March 5, 1678, declared that the sponsors in private baptism do contract the spiritual relationship and impediment of marriage.[581] (Regarding the requisites for valid sponsorship, cfr. above, Canon 765.) That the impediment of spiritual relationship is not multiplied by the fact that the same person acts as sponsor to several children of the same parents was declared by the Holy Office, April 29, 1894.[582]

1077. Can the minister of baptism be at the same time sponsor to the child he baptizes, and does he contract a double spiritual relationship? With reference to Confirmation, the Sacred Congregation of Rites decided on June 14, 1873, that if the

580 Vlaming, "Prælect. Jur. Matrim.," I, n. 376; the contrary is held by Cappello, "De Sacram.," III, n. 558.
581 Gasparri, "De Matrim.," I, n. 836.
582 Collect. de Prop. Fide, II, n. 1869.

bishop wishes to be sponsor for one of the persons to be confirmed by him, he must appoint a proxy to act as sponsor.[583] The same, Wernz remarks,[584] may perhaps be applied to the priest who wants to be sponsor to the child he baptizes. In this case there seems to be a double spiritual relationship between the minister of baptism and the person baptized. It is certain that the proxy does not contract any spiritual relationship.

In reference to the impediment of spiritual relationship contracted prior to the promulgation of the Code and now abolished by the Code (between the sponsor and minister of baptism and the parents of the one baptized, and the entire impediment of spiritual relationship from Confirmation), the Committee declared on June 2–3, 1918, that impediments arising from spiritual relationships which have been abolished by the Code cease to exist as impediments.[585]

13. Impediment of Legal Relationship

1078. Persons who by the civil law are declared incapable of marrying certain persons because of legal adoption are also by Canon Law declared incapable of contracting a valid marriage (**Canon 1080**).

Just as the Church in former times adopted many a law of the Roman Civil Code, she follows the same policy today with regard to the civil law on adoption in the respective countries. To know whether the canonical marriage impediment of legal adoption exists and how far it extends—whether it merely prohibits marriage between the person adopted and certain members of the family of the adopter or makes marriage invalid— we must consult the civil law of the country. As we said in our commentary on Canon 1059, no state in the American Union has an impediment of marriage arising from legal adoption.

---

[583] *Decreta Auth. S. R. C.*, n. 3305.
[584] *Jus Decretal.*, IV, n. 492, footnote **67**.
[585] *Acta Ap. Sedis*, X, 346.

CHAPTER V

OF THE MATRIMONIAL CONSENT

1079. Marriage is contracted by the legitimately manifested consent of two parties who are qualified by law to enter into such contracts: no substitute for this consent can be supplied by any human power. The matrimonial consent is an act of the will by which each party gives and accepts the perpetual and exclusive right to the body for the performance of actions that of their nature pertain to the procreation of children (**Canon 1081**).

As marriage is a state created by the contract of the parties, that contract must have all the essentials of a contract, namely, persons qualified to make it, an object for which the agreement is made, a consideration (or *quid pro quo*), offer and acceptance or the mutual agreement of the parties, freedom of consent (for it must be a voluntary agreement), and a legal form of agreement if (as in marriage) a special form of contract is required by law.

Here we are chiefly concerned with the offer and acceptance, or the mutual consent of the parties. The Code touches incidentally on the object of the marriage contract (the right to each other's body for the purpose of marriage, namely, the procreation of offspring). The Code does not speak at length of this matter here, because Canon 1013 has already dealt with the purposes of marriage.

The consent must be a free act of the will, and, whereas an act of the will as such is internal and invisible, it must be manifested by such external signs (either words or actions), as are in the common estimation of mankind considered sufficient to express one's will. It is evident that this act of the will cannot be supplied by any human authority, for it is not the authority or the law that makes the contract, but the parties. The competent authorities can dispense from the formalities and solemnities which the law ordinarily requires in the making of the marriage contract, but the natural essentials of the contract, of which the free consent is one, cannot be supplied by law or by any human power.[585a]

[585a] Insanity vitiating marriage consent, cfr. App. III, 46, a.

RATIONAL MARRIAGE CONSENT PRESUPPOSES KNOWLEDGE OF THE OBJECT OF THE MARRIAGE CONTRACT

1080. The matrimonial consent cannot be validly given unless the contracting parties know at least that marriage is a permanent union between man and woman for the procreation of children. Ignorance on this point is not presumed in persons who have attained the age of puberty (**Canon 1082**).

It is mere common sense that one cannot rationally will something of which one has no knowledge. The law states that the parties must not be ignorant of the fact that marriage is a permanent union between husband and wife for the purpose of begetting children. The Code does not enter into particulars regarding the requisite knowledge. Whether a general intention to get married and live like other married people without knowledge of the marital rights is sufficient, is not stated in the Code. The question is of importance for it turns on the object of the contract, the giving and accepting of the right over each other's body. If a girl or boy contracting marriage has no knowledge of the object of the contract (the right to sexual intercourse for the purpose of the marriage), it is difficult to understand how they can contract a valid marriage. Canonists commonly hold that it suffices if a person knows in general that marriage is a permanent union between man and woman for the purpose of having children, though they have no knowledge that sexual intercourse is necessary for the procreation of children. If the right to sexual intercourse is the object of the marriage contract (and Canon 1081 says so), the person who knows nothing about the object cannot contract a valid marriage. Nor will it help to say that he who wants marriage implicitly, wants all that marriage includes. The question is rather whether one can rationally want marriage, if one has no knowledge of the object of marriage.

Practically it will be difficult to declare a marriage null and void for lack of the necessary knowledge, because, as the Code states, the law presumes that knowledge in persons who are of the age of puberty (that is, a boy of fourteen and a girl of twelve years). The burden of proof rests with the person who asserts that he did not have the necessary knowledge.[586] If the

[586] A case in which marriage of a girl of twelve years and nine months

confessor gets such a case, he cannot decide it in confession only, unless he sees very clearly that there is no possibility to prove the case in the diocesan court. If the invalidity of the marriage cannot be proved, and there is no proof of a reason for a separation, the party is bound to live in marriage, and consequently is bound to validate the marriage by giving the consent that was wanting when the marriage was contracted. Canon 1136 rules that when a marriage is invalid for lack of consent, the marriage is validated if the party which had not consented does now consent, provided the consent of the other party continues. If the lack of consent was merely interior (as is the case in lack of consent for reason of absence of necessary knowledge concerning the object of marriage), it suffices that the party give the consent interiorly, without external manifestation of it.

Error which Vitiates Matrimonial Consent

1081. Error concerning the identity of the person with whom one wants to contract marriage, renders marriage null and void. Error concerning any *quality* of the person, though such quality caused one to contract marriage, renders marriage invalid only in two cases: (1) if the error concerning a certain quality amounts to an error in the person; (2) if one contracts with a person whom he believed to be free, while in fact that person is a slave strictly so called (**Canon 1083**).

Not without reason does the Church warn her children to be on their guard and to act with caution and prudence before contracting marriage, since they must bear the consequences if they let themselves be deceived or make a mistake. The Church does not admit deception and mistake as invalidating reasons of the marriage contract. The only mistake or error that is admitted by the Church as an invalidating cause of marriage is an error concerning the identity of the person whom one intends to marry. If another person substitutes himself, and succeeds in impersonating the party so well that the second party is deceived, there is of course no marriage. This case is almost impossible in countries where courtship usually precedes marriage. Mistakes

with a man of twenty-five years of age was declared null and void for lack of the necessary knowledge was decided by the Sacred Congregation of the Council, May 19, 1888 (*Acta S. Sedis*, XXI, 162).

concerning the identity of the person one intends to marry are indeed of rare occurrence anywhere. The case of a slave deceiving the other party into the belief that he or she is a free man or woman, may occur in those countries where slavery still exists. Other deceptions and mistakes (e.g., as to wealth, position, character, etc.) do not invalidate marriage.

THEORETICAL ERRORS ON THE NATURE OF CHRISTIAN MARRIAGE

1082. Mere error concerning the unity, indissolubility, and sacramental dignity of marriage does not invalidate the matrimonial consent, even if such error was the cause of the contract (**Canon 1084**).

What constitutes marriage, and what are its characteristics, does not depend on man's mind or on his understanding of marriage, but on the law of Christ. Canon Law supposes that a Christian who wants to contract marriage, is willing to contract marriage according to the law of Christ. As it is not a matter of choice but of strict obligation for all human beings to conform themselves to God's law, their ignorance or error concerning that law cannot change the law. In human contracts the same principle is recognized. A citizen who makes a contract is bound by the consequences and obligations of that contract as they are laid down by law, and he is not excused from them because he did not know these consequences or thought the obligations to be different from those laid down by law. Sound public policy demands that no attention be paid to a person's private opinions, errors or mistakes, regarding what the law actually rules in the matter.

Supposing that a non-Catholic contracting marriage with a Catholic is firmly convinced that he is at liberty to get a divorce for any of the reasons for which the civil law grants divorces, is that marriage a true marriage according to the teaching of the Catholic Church? Several cases on this point have been discussed by the Tribunal of the Roman Rota. It has been held, as stated here in the Code, that error or belief as to the character and obligations of marriage as defined by the law of God cannot affect the nature and character of the marriage contracted.[587] Only where a party has explicitly made his consent

[587] August 10, 1912; *Decisiones S. Rom. Rotæ*, IV, Decis. 35; March

dependent on a condition which is against one of the essential characteristics of marriage, and has exteriorly manifested his mind, is the marriage rendered null and void (cfr. below, Canon 1086).

KNOWLEDGE OR OPINION THAT MARRIAGE IS INVALID

1083. The knowledge or opinion of the nullity of a marriage does not necessarily exclude matrimonial consent (**Canon 1085**).

This is another instance of the principle that an error of opinion cannot affect the contract as ordained by law. First, it may happen that a valid marriage is not possible between two parties for reason of a diriment impediment, and that one or both parties know of the impediment at the time of the giving of the matrimonial consent. Secondly, it may happen that the opinion of one or both parties is wrong, either because actually there is a diriment impediment and they are ignorant of it, or because they think that a diriment impediment exists while actually there is no such impediment. In any case, the validity or invalidity of the marriage does not depend on what the parties think or believe in the matter, but on the actual and objective state of the case according to the law. The law, not private opinion, controls.

The Code states that there may be matrimonial consent, though the marriage is invalid and the parties know of its invalidity at the time of the contract, and that matrimonial consent may be present, though the parties erroneously think at the time of the contract that their marriage is invalid. Canon 1085 is supplemented by Canon 1139, which deals with the validation of such marriages.

MATRIMONIAL CONSENT PRESUMED IN LAW TO BE IN HARMONY WITH THE NATURE OF THE CONTRACT

1084. The internal consent of the mind is always presumed to correspond with the words or signs employed in the marriage ceremony. If, however, either one or both parties by a positive

I, 1913 (the famous Anna Gould-Boni de Castellane case), V, Decis. 16. Cfr. Gasparri, "De Matrimonio," II, 97, on civil marriage contracted with the understanding of getting a divorce if the marriage turns out badly. Also *Collectanea de Prop. Fide*, II, n. 1465.

act of the will refuse marriage itself, or all right to the conjugal act, or any of the essential qualities of marriage, the marriage is invalid (**Canon 1086**).

This Canon confirms the principles enunciated in the preceding Canons. The internal will or intention is presumed in law to agree with the external signs by which matrimonial consent is expressed. He who asserts that he did not mean what his words or other expression of matrimonial consent imported, must furnish proof of his assertion.

The Code states that, if either party by a positive act of the will does not want to contract marriage though exteriorly he pronounces the words of consent, or if by a positive act of the will he does not want to give the marriage rights to the other party, or does not want to contract marriage as defined in its essential qualities (unity, indissolubility) by the law of God, he does not contract marriage, but practises fraud and deceit by using words or signs which apparently express matrimonial consent, without actually giving it validly. We saw above that the validity of the marriage cannot be questioned if by mere error or mistake or want of knowledge of the law of God the parties are ignorant of the true principles of marriage. As to the object of the contract of marriage (the right to each other's body), we saw already that no marriage can exist without the giving and accepting of that right, as otherwise there would be a contract without an object, a contradiction in itself.

Now, the positive act of the will opposed to the nature of the matrimonial contract or against its essential qualities makes the marriage null and void. Whether the parties are able to prove that state of mind, is another question. If they cannot prove it, they are in law considered validly married and the ecclesiastical court will oblige them to live together; if sufficient reasons are present, it may indeed grant a separation, but the marriage bond remains. If they are obliged to live together, they are obliged to give the consent necessary to validate the marriage. Purely internal lack of consent is healed by giving such consent interiorly (cfr. Canon 1136).

Consent Vitiated by Force and Fear

1085. Marriage is also invalid if contracted under the influence of force or grave fear which an outside agency unjustly exercised over a person so that he was forced to choose marriage as a means to free himself from the force or fear. No other fear entails the nullity of marriage though it caused the contract to be made (**Canon 1087**).

The terms ''force'' and ''fear'' in Canon 1087 are connected with each other in the manner of cause and effect. Force (violence or molestation) is employed to intimidate another and weaken his will so that he may be made to do what he would not otherwise do of his own free choice. While nobody can absolutely force another to make an act of the will, the unjust use of force, violence and continued molestation inflicted for the purpose of overcoming the resistance of a person's will-power, is nevertheless a grave injustice and an interference with a person's natural right to freedom. The Code rules that, if one is forced to choose marriage in order to free oneself from grave molestation, force, or violence, unjustly inflicted by another, the marriage thus contracted is null and void.

The Code reads ''ab extrinseco et injuste incussum.'' The term ''ab extrinseco'' is easy to understand, for it means a human agency that causes the fear, not the elements of nature, or the spirit world, or one's own soul or fear brought on by motives of one's conscience. The term ''injuste'' is more difficult to interpret exactly. Before the promulgation of the Code it was commonly held by canonists and moralists that a person who had made a valid promise of marriage could be forced by the ecclesiastical court to keep his promise, supposing that there was no valid reason for breaking it. The Code, however, rules that the injured party has no right to initiate a suit in the ecclesiastical court to enforce the fulfillment of the promise. The only right which Canon 1017 gives to the injured party is to sue for damages, if any damages resulted from the breach of promise.

As to the justice of the threats, the case becomes practical in our country when a man is brought to court for having seduced a woman into fornication. In some states the judge is authorized by law to give the man the alternative of either marrying the woman or going to prison. If, to escape the prison sentence, the man consents to marry the woman, is such a marriage valid? Speaking of cases in which the man forced the woman to the sexual intercourse, Cardinal Gasparri holds that the action of the judge in giving him this alternative is not unjust, and that therefore the fear is justly inflicted and the marriage is valid.[588] There are canonists who do not admit that the judge has the right to give the guilty man the option only between marriage and prison, and contend that he should be given also a choice of compensating the woman by payment of damages. They thus claim that the action of the judge is unjust *in modo,* and the Code does not distinguish between fears which are unjust *quoad substantiam* and *quoad modum,* but speaks generally of fear unjustly inflicted.[589] Practically, the latter opinion is preferable for several reasons. First, such a law giving the judge the right to demand that alternative is not conducive to the public welfare but rather injurious, for happy marriages are not, as a rule, contracted in that fashion. Furthermore, often an outright injustice is done to the man, because in many cases the woman is equally guilty, according to the old axiom, *scienti et volenti non fit injuria.*

1086. Another disputed question is whether the grave fear must be caused precisely for the purpose of forcing a person to marriage. The commentators of the former Canon law are practically unanimous that the unjustified force, violence, or vexation must be inflicted for the purpose of forcing a person to contract marriage. The various texts of the old law on force and fear and the decisions of the Roman Rota justify that interpretation. The question is whether the Code has modified the law in this particular. It seems so, for the Code speaks of grave fear caused by unjust force or violence, "from which one has no escape except to choose marriage" (*a quo ut quis se liberet, eligere cogatur matrimonium*). The case is not very practical, for usually the marriage would be no escape from the unjust vexation, threats, etc., unless they had been inflicted for the purpose, directly or indirectly manifested, of forcing the party to contract a certain marriage. The commentators on the Code do not agree whether the Code in this particular modifies the former law.[590]

1087. The fear must be both grave and unjustly caused. Under this head commentators on the former law as well as those on the Code discuss the question of *reverential fear,* by

[588] *De Matrimonio,* II, n. 949.
[589] Cappello, "De Sacramentis," III, n. 606.
[590] Chelodi, "Jus Matrimoniale," n. 119.

which is meant fear of a subject to displease or offend his superior, father, or guardian by resisting a marriage which they want their subject to contract. In itself that fear cannot be called grave, but circumstances may be such that the continued vexation to which a young man or young lady is subjected becomes unbearably grave. Wherefore, there are several cases in recent years where the Roman Rota decided in favor of the nullity of marriage entered into through undue pressure of the parents.[591] If, together with importune urging and other undue interference, the threat of disinheritance is joined, or ill-treatment and violence used because of resistance to a marriage planned by the parents, it is evident that the fear is both grave and unjustly caused. Even here in the United States where, as a general rule, the states permit a parent to do with his goods as he likes and to will them to whomsoever he pleases —even cutting off a child with a nominal sum to prevent attacks on the last will for reason of "pretermitting a child" as it is called—even here such threats of a father to make his child marry as he wants are undue interference with the freedom of choice in marriage. In the decision of the Roman Rota handed down in a case of reverential fear, June 2, 1911, the Tribunal quotes with approval the words of Sanchez, that the lasting indignation alone of a parent does so interfere with the liberty of the child that in law consent to the marriage is considered to be wanting.

1088. The question whether the impediment of force and fear is an impediment of the natural law or of ecclesiastical law only, remains unsettled, for the Code does not decide the question and the authorities who wrote before the Code are divided. There is some force to the argument of those who hold that the natural law makes a marriage entered into by force and fear invalid, because the invalidity is the only remedy against the injustice inflicted: for, if it is admitted that the marriage is valid, there is no way of redressing the evil. However, this may be a very urgent reason why the legislator should make full freedom in the choice of person in marriage an essential requisite for validity of the contract, but it is not so certain that the contract of its very nature is invalid. Otherwise the

[591] April 26, 1916 (*Acta Ap. Sedis*, IX, 144); March 11, 1912 (*Acta Ap. Sedis*, IV, 503); June 2, 1911 (*Decisiones S. Rom. Rotæ*, III, Decis. 21). Cfr. also App. III, 46, b.

same should be said in case of deception and fraud practised by one party on the other as to position, goods and property, health, etc., and yet the marriage is held to be valid despite the fraud and deception.

CONSENT TO BE GIVEN IN EACH OTHER'S PRESENCE

1089. In order to contract marriage validly, the parties must be in each other's presence, either in person or by proxy. The parties shall express their marriage consent in words, and shall not use equivalent signs if they can speak (**Canon 1088**).

The presence of the parties making a contract is not of itself necessary; in fact, many important contracts are concluded daily by correspondence. However, in the marriage contract, the Church absolutely requires the simultaneous presence of the parties, either in person or by proxy. Canon 1089 gives special rules regarding the proxy. The matrimonial consent of the parties must be personal, that is to say, given by the parties as an expression of their own will, for Canon 1081 states that marriage is effected by the consent of the parties, and that no substitute for their consent can be supplied by any human power. In the former Canon Law it was disputed whether the consent given by a father or mother in the presence of their child was a valid marriage, if the child did not contradict.[592]

1090. Prior to the Council of Trent, it was commonly held that marriage could be contracted by letter. After the Council of Trent had demanded for the validity of the marriage that it take place before the proper pastor and at least two witnesses, canonists still disputed whether marriage under the Tridentine law could be contracted by letter, and many maintained that it could. The Roman Rota, January 19, 1910, upheld the validity of a marriage in which the man gave his consent by letter written to the girl, with which letter and witnesses the girl went to her pastor to express her consent; that marriage was contracted on August 15, 1900.[593] Since the promulgation of the Code marriage by letter is no longer possible.

1091. The Code explicitly states that marriage can be contracted by proxy. The commentators on the former Canon Law

---

[592] Schmalzgrüber, "Jus Eccl.," VIII, nn. 246, 247.
[593] *Acta Ap. Sedis*, II, 297–309.

were not agreed on the question whether marriage by proxy was valid after the Council of Trent. Some canonists held that the Chapter "Tametsi" of that Council had implicitly revoked the law of the Decretals which explicitly allowed the contracting of marriage by proxy.[594]

The Code further requires that the consent be expressed in words, and those who are able to speak are not allowed to express their consent by signs. The wording of the Code shows clearly that the verbal expression of consent is not required under pain of nullity of the marriage. The priest must ask for and receive the consent, and any signs which ordinarily suffice to express an affirmation are sufficient for validity. The Holy Office, August 22, 1860, declared: "The marriage is firm and valid, whenever marriage consent is expressed by nodding, or by other ceremonies before witnesses which in the common estimation of the country sufficiently express the mutual marriage consent."[595]

Rules for Marriage by Proxy

1092. For the validity of a marriage by proxy a special mandate to contract it with a specified person is required, which mandate must be signed by the party issuing the same and either the pastor or the local Ordinary of the place where the mandate is issued, or by a priest delegated by either pastor or local Ordinary, or by at least two witnesses. The diocesan statutes may demand additional safeguards. If the person issuing the mandate does not know how to write, this fact shall be noted in the mandate, and an additional witness shall be employed who must subscribe the mandate together with the others whose signatures are required; otherwise the mandate is null and void.

If the person who gave the mandate shall have recalled the same, or shall have become insane, before the proxy contracted marriage in the principal's name, the marriage is invalid, though neither the proxy nor the other party to the marriage knew about the revocation of the mandate. The proxy must in person fulfill his office, or otherwise the marriage is invalid (**Canon 1089**).

[594] c. 9, *De Procuratoribus*, lib. I, tit. 19, in Sexto; Reiffenstuel, "Jus Can. Univers.," I, tit. 38, n. 67; Ferraris, "Bibliotheca," V, *Matrimonium*, art. I, n. 34.
[595] *Collect. de Prop. Fide*, I, n. 1201.

The formalities required for the written mandate by which a proxy is appointed, are about the same as the formalities demanded in the engagement contracts by Canon 1017. There is some difference: for instance, a priest can be delegated as witness of the mandate by the pastor or the Ordinary of the place where the mandate is issued. With a few modifications, the Code repeats the law of Pope Boniface VIII, in the *Liber Sextus* of the Decretals referred to above. In the former law a written document was not required, nor was it necessary to give the mandate in the presence of witnesses, though even under the old law the proxy certainly could not lawfully be admitted to contract marriage in the name of another person unless he could prove his mandate. In the former law the principal could also authorize the proxy to appoint another to carry out the mandate. The Code demands that the proxy act in person, and seems to admit no power of subdelegation in the matter.

In the United States marriage by proxy is not recognized: the citizen has no power to authorize another to contract marriage for him, though it is merely to hasten an intended marriage or to bring about a marriage of parties already engaged.[596] As to marriages of foreign subjects actually resident in the United States, a recent decision of Federal Judge Lowell, of Boston, Mass., [597] upheld the validity of a marriage contracted by such a resident in Europe by means of a proxy. The person seems to have been a Portuguese subject, and had obtained from the Portuguese Consul at Philadelphia a certificate in which he named a person to act as his proxy in Portugal. This ruling is said to be unique in the history of American and English courts.

1093. Marriage can also be contracted through an *interpreter* (**Canon 1090**). This supposes that both parties are present, either in person or by proxy, and the interpreter is merely employed to translate the words of consent spoken by the parties.

The pastor shall not assist at a marriage to be contracted by a proxy or by an interpreter unless there is good reason for it, and provided he has no reason whatever to doubt the authenticity of the mandate exhibited by the proxy or the truthfulness of the interpreter; if time permits, the pastor must

---

[596] Clark, ''Contracts,'' 381.
[597] *Washington Post* (January 29, 1924), p. 4.

obtain the permission of his Ordinary to assist at such marriages (**Canon 1091**).

CONDITIONAL MARRIAGE CONSENT OF THE PARTIES

1094. Conditions attached to the marriage consent, and not revoked, are governed by the following rules:

(1) If the condition is of the future and either necessary, or impossible, or sinful, but is not contrary to the essence of marriage, it is considered as not added to the contract;

(2) If the condition is of the future and is contrary to the essence of marriage, it renders the marriage null and void;

(3) If the condition is of the future and licit, it suspends the validity of the marriage;

(4) If the condition is either of the past or the present, the marriage is valid if the condition is existent, but invalid if the condition is not realized (**Canon 1092**).

The Code repeats the former law on the matter of conditional consent in marriage. The first two paragraphs of Canon 1092 are taken in substance from the Decretals of Pope Gregory IX.[598] The conditional consent is not considered in the external forum, unless the condition is externally manifested in such a manner that full proof of it can be furnished in the ecclesiastical court. Besides, it must be proved that the party adhered to the condition up to the very moment of giving the marriage consent. A revocation of the condition may be construed, not only from express words contrary to the former condition, but also from the acts and conduct of the party who had previously expressed such condition.

As to future impossible, necessary, and sinful conditions, when the sinfulness of it is not against the essence of marriage (for instance, "I marry you provided you assist me in my dishonest business"), these conditions are disregarded in law, as though they were not made.

Conditions of the future against the essence of marriage render the marriage null and void. Pope Gregory IX gives some examples of these conditions in the chapter referred to above: If one party should say to the other: I contract with

---

[598] c. 7, *De conditionibus appositis in desponsatione vel in aliis contractibus*, lib. IV, tit. 5.

you if you avoid the procreation of offspring; or until I find another person richer and more honorable than you, or if for gain you give yourself to adultery.

1095. The condition against the purpose of marriage (if you avoid the procreation of offspring) is, according to some canonists, to be understood of avoiding it by sinful means. Whether marriage is null and void if one party consents to the marriage on condition only that they shall abstain from conjugal intercourse, is much debated among theologians. The object of the marriage contract is the right to each other's body for the acts necessary for the procreation of offspring. To contract with the condition that they shall not exercise the right to sexual intercourse, while the right thereto is nevertheless given, is said by some to be sufficient for a valid marriage. They say that the right itself is distinct from the use of the right; one is given and the other is excluded by the condition. The object of the marriage is precisely the right to a use; the distinction might be proper in the transfer of property rights in which the right, or title, or ownership can be and often is distinct from the right to use the property, but in marriage the distinction seems to have no application.[599]

1096. Greater practical difficulty arises frequently in marriages contracted with the understanding that, if the parties find they cannot get along peacefully, they are free to seek a divorce, and in marriages in which the parties agree to limit the number of children to one or two, or to have no children for the first few years, and the like sinful agreements. Are these conditions against the essence of marriage which, according to Canon 1092, render the marriage consent null and void? It is a well-known principle, clearly stated in Canon 1084, that theoretical errors of the parties as to the essentials of Christian marriage do not invalidate the marriage consent, but, when these errors against the essence of marriage are made conditions, or (as Canon 1086 has it) what is essential in marriage is excluded by a positive act of the will, there can be no valid marriage because in the same act of the will the person wants marriage and does not want marriage (that is, marriage as ordained by Christ).

One has to investigate in these cases whether the agreements

599 Benedictus XIV, "De Synodo Diœc.," lib. XIII, cap. 22, nn. 10–13.

are merely resolutions to commit sin, or whether one or both parties make them conditions under which they want to contract marriage. It must be noted, however, that it is not necessary that these points against the essence of marriage are made conditions, for Canon 1086 rules that, if there is a positive act of the will against the essentials of marriage, there can be no valid marriage.

1097. Regarding the licit conditions which a person may attach to the marriage consent (cfr. Canon 1092, nn. 3–4), one has to examine closely whether they were conditions properly so called, or merely an expression of a hope, a desire, an aversion, etc. In the case of a dope fiend where the girl had repeatedly asserted that she would never marry the man if the rumor about his being addicted to dope was true, the Roman Rota, December 18, 1913, decided in favor of the nullity of the marriage for reason of the *conditio sine qua non* not being verified.[600] Another illustration of a condition attached to the consent is found in the case decided by the Roman Rota, August 11, 1921. In this case, a Catholic girl had married a man who was known to have abandoned the practice of the Catholic faith, and had therefore declared that she would never marry him unless she was free to practise her religion and raise the children in the Catholic faith. The civil ceremony demanded by the law of France was followed immediately by the Catholic marriage ceremony, and at this the man showed already his disgust with things Catholic. He afterwards wanted to stop his wife from going to Church and from making her Easter duty. The Roman Rota declared the marriage invalid for want of fulfillment of the condition attached.[601]

1098. Though marriage was contracted invalidly for reason of an impediment, the consent given is presumed to persevere until there is certainty of its revocation (**Canon 1093**). The Code thus concludes its treatment of all the impediments and of those cases which affect the matrimonial consent (ignorance, error, positive will against the essence of marriage, force, and fear, conditions). There has been a controversy among canonists as to whether marriage consent could be present if at least one of the parties knew of the impediment, and thus knew that no valid marriage could be contracted. The Code declares

---

[600] *S. Rom. Rotæ*, V, Decis. 52.   [601] Cfr. App. III, 46, c.

in general that the marriage consent is presumed to be there, even though a diriment impediment makes such consent null and void, and that such consent is presumed in law to persevere until it can be proved with certainty that the consent was revoked. This Canon is important in the matter of validating invalid marriages, which matter is treated in Canons 1133–1141.

CHAPTER VI

OF THE FORM OF THE MARRIAGE CONTRACT

1099. Those marriages only are valid which are contracted either before a pastor or the local Ordinary or a priest delegated by either and at least two witnesses, in conformity, however, with the rules laid down in the following Canons, and saving the exceptions mentioned below in Canons 1098 and 1099 (**Canon 1094**).

This first Canon on the form of marriage is taken verbatim from the "Ne Temere" Decree, which went into force on April 19, 1908. Previously there had been no general law throughout the whole Church making the solemnization of the marriage before an authorized priest necessary for validity. The common law marriage was recognized as valid in all those dioceses and places where the law of the Decree "Tametsi" of the Council of Trent had not been promulgated in the manner prescribed by that Council, or introduced by ancient custom. For the United States, the Decree of the Holy Office, November 25, 1885, confirmed the finding of the Fathers of the Third Council of Baltimore in reference to the places in which the "Tametsi" was in force, and also determined the places to which the declaration of Pope Benedict XIV was extended concerning the freedom from the form of marriage in marriages between baptized non-Catholics and between Catholics and baptized non-Catholics.[602]

While there was no general law making the celebration of marriage before an authorized priest necessary for validity, the Church had since the early days of its existence forbidden secret marriages and insisted that they be celebrated publicly before the Church. St. Ignatius, Tertullian, St. Ambrose, and local

---

[602] *Decreta Concilii Baltimor. III*, p. CV. See also Sabetti, "Theol. Moral.," (ed. 1902), p. 698, on the impediment of clandestinity.

Councils of the early Church, cited by church historians and canonists, show sufficiently that the Church wanted her children to contract marriage publicly with the sanction and the blessing of the Church.

In the Oriental Church private or secret marriages were likewise forbidden, as can be seen from the Councils of Laodicea (343, 381) and St. John Chrysostom. In an Instruction to the Greek-Roumanian priests, the Sacred Congregation of the Propaganda discusses the question of clandestine marriages in the Oriental Church. It refers to Emperor Leo the Philosopher, who in 893 passed a law that marriages were null and void unless they were solemnized in the Church. The Sacred Congregation remarks that the emperor had no jurisdiction to pass such a law, and, though the law was accepted in many dioceses of the Oriental Church, the Congregation proves by references from Oriental authorities that this law was not accepted everywhere in the Oriental Church. It is perfectly in harmony with the tradition of the Church to insist on marriage being publicly celebrated in church, but, unless the competent ecclesiastical authority passes a law requiring the solemn form under pain of nullity, the clandestine marriages are valid.[603]

The ''Ne Temere'' Decree made the form of marriage obligatory for all Catholics of the Latin Rite, and they were bound by this law also in marriages with non-Catholics and with Catholics of Oriental Rites. An exception was allowed for mixed marriages in Germany and Hungary, but the Code makes no allowance for special laws in reference to the form of marriage. Some canonists considered the exception not as a particular law, but rather as a privilege, and maintained that as a privilege the exception continued. The question was put before the Holy See and the Cardinal Prefect of the Committee answered, March 30, 1918, that the Code abolished the exception.[604]

REQUISITES FOR THE VALID ASSISTANCE OF BISHOP AND PASTOR

1100. The pastor and the local Ordinary assist validly at marriages:

(1) from the day only on which they have taken canonical

---

[603] *Collectanea de Prop. Fide*, I, n. 1154.
[604] *Linzer Quartalschrift*, LXXI, 729.

possession of their benefice, according to Canons 334 and 1444, or have entered upon their office, provided they are not excommunicated, interdicted, or suspended from office by sentence, or declared as such;

(2) only within the limits of their respective territories, in which they assist validly at all marriages not only of their subjects but also of non-subjects;

(3) provided they are not constrained by force or grave fear to ask for and receive the marriage consent of the parties (**Canon 1095, § 1**);

The pastor and the local Ordinary who can validly assist at marriage may also give another priest permission to assist validly at marriage within the limits of their respective territories (**Canon 1095, § 2**).

The pastor and the local bishop (or other Ordinary) can assist at marriages in their respective territories from the day on which they take canonical possession of the parish or diocese (cfr. Canon 334, above, n. 245). Canon 1444 states that the taking of possession of a benefice is to be done in the manner pointed out by the particular law or legitimate custom, unless the local Ordinary for a good reason dispenses with the formality by written instrument, in which case the dispensation takes the place of the canonical introduction into the benefice (cfr. Canon 461, above, n. 337, on the taking of possession of parish by pastor).

There are other persons besides the local Ordinary and the pastor who by law obtain the same jurisdiction as the Ordinary and pastor, and can therefore assist at marriage from the day on which they enter into office. Amongst these are included the vicar-general, the administrator of a diocese (or a parish), the priest who takes the place of the pastor in his absence, disability, etc. As the phrase ''initi officii'' is nowhere defined in law, most commentators abstain from giving an explanation of it. It seems to mean the beginning of the actual exercise of the duties of the office to which they have been appointed.

1101. Within the limits of their respective territories the local Ordinary and the pastor can validly assist at all marriages of their own subjects as well as of non-subjects. They lose the power to assist validly if an excommunication, interdict, or suspension from office has been pronounced against them by a competent ecclesiastical court by a declaratory or condemnatory sentence. The mere fact that a local Ordinary or a pastor has committed an offence to which the law attaches *ipso facto* one of these censures, does not deprive them of the power to assist validly at marriages, unless the competent ecclesiastical court has taken up the matter and issued the declaration that they have incurred such censure.

Pastors who have charge over a certain territory together with other pastors (as is found frequently in the United States in the case of the foreign language parishes) occupy a peculiar position which is not clearly defined in the Code. The foreign language parishes frequently extend over several English-speaking parishes. Thus it happens that, in a town with possibly three English-speaking parishes with definite territories, a single Italian parish extends over the entire town, a Polish parish likewise extends the whole town, and there is still another German parish for all German-speaking Catholics. The question is whether these pastors of foreign language parishes can assist at marriage in any part of the town, and whether they can validly assist at marriages, not only of their respective nationals, but of any Catholics who come to them. Is their jurisdiction territorial, or is it personal and restricted to their nationals? The commentators of the Code are hopelessly divided on the question. De Smet, De Becker, Leitner, Augustine, Fanfani, and Cappello hold that it is territorial, and extends over the territory held in common with other pastors, so that they can assist at least validly at all marriages of Catholics.[605] Blat, Vlaming, Chelodi, Ayrinhac, and Creagh hold that it is personal, and restricted to their own nationals, so that they cannot validly assist at marriage, unless at least one of the parties is their own national.[606] The point is not decided by the Declaration to the "Ne Temere" of February 1, 1908, that pastors who have no exclusive proper territory, but hold it together with one or more pastors, can validly assist in the entire territory which they hold in common with other pastors. The question in the case of the language

---

[605] De Smet, "De Spons. et Matrim.," p. 94; De Becker, "De Spons. et Matrim.," 29, on the "Ne Temere"; Leitner, "Kath. Eherecht," 190; Augustine, "Commentary," V, 279; Fanfani, "De Jure Paroch.," 289; Cappello, "De Sacram.," III, n. 667.

[606] Blat, "De Rebus," III, 644–645; Vlaming, "Prælect. Jur. Matr.," II, n. 565; Chelodi, "Jus Matrim.," 142; Ayrinhac, "Marriage Legislation," n. 240; Creagh, "Ne Temere," 38.

parishes is precisely whether, in the creation of these parishes, the bishop assigned them any territory at all, or simply gave them a personal jurisdiction over their nationals. In the last analysis the answer to the question depends on the particular law of each diocese, or on the document of erection of the language parishes. The Code states that it does not change the status of the language parishes, and that the local Ordinaries shall not change their status without consulting the Holy See (cfr. Canon 216).

If chaplains of hospitals and other ecclesiastical institutions have received from the Ordinary of the diocese full parochial charge without any restriction as to marriages, they can validly witness marriages within the confines of such places and for their own subjects (cfr. Sacred Congregation of the Council, February 1, 1908).

1102. The assistance of the pastor or the local Ordinary is not valid, if he is constrained thereto by force or grave fear. The assistance must be voluntary and uninfluenced by threats or violence. The Code does not say, as in the case of the impediment of force and fear, that the fear must be caused by unjust means, but simply that pastor or bishop cannot be constrained to assist by force or grave fear. Neither does it suffice that the parties and witnesses take the pastor by surprise and declare themselves husband and wife, for it is essential to the validity of the marriage that the pastor be present not passively, but must actively ask for and receive the consent. This applies also to mixed marriages as we will see under Canon 1102.

Delegation of Priest to Assist at Marriage

1103. When permission is given to another priest to assist at marriage in accordance with Canon 1095, § 2, it must be granted expressly to a specified priest for a specified marriage. General delegations must not be given except to regularly appointed assistants for the parish to which they are appointed; otherwise the permission or delegation is invalid. The pastor and the local Ordinary shall not give permission to another priest to assist at a marriage until after all that which the law requires for the proof of the free state of the parties has been performed (**Canon 1096**).

In the first place, the local Ordinary or the pastor who wants to delegate another priest to assist at marriage must be himself entitled to assist validly. The Code further states that the permission or delegation must be given expressly. Thereby all tacit, implied, presumed, or interpretative permission is excluded. It must be expressly given either orally, or in writing, or by action. In all three ways an explicit giving of permission is possible. The last-named manner (by action) may or may not be an express delegation, according to the circumstances of the case. In a marriage case decided July 9, 1918, the Roman Rota discusses the various ways of giving a delegation to witness a marriage: it draws a distinction between a mere tacit permission or delegation and a permission which is expressed by acts, and states that actions are stronger to prove a person's intention than words. Such a permission given "tacite per facta vere concludentia et præcedentia" should according to the Roman Rota be called rather a *licentia expressa* or *quasi-expressa,* because it is expressed not by words or in writing, but by facts.[607] Raus, in a discussion on this point in the *Linzer Quartalschrift,* argues that such a permission granted by concluding facts suffices to answer the requirements of the Code (*licentia dari expresse debet*).[608]

1104. The next requirement in granting a priest permission to assist at a marriage is that it must be given to a specified priest (*sacerdoti determinato*). The priest may be designated either by name or by office, or in any other way in which it is made certain who the individual priest is whom the pastor or bishop delegates. The pastor or the Ordinary must do the determining of the priest, for it cannot be left to the parties or to another person to choose the priest who is to assist at the marriage. That such an indirect pointing out of the priest is not sufficient, is certain from the following recent declaration of the Committee: "Whether according to Canon 1096, § 1, the priest is specified if the pastor declares to the superior of a monastery in a particular case that he (the pastor) delegates for the marriage to be contracted on the following Sunday in the mission chapel attached to the parish that religious priest whom the superior of the monastery shall appoint to say Mass

607 *Acta Ap. Sedis,* XI, 154.
608 LXXVI (1923), 488.

in that chapel on next Sunday?'' The answer was that it is not a sufficient delegation.[609]

To provide in similar cases for valid assistance, the pastor should directly delegate the superior of the monastery and explicitly give him the right to subdelegate a priest. Commentators very generally agree that the Code does not invalidate, or even forbid, the delegation of a priest with the right to subdelegate. In fact, a decision on the ''Ne Temere'' Decree which required, even in stronger terms than the Code, that the permission to assist at marriage be given to a specified priest, declared that in reference to delegation nothing has been changed except that it has to be given to a certain and specified priest, and that it is restricted to the territory of the delegating priest or local Ordinary.[610] The Code has an additional restriction of delegation, namely, that it forbids general delegation, of which we shall speak presently (cfr. n. 1105).

There seems to be no conflict with the Code if a pastor or an Ordinary should delegate several specified priests for the same marriage. According to the rule of the Code, if several persons are delegated for the same affair, they may be delegated to act either individually or in a body. If nothing is said as to how they are to act, they are to be considered delegated to act individually in matters of the voluntary jurisdiction, and in a body in matters of judicial proceedings. When delegated individually for the same affair, he who first acts in the matter excludes the others, unless after having started to act he afterwards is prevented from continuing, or does not wish to continue (cfr. Canon 205).

1105. A further requirement in giving permission to assist at a marriage is that it must be given ''for a specified marriage,'' every kind of general delegation being excluded except in the case of the regularly appointed assistants within the limits of the parish. The marriage (or marriages) must, therefore, be sufficiently designated in the delegation so that it is specifically known for what marriage (or marriages) the delegation is given. Expressions such as ''the next two marriages in this parish,'' ''all the marriages to be celebrated on a certain day,'' etc., would

---

609 Cfr. App. III, 47, c.
610 Sacred Congregation of the Council, July 27, 1908; *Acta S. Sedis*, XLI, 510.

not specify the marriages sufficiently unless the individual marriages for which the delegation is given are identified by some record or note-book of the pastor, or from some other source.

As to assistant priests, administrators of parishes, and a priest who takes the place of a pastor in the latter's absence, the following may be said. First, as to assistant priests, the question was submitted to the Holy See whether the general faculties of priests in the diocese to administer all the sacraments confer a general delegation to assist at marriage in the parish in which they are assistants. The answer of the Holy Office was that they have no such delegation, unless they are *vice-parochi* who by custom of the diocese are considered to have that general delegation.[611] The term *vice-parochi* is not well defined in the old law, and may include assistants. Under the Code it is certain from Canon 1096 and Canon 476 that they may be delegated generally for all marriages, but they do not have that delegation *ipso facto,* and must be given it either by the statutes of the diocese or by the letters of appointment of the bishop. For Canon 476 states that the rights and duties of an assistant must be learned from the diocesan statutes, the letters of appointment of the Ordinary, and from the commission given them by the pastor. By law, therefore, they have no faculty to assist at marriages in the parish to which they are appointed.[612] The Sacred Congregation of the Sacraments has disapproved of the custom of assistants in a parish witnessing marriages without the express delegation of either the bishop or the pastor, and it forbade the assistants to witness marriages on the plea that the pastor had let them do so, seeing what they did and not interfering. After consulting the Supreme Pontiff, the Sacred Congregation told the bishop to acquiesce in the marriages thus witnessed.[613] If they are delegated generally for marriages, they can subdelegate in individual cases according to the general principles of delegated power (cfr. Canon 199).

1106. Regarding priests who occasionally take the place of the pastor, a declaration of the Committee rules as follows:

First, the *vicarius œconomus* (cfr. Canons 472–473) can assist at marriages in the parish and give permission to another priest

---

[611] Sept. 7, 1898; *Collect. de Prop. Fide,* II, n. 2020.

[612] Concerning substitutes of pastor and assistant priests, cfr. App. III, 47, a and b.

[613] March 13, 1910; *Acta Ap. Sedis,* II, 193.

to assist. This vicar is the administrator of the parish during a vacancy, and is in every sense of the term a pastor for the time being, with all the rights and duties of a pastor.

Secondly, the *vicarius substitutus* (cfr. Canon 465) can assist or delegate another priest to assist at marriage. This vicar takes the place of the pastor whenever the pastor is absent from his parish for more than a week. The pastor must get the bishop's permission for such an absence, must appoint a priest to take his place, and this substitute must be approved by the bishop. After the approval the substitute pastor has the rights of a pastor during the pastor's absence, unless the Ordinary limits his powers. An earlier declaration of the Committee had ruled that the priest substituting in the absence of the pastor may assist at marriages after his appointment by the pastor had been approved by the Ordinary, not before that approval.[614]

Thirdly, the *vicarius substitutus* of a religious pastor has the same rights as the *vicarius substitutus* of a secular pastor, in the absence of the pastor. Like the secular pastor, the religious pastor must also get permission to leave the parish for over a week, and must appoint a substitute with the approval of the Ordinary. He needs, besides, the permission of his religious superior, for the substitute must be acceptable to both the Ordinary of the diocese and to the religious superior, but the approval of the Ordinary only is essential for the valid parochial jurisdiction of the substitute. This also was decided in the declaration of the Committee of July 14, 1922.

Fourthly, the *vicarius substitutus* may assist at marriages and delegate other priests as long as the bishop who was notified of the appointment of the substitute by the pastor has not ruled otherwise. This substitute is the priest who is appointed by a pastor who has to leave his parish hurriedly for some sudden and grave reason which will keep him away for more than a week. He may leave without first asking the bishop's permission and proposing the substitute for the bishop's approval, but he must appoint a substitute and inform the bishop as soon as possible of the reason why he went away and whom he appointed as his substitute.

Fifthly, the Holy See was asked whether the priest who in Canon 475 is called the *vicarius adjutor* (appointed by the

---

[614] Cfr. App. III, 47, a.

bishop to assist a pastor who on account of old age, defect of mind, incompetence, blindness, or any other permanent cause is unable to govern the parish), has the right to assist at marriages. The committee answers that the second paragraph of Canon 475 contains the solution of the question. That section states that, if he takes the place of the pastor in all things concerning the management of the parish, the *vicarius adjutor* has all the rights and duties of a pastor except the obligation to apply Mass for the people. If, however, he only partly supplies the pastor, his rights and duties must be learned from the bishop's letter of appointment.[615]

1107. Finally, the second paragraph of Canon 1096 rules that the pastor and the local Ordinary shall not give permission to another priest to witness a marriage until after all has been done that is demanded by Canon Law to prove that the parties are free to marry. The reason for this rule is evident, since the pastor and the local Ordinary are in a better position to know the parties and to make the necessary investigations concerning impediments of marriage than a delegated priest. The Church is particularly stringent in demanding certainty that the parties are free from the impediment of *ligamen* (the bond of a still existing valid marriage). As divorces and separations of married people are frequent, it is important that a careful investigation be made if there is any reason at all to suspect that one or both are married persons, and inquiry must be made when the parties are practically unknown to the pastor, as so frequently happens in city parishes where many people change their residence every few months. In a Decree of March 6, 1911, the Sacred Congregation of the Sacraments insists on the gravity of the obligation of the pastor to make proper investigations.[616] The same Congregation has recently issued another Instruction on the same subject the substance of which is as follows:

Many bishops have complained that the pastors, especially in the foreign and distant countries to which many workingmen from Europe emigrate, assist at marriage without complying with the law which demands the investigation of the free state of the parties and the sending of notice of the marriage contracted to the parish where the parties were baptized. As a

615 Committee, May 20, 1923; *Acta Ap. Sedis*, XVI, 115.
616 *Acta Ap. Sedis*, III, 102.

consequence, it happens not infrequently that marriage is attempted by people who are already married. The Sacred Congregation refers to its own Decree of March 6, 1911, and says that it issues this new Instruction lest anyone claim that the Code has abolished the former Decree.

The local Ordinaries are to remind the pastors that they may not assist at marriages, not even under the pretext and with the intention of preventing the faithful from living in concubinage or of contracting a civil marriage, without having legitimately ascertained the free state of the parties. Canons 1020 and 1097 demand this of the pastor. He must also, in accordance with Canon 1021, demand the baptismal certificate of the parties if they have been baptized in another parish. The manner of conducting the investigation is not detailed in the Code, but Canon 1020 states that the local Ordinary is to prescribe special regulations for this investigation.

Canon 1103 requires that the pastor who witnesses the marriage shall send the record of the same to the pastor of the church where the parties were baptized. In order that the purpose of the law of that Canon be attained, the notice sent to the church where the parties were baptized must give the full names of both the parties and their parents, the age of the parties, place and date of the marriage, full names of the witnesses, full name of the pastor and the parochial seal. The notice shall be sent by registered mail. Letters between the pastors in reference to the parties shall be asked for and forwarded through the chancery of the local Ordinary of the respective pastor.

The marriages of some of the workingmen who come from other countries are to be considered like marriages of *vagi* (that is, persons with no domicile or quasi-domicile). Now, Canon 1032 rules that a pastor shall not assist at marriages of *vagi* without first obtaining permission from the Ordinary of the diocese. Even though they are not *vagi*, there is often no certainty of the absence of impediments in the case of immigrants, and, if there is a doubt about an impediment, Canon 1031, § 1, forbids the pastor to assist at the marriage without consulting the local Ordinary, except in a case of necessity or danger of death. If a pastor gets notice from another pastor of a marriage having been contracted, and he knows that one or both parties were already married, he shall at once notify the pastor through the chancery office of his diocese of the criminal attempt at a second marriage. The bishop shall see that this Instruction is carried out by the pastors and that offenders are punished. Thus far the recent Instruction of the Sacred Congregation of the Sacraments.[617]

1108. Another question arises from Canon 1096. Canon 1095 lays down certain rules to be complied with before the bishop and the pastor can validly assist at marriages in their respective diocese or parish. The question is whether these rules also apply to the priest delegated to assist at marriage— especially whether a priest excommunicated, suspended from office, or interdicted by a declaratory or condemnatory sentence of a competent ecclesiastical court can be validly delegated. The commentators of the Code are divided on the point. Augustine,[618] Cerato,[619] De Smet,[620] Linneborn [621] and Blat [622] hold that such a priest cannot be validly delegated. Vlaming,[623] Leitner,[624] Petrovits [625] and Wouters [626] hold that such a priest can be validly delegated.

The opinion which holds that a priest censured by the above penalties in an ecclesiastical court of competent jurisdiction cannot be validly delegated, seems to be better supported by arguments from both reason and law. For it would be rather strange if a censured priest could be delegated to witness marriage when the law rules that a censured bishop or pastor cannot validly witness marriages. Besides, the person excommunicated by sentence of an ecclesiastical court cannot validly exercise an act of jurisdiction in virtue of Canon 2264. Though the assistance at marriage is not strictly speaking an act of jurisdiction, still it partakes of the nature of a jurisdictional act, as is shown by the fact that the law applies to this delegation the rules on the delegation of jurisdiction. The "Ne Temere" Decree (art. VI) stated explicitly that the delegated priest was bound by

---

617 July 4, 1921; *Acta Ap. Sedis*, XIII, 348.
618 *Commentary*, V, 286.
619 *De Matrimonio*, 166.
620 *De Spons. et Matrim.*, n. 122.
621 *Grundriss des Eherechts*, 361.
622 *Commentarium*, lib. III, 646.
623 *Prælect. Jur. Matrim.*, II, n. 573.
624 *Kath. Eherecht*, 205.
625 *New Church Law on Marriage*, n. 474.
626 *De Forma Spons. et Matrim.*, 25.

the same rules with reference to valid and licit assistance as the delegating bishop or pastor. It seems that the Code did not think it necessary to reënact article VI of the "Ne Temere" Decree, since it is obvious that the delegated person cannot be in a more favorable position in law than the person delegating.

The Civil Law of the United States on Assistance of Priest at Marriages

1109. In all the states of the American Union the marriage ceremony may be performed by any minister of the Gospel, ordained or licensed according to the usages of his denomination; sometimes the law adds "in good standing with his church," or some such phrase. In several states there are certain conditions to be complied with by the minister of religion. In Delaware and Pennsylvania all religious celebrants must report their names and residences to a specified official, who shall register them. If the celebrant moves to another place, he must report that fact within thirty days. Oklahoma has gone farther, requiring all religious celebrants to file their credentials. In Oregon the credentials must be "approved," and then recorded. In eight other states (Arkansas, District of Columbia, Maine, Minnesota, Nevada, Ohio, Rhode Island, and Wisconsin), every religious celebrant must obtain a clergyman's certificate or license. In Kentucky, Virginia, and West Virginia he must give bond for the proper performance of his duties.

"In all but nine states a minister from any part of the United States may apparently solemnize a marriage. In a few states this wide range of authority is explicitly given. Thus, in Louisiana any minister of the gospel or priest of a religious sect qualifies as a celebrant, whether he is a citizen of the United States or not. Ordinarily, however, there is no reference to the territorial bounds of authority. The nine exceptional states which limit solemnization to ministers of the state are Indiana, Massachusetts, Michigan, Missouri, Nevada, New Hampshire, Ohio, Vermont, and Washington." [627]

---

[627] Hall and Brooke, "American Marriage Laws," 42 (Russell Sage Foundation, New York, 1919). As the statutes of the various states are subject to changes by the respective legislatures, the latest revised statutes of the various states must be consulted.

Canonical Requirements for Licit Assistance

1110. The pastor or the local Ordinary assist licitly at marriages under the following conditions:

(1) After they have legitimately ascertained the free state of the contracting parties, according to the rules of law;

(2) After they have ascertained that at least one of the parties has a domicile, or quasi-domicile, or one month's residence in the place of marriage. In case of *vagi* it suffices that they are actually staying in the place, that is to say, if one at least is a *vagus;*

(3) If neither party is subject to the pastor or the local Ordinary under the provisions of the preceding paragraph, the permission to assist at the marriage must be obtained from the pastor or local Ordinary of the parish or diocese where either party has a domicile or quasi-domicile or has resided one month, unless there is question of *vagi* who are actually travelling and who have no place of sojourn anywhere, or unless there exists a grave necessity for the immediate celebration of the marriage which excuses asking for the permission.

In every case it shall be the rule that the marriage is to be contracted before the pastor of the bride, unless a just reason excuses. Marriages of parties belonging to different Catholic Rites shall be contracted in the presence of the pastor of the groom and according to the ceremonies of his Rite, unless a particular law rules otherwise.

The pastor who assists at marriage without the permission required by law does not become the rightful owner of the stole fee but must forward it to the proper pastor of the contracting parties (**Canon 1097**).

It is important to ascertain who the proper pastor or local Ordinary is in a given marriage, not only for the purpose of licit assistance at the marriage, but also to insure its validity when there is question of dispensation from diriment impediments of marriage. For at least one of the parties must be a subject of the local Ordinary in order that he may validly grant the dispensation. This phase of the question has been treated sufficiently in our commentary on the Canons dealing with dispensations from impediments of marriage (cfr. above, Canons 1043–1057).

1111. The bishop and the pastor are forbidden by the divine and the ecclesiastical law to lend their aid to sacrilegious marriages, and they must, therefore, employ great diligence to discover the existence of any impediments which would render the marriage null and void. The Code speaks of the duty of both bishop and pastor, because both are by law entitled to witness marriages within the boundaries of their respective territories. As a rule, the pastor attends to this matter, for the bishop rarely witnesses marriages.

1112. As to the licit assistance at a marriage, the rule is that a pastor shall not marry a couple if neither party is his subject. The Code in this Canon determines how a person becomes a subject of the pastor with reference to marriage—viz., by domicile, quasi-domicile, or one month's sojourn in a parish. Persons who have neither a domicile, nor a quasi-domicile, nor one month's sojourn (immediately before marriage), become subject (as *vagi*) to the pastor of the parish where they actually stay. The rules as to what constitutes a domicile and quasi-domicile are given in Canon 92. If the intention to stay in a place permanently or for the greater part of the year is dependent on a future contingent condition (e.g., if I get a certain employment or position, if I get married, etc.), such an intention does not suffice to establish a domicile or quasi-domicile from the very moment that one takes up residence in a certain place. This is not an intention pure and simple to stay in a certain place, but a conditional intention in which the will to stay becomes absolute only after the condition is verified. In a marriage case in which the question of domicile was of importance to the decision, the Roman Rota declared that the taking up of residence with the intention to remain if marriage followed is not sufficient intention to establish a domicile.[628]

1113. *Vagi* become subject to the local Ordinary and pastor of the place where they actually stay. Canon 1032 rules that the pastor shall not assist at the marriage of such persons without having first referred the case to the local Ordinary or to a priest delegated by the Ordinary for that purpose. On the marriage of *vagi*, the Council of Trent declares as follows: "There are many persons who are vagrants, having no fixed homes; and being of a profligate character, they, after aban-

[628] May 5, 1914; *Acta Ap. Sedis*, VI, 387.

doning their first wife, marry another, and very often several in different places, during the life-time of the first. The Holy Synod, being desirous to prevent this disorder, gives this fatherly admonition to all whom it may concern not to admit this class of vagrants easily to marriage; and it also exhorts the civil magistrates to punish such persons severely. But it commands parish priests not to be present at the marriages of such persons, unless they have first made a careful inquiry, and, having reported the circumstances to the Ordinary, have obtained his permission." [629]

In a case of necessity Canon 1032 states that a pastor may marry *vagi*. The Decree of July 4, 1921, referred to above, does not admit as a case of necessity the danger of a civil marriage or the ending of actual concubinage or other sinful relations. It wants the case referred to the Ordinary whenever doubt remains as to a diriment impediment and especially about the bond of a former valid marriage.

1114. If neither party is subject to the pastor or the Ordinary (according to Canon 1097), the permission of the proper pastor or Ordinary of one or other of the contracting parties is necessary for licit assistance at marriage. In so far as the validity is concerned, the Ordinary and the pastor can within their respective territories witness the marriages of all Catholics, no matter where they have their residence. If both parties belong to some Oriental Rite united to the Holy See, their marriage before a pastor of the Latin Rite would be valid as a rule here in the United States. In some places of the Orient the form of marriage as prescribed by the Council of Trent has been received into the local law, and these Orientals can be married only by their own proper pastor. Most of the Oriental Catholics, however, were not under the law of the Council of Trent. The Syrians and the Ruthenians in Galicia were under the Tridentine law. When the "Ne Temere" Decree was promulgated, the Holy See extended that Decree to the Ruthenians in Galicia, and it was likewise made obligatory for the Ruthenians in Canada and in the United States. Those Orientals who are bound either by the "Tametsi" Decree of the Council of Trent or by the "Ne Temere" Decree, must contract marriage before the pastor who is their proper pastor either by domicile, quasi-

[629] Sessio XXIV, cap. 7, *De Reform. Matrim.*

domicile, or (in the case of the "Ne Temere") because of one month's residence. Other Orientals can validly contract a clandestine marriage, though it is illicit on account of the ancient prohibition of the Oriental Churches against clandestine marriages.[630]

1115. The Code retains the law of the "Ne Temere" Decree that marriage is to be contracted as a rule before the pastor of the parish where the bride has a domicile or quasi-domicile, or has resided one month, any of the three pastors being equally entitled to witness the marriage. The Code demands only a reasonable motive to entitle the pastor of the groom to perform the marriage ceremony; he is a proper pastor of the parties as well as the pastor of the bride. If there is a good reason why the marriage should be contracted in the parish of the groom, the pastor of the groom has the right to officiate at the marriage, and he does not need the permission of the pastor of the bride. Commentators on the "Ne Temere" Decree, which in this matter has the same rule as the Code, held that no grave obligation was imposed by the "Ne Temere" to have the marriage in the parish of the bride. Convenience and utility were considered sufficient reasons by Gennari to have the marriage in the parish of the groom, and the commentators on the Code hold quite generally that a slight reason is sufficient. That there is at least an obligation *sub levi* to have the pastor of the bride assist at the marriage, seems to be certain from the very fact that the Code wants this regulation to be the general rule and requires a good reason for a deviation. If there were no obligation at all, no reason would be required to justify a deviation.

1116. If the parties belong to different Rites, the general rule is to be that the marriage be contracted before the pastor of the groom. If the particular law approved by the Holy See for some Oriental Rite in marriages between persons of the Latin and an Oriental Rite rules otherwise, the particular law is to be followed. Thus in a convention between the Bishops of the Latin Rite of the ecclesiastical province of Leopoli or Lwow, in Galicia, and the Bishop of the Ruthenian Rite in the same province, approved by the Sacred Congregation of the

---

[630] Decree for the Ruthenians in the United States was issued August 17, 1914, and was to remain in force for ten years (*Acta Ap. Sedis*, VI, 458–463.).

Propaganda, October 6, 1863, the marriage was always to take place in the parish of the bride, whether she belonged to the Latin or to the Ruthenian Rite.

1117. If both parties have a domicile or quasi-domicile or have resided one month in a parish, and they ask to be married in a strange parish, the pastor of such parish is strictly forbidden by the Code to marry them without the permission of one of the proper pastors of the parties, except in a case of necessity. If a pastor without necessity marries parties who by right belong to another pastor, the Code rules that the marriage fee or offering does not become his own property, but he is bound to remit it to the proper pastor of the contracting parties. The difficulty is to know what proper pastor is to get the fee, when there are several proper pastors. Thus, if the bride lives in one parish and the groom in another, both pastors are equally proper pastors. It may also happen that the bride has several proper pastors (one of domicile, another of quasi-domicile, a third one by reason of one month's residence prior to her marriage). Should the fee be divided? The Code does not as much as hint at a division of the fee. Some commentators think that the bishop has the right to lay down a more precise rule to determine to whom the fee should go when there are several proper pastors and the marriage was performed by a pastor who had no right to marry the parties. It is doubtful whether the bishop has any power to supply what is wanting in the Code by way of interpreting a rule of the Code. Moreover, while it may be admitted from the necessity of the case that the bishop should have power to decide the conflicting claims of several pastors in his own diocese, he has no right to decide on the claims of a pastor of another diocese if one of the proper pastors of the parties belongs to another diocese. Nothing but a general ruling of the Holy See can cover all the cases arising under this head.

If the parties have merely a diocesan domicile or quasi-domicile, Canon 94 rules that their proper pastor is the pastor of the place where they actually stay. In the city life of today it happens frequently that people change their living quarters several times a year, and yet do not move out of the city, nor do they intend to leave the city. There is no doubt that they acquire a diocesan domicile or quasi-domicile (cfr. Canon 92), but they may have no parochial domicile or quasi-domicile. If they have a diocesan domicile or quasi-domicile, Canon 94 applies, and the pastor of the parish where they actually stay becomes their proper pastor.

1118. If the bride is a non-Catholic, doubt arises whether the marriage is to be performed by the pastor of the parish where the bride resides. A distinction should be made between the case of a bride who is a baptized non-Catholic and the case of one who is unbaptized. All baptized persons are subject to the Church, and therefore there is a ''parochus sponsæ'' in the case of a baptized non-Catholic bride; on the contrary, if the bride is unbaptized, one cannot speak of a ''parochus sponsæ.'' If the bride is a baptized non-Catholic, the pastor of the parish where the bride lives has the right to witness the marriage, for the Code without distinction rules that the marriage is to take place before the pastor of the bride. In a case decided by the Sacred Congregation of the Sacraments, January 28, 1916, this Congregation says that the ''Ne Temere'' Decree requires merely one month's residence of one or other of the contracting parties without any references as to their religion. In the case in question, the bride, while still a non-Catholic, had gone to a certain parish for a vacation, stayed there one month, and been received into the Church during that time. She returned to her home, and after three weeks at home was married by the pastor where she had stayed a month and been baptized and received into the Church. The Sacred Congregation ruled that the pastor had illicitly witnessed the marriage because the sojourn of one month must be the month before the marriage, and the three weeks were too long an interruption.[631] The ''Ne Temere'' Decree is identical with the law of the Code on this point. The case does not state whether the bride was baptized conditionally, but only that she was baptized and received into the Church. However, we believe that, unless the non-Catholic is subject to the Church by baptism (though its validity may be doubtful), the term ''parochus sponsæ'' cannot have any application, because the unbaptized bride cannot have a pastor.

---

[631] *Acta Ap. Sedis,* VIII, 64; *Ecclesiastical Review,* LXIII, 417.

Exceptions from the Canonical Form of Marriage

1119. If the pastor, or the local Ordinary, or a priest delegated by either, who should according to Canons 1095 and 1096 assist at the marriage, cannot be had, or the parties cannot go to him without great inconvenience, the following rules are to be observed:

(1) In danger of death, marriage may be validly and licitly contracted in the presence only of two witnesses; even apart from the danger of death marriage may be thus contracted, if it can be prudently foreseen that this state of affairs (namely, the great difficulty of getting an authorized priest to witness the marriage) will continue for a month;

(2) In both cases, if there is at hand another priest who can be present at the marriage, he should be called and should assist at the marriage together with the witnesses, without prejudice however to the validity of the marriage contracted only before the witnesses (**Canon 1098**).

When the Code lays down the general conditions under which marriage may be contracted without the presence of an authorized priest, it uses very far-reaching terms: *haberi vel adiri nequeat sine gravi incommodo.* There must be a grave inconvenience in having an authorized priest present at the marriage, so that neither the priest can go to the parties nor the parties to the priest without great inconvenience. That grave inconvenience is something which cannot be defined with mathematical accuracy, because much depends on conditions and circumstances of persons and places. Thus, for instance, what is very difficult for some persons may not be a great inconvenience to others. The poverty of the parties, the distance and conditions of the roads, the health of both priest and parties—all these matters may make it very difficult for the priest to reach the parties and for the parties to reach the priest.

That this difficulty of securing the presence of the priest at the marriage need not be a general or common difficulty, but may be a particular and individual difficulty of the particular priest and couple, is quite generally admitted by commentators on the Code, and rightly so, for, where the Code does not distinguish, we should not distinguish. As to the difficulty caused by the civil law which may under certain circumstances forbid the priest to witness the marriage, though physically speaking he could be easily present, we shall speak of this when discussing the second of the two cases where marriage may be entered into without the presence of the priest.

MARRIAGE IN DANGER OF DEATH

1120. If one of the parties to be married is in danger of death, and no authorized priest can be procured, the parties can contract marriage before two witnesses. Words which express mutual consent suffice, and also signs which manifest mutual consent, but Canon 1088 forbids the use of signs if the parties can speak. What constitutes danger of death cannot be defined by a general rule, nor can it be known in each and every case whether such danger objectively exists. The danger of death need not necessarily arise from illness only, for the Code speaks of danger of death generally, from any source. A *bona fide* belief of the parties that there is danger of death before an authorized priest can be had must suffice, because in many cases there is no possibility of ascertaining the objective danger of death. There need be no special reason why the parties want to get married in danger of death, for the Code does not require any; the "Ne Temere" Decree had "ad consulendum conscientiæ et (si casus ferat) legitimationi prolis," but the Code has dropped this clause.

Can there be a marriage if there is a diriment impediment, or does this impediment cease in danger of death? It is very doubtful whether the opinion stated by St. Alphonsus and followed by many theologians, that the impediments cease in a case of necessity by the presumed concession of the Church, can be upheld. Everything points to the contrary will of the Church, namely, not to dispense in a case of necessity from invalidating laws. Canon 1019 insists that the pastor who finds one of the parties in danger of death must investigate carefully about the impediments; other provisions in Canons 1043 and 1044 grant far-reaching faculties to dispense persons in danger of death. All of these regulations seem to negative the above opinion. Besides, the law gives special firmness to invalidating laws, not allowing ignorance of the laws as an excuse (cfr. Canon 16). However, it cannot be said that the Code closes the controversy.[632] If a priest is present and the marriage is necessary for the peace of conscience, he has in virtue of Canon 1044 far-reaching faculties, if there is no time to refer the matter to the bishop (cfr. Canons 1043 and 1044, above).

MARRIAGE IN ABSENCE OF PRIEST

1121. If the parties cannot go to an authorized priest nor the priest come to them without great inconvenience, and there is a reasonable prospect that this condition of affairs will last for a month, the parties may contract marriage before two witnesses without the priest. There are many places in the United States where one priest has charge of an immense district, far greater in territorial extent than large dioceses in Europe. He travels from mission to mission and is able to visit each only a few times a year. In these districts there must be some provision for Catholics to marry without the assistance of the priest. The Code provides quite satisfactorily for such circumstances, even more liberally than the "Ne Temere" Decree had done. Under that Decree the great difficulty of getting a priest had to have existed a month before the marriage could take place, while the Code rules that it suffices if it is prudently foreseen that the difficulty will last a month.

In judging whether or not it will be possible without great difficulty to have an authorized priest witness the marriage within a month, the ordinary and usual circumstances of the respective place must be taken into consideration. An unusual and unexpected visit of the priest in charge of the district need not be counted on. On the other hand, if the priest has not been in the place or near the place for a month or longer, but is expected to make his regular visit within a month, the parties cannot marry without him but must await his arrival. It need scarcely be remarked here that, when the parties are entitled to contract marriage without the presence of the priest, they are justified in going to a justice of the peace, or any other official of the government who is entitled to witness marriages, so that their marriage may have the recognition of the civil law. They can also marry before a non-Catholic minister, not as a minister of religion but as an official entitled by civil law to witness mar-

[632] Cappello, "De Sacramentis," III, n. 199.

riages; they must not allow him to use any religious ceremony, as may be seen from Canon 1063. If they can without great difficulty approach a civil official entitled to witness marriages, there is no reason to go to the non-Catholic minister, for the Code allows this only in case the civil law forces them to go to a minister. Here in the United States there is no such law, but indirectly the law may oblige them to contract marriage before a minister, if the non-Catholic clergyman is the only person in the place who is entitled to witness marriages. This might well happen in some of the sparsely settled districts in our country.

There is some difficulty in determining precisely from what moment the space of one month is to be figured. Is it to be reckoned from the date which the parties have set for their marriage, or does the month begin with the day on which the parties have decided to get married and begin preparations for it? It seems that the date which the parties have set for their marriage should be considered the starting point from which the absence of the priest, or the great difficulty of reaching him within thirty days, is to be computed. The law on this point is not sufficiently clear.

1122. Another question arises in connexion with the phrase of the Code, "si haberi vel adiri nequeat sine gravi incommodo." Supposing that, physically speaking, it is not difficult for the parties to approach the priest or for the priest to come to them, but on account of the civil law in the case the priest is forbidden under severe penalty to assist at the marriage. This can easily happen in a case in which the parties can contract a valid marriage under the law of the Church, but are forbidden to marry for reason of an impediment of the civil law —all the more easily because there is no provision in the civil law of the United States for dispensation from marriage impediments. May the parties in such a case for the sake of their conscience privately express their marriage consent before two trusted witnesses? The greater number of commentators, who seem to have the wording of the Code in their favor, hold that marriage can be validly contracted without an authorized priest, because the Code states that marriage can be thus contracted, whenever the priest cannot be had or cannot be approached without great inconvenience. The Code makes no distinction as to the reasons or causes from which the difficulty of obtaining the priest arises. Other authors hold that the marriage in question would not be valid—for instance, Noldin, Genicot-Salsman, Wouters, De Smet, and Linneborn.[633]

The few authors who hold the opinion that marriage cannot be validly contracted if the penalties of the law keep the priest from assisting at the marriage, base their opinion partly on a Decree of the Sacred Congregation of the Sacraments, January 31, 1916 (which said that, if the civil law kept the priest from assisting at the marriage, the case should be referred to the Holy See), and partly on a decision given privately to the Bishop of Paderborn, in Germany, by the same Sacred Congregation, March 9, 1916. The latter case dealt with marriages contracted privately, because, on account of the civil law, these marriages were not allowed and the priest was not allowed to assist. The Sacred Congregation wants the bishop to have recourse to the Holy See in such cases, but it grants the bishop the faculty to validate *in radice* marriages already contracted. Evidently, the Holy See does not favor these private marriages under those circumstances, but, until the Holy See rules otherwise by an official declaration, these marriages cannot be called invalid.

1123. Two witnesses are required both in danger of death and in the case where no priest can be had for a month. The qualifications of the witnesses are not specified in law, wherefore it suffices that they have the use of reason and are present in such a manner that they can testify to the fact that the marriage was contracted. As the Holy Office declared on August 19, 1891,[634] that persons belonging to a non-Catholic sect should not be employed as witnesses, they should not be requested to act except in case of necessity.

1124. If any priest is at hand in these two exceptional cases, the Code wants the parties to call him to assist at the marriage. Canonists discuss the question whether the parties are obliged to call a priest though they know that he is suspended, or other-

[633] Noldin, "Theol. Moral.," III, n. 652 (ed. 1920); Genicot-Salsman, "Theol. Moral.," II, n. 474 (ed. 1921), who is cited by some canonists as opposing the opinion, seems rather to favor it; Wouters, "De Forma Prom. et Celebr. Matr.," 41, follows Genicot-Salsman; De Smet, "De Spons. et Matr.," n. 137; Linneborn. "Grundriss des Eherechts," 372. Controversy settled by recent decision. cfr. App. III. 47, d.

[634] *Collect. de Prop. Fide*, II, n. 1765.

wise in bad standing. It is not very probable that the Code contemplated the calling of such a priest. In most cases, however, the parties may know nothing more about him than that he is a priest, and, if they have reason to suspect that he is not in good standing, they need not call him.

Persons Bound to the Canonical Form of Marriage

1125. The following persons are bound to observe the above-stated form of marriage:

(1) All persons baptized in the Catholic Church, and converts from heresy or schism (even though they afterwards lapsed from the Church), whenever they contract marriage among themselves;

(2) These same persons are bound to observe the canonical form of marriage also when they contract marriage with non-Catholics, either baptized or unbaptized, even after they have obtained a dispensation from the impediment of mixed marriage or of disparity of cult;

(3) Catholics of Oriental Rites, if they contract marriage with persons bound to observe this canonical form of marriage (**Canon 1099,** § 1).

Non-Catholics, whether baptized or unbaptized, who have never become converts to the Catholic Church, are never bound to observe the Catholic form of marriage if they marry among themselves. Exempt also from the canonical form of marriage are persons born of non-Catholics, who were baptized in the Catholic Church, but were raised from their infancy in heresy, schism, infidelity, or without any religion, whenever they contract marriage with non-Catholics (**Canon 1099,** § 2).

The phrase, "baptized in the Catholic Church" (taken from the "Ne Temere" Decree), has been a rich source of controversy as to the persons comprehended under that term. In the case of persons baptized as adults there is not much difficulty in determining whether they were baptized in the Catholic Church, for their own declared will and intention to become Catholics suffices to prove that they were baptized in the Catholic Church, though perchance a minister of some non-Catholic denomination deceived them by representing himself as a Catholic priest, or though, in a case of necessity, they were baptized by a non-

Catholic.   An adult cannot become a member of the Church as a divinely instituted organization except by his own free will. Wherefore, his declared will and intention in receiving baptism must decide whether he joins the Catholic Church or some other denomination.   In the case of an adult baptized in danger of death in an unconscious condition by a Catholic priest or a Catholic layman, some difficulty may arise as to that baptism. Canon 752 does not permit the baptism of an adult without his knowledge and consent.   If the person is unconscious, the same Canon rules that one may not baptize an adult unless he has given at least probable signs of his desire to be baptized; in this case only is it lawful to give conditional baptism.   If the person survives the danger, and, on being told of his baptism, protests against being received into the Church in that manner and does not want to belong to the Catholic Church, he does not become her subject, since the Church requires that he enter her communion of his own free will.

In the case of children baptized before they come to the age of discretion, it is frequently difficult to determine whether they are baptized in the Catholic Church.   Infants cannot exercise their own wills, wherefore the parents or the legitimate guardians are the persons entitled and obliged to procure the grace of baptism for their charges (cfr. commentary under Canon 1070).

1126. Catholics of the various Oriental Rites who contract marriage with Orientals, or with other persons not bound to observe the canonical form of marriage, are free from the law on the form of marriage.   If they, however, marry persons who are subject to this law of the Code, the marriage cannot be validly contracted without observing the canonical form.   In the law of the Council of Trent, the exemption of one person from the form of marriage as prescribed by the Decree "Tametsi" was communicated to the other contracting party. Under the law of the Code, however, the canonical form of marriage is obligatory, even though only one of the contracting parties is subject to its legislation.

In some countries Catholics of Oriental Rites are subject to the form of marriage as specified by the "Ne Temere" Decree —e.g., Catholics of the Greek-Ruthenian Rite in the United States and in Canada.[635]   Some of the Oriental Rites are sub-

635 Decree for Greek-Ruthenian Rite in United States, August 17, 1914

ject to the form of marriage, as demanded by the Decree "Tametsi" of the Council of Trent. Generally, however, clandestine marriages of Orientals are valid, though rigidly forbidden by their laws.

Non-Catholics, baptized and unbaptized, who contract marriage with persons who are not bound to observe the canonical form of marriage, are exempt from the law on the form of marriage. Are Catholics, who at an adult age have fallen away from the Church either by joining a non-Catholic sect or rejecting all religious creeds, to be called non-Catholics, and are they thus exempt from the canonical form of marriage when they marry other lapsed Catholics, or Protestants, or unbaptized persons? Blat[636] interprets Canon 1099 in such a way as to free lapsed Catholics when they marry non-Catholics properly so called, and considers them bound to observe the canonical form when they marry other lapsed Catholics. That opinion necessitates a twofold meaning of the term "non-Catholic" in the same Canon, for in Canon 1099, n. 1, lapsed Catholics are certainly bound to the canonical form of marriage. Canon 1099, n. 2, speaks of non-Catholics generally, but we believe that the term is restricted by the first portion of the Canon to those adults who were never Catholics. Wherefore lapsed Catholics are in all cases bound to observe the canonical form of marriage.

1127. Another difficulty is mentioned by Augustine,[637] who holds that children of two non-Catholics, baptized in the Catholic Church but raised from infancy in a non-Catholic faith or without any religion, are not bound to observe the Catholic form of marriage if they marry persons who were never Catholics at an adult age, and were not baptized in the Catholic Church, but he thinks that they are bound to the Catholic form of marriage if they marry persons who were baptized in the Catholic Church, though raised from infancy without any religion or in some non-Catholic denomination. It seems, however, that the Church considers the last-mentioned group as non-Catholics, and comprehends them in the last phrase of Canon 1099, "quoties cum parte acatholica contraxerint."

1128. In Germany and Hungary marriages between Catholics

(*Acta Ap. Sedis*, VI, 463); for Canada, August 18, 1913 (*Acta Ap. Sedis*, V, 393).

[636] *Commentarium*, lib. III, 652.

[637] *Commentary*, V. Appendix II. Cfr. Vol. II, App. III, 47, f.

and non-Catholics had by special law been exempted from the Catholic form of marriage—Germany by Decree of April 15, 1906, and Hungary by Decree of February 23, 1909. The greater number of commentators of the Code hold that the Code abolishes this special law which is contrary to the law of the Code (cfr. Canon 6, n. 1). Chelodi,[638] with a few other canonists, considers the exemption granted to Germany and Hungary as a privilege, and consequently holds that it has not been abolished by the Code. The President of the Committee declared on December 9, 1917, that the exemption granted to Germany and Hungary ceases when the Code of Canon Law comes into force.[639]

SACRED RITES OF THE MARRIAGE CONTRACT

1129. Except in the case of necessity, the sacred rites prescribed in the liturgical books approved by the Church, or by laudable and approved customs, shall be employed in the celebration of marriage (**Canon 1100**).

The pastor shall see that the contracting parties receive the solemn nuptial blessing, which can be given them even after they have lived for a long time in marriage. It can be pronounced only in Holy Mass with the observance of the special rubrics, and may be given on all days with the exception of the forbidden season, as specified in Canon 1108. The solemn nuptial blessing may be given only by the priest who has the right to witness the marriage validly and licitly, or by his delegate (**Canon 1101**).

The sacred rites of marriage are divided into the ceremonies which surround the essential feature of the marriage—the expression of consent of both parties—and the ceremonies which may be performed at any time after the marriage has taken place (namely, the nuptial blessing). The first-named ceremonies are obligatory, and may not be omitted except in a case of necessity; the ceremonies of the nuptial blessing are not strictly speaking obligatory, but the pastor is exhorted by the Code to see that the parties receive this blessing. The sacred rites of marriage are given in the Roman Ritual, but the Church permits dioceses and countries to follow the laudable and ap-

---

[638] *Jus Matrimoniale,* 169.
[639] Leitner, "Lehrbuch des kath. Eherechts," 211. Cfr. App. III, 3, f.

proved local customs. From this concession it does not follow that each pastor is at liberty to employ ceremonies and prayers according to his own liking. As a rule, the diocesan statutes (or the laws of Provincial and National Councils) have their regulations in the matter of the ceremonies at marriage. Apart from positive enactments, customs which have been generally adopted in a diocese and are of sufficiently long standing to merit the name of accepted customs, may be followed in reference to ceremonies at marriage.

1130. The nuptial blessing which the Church desires the parties to receive may be given either immediately after the marriage ceremony or at a later date. Ordinarily, the blessing can be given only in conjunction with Holy Mass and during the open season. However, Canon 1108 gives the local Ordinaries power to permit the nuptial blessing, *ex justa causa,* also during the forbidden season. The new faculties of the bishops of the United States empower the bishop to allow the giving of the nuptial blessing outside of Holy Mass. On the days on which the rubrics of the Roman Missal allow the votive Mass "Pro sponso et sponsa," this Mass is to be taken for the nuptial blessing. On the days on which the rubrics do not permit the votive Mass, the Mass of the day is to be taken and the oration from the Mass "Pro sponso et sponsa" is added to the oration or orations of the Mass of the day. If two or more couples wish to receive the nuptial blessing during the same Mass, the marriage ceremony preceding the Mass is gone through with each couple separately, but the prayers of the nuptial blessing which are said over the married couples after the *Pater Noster* and before the Last Blessing of the Mass may be said in the plural over several couples. If the woman is a widow and has received the nuptial blessing in a former marriage, she cannot again receive the nuptial blessing. If the man is a widower but the woman was not married before, or, if married, did not receive the nuptial blessing at her former marriage, the couple can receive the blessing.

1131. In marriages between Catholics and non-Catholics the questions eliciting the consent of the parties are to be put by the priest, as demanded by Canon 1095. All sacred rites, however, are forbidden, and the marriage ceremony is not to take place in the church. If from this prohibition greater evils are anticipated, the Ordinary may allow some of the usual sacred ceremonies, excepting always the celebration of Mass (**Canon 1102**).

The Church does not favor marriages of Catholics with non-Catholics, even in cases in which the non-Catholic is entirely willing to let the Catholic party practise his religion and baptize and raise the children in the Catholic faith. In such marriages no other ceremonies or sacred rites may be employed except what is essential to a valid marriage contract. From the earliest times of the Church to the present day, it has been forbidden to admit non-Catholics to take an active part in the liturgical functions of the Church. Wherefore, the Code rules that the marriage of Catholics with non-Catholics shall not be accompanied by any sacred rites, but the priest shall merely ask for the marriage consent of both parties and get their answer to his questions.[640] By other Decrees of the Holy See it has been made plain that the marriage must not take place in church, that the priest shall not wear any sacred vestments but only his clerical garb, and that he shall not bless the ring nor pronounce other liturgical prayers over the parties.[641]

By way of exception, the Code permits the bishops to allow some of the sacred ceremonies to take place in marriages of Catholics with non-Catholics, if the refusal of all sacred rites might occasion trouble, but the bishop cannot allow them to be married with a Mass, much less to receive the nuptial blessing in Mass. Here in the United States there is as a rule no reason why sacred rites should be employed at these marriages, and it has been done very rarely, if ever. In some countries in Europe, the Protestants felt very much offended if they were not permitted to marry a Catholic in church. It was, therefore, quite common in some places to have the mixed marriages in church, but there was always a distinction made between marriages of two Catholics and mixed marriages.

If the non-Catholic party absolutely refuses to give a guarantee that he will not interfere with the practice of religion by the Catholic party and have all the children baptized and raised in the Catholic faith, the Code (Canon 1061) states that

---

[640] Holy Office, November 26, 1919; *Linzer Quartalschrift*, LXXIV, 249.
[641] *Instructio Secretarii Status Jussu Pii PP. IX*, Nov. 15, 1858; *Collectanea de Prop. Fide*, I, n. 1169. Cfr. also App. III, 48, d.

in such cases the Church does not dispense the Catholic from the impediment of mixed religion or of disparity of cult, and consequently the bishop cannot make use of his faculties of dispensation. If, despite the refusal of the Ordinary to grant the dispensation, the Catholic party marries outside the Church but later on is truly sorry for his sin, the faculties of the American hierarchy empower the bishop to validate the marriage by the *sanatio in radice,* if it cannot be validated in the ordinary way, either because the non-Catholic party cannot without great danger to the Catholic be informed of the invalidity of the marriage before the Church, or because the non-Catholic refuses to make the promises, or refuses to go to the priest.

Recording of Marriages

1132. After the celebration of marriage the pastor, or the priest who takes his place, shall as soon as possible enter in the marriage record the names of the married couple and of the witnesses, the place and date, and other particulars prescribed by the ritual and the Ordinary of the respective diocese. The pastor or his substitute shall make the entry, even if another priest delegated either by himself or by the Ordinary assisted at the marriage.

The pastor shall also, in accordance with Canon 470, § 2, make a note in the baptismal record that the parties contracted marriage in his parish on such a day. If one or both parties were baptized in another parish, the pastor in whose parish the marriage took place shall send notice of that fact to the pastor where the parties were baptized, which notice he may send either directly or through the episcopal curia.

Whenever marriage was contracted without the assistance of the pastor or a delegated priest in places where an authorized priest could not be had for a month, or in danger of death (as described in Canon 1098), the priest who happened to be present, or otherwise the witnesses together with the contracting parties, are bound to see that the marriage is entered in the prescribed records as soon as possible (**Canon 1103**).

1133. The question is raised by this Canon whether the recording of the marriages is a personal duty of the pastor, which he cannot commit to others. The Roman Ritual orders that the pastor make the entry with his own hand (*manu sua*). It is a general rule of law that one can delegate another person to fulfill the duties of one's office unless they are of their nature of a personal character, or the law explicitly demands personal attention to a certain duty of one's office. From the words of the Code one cannot prove that the pastor is forbidden to commit that duty to somebody else. The Code merely commands that the pastor or the priest who takes the place of the pastor (e.g., during the vacancy of the parish, during the absence of the pastor, etc.) keep the record of marriages. Whether he writes that record himself, or commits it to somebody else, is immaterial in so far as the wording of the Code goes.[642] It is, however, generally held by canonists that the keeping of an exact marriage record is a grave duty, for the very purpose of the record indicates this gravity.

1134. The rule that the marriage record is to be entered also in the baptismal record of the parties was first enacted as a general law in the "Ne Temere" Decree, and that law is retained by the Code. If the parties were not baptized in the parish where the marriage takes place, the pastor is obliged to send a copy of the marriage record to the pastor (or pastors) of the place (or places) where the parties were baptized. He may send the notice either directly or through the chancery office of his own diocese. An Instruction of the Sacred Congregation of the Sacraments, June 26, 1921, supplements the Code by more specific directions as to the entry in the baptismal record, saying that the notice which the pastor of the place of marriage sends to the place of baptism must be a complete marriage record, and must be authenticated by the full name of the pastor and the seal of the parish.[643]

Chapter VII

THE MARRIAGE OF CONSCIENCE

1135. By a marriage of conscience is meant a marriage contracted without the publication of the banns and in secret, in accord with the following Canons. The local Ordinary may

---

[642] Cappello, "De Sacrm.," III, n. 718; Petrovits, "New Church Law on Marriage," n. 515; Linneborn, "Grundriss des Eherechts," 386; Ayrinhac, "Marriage Legislation," n. 267; De Smet, "De Spons. et Matrim.," n. 700.

[643] *Acta Ap. Sedis*, XIII, 348.

allow such a marriage for very grave and urgent reasons; the vicar-general cannot give permission for a marriage of conscience except by special mandate of his Ordinary (**Canon 1104**).

The laws of the Church in reference to the publication of the banns and other formalities to be observed in the celebration of marriage are intended to give marriage the character of a public contract. The publicity has the purpose of preventing parties from living together as husband and wife without due authorization of the Church. Furthermore, the publicity of the marriage contract prevents to a certain degree at least the deception of young ladies by unscrupulous men and *vice versa.* Wherefore, the Council of Trent states that the Catholic Church has always detested and forbidden secret marriages.[644]

In his Encyclical "Satis Vobis," of November 27, 1741, Pope Benedict XIV prescribed the rules to be observed in the secret marriages, and the Canons of the Code on the marriage of conscience are largely taken from that document.[645]

It may happen that two persons cannot publicly contract marriage, and at the same time circumstances may be such that the parties should be married to avoid secret sinful relations and the illegitimacy of their offspring. The Code requires a very grave and urgent reason before the local Ordinary may allow a secret marriage. Cases in which either the civil law prevents parties from getting married, or where there is unjust and violent opposition of the parents, and where at the same time the spiritual welfare of the parties calls for marriage, seem to be contemplated by the Code.

1136. The permission to contract a marriage of conscience imposes the promise and grave obligation to observe the secret on the priest who witnesses the marriage, on the witnesses, on the Ordinary and his successors, and also on the contracting parties as long as one of the parties does not consent to the publication of the marriage (**Canon 1105**).

The obligation of secrecy is demanded by the law of the Code in favor of the parties. If both parties consent to have their marriage made known, the obligation of secrecy imposed by the law on the persons mentioned in Canon 1105 ceases.

---

[644] Sessio XXIV, cap. 1, *De Reform. Matrim.*
[645] *Fontes Cod. Jur. Can.,* I, n. 319.

However, one of the married parties cannot without the consent of the other make the marriage known, for each party is equally entitled to the right of secrecy. From the common principles of moral theology it follows that, if any other persons besides those mentioned in the Code obtain knowledge of the secret marriage, they are bound by the obligation of secrecy, and are forbidden to make the marriage known without the consent of the parties. It is necessary that the parties who are secretly married conduct themselves in public in such a manner that they do not give scandal, for, if they are generally considered unmarried, they cannot conduct themselves as married persons before others. Wherefore the Code continues:

1137. The obligation of the promise to keep the marriage secret, which is imposed by law on the local Ordinary, does not bind him in cases wherein the keeping of the secret would cause scandal or gravely impair the sanctity of marriage, or if the parents do not have the children born of such a marriage baptized, or if they have them baptized under fictitious names without giving the Ordinary within thirty days notice of the birth and baptism of such children with a truthful statement of the names of the parents; nor does the secret bind the Ordinary if the parents neglect the Christian education of their children (**Canon 1106**).

This Canon enumerates the cases in which the local Ordinary is not bound to keep the secret imposed by law whenever he permits a marriage of conscience. The persons who are permitted by the Ordinary to contract a secret marriage must faithfully observe the law regulating such a marriage. Above all, they may not inflict the stigma of illegitimate birth on their offspring and make it impossible to prove in later years that the children were born of legitimate wedlock.

1138. The marriage of conscience is not to be entered in the ordinary records of marriage and baptism, but is to be entered in a special record kept in the secret archives of the diocesan Curia, in the manner directed in Canon 379 (**Canon 1107**).

Proof must be available of every marriage legitimately contracted, and for this purpose the Church demands that each pastor keep a marriage record. Besides, the marriage is also to be entered in the baptismal record in the parishes where the parties were baptized. The record of secret marriages is not entered in the common parish record, but in a special book kept in the secret archives of the diocesan Curia. The baptism of children born of a secret marriage is not to be entered in the ordinary baptismal record of the parish but in a special record kept in the secret archives of the diocesan Curia, unless both parties consent to have the baptism registered under their true names. If they give fictitious names for the entry of the baptism in the parish register, they must within thirty days after such baptism inform the Ordinary of the diocese in which they reside of the true names so that the bishop can enter the baptism in the secret archives of the diocese, and thus make it possible to prove the legitimate birth of the children.

If the Ordinary allows a marriage of parties who are forbidden by the civil law to marry for reason of some impediment of that law, great care must be taken that the marriage remains secret, because fine or imprisonment awaits the priest who witnesses a marriage forbidden by law. If the spiritual welfare of the parties demands that they be married, and such marriage is possible under the law of the Church but is not possible under the laws of the state, there is an unavoidable conflict between the duty of conscience and the law of the state. The words of St. Peter apply: "If it be just, in the sight of God, to hear you rather than God, judge ye" (Acts, iv. 19).

CHAPTER VIII

TIME AND PLACE OF THE CELEBRATION OF MARRIAGE

1139. Marriage may be contracted at any time of the year. Only the solemn nuptial blessing of marriage is forbidden from the First Sunday in Advent to Christmas Day inclusively, and from Ash Wednesday to Easter Sunday inclusively. The local Ordinaries may permit the solemn nuptial blessing during these seasons for a good reason, subject to the laws of the sacred liturgy, but they must admonish the parties to refrain from too much pomp (**Canon 1108**).[645a]

The forbidden seasons in the law before the promulgation of the Code ran from the First Sunday in Advent to the Epiphany inclusive, and from Ash Wednesday to the octave of Easter (Low Sunday) inclusive. The general law of the Church did not forbid Catholics to marry during these seasons, but

[645a] Concerning nuptial blessing, cfr. App. III, 48, a–c.

only forbade the solemn nuptial blessing and public wedding festivities on an elaborate style. The statutes of many dioceses were far stricter than the Church. Thus, many forbade the publication of the banns and simple marriage during the forbidden seasons; other statutes forbade people to marry on Sundays or holydays of obligation throughout the year, while some dioceses forbade marriage in the afternoon or evening. Commentators on the Code have discussed how far these laws of the various dioceses are modified or abolished by the Code. It is a well-known principle of law that an inferior legislator (the bishop in the case under discussion) cannot restrict or take away a right or liberty granted by the law of the Supreme Pontiff. If the inferior authority could do so, his power would be greater than that of the Supreme Legislator of the Church.

Now, the Code states that marriage may be contracted at any time of the year. The diocesan law cannot, therefore, forbid marriage on Sundays and holydays of obligation, or during Advent, Lent, or any other season. The banns can and must, therefore, be published at any time of the year, just as marriage is allowed any time of the year. The legality of the diocesan statutes forbidding marriage at certain hours of the day (viz., afternoon or evening) is also debated by commentators on the Code. At first sight, one is inclined to judge that such a diocesan law is in opposition to the law of the Code, and therefore void, because the Code without restriction or distinction allows marriage at any time of the year. Nevertheless, many commentators on the Code argue from Canon 1171 that the bishop can forbid marriage to be celebrated in the evening or at night. That opinion seems to be well founded, provided there is serious reason to fear abuses, for Canon 1171 states that the Ordinary of the diocese has the right to fix the hours for the performance of the sacred rites in churches and chapels of his diocese. The same commentators argue that in the former law there was also a prohibition to contract marriage in the evening or at night,[646] and that the law of the Code does not change the former law unless the wording of the Code is such that the correction of the old law is apparent. There is no doubt that the Church has always desired that the parties be married at Holy Mass, and that they receive Holy Communion at the Mass,

[646] Cappello, "De Sacrm.," III, n. 726.

but there seems to have been no general law forbidding the simple marriage ceremony at any hour of the day or night. Individual abuses are no reasonable motive for depriving the rest of the people of a liberty granted by the common law; otherwise we would soon be so hedged in by law that we could not possibly avoid violating it, and that would be the surest way to kill respect for all law.

The forbidden seasons are not so strict in the Code as they were in the former law. The Code grants the local Ordinaries power to permit the solemn nuptial blessing even during the forbidden seasons, and, if he permits it, the votive Mass "Pro sponso et sponsa" is to be said, unless the rubrics of the Missal forbid the votive Mass on that day; in the latter case the Mass of the day is to be said with the commemoration from the Mass "Pro sponso et sponsa," and the prayers to be read over the married couple after the *Pater Noster* and before the last blessing are also taken from that votive Mass.

PLACE WHERE MARRIAGE IS TO BE CONTRACTED

1140. Marriage between Catholics shall be contracted in the parish church, and cannot take place in another Church, public or semi-public oratory without the permission of either the local Ordinary or the pastor. The local Ordinary may not permit the celebration of marriage in private houses except in some extraordinary case and for a good reason. The Ordinary shall not permit marriages to take place in the churches or chapels of seminaries or of religious women, except in a case of urgent necessity and with due precautions.

Marriages between a Catholic and a non-Catholic shall be contracted outside the church. If, however, the Ordinary judges that this rule cannot be enforced without causing greater evil, it is left to his discretion to dispense with this prohibition but, as was stated in Canon 1102, he may never permit the celebration of Holy Mass at such a marriage (**Canon 1109**).[646a]

Since the witnessing of the marriage contract is a function reserved to the pastors by the general law of the Church, the marriage is to take place in the parish church and, as a rule, in the proper parish of the bride. The pastor and the bishop may delegate another priest to witness marriages, and they may

[646a] Concerning ceremonies in mixed marriages, cfr. App. III, 48, d.

permit the marriage to take place in another church or oratory, except those of seminaries and of religious women. As the Code restricts the power of the bishop to allow marriages in the last-mentioned places to cases of urgent necessity, it will be very rarely possible to grant such a permission.

1141. Marriage may not, as a rule, be contracted in private houses, but the Code gives the local Ordinary authority to allow it in extraordinary cases. This rule evidently applies to marriages between Catholics as well as to marriages between Catholics and non-Catholics, for the Code rules that marriage generally may not be contracted in private houses. Just what case is contemplated by the Code when it speaks of some extraordinary case, it is difficult to say. It does not seem to be a sufficient reason because the non-Catholic or the Catholic party is wealthy, and that his wishes should be granted. That offends the common people who have built thousands of churches, schools, convents and all kinds of Catholic institutions of charity at the cost of personal sacrifices far greater than any made by the rich. Marriage at home is not forbidden in a case of necessity—for instance, when one of the parties is unable to go to church without great difficulty—for such cases are usually not specially provided for in law.

1142. Marriages between Catholics and non-Catholics are not to take place in a church or any place of divine worship. The usual place for these marriages is the pastor's residence. The Code does not indicate where these marriages should be contracted, but here in the United States the diocesan statutes usually designate the pastor's residence as the place, for there is the office where the parishioners transact business with the pastor, and it is an appropriate place for such marriages. The bishop can allow mixed marriages in church with some religious ceremonies, if the prohibition of the common law might arouse the animosity of non-Catholics against the Church, or other serious troubles might result from the prohibition.

CHAPTER IX

OF THE CONSEQUENCES OF MARRIAGE

1143. From valid marriage there arises between the married couple a bond perpetual and exclusive of its very nature.

Christian marriage, moreover, bestows the grace of the sacrament on parties who place no obstacle in the way (**Canon 1110**).

We have already seen that it is the teaching of the Church that Christ restored marriage to its pristine dignity by giving marriage the character of a permanent union between husband and wife and abolishing polygamy and divorce. This applies to all marriages. Marriage between Christians has the additional dignity of a sacrament. If a Catholic gets a dispensation to marry an unbaptized person, it is a disputed question whether the Catholic party receives the sacrament. The better opinion seems to be on the side of the many theologians who hold that the Catholic party in such a marriage does not receive the sacrament, for, on the one hand, the parties administer the sacrament to each other, and, on the other, the traditional teaching of the Church does not give to unbaptized persons the power to administer any other sacrament than baptism in case of necessity.[647]

Mutual Rights of Husband and Wife

1144. Both married parties possess from the moment the marriage contract has been concluded equal rights and duties concerning the actions proper to conjugal life (**Canon 1111**).

The primary purpose of marriage is, according to the law of God, the procreation of children. To that end sexual intercourse of the married couple is necessary, and it is therefore understood that, by the marriage contract, each party gives to the other the right to sexual intercourse. Marriage as willed by God includes this right and duty of married persons, so much so that the parties cannot contract marriage and at the same time refuse to surrender to each other this right. As the direct object of the marriage contract, this right imposes a strict obligation of justice on each party not to refuse the exercise of that right when either party asks for it in a proper manner (I Cor., vii. 5).

Here may be mentioned a peculiar concession of the law of the Decretals, which is now indirectly revoked by Canon **1111**, namely, that either party had the right to refuse conjugal intercourse during the first two months after marriage, if the party was considering entrance into a religious order.[648]

[647] Wernz, "Jus Decretalium," IV. n. 44.
[648] Gasparri, "De Matrimonio," II, n. 1296.

1145. The Code continues: Unless the special law rules otherwise, the wife shares in the state of her husband as far as canonical effects are concerned (**Canon 1112**).

This Canon has reference to the standing of the husband in ecclesiastical affairs—not to his secular state or temporal goods and affairs, which are regulated by the civil law of the nations, and differ in the various countries. An illustration of what is meant by this rule of the Code is seen in Canon 93, which states that the wife shares the domicile of her husband; and in Canon 1229, which states that the burial place of the husband is also the burial place of the wife.

JOINT DUTIES OF MARRIED COUPLE TOWARDS THE CHILDREN

1146. The parents are bound by a most serious obligation to provide to the best of their ability for the religious and moral as well as the physical and secular education of their children and to care for their temporal welfare (**Canon 1113**).

The Canon just quoted summarizes the obligations which the natural law imposes on married persons with reference to their children. The spiritual, physical, and civic education, and the spiritual and temporal welfare of the children, are naturally in the hands of the parents. The parents are indeed subject to direction and control in these duties. In spiritual affairs they are controlled by the authority of the Church, in the physical and temporal affairs by the authority of the civil government of their country, but these two powers may not destroy the inherent right of the parents to the custody, care and education of their children. There is a tendency in these days on the part of the civil power to deprive the family of its inherent and inalienable rights over their children, which tendency is as dangerous as the attempts of the state to interfere with the inherent rights of personal freedom of its citizens. It is old-time slavery in another form.

RULES BY WHICH LEGITIMACY OF CHILDREN IS DETERMINED

1147. Legitimate children are those conceived or born in valid marriage, or in a marriage contracted in good faith though invalidly. If, however, married persons were forbidden to have conjugal intercourse at the time of the conception of a child, because one or both parents had after the marriage made solemn religious vows, or the husband had received major orders, the child conceived in this unlawful intercourse is illegitimate (**Canon 1114**).

It suffices that the child be born in legitimate wedlock. If a man has sexual intercourse with a woman before he is married to her and a child is conceived, the child is legitimate if at the time of its birth the man is validly married to the woman with whom he had intercourse before marriage. Even if a married man commits adultery with another woman and she conceives and his wife dies and he marries the woman with whom he committed adultery before the child is born, the child is legitimate because born in legitimate wedlock.

A child conceived or born in an invalid marriage is legitimate if that marriage was contracted in good faith. It suffices that one of the parties to the marriage was in good faith, so that the marriage has the effect of a valid union as far as the legitimacy of the children is concerned, until both parties know for certain of the invalidity of their marriage (cfr. Canon 1015, § 4).

The rule of the second part of Canon 1114 is an exception to the general principle that a child conceived or born in legitimate wedlock is legitimate. The Church under certain conditions gives permission to married persons to enter a religious order or to enter the priesthood. When such persons have made solemn religious vows or have received major orders, they are forever forbidden to live in marriage. If they have sexual intercourse after one or both have thus consecrated their lives to God, the child conceived of such intercourse is illegitimate.

1148. The father of a child is he who appears to be such by lawful marriage, unless there are manifest proofs to the contrary. The children who are born at least six months from the date of the marriage, or within ten months from the date of the dissolution of conjugal life, are in law presumed legitimate (**Canon 1115**).

The principle, "nemo malus nisi probetur," induces the Code to lay down the rule that without convincing proof the wife must not be considered to have conceived a child through adulterous intercourse with another man, and her husband is to be considered the father of the child.   The assertion of either the wife or the husband, or their united testimony, that the child is not legitimate, is no proof in Canon Law of the illegitimacy of the child.   Sound public policy demands that the honor and the future welfare of the child be absolutely protected by the law of the Church, and the laws of the various states of our country follow the same policy.   Very stringent proofs are required to prove the illegitimacy of a child born of a married woman.

1149. With reference to a child born soon after marriage, and a child born of a married woman after the death of her husband, or after the discontinuation of conjugal life for other reasons, the Code in the first case takes the shortest possible period of gestation (six months) and in the second case the longest possible period (ten months).   There is some difficulty in determining whether a child is legitimate, if a married woman gives birth to a child within less than six months after her marriage.   Some commentators apply the principle of Canon 1114 to the case, and say that the child is legitimate because it is born in legitimate wedlock.   If that rule of the Code decided the case, it was superfluous to add the second sentence to Canon 1115.   How can the Code suppose a child born three or four months after marriage to be legitimate, unless it build its legal presumption on the supposition that the present husband had sinful intercourse with his present wife before they were married?   The presumption may be very probable, but legal presumptions are not founded on the assumption of crime.   Wherefore, we believe that one may not speak of such a presumption in law.   Vlaming thinks that the newly wed husband can by his declaration that the child is his, establish the legitimacy of the child.[649].   However, if the law declares a child illegitimate when born to newly wed persons before six months have elapsed after marriage, it is difficult to understand how the mere declaration of the husband can overcome the contrary presumption of law.   One may argue that the Code does not declare a child born before six months of married life illegitimate, but merely states that, if six months of married life have elapsed, the child

[649] *Prælect. Juris Matrim.*, II, n. 688.

born is presumed to be legitimate. Canon 777 may perhaps be quoted in favor of thus establishing the legitimacy of the child, for there the Code speaks of the baptism of illegitimate children and rules that the name of the father may be entered in the baptismal record as the father of the child if of his own accord he requests in writing or before two witnesses that the pastor should enter his name.

LEGITIMATION BY SUBSEQUENT MARRIAGE

1150. Children born of unmarried persons who at the time of the conception, or during pregnancy, or at the time of birth, were free to contract a valid marriage, are rendered legitimate by a subsequent valid marriage and also by an invalid marriage contracted in good faith. It is immaterial whether the marriage is newly contracted, or a former invalid marriage is validated, and the legitimation of the children already born takes place even if the marriage is not consummated by conjugal intercourse (**Canon 1116**).

Illegitimate children are in law distinguished into two main classes, *natural* and *spurious*. The spurious children are subdistinguished into *adulterous, sacrilegious, incestuous,* and *nefarious*. The children born of unmarried parents who were not prevented by any invalidating impediment from contracting marriage at the time of conception, or pregnancy, or birth of the illegitimate child, are called *natural* children (*filii naturales*). If the parents were not at the times stated capable of contracting a valid marriage for reason of an invalidating impediment, the children are called *spurious* (*filii spurii*). The spurious children are called *adulterous,* if born from adulterous intercourse; they are called *sacrilegious,* if one or both parents were either in solemn religious vows, or if the father was in major orders; they are called *incestuous,* if the parents were blood-relations or relations by marriage in those degrees which invalidate marriage; they are called *nefarious,* if the parents of the illegitimate child were blood-relations in the direct line. Only the first class of illegitimate children (the *filii naturales*) are made legitimate by a subsequent marriage. However, Canon 1051 concedes that, by a dispensation from a diriment impediment of marriage granted by ordinary power or by power delegated by a general indult, the legitimation of the offspring of the parties who get the dispensation is *ipso facto* granted, with the exception of adulterous and sacrilegious children.

Children legitimated by subsequent marriage are, in so far as canonical effects are concerned, held equivalent in all things to legitimate offspring, unless the Canons explicitly rule otherwise (**Canon 1117**). Various Canons explicitly state that any person born outside of legitimate wedlock, though rendered legitimate by subsequent marriage, cannot be promoted to certain high ecclesiastical dignities, e.g., the cardinalate (cfr. Canon 232), the episcopate (cfr. Canon 331), an abbacy or prelacy *nullius* (cfr. Canon 320).

CHAPTER X

OF THE SEPARATION OF MARRIED PERSONS

ARTICLE I.—OF THE DISSOLUTION OF THE BOND OF MARRIAGE

1151. The valid marriage of Christians, consummated by the conjugal act, cannot be dissolved by any human authority for any reason; death alone can dissolve the bond (**Canon 1118**).

A non-consummated marriage between baptized persons, or between baptized and unbaptized persons, is dissolved automatically by law through solemn religious profession and also by a dispensation of the Holy See, when such is granted for a good reason at the request of both parties, or of one party, even though the other objects (**Canon 1119**).

This Canon states the two cases in which a valid marriage between Christians, or between a Christian and an unbaptized party, can be dissolved by the authority of the Holy See, provided such marriage has not been consummated by conjugal intercourse. The only kind of a marriage bond which cannot be dissolved is described in Canon 1118—a valid and consummated marriage between two Christians. Theologians point out that by the conjugal intercourse the words of Christ take effect "et erunt duo in carne una"; and that the absolute indissolubility of the Christian marriage—"let no man put asunder what God hath joined"—results only after conjugal intercourse following the marriage of two Christians.

1152. Solemn religious profession dissolves the unconsummated marriage of Christians and also of Christians with unbaptized persons. Theologians discuss whether the dissolution of the marriage bond by solemn religious profession rests on the natural law, or the ecclesiastical law, or the positive divine law. The official pronouncements of the Church do not decide the controversy, and the Council of Trent merely states: "If anyone saith that matrimony contracted but not consummated is not dissolved by the solemn profession of religion by one of the married parties; let him be anathema." [650]

The Supreme Pontiff can, in virtue of the plenitude of power resting with him, dissolve by dispensation an unconsummated marriage of Christians or of Christians and unbaptized persons. The dogmatic theologians discuss the history of this case and the reasons which prove that the Supreme Pontiff has this power. Whatever the weight of their argumentation may be, one thing is certain, namely, that the Head of the Church must have God's guidance when he proceeds to determine the extent of his power in a matter so vital to Christian morality.

The important prerequisite in both cases is to prove that the marriage was not consummated by conjugal intercourse. The whole procedure for the proof of the non-consummation of the marriage is reserved to the Holy See. The obtaining of the information on and proof of the facts must of necessity be committed by the Holy See to others. A lengthy Decree of the Sacred Congregation of the Sacraments outlines in detail the procedure for the proof of the non-consummation of the marriage, which Decree, together with the legal forms for the citation of the parties, interrogatory of the parties and the witnesses, etc., is given in the issue of the *Acta Apostolicæ Sedis* of August 1, 1923.

THE PAULINE PRIVILEGE

1153. The valid marriage of two unbaptized parties, though consummated, is dissolved in favor of the faith by the Pauline Privilege. This privilege does not apply in a marriage contracted between a baptized and an unbaptized party with the dispensation from the impediment of disparity of cult (**Canon 1120**).

[650] Sessio XXIV, can. 6, *De Matrimonio.*

This privilege is based on the words of St. Paul in the First Epistle to the Corinthians, vii. 12–15: "If any brother hath a wife that believeth not and she consent to dwell with him: let him not put her away. And if any woman hath a husband that believeth not and he consent to dwell with her: let her not put away her husband. . . . But if the unbeliever depart, let him depart. For a brother or a sister is not under servitude in such cases. But God hath called us in peace."

The first requisite is that the parties at the time of their marriage were both unbaptized; the second is that one of the parties be validly baptized after that marriage; the third is that the convert to Christianity interpellates the unbaptized party as stated in Canon 1121.

The author of the commentary on the thirteen Epistles of St. Paul, commonly called *Ambrosiaster,* who lived towards the end of the fourth century, speaks quite plainly of the Pauline Privilege. The passage referring to the Pauline Privilege is given in the *Decretum Gratiani,* but is erroneously ascribed to Pope St. Gregory I by Gratian.[651] The Pauline Privilege is again mentioned in the *Concilium Trullanum* (692). After that the authorities are numerous as can be seen from the list given by Wernz.[652] Finally, Pope Innocent III stated the law on this matter explicitly, and this law passed into the official collection of laws known as the "Decretals of Pope Gregory IX." [653]

THE INTERPELLATIONS

1154. Before the converted and baptized party can validly contract a new marriage, he must first interpellate the unbaptized party, without prejudice to the precepts of Canon 1125, and ask: (1) whether the unbaptized party wishes to be converted and baptized; (2) if the unbaptized party does not want to be baptized, whether he (or she) is willing to live peacefully in marriage without offence to God (i.e., without interfering with the religious obligations of the convert). These questions must always be put to the unbaptized party, unless the Holy See has declared otherwise (**Canon 1121**).

---

651 c. 2, C. XXVIII, qu. 2.
652 *Jus Decretalium,* IV, 1041.
653 cc. 7, 8, *De Divortiis,* lib. IV, tit. 19.

The interpellations should be made normally with the authority of the Ordinary of the converted party in at least in a summary and extrajudicial form, and the Ordinary is entitled to grant the unbaptized party at his (or her) request a certain length of time to reflect before making answer, with the warning, however, that failure to answer within the specified time will be taken as a reply in the negative. Interpellations made privately by the convert himself (herself) are valid, and, if the above-mentioned form cannot be observed, are also licit: but in the latter case proof of the interpellation in the external forum must be established by at least two witnesses, or by other evidence acknowledged in law (**Canon 1122**).

If the interpellations have been omitted by declaration of the Apostolic See, or if the unbaptized party has expressly or tacitly given a negative answer, the baptized party has the right to contract a new marriage with a Catholic, unless after the reception of baptism he has given the unbaptized party just cause for separation (**Canon 1123**). The dispensation of the Holy See is here called a declaration, because in many cases it is a mere declaration of the Pauline Privilege. Natural justice demands that the converted party should lose the right to abandon the party whom he married in infidelity and to marry another, if after his baptism he behaves in such a manner that the unbaptized party has just reason to separate from him.

The converted party does not lose the right to contract a new marriage with a Catholic, even though he has lived in marriage with the unbaptized party after his conversion. Wherefore, he can make use of his right to a new marriage with a Catholic if the unbaptized party afterwards changes his mind (as to peaceful cohabitation) and abandons the baptized party without a just cause, or does not live with the baptized party in peace and without blaspheming the Creator (**Canon 1124**). The purpose of the Pauline Privilege is to guarantee the converted party freedom to practise his religion and satisfy the obligations of Christian life assumed by baptism. If, therefore, the unbaptized party pretends to guarantee this liberty of the Catholic party, but afterwards violates his promise, the converted party is free to divorce him provided the interpellations have been duly made or a dispensation from the obligation of making them obtained.

On July 11, 1886, the Holy Office declared that the marriage of two unbaptized persons of whom one becomes a Christian after the marriage, is not dissolved by the mere fact that one party gets baptized, but only at the moment of the new marriage of the baptized party.[654] If, therefore, the other party also becomes a Christian before the first marries again, the Pauline Privilege does not apply.

1155. The interpellations or questions to be put to the unbaptized party are so necessary that without them the convert cannot validly contract a new marriage, as is evident from the wording of Canon 1121. It seems that the new marriage of the converted party is not valid without the interpellations, even though it is useless to make them—for example, when the unbaptized party has married again, or when it is impossible to make the interpellation because the converted party does not know where the other party lives. The facts themselves in these cases prove that the case of St. Paul is verified: "If the unbeliever depart, let him depart." Nevertheless, the Code states absolutely in Canon 1121 that the interpellations must always be made, unless the Holy See has declared otherwise. Cappello sums up the controversy on the necessity of the interpellations in cases where they are useless or impossible, and concludes that the necessity of making the interpellations ceases if there is moral certainty that the unbaptized party persists in abandoning the baptized party, and if the interpellations cannot be made except with great difficulty or danger, or are altogether impossible. He then adds that the Supreme Pontiff has reserved to himself the judgment on the facts that are claimed to make the interpellations useless, or impossible, or very difficult. Finally, he concludes that, if the interpellations were in such cases illegitimately omitted, the marriage of the converted party seems to be invalid. This invalidity he ascribes to the positive law of the Church inhabilitating the convert from contracting a new marriage. He thinks that it would be valid under the divine law as promulgated by St. Paul, if the Church had not added this invalidating condition to the use of the privilege.[655]

The position of Cappello is criticized by Arendt in the "Ephemerides Theologicæ Lovanienses,"[656] who explains that,

[654] Gasparri, "De Matrimonio," II, n. 1334.
[655] De Sacramentis, III, n. 776.
[656] I, 177.

though the Pauline Privilege is granted only on condition that the interpellations be made, it was not granted irrespective of the Supreme Authority of St. Peter and his successors, but rather subject to that authority: consequently, where the Pauline Privilege with its explicit conditions becomes inadequate, the Supreme Pontiff can supply the inadequacy in favor of the promotion of the faith.

The speculative question as to the necessity of the interpellations under the divine law in cases where they are useless or physically or morally impossible, remains unsolved. The commentators on the Code agree that, in practice, the declaration of the Holy See is necessary in these cases for the validity of a new marriage of the converted party. That declaration may be given either by law (e.g., in Canon 1125 for the cases there specified) or in individual cases at the application of petitioners.

DISPENSATION FROM THE INTERPELLATIONS

1156. In so far as they refer to marriage, the Constitutions of Pope Paul III ("Altitudo," June 1, 1537), Pope St. Pius V ("Romani Pontificis," August 2, 1571), and Pope Gregory XIII ("Populis," January 25, 1585), given to individual countries, are extended to all other countries in the same circumstances (**Canon 1125**). The parts of these Constitutions which refer to marriage are given in the Appendix of the Code (cfr. Documents VI, VII and VIII). By this Canon and the documents, the following concessions are made:

(1) In countries where polygamy is practised, a man who becomes a Christian and who had before his conversion married several wives and does not remember which one he married first, may after his conversion marry any one of them. If he remembers which one he married first, he shall dismiss the others and retain the first (Constitution "Altitudo");

(2) In countries where polygamy is practised and where a man has married and dismissed several wives, and finally he and one of his wives become Christians, he may retain the one who was baptized with him, though she be not his first wife (Constitution "Romani Pontificis");

(3) In certain countries it frequently happens that one of a married couple is carried off by the enemy to a remote place,

and cut off from all communication with his former spouse and relatives. If this captive or the party left behind becomes a Christian, and cannot without great danger or difficulty go or send messengers to question the other party whether he (or she) wants to be converted or at least live peacefully with the converted party, the Ordinaries and the pastors can allow the convert to marry any Catholic without the interpellation. The marriage is declared valid, even if later on it should become known that the other party had become a Christian before the second marriage took place, or that the other party had no chance to answer to the interpellation (Constitution "Populis").

The Code states that these Constitutions, given to particular countries, are now to be considered given to all countries, but it adds that these dispensations are good only "in iisdem adjunctis." They are thus applicable only when and where the circumstances or conditions are the same as those outlined in the said Constitutions. Wherefore, they are not very practical in Christian nations, although they are of practical utility in the missions in heathen countries. Nevertheless, there is a probable opinion that the Ordinary may allow marriage without the interpellation if the converted party cannot at all or only with grave danger and difficulty make such interpellation (Vermeersch-Creusen, "Epitome Iuris Canonici," II, ed. 1930, n. 436).

Point of Time of Dissolution of First Marriage

1157. The bond of the former marriage contracted in infidelity is dissolved only at the time when the converted party actually contracts a new and valid marriage (**Canon 1126**).

It is not the baptism of one of the parties that dissolves the marriage bond contracted by two unbaptized persons, but rather the new marriage entered into under the Pauline Privilege. Wherefore, the case must be such that the converted party can validly contract a new marriage—namely, that the other party remains unbaptized and that the baptized party has legitimately made the interpellation and received a negative reply. The interpellation may be dispensed with under certain circumstances by the Holy See. If the other party has also become a Christian (perhaps in some non-Catholic denomination) by valid baptism before the party first converted married again, the Pauline

Privilege no longer applies, for the words of St. Paul—"if the unbeliever depart, let him depart"—are no longer verified. Nevertheless, there is a good deal of controversy about the case where two unbaptized married persons were separated, and both, unknown to each other, became Christians. We have cases of that kind frequently in the United States. Here many people are not baptized, although in general they lead a Christian life; very frequently they get a divorce after the first marriage, drift apart and never hear of each other again. In such cases the making of the interpellation is practically impossible.

One group of theologians explains the above and similar cases of dispensation from the interpellation merely as an interpretation of the Pauline Privilege; another group explains them by saying that the Supreme Pontiff has power to dissolve the marriage contracted by two unbaptized persons when one party becomes a Christian, even though after the baptism of the one party they had conjugal intercourse. Also, when both parties have become Christians but have not had conjugal intercourse after both were baptized, the Supreme Pontiff must have the power to dissolve the marriage, for otherwise it would be difficult to understand the faculty given by the Constitution "Populis" of Pope Gregory XIII.[657]

In Doubtful Cases the Pauline Privilege Has the Favor of the Law

1158. In a doubtful matter the Pauline Privilege enjoys the favor of the law (**Canon 1127**). This principle of the Code is not new, for it is found in almost the same words in a Decree of the Sacred Congregation of the Holy Office, April 19, 1899: "Mens est ut in dubiis, judicium sit in fidei favorem." [658] When, therefore, it is questionable whether a convert to the Catholic faith can marry again under the Pauline Privilege, one must carefully investigate whether the state of facts is such that justifies the application of the said Privilege. If some fact essential to the application of the Privilege remains doubtful, the Privilege may nevertheless be applied. Cappello enumerates the matters concerning which doubt may arise: (1) about the

---

[657] On this controversy see Cappello, "De Sacramentis," III, 826–831.
[658] *Collectanea de Prop. Fide*, II, n. 2043.

validity of the marriage contracted in infidelity; (2) about the person of the first wife (i.e., which was the first of several wives); (3) about the validity of baptism of one party; (4) about the sincerity of the unbaptized party to live peacefully with the converted party; (5) about the sufficiency of the reason for dispensation from the interpellation; (6) about the existence of the marriage contracted; (7) about the verification of all the conditions required for the application of the Pauline Privilege.[659]

1159. The cases which are likely to come under the observation of the parish clergy in the United States will be cases where a non-Catholic becomes a convert to the Church, and where his baptism or the baptism of the other party to whom he was married before his conversion is doubtful. One may have one of the following cases: (1) both parties doubtfully baptized; (2) one party certainly baptized, the other unbaptized; (3) one party certainly baptized, the other doubtfully baptized; (4) one party unbaptized, the other doubtfully baptized.

In the first and fourth cases, there seems to be room for the application of the Pauline Privilege. Not to complicate matters, we suppose that the doubtful baptism was received in a non-Catholic sect, and that the marriage of the parties took place outside the Catholic Church and was valid. In either case both parties might be considered unbaptized, since it is doubtful whether any of the parties were validly baptized. If one of the parties becomes a Catholic and is baptized conditionally, as has to be done with a doubtfully baptized convert, he can, we believe, make use of the Pauline Privilege and marry again, provided he has first interpellated his partner in marriage and received a negative reply. If they are perhaps already separated by civil divorce and the interpellation is useless or cannot be made without great difficulty, a dispensation from the interpellation can be obtained from the Holy See.

There is a difficulty in these two cases about the doubtful baptism, for according to Canon 1070 a doubtful baptism is to be considered a valid baptism in the matter of marriage. Nevertheless, that rule of the Code does not seem to interfere with the Pauline Privilege, for Canon 1070 refers to the rule of Canon 1014, which states that marriage enjoys the favor of

659 *De Sacramentis*, III, n. 788.

the law, and that therefore one has to stand for its validity in case of doubt, but that same Canon 1014 immediately adds that the favor of the law given to the Pauline Privilege prevails. Arendt, who discusses the Pauline Privilege in the "Ephemerides Theologicæ Lovanienses," would rather dissolve a valid marriage of a doubtfully baptized non-Catholic and an unbaptized person (married after the Code became law) by dispensation of the Supreme Pontiff from the bond of a *matrimonium legitimum non ratum*. He supposes the dispensation is given after the conversion and conditional baptism of the doubtfully baptized non-Catholic.[660]

1160. As to the case in which both parties were doubtfully baptized and both became converts to the Catholic Church, Arendt (if we understand him correctly) would dissolve the bond of the marriage, not by the Pauline Privilege, but by a dispensation of the Supreme Pontiff from the *matrimonium ratum non consummatum,* provided the parties have not lived in marriage after both were baptized for certain.[661] He criticizes severely the statement of Cerato [662] that the marriage of two doubtfully baptized parties of whom one becomes a convert to the Catholic Church, can be dissolved by the Pauline Privilege. He argues that neither the Pauline Privilege nor a dispensation of the Supreme Pontiff can dissolve such a marriage, if the parties have had conjugal intercourse at all during their marriage. He holds that, through the doubtful baptism and the conjugal intercourse of the married couple, the marriage has probably become a *matrimonium ratum et consummatum*—that is to say, it is probably a consummated marriage of Christians from which the Pope cannot dispense.

The foregoing opinions on the meaning of Canon 1127 have been considerably upset by the recent Decree of the Holy Office which rules: (1) the Pauline Privilege cannot be applied to converts if a marriage was between two doubtfully baptized non-Catholics, and the doubt about baptism is insoluble; (2) if one party was unbaptized and the other doubtfully baptized, and the doubt about baptism is insoluble, the Ordinary cannot allow the use of the Pauline Privilege, but must in each case recur to the Holy Office (June 10, 1937; *Acta Ap. Sedis*, XXIX, 305).

[660] I, 174.   [661] *Ibid.*, 183, 31.   [662] *Matrimonium*, n. 127.

1161. When one party is certainly validly baptized and the other is unbaptized or doubtfully baptized, the case is commonly considered not to fall under the Pauline Privilege. The valid baptism of one party seems to take the marriage out of the case contemplated by the Pauline Privilege. Can such a marriage be dissolved by the Supreme Pontiff, when one of the parties becomes a convert to the Catholic faith? The question is important, for here in the United States we have many marriages between baptized non-Catholics and unbaptized persons, and since the impediment of disparity of cult no longer invalidates the marriages of baptized non-Catholics with unbaptized persons, the question whether the Holy See can dissolve that marriage bond is of practical importance. From the Papal documents (especially those quoted under Canon 1125), it seems that the only marriage which cannot be dissolved by the power of the Vicar of Christ is the consummated marriage of two Christians. On September 17, 1627, Pope Urban VIII stated that the marriages of infidels are not held to be so firm that they could not be dissolved "necessitate suadente." The same remark may be applied to a marriage of an unbaptized person and a baptized non-Catholic, since such a marriage is most probably not a sacrament. Recently the Holy Office dissolved *in favorem fidei* the bond of a marriage entered into in 1919 by a baptized Anglican and an unbaptized person. The parties had been divorced and one of them had married again, while the other wanted to become a Catholic and marry a Catholic. The Holy See dissolved the bond of the first marriage. This case has not been reported in the official organ of the Holy See, but it is certain that the dispensation was granted *in favorem fidei*, November 6, 1924.[663]

ARTICLE II.—OF THE SEPARATION OF MARRIED PERSONS

1162. Married persons are obliged to preserve the community of conjugal life, unless a just cause excuses them from this obligation (**Canon 1128**).

A separation from bed and board has been allowed by the Church for just reasons. After the Reformation the Lutherans,

---

663 *Homiletic and Pastoral Review*, XXV (Dec., 1924), 272–288; *Eccl. Review* (January, 1924), 59–66 (October, 1924), 404–406.

who availed themselves of every possible opportunity to blame the Church for her teaching and practice, said that the Church was acting contrary to the Gospel of Christ by allowing the separation of married people for many reasons, while Christ allows separation for adultery only (Matt., v. 19). The Council of Trent, however, upheld the practice of the Church, and stated that "if anyone says that the Church errs by allowing the separation of married persons from cohabitation for a definite or for an indefinite time, let him be anathema." [664] That controversy has long since died a natural death, for at the present time and for many years the Catholic Church has waged a singlehanded fight, not merely against unjustified separation, but against the dissolution of the marriage bond so freely asked for by non-Catholics and so liberally granted by the civil governments of so-called Christian nations.

The reasons for separation from cohabitation admitted by the Church may be classified under three heads: adultery, heresy or schism; any grave bodily or spiritual danger; and mutual consent.[665]

1163. If one party is guilty of adultery, the other has the right to dissolve even for all time the community life, although the marriage bond remains. This right is forfeited if the other party consented to the crime, was the cause of it, expressly or tacitly condoned it, or, finally, committed the same crime. Tacit condonation of the crime exists where the innocent party, after having learned of the crime, has continued to live with the other party in marital relations; such the law presumes to be the case, unless the innocent party within six months either expels or leaves, or brings legal accusation against the guilty partner (**Canon 1129**).

1164. The innocent spouse who, either upon sentence of the judge or on his own initiative, legitimately leaves the guilty party, is never again under the obligation to readmit the adulterer to the community of life. The innocent party, however, may admit or recall the guilty partner, unless he has in the meantime, with the consent of the innocent party, embraced a state of life inconsistent with marriage (**Canon 1130**).

Adultery gives the innocent party the right to a perpetual

---

[664] Sessio XXIV, Canon 8, *De Matrimonio.*
[665] Gasparri, "De Matrimonio," II, n. 1363.

separation. From the former law as well as from these Canons, it is certain that the innocent party can separate not only by the authority of the ecclesiastical court, but also privately without the intervention of the authorities. It is necessary, however, that there is certainty of the crime of adultery. Whether the crime must be public to entitle a married party to separate by private authority, or whether it suffices that the other party knows for certain of the crime, is disputed. The Code does not give an answer to this question, but states generally that a married person has the right to separate permanently because of the adultery of the other party. That seems to give the injured party the right to separate irrespective of publicity of the crime. Nevertheless, if the party accused of adultery denies the crime, objects to the breaking of the marital relations and demands that the party who wants to break away be forced by the ecclesiastical court to comply with the duties of the marital state, the other party must furnish proof of the adultery, for otherwise the judge has to order the resumption of cohabitation. Wherefore, it may be said that the crime need not be public to entitle the party to private separation for adultery, but the party charging his or her consort with adultery must be able to prove the charge. Sound public policy must stand for the preservation of the cohabitation of married persons, and the party who claims to have cause for separation must be able to furnish proof of such allegation.[666]

1165. The Code takes care to state that adultery is a reason for separation only in those cases in which the guilt of the crime is ascribable exclusively to one party, and the other is truly innocent. If the other party consented to the adultery, it is no ground for separation. If the other party knew of the evil intention of his consort and did not protest when protest was possible and obligatory, it amounts to tacit consent. Furthermore, the so-called innocent party may have been the cause of the adultery, in which case the crime is no cause for separation. Thus, if the wife refuses her husband the marriage rights for a long time and without a valid excuse, she may indirectly cause the husband to commit adultery. If both parties are equally guilty of adultery, the Code rules that adultery is no cause for separation.

666 Gasparri, "De Matrimonio," II, n. 1368.

Canon Law as well as civil law favor the condoning of adultery by the innocent party for the sake of keeping together the family. The law presumes condonation if the innocent party has not taken any steps to avail himself of the right of separation within six months after becoming certain of the adultery.

It is not admitted by all theologians that the indirect causing of the adultery by refusal of the marriage rights without a legitimate cause deprives the innocent party of the right to separate. Gasparri holds that the party refusing does not lose the right to separation, provided that the marriage rights were not refused with the intention that the other should be forced into committing adultery.[667] Reiffenstuel, Schmalzgrüber, and other canonists whom Gasparri follows, argue from some of the Decretals, but there seems to be no text that covers the case. The Code states that the adultery of one party is no ground for separation if the innocent party gave the cause for the adultery. No distinction is made between direct or indirect cause; in fact, the nature of the case is such that one party can rarely, if ever, directly cause the adultery of the other party.

The adultery as a cause of separation evidently favors the innocent party only, for otherwise the adulterer might benefit by his crime. The guilty party, therefore, has no right to separate, and must stay with the innocent party if the latter desires. Once the innocent party has decided to continue to live in conjugal relations with the guilty party, the adultery ceases to be a cause for separation, and the innocent party may not at some future disagreement or quarrel threaten to separate because of the adultery. Even though the innocent party separates from the adulterer, he or she has the right to recall the adulterer at any time. The only exception the Code admits to this right of the innocent party is when the adulterer has with the consent of the innocent party embraced a state of life foreign to marriage—that is to say, has taken religious vows or received major orders.

SEPARATION FOR VARIOUS CAUSES

1166. If one party joins an heretical sect, if he educates the offspring as non-Catholics, if he leads a criminal and despicable

---

[667] *De Matrimonio*, II, n. 1366.

life, if he threatens great bodily or spiritual danger to the other party, or if through cruelties or in any other way he makes the common life too difficult, the other party may legitimately leave the guilty party. This should ordinarily be done with the intervention of the local Ordinary, but may be done also on one's own initiative if the reason for separation is certain and there is danger in delay.

In all these cases the common life must be resumed when the reason for the separation ceases. If, however, the separation was pronounced by the Ordinary either for a time or indefinitely, the innocent party is not obliged to return except when the time specified by the Ordinary has elapsed or the Ordinary gives written orders to return (**Canon 1131**).

This Canon summarizes the various other reasons which justify the separation of a married couple. Regarding apostasy as a cause for separation, the Code presumably refers only to the case where a Catholic joins an heretical sect. Thus, Pope Urban VIII decreed that, if a woman on her own initiative leaves her husband because of his lapse into heresy, she is obliged to return to her husband after his reconciliation with the Church; if, however, she leaves him by the authority of the Church without the hope of resumption of conjugal life, she is not to be forced to live again with him.[668] The law of the Decretals is generally understood to have granted the right to the innocent party to leave the party guilty of heresy without the intervention of the local Ordinary. The Code ordinarily does not allow separation by private authority, except when delay entails danger for the innocent party.

1167. *Educating Children as non-Catholics.*—If **both** married parties are Catholics, their obligation to raise the children in the Catholic faith is evident. If a Catholic with the permission of the Church marries a baptized or unbaptized non-Catholic, the Church gives that permission only on the condition that the non-Catholic party and the Catholic promise to baptize and raise the children in the Catholic faith. The violation of the assumed obligation is a cause for separation. Usually the opposition of the non-Catholic begins to show itself when there is question of baptizing the first child. Again and again one meets with cases in which the non-Catholic prevents the Catholic baptism of the

[668] *Decretal. Greg. IX*, c. 6, *De Divortiis*, lib. IV, tit. 19.

child, and comparatively few are the cases where the Catholic party has sufficient faith and courage to make the non-Catholic party stand by his promise or leave him. The Code speaks only of the refusal to educate the child in the Catholic faith, which has a broader implication than mere baptism in the Catholic Church.

1168. *Criminal and Disgraceful Life.*—It is but reasonable that the Church should allow separation if one of the parties contracts criminal habits and leads a disreputable life. The ruin of the innocent party's life is enough suffering without subjecting this party to lifelong and continual torture and mental agony. An individual criminal or disgraceful act is not regarded by the Code as a cause for separation, for, painful as it may be to the innocent partner in marriage to have to share the disgrace before the public, still honor and good reputation can be regained if the guilty party truly amends.

1169. *Danger of Grave Bodily or Spiritual Harm.*—Under this head many cases may arise which give the party exposed to such danger the right to separate. Quite frequently a party succeeds in concealing bad moral habits and physical defects during the time prior to marriage, and the other party finds out the truth too late to save his or her freedom from the marriage bond. The innocent party, however, should not be put to the additional suffering of living with a person of that kind. It may be, and very likely frequently is, partly the fault of this party not to have taken the marriage as seriously as its importance demands, but that is no excuse for the other who succeeded in hiding his true character or some physical defect or ailment (like syphilis, tuberculosis, etc.)

1170. *Cruelty which Makes the Common Life too Difficult.*— The term "cruelty" is stretched to its breaking point in divorce proceedings in our civil courts so that certain incompatibilities of temperament and differences of character, which humanly speaking are unavoidable, are put down as cruelty. The Code uses a very significant term "sævitiæ" (corresponding to our savagery or ferociousness) to denote cruelty. The Code, therefore, means real cruelty.

The Code gives the above reasons for separation merely as examples or illustrations of cases that entitle the injured party to separation; it does not restrict separation to those cases.

There is no doubt that the welfare of all parties concerned, and indirectly the welfare of society at large, demands the separation of married people when matters have taken such a turn that no sincere reconciliation between husband and wife can be hoped for. Continued severe quarrels and enmities between them endanger their souls, and, if there are children to raise, there is no possibility of raising them properly in a family thus disrupted. Inadequate as the raising of children in homes and boarding schools may be (for their natural place is in the family), still in cases where they see nothing but scandal, or bitter quarrel and enmity between father and mother, it is preferable to break up the family which has failed in the purpose for which it was established.

1171. The reader will notice from the above-quoted Canons that the Church does not allow married people to separate on their own initiative except in the case of adultery and where one of those other reasons has become so urgent that immediate action is necessary for the safety of the injured party. Otherwise, the aggrieved party must submit his (or her) complaint to the judgment of the local Ordinary. If the bishop finds the complaint justified and judges that it is best for the parties to separate, he may decree the separation either for a fixed length of time, or he may order separation indefinitely. It should be noticed, however, that the Code rules that, in all separations for causes other than adultery, the separation cannot be permanent, but is conditioned on the continuance of the cause for separation. If the cause ceases, the parties are obliged to resume the marital relations. If the decree of the local Ordinary was in favor of an indefinite separation, the injured party may delay the return to marital life until the Ordinary orders the return. The Ordinary, however, is obliged by law to order the resumption of the marital relations when it is proved that the cause for separation has ceased.

1172. Here the question arises whether the party who has a genuine reason for separation recognized by the Church may ask for a civil divorce. From the exclusive jurisdiction of the Church over the marriage of Christians, one must necessarily conclude that Catholics do wrong in asking for a civil divorce before they have submitted their case to the bishop of the diocese of their domicile. But can they in conscience ask for a civil divorce after the Ordinary has declared that they have a true cause for separation? The question squarely confronts the party and must be answered, for, if the other party objects to the separation allowed by the Ordinary, the injured party cannot break the marital relations without coming into conflict with the civil law, which gives either married party the right to force the other to cohabitation. The difficulty is accentuated by the fact that some of the states of the American Union do not grant a separation but only an absolute divorce *a vinculo* (the very expression used by some of the statutes of the states). In other states for the same specified reasons the party may sue either for separation or for an absolute divorce; in still other states one set of reasons is specified for absolute divorce, and another set for separation.

The same difficulty confronts Catholics also in many other countries where the civil law attempts to dissolve the bond of marriage. Application has been made repeatedly to the Holy Office and to the Sacred Penitentiary (especially by French bishops) to declare whether a Catholic judge and a Catholic lawyer can handle these cases, and whether persons who have cause for separation and obtain permission from the Church to separate, can apply for a divorce. The Holy See has invariably given an evasive answer, which shows clearly that the Church does not as yet want to decide the question definitively. The answers which have been given are worded in such a manner that nothing certain can be concluded from them.[669]

1173. Practically there is nothing else to be done than to suffer the interference of the civil power in a matter which does not belong to its jurisdiction. If these civil powers pretend to dissolve the bond of a valid marriage of Christians, they are attempting the impossible; all that the civil power can do is to release the parties from the civil consequences of the marriage contracted, and it seems that a Catholic who, according to the law of the Church, has a right to separation but cannot make his right effective unless he gets the civil divorce, has a right to apply for it. We believe that no attention should be paid to the pretensions of the civil power to dissolve the bond of marriage, for that power can do only so much as its inherent

[669] See the proposed questions and answers in Cappello, ''De Sacramentis,'' III, 875–884.

power permits, namely, free the parties from the civil obligations and effects of the marriage contract, and to that extent only attention need be paid to its decree. If the other party has no conscience, and takes advantage of the pretension of the civil power and under its protection marries again, this wickedness should not prevent the innocent party who has a right to separation from making its right effective by getting a civil divorce.

Custody of the Children After Separation

1174. After the separation, the children are to be placed in the custody of the innocent party, and, if one of the parties is a non-Catholic, the Catholic party is to have the custody, unless the Ordinary in either case decides otherwise for the sake of the welfare of the children, always safeguarding their Catholic education (**Canon 1132**).

This is what the Church wants done in a case of separation, but the civil power usually decides in a divorce case who shall have the custody of the children, and the policy of the various states of our Union has been to give the custody of the children to the person who, in the judgment of the court, is best qualified to take proper care of the children, whether it be one of the parents or a stranger appointed as legal guardian. This rule is so closely adhered to that the other question of the religion of the children takes a secondary place in the eyes of the law. In fact, it is doubtful whether under the American relation of the state to religion, all religions being considered equal before the law, attention can be paid by the court to any agreements giving preference to one religion over another. To recognize an agreement by which one religion gets preference over the other (as in the case of marriage between Catholics and non-Catholics) does not seem possible under our Constitution. There is the additional difficulty of safeguarding the Catholic education of the children by agreement of the parents, for it is generally held by our courts that contracts and agreements regulating the duties of husband and wife in matters pertaining directly and exclusively to the home, cannot be made the subject of public inquiry, and that it is contrary to public policy to recognize and enforce them.[670]

[670] Clark, ''Contracts'' (ed. 1914), 384.

1175. *Separation by Mutual Agreement.*—The Code has no other explicit ruling on this point except that it indirectly permits separation for just cause by stating in Canon 1128 that married persons are obliged to live together unless a just cause excuses them from this obligation. It is generally admitted by canonists and moralists that, by mutual consent and for a just cause, the parties may separate for a time or even permanently. However, the parties must avoid any scandal that might come from such separation, and must take care not to expose each other to the proximate occasion of sin. Here in the United States it happens frequently that poor people immigrate from European countries and, not having enough money to move the whole family at one time, the husband comes first to work for some time to get the necessary means to pay for the transportation of the wife and children. In some dioceses the statutes have been rather severe in reference to such cases, ordering the confessors to refuse absolution if the separation had lasted two or three years. It is very doubtful whether the Ordinary of the diocese can pass such a law, for, where the Common Law of the Church grants liberty, the inferior legislator must respect that liberty. The question of conscience arising from possible abuse of the liberty granted by the Common Law can best be dealt with by the confessor in the individual cases.

CHAPTER XI

OF VALIDATION OF MARRIAGE

ARTICLE I.—OF SIMPLE VALIDATION

1176. To validate a marriage which is invalid on account of some diriment impediment, it is necessary that the impediment shall either cease or be dispensed, and that at least the party conscious of the impediment shall renew the consent. This renewal of consent is required by ecclesiastical law for the validation of the marriage, even though in the beginning both parties gave their consent and have not revoked it since (**Canon 1133**). The renewal of consent must be a new act of the will for a marriage that is known to have been invalid from the beginning (**Canon 1134**).

If the impediment is *public,* the consent must be renewed

by both parties in the form prescribed by law. If the impediment is *occult* and known to both parties, it suffices that the consent be renewed privately and secretly by both parties. If the impediment is *occult* and known only to one party, it suffices that the party who knows of the impediment shall privately and secretly renew the consent, provided the consent of the other party given at the time of the invalid marriage continues (**Canon 1135**).

The rules given by the Code are plain. First, the Code speaks of the validation of a marriage made invalid by a diriment impediment of ecclesiastical law, for, if the marriage is invalid for reason of a diriment impediment of the divine law, the marriage cannot be validated as long as that impediment lasts. Now, if the marriage was invalid through a diriment impediment, it may be that the impediment has since ceased, and if it has not ceased a dispensation may be obtained.

1177. As to the renewal of consent, the marriage must be contracted before the pastor or a delegated priest and two witnesses, if the marriage was not contracted in legal form in the first place (cfr. below, Canon 1137). If the marriage was made invalid through some impediment, one must inquire whether that impediment is public or occult (cfr. Canon 1037, above, n. 1007). If the impediment is public, the marriage must be contracted over again before the pastor and two witnesses. If the impediment is occult, the party (or parties) having knowledge of the impediment must renew the consent, but this may be done privately and secretly. The Church demands a new act of the will for the validity of the marriage. Formerly there was greater difficulty in validating a marriage when it had been invalidly contracted because of an occult impediment, since the Sacred Penitentiary demanded that the other party be informed of the invalidity of the marriage: this is no longer necessary under the law of the Code, which states that the private and secret renewal of consent by the party (or parties) having knowledge of the invalidity suffices.

However, the consent of the party ignorant of the invalidity of the marriage must still continue. As a rule, this point will give little trouble, for the consent once given is by law supposed to persevere until its revocation is apparent (cfr. Canon 1093).

Validation of Marriage Made Invalid by Lack of Consent

1178. A marriage which is invalid through lack of consent is validated if the party who did not consent now gives his consent, provided the consent of the other party continues. If the lack of consent was merely internal, it suffices that the party who did not consent now gives consent by an internal act. If the lack of consent was manifested also outwardly, it is necessary to renew the consent outwardly, either in the form prescribed by law, when the absence of consent was public, or in some private and secret but external manner if the lack of consent was occult (**Canon 1136**).

In the chapter dealing with matrimonial consent (Canons 1081–93), the Code treats of the various forms of defective consent: consent vitiated by ignorance, by error, by fear and force, by a condition attached. Now, if the marriage was rendered invalid through lack of that consent which in law is required for a valid marriage, and the party whose consent was either altogether absent or vitiated is willing to validate the marriage, one must first be certain that the other party has not in the meantime revoked his consent, and then inquire in what manner the lack or defect of consent came about. If the lack of consent or the defective consent was not external, but entirely internal, nothing more is required to validate the marriage than that internal consent be now given. If the defective consent was manifested outwardly, one must again inquire whether the defect was public or whether it remained occult. If it was public, the consent must be renewed in legal form —that is to say, the parties must give their consent before an authorized priest and two witnesses. If the defect of the consent was manifested but remained occult, it suffices that the consent be now given by some outward sign, words or act, but it suffices to do so privately and secretly.

1179. There is some difficulty in determining when the defect of consent is public and when it is occult. The same terms, public and occult, are employed in Canon 1135 when the Code speaks of the validation of a marriage made invalid through a diriment impediment. There we remarked that public and occult must be understood in the sense of Canon 1037, which rules that an impediment is to be considered public if it can be proved in the external forum.   It seems the commentators of the Code quite generally apply Canon 1037 also to public and occult defects of consent.   That seems to be correct, for, when two competent witnesses can prove the defect of the consent (e.g., ignorance, force or fear, faked consent, a condition unverified), the marriage can and must be declared null and void, if the matter is brought before the ecclesiastical court.   The private renewal of consent could not change the status of the marriage in the external forum.

1180. To validate a marriage which was nullified by a defect in the form, it must be contracted again in the legitimate form (**Canon 1137**).

If the parties were married outside the Church, if the priest who witnessed the marriage was not properly qualified, or if two qualified witnesses were not present, the marriage is null and void, and such a marriage can be validated in no other way than by the observance of the prescribed form of marriage. The rule here stated is now of general application for all marriages in which at least one of the parties is subject to the law of the Code on the form of marriage (cfr. above, nn. 1123–1126). If one of the parties cannot be persuaded to validate the marriage before the authorized priest and witnesses, as happens quite frequently in mixed marriages contracted outside the Church, nothing remains but to get the *sanatio in radice* to validate the marriage.

ARTICLE II.—OF THE "SANATIO IN RADICE"

1181. The *sanatio in radice* of a marriage is a validation that entails, besides a dispensation from or a cessation of an impediment, a dispensation from the law of renewing the consent, and has also by a fiction of law a retroactive force which gives the marriage the same canonical effects as though it had been valid from the beginning.   The validation of the marriage takes place at the moment of the granting of the favor; the retroactive effect, however, is to be understood to reach back to the beginning of the marriage, unless it is expressly stated otherwise in the rescript.   This dispensation from the law of renewing the consent can be given even without the knowledge of one party or of both (**Canon 1138**).

The Code explains the concept of the *sanatio in radice*. From this explanation it can be seen that the *sanatio* is a great favor, for it enables the priests engaged in the care of souls to straighten out marriages which could not otherwise be rectified (e.g., in cases where one or perhaps both parties refuse to contract marriage again in the usual form of the Church). The *sanatio* can be granted if both know of its concession, or if both are ignorant of it, or if one party only has knowledge of it.

1182. Any marriage which has been contracted with the naturally sufficient consent of both parties, even though this consent is juridically inefficacious because of a diriment impediment of ecclesiastical law or the lack of the prescribed form, can be validated by the *sanatio in radice,* provided the consent endures. If the marriage was contracted under an impediment of the natural or the divine law, even though the impediment should have ceased afterwards, such marriage is not validated by the Church by means of the *sanatio in radice,* even from the moment of the cessation of the impediment (**Canon 1139**).

It is evident that there must have been matrimonial consent, and that such consent perseveres, if the Church is to grant a *sanatio in radice,* for the Church can dispense from her laws and from the effects of these laws, but she cannot supply the consent. Matrimonial consent given in any form or manner, provided it is naturally sufficient to constitute a marriage consent, suffices for the application of the *sanatio in radice.* Thus, marriages contracted outside the Church, and even the so-called "common-law marriage," may be validated by the *sanatio in radice.* A "common-law marriage" may be defined as a marriage consummated by the consent of the parties without a religious or civil ceremony.[671] There is difficulty at times in distinguishing between a common-law marriage and concubinage. The intent of the parties to be man and wife is the fundamental essential of common-law marriage. Besides the sexual intercourse, there must be some indication of the intent to marry and to be considered as married persons, for, while it is certain that the expression of consent by words is not essential to matrimonial consent, the mere fact of living together in sexual intercourse is not a sufficient manifestation of matrimonial consent,

[671] *Digest of the Law Relating to Common Law Marriage in the U. S.* (Washington, Government Printing Office, 1919).

because such intercourse may or may not proceed from an intention to be man and wife.

1183. A union that is adulterous or otherwise contrary to the law of nature or the positive divine law, is not validated by the Church after the cessation of the impediment. If it is to become a valid marriage after the cessation of the impediment, a new consent in legal ecclesiastical form is necessary. What is to be said about those diriment impediments of marriage concerning which it is doubtful whether they are of the natural or divine law or of ecclesiastical law? It seems to us that the power of the Church is not to be questioned. The Supreme Pontiff's power is limited only in those matters which are known with certainty to have been fixed by the law of God (whether the natural or the positive divine law); it has no other limitations in all matters pertaining to the jurisdiction of the Church. The Code says that the Church does not grant a *sanatio* of marriages contracted with an impediment of the natural or divine law even after the impediment has ceased. There can be no doubt that the Church has power to grant the *sanatio* from the moment that the impediment ceased, but, if one speaks of a complete *sanatio* (namely, from the very beginning of the invalid union), the Church cannot grant a *sanatio* for marriages contracted invalidly for reason of a diriment impediment of the natural or divine law, because she could not remove that impediment from the beginning. The Decree of the Holy Office which said that such marriages *cannot* be validated by a *sanatio in radice* does not conflict with the Code, nor with dispensations granted by the Sacred Penitentiary, if one understands the *sanatio in radice* in its perfect form, as defined in Canon 1138.[672]

1184. If consent is lacking in either both or one of the invalidly married parties, the marriage cannot be validated by the Church through the *sanatio in radice*, whether there was no consent from the beginning, or when it was given in the beginning but afterwards revoked. If, however, consent was wanting from the beginning but was given later on, the *sanatio* can be conceded from the moment that consent was given (**Canon 1140**).

672 March 2, 1904; *Collect. de Prop. Fide*, II, n. 3188. Cfr. Gasparri, ''De Matrimonio,'' II, n. 1444.

This rule is a logical conclusion from the preceding Canons. The very idea of the *sanatio in radice* supposes that, when the *sanatio* is applied there is present then and there a consent which can be cured of its legal insufficiency. In two cases, therefore, the *sanatio* is not granted: (1) if there is no existing matrimonial consent at the time the *sanatio* is to be granted; (2) even though matrimonial consent is present, if the attempted marriage was invalid because of an impediment of the natural or the divine law.

POWER TO GRANT THE "SANATIO IN RADICE"

1185. The *sanatio in radice* can be granted by the Holy See alone (**Canon 1141**).

The *sanatio in radice* always contains a dispensation from at least one general law of the Church, namely, the required canonical form of marriage, and frequently also from a diriment impediment of marriage. Wherefore the *sanatio* is reserved to the Holy See. Delegated power is given to the bishops of the United States to grant the *sanatio in radice* for marriages attempted before a civil magistrate or a non-Catholic minister, if one of the parties is a non-Catholic (baptized or unbaptized), and the ordinary way of validating the marriage is not possible because either the non-Catholic cannot be informed of the invalidity without the danger of great harm or trouble to the Catholic party, or because the non-Catholic cannot be persuaded to fulfill the canonical form of marriage, or to make the necessary promises. If any other diriment impediment is found in the case, the Ordinary can grant the *sanatio* only if he has a faculty to dispense from that impediment. He may subdelegate pastors to grant the *sanatio,* but he cannot give them a general subdelegation, but only in individual cases. The tax for the *sanatio in radice,* for mixed religion, and for disparity of cult, is three dollars: the Ordinary may retain one-fifth of this sum for the needs of the diocese, and the rest is to be forwarded at the end of each year to the Holy Office.

The Sacred Congregation of the Sacraments grants to the bishops of the United States power to grant the *sanatio in radice* for marriages made invalid by a diriment impediment of lesser degree (cfr. Canon 1042), if it would cause great inconvenience to require the renewal of consent from the party ignorant of the impediment. The party who knows of the impediment and the invalidity is to be informed of the effects of the *sanatio*, and the validation of the marriage is to be recorded in the marriage record.

CHAPTER XII

OF SECOND MARRIAGES

1186. Though chaste widowhood is more honorable, second and further marriages are valid and licit, provided that, in accordance with Canon 1069, the nullity or dissolution of the previous marriage be legally proved (**Canon 1142**). A woman who has once received the nuptial blessing, cannot again receive it in a subsequent marriage (**Canon 1143**).

St. Paul says: "A woman is bound by the law as long as her husband liveth: but if her husband die, she is at liberty. Let her marry to whom she will: only in the Lord. But more blessed shall she be, if she so remain, according to my counsel" (I Cor., vii. 39 and 40). The Roman Law forbade marriage within a year from the death of the spouse, and inflicted *infamia juris* on those who married before the lapse of one year. When Pope Urban III was asked whether a person remarrying before the lapse of one year from the death of the former spouse was also marked with infamy under the Canon Law, he replied that the words of the Apostle are sufficient to prove that no disgrace is attached to a second marriage.[673]

TITLE VIII

OF SACRAMENTALS

1187. Sacramentals are sacred objects and actions which the Church, in a certain imitation of the sacraments, employs for the purpose of obtaining especially spiritual favors through her intercession (**Canon 1144**). The description of the sacramentals as here given by the Code explains the difference between sacraments and sacramentals. The sacramentals are created by

[673] *Decretal. Greg. IX, c. 4, De Secundis Nuptiis*, lib. IV, tit. 21.

the Church and their efficacy in obtaining divine favors, spiritual or temporal, is not inherent as in the case of the sacraments, but depends on the intercessory power of the Church.

The Holy See alone has the power to institute new sacramentals, to interpret authentically those in use, and to abolish or change any of them (**Canon 1145**).

The legitimate minister of the sacramentals is a cleric who has received the faculty for this purpose, and who has not been forbidden by the competent ecclesiastical authority to exercise it (**Canon 1146**).

There are many blessings in the Roman Ritual, some for the purpose of constituting an object a sacred article so that by its pious use spiritual or temporal benefits may accrue to the user. Others are formulæ for invocations and blessings of persons; still others are for the blessing of animals or of inanimate things to invoke God's blessing on those who own or use them. The Ritual itself usually indicates whether every priest may give the blessing, or whether it is reserved and a special faculty is needed to bestow it. Thus, the section ''De Benedictionibus'' of the Roman Ritual begins with the ''Benedictiones non reservatæ.''

1188. The Code gives the following rules regarding the various kinds of blessings:

(1) Consecrations can be validly performed by none but a consecrated bishop, unless the faculty is given to an inferior cleric either by law or by apostolic indult;

(2) Blessings, with the exception of those reserved to the Roman Pontiff, or to bishops, or to others, may be given by any priest;

(3) A reserved blessing, when given by a priest without the necessary permission, is illicit but valid, unless in the reservation the Holy See has expressly stated that it cannot be validly given except by those to whom the blessing is reserved or by those who have received a special faculty;

(4) Deacons and lectors can give validly and licitly only those blessings which are explicitly permitted to them by law (**Canon 1147**).

Rites to be Observed in the Sacramentals

1189. In the preparation and administration of the sacramentals the rites prescribed by the Church must be accurately observed. Consecrations and blessings, both constitutive and invocative, are invalid if the formula prescribed by the Church is not employed (**Canon 1148**). Invocative blessings are those by which God's blessing is invoked on a person, object, or place (e.g., the blessing of an infant, of edibles, of a house); *constitutive* blessings are those consecrations and benedictions which render a person, object, or place sacred (e.g., the blessing of an abbot, consecration or blessing of a church or sacred vessels, the blessing of prayer beads and other religious articles).

Persons who May Receive the Sacramentals

1190. Blessings are to be given primarily to Catholics; they may also be given to catechumens, and, where there is no prohibition of the Church, also to non-Catholics so that they may obtain the light of faith, or together with it bodily health (**Canon 1149**).

The Sacred Congregation of Rites recently declared that catechumens may be admitted also to the sacramentals which are publicly administered in church, as the ashes on Ash Wednesday, candles on Candlemas Day, and palms on Palm Sunday.[674] As to the private use of many of the sacramentals of the Church (e.g., holy water, prayer beads and other blessed articles), there is no prohibition of the Church preventing non-Catholics from using them. Persons excommunicated or interdicted by declaratory or condemnatory sentence of a competent ecclesiastical court are forbidden the use of the sacramentals (cfr. Canons 2260 and 2275).

Consecrated objects, and objects rendered sacred by the so-called constitutive blessing, must be treated with reverence, and they are not to be used for profane purposes nor for purposes for which they are not intended, even though these objects be kept in private houses (**Canon 1150**).

[674] On various declarations concerning Ash Wednesday and blessing of St. Blase, cfr. App. III, 49, a–d.

Regulations Concerning Exorcisms

1191. Nobody who has the power to pronounce exorcisms can lawfully read them over persons possessed by the devil unless he has received special and explicit permission from the Ordinary. This permission shall be granted by the Ordinary only to a priest who is distinguished for piety, prudence and integrity of life. The priest shall not pronounce the exorcisms until he has ascertained by careful and prudent investigation that the person is really possessed by the devil (**Canon 1151**).

Exorcisms can be pronounced by the authorized ministers, not only over the faithful and over catechumens, but also over non-Catholics and excommunicated persons (**Canon 1152**).

The ministers of the exorcisms which occur in baptism, and in consecrations and blessings are the clerics who legitimately perform these sacred rites (**Canon 1153**).

The difficult problem of determining whether a person is really possessed by one of the evil spirits, needs much prudence and prayer. On account of the importance of this exercise of the sacred ministry, the Church does not permit the priest to act on his own authority, but each case must be referred to the proper Ordinary of the priest who encounters a case that seems to have no other explanation than the influence of some evil spirit. Two extreme tendencies have to be guarded against— over-hastiness in pronouncing the case one of diabolical possession, and an *a priori* assumption that such cases of diabolical possession do not happen, and that therefore the afflicted person is merely suffering from some nervous disease. To be too credulous is bad, but to deny the possibility and probability of diabolical possession manifests either ignorance of or lack of belief in the Gospel.